PRAISE FROM OUR READERS

Mastering Access 97

"I read this book from cover to cover and found each page loaded with very practical information and explicit examples. I commend the authors for their ability to communicate otherwise very technical detail in understandable 'user friendly' language. I highly recommend this book."

Jim Shannon, Montana

Mastering FrontPage 98

"Best of the 9 FrontPage 98 books I own. Sybex does it again! I have been reading computer books for the last 10 years and Sybex has been a great publisher—putting out excellent books. After reading 3/4 of the book so far, I know that the publisher and the authors take pride in their product. It's a wonderful book!"

Mike Perry, New Jersey

"This is THE book for mastering FrontPage 98! I skimmed through 4 other books before deciding to buy this one. Every other book seemed like a larger version of the weak documentation that comes with the software. This book provided the insight on advanced subjects necessary for administering a web. A must buy for FrontPage users."

Richard Hartsell, Utah

Mastering Windows 98

"The first book I've read that does what it says it will do! I learned more about Windows 98 in the first one hundred pages of this book than in all of the previous books I had read. My copy lies, dog-eared, beside my computer as a constantly ready source of easy to understand information. It really does show you how to Master Windows 98."

Steven Dean, Arizona

SYBEX

www.sybex.com

MASTERING

QUICKEN 2000

MASTERING™
QUICKEN® 2000

Stephen L. Nelson

SYBEX®

San Francisco • Paris • Düsseldorf • Soest • London

Associate Publisher: Amy Romanoff
Contracts and Licensing Manager: Kristine
O'Callaghan
Acquisitions & Developmental Editor: Sherry Bonelli
Editor: Linda Recktenwald
Project Editor: Susan Berge
Technical Editor: Maryann Brown
Book Designers: Patrick Dintino, Catalin Dulfu, and
Franz Baumhackl
Electronic Publishing Specialists: Kris Warrenburg and
Grey Magauran
Project Team Leader: Leslie Higbee
Proofreaders: Carrie Bradley and Rich Ganis
Indexer: Matthew Spence
Cover Designer: Design Site
Cover Illustrator: Sergie Loobkoff, Design Site

SYBEX is a registered trademark of SYBEX Inc.

Mastering is a trademark of SYBEX Inc.

Screen reproductions produced with Collage Complete.

Collage Complete is a trademark of Inner Media Inc.

TRADEMARKS: SYBEX has attempted throughout this
book to distinguish proprietary trademarks from
descriptive terms by following the capitalization style
used by the manufacturer.

The author and publisher have made their best efforts
to prepare this book, and the content is based upon
final release software whenever possible. Portions of
the manuscript may be based upon pre-release versions
supplied by software manufacturer(s). The author and
the publisher make no representation or warranties of
any kind with regard to the completeness or accuracy
of the contents herein and accept no liability of any
kind including but not limited to performance, mer-
chantability, fitness for any particular purpose, or any
losses or damages of any kind caused or alleged to be
caused directly or indirectly from this book.

Library of Congress Card Number: 99-65749
ISBN: 0-7821-2596-4

Manufactured in the United States of America

10 9 8 7 6 5 4 3

ACKNOWLEDGMENTS

A lot of people at Sybex worked hard to see that this book provides you with maximum value. They spent weeks and, in some cases, months of their time thinking about you and how to make one part of your life—using Quicken 2000—easier.

Many thanks to Contracts and Licensing Manager Kristine O'Callaghan, Developmental Editor Sherry Bonelli, Editor Linda Recktenwald, Project Editor Susan Berge, Technical Editor Maryann Brown, Electronic Publishing Specialists Kris Warrenburg and Grey Magauran, Project Team Leader Leslie Higbee, Proofreaders Carrie Bradley and Rich Ganis, and Indexer Matthew Spence.

Thanks also to Kaarin Dolliver, who helped revise and review chapters for the latest version of Quicken.

CONTENTS AT A GLANCE

PART IV • QUICKEN IN A SMALL BUSINESS

APPENDIXES

TABLE OF CONTENTS

PART II • QUICKEN AND YOUR PERSONAL FINANCES

PART IV • QUICKEN IN A SMALL BUSINESS

APPENDIXES

INTRODUCTION

Mastering Quicken 2000 is not like other Quicken books you have seen. Other books are organized by product feature or menu command, but this book is *task-oriented*. It describes how you can accomplish key personal, investment, and business financial tasks using Quicken.

How to Use This Book

If you haven't yet installed Quicken, start with Appendix A to find out how to install the software and set up your first account.

If you're totally new to Quicken, you'll want to start with Part I, "The ABCs of Quicken," which covers the mechanics. You need this information before you can truly unleash the power of this simple yet sophisticated product. Once you're familiar with the basic operations, you're ready to begin using it for your personal, investment, or business financial management.

If you use Quicken at home, turn to Part II, "Quicken and Your Personal Finances." It describes how Quicken can help you with a variety of personal financial record-keeping and management tasks: credit cards, loans, mortgages, insurance, taxes, and even saving for retirement.

If you're an active investor, turn to Part III, "Quicken for Investors." You'll find information and advice about using Quicken to track investments in mutual funds, stocks, bonds, and real estate.

If you're an entrepreneur, professional, or bookkeeper using Quicken in a business setting, turn to Part IV, "Quicken in a Small Business." It covers topics important to anyone who uses Quicken as a business-accounting system.

At the end of the chapters in Parts II, III, and IV is a "Mastering Financial Success" sidebar. These sections discuss financial management concepts and techniques related to the material covered in the chapter. You'll find tips and tricks on achieving financial independence, becoming a smart investor, simplifying your financial affairs, being a good business owner, and more. You can skip this material if you're interested only in the mechanics of using Quicken. But if you have time even to skim one or two of these sections, you'll find them well worth your while.

At the end of this book, I've provided two appendices. Appendix A describes how to install the Quicken 2000 program. Appendix B describes how to use Quicken in Canada.

Finally, a glossary at the end of the book provides a handy financial dictionary. In this glossary, you can look up just about any financial term or phrase you read in this book or in a newspaper or hear on the radio or the evening news.

Versions of Windows, Versions of Quicken, and This Book

In this book, the Quicken windows and dialog boxes show Quicken Deluxe 2000 in the Windows NT and Windows 98 environments. Does that mean you can't use this book if you're running Windows 95 or Windows 2000 or if you're using a different version of Quicken 2000? Of course not. All versions of Quicken 2000 work with Windows 95/98, Windows NT, and Windows 2000.

I do need to point out that not all features are implemented in all versions of Quicken. For example, if you recently bought a new computer and Quicken came with it, you probably have some form of Quicken Basic 2000, which does not include the planners and a few other features, such as Alerts, QuickEntry, WebEntry support, and some reports. You'll need to remember this as you work through this book.

Conventions Used in This Book

The early chapters of this book give explicit directions for making menu selections and filling out dialog boxes with both the mouse and the keyboard. In later chapters, I simply tell you to select, click, or enter, and I leave it to you to choose the method that works best for you.

To indicate how you choose a menu command, this book uses the symbol ➢. For example, to instruct you to select the Open command from the File menu, the text says, "choose File ➢ Open."

Material that you need to type is in **boldface,** and optional steps in the procedures are *italic.*

To highlight important aspects of Quicken operations, you'll see Notes, Tips, and Warnings.

NOTE   Notes give you a little more information about a topic.

 TIP   Tips tell you a technique for getting something done more efficiently.

 WARNING   Warnings alert you to problems you may encounter in carrying out a function discussed in the text.

You will also find sidebars—short essays that relate to using the program—throughout this book. Sidebars provide useful advice and suggest how to make important decisions. Each sidebar has a title and appears in a box with a shaded background.

PART I

The ABCs of Quicken

LEARN TO:

- **Work with the Quicken Interface**

- **Record Transactions in the Quicken Register**

- **Write and Print Checks**

- **Produce Financial Reports and Charts**

- **Balance Your Bank Accounts**

CHAPTER 1

Getting Started

Y ou'll find it helpful to learn a few things about Microsoft Windows and the Quicken product before you start using Quicken. In this chapter, you'll learn the basics: how to start Quicken, how to find your way around Quicken's areas and dialog boxes, and how to get help as you use Quicken. If you've already worked with Quicken or if you're comfortable using another Windows application, you can skim this chapter—you may know most of the information, but you may likely learn something new as well.

Before You Start

In this chapter, I assume you've already done the following two things:

- You have installed the Quicken software.
- You have set up at least one bank account.

If you haven't done either of these things, refer to Appendix A. It tells you how to install Quicken and how to set up your first account.

 NOTE If you're just starting to use Quicken in a business setting—say you're the new bookkeeper—these two things will almost certainly have already been done. This chapter is the right place for you to begin.

Starting Quicken

Once you (or someone else) has installed Quicken, starting Quicken is easy. When you turn on your computer, Windows starts and then displays the Desktop, as shown in Figure 1.1. To start Quicken, double-click the Quicken shortcut.

FIGURE 1.1

The Windows Desktop

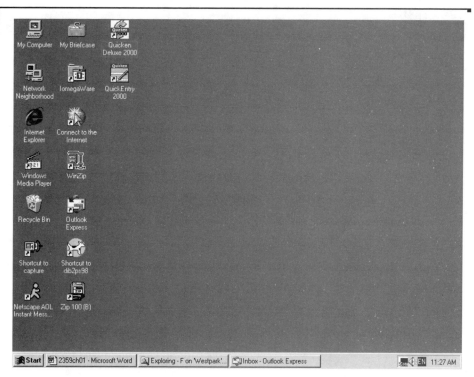

 NOTE Your Desktop probably looks a little different from the one shown in Figure 1.1 because you most likely have different software installed on your computer. You may also have a wallpaper pattern on your Desktop. If you're using the Deluxe version of Quicken 2000, your Quicken shortcut will say Quicken Deluxe 2000, as shown in the figure. If you're using a different version, the Quicken shortcut will have a slightly different name.

When you first open Quicken, you'll see the Quicken Home Page, called My Finances, as shown in Figure 1.2. From this page, you can access almost every area of Quicken and immediately accomplish most tasks. Your screen will look different from the one in Figure 1.2 depending on the number and type of accounts you've set up.

FIGURE 1.2

The Quicken Home Page

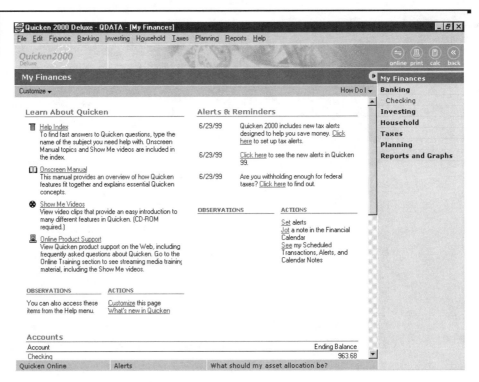

TIP To return to the Quicken Home Page at any time, click the My Finances QuickTab on the right side of your screen.

Now, let's get to the heart of the matter—the Quicken application window. Choose Finance ➤ Account List to open the Account List, as shown in Figure 1.3.

To navigate in Quicken, you can either choose commands from the menu or you can click QuickTabs. From the areas displayed, you can also click hyperlinks to move around.

NOTE Which QuickTabs you have displayed depends on where you or someone else last worked in Quicken.

FIGURE 1.3

The Account List in the Quicken application window

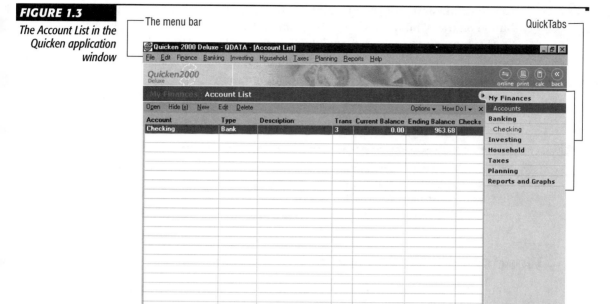

A Quick Geography Lesson in Quicken

If you haven't worked with a Windows application before, you need to learn about three things in the Windows interface: windows, menu commands, and dialog boxes. This knowledge will make using Quicken—and any other Windows application—easy and straightforward.

The Quicken Application Window

All the information Quicken displays for you appears in an *application window*. The layout of the Quicken application is very simple: The Quicken title bar and menu bar are at the top of the application window.

You can resize and relocate the Quicken application window. To do this, you use the window buttons in the top-right corner of the application window. The button that looks like a bar or hyphen minimizes the application window so it appears as a button on the Windows Taskbar. (To "unminimize" the application, simply click its Taskbar button.) The button that looks like a box with a dark top edge or a couple of boxes with dark top edges either maximizes the application window to fill the entire screen or restores a window to its previous, unminimized size. The button with the × closes the application window (which is the same thing as closing the application). To move a window, drag its title bar.

 TIP If you want more information about resizing and relocating windows and how to use the Control menu commands, refer to a good book on Windows, such as Robert Cowart's *Mastering Windows 98* (Sybex, 1998).

Working with Menus and Commands

To tell Quicken what you want it to do, you issue *commands*. For example, if you want Quicken to open a document, you choose File ➤ Open (open the File menu and select Open). A *menu* is simply a list of commands.

Much of this book talks about how you use commands to accomplish specific personal finance, investment, and business-management tasks with Quicken. To use the commands, you'll need to know how to choose commands in Quicken.

In the Windows operating environment, there are usually at least three ways to choose most commands. Let's look at these methods now. In subsequent chapters, I'll assume you've already selected the method you want to use, so I won't describe mouse-clicking or keystroke mechanics.

Using the Mouse to Select and Deselect Commands

To choose a command with a mouse, point to the menu you want to display and click the mouse's left button. (This action is called "clicking the object.")

Once you click the menu, Quicken displays it. Next, you simply click the command you want to use. For example, choosing File ➤ Print List in the Account List requires two clicks:

1. Click the File menu name.

2. Click the Print List command.

Quicken then displays the Print dialog box, as shown in Figure 1.4.

FIGURE 1.4

The Print dialog box

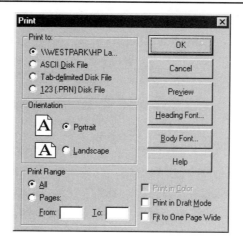

To deselect a command you've selected with the mouse, you can press the Esc key on your keyboard or click an empty area of the screen. If choosing a command causes Quicken to display a dialog box, you can close the dialog box by clicking the dialog box's Close button (the × symbol, located in the upper-right corner of the dialog box). I'll talk more about the Close button and the other Windows command buttons later in the chapter.

Using the Keyboard to Select and Deselect Commands

You can select any command using the keyboard. To do this, you perform three actions: activate the menu bar, display a menu, and then choose a command. To illustrate this, let's suppose you want to choose the File ➤ Print List command. (Go ahead and follow along with the discussion here; you can't hurt anything or damage your data.)

1. Press the Alt key and the underlined letter in the menu you want to display. For example, to activate the File menu, press Alt and then F. This activates the selected menu. To show you've selected the menu, Quicken drops down the menu, or activates it, as shown in Figure 1.5.

2. Select the command you want. You can use the ↑ and ↓ keys to highlight the command and then press Enter, or you can press the underlined letter of the command name. To select the Print List command once the File menu is displayed, you can press P.

Some menu items contain additional commands. If a command name is followed by a triangle, that command displays a menu of additional commands. For example, on the File menu, the File Operations command is followed by a triangle. This tells you that choosing the File Operations command actually displays another menu of commands.

FIGURE 1.5

The activated Quicken File menu

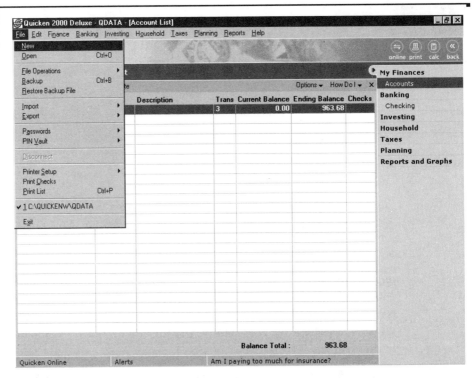

Not every command makes sense in every situation. Quicken disables commands that you shouldn't or can't choose. To identify these disabled commands, Quicken displays their names in gray letters.

NOTE You don't need to stick to one command-selection method. You can mix and match the keyboard, shortcut, and mouse methods. For example, you can display a menu using the mouse and then use the keyboard to select a command.

Using Shortcuts to Choose Commands

Take another look at Figure 1.5, which shows the Quicken File menu. To the right of some of the commands, the File menu shows key combinations. For example, to the right of the File ➤ Open command, you see the key combination Ctrl+O. To the right of the File ➤ Print List command, you see the key combination Ctrl+P. When you see such a key combination listed in a menu, this means that you can select this command in a way that bypasses the menu: Press Ctrl and hold it down, and then press the letter key. The menus must be closed and the menu bar deselected for these key combinations to work.

In Windows applications, these key combinations represent *shortcuts*; you can press a key combination to choose a command. In effect, pressing a command's shortcut key combination does two things at once: It activates the menu, and it chooses a command. If you press Ctrl+P, you choose the Print List command from the File menu. Quicken displays the Print dialog box.

You'll want to learn the shortcuts for those commands you choose over and over. You can do this just by paying attention to the menus you display. Key combinations appear to the right of many menu commands.

Navigating Quicken's Areas

Quicken uses the area beneath the menu bar to display a variety of areas. The main areas (Banking, Investing, Household, Taxes, Planning, and Reports and Graphs) contain numerous hyperlinks you can click to perform common financial tasks within the area. For example, click the Banking QuickTab and click an account's hyperlink, and Quicken displays that account's register, as shown in Figure 1.6 (which shows a checking account register). Quicken's areas display many other kinds of information as well.

FIGURE 1.6

You can display various areas within the Quicken application window. In this case, a checking account register is displayed.

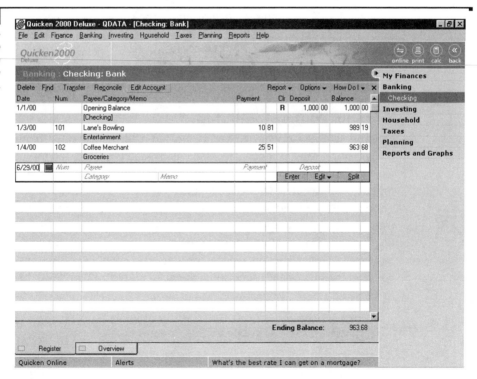

Moving Around in an Area

If the dimensions of your screen aren't big enough to display everything in an area, Windows puts a *scroll bar* along the right and bottom edges of the area. Look at the register in Figure 1.6; you'll see a vertical scroll bar along the right edge.

You can move up and down by pressing the Page Up and Page Down keys. You can also use your mouse to move up, down, left, and right. You can move up one line by clicking the up arrow at the top of the vertical scroll bar. You can move down one line by clicking the down arrow at the bottom of the vertical scroll bar. As you move up and down, Quicken moves the scroll bar marker (it's the square in the scroll bar) up or down the scroll bar. This marker shows your position relative to the entire area.

To use your mouse to move left and right, use the horizontal scroll bar. Mechanically, it works the same way as a vertical scroll bar. You can click the arrows at either end of the horizontal scroll bar to move one column to either the left or the right.

You can also *drag* the scroll bar marker in the direction you want to go. To do this, place the mouse pointer on the scroll bar marker, hold down the left mouse button, and then move the mouse up or down (or right or left). As you drag the mouse, Quicken scrolls the contents of the area.

There's still another way to scroll through an area with a mouse. You can click the scroll bar itself. For example, clicking above the vertical scroll bar's marker does the same thing as pressing the Page Up key. Clicking below the vertical scroll bar's marker does the same thing as pressing the Page Down key. Clicking to the right of this marker on the horizontal scroll bar moves to the right one screen, and clicking to the left moves to the left one screen.

Working with Multiple Areas

Quicken displays only one area at a time, but it allows you to keep multiple areas open at once. After you open an area, Quicken adds a QuickTab for it along the right edge of the application window so that you can quickly access it again. When you move to another area, Quicken displays it on top of any other open areas.

To move to another open area, you simply click its QuickTab. For example, if you want to schedule a payment, you can choose Finance ➤ Financial Calendar. Quicken displays the Financial Calendar, as shown in Figure 1.7. The QuickTabs show that the Account List and Checking register areas are also open, in addition to the main areas, which are always open. To redisplay the Account List or Checking register, just click its QuickTab.

Working with Dialog Boxes

Quicken often needs additional information from you when you tell it to execute a particular command. To get that information, the program displays a *dialog box*. Figure 1.8

shows the parts of the Print Register dialog box, which Quicken displays whenever you choose the Print Register command from the File menu. (For the Print Register command to be available on the File menu, you must display an account register.) Dialog boxes contain boxes, lists, and buttons that allow you to provide additional information.

FIGURE 1.7

The Quicken application with three extra areas open: the Account List, the Checking account register, and the Financial Calendar on top

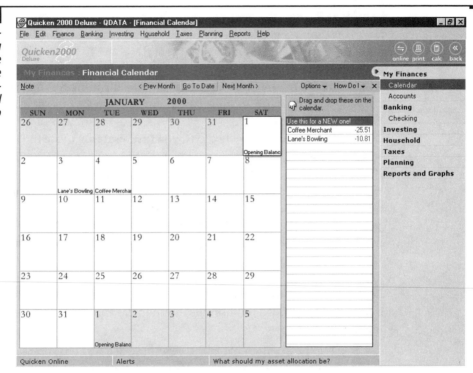

FIGURE 1.8

Elements of a dialog box

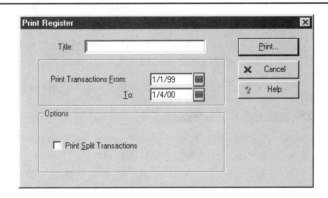

TIP You can tell which menu commands display dialog boxes. Whenever a command name is followed by three periods (...), choosing that command displays a dialog box.

Text Boxes

A *text box* is simply a blank you fill in. In the Print Register dialog box shown in Figure 1.8, the Title, the Print Transactions From, and the To blanks are text boxes. You use them to add a title or label to a register and to tell Quicken the range of dates you want a register to include. (I'll talk about actually using this dialog box to print your register in Chapter 2; for now, just focus on the mechanics of using dialog box elements.)

To enter information into a text box, you first need to activate the text box. You can do this either by clicking the text box with the mouse or by pressing Tab or Shift+Tab until the text box is highlighted.

Once you've activated the text box, you're ready to enter data in it. If a text box is empty (like the Title text box in Figure 1.8), selecting the text box simply causes Quicken to put the insertion bar (a flashing vertical I-beam) at the start of the text box.

If the text box already holds data, Quicken selects and highlights the current contents. When this is the case, you can replace the selected contents of the text box by just typing over it.

If you don't want to replace text box contents but instead want to insert or add to the current contents, you position the insertion bar at the position where you want to add new text, as follows:

- To place the insertion bar at the beginning of a text box, press the Home key or click the very first character position in the text box.

- To insert characters into the middle of the text box, you can use the ← and → keys to move the insertion bar to the point where you want to insert characters, or you can click the mouse to move the insertion bar there.

- To place the insertion bar at the end of the text box, press the End key or click after the very last character in the current text box.

Once you've positioned the insertion bar, begin typing.

Command Buttons

Command buttons tell Quicken what you want it to do with the information you've entered into the dialog box. Most dialog boxes have an OK command button, which tells Quicken to proceed to the next step. If a dialog box is displayed to collect information for a command, selecting OK initiates the command.

In some cases, the OK command button is replaced by an equivalent command button that names the action that occurs when the command is executed. For example, the Print Register dialog box doesn't provide an OK command button, but it does provide a Print command button. In this case, the Print command button is equivalent to an OK command button.

Most dialog boxes have a Cancel command button, which tells Quicken not to accept any information you've entered and to return to what you were doing before. Dialog boxes commonly provide other command buttons, too.

You can select command buttons in several ways. You can click the command button, or you can highlight the command button using the Tab and Shift+Tab keys and then activate it by pressing Enter. If a command button shows a thick, dark border—and one of the commands usually does—you can select it by pressing Enter. (The command button with the thick, dark border is the *default* command button.) If a command button's name contains an underlined letter, you can press the Alt key and the underlined letter to select the command button.

Option Buttons

Earlier in the chapter, I mentioned that Quicken displays the Home Page when you start the program. If you don't want it to do this, you can instead choose to display reminders at startup or to go straight to the area you last visited and not display either one.

 NOTE   Chapter 6 describes the ways you can customize Quicken.

When you have a mutually exclusive set of choices such as this, Quicken uses *option buttons* to present your choices. For example, in the Startup tab of the General Options dialog box, shown in Figure 1.9, the option buttons let you choose what you want displayed at startup. (To display the General Options dialog box, choose Edit ➢ Options ➢ Quicken Program.)

To mark an option button with the mouse, click it. To indicate your choice, Quicken inserts a black dot, or bullet, in the button you choose. Figure 1.9 shows the Quicken Home Page When Starting Quicken option button marked with the bullet.

To mark an option button with the keyboard, highlight the selected option button by using the Tab or Shift+Tab keys. Then use the ↑ and ↓ keys to move the bullet to one of the other option buttons. Quicken then moves the bullet to mark your choice.

FIGURE 1.9

The Startup tab in the General Options dialog box

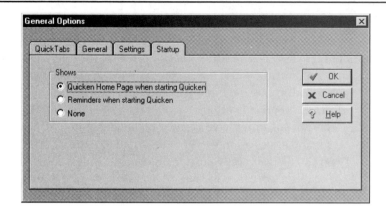

Checkboxes

Checkboxes amount to on/off switches. Figure 1.8 shows one checkbox for printing split transactions. (Don't worry if you don't understand what this checkbox does right now; I'll talk about it in a later chapter.)

The easiest way to turn on (or turn off) a checkbox is by clicking the mouse. If you click a checkbox that's turned on—indicated by a checkmark in the box—Quicken turns off the checkbox and removes the checkmark. If you click a checkbox that's turned off—one that is empty—Quicken turns on the checkbox and adds a checkmark to it.

You can also turn checkboxes on and off using the keyboard. For example, you can highlight the checkbox using the Tab and Shift+Tab keys; then you can use the spacebar to alternately turn the checkbox on and off. Or, you can press the Alt key and then the underlined letter in the checkbox name to alternately turn the checkbox on and off. Pressing Alt+S, for example, toggles the Print Split Transactions checkbox on and off.

List Boxes

If you want to choose from a series of items, Quicken uses a *list box* to display your choices. If you click the Settings tab in the General Options dialog box, you can see a variety of list box called a drop-down list box. To change the starting month of your fiscal year, you click the down arrow on the right side of the Starting Month box. This drops down the list box's list, and then you select one of the list entries by clicking it.

 NOTE Other list boxes don't require dropping-down. Instead, you just select a list entry by clicking it.

To drop down a list box, you can also select it by using the Tab or Shift+Tab keys and then press Alt+↓.

To select an entry in a drop-down list, click the entry with the mouse or highlight the entry with the arrow keys and press Enter.

When a list box is active, pressing a letter key, such as *S*, selects the first entry that starts with the letter. If a list box's entries don't fit within the list box, Quicken adds a vertical scroll bar to it. You can use it to scroll through the list box's entries.

Finding Help When You Need It

Quicken provides a couple of easy ways to access help when you need it. One method allows you to find quick answers to pressing questions, while the other allows you to browse through help information.

Getting Quick Answers in an Area

If you're struggling with a task in an area, you can find out how to accomplish it by clicking the How Do I? button. This displays a drop-down menu of common tasks in the area you're currently in, as shown in Figure 1.10. To find out how to accomplish a task listed in the menu, just select it. Quicken displays the topic in the Quicken Help window.

FIGURE 1.10

The How Do I? menu for an account register

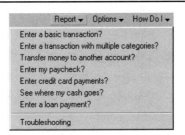

Using the Help Menu

To start the Help application, choose Help ➢ Index. This displays the Help Topics window shown in Figure 1.11, which has three tabs:

- Contents lists "books" that provide information about Quicken procedures, examples of how to set up Quicken to suit your financial needs, and expert financial advice.

- Index allows you to scroll through the index of Help topics or search for a term.

- Find allows you to search for help by entering keywords.

FIGURE 1.11

The Help application window

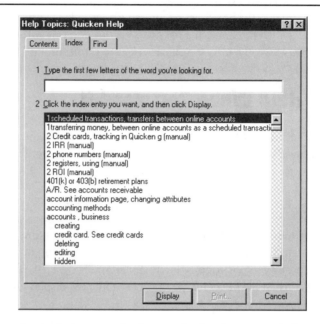

The Help menu also includes several other methods of accessing help:

Current Window   Describes the current area and contains links for accessing help in the area.

Troubleshooting This Window   Provides solutions for frequently encountered errors or difficulties in the current area.

Show Me Videos   Opens the Show Me Videos area. To play a video demonstration, insert your Quicken CD-ROM and click a hyperlink. Quicken displays a VCR-like screen that has a Play button (the one with the triangle), a Stop button (the one with the square), and a vertical slider that moves across the screen as the video plays. (Once you click the Play button, the Pause button becomes activated.)

Onscreen Manual   Lets you read through brief tutorials about using Quicken in your day-to-day record keeping and in your long-term financial planning. Just click the hyperlinks to display topics.

Product Support   Displays the Product Support dialog box, as shown in Figure 1.12. The buttons provide several options for accessing technical support:

- Troubleshoot displays troubleshooting topics for the active window.

- Go to Web connects to the Quicken Web site and lets you view answers to frequently asked questions.
- Learn More by Fax lets you request technical support via fax.
- Call for Support displays a dialog box that lists the information that Quicken's support team might ask for if you call technical support.
- System Info displays information about your hardware and operating system that can help technical support technicians diagnose and solve your technical problems.

FIGURE 1.12

The Product Support dialog box provides several options for accessing technical support.

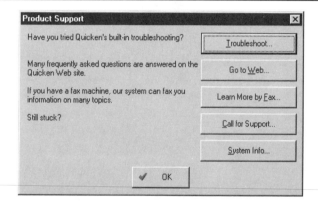

Intuit Business Solutions MS   Displays a list of other Quicken products by business category, such as Payroll and Project Costing.

About Quicken   Displays the Quicken copyright notice and the version and release numbers. To close the dialog box, just press Esc.

CHAPTER **2**

Using the Quicken Register

First things first: You'll probably want to start using Quicken by tracking the money that flows into and out of the bank account that you use most frequently. You'll be able to summarize your financial affairs in a way that you've never done before, and you'll learn the basics of working with the Quicken program.

Before You Start

Before you can use the Quicken register to track the money that flows into and out of your bank account, you need to do the following:

- Install and set up Quicken, which really means that you need to copy the Quicken application onto your hard disk and set up your first bank account. If you haven't already done these two things, refer to Appendix A.
- Learn how to work with the Windows operating environment. If you don't already know how to do this, take the time to review Chapter 1.

Recording Checks, Other Payments, and Deposits

To record transactions, you first need to display the register for the bank account you want to work with. Click the account's hyperlink in the Banking area to open that account's register.

Figure 2.1 shows a checking register in Quicken. Quicken highlights the first empty row in the register. (If the next empty row of the register isn't highlighted, you can use the ↑ and ↓ keys to highlight it, or choose Edit ➢ Transaction ➢ New.)

To record a payment from an account into the empty register row, follow these steps:

1. Enter the payment date in the Date field (text box). You may need to highlight the Date text box if it isn't already selected. Quicken automatically enters the present date based on your computer's internal clock. If the date shown isn't the transaction date, enter the date in MM/DD/YY fashion. (You don't need to enter the year number if the one Quicken already shows is correct.) When the Date text box is selected, Quicken provides several shortcuts for quickly changing the display date:

   - Press + or – to adjust the date ahead or back one day at a time. (If you press the key that shows the = and the + symbols, you don't need to hold down the Shift key; Quicken assumes you mean +.)

FIGURE 2.1

An account register

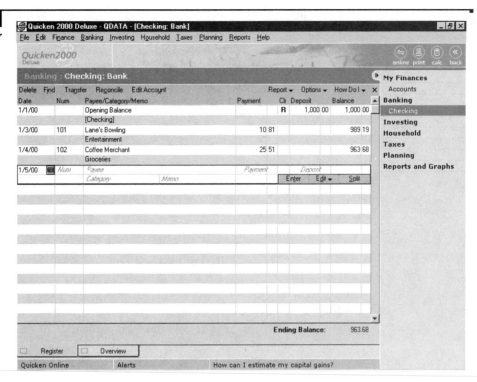

 NOTE If the current date is not correct, consult your Windows documentation for information about resetting the clock and calendar.

- Press **T** to set the date to today's date. Press **M** to adjust the date to the first day in the month and **H** to adjust the date to the last day in the month. (Quicken uses M and H because *M* is the first letter in the word *month* and *H* is the last letter.) Press **Y** to adjust the date to the first day in the year and **R** to adjust the date to the last day in the year. (*Y* is the first letter in the word *year* and *R* is the last letter.)

 NOTE You can use upper- or lowercase letters. In this case, Quicken is not case-sensitive.

- Click the button at the right end of the active Date field to open a small calendar. The calendar highlights the current month and day; you can change months by clicking the arrows at the top of the calendar and change dates by clicking the mouse directly on the date.

2. Once the date is correct, press Tab or click the Num field, which is a combo box. Quicken activates a list box that contains abbreviations for the different bank account transactions.

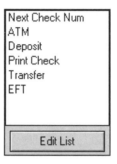

- *If you're recording a handwritten check,* type the check number, or select the Next Check Num entry to calculate the handwritten check's number by adding one to the previous check number.

- *If you're recording a cash machine withdrawal,* select the ATM entry from the list box.

- *If you're recording a deposit,* select the Deposit entry from the list box (discussed later in the chapter).

- *If you want to print checks,* use the Print Check entry to identify which checks you want to print, as described in Chapter 3.

- *If you're recording an electronic funds transfer,* select the EFT entry from the list box.

3. Move to the Payee field by clicking it or pressing Tab until you reach it. Enter the name of the payee. If this is the first time you've recorded a payment to this payee, type the payee's name. If you've paid this payee before, you can select the payee's name from the Payee drop-down list.

 TIP Using the Payee drop-down list makes it easy to use the same exact payee name every time you record a transaction from any given payee. Then you'll find it easy to summarize your spending by payee.

---

4. Move to the Payment field and enter the amount of the payment. You don't need to enter dollar signs or commas. You must use a period, however, to identify any cents.

When you enter the Payment or Deposit text box, a small calculator icon appears at the right end of the field. Clicking the calculator icon opens a small calculator. You can enter numbers by clicking the calculator's keys or by using the number keys on your keyboard. The result of the calculation appears in the Payment or Deposit field. If you use the numeric keypad on your keyboard, be sure that NumLock mode is on.

5. If you want to mark the transaction as already cleared by the bank, click in the Clr box, and a c will appear. The c indicates that you have manually cleared the transaction. When Quicken reconciles a transaction, an R appears.

Normally, you mark checks as cleared as part of reconciling a bank account (discussed in Chapter 5). If you're entering old transactions—say you're starting your Quicken record keeping as of the start of the current year and so you have some old, cleared transactions to enter—you can mark these transactions with a c in the Clr column to make your reconciliation easier.

6. Categorize the transaction by moving the cursor to the Category combo box. From the list of existing categories that appears, select the category that best describes the payment.

A check to your landlord for rent, for example, might be categorized as Rent. If you can't find an expense category that describes the payment, you can enter a short category description directly into the Category text box. If you want to create a category named, for example, Software, type **Software**, and press Tab to open the Set Up Category dialog box, as shown in Figure 2.2. The new category name you entered shows in the Name text box. If you want, enter a description of the category in the Description text box. Verify that the Expense or Subcategory Of option button is marked so Quicken knows this is a category used to track spending. Finally, mark the Tax-related checkbox if this expense category is tax deductible, and mark the Spending Is Not Discretionary checkbox if that also describes this expense.

The Subcategory Of drop-down list box allows you to create more detailed categorization. In Figure 2.2, Software is a subcategory of the category Entertainment. (Entertainment is an expense category.) When you enter software in the register, Quicken lists the category as Entertainment:Software. When you create reports, the expense accumulates in the Entertainment category. In other words, the definition of the parent category as either expense or income sets the definition for subcategories.

FIGURE 2.2

*The Set Up Category
dialog box*

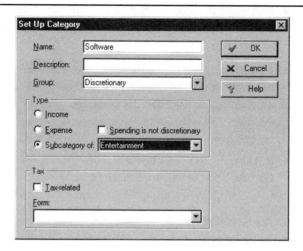

 NOTE I'll talk more about categories in later chapters. See Chapter 14 for help on setting up category lists that support your income tax planning and preparation. See Chapter 15 for a discussion about how to use categories and subcategories as budgeting tools.

7. If you want to add a memo description of the transaction, highlight the Memo text box by clicking it or by pressing Tab. Then enter a brief description. You can enter anything you want in the Memo text box, but there's no reason to duplicate information you've entered or will enter someplace else.

8. Click the Enter button (it appears just below the Deposit text box) to enter the transaction data into the register.

Quicken updates the bank account balance and highlights the next empty row in the register.

 NOTE Quicken also records transactions into the register if you press Enter when the Memo box is highlighted or if you press Ctrl+Enter when any of the text or combo boxes are highlighted.

Figure 2.3 shows a register with four checks, including a check for $51.20 to Frank's Place for software and another for $500, written to Armstrong Commons to

pay January's rent. The box at the bottom of the screen shows transactions that Quicken has memorized and now displays in the memorized transactions list.

FIGURE 2.3

Recording checks in the register

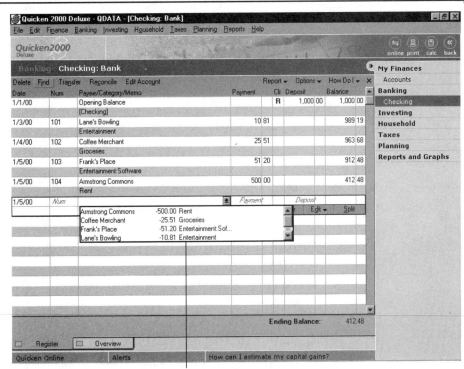

Memorized transactions list

Using QuickFill to Speed Data Entry

Quicken provides QuickFill, a data-entry aid that you run into as soon as you start recording transactions. QuickFill keeps lists of the entries you make in the Payee and Category combo boxes. (In fact, it's QuickFill's list that Quicken displays in the Payee and Category drop-down list boxes.) When you make a new entry in a text box, QuickFill matches your new entry against the first entry that looks similar in its list. Then it fills the text box with this similar-looking entry.

This sounds unwieldy, but it works wonderfully. If, for example, you enter the Payee name Armstrong Commons, the next time you begin typing something into the Payee combo box that starts out with the letters *Arm*, QuickFill completes the combo box so it shows Armstrong Commons. You can then move to the next field if

QuickFill's guess is correct. If you're typing something different from what QuickFill guesses, it's not a problem. Just keep typing. What you type replaces whatever Quick-Fill supplies.

In the case of a payee name, QuickFill does even more than fill in the Payee field. If you accept the payee name supplied by QuickFill and move to the next field, Quick-Fill fills in the rest of the transaction's fields using the previous transaction's information. For example, if you let QuickFill fill in the payee name Armstrong Commons, and then you press Tab to move to the Payment text box, QuickFill uses the amount, memo, and category information from the previous Armstrong Commons transaction. Because checks you write to the same payee usually have similar features, Quick-Fill's automatic completion saves lots of data-entry time.

Recording Deposits

To record the money that flows into an account, you record a deposit transaction into the next empty row of the register. Follow these steps:

1. To enter the deposit date, highlight the Date text box, if necessary. Enter the date in MM/DD/YY fashion. Again, you don't need to enter the year number if it's already correct.

2. To identify the transaction as a deposit, highlight the Num combo box and select the Deposit entry.

3. To enter the person or company from whom you received the money you're depositing, move to the Paid By combo box.

- *If this is the first time you've recorded a payment from this person or business*, type the person's or firm's name.

- *If you've previously recorded a check from the person or business*, type the first few letters of the payer's name. Quicken attempts to complete the name for you using QuickFill. If Quicken selects the correct name, press Tab to accept it and continue describing the transaction.

4. Highlight the Deposit text box and enter the amount. Don't enter dollar signs or commas. Do enter a period to identify the cents.

5. If the bank has already recorded the deposit you're entering into the register, click in the Clr (Clear) text box. You would probably do this only if you're entering an old transaction or the transaction is an automatic deposit, such as an automatic payroll deposit.

6. Categorize the deposit using the Category drop-down list.

A check from your employer, for example, might best be categorized as Salary. A check from a customer might best be categorized as Sales. If you can't find an income category that describes the deposit, enter a short category name directly into the Category combo box and press Enter. Quicken asks if you want to create a new category. If you do, click the Yes button. Quicken displays the Set Up Category dialog box (see Figure 2.2). Enter the category name you want to use in the Name text box. If you want, enter a description of the category in the Description text box. Verify that the Income option button is marked so that Quicken knows this is a category used to track income. Finally, mark the Tax-related checkbox if this income category is taxable (it probably is).

7. If you want to add a memo description, click in the Memo text box. Then enter a brief description. If you're depositing a payroll check, you might want to record the payroll check date or payment period. Or, if you're depositing a customer or client check, you might want to record the invoice being paid.

8. Click the Enter button to record the deposit into the register. Quicken updates the bank account balance and highlights the next empty row in the register.

Figure 2.4 shows a $1,000 payroll deposit from your fictitious employer, The Meteor Group. Note that the check is categorized as Salary.

FIGURE 2.4

The register after categorizing a deposit as Salary

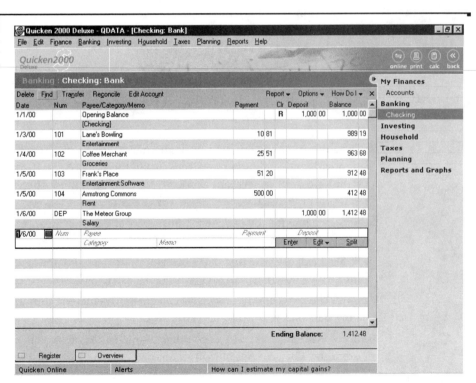

Using the Paycheck Wizard

You have two options for recording paychecks. If you want to make less work for yourself, you can record a paycheck as a simple deposit in the amount of your net earnings, as described in the preceding section. This method suffices for most people, because you really need to track only your net income, not your deductions and withholding. (Your employer keeps track of these things for you, and you need to use your employer's figures when you file your taxes.) But if you want to keep track of your deductions yourself—perhaps to monitor whether you're withholding enough in federal income taxes or to track the progress you're making in your IRA (Individual Retirement Account)—you can use Quicken's Paycheck Wizard.

The Paycheck Wizard is simple to use. Once you specify how often you get paid and describe your deductions, the Paycheck Wizard creates a scheduled transaction for your regular paychecks, so that you can record the paycheck deposit and all of the deductions withheld from the check in your Quicken register with a single mouse click. To set up a paycheck, follow these steps:

1. Choose Banking ➤ Banking Activities ➤ Set Up My Paycheck As A Register Transaction to display the Paycheck Setup dialog box. Click Next to start the Paycheck Wizard.

 TIP If you categorize a deposit as Salary, Quicken automatically prompts you to set up a paycheck. Just click Yes to launch the Paycheck Wizard.

2. Describe any additional amounts deducted from your paycheck besides the standard taxes (Quicken tracks those), and then click Next. If you regularly contribute to your retirement account, for example, mark the 401(k) Or Other Retirement Plans checkbox, as shown in Figure 2.5.

3. Enter a name for the paycheck transaction and specify how often you get paid in the dialog box Quicken provides. Click Next to continue.

4. Enter the date of the first paycheck you want to record and specify the account into which you'll deposit your paychecks. Then click Next.

5. Enter the gross and net pay, and categorize the income from the paycheck, as shown in Figure 2.6, and then click Next.

6. If you have sources of income other than straight salary (such as bonuses, for example), click the Yes button, categorize them, and enter the amounts. Click Next to begin describing your paycheck deductions.

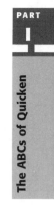

FIGURE 2.5

The Paycheck Wizard lets you specify which deductions you want to track.

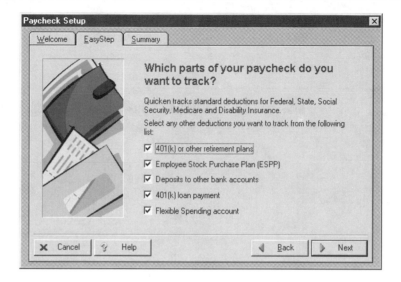

FIGURE 2.6

Entering the gross and net pay amounts from the paycheck

7. Describe the taxes deducted from your gross pay by entering the amount withheld for each tax in the corresponding Amount text box, as shown in Figure 2.7. If you don't pay a certain tax (if your state doesn't collect income taxes, for instance), leave the amount as zero. Quicken suggests categories for describing the taxes in the Category drop-down list boxes. If you want to select a different category for describing a tax, you can select one from the drop-down list. Click Next to continue.

FIGURE 2.7

Describing the taxes withheld from the paycheck

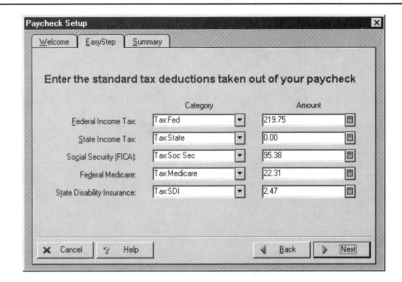

8. If other taxes are withheld from your paycheck, describe these taxes in the next dialog box Quicken displays. Then click Next.

9. If you specified in step 2 that you wanted to track any deductions beside the standard taxes, Quicken displays dialog boxes where you can describe these deductions. Click Next to describe each deduction.

10. If you had other amounts deducted from your paycheck that were not listed in step 2 and have not been accounted for, use the dialog boxes Quicken provides to describe these deductions. Then click Next.

11. Specify whether or not you want Quicken to remind you of your paycheck transaction. Then click Next to display a summary of your paycheck transaction, as shown in Figure 2.8, and click Done to record the transaction.

The scheduled paycheck transaction appears in the Reminders window whenever the paycheck deposit approaches. To enter the paycheck transaction in the register, just click the Enter in Register button.

FIGURE 2.8

Quicken displays a summary of your deductions.

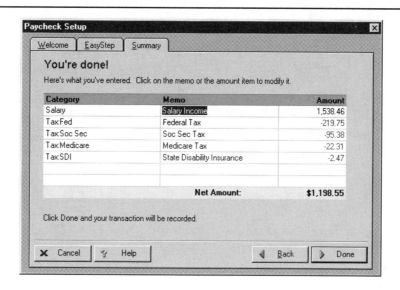

Scheduling Recurring Transactions

If you have bills you want to pay without fail every month or a paycheck you need to record every other week, Quicken's scheduled transactions feature can help you. To tell Quicken that it should automatically record a transaction, you *schedule* the transaction in one of two ways: with the Banking ➤ Scheduled Transaction List command or by using the Financial Calendar.

Scheduling a Transaction Using the Financial Calendar

To schedule a transaction using the Financial Calendar, you must first enter the transaction once in the register so that Quicken memorizes it. Then follow these steps:

1. Choose Finance ➤ Financial Calendar to display the Financial Calendar window, as shown in Figure 2.9.

The main part of the Financial Calendar window shows the current month's calendar. You can move backward and forward a month at a time by clicking the Prev Month and Next Month buttons. The list box on the right half of the window shows the memorized transactions.

FIGURE 2.9

*The Financial
Calendar*

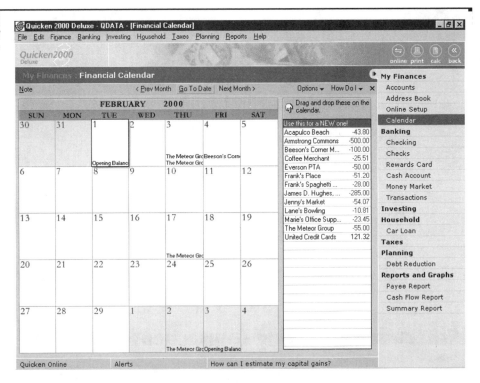

2. Display the first month you want to schedule the transaction by using the Prev Month or Next Month button.

3. Select the transaction by clicking it. Then drag the transaction to the first day it should be scheduled. Quicken displays the New Transaction dialog box, as shown in Figure 2.10. The information displayed in the dialog box describes the transaction you've just dragged.

4. Activate the Account to Use drop-down list box and choose the account into which the transaction should be recorded.

5. Activate the Type of Transaction drop-down list box to indicate whether you want Quicken to record a check, a deposit, or another type of transaction.

6. Use the next section's drop-down lists and text boxes to change any part of the recurring transaction.

7. Mark the Scheduled Transaction option.

8. Activate the How Often drop-down list box to indicate the frequency of the transaction: Only Once, Weekly, Every Two Weeks, Twice a Month, or another time period.

FIGURE 2.10

The New Transaction dialog box

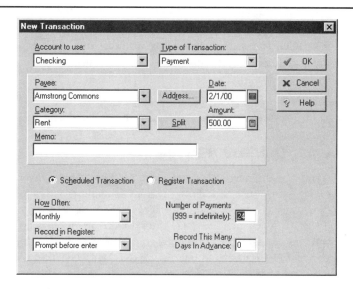

9. Use the Number of Payments text box to enter the number of payments you want Quicken to enter.

10. Use the Record in Register drop-down list box to specify whether you want Quicken to automatically enter the transaction or prompt you to enter the transaction.

11. If you want Quicken to remind you of unprinted checks, investment reminder notices, and scheduled transactions, use the Record This Many Days in Advance text box to specify the number of days of advance warning you want for this scheduled transaction.

12. Click OK.

Quicken schedules the transaction. To show the scheduled transaction, it puts the payee name on the calendar for each day the transaction will be recorded. Quicken also reminds you of scheduled transactions in the Reminders window. You can view the Reminders window by choosing Finance ➣ Reminders. With the Reminders window displayed, you can enter a scheduled transaction by selecting it and clicking the Enter In Register button. Or, you can skip the individual occurrence by clicking the Skip Payment button.

Using the Scheduled Transaction List

If you want to delete or edit a scheduled transaction, choose Banking ➣ Scheduled Transaction List. Quicken displays the Scheduled Transaction List, which lists all your scheduled transactions.

To delete a scheduled transaction, select it, click Delete, and click OK. To edit a scheduled transaction, select it, click Edit, and make your changes using the Edit Scheduled Transaction dialog box. You can also add new scheduled transactions using the Scheduled Transaction List window's New button.

MASTERING THE OPPORTUNITIES

Using QuickEntry 2000

If you need to enter only a transaction or two and don't want to start the Quicken program, you can use QuickEntry, a small, separate program that allows you to enter register transactions. To start QuickEntry, click the Windows Start button and choose Programs ➤ Quicken ➤ QuickEntry 2000. This displays an empty register for one of your Quicken accounts. You enter transactions in the QuickEntry register the same way you enter transactions in the regular Quicken register, as shown below. If you want to enter transactions into a different account, click the Accounts menu, choose an account group from the submenu, and then choose the specific account.

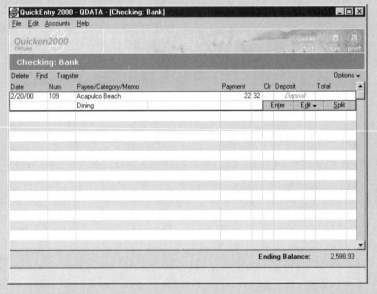

When you've finished entering transactions, click the QuickEntry application window's Close button. The next time you start Quicken, it displays the Accept Transactions dialog box shown on the facing page. Use this dialog box to accept, edit, or delete transactions entered with QuickEntry.

Continued ▐▶

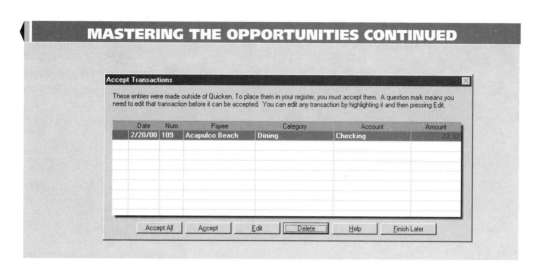

What to Do If You Make a Mistake

Your typing skills aren't perfect, of course. What's more, you will sometimes enter transactions into your registers using bad source documents (an erroneous deposit slip, for example). These little errors shouldn't cause you much concern, because Quicken provides a rich set of tools for fixing data-entry mistakes.

Fix-It Basics

If you make a mistake entering a transaction, all you need to do is change the erroneous piece of data. If you haven't yet recorded the transaction, you can move the selection cursor to the incorrect field. If you have recorded the transaction, you need to find the transaction and then highlight it either by clicking it with the mouse or by using the ↑ and ↓ keys. Then, you highlight the incorrect field by clicking it or by using the Tab and Shift+Tab keys. At this point, you can replace the incorrect entry by typing over it.

You can also edit the incorrect entry rather than replacing it altogether. Use the Backspace key to erase characters to the left of the insertion bar and then type the correct data. You can also reposition the insertion bar with the arrow keys, erase characters to the right with the Delete key, and then type the correct data.

Once you make your fix, record the transaction with the new, updated information—for example, by pressing the Enter button.

Two Fix-It Tools Everyone Should Use

Two of the fix-it tools Quicken provides are so easy and so handy that everyone—even new users—should learn to use them. The following descriptions are intentionally brief, by the way. Your best bet for learning these tools is to just start using them as soon as possible.

Tool	Why You Use It
Edit ➤ Transaction ➤ Void Transaction	To void a transaction already entered into the register. Quicken marks the transaction as void so it isn't included in account balances or category titles but leaves the transaction in the register so that you have a record of the transaction's existence.
Edit ➤ Transaction ➤ Delete	To permanently remove a transaction from the register. Quicken asks you to confirm the deletion with a message box.

Delete appears as a command button at the top of the account register and as an Edit menu command, and Delete Transaction appears as a command on the shortcut menu that you see when you select the entry in the register and click the Edit command button. Likewise, Edit Transaction appears on this shortcut menu.

 NOTE Alongside the Enter and Edit command buttons, the account register contains a Split button. I'll talk about how to use this button in the "Split Transactions" section later in this chapter.

More Editing Tools

Once you're comfortable with the two fix-it tools just described, you may want to use the more powerful fix-it commands Quicken provides: Copy, Cut, Paste, Find, Find/ Replace, and Recategorize.

Cutting, Copying, and Pasting Data

With the Copy, Cut, and Paste commands, you can copy or cut the contents of one text or combo box and paste them into another text or combo box. This means that you can move text easily if you've stuck something into the wrong text box. It also means you can type something once and then copy it (or a portion of it) as many times as you need.

To copy and cut text box contents, you follow the same basic process:

1. Select the text box containing the text.

2. Highlight the chunk of text by dragging the mouse over it or by positioning the insertion bar at the start of the text and holding down the Shift key while using the right arrow key.

3. Once you've selected the text, choose the Edit ➤ Copy or Edit ➤ Cut command. Copying duplicates the selected text and stores the duplicate copy in the Windows Clipboard, a temporary storage area. Cutting moves the selected text to the Windows Clipboard.

4. To indicate where you want to place the copied or cut item, first identify the text or combo box by selecting it. Then use the mouse or the arrow keys to move the insertion bar within the text or combo box to the location where you want to place the text.

5. Once you've indicated the destination location, choose Edit ➤ Paste.

NOTE The Cut, Copy, and Paste commands are supported by the Windows operating environment, and they appear in most Windows applications. This means you can copy and cut chunks of text among different Windows applications. For example, you can select a chunk of text in Quicken, copy or cut the text to store it in the Clipboard, switch to another application, and then use that application's Paste command to move the text stored in the Clipboard to a text box there.

Finding a Transaction

If you know you made a mistake but don't know where, you can use the Find and Find/Replace commands. Let's look at the Find command first.

Find locates transactions within a register. To choose this command, choose Edit ➤ Find & Replace ➤ Find or click the Find command button at the top of the register. Quicken displays the Quicken Find dialog box, as shown in Figure 2.11. Enter whatever it is you're looking for in the Find text box. In the case of an error, for example, this might be a name you misspelled.

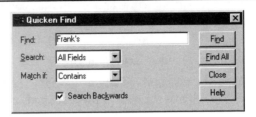

Use the Search drop-down list box to specify which fields you want to search. If you activate the drop-down list, you can choose any or all of the fields you fill in as part of recording a transaction into your register.

Use the Match If drop-down list box to specify what constitutes a match:

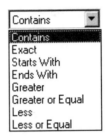

You can specify, for example, that the match be exact—in other words, that the bit of text or the number you entered in the Find text box must exactly match a field's contents in order for Quicken to consider the pair as matched. Or, you can specify that the text you entered in the Find box only match what starts or ends a field's contents. The Match If drop-down list also provides a complete set of mathematical operators such as greater, less, greater or equal, less or equal, and so on, just in case you want to search for an amount.

Quicken also provides three wildcard characters that you can use in the Find text box:

- A question mark (?) can stand for any single character. If you specify **?at**, for example, Quicken will find *bat*, *cat*, *hat*, and so on—any three-letter word that ends with the letters *at*.

- Two periods (..) stand for any group of characters. You can use the two periods at the beginning, in the middle, or at the end of the word or text. If you specify **..ville**, for example, Quicken will find *Marysville*, *Seville*, *Coupe de ville*, and so on.

- The tilde character (~) indicates you want to find a field that doesn't contain an entry. For example, if you want to find a transaction that doesn't use the category Household, enter **~Household**.

You can also combine wildcard characters. For example, the Find text entry ~**?at** will find fields that don't contain three-letter words ending with the letters *at*.

Once you've described the search criteria, choose the Find command button. Quicken searches from the selected transaction backward. (You can unmark the Search Backwards checkbox if you want to search from the selected transaction forward.) If Quicken finds a transaction that matches your search criteria, it activates the register but leaves the Find dialog box open in case you want to use it again. You can click the transaction to make a change to it. You can continue your search by clicking in the Find dialog box and selecting the Find command button again. When you finish with the Find dialog box, click its Close button.

If you want to build a list of all the transactions that match the search criteria, select the Quicken Find dialog box's Find All command button. Quicken displays a list of matching transactions in the Quicken Find document window, as shown in Figure 2.12.

FIGURE 2.12

When you choose the Find All command button in the Quicken Find dialog box, Quicken builds a list of transactions that match your search criteria.

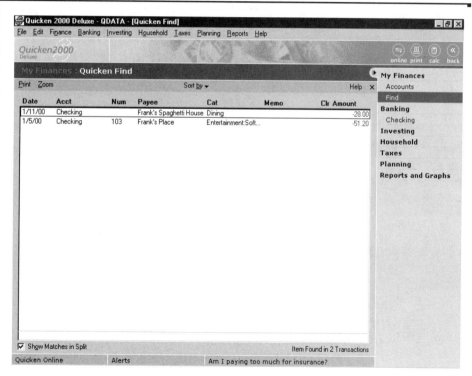

To edit a transaction or see it in complete detail, double-click it in the list or select it with the arrow keys and then press Enter. (This tells Quicken to select the transaction in the register.) When you've finished, choose the Close button to remove the matching transactions list and the Quicken Find document window.

You can also sort a register to find a transaction by clicking on a column heading to sort by that column.

The Replace Command for Making Many Transaction Changes

Edit ➤ Find & Replace ➤ Find/Replace lets you change a field in all the transactions that match your search criteria. When you choose Edit ➤ Find & Replace ➤ Find/Replace, Quicken displays the Find and Replace dialog box, as shown in Figure 2.13.

FIGURE 2.13

The Find and Replace dialog box lets you make editing changes to a set of transactions that match your search criteria.

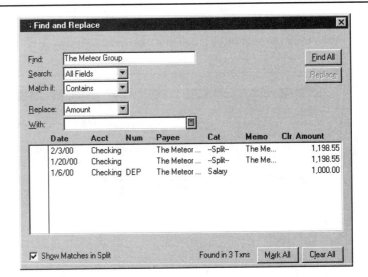

In the Find and Replace dialog box, you can use the Find, Search, and Match If boxes in the same way you use their counterparts in the Quicken Find dialog box. Once you've entered the search criteria using these boxes, you select the Find All command button to locate all the transactions that match your search criteria. Quicken then displays these matching transactions in a list box at the bottom of the dialog box. You use the Replace drop-down list box to specify which field in the matching transactions you want to change. If you want to change the amount, for example, activate the Replace drop-down list box and select Amount. Use the With text box to specify the replacement text or value.

If you enter a value in the Find text box, Quicken assumes that you are trying to find an amount and makes Amount the default selection in the Replace drop-down list. Once you enter the value in the Find text box, press Enter or click Find All to locate all the Amount transactions.

To specify which matching transactions you actually want to replace with the contents of the With box, click each transaction to mark it with a checkmark. Use the Mark All button to add a checkmark to all the matching transactions. Use the Clear All button to remove checkmarks from all the matching transactions.

When only the transactions you want to change are marked with checkmarks, click the Replace button. Quicken displays a message box asking you to confirm your change. Select OK. Quicken then makes the replacements and displays a message box that tells you the number of replacements made.

Using the Quicken Calculator

Quicken includes a simple pop-up calculator. You can start the calculator by clicking the calc button in the upper-right corner above the QuickTabs. Quicken starts the calculator shown in Figure 2.14 and displays it on top of the Quicken application window.

The Quicken calculator

To add two numbers, such as 24 and 93, type the first number, the plus symbol, the second number, and then click the equal sign or press Enter:

24+93=

If you want to use the mouse, click the calculator's keys. For example, to enter the value 24, click the 2 and then the 4. (The calculator displays 24 if you do this.)

To subtract one number from another, such as 5 from 25, enter the first number, the minus symbol, the second number, and then the equal sign:

25–5=

To multiply or divide numbers with the calculator, simply use the times symbol as the multiplication operator or the slash symbol as the division operator. For example, to multiply 25 by 1,250, enter the following:

25×1250=

And to divide 32,000 by 4, enter the following:

32000/4=

The MR, MS, and MC buttons recall, save, and clear entries from the calculator memory.

To place the value shown on the calculator display into a text box in the application window, select the text box and then select the calculator's Paste command button.

When you've finished working with the calculator, you can click the calculator's Close button, or you can click anywhere on the Quicken application window to make Quicken the active window. If you make the Quicken application window active, the calculator remains visible on your screen.

Setting Up Additional Bank Accounts

As part of installing Quicken, you set up at least one bank account. You'll want to set up additional accounts in Quicken for each of your other bank accounts so that you can track the account balances and the money flowing into and out of all of them.

Adding a New Bank Account

To set up another bank account, follow these steps:

1. Click the Banking QuickTab and then click the Create A New Account hyperlink to display the Create New Account window, as shown in Figure 2.15.

2. Click the Checking, Savings, or Money Market option button to tell Quicken that you want to set up another bank account and then click Next. No matter which button you choose, the process works the same: Quicken next displays the Checking Account Setup dialog box, Savings Account Setup dialog box, or Money Market Account Setup dialog box.

Later chapters describe how you set up and why you use the other account types shown in Figure 2.15. For now, concentrate on setting up a checking, savings, or money market account.

3. Click the Summary tab so that Quicken displays in just one place text boxes and buttons for all the information you need to collect, as shown in Figure 2.16.

4. In the Account Name text box, enter a bank account name.

5. In the Description text box, you have the option of describing the account in more detail, such as by providing the bank name or account number.

6. Enter the bank account balance and bank statement date information in the text boxes provided. As noted in Appendix A, unless you have meticulous records, the best approach is usually to use the current balance from your bank statement and then adjust this balance (so it's correct) by recording any uncleared transactions.

7. Indicate whether this account is one you'll use for online banking or bill paying. If you do this, Quicken will ask you for some additional information about the bank. See Chapter 9 for more information about online banking and bill paying.

FIGURE 2.15

The Create New Account window

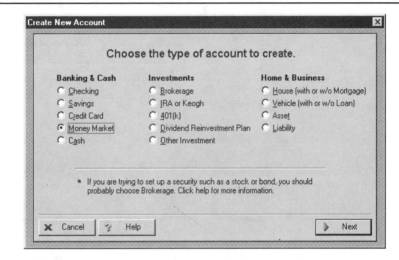

FIGURE 2.16

The Summary tab of the Account Setup dialog box lets you enter all the information needed to set up a typical account.

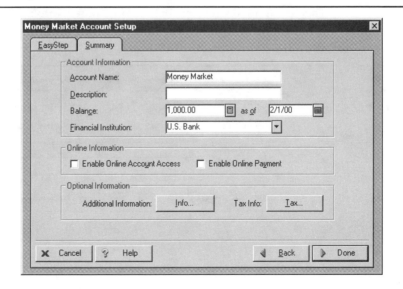

8. Optionally, click the Info button to display the dialog box shown in Figure 2.17. This lets you collect and store more information about the account, including the bank name, the account number, the name of the person you deal with at the bank (such as a personal banker, private banker, or loan officer), the telephone number, and so forth. You can typically get all of this information from your last bank statement. When you finish entering this information—if you do enter it—click OK.

FIGURE 2.17

*The Additional
Account Information
dialog box*

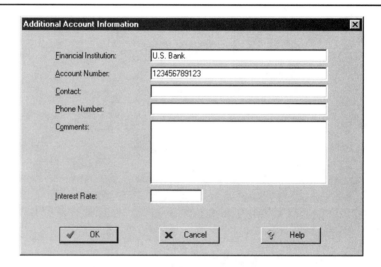

9. If you like, you can also add information about taxes. Click the Tax button in the Account Setup dialog box to display the dialog box shown in Figure 2.18. This lets you tell Quicken that moving money into and out of this checking account has an impact on your income taxes.

FIGURE 2.18

*The Tax Schedule
Information dialog box*

Most people won't need to worry about the Tax button. However, if your transactions affect your taxes, you should keep track of that information. For example, if you're keeping IRA money in a checking account or money market account and then writing checks on this account as a way to withdraw money from the IRA account, you probably want to click the Tax button. When Quicken displays the Tax Schedule Information dialog box, mark the Tax-Deferred or Tax-Exempt Account checkbox. Then use the Transfers In drop-down list box to specify which tax form and line transfers into this account should be reported. Use the Transfers Out drop-down list box to specify which tax form and line transfers (or withdrawals) from this account should be reported. When you finish entering this information, click OK.

10. Click Next if you indicated that you will use online banking or online bill payment. (Quicken provides a Next button only if you indicated you will do this.) Quicken prompts you for the information it needs to connect to your bank electronically. If you're banking online or paying bills online, you'll have received a welcome letter from your bank. This welcome letter provides the information you need to answer the questions that Quicken asks.

11. Click Done.

When you're displaying an account register, you can click the Overview tab at the bottom of the screen to display and edit the details of the account.

Copying Transactions into an Account

You can copy transactions from an existing account into a new account (or a new file). If you need to copy only a few transactions, the easiest way is to print a copy of the account register (see "Printing an Account Register" later in this chapter), and then enter the transactions individually into the new account.

When you want to copy a number of transactions, you can save time by exporting the transactions as a QIF file and then importing them back into the new account:

- To export the transactions, choose File ➤ Export ➤ QIF File. In the QIF Export dialog box, enter a name for the QIF file in the QIF File to Export To text box, select the account from which you want to export transactions, and enter the date range of transactions you want to export. Mark the Transactions checkbox, and then click OK.

- To import transactions into an account, open the Quicken file containing the account and choose File ➤ Import ➤ QIF File. In the QIF Import dialog box, enter the name of the QIF file you exported in the QIF File to Import text box, select the account to which you want to import the transactions, and click OK. Quicken copies the transactions into the account.

Transferring Money between Accounts

Once you start working with multiple accounts, you'll need to know how to record account transfers—movements of money from one account to another account.

Recording account transfers in an account register is very easy. Enter the date in the Date field, and then press Tab to move to the Num field. When you do, the Num field becomes a drop-down list box. Click the arrow button and select Transfer, and then enter the amount in the Payment or Deposit field, depending on whether you're transferring the money out of or into the account whose register you currently have displayed. Tab to the Xfer Acct field (Quicken replaces the Category field name with Xfer Acct when you choose Transfer in the Num field) and select the account to or from which you wish to transfer the funds from the drop-down list. Figure 2.19 shows an account transfer: $250 deposited into the money market account from the checking account. To identify the transaction as an account transfer, Quicken places brackets around the account name.

FIGURE 2.19

The last entry in the register is an account transfer transaction, with money transferred from the checking account to the money market account.

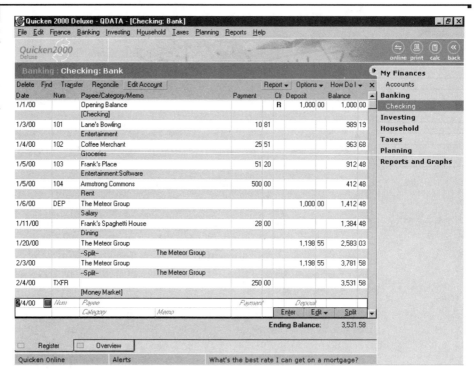

You can also use the Transfer dialog box, shown in Figure 2.20, to record account transfers. To use the Transfer dialog box, select the Transfer button that appears at the top of the register. Then, use the text and combo boxes it provides to give the transfer date and amount as well as the names of the accounts the money moves between. Using the Transfer dialog box to record transfers has a couple of advantages over using the account register to record transfers:

- The Transfer dialog box visually shows you that only four pieces of information are necessary to record a transfer.

- You aren't limited to recording a transfer transaction from or to the account shown in the active register. You can specify any source or destination account.

FIGURE 2.20

The Transfer dialog box

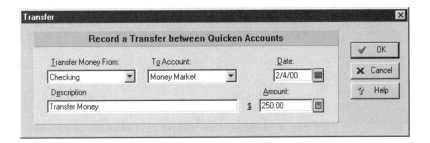

Quicken is clever about how it records account transfers. If you enter a transfer transaction into, say, the checking account, and the transaction shows the money as going into the money market account, Quicken also enters the transfer transaction into the money market account. For example, if you did enter the transfer transaction shown in Figure 2.20, Quicken would record the related transfer transaction into the money market account register, as shown in Figure 2.21.

If you edit a transfer transaction in one register, Quicken may even update the matching transfer transaction in the other register. Changes to a transfer transaction's date or amount, for example, are made to the matching transfer transaction, too. (However, changes to a transfer transaction's other fields—such as its check number, memo description, and cleared status—don't get made to the matching transfer transaction.)

 TIP You can flip between the two sides of a transfer very easily. If the highlighted transaction in a register is a transfer, choose Edit ➤ Transaction ➤ Go to Transfer to move to the other side of the transfer.

FIGURE 2.21

The other side of the
transfer transaction

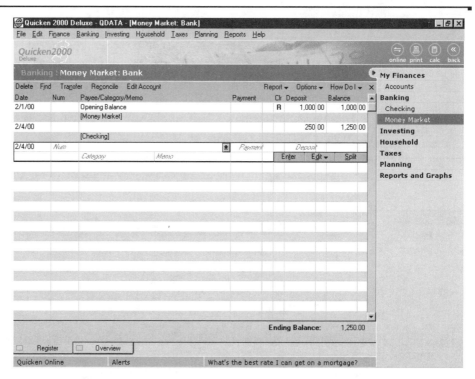

Split Transactions

Not every check you write can be fairly categorized using a single category. For example, a check written to a particular supermarket covering both groceries and automobile supplies can't be described using a single category.

Similarly, not every deposit you make can be fairly categorized using a single category. A check that includes your regular wages and a reimbursement for travel expenses can't be described entirely as wages (or as expense reimbursement). Fortunately, Quicken provides a handy way to deal with this record-keeping reality: split transactions.

Making a Split Transaction

Suppose you want to record a $100 check that pays $75 of groceries and $25 of birthday gifts. To record this check, you follow the same steps you use to record any other check. But when you get to the step where you're supposed to enter the category, you select the Split button, which appears in the row for the transaction (just below the Balance column) when the transaction is selected. When you select Split, Quicken displays the Split Transaction Window, as shown in Figure 2.22.

Here's what you do to use the Split Transaction Window:

1. Categorize the first expense paid with the check: Place the cursor in the first Category combo box. Activate the drop-down list. Then, choose the first spending category—in this case, it's Groceries—paid with the check.

2. If you want a memo description of the expenditure, place the cursor in the first Memo text box. Then enter a description of the expenditure.

FIGURE 2.22

The Split Transaction Window

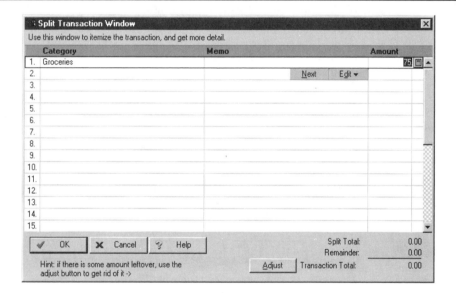

3. Enter the first expense category amount: Place the cursor in the first Amount text box and enter the amount. (Because the first spending category is Groceries and you spent $75 on groceries, type **75**.)

 TIP You don't need to enter split amounts in dollars. If you enter a percentage amount, such as **75%**, Quicken calculates the split amount by multiplying the split percentage by the transaction total. If the transaction total is $100 and you enter a split transaction amount as **75%**, Quicken calculates 75 percent of 100 and enters $75 as the split transaction amount.

4. Repeat steps 1 through 3 for the other spending category, Gifts Given.

To record a transaction with more than two spending categories, repeat steps 1 through 3 as many times as necessary. If you need more than eight categories to split the transaction, use the vertical scroll bar in the Split Transaction Window to page down to more split transaction lines. You can split a transaction into as many as 30 categories.

5. Verify that the split transaction lines agree with the register.

When you finish describing each of the spending categories for a check, the total of the individual split transaction lines you've entered should agree with the payment you entered. If it doesn't, you can click the Adjust button in the Split Transaction Window to adjust the Payment amount shown in the register to whatever the split transaction lines total. In addition, you can either enter additional split transaction lines or adjust one of the split transaction lines already entered.

 TIP You can easily tell whether the total of the split transaction lines equals the payment amount entered in the register. Quicken uses the empty split transaction line beneath the last split transaction you entered to show the difference between the payment amount and the total of the individual split transaction lines.

Figure 2.23 shows the Split Transaction Window filled out to record a $100 check that pays $75 for groceries and $25 for gifts.

FIGURE 2.23

A completed Split Transaction Window, recording $75 of groceries expense and $25 of gift expense

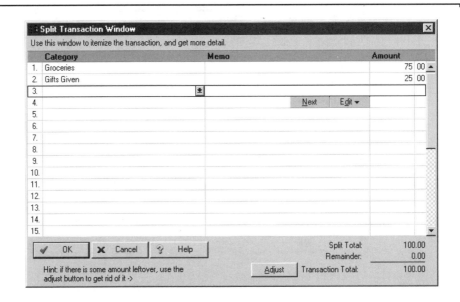

Removing a Split Transaction

To remove a split transaction—a split category and amount shown in the Split Transaction Window—select Split in the Category field and click the X button next to it. You might use this technique, for example, to delete an erroneous split transaction line. You can click the checkmark button to go back to the Split Transaction Window.

 NOTE Splitting deposit transactions works the same way as splitting payment transactions. You enter the deposit in the usual way, including the deposit amount. Then, when you get to the Category combo box, click the Split command button. Quicken displays the Split Transaction Window, and you describe each of the income categories in a deposit using different split transaction lines.

Splitting Combined Transactions

You now know how to use more than one expense category to describe a payment and how to use more than one income category to describe a deposit. But you aren't limited to using just expense or just income categories on a split transaction. You can, in effect, mix and match your categories.

For example, if you go to the bank and deposit your $1,000 payroll check but keep $25 of cash for Friday-night fun, you would fill out the Split Transaction Window as shown in Figure 2.24. Your net deposit is really $975. You would record the deposit amount as $975, of course.

One thing that's initially tricky about splitting combined income and expense transactions is the sign of the split transaction line amounts. In Figure 2.24, for example, the $1,000 of salary shows as positive and the $25 of recreation shows as negative. (On a color monitor, the negative $25 also shows in red to further identify the value as a negative number.) However, this isn't because salary income increases the account balance or because recreation expense decreases the account balance. Quicken just adds up the amount of the split transaction lines. So you use negative split transaction amounts, such as the $25 of recreation expense, to reduce the total split transaction lines.

Say, for example, you want to record the purchase of an item your employer manufactures—a new $1,500 hot tub. If you'll pay $500 by writing a check and will also forfeit a $1,000 payroll check, you would record this split transaction as shown in Figure 2.25.

NOTE You can also use the Split Transaction Window to describe account transfers. Chapter 20 shows how you split transactions between expense categories and account transfers as part of preparing employee payroll.

FIGURE 2.24

A completed Split Transaction Window, recording $1,000 of salary income and $25 of recreation expense

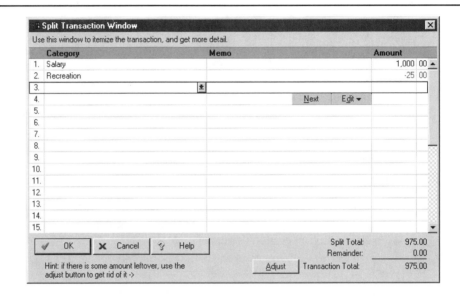

FIGURE 2.25

A completed Split Transaction Window, recording $1,000 of salary income and $1,500 of household expense

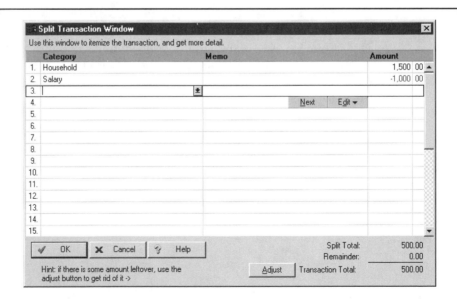

Changing a Split Transaction

Editing the details of a split transaction works very much like you might expect, with one minor exception.

To display the Split Transaction Window so that you can make changes, click the Split button or click the button that has a checkmark. In the Split Transaction Window, you can make whatever changes you want by replacing categories, memo descriptions, or amounts. You make these changes by clicking the text box you want to change and then typing the new information.

You can also remove the splits from a transaction. In other words, you can tell Quicken you want to "unsplit" a transaction. To do this, click the Cancel button—it looks like a small *X*—that appears next to the Category drop-down list, as you can see in Figure 2.26.

FIGURE 2.26

Quicken adds buttons next to a split transaction.

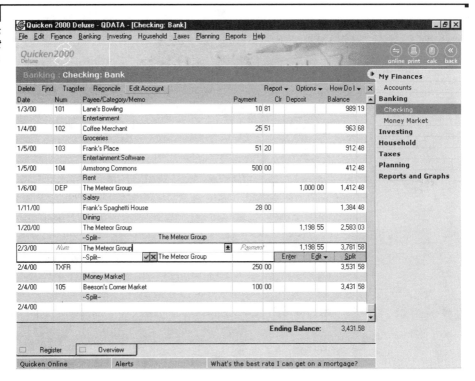

The most common reason that you will want to "unsplit" a transaction is that QuickFill has filled out the Split Transaction Window for you even though it shouldn't have. For example, if you write a $100 check to Beeson's Corner Market and split the check as $75 groceries and $25 gifts, Quicken's QuickFill feature memorizes this information. The next time you write a check to Beeson's Corner Market, QuickFill copies all the information you used to describe the last check, including the split-transaction information. If the new check to Beeson's, however, is only for groceries, you'll want to "unsplit" the transaction.

 NOTE There's nothing wrong with having only a single split transaction line. Everything still works correctly within Quicken. The only disadvantage of this single split transaction line is that you need to select the transaction and open the Split Transaction Window to see how a check or a deposit was categorized.

Register Record-Keeping Tricks

If you're just getting started with a checkbook program like Quicken, incorporating the program into your record-keeping routines can be a little awkward. To ease this process, here is a handful of helpful ideas:

- Batch your payment and deposits together so that you can enter them as a group. Starting Quicken and displaying an account register isn't difficult, but doing it several times a day for every transaction is time-consuming. You'll find it works best to sit down, say, once a week and enter the previous week's transactions. This should also work fine for businesses. Even large businesses don't pay bills every day. They batch them and then process them together once or twice a week.

- Keep documentation of the checks you write by hand so that you can remember, for example, what you paid with check 1245. (Duplicate checks are handy because you always create a record of the checks you write by hand.)

- Be sure to keep the documentation—deposit slips, ATM receipts, and so forth—that describes the other transactions you'll want to enter into your register. Again, because you won't be carrying your computer around with you everywhere you go, you'll want some paper documentation you can review whenever you do sit down at your computer to do financial record keeping.

Printing an Account Register

It's a good idea to print an account register at the end of the month. This paper record provides a hard copy of the transactions you've entered and acts as a permanent backup copy of your financial records. You can keep this copy with the bank account statement you receive. (You probably won't need the register unless you someday need to restore your financial records from a backup copy.)

To print an account register, first display the account in the register. Then follow these steps:

1. Choose File ➤ Print Register to display the Print Register dialog box, as shown in Figure 2.27.

FIGURE 2.27

The Print Register dialog box

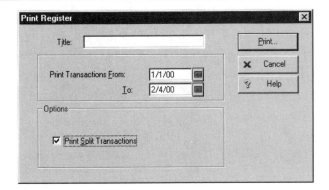

2. If you want to enter a title for the register, use the Title text box. If you don't enter a title, Quicken uses Account Register for the title.

3. Enter the range of dates you want the register to include using the Print Transactions From and To text boxes.

 TIP If you look closely at the Print Transactions From and To text boxes, you'll see something that resembles (sort of) a small calendar. Click this calendar to display a pop-up calendar you can use to quickly enter a date into the text box. The calendar highlights the date already shown in the text box, but you can change the month by clicking the arrows at the top of the calendar and change the date by clicking the mouse directly on the date.

4. If you want to print split transaction information—and you probably do if you've been splitting transactions—mark the Print Split Transactions checkbox.

5. Click the Print command button when you're ready to print. Quicken displays another Print dialog box, as shown in Figure 2.28. (See Chapter 4 for information about how to use the Print dialog box to control the way Quicken prints reports such as the register.)

6. Click OK. Quicken passes the register information to Windows, and it prints your register. Figure 2.29 shows a printed Quicken check register.

FIGURE 2.28

The Print dialog box

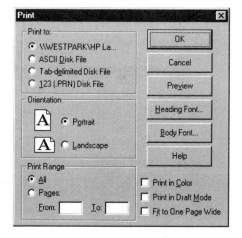

FIGURE 2.29

A printed Quicken check register

Check Register

Page 1

Checking
2/4/2000

Date	Num	Transaction	Payment	C	Deposit	Balance
1/1/2000		Opening Balance cat: [Checking]		R	1,000.00	1,000.00
1/3/2000	101	Lane's Bowling cat: Entertainment	10.81			989.19
1/4/2000	102	Coffee Merchant cat: Groceries	25.51			963.68
1/5/2000	103	Frank's Place cat: Entertainment:Software	51.20			912.48
1/5/2000	104	Armstrong Commons cat: Rent	500.00			412.48
1/6/2000	DEP	The Meteor Group cat: Salary			1,000.00	1,412.48
1/11/2000		Frank's Spaghetti House cat: Dining	28.00			1,384.48
1/20/2000		The Meteor Group SPLIT Salary memo: The Meteor Group			1,198.55	2,583.03
		Salary Salary Income			1,538.46	
		Tax:Fed Federal Tax	219.75			
		Tax:Soc Sec Soc Sec Tax	95.38			
		Tax:Medicare Medicare Tax	22.31			
		Tax:SDI State Disability Insurance	2.47			
2/3/2000		The Meteor Group SPLIT Salary memo: The Meteor Group			1,198.55	3,781.58
		Salary Salary Income			1,538.46	
		Tax:Fed Federal Tax	219.75			
		Tax:Soc Sec Soc Sec Tax	95.38			
		Tax:Medicare Medicare Tax	22.31			
		Tax:SDI State Disability Insurance	2.47			
2/4/2000	TXFR	cat: [Money Market]	250.00			3,531.58
2/4/2000	105	Beeson's Corner Market SPLIT Groceries	100.00			3,431.58
		Groceries	75.00			
		Gifts Given	25.00			

CHAPTER **3**

Printing Checks

Once you've worked a bit with a Quicken register and used it to track a bank account balance and the money that flows into and out of an account, you'll want to consider printing checks using Quicken. Doing so will save you time, particularly if you now handwrite a lot of checks. What's more, printing checks with Quicken lets you produce professional-looking, accurate checks.

Before You Begin

Before you can print checks in Quicken, you need to do the following:

- Install the Quicken program, through Windows, and set up a bank account (see Appendix A).
- Order and receive the check forms you'll print. You'll find check order-form information in your Quicken packaging. You can also order checks online. Choose Banking ➢ Banking Activities ➢ Order Checks To Print With Quicken.

Collecting Check Information

Once you've completed the prerequisites, you're ready to begin describing the checks you want to print. You'll find it much easier to print checks if you're already familiar with the Quicken register. If you've been using the Quicken register to track a bank account, you'll notice that many of the steps are identical; the only difference is that Quicken supplies a different area for you to use.

Telling Quicken You Want to Write Checks on an Account

To tell Quicken you want to write checks, open the register for the account that you want to use, and then choose Banking ➢ Write Checks. Figure 3.1 shows the Write Checks area for a checking account. At the bottom of the Write Checks area, you can see tabs for each of your bank accounts. To choose another account on which you want to write a check, just click that account's tab.

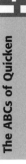

FIGURE 3.1

The Write Checks area

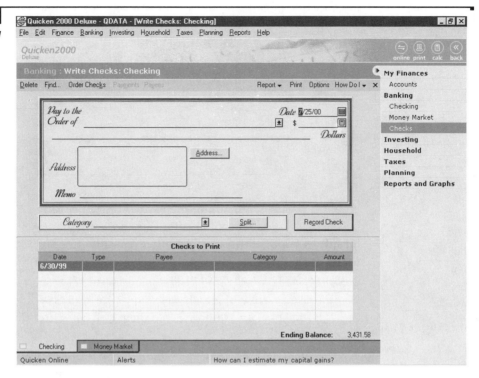

Describing a Check You Want Quicken to Print

Once you've identified the account and displayed the Write Checks area, you're ready to start writing checks. This process largely mirrors the process you use for recording a handwritten check into the Quicken register.

To describe a check you want Quicken to print, follow these steps:

1. If the date shown in the Date field (which automatically shows the current date) isn't the date that you want to print on the check, highlight the date and enter the correct date in MM/DD/YY format. You don't need to enter the year number unless the one Quicken already shows is incorrect.

 NOTE Quicken provides shortcuts you can use to set the date. They are described in Chapter 2.

2. Enter the name of the payee in the Pay to the Order of field. If this is the first time you've recorded a payment to this payee, just type the payee's name. If you've written a check to this payee before, you can activate the Pay to the Order of drop-down list by clicking the button at the right side of the field. Then you can choose the payee name from the list of payees.

3. Enter the payment amount in the Payment field beneath the date. You don't need to enter a dollar sign or comma (to separate thousands), but you must include a period to identify cents. After you enter the payment amount, press the Tab key. Quicken writes out the payment amount in words on the line below the Pay to the Order of field.

4. If you'll use an envelope with a window (the address you enter will show through the envelope window), type the payee name and the address in the Address block.

5. If you want to add a memo description, move to the Memo line and enter a brief description. You can enter anything you want into this field. (Note that there's no reason to duplicate information you've entered or will enter some-place else.) If a check pays a particular invoice or involves a specific account, consider using the Memo field to record this bit of information.

6. Categorize the transaction by using the Category drop-down list:

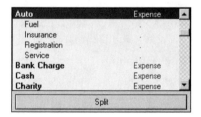

If you can't find an expense category that describes the payment, you can enter a category description directly into the Category field and press Tab to open the Set Up Category dialog box, as shown in Figure 3.2. Optionally, enter a description of the category in the Description text box. Verify that the Expense option button is marked so Quicken knows this is a category used to track spending.

Finally, mark the Tax-related checkbox if this expense category is tax deductible. (See Chapters 2 and 14 for more information about setting up and using categories.) Click OK when you've finished.

FIGURE 3.2

The Set Up Category dialog box

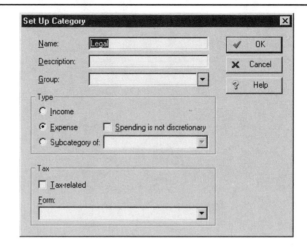

7. Click Record Check to record the check.

Quicken updates the bank account balance and displays a new blank check for you to write. Quicken also tells you the total value of the checks you have to print on the To Print line. In addition, if you've set the display properties of your monitor to a resolution higher than 640 × 480, Quicken even displays a Checks to Print box that lists the important information about each check. Figure 3.3 shows a $285 check written to James D. Hughes, Attorney, to pay a legal bill. The check is categorized as Legal. (A little later in the chapter, you'll see what this check looks like when it's printed.)

 TIP Changing your monitor resolution to 800 ¥ 600 or better allows you to fit more elements on your screen at once. To change your monitor's display properties, minimize all open application windows and right-click on your Desktop. Then choose the shortcut menu's Properties command. Click the Settings tab and move the Desktop Area slider to the right so that it reads 800 by 600 pixels. (If it won't slide past 640 ¥ 480, your monitor cannot work at a higher resolution.) Then click OK twice. Windows resizes your Desktop. Click Yes to keep the new resolution setting.

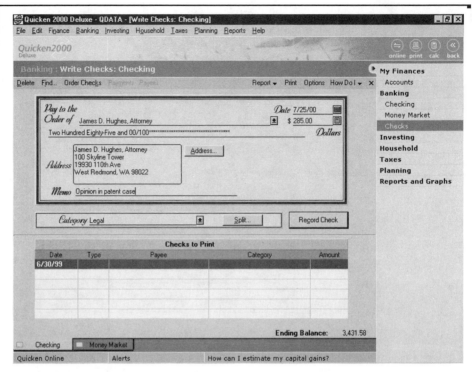

FIGURE 3.3

*A completed
check form*

Some Notes about Check Writing

When you click the Record Check command button or press Enter to signal to Quicken that you're finished describing a check, Quicken actually records the check into your register. So don't be concerned if you later open the register and see the check there.

If you do flip to the register, you'll notice that the Num text box for the check shows Print. This is what identifies the check as one Quicken will later print. In fact, you can enter checks you want to print directly into the register by typing **Print** in the text box. You can't, however, record a payee address into the register, so you probably won't want to use the "directly into the register" approach.

Another thing to note is that Quicken provides almost all of the same helpful features and capabilities for the Write Checks area that it does for the register, as described in Chapter 2. Here are the most important features of the Write Checks area:

• QuickFill is available, and you can use it to help enter payee names and category names.

- Split categories are available. You can display the Split Transaction Window simply by clicking the Split command button in the Write Checks area.
- Checks you write for deposit to another account can be recorded as account transfers. Just choose Transfer To/From and the name of the account from the Category combo box.
- Edit menu commands available for the register are also available for the Write Checks area (see Chapter 2).

Printing Your Checks

After you've entered the checks you want to print, you're ready to print some or all of them. Printing checks on an impact printer works in roughly the same way as printing checks on a laser or ink-jet printer. The only difference is that some of the dialog boxes look slightly different. The following steps are for a laser or ink-jet printer:

1. Load the preprinted check forms into your printer. If you're using a manual feed, place the appropriate number of check form sheets on the feed tray. If you're printing a lot of checks or just want to use the paper tray, open the paper tray and insert the check forms. If you use an impact printer with tractor feed, unload the paper you currently have loaded and replace this paper with your check forms.

2. Choose File ➤ Print Checks to display the Select Checks to Print dialog box, as shown in Figure 3.4.

FIGURE 3.4

The Select Checks to Print dialog box

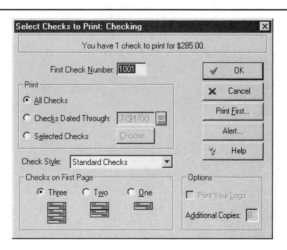

3. Move the cursor to the First Check Number text box and enter the number preprinted on the first check form you'll print. This is important! You want to make sure that the way Quicken numbers your checks is the same way that the bank numbers them on your bank statement.

4. Use the radio buttons in the Print section to indicate which checks you want to print, as follows:

- Mark the All Checks button to tell Quicken you want to print all the checks you entered.

- Mark the Checks Dated Through button to print checks only through a specified date. Specify this date using the text box that appears to the right of the option button.

- Mark the Selected Checks button if you want to print some but not all of the checks you entered. Then click the Choose command button. Quicken displays the Select Checks to Print dialog box, shown in Figure 3.5, which lists all the checks Quicken can print. Initially, all the checks are marked with a checkmark, meaning Quicken thinks it should print them. To indicate you don't want to print a check, click the check to remove the checkmark. When you've unmarked each of the checks you don't want to print, click the Close button to return to the dialog box shown in Figure 3.4.

FIGURE 3.5

Quicken lists the checks to print.

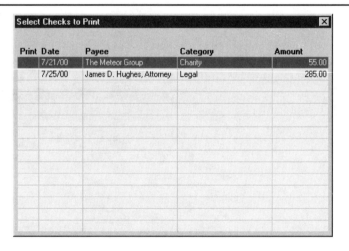

Print	Date	Payee	Category	Amount
	7/21/00	The Meteor Group	Charity	55.00
	7/25/00	James D. Hughes, Attorney	Legal	285.00

5. To tell Quicken which check-form style you'll use, activate the Check Style drop-down list box and choose the check style—the one you ordered and will print on—from the list. If you ordered regular laser printer checks, for example, choose the Standard Checks option.

6. Click the appropriate Checks on First Page button to indicate how many check forms appear on the first page of the laser check forms you loaded into your printer. If there's only one check form per page, only the One button will be enabled. It will be the default—and only possible—choice. If you're using trac- tor forms on your printer, the Checks on First Page buttons in the Select Checks to Print dialog box will be grayed out (unavailable).

7. If you're printing on a laser printer and want a copy of the check forms you print, enter the number of copies you want in the Additional Copies text box. (This text box is not available when you're using an impact printer, because an impact printer can produce multiple copies using multipart check forms.)

8. Click OK. Quicken prints the checks and displays a message asking if the checks printed correctly, as shown in Figure 3.6.

9. If the checks printed correctly, click OK. If they didn't (for instance, if the forms were misaligned or jammed in your printer), enter the check number of the first check that printed incorrectly in the text box provided in the Did Checks Print OK? message box, and click OK. Quicken redisplays the Select Checks to Print dialog box. Then repeat steps 1 through 8 to reprint the checks correctly. (See the next section for information about correcting check-printing problems.)

Figure 3.7 shows an example of a printed check, which uses the data from the com- pleted check form shown earlier in Figure 3.3.

FIGURE 3.6

The Did Check(s) Print OK? message box

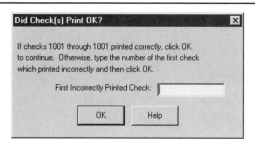

FIGURE 3.7

*A sample check using
the data shown in
Figure 3.3*

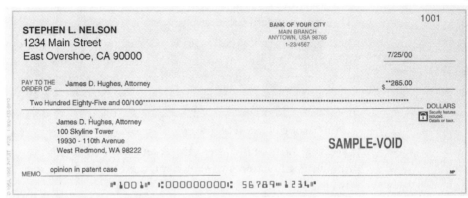

Check-Printing Problems

One common problem you can have with check printing is misaligned forms. It may
be that the printed information appears a character or two too far to the left, too
high, or too low.

To correct check-alignment problems, choose the File ➢ Printer Setup ➢ For Printing Checks command. When Quicken displays the Check Printer Setup dialog box,
shown in Figure 3.8, click Align.

FIGURE 3.8

*The Check Printer
Setup dialog box*

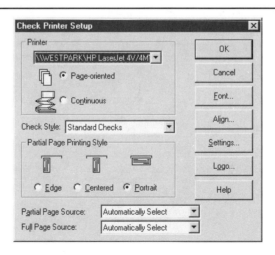

Quicken displays the Align Checks dialog box, shown in Figure 3.9. Choose one of the Checks on Page buttons—Full Page of Checks, Two Checks on Page, or One Check on Page—to tell Quicken how many checks you're printing per page. Quicken displays the Fine Alignment dialog box, shown in Figure 3.10.

 NOTE The number of checks on the page is the first, and most basic, thing you need to check. If Quicken thinks it can print, for example, three check forms on a page that has only two check forms, it's a sure recipe for printer-alignment troubles.

FIGURE 3.9

The Align Checks dialog box

FIGURE 3.10

The Fine Alignment dialog box

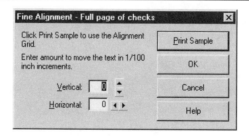

To correct the alignment, you can use either the Vertical and Horizontal text boxes or the mouse. Using the mouse is the easiest way. You simply click the buttons to the right of the Vertical and Horizontal text boxes to move the check data to its correct position. Is the text printing a bit too high? Click the button with the down arrow. Too far to the left? Click the button with the right arrow. You get the idea.

A more precise (but more cumbersome) way to change the alignment is to enter the correct horizontal and vertical alignment values for your printer in the Horizontal and Vertical text boxes. Enter values in hundredths of an inch. Positive values move the text right or up. Negative values (preceding the number with a minus sign) move the text down or to the left.

You can check the alignment by clicking the Print Sample button in the Fine Alignment dialog box. Quicken prints a sample check that fills up each of the fields on a check form. You can use this check to make sure that Quicken is printing the information that it's supposed to print in the right places. When the check's alignment is satisfactory, click OK to save the setup.

TIP If you're really having troubles and don't mind using up a few check forms, you can try printing another sample check form. A cheaper way is to print samples on plain paper and then hold them over the real checks to verify the alignment.

CHAPTER 4

Tracking Your Finances with Reports

The information you collect using the Quicken registers and Write Checks area creates a database that describes your personal or business financial affairs. Although you don't ever need to "do anything" with this financial database, Quicken's powerful reporting and graphing features let you review, summarize, and organize it in ways that almost surely will provide valuable and interesting insights.

This chapter shows you how to produce and use Quicken reports and how to customize these reports so that they more closely fit your needs. There's only one prerequisite to using Quicken's reporting and charting features: entering transactions into its registers. If you've done this, you're ready to begin producing reports and graphs.

 NOTE Chapter 8 explains how you produce graphs that can often show you things that reports never will.

Quicken's Simple Reports

Quicken provides three simple-to-use reports that new users will want to make immediate use of: QuickReports, Snapshots, and EasyAnswer Reports. Let's look at these reports first.

QuickReports for Summarizing Register Information

QuickReports summarize information in a register. The easiest way to illustrate how they work is with an example. Suppose that you're reviewing the checks you've written to various merchants. You see a large deposit from The Meteor Group, then another, and then you wonder how much money you've received from The Meteor Group over the year.

To answer this question with a QuickReport, select a transaction where the payee is The Meteor Group, and then select the Report button at the top-right of the register. Quicken displays a menu with commands corresponding to the various QuickReport options available for the selected transaction. (One option will be Payments Received from the Meteor Group.) When you select one of the QuickReport options, Quicken produces the report and displays it in a separate area on your screen, as shown in Figure 4.1.

FIGURE 4.1

QuickReports make it easy to summarize account information.

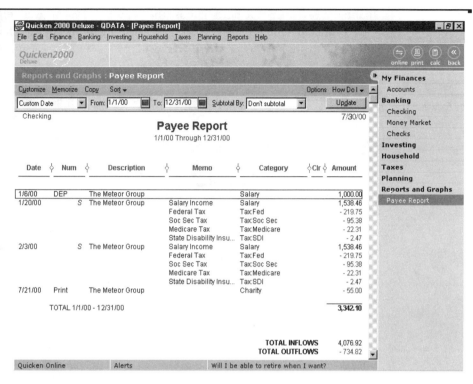

You can create QuickReports that summarize your information by payee or by category and that plot expense category information in a chart. If you want to print a QuickReport report (but not a graph), select the Print command button at the top of the Report area (see the "Report-Printing Basics" section later in this chapter for details on printing reports). To remove the QuickReport area from your screen, select its Close button.

Snapshot Reports with Summary Graphs and Tables

A great report for new users is the Snapshot report. You produce Snapshot reports in your Home page. You'll find details and instructions for doing this in Chapter 6.

EasyAnswer Reports for Answering Financial Questions

EasyAnswer Reports work by letting you ask a question. Quicken then selects the report that best answers your question.

To use the EasyAnswer Reports, choose the Reports ≻ EasyAnswer Reports and Graphs command. Quicken displays the EasyAnswer Reports and Graphs tab of the Reports and Graphs area, as shown in Figure 4.2.

FIGURE 4.2

The EasyAnswer Reports and Graphs tab

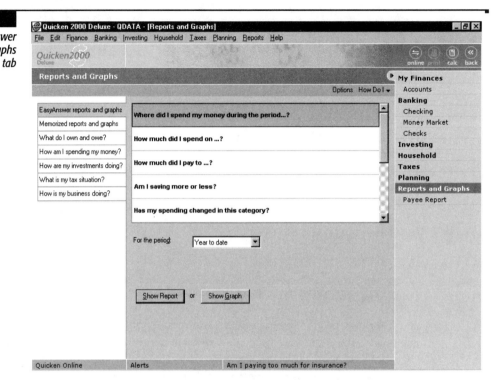

To produce an EasyAnswer Report, click the question you want to ask, and then click the Show Report button. Quicken displays a report that answers the question.

You can change the nature of the question by activating the details drop-down list box that provides key words or phrases to the question text, and then selecting a new key word or phrase. For example, if you want to ask the first question, "Where did I spend my money during the period...?" you can specify the last part of the question as "Last Year," "Last Month," and so on.

Quicken's Advanced Reports

In addition to the simple reports such as Snapshots and EasyAnswer Reports, Quicken produces dozens of more advanced reports that are preformatted to save you time. On the Reports menu and in the Reports and Graphs main area, these advanced reports are grouped into five sets:

- Own & Owe reports summarize your financial assets and liabilities.
- Spending reports summarize money going in and money going out.
- Investing reports summarize investment account information.
- Tax reports summarize tax-related information.
- Business reports summarize business financial information.

These reports are summarized in Tables 4.1 through 4.5.

 NOTE Until you start collecting investment record-keeping information with Quicken, it won't make much sense for you to produce investment reports. Chapters 17 and 18 describe how to perform investment record-keeping in Quicken.

TABLE 4.1: QUICKEN OWN & OWE REPORTS

Report	When You Use It
Account Balances	To create a list of all your assets and liabilities.
Net Worth	To show the account balances in all your accounts. A Net Worth report is unusual in that it doesn't summarize financial activity for a period of time but rather your financial condition at a specific point. Therefore, instead of entering a range of dates when you create the report, you enter a specific date on which you want to know account balances.

TABLE 4.2: QUICKEN SPENDING REPORTS

Report	When You Use It
Cash Flow	To summarize the money that flows into and out of bank accounts. If you've set up cash or credit card accounts, the money that flows into and out of these accounts is summarized by category too.
Cash Flow Comparison	To compare transaction totals for two time periods. For example, you can use a Cash Flow Comparison report to compare your spending by category last month with your spending by category this month.

Continued ▶

TABLE 4.2: QUICKEN SPENDING REPORTS (CONTINUED)

Report	When You Use It
Transaction	To create a list of transactions and their total according to a time period you specify.
Itemized Categories	To summarize all the transactions in all your accounts by income and expense category. The difference between an Itemized Categories report and a Cash Flow report is that a Cash Flow report doesn't include transactions from Quicken's special liability, asset, and investment account types.
Banking Summary	To summarize transactions by category or some other method that you specify.
Income and Expense Comparison	To compare income and expenses by category for two time periods. For example, you can use an Income and Expense Comparison report to compare your spending in one category last month with your spending in that category this month.
Budget	To compare your annual actual income and spending against your budget.
Monthly Budget	To compare your actual income and spending by category with the budget you've assigned for each income and expense category. This report summarizes income and expense categories for bank, cash, and credit card accounts.
Missing Checks	To identify checks that have not been cleared. This includes transactions from all the accounts you've set up—not just your bank, cash, or credit card accounts.
Reconciliation	To print a copy of a reconciled account.

TABLE 4.3: QUICKEN INVESTING REPORTS

Report	When You Use It
Capital Gains	To calculate your realized capital gains and losses.
Investment Performance	To calculate the returns on the individual securities you hold in an investment portfolio.
Portfolio Value	To summarize the current market value of each of the securities you hold in an investment portfolio—individual stocks, bonds, shares of mutual funds, and so on.
Investment Income	To summarize financial transactions by income for an investment account or multiple investment accounts.
Investment Transactions	To list all the transactions you've entered into an investment account register.

TABLE 4.4: QUICKEN TAX REPORTS

Report	When You Use It
Tax Summary	To summarize your taxable income and tax deductions. The difference between an Itemized Categories report and a Tax Summary report is that the Tax Summary report includes only those categories you (or Quicken) marked as tax-related.
Capital Gains	To calculate realized gains on securities that you have sold.
Tax Schedule	To summarize your tax-related categories by input line on your personal or business federal income tax return. You don't need to be concerned with which tax return line a category is reported on, unless you're exporting data directly to a tax-preparation package.

TABLE 4.5: QUICKEN BUSINESS REPORTS

Report	When You Use It
P&L Statement	To summarize the financial activity by income and expense category. A P&L, or Profit and Loss, Statement shows transactions from all the accounts you've set up—not just your bank, cash, or credit card accounts.
P&L Comparison	To summarize the financial activity by income and expense category for two periods so you can compare them.
Job/Project	To summarize your transactions from all your accounts by income and expense categories and by classes.
A/P by Vendor	To see the unprinted checks stored in each of the bank accounts. (A/P stands for accounts payable.)
A/R by Customer	To see the uncleared transactions in each of the asset accounts you've set up. (A/R stands for accounts receivable.)
Payroll	To summarize all payroll-related transactions, such as when you need to prepare quarterly and annual payroll tax reports and returns.
Balance Sheet	To show the account balances in all your accounts. Like the nearly identical Net Worth report, a Balance Sheet report doesn't summarize financial activity for a period of time, but rather your financial condition at a certain point. You don't enter a range of dates when you create the report, but rather a specific date on which you want to know account balances.

Continued

TABLE 4.5: QUICKEN BUSINESS REPORTS (CONTINUED)	
Report	**When You Use It**
Missing Checks	To identify checks that have not been cleared. Transactions are presented in date order, with uncleared checks highlighted in red on your screen.
Cash Flow	To summarize the money that flows into and out of bank accounts. If you've set up cash or credit card accounts, the money that flows into and out of these accounts is summarized by category too.
Cash Flow Comparison	To compare transaction totals for two time periods. For example, you can use a comparison report to compare your sales revenue by category last month with your sales revenue by category this month.

Report-Printing Basics

To print any report, follow these steps:

1. Click the Reports and Graphs QuickTab. Quicken displays the Reports and Graphs area, as shown in Figure 4.3. Choose a report group by clicking a tab on the left side.

2. Select the specific report you want to produce. For example, if you want to print a Cash Flow report, click the How Am I Spending My Money? tab and select Cash Flow Report.

3. Quicken assumes that the reports you produce should describe financial activity from the start of the year through the current date. If you want to describe some other period of financial activity, select a different time frame from the Dates drop-down list box or enter custom dates in the From and To boxes. Clicking the calendar icon next to the From and To combo boxes opens small calendars you can use to change to any month and select any date.

4. Click Create Now to produce the report.

Quicken opens a Report area for the report you request. Figure 4.4 shows a personal Cash Flow report in a new area. This is the same report Quicken produces if you choose Reports ➤ Spending ➤ Cash Flow Report.

 NOTE To remove a report's QuickTab from the Quicken application window, click the Close button at the top-right corner of the report.

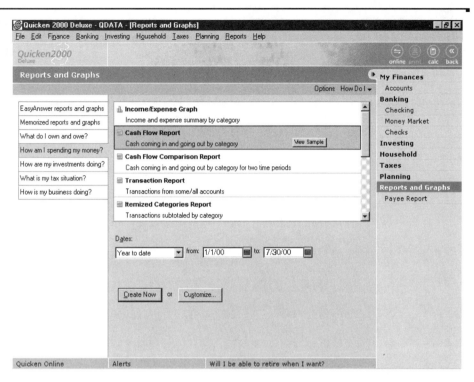

FIGURE 4.3

The Reports and Graphs area with the Cash Flow Report selected

5. To print a paper copy of the report displayed in the active area, click the Print command button in the row of command buttons at the top of the Report area. The Print dialog box appears, as shown in Figure 4.5.

6. Use the Print To option buttons to indicate how a report should be printed:

- If you want to print a report on paper (which means sending it to your printer, the most common choice), click the first option button.

- If you want to print to exportable file formats, such as ASCII and Lotus 1-2-3, choose one of the other Print To option buttons.

TIP If you're proficient with a spreadsheet, you can print a Quicken report as a disk file and then import it into just about any spreadsheet program, such as 1-2-3, Excel, Quattro Pro, Works, and so on. You might want to do this to tap a spreadsheet's more powerful and more flexible modeling tools.

FIGURE 4.4

A Cash Flow report summarizing data entered in Quicken's registers

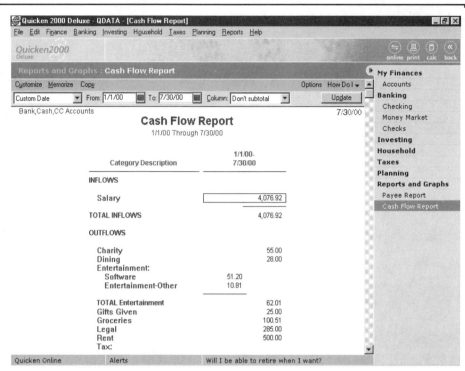

FIGURE 4.5

The Print dialog box

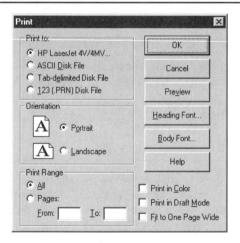

7. Use the Orientation option buttons to specify how Quicken should print the report on the page: Portrait or Landscape.

8. If you want to print only a page or range of pages of the report, mark the Pages option button in the Print Range area. Then use the From and To text boxes to specify the page range.

9. If you are using a color printer, check the Print in Color box to see your financial red ink in printed red ink or to see other color effects similar to those you see on your screen.

10. If you want to accelerate printing speed when print quality isn't important, click the Print in Draft Mode checkbox.

11. If you want Quicken to fit the report's information across the width of a single page, mark the Fit to One Page Wide checkbox.

 TIP To preview what you are about to print, click the Preview button, which displays a screen preview of your paper report.

12. Select OK when the Print dialog box is complete.

If you're printing to a printer, Quicken sends the report to Windows, which manages the actual work of printing the report. If you indicate that you want to print to a disk file, Quicken displays the Create Disk File dialog box, as shown in Figure 4.6.

FIGURE 4.6

The Create Disk File dialog box

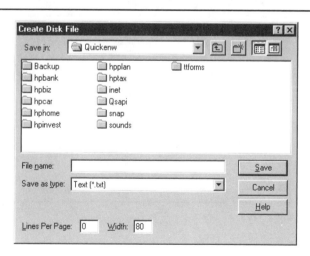

13. If you're printing to disk, use the Create Disk File dialog box to indicate the path and filename for the disk file. For example, to create a file named REPORT.TXT in the Quicken directory on your C hard drive, locate the QUICKENW folder from the list box and then enter the name REPORT.TXT in the File Name text box.

Zooming In on a Report

Quicken provides QuickZoom, a handy feature that you can use in any Report area. Here's how it works: Say you have a question about a figure that appears on a report. You simply point to the figure with the mouse. (Quicken changes the mouse pointer to a magnifying glass with a Z where the magnifying glass lens should be.) Then you double-click the mouse. Quicken prepares a list of the individual transactions that, collectively, make up the figure that you've clicked and displays it in its own Report area. (If you wish to look at a transaction underlying the report, you can double-click again to be taken to that specific transaction in the register.)

With QuickZoom, you never need to wonder why some expense category is so high or what income transactions go into a sales figure; a double-click of the mouse produces a report that answers the question. Figure 4.7 shows a QuickZoom report created by double-clicking the Groceries total in Figure 4.4 (the Cash Flow report shown earlier in the chapter).

FIGURE 4.7

A QuickZoom report shows the individual transactions that go together to explain a summary figure on a report.

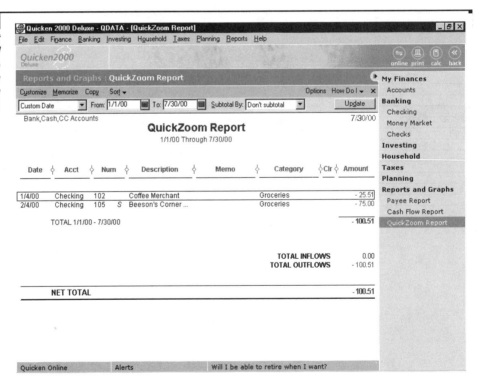

Changing the Way Your Reports Are Printed

Quicken lets you have it your way when it comes to printing your reports. You can choose the font, font style, and font size for your reports. To make this change, click the Heading Font or Body Font command button in the Print dialog box. Quicken displays a dialog box like the one shown in Figure 4.8 (if you click the Heading Font command button) or a similar dialog box (if you click the Body Font command button).

Use the Font text box or list box to select a font or typeface. Use the Font Style text box or list box to add boldfacing or to italicize the report header. Use the Size text box or list box to select a point size (one point equals 1/72 inch). You can see the effect of your font, font style, and point size changes in the Sample box.

FIGURE 4.8

The Select Heading Font dialog box

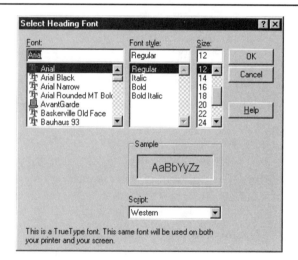

Describing Your Report Preferences

To customize a report, you change the report preferences settings: Choose Edit ➢ Options ➢ Reports and Graphs. When Quicken displays the Report and Graph Options dialog box, shown in Figure 4.9, make the changes you want.

The settings in the Report and Graph Options dialog box work as follows:

> **Default Date Range and Default Comparison Date Range text boxes**   Here, you can tell Quicken what it should suggest as the range of dates covered in the report.

FIGURE 4.9

*The Report and Graph
Options dialog box*

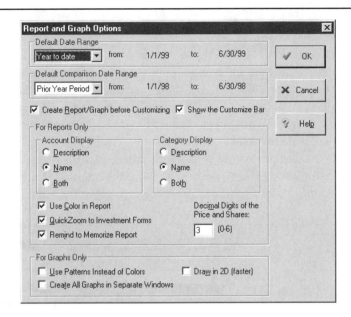

Create Report/Graph before Customizing checkbox   Mark this if you want to use the default settings and go straight to creating the report. If you don't mark the checkbox, Quicken displays the Create Report dialog box, which you can use to customize the report Quicken produces.

Show the Customize Bar checkbox   Mark this to display the Customize bar in Report areas. The Customize bar allows you to change the report time frame directly from the Report area.

Account Display option buttons   This section indicates whether you want Quicken to display the account name, a description, or both. Note that this preference setting has no effect when you've chosen to display more than one account. In this case, Quicken uses the description All Accounts or Selected Accounts.

Category Display option buttons   This section indicates whether, when Quicken summarizes by categories, it should use the shorter 32-character category name, the longer 54-character category description, or both the name and the description. Note that when a category doesn't have a description, Quicken uses the category name, regardless of what the Category Display option buttons show.

Use Color in Report checkbox   Mark this if you want Quicken to use color in the Report areas. (Of course, this setting can't add color to reports printed on a black-and-white printer.)

QuickZoom to Investment Forms checkbox   Mark this to jump from a specific investment transaction to an investment form for that transaction.

Remind to Memorize Report checkbox   Mark this to have Quicken remind you to memorize reports you've customized.

Decimal Digits of the Price and Shares text box   Enter the number of decimal places you want Quicken to display for security prices and share amounts in your investment reports. Quicken can display up to six decimal places (prices to one ten-thousandth of a cent).

Creating Customized Reports

The standard reports provided by Quicken almost always provide you with the information you need. But you aren't limited to viewing the information in your financial database (the transactions you've collected in the Quicken registers) using these standard reports. You can customize any of them, and you can change the contents of your report while creating it or while it is displayed on your screen.

Before you begin customizing a report, however, it's helpful if you understand that all Quicken reports are derived from one of five basic report types:

Report Type	What It Does
Summary	Summarizes register transactions
Transaction	Lists register transactions
Comparison	Shows two sets of summary numbers, such as last year's category totals and this year's category totals, as well as the difference between the two sets
Budget	Shows actual category totals, budgeted category totals, and the difference between the two
Account Balances	Shows account balance information

 NOTE   Although customizing reports in Quicken isn't difficult, you may want to postpone it until you're comfortable entering transactions into registers. Most of what you do when you customize a report is simply describe how you want register information organized and summarized. The more familiar you are with the information that goes into a register, the easier it is to customize.

Customization is similar for all types, so I'll describe the general procedures and then comment on the items that vary by report type. The action begins from the Create Report dialog box, which you open by choosing the command for the type of report you want to customize. The Create Report dialog box for any report type includes a Customize button.

Click the Customize button to open the customization dialog box. Figure 4.10 shows the dialog box for customizing a Summary report, which is similar to the other report customization dialog boxes. By clicking the dialog box tabs—Display, Accounts, Include, and Advanced—you reach boxes and option buttons for customizing the reports in various ways. In the following sections, I'll explain the customization options (by tab) for each major type of report.

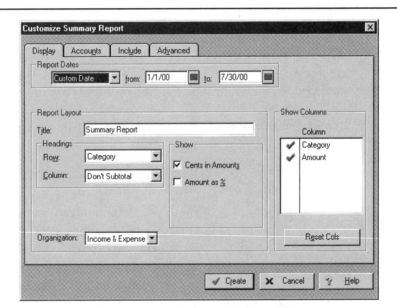

FIGURE 4.10

The Customize Summary Report dialog box

Customizing a Summary Report

To begin customizing a Summary report, choose Reports ➤ Banking ➤ Summary. Click the Customize command button to open the Customize Summary Report dialog box (Figure 4.10).

Changing Summary Report Display Settings

In the Customize Summary Report dialog box, the Report Dates boxes let you specify the range of dates that the report covers. You can specify a date range either by typing a starting and ending date in the From and To boxes or by selecting a report duration from the Report Dates drop-down list box:

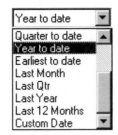

The Report Layout settings let you change the report name, select headings for rows and columns, and reorganize the summary structure of your report.

You can use the Title text box to replace the generic report title with a more specific description. Highlight the text box and enter the desired report title or description.

In the Headings area, the Row drop-down list box offers choices to create a row for each category, class, payee, or account. The Column drop-down list box provides a Don't Subtotal entry, a series of time-related subtotaling entries (a week, two weeks, half a month, and so on), and the Category, Class, Payee, and Account column subtotaling options.

The Show section contains two checkboxes. The Cents in Amounts box, if marked, displays amounts in dollars and cents. If unmarked, the amounts are shown rounded to the nearest dollar. The Amount as % checkbox, if marked, shows amounts as percentages of the total. Leaving the box unmarked shows amounts as dollars and cents.

Use the Organization drop-down list box to tell Quicken how it should arrange the report's information: by income and expense or on a cash-flow basis. Select Income & Expense if you want to organize the report into three parts: income category summaries, expense category summaries, and account transfer summaries. Select Cash Flow Basis if you want to organize the report into two parts: cash inflows and cash outflows. Select Category if you want to group and total report information by categories.

Changing Summary Report Account Settings

Clicking the Accounts tab of the Customize Summary Report dialog box displays options for specifying which accounts' transactions should be included in the report, as shown in Figure 4.11.

If you want to change the account selection, click an Account Type button to include all accounts of that type. Click the Mark All button to put a checkmark next to all listed accounts, or click individual account names to deselect or reselect them until you have the selections you want.

FIGURE 4.11

The Accounts tab of the Customize Summary Report dialog box

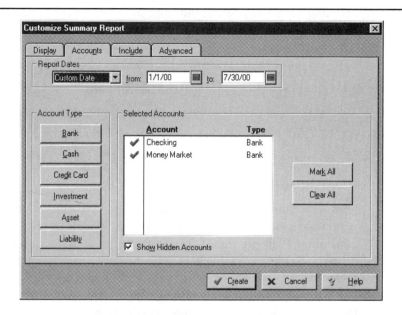

Changing Summary Report Include Settings

The Include tab lets you filter the transactions in a register so that only those that conform to your description appear in the report. The Include tab of the Customize Summary Report dialog box is shown in Figure 4.12.

FIGURE 4.12

The Include tab of the Customize Summary Report dialog box

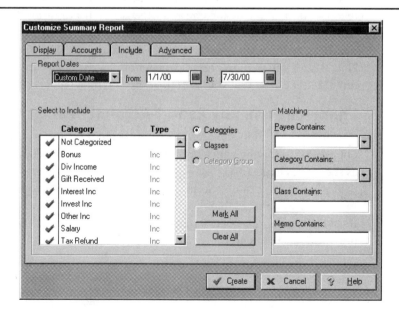

Here are some situations in which you might filter transactions in this way:

- You're looking for a specific transaction (such as grocery checks for more than $50).

- You want to build a report that includes only a subset of the information in a regular Summary report (perhaps just your housing and household expenses).

- You want to slice your data in a way that's slightly different from what your existing categories and classes allow (you want to see what you're spending on groceries at Beeson's Corner Market).

The list in the Select to Include area initially includes all categories as well as a Not Categorized category. Clicking a category alternately selects or deselects it. Clicking the Mark All button selects all categories. Clicking the Clear All button deselects all categories.

Click the Classes button to display defined classes in the list. Classes are selected and deselected the same way categories are.

NOTE If you're confused by this "class" business, don't worry—you haven't missed something. Classes are another tool you can use to summarize financial information. I'll describe how to use classes to track individual real estate investments in Chapter 19.

You can also limit, or *filter*, the information included in a Summary report. For example, you might want to see a report that includes only checks categorized as Entertainment if you were reviewing ways to reduce your spending in that area. To limit the information in a Summary report, use the Matching boxes: Payee Contains, Category Contains, Class Contains, and Memo Contains.

To use the Matching boxes, follow these steps:

1. Enter the name of the payee whose transactions you want to show. For example, to include only those transactions with the payee name Armstrong Commons, type **Armstrong Commons** into the Payee Contains text box or use the drop-down list box.

TIP To include names that start with the word Armstrong, type **Armstrong..** instead. To include payee names that end with the word Armstrong, type **..Armstrong**. To include payee names that use just the word Armstrong, type **=Armstrong**. To exclude payee names that show or use Armstrong, you use the tilde (~). For example, to exclude payee names that start with Armstrong, type **~Armstrong**. These tricks—using two periods and the tilde, which Quicken calls match characters—also work for the Category Contains, Class Contains, and Memo Contains drop-down boxes.

2. Enter the category you want included transactions to show. For example, to include only those transactions with the category Salary, type **Salary** in the Category Contains text box or select it from the drop-down list box.

3. Enter the class you want the included transactions to show. For ex`mple, to include only those transactions with the class Winston, type **Winston** into the Class Contains text box.

4. Enter the memo description you want the included transactions to show. For example, to include only those transactions with the memo description Payroll, type **Payroll** into the Memo Contains text box.

Changing Summary Report Advanced Settings

In addition to the Display, Accounts, and Include settings, Quicken also provides an eclectic set of additional customization options. These options allow you to further filter the transactions appearing on the report by choosing transactions by amount or type. The Advanced tab of the Customize Summary Report dialog box is shown in Figure 4.13.

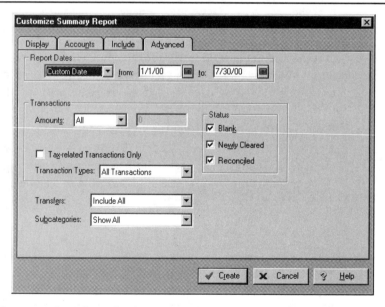

FIGURE 4.13

The Advanced tab of the Customize Summary Report dialog box

The Amounts drop-down list lets you include all transactions or only those less than, equal to, or greater than the number you enter in the adjacent text box.

The Tax-Related Transactions Only checkbox, if marked, shows only transactions you have assigned to tax-related categories in Quicken's category lists. Leaving it unmarked shows all transactions.

The Transaction Types drop-down list lets you choose to include all transactions or to show only payments, deposits, or unprinted checks in your report.

The Status checkboxes allow you to prepare a Summary report that focuses on blank, newly cleared, or reconciled checks. Normally, to show all items in your reports, you leave all three boxes marked (their default state). Selectively unmarking the boxes produces specialized reports focusing on only the marked type of item.

The Transfers drop-down list lets you include all or exclude all transfer transactions from the report. You can also choose Exclude Internal to hide transfers between accounts included in the report.

The Subcategories drop-down list shows all subcategories when Show All is selected. You can also choose Hide All to not display subcategories or Show Reversed to group categories under subcategories, which has the effect of grouping subcategories that are normally separated under different categories.

Customizing a Transaction Report

Like the Summary report, the Transaction report has a variety of customization options.

To begin customization, choose Reports ➢ Banking ➢ Transaction. In the Create Report dialog box, click the Customize command button to open a Customize Transaction Report dialog box.

Changing Transaction Report Display Settings

The Customize Transaction Report dialog box's Display tab works in the same basic way as the Customize Summary Report dialog box's Display tab. You can change the report name, select headings for rows and columns, and reorganize the summary structure of your report.

In the Title text box, replace the generic report title with a more specific description: Highlight the text box and enter the desired report title or description.

In the Headings area, the Subtotal By drop-down list defines an additional column for a variety of time periods. A Don't Subtotal entry creates only a single column.

The Sort By drop-down list contains six options:

None   Sorts by account type, account name, and date.

Date/Acct   Sorts by date and then by account type and account name.

Acct/Chk#   Orders entries by account type and then by check number.

Amount Sorts from the smallest to the largest amount.

Payee Sorts alphabetically by payee.

Category Sorts alphabetically by category.

In the Organization drop-down list box, you can tell Quicken how to arrange the report's information: by income and expense or on a cash-flow basis. Select Income & Expense if you want to organize the report into three parts: income category summaries, expense category summaries, and account transfer summaries. Select Cash Flow Basis if you want to organize the report into two parts: cash inflows and cash outflows.

The Show area contains three checkboxes:

Cents in Amounts Displays amounts in dollars and cents. If unchecked, the amounts are shown rounded to the nearest dollar.

Totals Only Shows only the total amount of the transactions meeting the other report criteria.

Split Transaction Detail Includes detail from split transactions.

Changing Other Transaction Report Settings

With the exception of the layout settings noted in the previous section, the procedures and options for customizing a Transaction report are similar to the procedures described for customizing a Summary report. Refer to the Summary report sections earlier in this chapter that discuss the Accounts, Include, and Advanced customization options.

Customizing Other Reports

You can customize three other types of basic reports:

- Comparison
- Budget
- Account Balances

If you've reviewed the options described in the preceding discussion of customizing a Summary report, you will have no surprises as you approach these three. They're all somewhat simpler than either the Summary or Transaction type of report; in many cases, you have fewer options to deal with.

There are one or two wrinkles, though. The Comparison report has Difference as % and Difference in $ checkboxes in its Display tab. Marking these boxes generates columns that show the percentage and dollar differences between the categories chosen for the report.

The Account Balances report has a setting called Interval, which creates a column with totals for the time period you select from a drop-down list. The Account Balances report also has two choices in the Organization layout area. You can choose Net Worth to print your net worth as the last item on the report. Choose Balance Sheet to print net worth as a liability with total liabilities and equity following.

Memorizing the Customized Reports You Create

You can go to quite a bit of effort to create customized reports that summarize the information you've collected in the Quicken registers. Sometimes, you'll be creating a customized report for one-time use. However, other times you will be creating a customized report that you'll want to use repeatedly. In these cases, you can *memorize* the customization settings, filters, and options. This means that when you want to produce the report, you can reuse the memorized report.

Memorizing a Report

Memorizing a report is simple. After you've generated the report, click the Memorize command button, which appears in the command button row at the top of every Report area. Quicken displays the Memorize Report dialog box, shown in Figure 4.14.

FIGURE 4.14

The Memorize Report dialog box

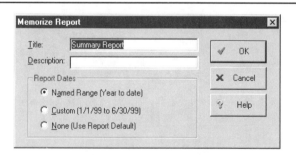

Enter a name for the report to be memorized in the Title text box. Then use the Report Dates option buttons to indicate whether you want to use the textual description of the report date range (the Named Range option button) or the actual fixed date description (the Custom option button). Or, click None to use the default report date ranges. (You can specify and change this range using the Edit ➤ Options ➤ Reports command, as described earlier in this chapter.)

Optionally, use the Description box to provide additional information about the report, such as why you've created the memorized report or when it should be used.

Using a Memorized Report

Once you have Quicken memorize a report, you can produce a new copy of the memorized report any time by clicking the Memorized Reports and Graphs tab in the Reports and Graphs area. Figure 4.15 shows what this tab looks like with a single memorized report named Summary Report.

FIGURE 4.15

The Memorized Reports and Graphs tab of the Reports and Graphs area

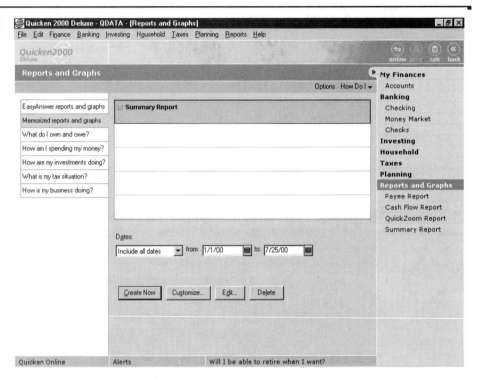

NOTE Printing a report that appears on the Memorized Reports menu works just like printing a report that appears on the Banking, Planning, Business, Taxes, or Investments Report menu.

Rules for Retaining Documents

You've probably wondered how long you should keep your canceled checks and how long it makes sense to hang onto old tax returns. Now that you have Quicken producing all these handy reports, see Table 4.6 for some guidelines for determining how long you should hold onto these things. This table summarizes the usual document-retention rules for Quicken reports and for several other business documents and forms as well. These rules are based on conservative applications of the relevant statutory and regulatory requirements, as well as statutes of limitations.

TABLE 4.6: DOCUMENT-RETENTION RULES AND GUIDELINES

Document or Form	Years Retained
Asset purchase records	Seven years after asset is sold or disposed of (including investment registers)
Backup files	One year
Checks, canceled	Permanently
Check registers	Permanently
Monthly home tax summaries and schedules	Three years
Yearly home tax summaries and schedules	Seven years after filing a return based on report
Other home reports (including investment reports)	One year
Monthly business P&L and tax reports	Three years
Yearly business P&L and tax reports	Seven years
Other business reports	One year

CHAPTER **5**

Balancing Bank Accounts

From time to time, you'll need to balance the bank accounts you track with Quicken. Balancing an account entails explaining the difference between what your records say you have in a bank account and what the bank says you have in that bank account. By regularly balancing bank accounts, you catch both the errors you've made and the errors the bank has made, and you can thereby ensure the accuracy of your financial record keeping.

There's no magic in this, of course. All Quicken does is automate and expedite the balancing you would (or should) normally do by hand. With Quicken, balancing a bank account takes only minutes.

Before You Begin

To balance a bank account with Quicken, you must have your most recent bank statements. In addition, you must have the following:

- A record of the bank account's activity—your payments and deposits—stored in Quicken.
- An accurate starting balance for the bank account when you originally set it up.

 NOTE If you didn't provide an accurate starting balance when you originally set up the bank account, all is not lost. You can still balance your account, as explained later in the chapter.

Understanding the Reconciliation Process

Balancing a bank account has a simple premise: The difference between what your records show as an account balance and what the bank's records show as an account balance should equal the sum of your uncleared payments and deposits.

Let's set up a simple example to show how the reconciliation process works. Suppose your records of a bank account show the account balance as $50, and the bank's records show the account balance as $95. Furthermore, suppose your records show a

$50 check that you've written but that has not yet cleared the bank, and suppose the bank's records show a $5 monthly service charge that you haven't yet recorded into the Quicken register.

Clearly, the $50 balance in your register doesn't equal the $95 balance shown on the bank account statement. But this will almost always be the case. The real question is whether the difference between the two balances can be explained. If it can, the account balances. If the difference can't be explained, the account doesn't balance.

Determining whether an account balances requires four simple steps:

1. Record any transactions shown on the bank statement that should be but aren't shown in your register. For example, if the bank statement shows a $5 monthly service charge, you'll need to record this payment in your register. In the simple example we're using, recording this transaction adjusts the balance shown in your records to $45, because $50 minus $5 equals $45.

 NOTE Your bank statement may show other transactions that your records don't: payments for bank services, credit card fees, and deposits for items like monthly interest income. Your bank statement may also show transactions that you initiated but forgot to record, such as automated teller machine (ATM) withdrawals.

2. Add up the uncleared transactions. (Subtract the total of the uncleared deposits from the total of the uncleared checks.) In our example, there's just one uncleared transaction—the $50 check—so the sum of the uncleared transactions is $50. In a more typical case, you might have recorded numerous checks that the bank hasn't recorded, or there might be deposits that you've recorded but that the bank hasn't.

3. Determine the difference between what your records show as the account balance and what the bank's records show as the account balance. In the example, your records now show $45 as the account balance. The bank's records show $95, so there's a $50 difference between your records and the bank's.

4. Verify that the uncleared transactions total (calculated in step 2) equals the difference between your records and the bank's records (calculated in step 3). In our example, we know that $50 equals $50; so we've now explained the difference between the two accounts.

MASTERING TROUBLESHOOTING

When an Account Won't Balance

Sometimes, of course, an account won't balance. Although an account that doesn't balance can be perplexing and even infuriating, the basic reasons for imbalance are usually straightforward:

- The bank's balance is wrong because its starting balance is wrong or because one or more transactions are wrong or missing.
- Your account balance is wrong for one of the same reasons.
- The uncleared transaction total is incorrect.

In my experience, it's unlikely that the bank's balance is wrong or that the bank missed or incorrectly recorded a transaction. Whatever else may be true about banks, they generally do a very good job of financial record keeping.

So when there's a problem with a bank account, it usually stems from one of two situations: Either you've come up with an incorrect uncleared transaction total, or your records' account balance is wrong. To get the account to balance, you need to find the error in your records or the error in the uncleared transaction total. A little later in the chapter, I'll describe tricks for finding errors in your record keeping.

Balancing an Account in Quicken

To balance a bank account in Quicken, display the bank account register (shown in Figure 5.1).

As discussed in the previous section, be sure that the bank statement doesn't show any payments or deposits that you need to record in the register. The only bank account transactions you don't need to record are the monthly service charge and the interest income; Quicken lets you record these as part of reconciling the account. Any other new transactions that the bank account statement shows need to be recorded.

FIGURE 5.1

Getting ready to balance a bank account

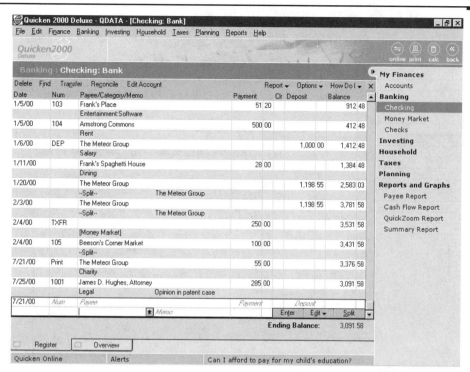

MASTERING TROUBLESHOOTING

Crime-Stopper's Textbook: Catching Forgers

When you reconcile your bank accounts, review the canceled checks to be sure that they haven't been altered and that whoever was supposed to sign the check really did sign it. Fraudulently altering or marking a document (such as a check form) to change another person's liability constitutes forgery, and reviewing canceled checks may be the only way you'll catch a forger.

As long as you immediately report forgery to the bank, you probably won't suffer any losses. This may not be true, however, if you've been careless (for example, you left a checkbook on the dashboard of your car and left your car's windows open, or you hired someone whom you knew to be a convicted check-forging felon) or if you delay reviewing the canceled checks or reporting forgery you've discovered to the bank.

Here's an example from personal experience: Long after I began telling people to review their canceled checks, a new employee of mine stole a sheet of blank checks and wrote himself extra weekly payroll checks. I caught him when I reviewed my canceled checks and realized that he had forged my signature.

Reconciling the Account

Once you've entered the missing transactions shown on the statement, follow these steps:

1. Click the Reconcile button to display the Reconcile Bank Statement dialog box, as shown in Figure 5.2 (for balancing a checking account).

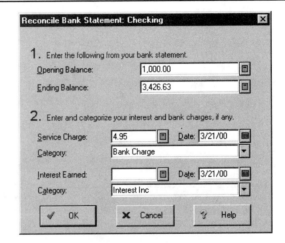

2. Verify that the figure shown in the Opening Balance text box is the starting bank account balance on your bank statement. If it isn't, correct it.

The first time you reconcile an account, Quicken uses your starting account balance. The subsequent times you reconcile an account, Quicken uses the Ending Balance from the previous reconciliation.

3. Enter the ending bank account balance from your bank statement in the Ending Balance text box. Simply place the cursor in the text box and type the figure.

4. In the Service Charge box, enter the monthly service charge shown on the bank statement (if you haven't already entered this directly in the register).

5. In the Service Charge Date box, tell Quicken when the service charge occurred.

6. In the Category box, Quicken categorized the service charge. If you want to use a different category, click the arrow at the right of the box and select the category you want from the drop-down list.

7. In the Interest Earned box, enter the monthly interest income shown on the bank statement (if you haven't entered this directly in the register).

8. In the Interest Earned Date box, enter the date the bank added the interest to your account.

9. Quicken categorizes the interest in the Category box. If you want to use a different category, click the arrow at the right of the box and select a category from the drop-down list.

10. Click OK. You'll see the Reconcile Bank Statement area, as shown in Figure 5.3.

FIGURE 5.3

The Reconcile Bank Statement area

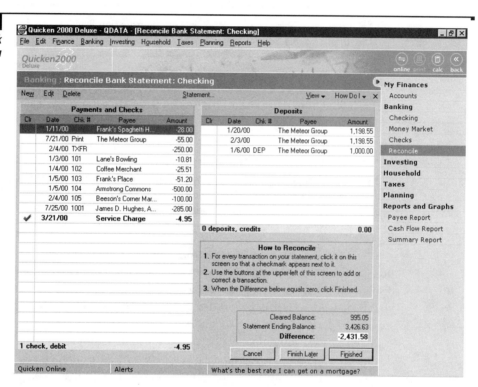

If you have a question about a transaction shown in the Reconcile Bank Statement area, select the transaction either by using the arrow keys or by clicking the mouse. Then select the Edit command button. (It's the second button from the left.) Quicken displays the bank account's register, with the cursor in the transaction. You can examine the transaction in more detail, including the split transaction lines. When you're ready to return to the Reconcile Bank Statement area, click the Reconcile QuickTab.

11. Review the list of transactions shown in the Reconcile Bank Statement area and mark each transaction that has cleared by highlighting it. Quicken places a checkmark next to it. (If you accidentally mark a transaction as cleared when it shouldn't be, click it with the mouse or press the spacebar.)

As you indicate which transactions have cleared, Quicken continually calculates a Cleared Balance figure at the bottom of the screen. The Cleared Balance is just your records' bank account balance minus all the uncleared transactions. When this Cleared Balance equals the bank statement balance, your account balances, because the uncleared transactions total explains the difference between your records and the bank's records.

TIP You can rearrange the entries in the reconciliation lists by date, payee, or amount rather than by check number. To do so, choose one of these options from the View menu.

12. Select Finished when the difference between the cleared balance and the bank statement balance is zero. Figure 5.4 shows how the Reconcile Bank Statement area should look when you've successfully reconciled an account.

TIP If you made a mistake entering your ending bank account balance, you can return to the Reconcile Bank Statement dialog box (Figure 5.2) by clicking the Statement button at the top of the Reconcile Bank Statement area.

When you select the Finished button, Quicken updates the status of the transactions you marked as cleared by placing an R in the Clr column of the register. Then it displays a message box congratulating you on finishing the reconciliation and asking you if you want to print a report describing the reconciliation. The message box is shown in Figure 5.5.

In most cases, you probably don't need a reconciliation report. The report simply documents the fact that you reconciled an account. And after all, you already know that you reconciled the account. In this case, select No in the Reconciliation Complete dialog box.

The one time it probably does make sense to print a reconciliation report is when you're reconciling an account for someone else. For example, if you're a bookkeeper and you use Quicken in your work, it makes sense for you to document that you've completed a reconciliation so that you can show your employer that you've balanced the account. Continue with the instructions in the next section to create this report.

FIGURE 5.4

The Reconcile Bank Statement area showing a difference of zero

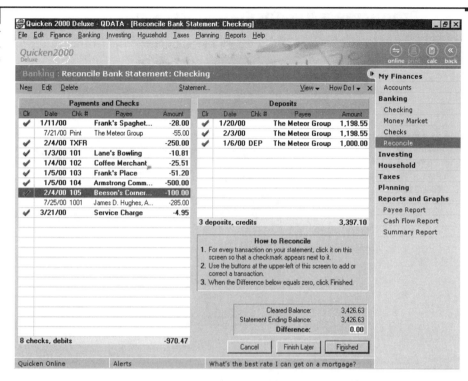

FIGURE 5.5

The Congratulations message

Producing a Reconciliation Report

If you want to produce a report that summarizes the reconciliation, follow these steps:

1. Select Yes in the Reconciliation Complete dialog box to display the Reconciliation Report Setup dialog box, shown in Figure 5.6.

FIGURE 5.6

The Reconciliation Report Setup dialog box

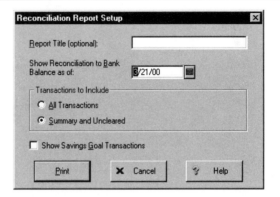

 TIP If you don't want to print a report immediately after reconciling an account, you can do so later by choosing Reports ➢ Banking ➢ Reconciliation.

2. If you want to record a title or description for the report, enter it in the Report Title text box.

3. In the Show Reconciliation to Bank Balance As Of text box, enter the date (in MM/DD/YY format) through which cleared and uncleared transactions should be reported.

4. Use the Transactions to Include option buttons to indicate what you want to show on the report:

- Mark the All Transactions option button if you want all the transactions from the last reconciliation through the Show Reconciliation to Bank Balance As Of date to show on the report. (You usually won't need to show this level of detail.)

- Mark the Summary and Uncleared option button if you want summary information and the individual uncleared transactions to show. (This is the option you'll usually want; it individually lists the uncleared transactions that explain the difference between your records and the bank's.)

5. Select Print to produce the reconciliation report, and use the Print To option buttons to indicate where Quicken should send the reconciliation report. Quicken sends the reconciliation report to Windows so that your report can be printed, or if you clicked any of the three Disk option buttons, Quicken prompts you for the complete path name of the reconciliation report disk file.

What to Do If You Can't Reconcile an Account

If you can't get a bank account to reconcile, you have a choice: You can tell Quicken to force your records to agree with the bank's (this isn't a very good idea), or you can suspend the reconciliation, attempt to find the error that's causing you problems, and then restart the reconciliation. I'll describe both approaches here, although the former should be used only as a last resort or when you haven't been able to get an account to reconcile for several months in a row.

Postponing a Reconciliation So You Can Find Your Error

If you diligently entered each of the new transactions your bank statement showed and carefully marked each cleared transaction in the Reconcile Bank Statement area, and your account won't reconcile, here's what you should do:

First, click Finish Later in the Reconcile Bank Statement area. This tells Quicken not to complete the reconciliation. Quicken closes the area but leaves intact the transactions you've marked as cleared. (It does this by putting an R in the Clr text box in the account register.)

Next, review your records—particularly the transactions you entered since the last reconciliation—for any errors. The most common causes of reconciliation problems are transactions that you haven't yet entered into the register and transactions that you incorrectly marked as cleared or uncleared. If you've double-checked your records for these errors, consider these other potential errors:

Backward numbers   Look for transactions you may have entered backward—deposits you entered as payments or vice versa. These can be tricky to spot because every transaction looks right except for one tiny thing: the sign of the amount is wrong. But you can often find backward transactions by dividing the unexplained difference by 2 and then looking for a transaction equal to the result. If the unexplained difference is $101.50, for example, it may be that you entered a $50.75 transaction backward.

Transposed numbers   Look for amounts with transposed numbers. These errors are also tricky to locate because all the digits appear correct, but they aren't in the right order; $46.25 might have been entered as $42.65, for example. If the difference is evenly divisible by nine, look for transposed numbers in the amount. For example, if you did enter 42.65 instead of 46.25, the difference in the Reconcile Bank Account area will equal $3.60. The $3.60 amount is evenly divisible by nine, so the difference suggests a transposition error.

Transactions entered twice   Look for transactions you've erroneously entered twice. These are usually pretty easy to spot. A telltale sign is that the difference shown equals the amount of a transaction correctly marked as cleared or left as uncleared.

Once you find and correct the error causing the discrepancy, restart the reconciliation process by clicking the Reconcile button. Fill out the Reconcile Bank Statement dialog box and the Reconcile Bank Statement area to continue marking transactions as cleared (or uncleared). Then, when the difference equals zero, click Finished.

Forcing Your Records to Agree with the Bank's

If you can't get an account to reconcile, you can force your records to agree with the bank's. The one time it is reasonable (at least in my opinion) to force your records to agree with the bank's is when you've attempted to reconcile your account for two or three or (better yet) four months and find that you always have the same unexplained difference. In this case, you know that the uncleared transactions total explains the difference; so the problem you can't find is either in the bank's records (which is unlikely) or yours. By forcing your records to agree with the bank's, you implicitly admit that the problem is yours and not the bank's.

To make this adjustment, just click the Finished command button in the Reconcile Bank Statement area, even though the difference doesn't equal zero. Quicken displays the Adjust Balance dialog box, as shown in Figure 5.7.

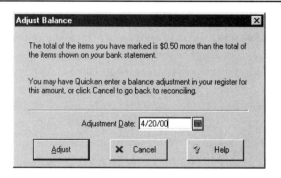

To make the adjustment, simply enter the date on which the adjustment transaction should be recorded, and then click Adjust. Quicken records an adjustment transaction that forces your records to agree with the bank's. For example, if your records show the account balance as $3 too high, Quicken just adds a payment transaction for $3 and marks the transaction as cleared.

Quicken doesn't categorize adjustment transactions, but you may want to do so. Because you never found the error, you don't actually know which category should be used. Here are two things you can do:

- You can use the category you use for the largest share of your spending. As a practical matter, the adjustment transaction will then have the least effect on this category's totals (because this category will show the largest category totals). What's more, there's a pretty good chance the record-keeping error affects this category.

- You can set up a Balance Adjustment category that you can use to summarize your reconciliation balance adjustments. This doesn't actually make your category reporting any better, but it does make it easy to see just what portion of your spending is unknown.

CHAPTER **6**

Customizing the Way Quicken Works

You can make a whole series of changes to the way Quicken works. Many of the changes are largely cosmetic; they affect only the way Quicken appears. But some of the changes are more structural; they affect either the way Quicken works or the way you work with Quicken. I'll describe each of these sets of possible changes in this chapter.

 NOTE The only prerequisite for this chapter is to know how to work with Windows.

Changes to Consider As Soon As You're Comfortable

Three of the changes you can make are so easy you can (and should) consider making them as soon as you're comfortable working with Quicken and entering transactions into a register. These include customizing your Home page, switching to a one-line view of the register, and saving your Desktop arrangement.

Customizing Your Home Page

When you start Quicken the first time, you see a screen similar to the one in Figure 6.1. The graphs, charts, and tables you see when you scroll down the page are colorful and attractive, but these particular representations probably won't make any sense to you, and it's unlikely that they'll be of any use to you. You can tell Quicken that you don't want to see this page by following the instructions in the "Saving a Desktop" section that follows or in "Changing Quicken's General Options," later in this chapter.

FIGURE 6.1

The default Quicken Home page

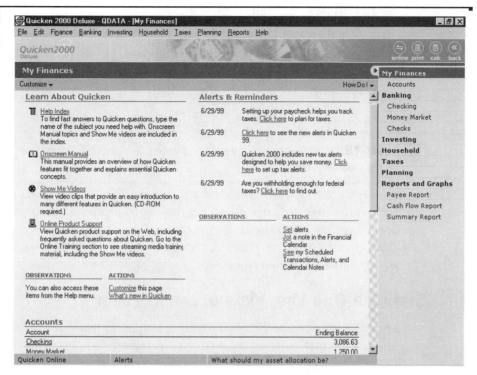

If you like this page, though, you can customize what it contains so that it is meaningful to you. To customize the current view, follow these steps:

1. From the Home page, click the Customize button, and from the drop-down menu, choose Customize This View to open the Customize View dialog box.

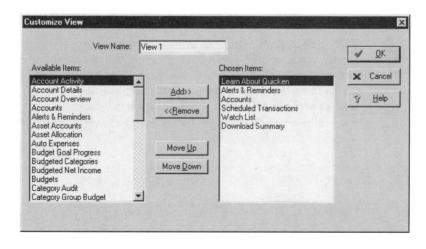

2. To remove an item from the display, select it and click Remove.

3. To add an item to the display, select it in the Available Items list and click Add.

4. To change the order in which items are displayed, select an item and click either Move Up or Move Down.

5. When the arrangement suits you, click OK.

 NOTE By default, your view is named View 1. To rename it, simply type a new name in the View Name box.

To create an entirely new view, click the Customize button, and from the drop-down menu choose Create a New View to open the Customize View dialog box. Select items from the Available Items list, click Add to add them to the Chosen Items list, arrange them to suit your fancy, name your view if you want, and click OK.

Getting a One-Line View of the Register

Switching to a one-line view of the register is another change you may want to make. This lets you pack more information into the register. To switch to a one-line view, just click the Options button in the top right of the register, and then choose One-Line Display. Quicken condenses all the information normally shown in two lines into one line by using shorter text boxes and omitting the Memo text box. If you click the Options button again, you will find that Quicken has placed a check next to One-Line Display to indicate that it is active. Choose One-Line Display again to switch back to the two-line view. Figure 6.2 shows the one-line version of the register.

 TIP The Options menu also provides commands for sorting the transactions that appear in the register: Sort by Date/Amount, Sort by Amount (Largest First), Sort by Amount (Smallest First), Sort by Check Number, Sort by Payee, and so on. If you're reviewing the contents of your register (rather than entering data into it), you can often use these sorting commands to organize your register and to more easily locate specific transactions.

FIGURE 6.2

*The one-line view of a
Quicken register*

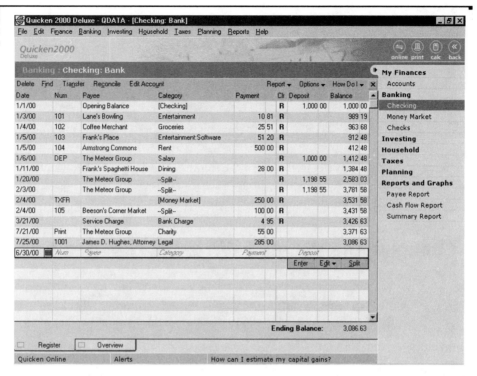

Saving a Desktop

Quicken calls the application window area beneath the menu bar the *Desktop*. Whenever you start Quicken, it displays the Desktop just the way you left it, with the same areas open and QuickTabs showing. You can change this arrangement, however, and have Quicken use a standard Desktop whenever you start.

First, arrange the Desktop exactly the way you want it to appear. Select the areas you want displayed and arrange them the way you want. Then choose the Edit ➢ Options ➢ Desktop command. Quicken displays the Save Desktop dialog box, as shown in Figure 6.3.

Selecting the Save Current Desktop button tells Quicken to preserve the arrangement of the Desktop as it is. When you select Save Current Desktop, the Save Desktop on Exit button is deactivated, which makes sense because you want to freeze your present configuration, not save whatever you have when you exit.

FIGURE 6.3

*The Save Desktop
dialog box*

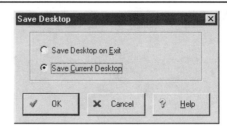

If you prefer to start with the Desktop looking as you left it upon exit, click the Save Desktop on Exit button. When you quit Quicken, the area arrangement is saved and will be restored when you return.

Changing the Way the Write Checks Area Works

You can make several changes in the way the Write Checks area works. For example, you can fine-tune aspects of check printing, control QuickFill's operation, and tell Quicken how it should validate the transactions you enter.

Fine-Tuning the Check-Printing Feature

You can control which information Quicken prints on a check and the appearance of that information. To do this, display the Write Checks area (by clicking the Write A Check hyperlink on the main Banking area), and then click the Options button. Quicken will display the Check Options dialog box, as shown in Figure 6.4.

FIGURE 6.4

*The Checks tab in the
Check Options
dialog box*

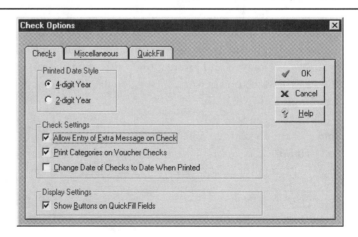

TIP The Options button is on the right side of the row of buttons at the top of the Write Checks area. This row of buttons changes according to the active area. Although the buttons correspond to menu commands, you can often save yourself a few steps by using the buttons. That can add up to a lot of saved time after a while, so try to get in the habit of using these buttons whenever they are available.

Use the Printed Date Style option buttons to specify how you would like Quicken to print the year on your check forms. The two option buttons show how a particular year appears. If the check date is July 4, 1999, for example, you have these choices:

Button	What You See
4-digit Year	7/4/2000
2-digit Year	7/4/00

The Allow Entry of Extra Message on Check checkbox tells Quicken to add another text box to the Write Checks area so that you can include another piece of data on the check form. Figure 6.5 shows the Write Checks area after the Allow Entry of Extra Message on Check checkbox has been marked. The extra message will appear on the printed check in roughly the same position as the message box shown in the Write Checks area.

FIGURE 6.5

The Write Checks area with an extra message box added

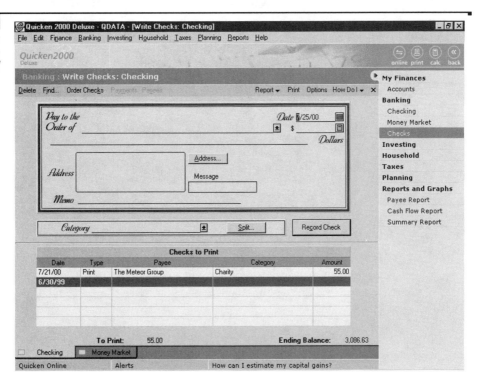

The Print Categories on Voucher Checks checkbox tells Quicken to print what you've entered as a check's category or split category information on the voucher portion of a check. You'll want to mark this box if you use Quicken to prepare employee payroll checks. You can use the split category information to describe an employee's gross wages and payroll deductions.

The Change Date of Checks to Date When Printed checkbox lets you exercise control over which date is printed on a check: the system date at the time you print the check or the date you (or someone else) entered in the check register. To use the system date as the date printed on the check, mark this checkbox. To use the date you entered in the Write Checks area, leave the checkbox unmarked.

The Show Buttons on QuickFill Fields checkbox lets you remove the down arrows, calculator, and calendar buttons at the end of the Pay to the Order of, Date, Amount, and Category fields.

Controlling How QuickFill Works

To change the way QuickFill works, display the Check Options dialog box as described earlier and click the QuickFill tab. Quicken displays the Check Options dialog box with the QuickFill settings, as shown in Figure 6.6.

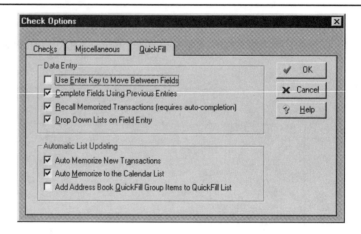

Turning QuickFill Field-Filling On and Off

QuickFill is such a handy feature and time-saver that I can't imagine why you wouldn't want to use it. However, if you do want to turn it off, unmark the Complete Fields Using Previous Entries checkbox. When you check this box, QuickFill automatically fills in the payee, category, amount, address, and memo if what you're typing looks like it might be the start of a payee or category that you've used before. Unmark the checkbox if you don't want QuickFill to fill in these fields automatically. QuickFill is a valuable feature, but it can be a little overzealous. If you want, you can limit when and how QuickFill works.

 TIP The Use Enter Key to Move Between Fields checkbox tells Quicken that it should treat the Enter key like the Tab key. When this checkbox is marked, pressing Enter will highlight the next text box—just as pressing Tab does.

Using Memorized Transactions

To tell QuickFill to find a memorized transaction with the same payee that you entered into the Payee text box and to then use this memorized transaction to fill the rest of the transaction's text boxes, leave the Recall Memorized Transactions checkbox marked. If you don't want QuickFill to retrieve memorized transactions, remove the checkmark from the box.

 NOTE To use a memorized transaction's data to enter a new transaction quickly, just display the Memorized Transaction List area (choose Banking ➤ Memorized Transaction List), select the memorized transaction you want to enter on the check, and click the Use button. You can enter memorized transactions into the register in the same way. Just display the account you want to use in the register, select the next empty row of the register, and then select the memorized transaction from the Memorized Transaction List area.

Controlling the Num, Payee, and Category Drop-Down Lists

Whenever you highlight the Num, Payee, or Category combo box in either the register or the Write Checks area, QuickFill displays a drop-down list. For the Register area's Num combo box, QuickFill displays a drop-down list of transaction codes. For the Payee and Category combo boxes, QuickFill displays drop-down lists of previously used payee names and of the categories you've set up.

Normally, you'll find the display of these drop-down lists very helpful. If they aren't useful to you, you can tell Quicken that you don't want to see them. Just unmark the Drop Down Lists on Field Entry checkbox.

Memorizing Transactions Automatically

Unless you tell it otherwise, QuickFill copies every new transaction's information to a list called, appropriately enough, the Memorized Transactions List. You can then set up QuickFill to automatically use memorized transactions to enter new transactions. If you don't want QuickFill to automatically memorize transactions—for example, because you want to conserve memory and disk space—unmark the Auto Memorize New Transactions checkbox.

For the average Quicken user, it's easiest to let QuickFill memorize transactions. But you can also memorize an individual transaction by choosing the Edit ➢ Transaction ➢ Memorize command.

Adding Transactions to the Financial Calendar

If you mark the Auto Memorize to the Calendar List checkbox, Quicken adds check transactions to the Financial Calendar's list of transactions. (Chapter 20 describes how you can use the Financial Calendar for monitoring important payroll transactions.)

Retrieving Names and Addresses from the Address Book

If you place a checkmark in the Add Address Book QuickFill Group Items to QuickFill List checkbox, Quicken will "QuickFill" the Payee and Pay to the Order of fields using the names and addresses that you've stored in the Financial Address Book that comes with Quicken Deluxe. (Chapter 10 describes Quicken Deluxe features and how to use them.)

Error-Checking Transactions

You can determine what safety measures Quicken should take to minimize the chances that you'll enter erroneous transactions into the Write Checks area. To address these information safety issues, display the Check Options dialog box as described earlier and then click the Miscellaneous tab. Quicken displays the Check Options dialog box with the Miscellaneous settings, as shown in Figure 6.7.

Mark the When Recording Out of Date Transactions checkbox if you want Quicken to display a warning message if you try to record a transaction for a different year.

Mark the Warn of Unsaved Transactions checkbox if you want Quicken to display a message box that warns you if you attempt to leave the Write Checks area without saving the check you're working on.

To make sure you categorize all your transactions, mark the When Recording Uncategorized Transactions checkbox. If you later try to record a transaction that doesn't show a category, Quicken displays a message box asking you to confirm that you want to record the transaction without a category. (You can still record transactions without categories if you mark this checkbox, but it will be more work.)

FIGURE 6.7

The Miscellaneous tab of the Check Options dialog box

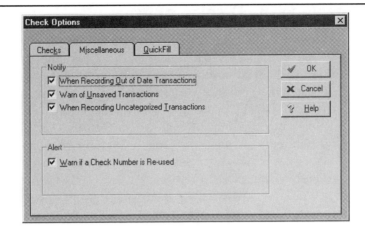

The Warn If a Check Number Is Re-used checkbox tells Quicken to display a message box that warns you whenever you enter a check number that has already appeared in the register. Because a check number should uniquely identify a check, you should use a given check number only once, so leave this checkbox marked.

Changing Quicken's General Options

You can make several additional preference-setting changes through the General Options dialog box. To display this dialog box, choose Edit ➤ Options ➤ Quicken Program. The General Options dialog box has four tabs: QuickTabs, General, Settings, and Startup. If it is not already showing, click the QuickTabs tab to display the options shown in Figure 6.8.

FIGURE 6.8

The QuickTabs tab of the General Options dialog box

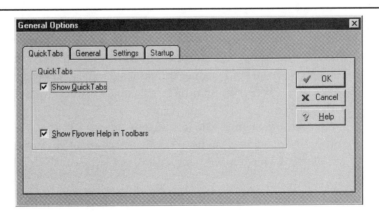

Controlling the Display of Areas

You use the QuickTabs options to specify how Quicken will display its areas. Initially, Quicken provides areas that fill the Quicken application window. QuickTabs appear to the side of the area and allow you to page through the open areas quickly.

By unmarking the Show QuickTabs checkbox, you can instruct Quicken to use normal, Windows-style document windows rather than QuickTabs.

When you check Show Flyover Help in Toolbars, Quicken displays a short description of the button's function whenever you leave the pointer over a toolbar button. You probably want to leave this checkbox marked, unless you know Quicken extremely well.

Changing General Settings

As you can see in Figure 6.9, clicking the General tab of the General Options dialog box displays even more options for customizing Quicken.

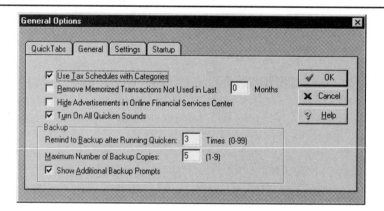

FIGURE 6.9

The General tab of the General Options dialog box

If you want to export Quicken data directly to a tax-preparation package, leave the Use Tax Schedules with Categories checkbox marked. This tells Quicken that it should ask you on which tax schedule and on which line a tax-related category should be placed. (See Chapter 14 for information about estimating and preparing income taxes with Quicken.)

The Remove Memorized Transactions Not Used in Last [*Number*] Months checkbox and text box let you clean up and reduce the size of your memorized transactions list. To remove old memorized transactions, mark the checkbox and then, in the text box, enter the number of months after which an unused memorized transaction should be deleted.

If you use Quicken's online services and don't want to be bombarded with commercial messages, check the Hide Advertisements in Online Financial Services Center checkbox.

By default, the sounds associated with actions you take in Quicken are turned on. If you want to turn them off, uncheck the Turn On All Quicken Sounds checkbox.

When you first install Quicken, Quicken asks you after every third time you exit the program if you want to back up your files. To be reminded more or less often (or never), enter a number in the Remind to Backup after Running Quicken box.

 TIP It's a good idea to back up your data files frequently. The more often you change your data, the more often you should back up your changes.

By default, Quicken automatically makes five copies of your data files every seven days and stores these backup files on your hard drive in the \BACKUP directory. To change this, type a number in the range 1 through 9 in the Maximum Number of Backup Copies box.

Changing Keyboard and Calendar Settings

You can also adjust some of Quicken's keyboard and calendar settings. Click the Settings tab to view the set of options shown in Figure 6.10.

FIGURE 6.10

The Settings tab of the General Options dialog box

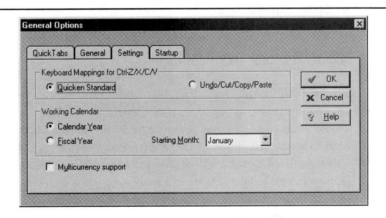

The Keyboard Mappings for Ctrl-Z/X/C/V options tell Quicken whether you want to use the command shortcuts Ctrl+Z, Ctrl+X, Ctrl+C, and Ctrl+V in the Quicken way or in the Windows way. If you want to adjust this setting, you'll know it. If you're someone who uses command shortcuts regularly (either in Quicken or in other Windows applications), you'll want the shortcuts to work the way you expect.

The Working Calendar option buttons let you use a fiscal (or accounting) year that's different from the calendar year. Individuals who use Quicken probably don't need to worry about this, but some businesses and many nonprofit organizations use a non-calendar fiscal year. If you want to do this, mark the Fiscal Year option button, and then use the Starting Month drop-down list to indicate when your fiscal year starts.

If you have accounts that use a foreign currency, check the Multicurrency Support checkbox. When you then click OK, Quicken places the currency symbols for all your accounts in the Balance field.

 TIP For much more information on using foreign currencies, choose Help ➤ Index, and search on *multicurrency*. See your Windows documentation for how to view or change your default currency.

Changing the Way Quicken Starts

As I mentioned earlier, by default Quicken displays the Home page when you open the program. To change this, you use the Startup tab of the General Options dialog box.

If you don't want to display the Home page, unmark the Home Page When Starting Quicken button. To display reminders instead (as discussed in the next section), mark the Reminders When Starting Quicken button. Choose None if you don't want to display either.

Using Reminders and Alerts

Just as you might place a sticky note on your printed calendar or pencil in a message to remind yourself to pay a bill on a certain date, you can ask Quicken to remind you to take action on upcoming financial matters. Quicken's Reminders feature lists transactions you've scheduled and notes you've entered in the Financial Calendar, checks you have listed to print, online payments you have set to send, and investment actions you've indicated you want to take. To display Quicken's Reminders, choose Finance ➤ Reminders.

You can customize the reminders Quicken displays by clicking the Options button and choosing Reminders ➤ Days Shown. In the Days In Advance box, enter the number of days in advance you want to be reminded of a scheduled transaction. In the

Show Notes For drop-down list box, select the time range for which you want to view reminders. For example, if you want to see only overdue transactions for the previous week, choose Last Week.

You can set up Alerts in Quicken to warn you of situations such as approaching a bank account's minimum balance, reaching your credit limit, spending over budget, or withholding too little tax. You can also set up Quicken to alert you if your insurance policy is about to expire or if a stock price hits a low or high limit you've specified. To set up alerts, choose Finance ➤ Alerts. Select checkboxes from the list in the left to turn an alert on. Use the list in the right to specify the alert.

Quicken 2000 can now alert you when a bond is about to mature or a CD is about to expire. The new Insider Trading alert notifies you if an individual buys or sells a large volume of shares. The New Research Report Available alert lets you know if the securities you're tracking have new research reports available. The new Moving Averages alert can help you spot changing trends in a stock's price.

Changing the Way the Register Looks and Works

Quicken lets you change the way the account register looks and works. Many of the changes you can make are identical to the changes you can make in the Write Checks area.

Changing the Register Display Options

To make changes to the register preferences, choose Options ➤ Register Options to open the Register Options dialog box, shown in Figure 6.11.

FIGURE 6.11

The Register Options dialog box

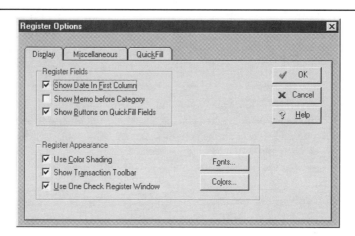

The checkboxes in the Display tab work as follows:

Show Date in First Column Acts as a toggle switch. Mark this checkbox if you want to see the Date field first and the Num (transaction number) field second. Unmark this checkbox if you want to see the transaction number first and the date second.

Show Memo before Category Also acts as a toggle switch, flip-flopping the position of the Memo and Category boxes in the register.

Show Buttons on QuickFill Fields Turns on and off the drop-down list that appears at the end of all fields that work with QuickFill.

Use Color Shading Turns on and off the shading that appears on the second line of each transaction.

Show Transaction Toolbar If marked, tells Quicken to display the Record, Enter, Edit, and Split buttons in the selected transaction's row of the register.

Use One Check Register Window If left unmarked, Quicken opens a new window for every register you open. If it is marked, only one register window is opened at a time, but it will change to whatever account register you wish to examine.

Changing Font Preferences

Quicken adds the ability to change the font and font size for the screen display of registers and lists.

Choose Options ➤ Register Options to display the Register Options dialog box and click the Fonts button. Quicken displays the Choose Register Font dialog box, as shown in Figure 6.12. Scroll through the font list and highlight a font to select it. Choose a size and, if desired, check the Bold checkbox. Choose carefully, with regard to legibility. You can see how your choices look in the preview box at the bottom of the dialog box. Click OK to set a new default. If you do not like the new default, you can later return to MS Sans Serif by choosing the Reset button in this dialog box.

 WARNING Again, be careful when you make changes, because this option can leave you worse off than when you began. The default font is MS Sans Serif, a Windows font created for legibility on the computer screen. Other fonts, which may look elegant on paper, can be difficult to read on the screen.

FIGURE 6.12

The Choose Register Font dialog box

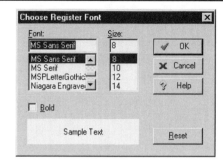

Changing Register Colors

Another choice in the Register Options dialog box (choose Options ➤ Register Options) lets you change register colors. Click the Colors button to display the Choose Register Colors dialog box, shown in Figure 6.13. There are six possible account types in Quicken. Assigning colors to registers can help you distinguish them from one another and prevent mistaken entries in the wrong register.

FIGURE 6.13

The Choose Register Colors dialog box

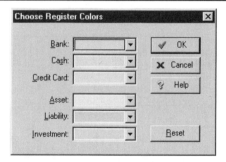

To set a color for an account type, activate one of the drop-down list boxes—Bank, Cash, Credit Card, Asset, Liability, or Investment—and click your color of choice. Click OK to complete the selection. The Reset button allows you to return to Quicken's preset color scheme.

CHAPTER 7

Protecting Your Financial Records

I f the information you're collecting with Quicken is important—and it almost certainly is—you'll want to take steps to protect that information. After all, if you're using Quicken as a personal financial record-keeping system, the Quicken data files may describe things such as your net worth, the cash you have available for things like retirement and next week's groceries, and which tax deductions you're entitled to. If you're using Quicken as a business record-keeping tool, the Quicken data files describe the assets you own and the liabilities you owe. They also contain the information necessary to calculate your profits.

Backing Up and Restoring Your Data

You've heard it perhaps a hundred times before, but I'm going to say it again: You need to back up your data files. You don't want to lose your financial records just because your hard disk fails or someone accidentally or intentionally deletes or corrupts the data files.

MASTERING TROUBLESHOOTING

Quicken's "Hidden" Backup

Quicken has an elegant feature you may never be aware of unless you suffer a data loss disaster or are the type who likes to poke around on your hard disk. When Quicken is installed, it creates a subfolder named Backup. Periodically, as you leave a session with Quicken, your data is copied to the Backup folder without any notice to you.

This is a fine feature for those who delay or forget to make backups. If you lose or damage your main data file, you can use the File ➢ Restore Backup File command, as described later in this chapter, to copy the Backup data to your Quicken folder. Remember, however, that this data will not survive the loss of your hard disk or computer. Keep on making backups to removable media so the data won't be lost if the computer is damaged or destroyed.

When you look at the Backup folder, you'll notice several different copies of your files there. If you're running low on disk space, you might want to delete all but the most recent copy of your files.

Backing Up Your Files

It's easy to back up the Quicken data files that contain your financial records. All you need to do is copy the data files to a floppy disk and store the floppy disk in a safe place.

 WARNING Store the backup floppy disk at another location. You don't want whatever corrupts or destroys your original Quicken data files—a fire, a nefarious employee, a burglar, or whatever—to also corrupt or destroy your backup copy of the data files.

To back up your Quicken data files, follow these steps:

1. Insert a formatted floppy disk into the drive you will use to create the backup.

2. Choose File ➢ Backup and click Yes to display the Select Backup Drive dialog box, as shown in Figure 7.1.

3. Use an option button in the File to Back Up box to indicate which file you want to back up: the current file or another file, to be selected from a list.

4. In the Backup Drive drop-down list box, select the floppy drive you'll use to create the backup. Click OK.

FIGURE 7.1

The Select Backup Drive dialog box, showing drive A: as the backup drive

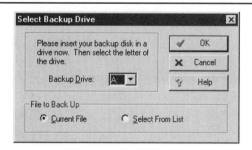

5. If in step 3 you indicated that you want to select the file that should be backed up, Quicken displays the Select a Quicken Data File to Back Up dialog box, shown in Figure 7.2. If you know the complete path name of the file you want to back up—the drive, the folder location, and the filename—you can enter this information directly into the File Name text box, and then click OK. Alternatively, use the Look In drop-down list box to select the drive where the original Quicken data file you want to back up is stored. Use the list box to locate the folder location of the original Quicken data file you want to back up. Select the Quicken data file you want to back up and click OK.

FIGURE 7.2

The Select a Quicken Data File to Back Up dialog box

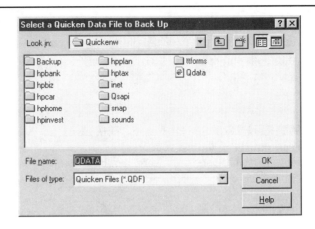

If you've backed up the data on the same disk previously, Quicken will display a message box asking you to confirm the backup before Quicken replaces the old file with the newer one.

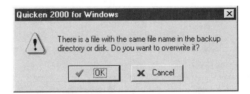

As Quicken backs up the data files, it displays a message box to tell you what it's doing. When it finishes, it displays another message box to tell you it has completed the backup. Click OK in this dialog box.

TIP It's a good idea to have "backup backups"—in other words, different copies of files you've backed up. Let's say you back up every week and something (perhaps a power surge) happens that damages your Quicken data files. If you try to use the most recent week's backup floppy disk to restore your financial records, you may find that it also has a problem. (Floppy disks are more unreliable than hard disks.) But if you also have a backup copy from the previous week's backup operation, you can try it as a last resort. You can make backup backups by using two or three floppy disks for your backups and then alternating your use of these floppy disks. Use one disk for week 1, a second disk for week 2, and a third disk for week 3, and then start the cycle over again by using the first disk for week 4.

Backup Reminder Messages

If you haven't recently backed up your file, Quicken displays a reminder message when you choose File ➢ Exit.

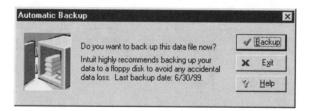

You can choose to start the backup process described in the preceding paragraphs by selecting the Backup command button, which appears in the message box. Or, you can exit without backing up by choosing the Exit command button, which also appears in the message box.

 NOTE One common data file problem is corruption of the index file that Quicken uses to organize your transaction data. Fortunately, if this index file becomes corrupted—if, for example, your computer resets while Quicken is running—Quicken automatically rebuilds the index for you without requiring you to restore the entire set of Quicken data files. You will know if this happens; Quicken displays a message box telling you the index file is damaged and that it is rebuilding the file for you.

How to Restore from a Backup in Seven Easy Steps

If your Quicken data files are corrupted, your problems are pretty minor as long as you have a recent backup copy of the data files to work with. To restore a damaged file, copy the contents of the backup data files to your hard disk.

 WARNING If you don't back up your data and you lose your Quicken data files, you'll need to reenter all your transactions.

To restore Quicken data files from the backup copy of the files, follow these steps:

1. Insert the disk with the backup copy of the Quicken data file into your floppy drive.

2. Choose File ➤ Restore Backup File. In the Select Restore Drive dialog box, choose the letter of the drive containing the backup disk. Click OK to display the Restore Quicken File dialog box, as shown in Figure 7.3.

FIGURE 7.3

The Restore Quicken File dialog box

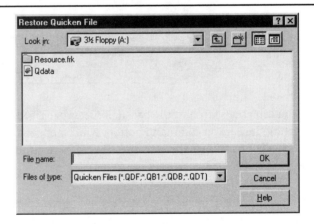

3. If necessary, activate the Look In drop-down list box and select the floppy drive containing the backup disk.

4. Click the data file you want to restore.

5. Click OK. Quicken displays a message box asking you to confirm that you want to overwrite the current version of the file.

6. To restore the data file by replacing the current, hard-disk version of the data file with the backup copy stored on the floppy disk, click OK. Quicken displays a message box telling you that it's restoring the data file.

7. When the restoration is complete, click OK in the message box telling you that the file has been restored successfully.

Once you've copied the contents of the backup data files to your hard disk, you'll need to reenter each transaction that you recorded after you last backed up. If you've been printing registers, you can use them to get the information you need to reenter the transactions. If you haven't been printing registers, you'll need to use whatever other source documentation you have, such as bank statements, invoices, canceled checks, and so on.

 TIP Back up your Quicken data files immediately after you finish the restoration. It may be that whatever corrupted or damaged the original data file will again corrupt or damage it. This would be a good opportunity to start that second backup disk I suggested earlier in this chapter.

Using Other Backup Utilities

You can use other backup utilities, such as a tape backup utility, to back up your Quicken data files. Simply follow the specific utility's instructions.

If you use another utility, keep in mind that you don't need to back up any of the Quicken program files (any files with the extension .BAT, .EXE, or .DLL). Just back up the Quicken data files—several individual files that make up the complete set of data files Quicken uses to store your financial records. Quicken uses the same filename as it uses for the Quicken program files, such as QDATA, but different extensions, such as .ABD, .QDB, .QDF, .QEL, .QSD, and so on. Therefore, make sure that you back up all the files that have either the QDATA filename Quicken supplies or the filename you've supplied.

Using Passwords to Restrict Access to Financial Data

Quicken also lets you assign passwords to files. Once you've done so, a person can neither use a file nor view its contents without first supplying the password. Quicken also lets you create a special type of password that limits the transaction dates that a person can use when entering transactions.

Locking Up a File by Assigning a Password

To lock up a file so no person without the password can access that file, assign a file-level password to the file. Simply follow these steps:

1. Choose File ➢ Passwords ➢ File to open the Set Up Password dialog box, shown in Figure 7.4.

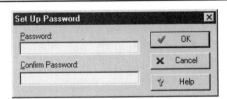

2. Enter the password you want to use in the Password text box, enter the same password in the Confirm Password text box, and then click OK.

You can use any combination of characters, but Quicken won't differentiate between uppercase and lowercase characters. From Quicken's perspective, GLADIOLA, Gladiola, and gLADiola are all the same password.

As you type the password, Quicken displays asterisks instead of the actual characters you type. This helps to prevent someone from looking over your shoulder and learning your password. But you should still be careful, because someone might be able to learn your password by watching which keys you type on your keyboard.

Quicken compares what you entered in the Password text box with what you entered in the Confirm Password text box. As long as the two passwords are identical, Quicken closes the Set Up Password dialog box. You now have a password.

If the two entries aren't identical, Quicken displays a message box alerting you to the error, and then Quicken redisplays the Set Up Password dialog box. You'll need to enter the same password in both the Password and Confirm Password text boxes.

 WARNING Don't forget your password! Forgetting a password has the same consequences as losing or corrupting your data files and not having a backup copy of the files: You will need to start all over from scratch. Keep a copy of your file password someplace safe. For example, if you use Quicken at work, you might want to keep a record of your password at home.

You won't need to use the password as part of the current session. But the next time you or someone else tries to access the file (probably the next time you start Quicken), Quicken will display a dialog box like the one shown in Figure 7.5. You'll need to enter your password in order to access the file.

FIGURE 7.5

The Quicken Password dialog box

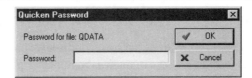

Using a Transaction Password

Quicken also supplies another type of password, called a *transaction password*. This password prevents people who don't have the transaction password from entering transactions that fall before a certain date. For example, you might use a transaction password so that a new user can't accidentally foul up last year's financial records while entering this year's transactions.

To set up a transaction-level password, follow these steps:

1. Choose File ➤ Passwords ➤ Transaction. Quicken displays the Password to Modify Existing Transactions dialog box, shown in Figure 7.6.

FIGURE 7.6

The Password to Modify Existing Transactions dialog box

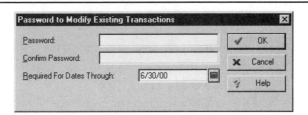

2. Enter the password you want to use in both the Password and Confirm Password text boxes. As with file-level passwords, you can use any combination of characters, and Quicken doesn't differentiate between uppercase and lowercase characters.

3. Enter the transaction date on or before which the user must supply the transaction-level password. Clicking the button at the right end of the text box opens a pop-up calendar you can use to choose a date. Click OK.

Quicken compares what you entered in the Password text box with what you entered in the Confirm Password text box. As long as the two passwords are identical, Quicken closes the Password to Modify Existing Transactions dialog box. Now Quicken will require you (and anyone else) to enter the transaction password before recording or editing a transaction dated on or before the specified transaction date.

Changing File-Level and Transaction-Level Passwords

You can change file-level and transaction-level passwords in the same way you add them. One change you can make is to replace a password with a blank password, which is the same as telling Quicken you no longer want to use a password.

Changing a File-Level Password

To change the file-level password, follow these steps:

1. Choose File ➤ Passwords ➤ File to display the Change Password dialog box, shown in Figure 7.7.

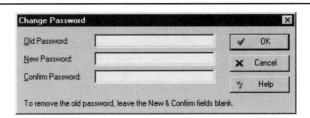

2. Enter the current file-level password in the Old Password text box.

3. Enter the replacement file-level password in the New Password text box and the Confirm Password text box. (If you want to just get rid of the file-level password and not supply a replacement, leave the New Password and the Confirm Password text boxes blank.) Click OK.

From this point forward, the new replacement password will control access to the file.

Changing a Transaction-Level Password

To change the transaction-level password, follow these steps:

1. Choose File ➤ Passwords ➤ Transaction to display the Change Transaction Password dialog box, shown in Figure 7.8.

FIGURE 7.8

*The Change
Transaction Password
dialog box*

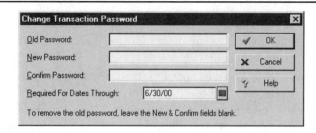

2. Enter the current transaction-level password in the Old Password text box.

3. Enter the replacement transaction-level password in the New Password text box and in the Confirm Password text box. (If you want to just get rid of the transaction-level password and not supply a replacement, leave the New Password and Confirm Password text boxes blank.)

4. In the Required For Dates Through text box, enter the date that determines when a transaction-level password is required.

5. Click OK.

From this point forward, Quicken will require the new transaction password whenever anyone attempts to enter a transaction or modify a transaction that falls on or before the cut-off date you specified in step 4.

Physical Security Measures

In terms of computer security, it's easy to focus on things like file backups and passwords. But don't forget about other physical security measures.

If you're using Quicken in a business, for example, it's a good idea to restrict access to the computer that runs the Quicken program and on which the Quicken data files are stored. With computers as relatively inexpensive as they are, for example, you might want to dedicate a computer to Quicken and prohibit people from using the computer for other things. (Large businesses routinely restrict access to their computer systems by providing tighter security and controlled access to their management information systems areas.)

You might want to put the computer that runs Quicken and stores the data files in a locked office. This deterrent wouldn't stop a determined criminal, of course; but with every obstacle you put in the path of a thief, you decrease your chances of becoming a victim.

Another physical measure relates to the check forms you use. Be sure to use a signature that's not easily duplicated (forged). Signatures that consist of a wavy line and a couple of i-dots (or are those t-crosses?) aren't going to be easily detected as forgeries by anyone—including yourself.

And while you don't need to worry about the way Quicken fills out a check, be sure to carefully and completely fill out the check forms you write by hand. Figure 7.9 shows a check form that I've purposely filled in sloppily, with blank spaces in the amount box and on the amount line. Figure 7.10 shows the same check form with some minor changes.

FIGURE 7.9

A check form that's been completed so sloppily that it's easy to alter

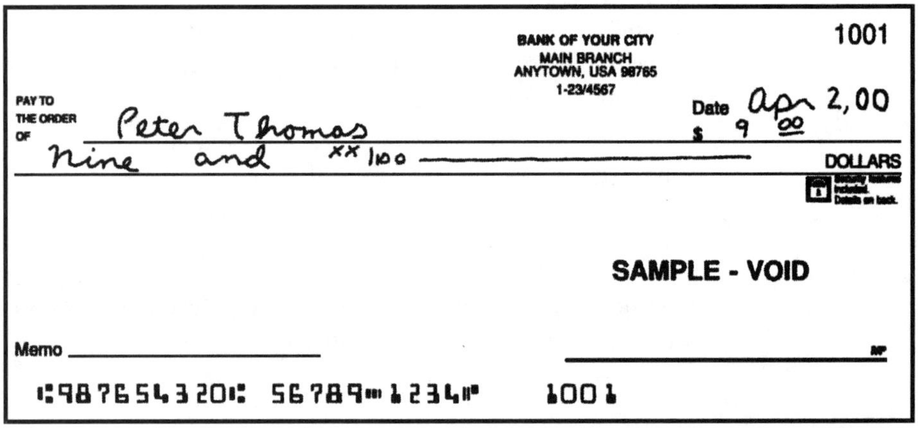

FIGURE 7.10

The same check form as shown in Figure 7.9 after it has been altered

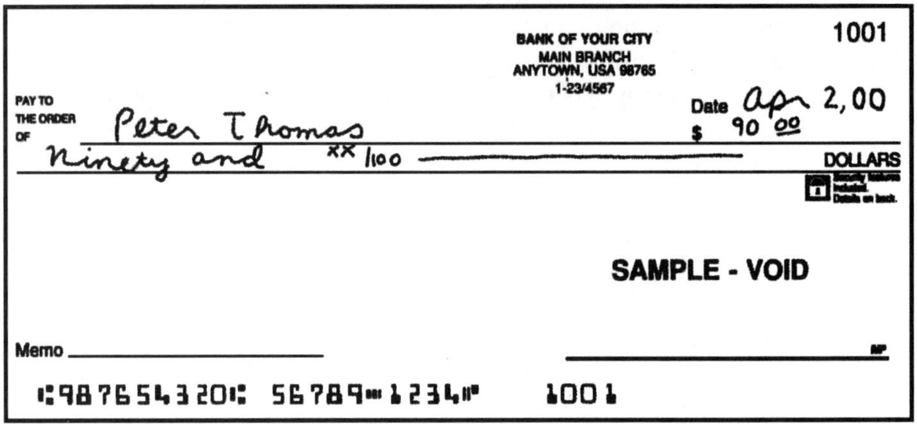

NOTE It's usually the bank's responsibility, not yours, to detect check forgeries. Forgery is any altering or marking that changes your liability, so filling in extra words and numbers on a check form, as in the example in Figure 7.10, constitutes forgery. It might not be you who suffers the loss if you are a victim of check forgery. However, you may need to absorb some of the loss if you're negligent or if you delay reporting a forgery to the bank.

CHAPTER **8**

Graphing Your Finances

Tabular presentations of quantitative information, such as the Quicken reports with their rows and columns of data, work well when you want access to the details or when you want to-the-dollar or to-the-penny precision. Sometimes, though, a graph works better. Graphs summarize your financial data in a picture, often display trends you might otherwise miss, and sometimes let you see—or at least detect—relationships in the graphed data that otherwise would remain hidden.

 NOTE You don't need any special skills or knowledge to graph data with Quicken. You do, however, need to have collected the data you want to graph by keeping records of your financial affairs using the Quicken registers.

How to Create Your First Graph in 60 Seconds

To create a graph, you simply choose a few commands from menus and tell Quicken which information you want it to graph. To illustrate how this approach works, suppose that you want to plot a graph that shows your income and expenses over several months.

Drawing an On-Screen Report

To create an on-screen report, follow these steps:

1. Click the Reports and Graphs QuickTab and click the How Am I Spending My Money? tab to display the list of spending reports and graphs, as shown in Figure 8.1.

2. Select Income/Expense graph.

3. Tell Quicken which months' data it should graph, using either the drop-down list box or the From and To text boxes.

FIGURE 8.1

*Creating a
Spending graph*

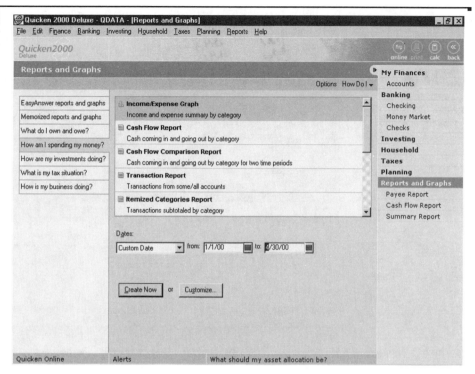

The drop-down list box contains descriptions such as Year to Date or Current Quarter. Choosing one of these will automatically change the From and To text boxes appropriately. You can also change the From and To text boxes directly. For example, to plot monthly income and expense data for January through April 2000, type **1/1/00** in the From text box and **4/30/00** in the To text box (see Figure 8.1). The drop-down list box automatically changes to Custom Date.

4. Quicken assumes that all the accounts in a file should be included in a graph. If you want to select specific accounts, click the Customize button to open the Customize Graph dialog box. If it is not already showing, click the Accounts tab, which is shown in Figure 8.2. Select and deselect the accounts to use by clicking each account or pressing the spacebar. The spacebar and clicking act as toggle switches: They alternately mark an account to be included and then not to be included.

5. Quicken assumes that all your categories should be included in a report. If you want to designate categories to plot, click the Categories tab in the Customize

Graph dialog box, which is shown in Figure 8.3. Select and deselect the categories to use by clicking each category or pressing the spacebar.

FIGURE 8.2

The Accounts tab of the Customize Graph dialog box

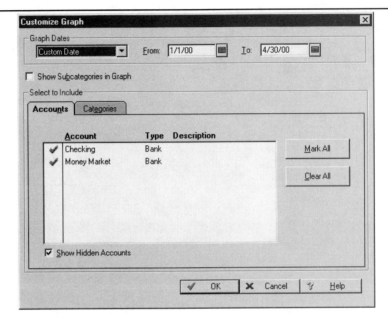

FIGURE 8.3

The Categories tab of the Customize Graph dialog box

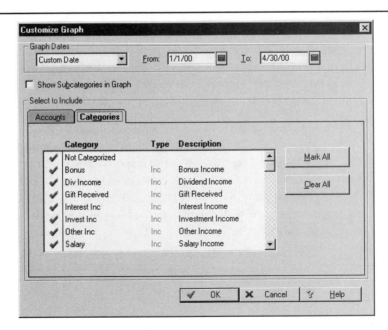

6. If you want to plot subcategories separately from their parent category, click the Show Subcategories in Graph checkbox.

7. Quicken assumes that you want to graph data from all classes. If you want to designate classes to graph, click on the Classes tab in the Customize Graph dialog box. (This tab appears only if you have created any classes.) Designate classes in the same way that you select specific accounts or categories.

8. When your selections are complete, click OK. Quicken creates the graph using just the data you specified. Figure 8.4 shows an Income and Expense graph.

FIGURE 8.4

The Income and Expense Graph area

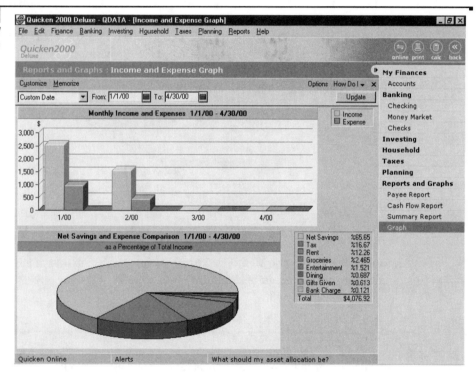

In the top half of the Graph area, Quicken displays a bar graph of total income and total expenses by month. In the bottom half of the Graph area, Quicken displays a pie graph of the expense categories as percentages of the total expenses.

TIP To change the dates for which a graph is plotted after you've displayed it, enter new dates in the From or To boxes and click the Update button in the upper-right corner of the Graph area.

Memorizing Graphs

Just as you can "memorize" reports, you can memorize graphs. By doing so, you can save any special graph-creation settings, such as the accounts or categories you want to use. The graph-memorization process works in the same way as the report-memorization process. Once you've produced a graph you want to save for future use, click the Memorize button in the Graph area. When Quicken displays the Memorize Graph dialog box, give the memorized graph a name and select OK.

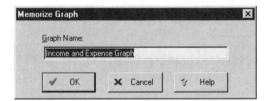

The next time you want to display the graph, choose the Reports and Graphs QuickTab and click the Memorized Reports and Graphs tab on the left side. Then select the memorized graph from the list that Quicken displays. The list in Figure 8.5 shows one graph listed.

 NOTE Three-dimensional graphs like the one shown in Figure 8.4 may look more interesting than the two-dimensional variety, but they are also less precise visually. If you want to add precision to your graphs by plotting them in 2-D, see the last section of this chapter, "Customizing Quicken's Graphing."

FIGURE 8.5

Memorized reports and graphs

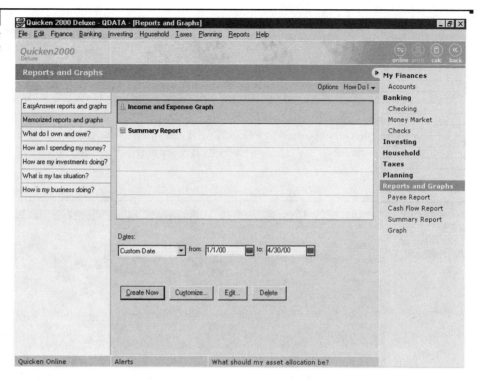

Printing Graphs

To print the graph currently displayed, choose File ➤ Print Graph. Quicken sends the graph to Windows to begin the work of printing your graph.

Graphs are more work to print than text, so it takes longer to print a page of graphs than a page of report information. As Quicken and Windows work to print your graph, you'll see a message box on your screen telling you that the graph is being printed.

QuickZooming on a Graph's Data Markers

Data markers are the symbols that a graph uses to show its information. These include the bars in a bar graph, the slices in a pie graph, and so on. If you want more information about a particular data marker's data—say, you want to see another graph that further describes a slice of a pie graph—you can use *QuickZoom*. The cursor changes to a magnifying glass when it points to a data marker. Just double-click the data marker you want to further explore. Quicken draws another graph, which shows information about the selected data marker. If you use QuickZoom on a pie graph to get more information about your net savings, for example, QuickZoom produces a bar graph of net income by month, as shown in Figure 8.6.

You can even QuickZoom on a QuickZoom graph. In this case, QuickZoom produces a Net Income by Month report showing the individual transactions that make up the values plotted in a QuickZoom graph. Figure 8.7 shows the QuickZoom report that describes the January income category data plotted in the QuickZoom graph in Figure 8.6.

FIGURE 8.6

A QuickZoom graph lets you see details of the graph data.

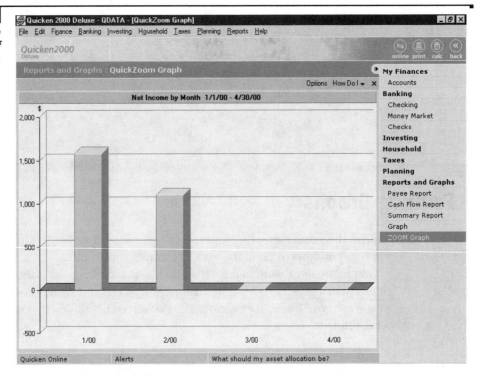

FIGURE 8.7

A QuickZoom Net Income by Month report shows transactions plotted in the QuickZoom graph in Figure 8.6.

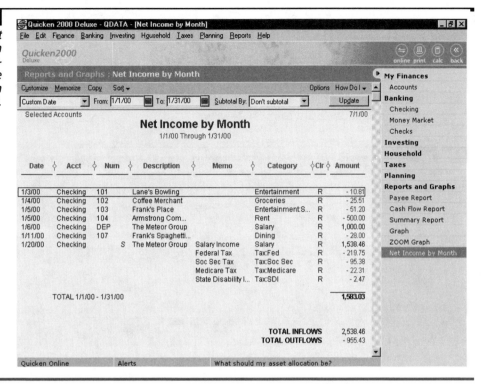

 TIP If you begin using QuickZoom to create QuickZoom reports, you'll very quickly create a collection of graph areas. Remember that you can individually close an area by clicking the Close button. This is the little X button in the upper-right corner.

Looking At the Other Graphs

Quicken produces several graphs in addition to the Income and Expense graph just described. You can choose one from the various tabs of the Reports and Graphs area.

The Budget Variance Graph

A Budget Variance graph compares your actual income and expense to your budgeted income and expense. To create this graph, you must first have created a budget (see Chapter 15, which explains how to create budgets). Then you follow a procedure similar to that used for creating an Income and Expense graph. Click the How Am I Spending My Money? tab in the Reports and Graphs area and then select Budget Variance

Graph from the list. Indicate which actual and budget data you want plotted, in the same way you select data for an Income and Expense graph, and click the Create Now button.

Figure 8.8 shows the Budget Variance graph. The top half of the area shows a bar graph of the monthly variances (difference) between the total actual income and the total budgeted income. The graph in the bottom half of the area compares actual and budgeted amounts, category by category.

FIGURE 8.8

A Budget Variance graph

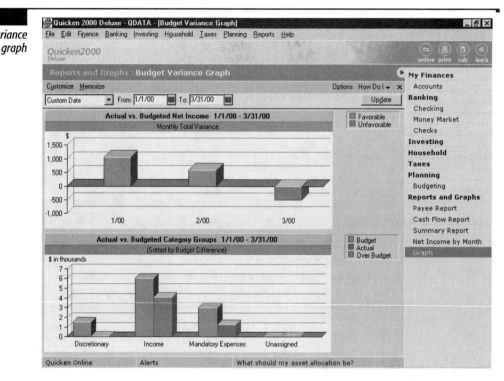

You can print, QuickZoom on data markers, and close Budget Variance graphs in the same way that you print, QuickZoom, and close Income and Expense graphs.

The Net Worth Graph

A Net Worth graph shows your total assets, total liabilities, and resulting net worth on a month-to-month basis. To create this graph, follow the same basic procedure you use to create Income and Expense and Budget Variance graphs. First, click the Reports and

Graphs QuickTab. Then click the What Do I Own and Owe? tab on the left side and select Net Worth Graph. Click the Customize button to indicate which accounts, categories, and classes you want plotted in the Net Worth graph, as explained earlier in the section "Drawing an On-Screen Report" about creating an Income and Expense graph.

When you click Create Now, Quicken draws the graph. Figure 8.9 shows an example of a Net Worth graph. Quicken uses bars to show your total assets and your total liabilities. It uses a small square to represent the net value, or your net worth, within each bar. It then draws a line to plot your net worth.

 TIP You can move the mouse over any area of a graph to display the exact amount of the data being plotted.

You can print, QuickZoom on data markers, and close the Net Worth graph in the same way that you print, QuickZoom, and close other graphs.

FIGURE 8.9

A Net Worth graph

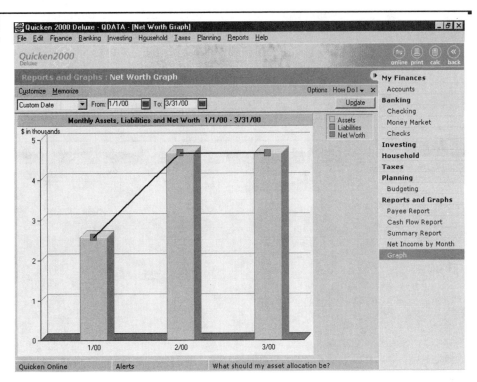

The Investment Graphs

If you're using Quicken for your investment record keeping, you can produce a bar graph that shows your total investment portfolio values by month, as well as the annualized average return. You can also produce a pie graph that summarizes your holdings by investment class. (You need to have begun using Quicken for investment record keeping to produce an investment graph, as explained in Chapters 17, 18, and 19.)

To produce an Investment Performance graph, follow these steps:

1. Click the Reports and Graphs QuickTab, click the How Are My Investments Doing? tab on the left side, and choose Investment Performance Graph.

2. Tell Quicken which months' investment data it should graph using the From and To text boxes. For example, to plot investment portfolio values and returns from January 2000 through March 2000, type **1/1/00** in the From text box and **3/31/00** in the To text box.

3. Quicken assumes that all the accounts in a file should be included in a graph. If you want to select specific investment accounts, click Customize. When the Customize Graph dialog box opens, click the Accounts tab, and then select and deselect the investment accounts to use.

4. Quicken assumes that all your securities should be included in the graph. If you want to select which securities should be plotted, click the Securities tab in the Customize Graph dialog box and mark the securities in the dialog box, as shown in Figure 8.10. Click OK to have Quicken create the graph.

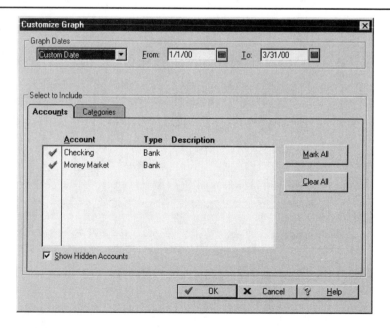

FIGURE 8.10

The Accounts tab of the Customize Graph dialog box

Figure 8.11 shows an Investment Performance graph. The top half shows a bar graph of the total investment portfolio value by security at the end of each month. The bottom half shows a bar graph of the average annual total return for the portfolio.

FIGURE 8.11

An Investment Performance graph

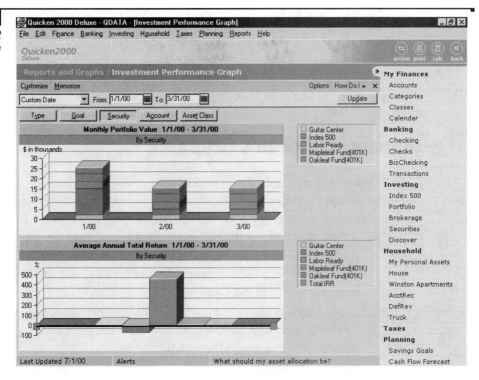

Along the top edge of the Investment Performance graph, Quicken adds several buttons you can use to rearrange the plotted data:

Button	When You Use It
Type	To plot your investment data by investment type
Goal	To plot your investment data by investment goal
Security	To return to the original, by-security plotting
Account	To plot your investment data by investment account
Asset Class	To plot your investment data by the security's asset class, such as Money Market or Domestic Small Cap

To produce an Investment Asset Allocation graph, follow the same basic procedure: Click the Reports and Graphs QuickTab, click the How Are My Investments Doing? tab on the left side, and select Investment Asset Allocation Graph. Then specify the date as of which you reported the allocation information. If you wish to include only specific accounts or securities in the graph, click the Customize button and customize the graph in the same way that you customize an Investment Performance graph. Then click Create Now to generate a pie graph that shows your investment holdings by asset class.

You can print, QuickZoom on data markers, and close investment graphs in the same way that you print, QuickZoom, and close other Quicken graphs.

Customizing Quicken's Graphing

Once you're comfortable using Quicken graphs, you can change the way Quicken draws and prints your graphs. To change the way Quicken draws many of the graphs you see and the way it prints them, click the Options button in the Graph area. The drop-down menu gives you the following choices:

Hide Customize Bar   If you want to hide the Customize bar in Graph areas, select this option. The Customize bar allows you to change the graph time frame directly from the graph.

Draw in 2D (faster)   If you want to use more precise, two-dimensional pie and bar graphs, select this option. The next time you click the Options button, this selection changes to Draw in 3D.

Draw in Patterns   By default, Quicken displays graphs on-screen with colored segments. When you select this option, Quicken displays all graphs using black-and-white patterns on the screen. Figure 8.12 shows an Income and Expense graph with cross-hatching.

Create Graphs in Separate Windows   The typical Quicken graph has two parts—for example, a bar graph and a pie graph. Selecting this option causes Quicken to print each part in its own area, which you can move and size separately. By default, both graphs print in a single area.

FIGURE 8.12

A two-dimensional Income and Expense graph with cross-hatching rather than color

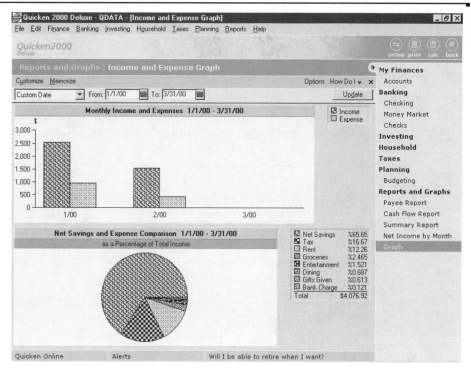

 NOTE Some people feel that pie graphs don't do a very good job of summarizing data because they can be used to visually depict only small data sets. A report is usually a much better way to show a small data set. Also, making pie graphs three-dimensional distorts the slices of the pie; those in the background appear smaller than they are, while those in the foreground appear larger.

CHAPTER **9**

Online Payment and Account Access

Quicken lets you simplify your financial affairs using its Online Payment and Online Account Access features. With Online Payment, you can automatically make payments for items you record in your Quicken registers. In essence, you tell either Intuit's computer or some bank's computer to use the information you've recorded about a particular payment to actually make the disbursement. With Online Account Access, you can transfer money between accounts set up for online banking and download account transaction information. This chapter describes both Online Payment and Online Account Access.

Before You Begin

To use Quicken's Online Payment and Online Account Access features, you need the following:

- Your computer must have a connection to the Internet. (See Chapter 11 for details on setting up an Internet connection.)
- To use the Online Account Access feature, your bank must support Quicken's online banking functions.

 NOTE Currently, about 75 banks and credit unions support online banking with Quicken, and this number is constantly increasing. In fact, in an effort to increase the number of banks offering this service, Intuit, Microsoft, and CheckFree (another online bill payment service) have created an alliance, called the Open Financial Exchange. The objectives of this alliance are to make online exchange of financial information easier and to encourage greater numbers of financial institutions to participate in online banking.

Online Payment

Quicken lets you pay bills electronically using Online Payment. With Online Payment, you use a modem to transmit information to another computer about the bills that you need to pay. Then the computer writes a check from your account to pay your bills for you.

Is Online Bill Payment for You?

Why would you use a service like Online Payment? Online bill payment delivers a major benefit. For the same work you go through to record payments in a Quicken register, you can also pay a bill. If you pay a bill with a check, you still need to print or handwrite that check, and then stuff, address, and mail the envelope.

 NOTE The cost of the online bill payment service varies, depending on your bank. Currently, my bank charges $5.95 a month for both online bill payment and online account access ($2 a month more than online account access alone). Does the price of the service seem expensive? If you consider how much it costs to mail in a payment ($.33), it's not so bad. And the check form you use to pay a bill may not be cheap. (For business checks and computer checks, you can easily pay a dime a form.) Using Online Payment can actually save you money.

There are only two potential drawbacks to using an online bill payment service. One is that it does require you to be a bit more organized in your bill paying. You need to transmit electronic payment information to the online bill payment service a few days early so that the service has time to process your payment. If you're always juggling those last few bills, this might not work. If you pay the mortgage with a handwritten check, for example, you may want the option of paying the mortgage on the last day and personally running the check down to the bank.

Another potential drawback is that some merchants don't like to deal with electronic payments. Reportedly, some banks with their own online bill payment services have balked at accepting electronic bill payments through Intuit or another financial institution. To be quite candid, I have had trouble paying some of my bills electronically, which is somewhat understandable. Electronic payments can be a little confusing to merchants. The checks don't look exactly like regular checks. (They aren't signed, for example.) And there's no way to include a remittance advice or payment coupon.

 MASTERING THE OPPORTUNITIES

An Online Bill Payment Service Choice

As of this writing, Quicken 2000 also includes CheckFree, another online bill payment service. Intuit (the company that makes and sells Quicken) has said that Online Payment is a better value for customers. Here are a few reasons why Online Payment might be the better choice:

- The financial transactions in Online Payment are handled directly by your bank, rather than by the CheckFree Corporation. If you are also using Online Account Access, this makes one less company to deal with. It also means that you work with a local service.

Continued

> ## MASTERING THE OPPORTUNITIES CONTINUED
>
> - Online Payment implements several helpful details in the service, such as automatic confirmation of payments and automatic adjustment of lead time, depending on the method of payment.
>
> Note, however, that Intuit recently sold the Online Payment service to the same company that owns and runs CheckFree. So, in practice, there probably will be less and less difference between the two services as time goes by. CheckFree operates in a manner very similar to Online Payment. You can use CheckFree by choosing the Banking ➢ CheckFree command.

Signing Up for Online Bill-Payment Services

You sign up for an online bill-payment service by filling out the Online Services Agreement that comes in the Quicken package or by filling out forms that are available through your bank. You may need to include a voided check with your sign-up paperwork.

A few days after you mail in your signed service agreement, you will get a welcome letter from either your bank or Intuit Services Corporation. The letter provides the information you need to set up Quicken for the online bill payment service.

Using Online Payment

If you know how Quicken works, you'll have no trouble with Online Payment. Once you've told Quicken that you want to use the Online Payment feature with a particular account, the only extra tasks you need to complete are building a list of electronic payees (the merchants, banks, and individuals that the online bill payment service pays) and learning to electronically transmit payment instructions to the online bill payment service center.

Marking an Account for Online Payment

To tell Quicken you want to use Online Payment with an account, follow these steps:

1. Display the account's register and click the Overview tab.

2. Click the Available, Not Enabled hyperlink beside Online Payment. This displays the Online Setup area shown in Figure 9.1.

FIGURE 9.1.

The Online Setup area

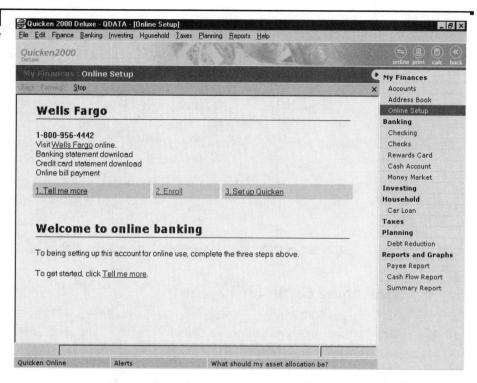

3. If you've selected a financial institution that Quicken recognizes, Quicken displays the online service information. If you haven't selected a financial institution that Quicken recognizes, it displays a list of participating institutions. Click a participating bank's hyperlink to see the online services it offers. Click the Tell Me More hyperlink to learn more about the services your bank offers. Click the Enroll hyperlink to apply for online services online. After you've applied and received any necessary setup information from your bank, click the Setup Quicken hyperlink. Quicken Displays the Edit Bank Account dialog box shown in Figure 9.2.

4. Select the Enable Online Payment check box and click Next.

5. Enter your bank's routing number and click Next. (The welcome letter that you got from your bank or Intuit supplies this information.)

6. Enter your account number and select an account type from the drop-down list box.

7. Enter your customer ID number (this is usually your social security number) and click Next twice to review the information that you provided.

8. Click Done.

FIGURE 9.2

The Edit Bank Account dialog box

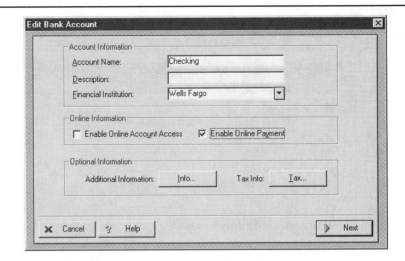

Describing Electronic Payees

To set up Online Payment, you need to create a list of the merchants you pay regularly. To do this, choose Banking ➤ Online Payee List. Quicken displays the Online Payee List, as shown in Figure 9.3.

FIGURE 9.3

The Online Payee List

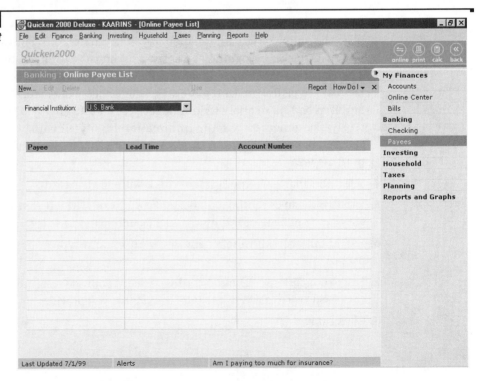

To describe an electronic payee, click the New button. Quicken displays the Set Up Online Payee dialog box, as shown in Figure 9.4. Fill in the dialog box and click OK. Then review the information in the Confirm Online Payee Information dialog box and click Accept. If you have additional payees to describe, click the New button in the Online Payee List and go through the process again.

FIGURE 9.4

The Set Up Online Payee dialog box

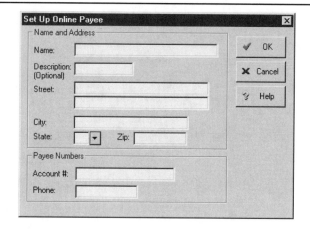

Paying a Bill with Online Payment

To pay a bill with Online Payment, choose Banking ➤ Online Banking. When Quicken displays the Online Center, click the Payments tab. Figure 9.5 shows this tab.

Notice that the form is very similar to a check, with a few important differences: There is a drop-down list box for selecting the account that you're using, the Delivery Date is automatically shown as ASAP, and the Pay to the Order Of line is labeled Payee.

You enter an electronic payment in almost the same way that you enter a regular check, with two differences: You must select which bank account you're using for the payment, and when you get to the Payee line, you must specify an electronic payee.

You can specify an electronic payee by entering a name into the Payee text box. As you type, if the payee is on your Online Payee list, Quicken will attempt to automatically fill in the rest of the name. If the name is not on your list, when you click Enter, Quicken displays the Set Up Online Payee dialog box (see Figure 9.4) so you can supply the information necessary to make an electronic payment. Figure 9.6 shows the Online Center describing an electronic payment. As you can see, you fill in an electronic payment form in the same way that you complete a check that you want to print.

FIGURE 9.5

The Payments tab of the Online Center

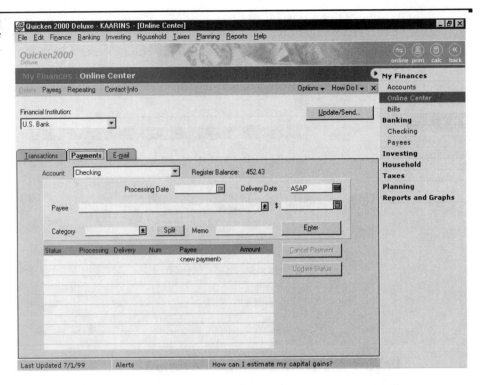

FIGURE 9.5

The Payments tab of the Online Center

After you have filled out the form, click the Enter button. Quicken adds your payment to the list and displays its current status in the text box at the bottom of the window. Note that Quicken has not sent the payment to your bank yet. It is stored on your computer until you send your transactions to the bank by clicking Update/Send, as explained in the next section.

TIP Before you start using Online Payment to pay your bills, experiment with the feature by sending yourself an electronic payment for some nominal amount, such as $1.00. You'll learn how long the online bill payment service takes to get payments to the payee. And you'll understand how the service uses the electronic payee information you provide.

FIGURE 9.6

The Online Center describing an electronic payment

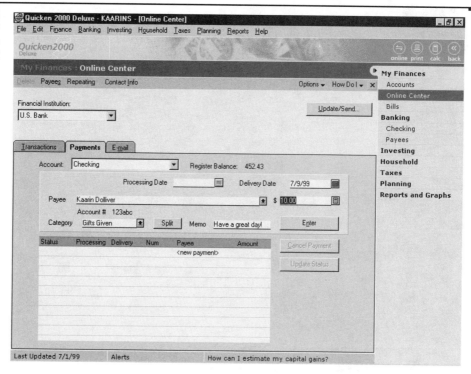

Sending Electronic Payments

Once you've described all of your electronic payments, making the actual payments is a snap. Simply display the Online Center, and then click the Update/Send button at the top right of the window. Quicken connects to the Internet; as it does so, you will see a series of message boxes.

Through the Internet, Quicken connects to the online bill payment service computer and displays the Instructions to Send dialog box, as shown in Figure 9.7. This dialog box shows a list of the online payments you have recorded up to that point, along with any other online transactions waiting to be sent.

If you see an electronic payment in the Instructions to Send dialog box that you don't want to transmit—or at least not yet—click it. This unmarks the electronic payment so Quicken won't send it. When you want Quicken to send an unmarked electronic payment, click that payment to mark it again.

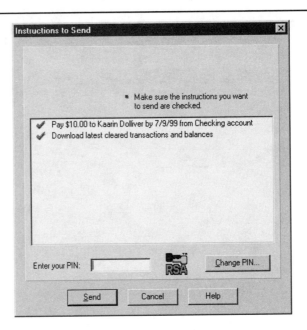

 NOTE The first time you attempt to use online services in Quicken, Quicken prompts you to set up an Intuit Membership. It also sets up your modem. The Intuit Membership is free and simply identifies you to the computer system that provides Quicken's online services. Typically, Quicken takes care of everything, so just follow the on-screen instructions that Quicken provides.

If this is the first time you're using Online Payment, the dialog box will look something like the one shown in Figure 9.7, though it might vary depending on your bank. Click Send. Quicken asks you for your existing PIN (Personal Identification Number) and prompts you to change it to a new PIN for your Online Payment account. (Usually, on your first call-in, you use your ATM card PIN.) If this isn't your first time using Online Payment, the dialog box shown in Figure 9.7 has an extra text box for your PIN. Just type your PIN in the Enter Your PIN text box, then click Send. Quicken sends your payment instructions. After the transmission is complete, Quicken displays the Online Transmission Summary dialog box.

PART

I

The ABCs of Quicken

MASTERING THE OPPORTUNITIES

PINs for Security

Online Payment uses a PIN as a way to keep your account information private. When you instruct the online bill payment service computer to actually process payments, Quicken supplies your account number and you supply your PIN. The online bill payment service computer then verifies the numbers you and Quicken provided and lets you transmit payment instructions. While this process may sound dangerous—after all, someone only needs to know your account number and PIN to start tapping your account—this security system is the same one you now use with your automated teller machine (ATM) card.

As an extra measure of security, some of the banks that provide online bill payment services require you to change your PIN every time you transmit payment information. This little gambit means that even if someone discovered the PIN that you were using last week, it wouldn't be any help this week. What's more, if a miscreant did access your Online Payment account, he or she would need to change your PIN. And in that case, the next time you tried to send payments, you would find that someone had accessed your account and changed your PIN. The bottom line is that PINs work very well as long as you keep the number a secret and don't forget it.

Using the PIN Vault

If you have online accounts with more than one bank, you can use Quicken's PIN Vault feature to store your account PINs in one place and enter a single password to connect to all of the banks. To set up the PIN Vault, choose File ➢ PIN Vault ➢ Setup. Click Next to begin the setup wizard. For each bank with which you have online services set up, select the bank from the drop-down list and enter the PIN in the two text boxes provided. Then enter and confirm the password you want to use for all of your accounts. Review the summary the wizard provides and click Done. The next time you use online services, you'll need to enter only the single password you specified.

To update your Internet information, pay bills, and download transactions for all of your online accounts at once, choose Finance ➢ One Step Update.

Making Regular Payments with Online Payment

You most likely pay some bills regularly, such as on a monthly basis. For example, mortgage, rent, car loan, and medical insurance payments are made regularly. To make it easier to pay this type of repeating transaction, Quicken lets you schedule a transaction so that it is paid automatically until you tell the Online Payment service to stop paying it. For example, if you're supposed to pay, say, an $800-per-month mortgage payment by the tenth of every month and you have 30 years of these monthly payments, you can tell Online Payment to send in your $800 every month by the tenth of the month.

To create such a repeating transaction, follow these steps:

1. Display the Online Center by choosing Banking ➢ Online Banking. Click the Payments tab.

2. Click the Repeating button. Quicken displays the Create Repeating Online Payment dialog box, as shown in Figure 9.8.

3. In the First Payment text box, enter the date of the first repeating payment you'll make using the Online Payment service.

4. If you have more than one account set up for Online Payment, select the account that will be used for the payment from the Account drop-down list box.

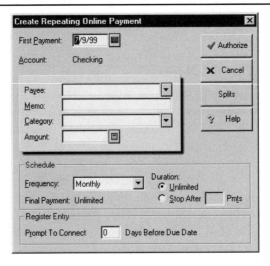

5. Select the electronic payee from the Payee drop-down list box.

6. Optionally, provide a memo description of the payment using the Memo text box.

7. Use the Category drop-down list box to describe the payment as falling into some expense category. If you want to split the payment, click the Split command button and then fill out the Split Transaction Window (see Chapter 2 for information about splitting transactions).

8. In the Amount text box, provide the payment amount.

9. Activate the Frequency drop-down list and select a payment frequency: every two weeks, twice a month, monthly, every two months, and so on.

10. Use the Duration option buttons and the Stop After [x] Pmts text box to describe how many payments you'll make. For example, if you have a $500 rent check you'll pay each month indefinitely, mark the Unlimited option button. If you have a $750 mortgage payment you'll pay monthly for 30 years, mark the Stop After option button and enter **360** in the text box. (As you probably know, 30 years of monthly payments is the same thing as 360 payments.)

11. Use the Prompt to Connect text box to specify how far in advance Quicken should remind you to transmit this payment. In general, you should transmit payments about five days before they're due.

12. Click the Authorize command button. Quicken closes the Create Repeating Online Payment dialog box.

To create additional online repeating payments, repeat steps 2 through 12.

If You Have Problems with Electronic Payments

When you have problems with an electronic payment, you do the same things you would do if the payment had been made with a paper check. If you've transmitted an electronic payment by mistake, you can try to stop payment. If you have questions about a particular payment, you can contact the bank or the Online Payment service.

Stopping a Payment

To stop payment, open the Online Center window by choosing Banking ➤ Online Banking. Check the status of your payment in the list at the bottom of your screen. If it says Unsent in the Status column, highlight the transaction by clicking it, then click the Delete button. When Quicken asks you to confirm the deletion, click Yes.

If it says Sent, click the transaction to highlight it, then click the Cancel Payment button. Quicken asks you to confirm your stop-payment request, then adds the payment cancellation to your list of instructions to send. The next time you connect to your bank, Quicken sends the instruction to cancel the payment. (This works only if the payment hasn't already been made by your bank, of course.) If the stop-payment request works, Quicken voids the electronic payment.

Getting Electronic Payment Information

To see electronic payment information, open the Online Center by choosing Banking ➤ Online Banking. The list box at the bottom of the screen lists any current online transactions.

To inquire about an earlier payment, click the Payments tab of the Online Center. Select a payment from the list and click the Update/Send button to get the current status of a payment.

Getting Help from Your Bank

There are two ways you can get help from your bank regarding electronic payments:

- Call the bank at the number listed on your bank's welcome letter.
- Send the bank an e-mail message.

To send an e-mail message to your bank, follow these steps:

1. Choose Banking ➤ Online Banking to open the Online Center and click the E-mail tab, which is shown in Figure 9.9.

FIGURE 9.9

The E-mail tab of the Online Center

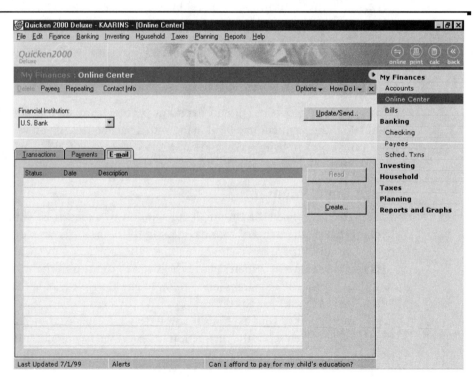

2. Click Create. Quicken opens the Create dialog box.

3. Select the E-mail About an Online Payment option button.

4. Select the Online Payment account on which you made the payment from the drop-down list box.

5. Select the individual online payment from the list box.

6. Click OK. Quicken opens the E-Mail About an Online Payment dialog box, as shown in Figure 9.10.

7. Write your message in the Message text box, and enter your name in the Sincerely text box, and then click OK to add the message to the list of instructions to send to your bank.

Replies to your inquiries and any other e-mail messages from your bank are automatically "mailed" to you whenever you connect to your bank to do your online banking. Incoming messages are listed on the E-mail tab of the Online Center.

FIGURE 9.10

Sending an e-mail inquiry to a bank

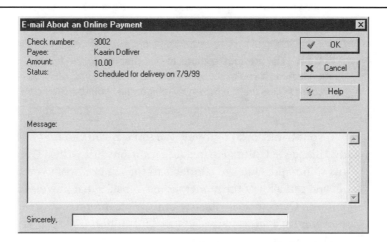

To read a mail message listed on the E-mail tab, select it in the first list box by clicking it, then click the Read button. Quicken displays the message text in the Message box. To delete a message after you've read it, select the message and click the Delete command button.

Online Account Access

With Online Account Access, you can move money between accounts and even pay a credit card bill, if the credit card is issued by the bank with which you do your online banking. You can also receive your bank statement electronically.

There aren't any hard-and-fast prerequisites for using Online Account Access. However, you'll find Online Account Access easiest if you've been using Quicken for at least a few weeks and have performed one or two reconciliations on the accounts that you want to use. Of course, you'll also need to sign up for online banking services with your bank and have an Internet connection.

Signing Up for Online Banking Services

Signing up for online banking isn't difficult, but you do need to work with a bank that supports Quicken's Online Account Access feature. Telephone your bank and ask whether your bank provides online banking services using Quicken.

 NOTE The previous sections in this chapter explain how to use Quicken's Online Payment feature. If you're set up for Online Payment, you can probably sign up for the Online Account Access feature by simply telephoning your bank.

If your bank doesn't provide the service, you can find a bank that does by choosing Finance ➢ Online Financial Institutions List within Quicken. When you choose this command, Quicken connects to the Quicken.com Web site through the Internet and gets a list of the numerous major banks that provide online services in cooperation with Quicken. (See Chapter 11 for more information about the Quicken.com Web site.) This list appears in the Financial Institution Directory, as shown in Figure 9.11. Read through the information to learn which services your bank or other banks in your area offer and how to contact a bank.

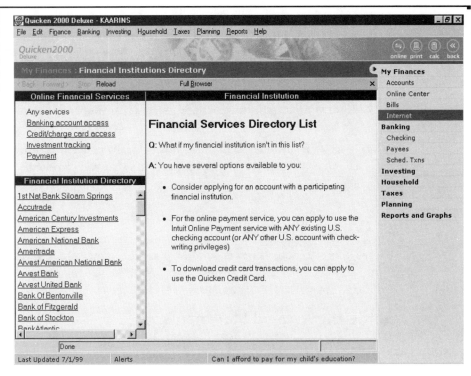

FIGURE 9.11

The list of financial institutions providing online services in cooperation with Quicken

Setting Up Quicken for Online Account Access

To tell Quicken you want to use Online Account Access with an account, follow these steps:

1. Display the account's register and click the Overview tab.

2. Click the Available, Not Enabled hyperlink beside Online Account Access. This displays the Online Setup area (refer to Figure 9.1).

3. If you've selected a financial institution that Quicken recognizes, Quicken displays the setup page for that institution. If you haven't selected a financial institution that Quicken recognizes, Quicken displays a list of participating institutions. Click a hyperlink to see the online services offered at an institution.

4. After you've selected an institution, click the Tell Me More hyperlink to learn more about the services your bank offers. Click the Enroll hyperlink to apply for online services online. After you've applied and received any necessary setup

information from your bank, click the Set up Quicken hyperlink. Quicken Displays the Edit Bank Account dialog box (refer to Figure 9.2).

5. Check the Enable Online Account Access check box and click Next.

6. Enter your bank's routing number and click Next. (The welcome letter that you got from your bank supplies this information.)

7. Enter your account number and select an account type from the drop-down list box.

8. Enter your customer ID number (this is usually your social security number) and click Next twice to review the information that you provided.

9. Click Done.

Using Online Account Access

Using Online Account Access is quite simple. When you want to get account balance information or move money between accounts, choose Banking ➤ Online Banking. Quicken displays the Online Center.

Retrieving Account Statements

To retrieve your account balance and cleared transactions for all your online accounts, including bank accounts and credit card accounts, follow these steps:

1. Click the Update/Send button in the upper right of the window. Quicken opens the Instructions to Send dialog box, as shown in Figure 9.12.

2. The Instructions to Send dialog box shows all of the transactions that Online Account Access will send once it goes online. (Quicken automatically assumes that you will want to send any transactions.) If you do not want Quicken to send a particular transaction while online, click the transaction. Quicken removes the checkmark to indicate that the transaction will not be sent.

3. Click in the Enter Your PIN text box and type in your PIN. (The bank included your PIN with the information it sent when you activated Online Account Access.)

4. Click Send. Quicken connects to the bank and transfers the information from your computer to the bank. At the same time, Online Account Access retrieves transactions from your bank and picks up any new transactions it can't find in your register. Online Account Access also indicates which transactions have cleared the bank.

FIGURE 9.12

The Instructions to Send dialog box with Online Account Access transactions

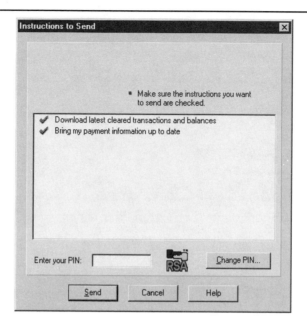

Approving Online Transactions

Quicken holds the transactions that it has downloaded so you can approve them before you put them in your account registers. To examine the transactions, click OK in the Online Transmission Summary dialog box, and then click the Transactions tab in the Online Center. This tab is shown in Figure 9.13.

If you have more than one account at the financial institution, you can use the list box at the top of the tab to choose an account. Click the name of the account that you want to examine, and Quicken will display the data in the window below the list box.

 NOTE In Figure 9.13, you can see one disadvantage of online banking. Because banks don't keep track of the names on the checks, all checks (like check number 1567 in Figure 9.13) look as though they're made out to Check. If the check doesn't match with one you've already entered in the register, you can enter the Payee name and assign the category as you enter the downloaded transaction in the register. Online Account Access *does* supply the Payee name for your credit card accounts or for debit purchases. Different banks handle the register details differently, however.

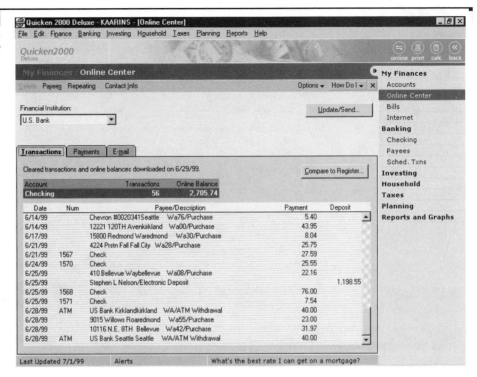

FIGURE 9.13

The Transactions tab of the Online Center

To compare the downloaded data with your register, click the Compare to Register button. Quicken splits the window, with the register showing in the top half and the list of transactions underneath, as shown in Figure 9.14. Use the scroll bars in each section to move through the lists and compare transactions. To accept a single transaction and add it to your register, highlight the transaction by clicking it, and then click the Accept button. To accept all of the transactions at once, click Accept All. To remove a transaction without adding it to your register, click the transaction, and then click Delete.

FIGURE 9.14

Comparing the online transactions with the account register

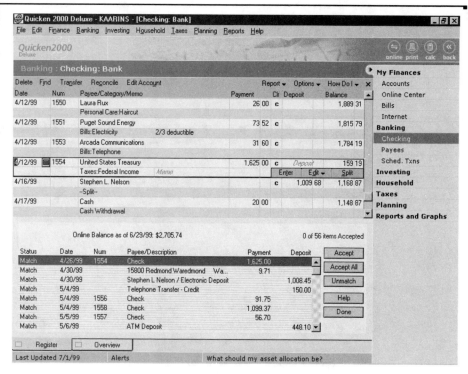

Quicken 2000 now recognizes more payee matches than in previous versions. For example, if you shop at Safeway store #123456, Quicken recognizes it as the same payee as Safeway store #654321.

Transferring Funds between Accounts

If you have two or more accounts at the same institution and you want to transfer money between accounts, open the Online Center (by choosing Banking ➤ Online Banking), then click the Transfers tab. Quicken displays the dialog box shown in Figure 9.15.

Use the Transfer Money From and To drop-down list boxes to identify the accounts you're moving money between. Use the Amount text box to give the amount of the transfer. Click the Enter button to add the transfer to the list of transactions to be sent to the financial institution.

The text box at the bottom of the tab lists all of the transfers you have recorded. To remove a transfer, click the transaction and then click Delete.

NOTE Some financial institutions do not process transfers electronically; instead, they process the transfers manually at central clearinghouses. This procedure may cause a time lag between the time you send your transfer in and the time the bank actually processes it.

FIGURE 9.15

The Transfers tab of the Online Center

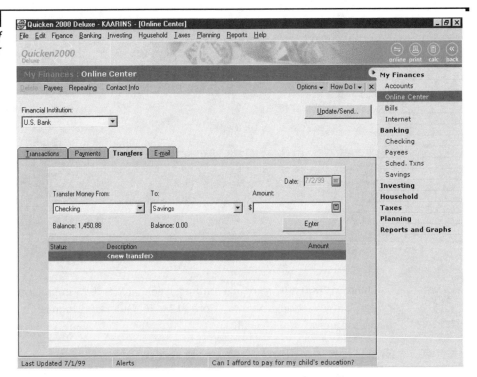

Corresponding with the Bank

As with Online Payment, if you have any questions, comments, or problems about your Online Account Access transactions, you can correspond directly with your bank via e-mail. Your messages are automatically transferred with your transactions.

To begin, click the E-mail tab of the Online Center. To send a message to your bank, click the Create button in the E-mail tab. In the next dialog box, click the E-mail about Online Account option button to send your bank a message regarding its online banking services. After you click OK, Quicken opens the Message to [*Your*

Financial Institution] dialog box, like the one shown in Figure 9.16. Fill in the text boxes to identify yourself, the subject of your message, and the account in question. Enter your message. To send your message, click OK. Quicken adds your message to the list of transactions. Quicken does not actually send your message to the bank until the next time you click Update/Send to transfer your transactions.

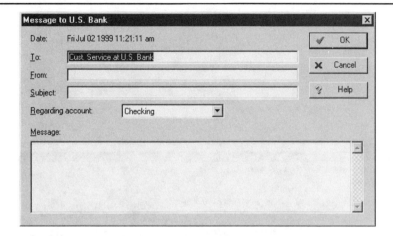

FIGURE 9.16

Writing a message to your financial institution

Replies to your inquiries and any other e-mail messages from your bank are automatically "mailed" to you whenever you connect to your bank to do your online banking. Incoming messages are listed on the E-mail tab of the Online Center. To read a message, highlight it by clicking it, then click Read. Quicken opens a window containing your message. You can print the message by clicking the Print button.

Reconciling an Online Bank Account

You reconcile, or balance, online bank accounts in a manner very similar to the way you balance other bank accounts. When Quicken then displays the Reconcile Online Account dialog box (see Figure 9.17), you indicate whether you want to balance against a paper statement you've received through the mail or against the most recent online balance you've retrieved.

Once you choose which balance you want to reconcile against, Quicken displays the Reconcile Bank Statement area, as shown in Figure 9.18. You use this area to indicate which transactions have cleared the bank. As you do, Quicken calculates a cleared balance figure at the bottom of the screen. When this amount equals the statement balance, you've reconciled your account. Note that the steps you take to reconcile, or balance, a bank account are described in detail in Chapter 5. Chapter 5 also describes what to do when an account won't balance.

FIGURE 9.17

*The Reconcile Online
Account dialog box*

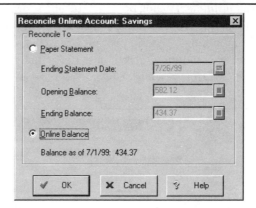

FIGURE 9.18

*The Reconcile Bank
Statement area*

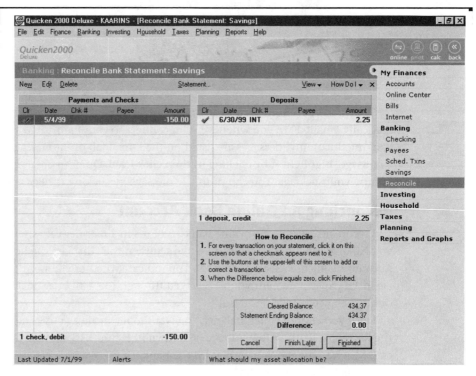

CHAPTER **10**
_____

Using the Address Book

Quicken Deluxe provides an address book. Regular users of Quicken may want to use this feature to keep track of people's names, addresses, e-mail aliases, and related information. This short chapter describes how to do this by showing how to add contacts to the Address Book, group contacts, and print labels.

Adding Contacts to the Address Book

Quicken comes with an address book you can use to maintain a database of names, addresses, and telephone numbers. To display the Address Book, click the Household QuickTab and then click the Record Important Addresses hyperlink. Figure 10.1 shows the Address Book with one payee entry.

FIGURE 10.1

The Address Book

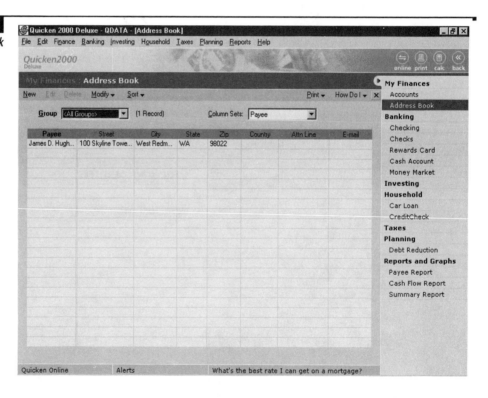

TIP You can also start the Address Book by choosing Finance ➢ Address Book.

To add a person to your address book, click the New button to display the Edit Address Book Record dialog box shown in Figure 10.2. Fill in the text boxes on the tabs of this dialog box. When you've finished describing someone, click OK. The Address Book adds the name and address to the list, as shown in Figure 10.1

 NOTE To record notes for an individual, click the Miscellaneous tab and use the Notes text box.

FIGURE 10.2

Enter contact information for a person

Edit Address Book Record

| Payee | Contact | Secondary | Personal | Miscellaneous |

Payee:

Street:

City:

State:

Zip Code:

Country:

Attn Line:

E-mail:

☐ Include this Payee in QuickFill List

✓ OK

✗ Cancel

? Help

Group...

Format...

Groups: None

To see the name and address information you've collected on an individual, just click his or her name in the list. If you've collected many names and addresses, you may need to scroll through the list to get to the person's record.

You can edit an existing name and address by selecting the person in the list box, clicking Edit, and then using the text boxes to make your changes. After you've made your changes, click OK. You can delete someone from the Address Book by selecting the person's name and clicking Delete.

Grouping Contacts

If your address book grows to dozens or even hundreds of names and addresses, you may want to organize the people in your address book into groups. For example, you can assign one person to the Family group, another to the Work group, another to the Friends group, and another to the Christmas List group. (The Address Book supplies these four groups initially, but you can add others.) To create a group, select New from the Group drop-down list box. In the New Group dialog box, shown in Figure 10.3, enter a group name and click OK.

FIGURE 10.3

The New Group dialog box

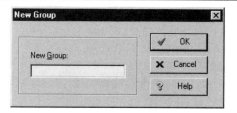

To assign a contact to an existing group, click the Modify button and choose Assign To Groups. This displays the Assign To Groups dialog box shown in Figure 10.4. You can select multiple groups from the list. When you're finished, click OK. To show only those contacts included in a specified group, select the group from the Group drop-down list box.

FIGURE 10.4

The Assign To Groups dialog box

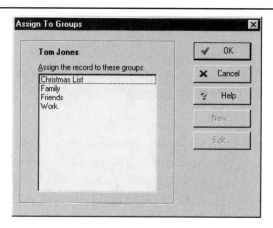

Essentially, Quicken's online Address Book is like a handwritten address book. Unlike a handwritten name and address list, however, a computerized name and address list provides several advantages:

- You can use the Sort menu's commands to arrange and rearrange the names and addresses. For example, choose Sort ➤ By Organization to arrange your address book alphabetically by the entries in that field.

- You can print the names and addresses in your list after you've sorted them or grouped them. To print names and addresses, click the Print command button and choose List.

Printing Labels

With the Address Book, you can quickly print mailing labels for your contacts. Just follow these steps:

1. If you want to print labels for only selected contacts and not the entire list, select the contacts for whom you want to print the labels.

2. Click the Print button and choose Labels. This displays the Print Labels dialog box shown in Figure 10.5

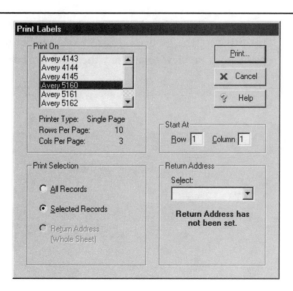

3. Select the type of label you have from the Print On list box.

4. Click the All Records option button or the Selected Records option button depending on which labels you want to print.

5. Load your labels in your printer and click Print. This displays the second Print Labels dialog box, shown in Figure 10.6.

FIGURE 10.6

The second Print Labels dialog box

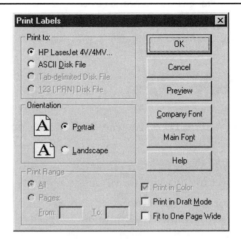

6. Verify the printer and the paper orientation. If you want to change the font used for printing the labels, click one of the font buttons. When you're ready to print, click Preview to preview the labels and or click OK to print them.

CHAPTER **11**

Quicken and the Internet

The Internet contains a wealth of personal finance information, much of which you can access from within Quicken 2000. In this chapter, you'll learn how you can use Quicken, the Quicken Financial Network, and Intuit's Web site to access financial information on the World Wide Web. The chapter also introduces you to a few other Internet sources of information about personal finances.

Internet Basics

If you have not yet explored the Internet, you are probably wondering what the hullabaloo is about. People are excited about the Internet for two basic reasons: It allows them to access and distribute information worldwide, and it allows them to communicate instantly and affordably with others across the globe.

Before you can explore the Internet, you need to set up your connection to the Internet.

How Do You Get Connected?

For your Internet connection, you need three things:

- A modem (unless you have a permanent connection through your work or school)
- An account with an Internet service provider (ISP), who will give you the telephone numbers and directions you need to make your connection
- A Web browser installed on your computer

Your Physical Connection

In order for your computer to become a part of the Internet, you need some sort of physical connection to the Internet. Usually, this takes the form of a telephone line, but sometimes (perhaps at your workplace, for instance), it takes the form of a full-time cable connection. If you want to connect a computer to a telephone line, you need a modem.

Most computers that you buy today come with a modem, but if you have a computer and don't have a modem, you can buy one at your local computer store. They come in several varieties, depending on the kind of computer you have. Some modems fit inside your computer; others sit outside your computer and connect to your computer via cable. Laptop computers often use a different type of modem as well. If you're not sure what type of modem you need, ask a salesperson for help.

The most important thing to remember when you buy a modem is that you should purchase the fastest one you can afford. This will save you time and money in the long run, because you will spend less time waiting for information to transfer between your computer and the Internet. And if you're in the market for a new computer, be sure to check the modem speed and get the fastest one you can afford.

Your Internet Account

Once you have a physical connection to the Internet, you need to have an Internet account. If you don't already have an Internet account through your work or school, you need to purchase an account with an ISP.

The ISP will provide you with the instructions and telephone numbers you need to access its server computer. This server plays an important part in your Internet connection. It functions almost like a switchboard. It processes the information you send out and routes it in the correct direction. It also stores information that others send you until you call the server to access it.

Depending on your location, there may be many ISPs to choose from if you need an Internet account. Some are large, national companies you've probably heard of before, such as America Online, CompuServe, and the Microsoft Network. Others are small, local companies, which you can find in the telephone book. Most ISPs offer several service plans varying in price depending on how much time you think you'll spend online. Increasingly, however, many ISPs offer unlimited access for a set fee. This is what you want if you can get it. If you have little or no experience with the Internet, you might want to get an account with one of the larger ISPs because their software is almost always of high quality and they can assist you if you have trouble making Internet connections.

Your Software

To view the information on the World Wide Web (the most popular part of the Internet), you need a Web browser. Often, your ISP provides you with a Web browser, and in some cases your computer may have come with a Web browser when you bought it. In addition, you already have a Web browser if:

- You chose to install Internet Explorer 5 when you installed Quicken 2000.
- You are running Windows 98 or a later version of Windows 95. Internet Explorer 4 is included with these products. If you've used Internet Explorer 4, chances are you've been prompted to upgrade to Internet Explorer 5 when you've gone online.

 WARNING   You must be running Internet Explorer 4 (or later) to be able to use all of Quicken's Internet features.

If you didn't install Internet Explorer when you installed Quicken, you can do so at any time. Follow these steps:

1. Close Quicken 2000 if it is open.

2. Place your Quicken CD in the drive and run Install.

3. Select Custom as the type of installation.

4. Remove the checkmarks from all items on the list of programs except Internet Explorer.

5. Follow the onscreen instructions.

If you want to use the Internet to write and receive electronic letters, or e-mail, you also need an e-mail program. Once again, your ISP most likely provided you with this software when you purchased your account. If you have Internet Explorer 5, you can use Outlook Express, which is an e-mail program that comes with it.

What Can You Do on the Internet?

If you consider the Internet as a vast library, millions of times the size of any library you've ever seen, it can get rather overwhelming. But basically, you can do the same things on the Internet as you do in the local library:

- Post notes on the bulletin board and read what others have posted.
- Chat privately in a secluded corner.
- Participate in meetings discussing current issues.
- Read and view all sorts of material, some of high quality and from a reputable source, and some of lesser quality or plain poor taste.

Like a library, the Internet is a superb place to conduct research. You can browse library card catalogs from your computer, and you can download entire books and read them on your computer. You can even visit companies, organizations, institutions, and governments using the World Wide Web.

Unfortunately, the Internet isn't nearly as organized as a library. Nor does it scrutinize and filter information as much as a library must. You might find this delightful if, for instance, you finally discover information that you have been seeking for years. But other times, you might be disgusted by what you see. Whatever your tastes, however, the Internet has a place for you, where you can communicate with other people who share your interests, your beliefs, and even your problems.

It would take an entire book to describe everything you can do on the Internet (and, in fact, many books are devoted to just that topic). Here, I will briefly introduce the two most popular features of the Internet: e-mail and the World Wide Web. You can refer to an Internet book for more information or use the Internet itself to discover more about it.

E-mail

One popular feature of the Internet is e-mail. Using e-mail, you can write messages and even send files electronically, including files that contain pictures and sound, to people around the world.

The only prerequisites for e-mail are that both people have some sort of computer access and an e-mail account. With an e-mail account, you can also subscribe to a mailing list, so that you regularly receive a particular organization's newsletter or memos about the activities of a particular society or club, in e-mail messages.

The World Wide Web

The World Wide Web is probably the most popular part of the Internet because it is so lively, colorful, and easy to navigate. Some of the more elaborate features of the Web allow you to have online conversations or play online games with other people in real time, even if oceans and time zones separate the participants.

The simple definition of the World Wide Web—also known as the Web, WWW, and W3—is a group of documents, accessible from almost any Internet connection in the world, that are linked together. Each document contains *hyperlinks* (sometimes called just *links*) to other documents by way of a format called *hypertext*. When you are looking at a Web document about Shakespeare, for example, the words *Globe Theatre* may be underlined or highlighted. By clicking those words, you are sent to another document relating to the Globe Theatre. It may have pictures, historical information, or just about anything else you can imagine. That document, in turn, may have links to other topics.

As a result, the World Wide Web is structured a bit like a spider web. To get to any point on a Web, there are many paths. One point links to another, which links to another, and so on. By traveling through these links, you can go to many points on the way to your final destination. And, in theory, you can get from any point in the entire system to any other point simply by following these links.

A *uniform resource locator*, or URL, describes each World Wide Web document. The URL includes the document's name and its location on the Internet. When you enter a URL in your Web browser, what you're really doing is telling a server computer (such as Intuit's server or your ISP's server) to display the document on your computer.

While URLs might at first glance seem to be just an indecipherable and arbitrary string of letters, dots, and slashes, once you become more familiar with them, you'll probably get an idea of how they are structured. For example, if you know the name of a large company, like Intuit, you can often just type **www.*name-of-company*.com** in your Web browser's Location or Address text box to display the company's home page, as in www.intuit.com. (The *www* stands for World Wide Web, of course, and the *.com* ending refers to commercial.) If you want to visit a local university, you can usually type **www.*name-of-university*.edu**, as in www.yale.edu. (The *.edu* stands for educational.) Or, if you want to visit a government organization, like the IRS, you can usually just type **www.*name-of-organization*.gov**, as in www.irs.gov. Once you get to the home page, you can then access other related pages in the company or organization's Web site, or group of Web documents.

Accessing the Web from Quicken

Within Quicken 2000, you can access the World Wide Web from the Online menu. You don't need to launch your Web browser to view the Quicken Financial Network. Before you can access the Quicken Financial Network directly from within the Quicken application window, however, you need to set up this feature in Quicken.

Setting Up Your Internet Connection

To set up your Internet connection in Quicken, choose Edit ➣ Internet Connection Setup. Quicken takes you through a wizard to set up your dial-up connection and your browser. To complete the wizard, follow these steps:

1. Click the option button that corresponds to your Internet connection and click Next. If you dial up using a modem, click the first option.

FIGURE 11.1

The Internet Connection Setup dialog box

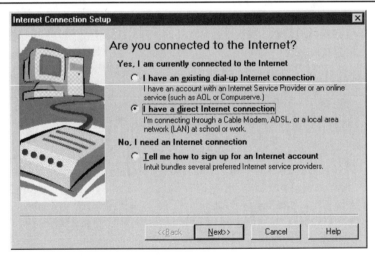

2. If you indicated that you use a dial-up connection to access the Internet, Quicken searches for your dial-up account. Select the account you want to use from the list box and click Next.

3. Quicken displays a message reminding you that to use all of Quicken's Internet features, you must be running Internet Explorer 4 (or later). Click Next.

4. Quicken searches for the browsers you have installed on your computer. Select the browser you want to use from the list box, as shown in Figure 11.2. Then click Next.

5. Quicken offers you a chance to try to improve your connection. If you want to do this, click Yes, I Want to Send Diagnostic Data to connect to Intuit's online site and have your connection information analyzed there. If you do not want to send data about your system to Intuit, click No, I Do Not Want to Send Diagnostic Data. Click Next.

6. Review the summary Quicken displays, and then click Finish.

FIGURE 11.2

Choose a Web browser

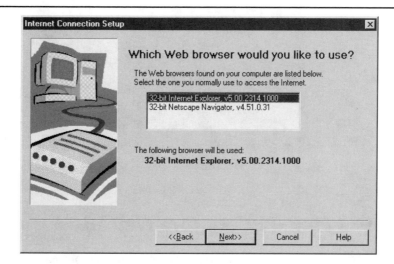

Customizing Your Internet Connection

Once you have configured your Internet connection, you can specify some connection options using the Customize Quicken 2000 Download dialog box, as shown in Figure 11.3. Choose Edit ➢ Options ➢ Internet Options.

• If you're using a dial-up connection (and not a permanent connection over a network), use the After Downloading Quicken Data options to specify whether you want Quicken to disconnect from the Internet or to remain connected after it updates your Quicken data.

• Use the Background Downloading options to specify whether you want to download in the background, which is faster.

• Check the box in the Download at Quicken Startup section if you want to be reminded to update when you start Quicken.

- Check the box in the Quicken.com Login section if you want to save your login and use it when updating.
- If you're using a dial-up connection, check the Warn Me Before Browsing To Remote Pages box if you want to be notified before accessing an Internet Web site.

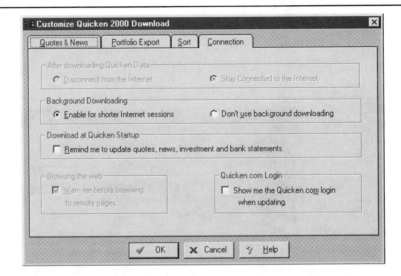

Accessing the Quicken.com Web Site

Over the past year, Intuit has vastly expanded the Quicken.com Web site. It now covers a much wider range of services, with information about everything from personal banking to small-business finances and investments.

Connecting to the Quicken.com Web Site

You can get to the home page of the Quicken.com Web site in two ways:

- If you're in the Quicken application window, choose Finance ➢ Quicken on the Web ➢ Quicken.com. Quicken runs your Web browser in the background and opens the home page of the Quicken.com Web site, as shown in Figure 11.4. (If you're not currently connected to the Internet, Quicken may prompt you to dial your service provider and log on.)
- If you're not running Quicken at the moment, start your Web browser and type **http://www.quicken.com** (the URL for the Quicken.com home page) in the Address or Location text box.

FIGURE 11.4

The Quicken.com
home page

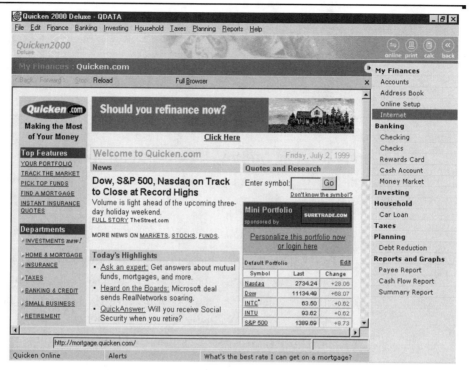

 TIP To access technical support online or to browse through a list of frequently asked questions about Quicken, choose Finance ➢ Quicken on the Web ➢ Quicken FAQs.

Exploring the Quicken.com Web Site

From the Quicken.com home page you can go to lots of places. Run your mouse across your screen a couple of times and see how often your mouse pointer turns into a little pointing hand. It does this whenever it rests on top of a hyperlink. If you click one of these hyperlinks, you will go to another page. You can use the Forward and Back buttons in Quicken or in your Web browser to move back and forth between the Web pages you last visited.

The Quicken.com page has two main sections, both of which contain several hyperlinks. From the pane on the left, you can click hyperlinks to access different parts of the Quicken.com Web site. In the main area of the Quicken.com home page, you can click hyperlinks to access a wealth of up-to-date financial information, including market quotes, news, and feature articles.

TIP Don't be concerned if you have different hyperlink options than the ones described here or if your screen doesn't look exactly like the one in Figure 11.4, because Intuit constantly updates the Quicken.com Web site. If you're curious about a link, go ahead and try it. Part of the fun is poking around and finding out what is available. If you find that it is something you're not interested in, remember that you can always click the Back button to return to the Quicken.com home page.

Getting Market Quotes, News, and Information

From the Quicken.com home page, the latest market news and information are only a click away:

- To get the latest price on a stock, enter a stock ticker symbol and click the Go button. Figure 11.5 shows an example of a quote page.

- To get the latest business news, just click a headline in the News section.

- To read a feature article on a financial topic, click a Today's Highlights hyperlink.

- To order or review a best-selling personal financial book, click a book title in the Amazon.com's Personal Finance Bestsellers section.

- To trade online, click a button for one of Quicken's online trading sponsors.

 FIGURE 11.5

Clicking the Go button displays the latest stock price information.

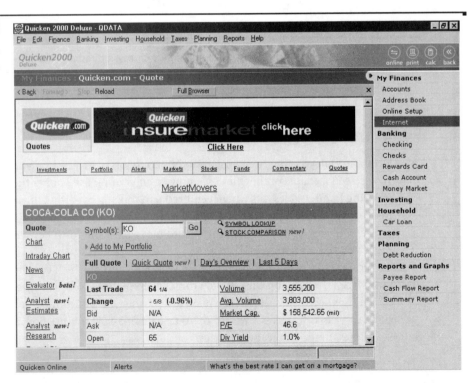

Entering Quicken Data Away from Home Using the Quicken.com Web Site

Quicken includes a feature called WebEntry that allows you to enter Quicken data from any PC with Internet access, even if that computer doesn't have the Quicken program on it, much less your Quicken file. To use WebEntry, access the Quicken.com Web site using a Web browser by entering **www.quicken.com** in the Address or Location box, then click the Quicken Web Entry hyperlink under Quicken Solutions in the left pane. If you haven't already logged on to the Quicken Web site, click the hyperlink to do so. You must log on before you can enter transactions. Then enter your transaction in the Web page form and click Enter Transaction. If you make a mistake, click Clear Form. Quicken.com stores and password-protects your transactions until you download them into your Quicken file. When you've finished entering transactions, click the Logout from Quicken.com hyperlink at the bottom of the page. To download WebEntry transactions in Quicken when you return home, open the Quicken file and choose Finance ➤ One Step Update. Then select the WebEntry Download item from the list and click Update Now. To enter the downloaded transactions into your account, choose Banking ➤ Banking Activities ➤ Accept Transactions Entered On The Web.

Visiting Quicken's Financial Centers

There are also departments, or areas of personal finance, you can visit by clicking the hyperlinks in the Departments list. Clicking a department header hyperlink takes you to the home page of that department. From there, you can click other hyperlinks to go to specific topics within the department or to related Web pages outside the Quicken.com Web site.

The Investments Page   This department highlights investment information, especially information about stocks and mutual funds. Several services are available from this page. Click the Portfolio hyperlink to customize your current portfolio or to create a new portfolio so that every time you return to the Quicken.com home page, you can see the investment information that you want.

 NOTE   Before you can create or customize your portfolio, you must register with Quicken.com. On the Investments page, click the Portfolio link at the top of the page, click on Register Now, fill in the information that Quicken.com requests, and click the Submit Registration button.

Click the Stocks hyperlink for links to the latest industry news and profiles of hot stocks. Click the Mutual Funds hyperlink to access the online Fund Finder or to read about Quicken's Featured Fund Family. You can also search for top mutual fund performers in the category you specify. To do this, click the Top 25 Funds hyperlink, select a mutual fund category from the drop-down list, select a time frame from the drop-down list, and click View Top 25 Funds. In Figure 11.6, you can see a list of the 25 best-performing mutual funds in the Diversified Emerging Markets category.

FIGURE 11.6

Top performers over the past five years in the Diversified Emerging Markets category

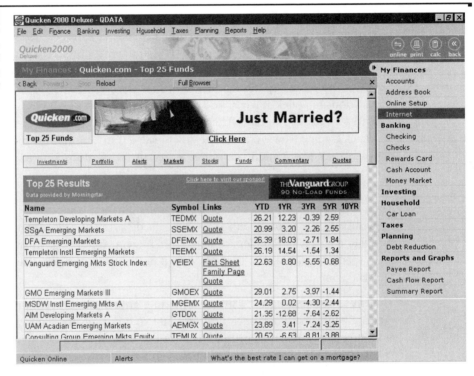

The Home & Mortgage Page

This page provides information on buying, selling, and refinancing a home. You can use the hyperlinks on this page to access a wealth of articles on these topics or to comparison-shop for loans. You can also view the average rates for mortgages in the United States. Click the Home Affordability hyperlink to find out what price house you can afford, as shown in Figure 11.7. Then you can proceed to compare loans from several lenders and print a pre-qualification letter.

FIGURE 11.7

Determining what home price and loan you can afford

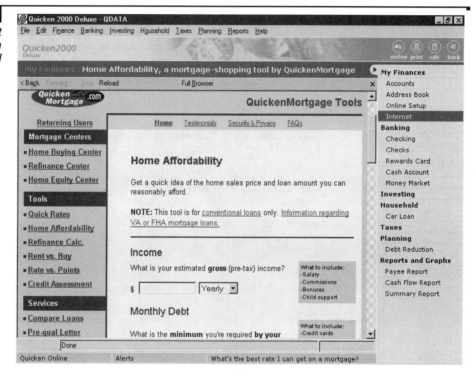

The Insurance Page This area serves as a clearinghouse for life, automobile, and home insurance information. The hyperlinks on this page link you to Web pages that can help you determine your insurance needs and choose which type of insurance is right for you. To compare term life insurance quotes, enter your zip code in the text box on the Insurance page and click the Go button. On the EasyQuote Term Life page, click the Get Quotes button, and then fill in the boxes on the InsureMarket - Four Minutes to Personalized Term Life Quotes page, as shown in Figure 11.8, to find which companies have the best life insurance policies for you.

 NOTE See Chapter 16 for information about how Quicken's built-in tools can help you make smarter insurance choices.

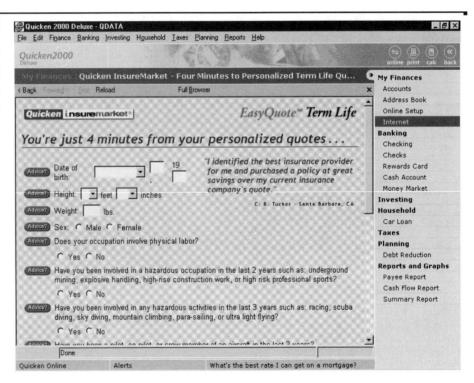

FIGURE 11.8

The InsureMarket - Four Minutes to Personalized Term Life Quotes page helps you find a life insurance policy that fits your needs.

The Taxes Page   This page, as shown in Figure 11.9, is a springboard into volumes of tax information. The Taxes page links you to tips on lowering your taxes, details of the latest tax law changes, and the Tax Calendar, which you can use to review the important tax dates in the previous and coming year. Click the Tax Estimator hyperlink to estimate your taxes, and then click the IFPN hyperlink to connect you to the Intuit Financial Professional Referral page, which helps you find accountants and tax advisors in your area.

 NOTE   See Chapter 14 for information about using Quicken to estimate and prepare income taxes. You'll find information about using the Tax Planner and TurboTax.

FIGURE 11.9

Start your search for answers to tax questions at the Taxes page.

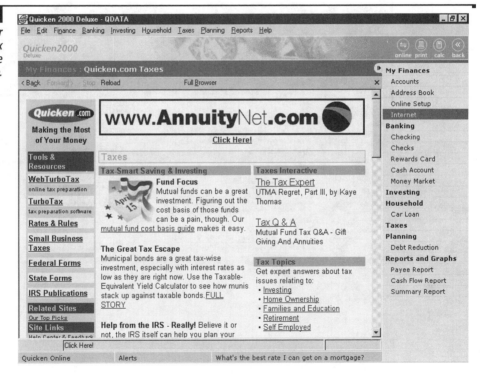

The Banking & Credit Page This page provides information about loans and bank accounts. It lists the national averages of interest rates for loan, savings, and credit card accounts. By clicking hyperlinks, you can compare rates, fees, and requirements for different accounts at banks in your area. You can also click hyperlinks on this page to learn more about online banking or to pick a credit card that's best for you. To begin monitoring your credit report, click the Credit Reports hyperlink to open the Credit Reports page, shown in Figure 11.10.

FIGURE 11.10

The Credit Reports page

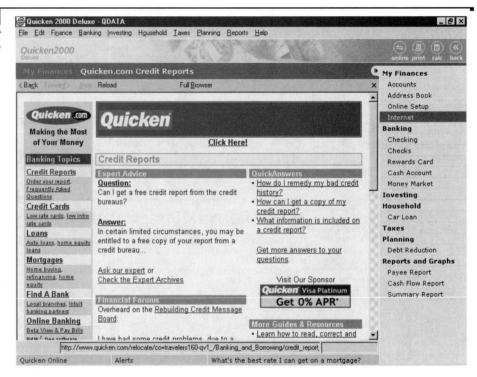

The Small Business Page   If you own and operate a small business or are thinking about starting one, you'll want to check out this page, which is shown in Figure 11.11. It includes information on outfitting your office, taxes and accounting, legal issues, business travel, and more. If you have job openings, you can post them here.

FIGURE 11.11

The Small Business page

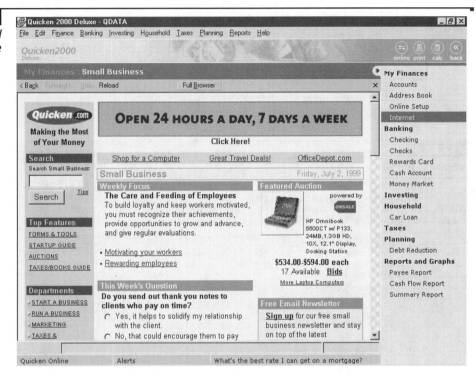

The Retirement Page   This page, shown in Figure 11.12, provides information about planning and saving for retirement. You can click hyperlinks on this page to learn about different types of retirement investment accounts, about the Social Security program, or about pension plans. Click the Build Your Plan hyperlink to access a Web page that you can use to calculate how much you will receive in Social Security and pension plan benefits and how much you need to save on your own for retirement.

NOTE   See Chapter 15 for information about planning your retirement using Quicken's built-in Retirement Planner feature.

FIGURE 11.12

The Retirement page links you to information that helps you achieve your retirement goals.

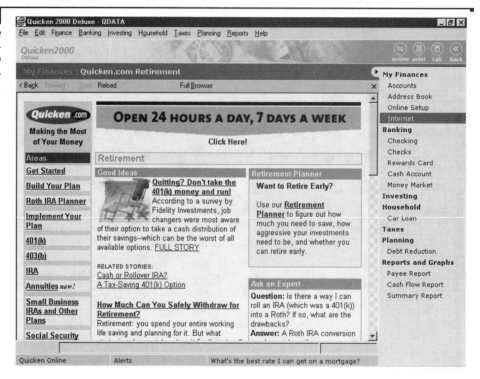

The Saving & Spending Page   This page includes tips on saving and downsizing your debt. It also has links to several planners you can use to help reach your savings goals and to control your spending. Click the Financial Health Checkup hyperlink to go through a check-up and find out if you're achieving your financial objectives. Or, click the Financial Fitness Quiz to fill out a survey that returns tips about where you can improve in your financial planning.

Message Boards Page   This page connects you to message boards and chat groups, where Quicken users can share questions, commentary, and advice on financial topics. The Message Boards page also links you to the Armchair Millionaire, an online collection of saving and investing techniques.

The Intuit Web Site

The Intuit Web site provides product-specific information regarding all of Intuit's products. Intuit is constantly updating the Web site, using it as a primary means of communicating with Quicken users around the world. For example, you may find the following on this Web site:

- Current information about Intuit products
- Facilities for asking questions about and ordering Intuit software
- Updates to Intuit software (which any user with World Wide Web access can download)
- Samples of Intuit products

Even if you don't enjoy spending much time on the Web, it's worth the effort to check out the site every once in a while. You can get to the Intuit Web site in two ways:

- If you're currently running Quicken, you can get there by choosing Finance ➤ Quicken on the Web ➤ Quicken Store and then clicking the Intuit hyperlink.
- Type **http://www.intuit.com** in the Address or Location text box of your Web browser.

Figure 11.13 shows the Intuit Web site's home page. As you can see, the information is organized by product. Although you can go directly to Quicken topics, you should take a look at the other product sections, even if you are not interested in the products themselves. The Small Business section, for instance, contains information relating to small businesses, and the TurboTax section contains advice on personal taxes. You might pass up some useful information if you stick to just the Quicken section. Besides, you miss out on half of the fun of the World Wide Web if you don't let curiosity get the best of you every once in a while.

FIGURE 11.13

The home page of the
Intuit Web site

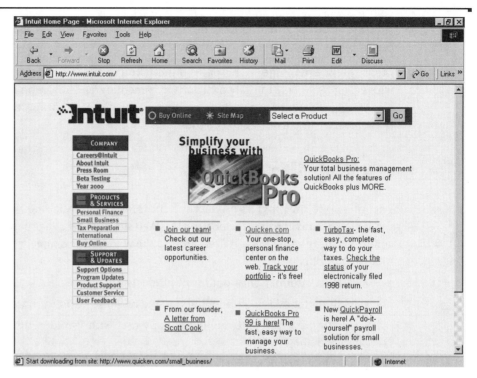

Finding Other Financial Information on the Internet

Of course, there is much more financial information on the Internet than what is available on the Quicken and Intuit Web sites. The following sections describe some ways to find that information.

NOTE To use the resources discussed here, you need access through an ISP to the World Wide Web and Internet newsgroups. In some cases, you also need an e-mail account. For more information, see the "How Do You Get Connected?" section at the beginning of this chapter.

Finding Information on the World Wide Web

Often, the most useful way to begin surfing the World Wide Web is by using a search engine. A *search engine* is an Internet tool that allows you to search the entire Web for information about a particular topic. To use a search engine, just type its URL in the Location or Address box of your Web browser. Then enter your search text in the box provided and click Search.

You can choose from countless search engines. Table 11.1 lists some of the more popular search engines with their URLs. Which one you decide upon depends on what you're trying to accomplish and also, frankly, on which one suits your fancy. There are two main styles of search engines: directory-style and index-style.

TABLE 11.1: ADDRESSES OF POPULAR SEARCH ENGINES	
Search Engine	**URL (Address)**
Directory-style	
Yahoo!	`http://www.yahoo.com/`
Magellan	`http://www.mckinley.com/`
Index-style	
AltaVista	`http://www.altavista.com/`
Lycos	`http://www.lycos.com/`
Infoseek	`http://www.infoseek.com/`
Excite	`http://www.excite.com/`

Directory-Style Search Engines

If you're looking for information about a general topic, or if you just want to do some Web browsing but don't have any specific destination in mind, you might want to use a directory-style search engine. Directory-style engines work like a table of contents or like the subject card catalog at the library. Yahoo! and Magellan are two well-known directory-style search engines (see Table 11.1 for their addresses). These search engines tend to be very user-friendly and good at finding the most relevant Web sites or categories of Web sites that meet your search criteria. For example, Figure 11.14 shows the result of entering *gold+commodities* in the Yahoo! Search text box.

TIP The plus sign in the *gold+commodities* search query tells Yahoo! to return only a list of sites about both gold and commodities. This plus sign is called an *operator*, and each search engine has different rules about the way it uses operators. If you're uncertain about which operators a search engine recognizes, look for a button on the search engine's home page called Search Tips, Help, or something similar. Click that button to read about how to enter your search question.

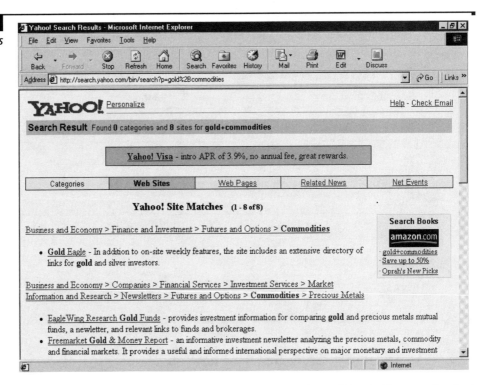

Index-Style Search Engines

If you're looking for very specific, or even obscure, information, you probably want to use an index-style search engine. Index-style search engines work like an index in a book or like a library search by keyword. Basically, an index search engine indexes every word in a Web page. These indexes can include more than eight billion words. This means that if you were to enter the words *gold* and *commodities*, the search engine would return thousands of matching sites. But if you were to enter the words *"utility deregulation" "municipal bonds"*, you would have much more luck with an index-style search engine than you would with a directory-style search engine. Figure 11.15 shows the results of this search using a popular index-style search engine, AltaVista. If you like index-style searching, you might also want to try Lycos, Infoseek, and Excite. The URLs for these search engines are listed in Table 11.1.

FIGURE 11.15

AltaVista search results

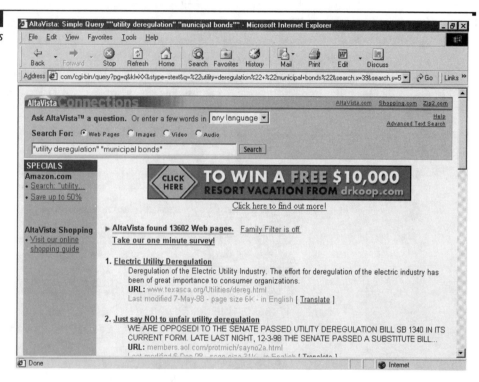

Reproduced with the permission of Digital Equipment Corporation. AltaVista and the AltaVista logo and the Digital logo are trademarks of Digital Equipment Corporation.

 MASTERING THE OPPORTUNITIES

Four Financial Web Sites

Here are some sites that may be interesting to you, along with their URLs:

- The Vanguard Group (`http://www.vanguard.com`) has one of the best sites for financial information. Vanguard is a no-load mutual fund management company. This Web site seems to be designed primarily to help investors, rather than to merely push Vanguard's products. The Investor Education section contains entire "courses" on investor-related subjects.

Continued

MASTERING THE OPPORTUNITIES CONTINUED

- Financenter (http://www.financenter.com) provides information about purchasing or financing homes and automobiles. This site also has some interesting credit card information, including a calculator that can compare all those offers you get in the mail from competing credit card companies.

- The Securities and Exchange Commission has a Web site named Edgar (http://www.sec.gov/edgarhp.htm) that provides the quarterly and annual reports that all U.S. publicly held companies must file.

- Of course, the IRS has a Web site as well (shown below), where you can download tax forms and information. To access this site, just type **http://www.irs.gov** in the Location or Address text box.

 WARNING Keep in mind that marketing on the Web has become big business and the ratio of advertising to useful information can be overwhelming if you're not ready for it. Confirm important information from independent sources before taking action. And be prepared to look through a lot of garbage until you find sites you like or develop search techniques of your own.

Joining Internet Newsgroups

A *newsgroup* is the cyberspace equivalent of the office water cooler; it's a place where people gather and chat about common interests. There are newsgroups for just about anyone, from fans of Mystery Science Theater 3000, to amateur and professional astronomers, to people looking for fat-free recipes. Anyone can start a discussion of a subject in a newsgroup by posting a message. And anyone can respond to an existing topic by replying to someone else's message.

How you access Internet newsgroups depends on the browser you use. I'll use Internet Explorer as an example here, but other Web browsers work in a similar way.

In Internet Explorer, click the Mail button and choose Read News from the drop-down menu to display Outlook Express. Then click the Newsgroups button to display the list of newsgroups available from your ISP's news server, as shown in Figure 11.16. (If you are having trouble getting this to work, you might need to contact your ISP for help.) To display only the newsgroups containing a certain word, enter that word in the text box at the top of the window.

FIGURE 11.16

An Outlook Express list of newsgroups

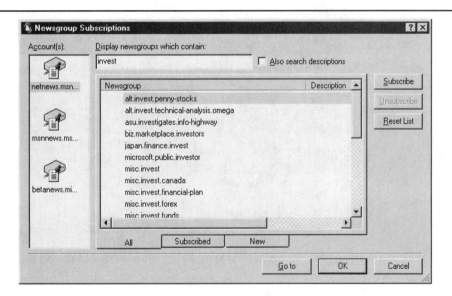

You can shorten your list of newsgroups by subscribing to the ones you prefer. To subscribe to a newsgroup, scroll down the list of newsgroups until you find one you think might interest you, then select the newsgroup's name and click the Subscribe button. Internet Explorer places a newspaper icon beside the newsgroup to indicate that you are now subscribed. Repeat this with each group you are interested in. When you're finished, click the OK button.

It's often difficult to tell exactly what a newsgroup is about by looking at its name. If you think it sounds interesting but are unsure if it's what you're looking for, you can try it out and unsubscribe later. To view the newsgroups to which you have subscribed, click the Subscribed tab. To unsubscribe from a newsgroup, select the newsgroup's name and click the Unsubscribe button.

To view the messages in a newsgroup, select the newsgroup from the list of newsgroups and click the Go To button. Internet Explorer lists the articles people have posted to that newsgroup, with the most recent ones at the bottom of the list. Scroll up and down the list to find an article that interests you. Once you see an interesting message, just double-click it to open it and read it. Figure 11.17 shows a typical newsgroup posting.

FIGURE 11.17

A newsgroup posting

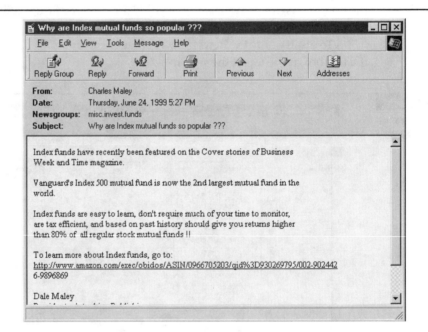

To reply to a message you are reading, click the Reply Group button. Internet Explorer opens a window that you can use to write your reply.

The original message is automatically included in your reply, and it is indicated with right arrows in the left margin. (By the way, it's considered common courtesy to delete any quoted sections that do not pertain directly to your reply.) The message is also automatically addressed to the newsgroup, and the subject line is filled in. After you have composed your reply, click the Post Message button to post your message to the newsgroup.

MASTERING THE OPPORTUNITIES

Ten Financial Newsgroups

The Internet provides more than 10,000 newsgroups, many of which touch on financial matters. The list below gives the names of those that are probably most germane to individuals interested in personal finance:

- alt.invest.penny-stocks
- clari.biz.currencies.misc
- clari.biz.currencies.us_dollar
- clari.usa.gov.policy.financial
- misc.invest
- misc.invest.canada
- misc.invest.futures
- misc.invest.real-estate
- misc.invest.stocks
- misc.invest.technical

New newsgroups are created daily, so there likely will be other groups by the time you read this. When a new one is created, an announcement of some kind is usually made in all newsgroups of related interest.

WARNING It is impossible to know anything about the people who post messages in a newsgroup, so treat whatever information you get with a grain of salt. Be sure to spend some time reading the group's messages before you post any messages yourself. Not only is this considered good etiquette, but it can also save you embarrassment. Also, consider the fact that any message you post is probably going out to an audience of thousands. It's a heady experience, when you think about it, and with that power comes a certain amount of responsibility. Treat people the same way you would if you were face-to-face with them—with respect and graciousness.

Internet Mailing Lists

A *mailing list* is similar to a newsgroup, except that the messages are sent by e-mail. Anyone with an e-mail account can take part in a discussion on a mailing list. Moreover, every message sent to the mailing list ends up in your mailbox, so if your ISP charges you according to the number of messages you receive, being on a mailing list can be costly.

You subscribe to a mailing list by sending an e-mail message containing your pertinent information to a list server. For a list of the publicly accessible mailing lists out there, take a look at the Web site at http://www.liszt.com.

 NOTE The first message you usually get when you sign on a mailing list contains an acknowledgment of your subscription and instructions on how to use the list and unsubscribe if you need to. Print out these documents and keep them in a file folder somewhere. It's frustrating both to you and to the other subscribers when people can't figure out how to unsubscribe and end up sending messages to everyone on the list for instructions.

 MASTERING THE OPPORTUNITIES

Three Financial Mailing Lists

Here are three mailing lists that might provide useful information.

- The Timely Investment Information list recommends stocks and provides economic commentary. Mail to bobbose@stockresearch.com, with the subject Subscribe.
- The Personal Finances list discusses personal finances. Mail to majordomo @shore.net, with the message subscribe persfin-digest.
- The Direct Invest list provides a forum for investors to discuss share opportunities and for business owners to exchange advice in offering stocks directly to the public. Mail to dpo@abiogenesis.com, with the message SUBSCRIBE your e-mail address (your own e-mail address, including what comes before and after the @ symbol).

Your mailbox will soon be regularly filled with messages. You may need to sift through all of them, but you'll be surprised at how quickly you can find information.

PART II

Quicken and Your Personal Finances

LEARN TO:

- **Record Credit Card and Cash Spending**

- **Track Loans and Mortgages**

- **Estimate and Prepare Income Taxes**

- **Use the Quicken Financial Planners**

- **Estimate Your Life Insurance Needs**

CHAPTER 12

Cash or Charge?

Y ou can use Quicken not only to track bank accounts but also to track just about any personal asset, most business assets, and just about any liability. This chapter describes how to use Quicken to track credit and debit cards as well as the cash you carry and spend (such as the money in your wallet or a business's petty cash fund). This chapter also describes how you can use the Quicken Debt Reduction Planner to calculate how long it will take you to pay off credit card balances.

Before You Begin

Here are the prerequisites for using Quicken for credit card tracking:

- Know how the Quicken register works and how to record payments and deposits into it (see Chapter 2).

- Know your current credit or debit card balance and, ideally, your credit limit. (You should be able to get some of this information from your most recent credit card or debit card statement. If you've saved your transaction slips since the most recent credit card or debit card statement, these will be useful too.)

- Have applied for a credit card with a bank that supports Quicken's online banking feature, if you want to retrieve your credit card statements by modem over the telephone line. You'll also need a modem, of course.

Paying Off a Credit Card

Credit cards can simplify and improve your financial life. You don't need to carry large sums of cash around, just a tiny rectangle of plastic. If you need a short-term loan—say a car breaks down or a child needs stitches—you have immediate funding at your fingertips.

Despite all the positive ways consumer credit influences our lives, it's easy for too much of a good thing to turn bad. To get into trouble, simply make that tempting minimum payment a few times on a credit card with a painfully high annual interest rate. Before you know it, you have hefty credit card balances, and you're paying hundreds or even thousands of dollars in annual interest charges.

If you find yourself in this predicament and want to get out of the credit card trap, you can use the Loan Planner to estimate what size payment will pay off a credit card over a specified number of years. Just follow these steps:

1. Choose Planning ➢ Financial Calculators ➢ Loan to display the Loan Calculator dialog box, as shown in Figure 12.1.

2. Click the Payment Per Period option button in the Calculate For section at the bottom of the dialog box, and use the Loan Amount text box at the top of the dialog box to enter the amount you currently owe on a credit card.

3. In the Annual Interest Rate text box, enter the annual interest rate charged on the card balance. If a card charges 18 percent annually, for example, type **18**.

The Loan Calculator dialog box

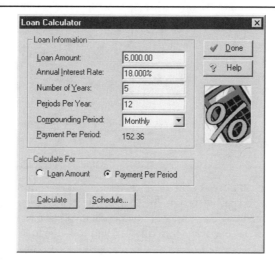

4. In the Number of Years text box, enter the number of years over which you want to pay off the credit card balance. If you want to have the balance paid off in five years, for example, type **5**.

5. Verify that the Periods Per Year text box shows 12, which indicates that you'll be making monthly payments.

6. Click the Calculate button.

Quicken calculates the monthly payment that repays the credit card balance over the specified number of years and displays it at the bottom of the Loan Information section. If you currently owe $6,000 on a credit card charging 18 percent annual interest, for example, paying off the $6,000 over five years will require monthly payments of $152.36.

If you want to see a breakdown of payments to principal and interest, click the Schedule command button to display a schedule of payments based on your figures. Figure 12.2 shows an example of a schedule of future payments.

PART

II

Quicken and Your
Personal Finances

FIGURE 12.2

The Approximate Future Payment Schedule area shows how your regular monthly payment will repay the credit card debt.

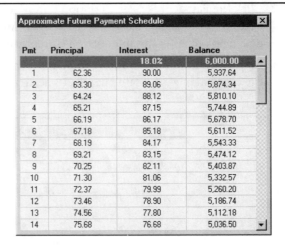

Approximate Future Payment Schedule				
Pmt	Principal	Interest	Balance	
		18.0%	6,000.00	
1	62.36	90.00	5,937.64	
2	63.30	89.06	5,874.34	
3	64.24	88.12	5,810.10	
4	65.21	87.15	5,744.89	
5	66.19	86.17	5,678.70	
6	67.18	85.18	5,611.52	
7	68.19	84.17	5,543.33	
8	69.21	83.15	5,474.12	
9	70.25	82.11	5,403.87	
10	71.30	81.06	5,332.57	
11	72.37	79.99	5,260.20	
12	73.46	78.90	5,186.74	
13	74.56	77.80	5,112.18	
14	75.68	76.68	5,036.50	

 TIP If a credit card issuer charges you interest from the date of the charge transaction, you also pay interest on the charges you make over a month rather than only the balance outstanding at the start of the month. It will take longer to repay the credit card balance than the Loan Planner calculates if you continue to use the credit card.

Checking Your Credit

We've all heard the horror stories about credit bureaus that, for some reason or another, have incorrect information that results in some temporary catastrophe. Since credit bureaus are responsible for keeping a considerable amount of information about your financial well-being, it's a good idea to check periodically to make sure that the information they have is accurate. This is especially true when there is some impending event that will affect you financially, such as buying a house or changing your marital status. At the very least, you should check your credit reports once a year.

 TIP You can order a copy of your credit report from Experian, a major credit bureau. You can also subscribe to a credit-monitoring service. There are many credit-reporting and credit-monitoring services available, but note that many are—at least in my opinion—rather expensive.

To check your credit, click the Banking QuickTab and click the Free Credit Report hyperlink. Quicken opens the CreditCheck area. Click the appropriate options to select the credit check options you desire.

Tracking Credit Cards

To track a credit card in Quicken, you need to set up an account for the credit card, and then you need to record the charges and payments you make. If you've set up bank accounts before and worked with these accounts, you'll find credit card accounts easy to use.

When to Set Up a Credit Card Account

Do you need to set up a credit card account? Even if you use a credit card, you may not need to track it with Quicken. If you pay off your credit card in full every month, you can categorize your credit bill when you write the check to pay the credit company by using the Split Transaction Window. And if you always charge nominal amounts that you don't need to keep careful track of, you probably don't need to set up a credit card account.

On the other hand, if you carry a substantial credit card balance, you'll want to set up a credit card account to categorize your credit card spending. You'll also want to set up a credit card account if you want to track your spending by merchant—the businesses that accept your credit card charges—even if you always pay off the credit card bill in full each month. Merchant information can't be recorded anywhere as part of writing a check to the credit card company. Finally, you'll want to use a credit card account if you need or want to track your credit card balance.

Setting Up Credit Card Accounts

You set up a credit card account in Quicken for each credit card you use. If you have both a Visa and an American Express card, you should set up two credit card accounts: one to track the Visa card and one to track the American Express card. To set up a credit card account, follow these steps:

1. Click the Banking QuickTab to display the Banking area, as shown in Figure 12.3.
2. Click the Create A New Account hyperlink to display the dialog box you use to set up a new account, as shown in Figure 12.4.
3. Select Credit Card, and then click Next.

4. When Quicken displays the Credit Card Account Setup dialog box, click the Summary tab. (If you've been working with Quicken a bit, you won't need the extra hand-holding the other tab in the Credit Card Account Setup dialog box provides.) Figure 12.5 shows the Summary tab in the Credit Card Account Setup dialog box.

5. In the Account Name text box, enter a short name for the credit card account, such as **Visa** or **AMEX**.

FIGURE 12.3

The Banking area

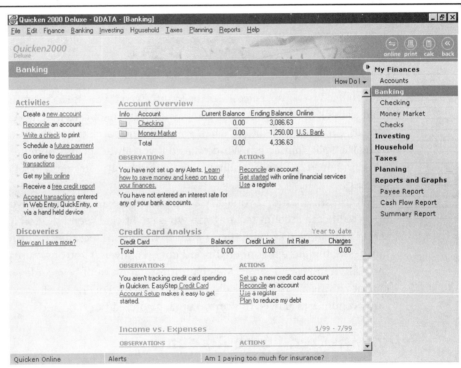

FIGURE 12.4

Setting up a new account

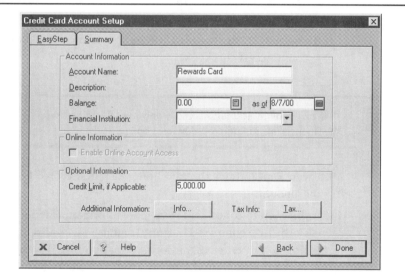

FIGURE 12.5

The Summary tab of the Credit Card Account Setup dialog box

 NOTE   If you have more than one credit card of the same kind—such as two Visa cards—consider using the credit card name and the issuer name to identify the credit card. For example, if you have Visa cards from Chase Manhattan and from Wells Fargo, you might name one credit card "Visa–Chase" and the other "Visa–Wells."

6. If you want to provide an account description, click in the Description text box. Enter a description of the credit card account or additional account information, such as the account number or the credit card company. You can enter a maximum of 54 characters.

7. In the Balance text box, enter the account balance on the day that you'll start keeping records for the credit card.

 NOTE You can enter the credit card balance as of the last statement date, but this figure won't include the payments you've made since the last statement or any charges you've incurred. Therefore, if you do enter the balance as of the last statement date, be sure to enter the transactions that have occurred since the last statement date when it is time to reconcile.

---

8. In the As Of (date) text box, enter the date on which you want to start keeping records for this account, in *MM/DD/YY* fashion. For example, type July 4, 2000, as **7/4/00**.

9. If you will retrieve your statements via modem, mark the Enable Online Account Access checkbox.

 NOTE Online Account Access is only available if you select a participating bank from the Financial Institution drop-down list box.

---

10. If you want to track the card limit, click in the Credit Limit text box and enter the amount.

11. If you want to collect and store more information about the credit card account, click the Info command button. Then use the Additional Account Information dialog box to enter this information. You might want to use the Additional Account Information dialog box, for example, to store the credit card number and the telephone number you use to report a lost or stolen credit card. When you have completed this screen, click OK.

12. If you're not using online banking, click Done to tell Quicken that the Credit Card Account Setup dialog box is complete. Quicken displays the Banking area (see Figure 12.3), and this time it includes your new credit card account. You're finished, and you can skip the rest of the steps described here.

13. If you checked Enable Online Account Access, click Next. Quicken displays several messages and then, ultimately, a window that lists the financial institutions that support online banking. Click the name of the financial institution that issued the card from the list, and then follow the on-screen instructions for applying. Note that to view the list of financial institutions, you need to have an Internet connection. Once you select the financial institution, Quicken displays additional message boxes, including one that asks you to confirm you've selected the right financial institution. And then it displays the Edit Credit Card Account dialog box shown in Figure 12.6.

14. Enter your credit card number in the Credit Card Number text box. You can get it right off the face of your credit card or your credit card bill.

15. Verify that the Account Type drop-down list box shows Credit Card as the account type. If it doesn't, activate the drop-down list box and then select Credit Card. Click Next.

16. Enter your I.D. number in the Customer I.D. text box.

17. Enter the 9-digit routing number in the Routing Number text box. You can get this number from the online banking welcome letter that you received from the financial institution issuing your credit card.

18. Click Next to review the information you provided, and then click Next again.

19. Click Done.

PART

II

Quicken and Your
Personal Finances

FIGURE 12.6

The setup information needed for an online banking credit card

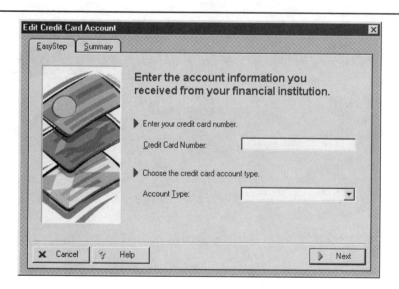

Quicken displays the Banking area, which includes your new credit card account in the list of accounts. This account has a lightning bolt next to the account type to indicate that it is an online banking account.

Telling Quicken Which Credit Card Account You Want to Work With

As you may know, Quicken displays different registers for different accounts and different credit card accounts. To record charges and payments related to a specific credit card, you'll need to display that credit card's register.

If you can see the credit card register's QuickTab in the Quicken application window, you can tell Quicken that you want to work with the account simply by clicking its QuickTab.

If you can't see a credit card register's QuickTab, display the Account List, select the account, and click the Open button in the Account List. (You can also double-click the account name.) Quicken then displays a register for the credit card account, and you're all set to begin entering credit card charges and payments. Figure 12.7 shows a sample credit card register

FIGURE 12.7

A credit card register

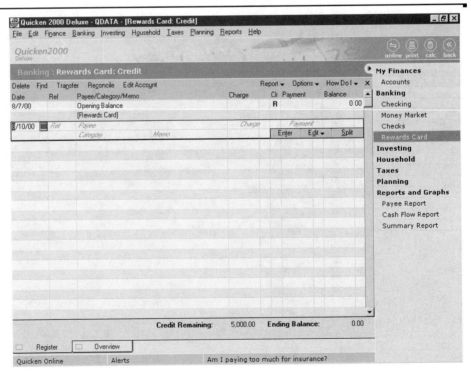

Recording Credit Card Charges

As long as you're not working with an online banking account, you record credit card charges in the same way you record payments made from a bank account. (Because recording transactions into an online banking account is a little different, I'll describe that process later in this chapter.)

To record a credit card charge, use the arrow keys or the mouse, or choose Edit ➤ Transaction ➤ New to move to the next empty row of the register. Then follow these steps:

1. Enter the credit card charge date in the Date text box. If the date shown isn't the correct transaction date, enter the date in *MM/DD/YY* format. You typically don't need to enter the year number; the one Quicken already shows is usually correct.

2. If you want to enter a credit card reference number, enter the number in the Ref text box. You can do this in the same way that you enter check numbers. (You might choose, for example, to enter a portion of the credit card transaction number.)

3. Enter the name of the merchant who accepted the credit card charge. Place the cursor in the Payee combo box. If this is the first time you've recorded a charge with the merchant, type the payee's name. If you've recorded a charge before or written a check, you can activate the Payee drop-down list and select the merchant's name from it.

4. Enter the amount in the Charge or Payment text box. You don't need to enter currency punctuation—such as dollar signs or commas—but you should include a decimal to identify any cents.

5. If you want to mark cleared transactions manually and the transaction you're entering into the register has already cleared or been recorded by the credit card company, click in the Clr text box to place an R there.

Normally, you won't mark cleared transactions. Marking charges and payments as cleared is something you do as part of reconciling a credit card account, which is discussed a little later in this chapter. If you're entering old transactions—say you're starting your record keeping as of the previous credit card statement—you can mark cleared transactions to make your reconciliation easier.

6. To categorize the transaction, highlight the Category combo box and activate the Category drop-down list. Then select the category that best describes the charge. A charge at the office supplies store, for example, might fall into the Office category.

A payment will usually be recorded as a transfer from the bank account you'll use to write the check that pays the bill (see Chapter 2). If you can't find an expense category that describes the charge, you can enter a short category description directly into the Category combo box. If you want to create a category named Office Supplies, for example, type **Office Supplies**. (See Chapter 14 for information about setting up category lists that easily support your income tax planning and preparation.)

7. If you want to enter a short description, click in the Memo text box and enter the description. You can enter anything you want in this field, but there's no reason to duplicate information that you've entered or will enter someplace else.

8. Select Enter to record the credit card charge or payment.

Quicken updates the credit card balance and the remaining credit limit and then highlights the next empty row in the register. Figure 12.8 shows several credit card charges.

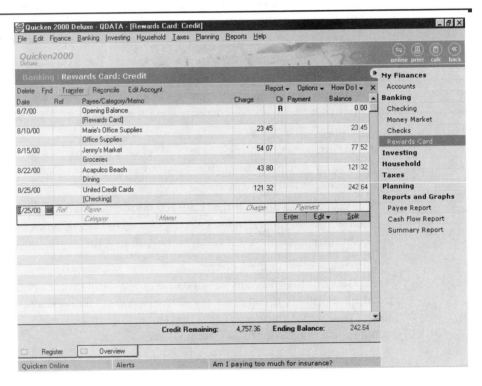

FIGURE 12.8

A credit card register with several charges

Paying a Credit Card Bill the Easy Way

The easiest way to pay a credit card bill is to just record a transfer transaction to the credit card account. If you write a check, for example, you must open the checking register and enter the check transaction as a payment to the credit card company, categorizing it as a transfer to the credit card account. When you do this, the transaction shows in the credit card register like the last transaction in Figure 12.8. (Chapter 2 explains how transfer transactions work.)

Paying and Reconciling a Credit Card Bill

You can also pay a credit card bill as part of reconciling a credit card statement. To do so, you go through the steps for analyzing the difference between your credit card records and the credit card company's records. (This process works just like a bank account reconciliation.) Then, at the end, you tell Quicken how much you want to pay.

To reconcile and pay a credit card bill, display the register for the credit card account. Then follow these steps:

1. Click Reconcile to display the Credit Card Statement Information dialog box, as shown in Figure 12.9.

PART

II

Quicken and Your
Personal Finances

FIGURE 12.9

*The Credit Card
Statement Information
dialog box*

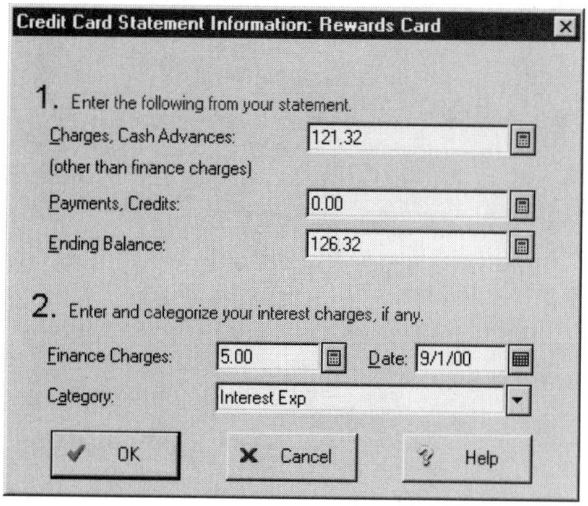

2. Using the Charges, Cash Advances text box, enter the amount your credit card statement shows as the total charges and cash advances.

3. Using the Payments, Credits text box, enter the amount your credit card statement shows as the total payments and credits.

4. Enter the ending credit card account balance from your statement in the Ending Balance text box.

5. Enter the monthly finance charge shown on the statement (if you haven't done so already) in the Finance Charges text box.

6. Tell Quicken when the finance charge occurred using the Date text box.

7. Categorize the finance charge by using the Category text box. (If you don't remember which category you want to use, click the down arrow on the Category drop-down list box to display a list of categories.)

8. Click OK to display the Reconcile Credit Statement, as shown in Figure 12.10.

 TIP If you have a question about a transaction shown in the Reconcile Credit Statement, double-click the transaction to display the credit card account's register with the transaction highlighted. You can examine the transaction in more detail—for example, by reviewing the split transaction information. When you're ready to return to the Reconcile Credit Statement, click the Return to Reconcile command button.

FIGURE 12.10

The Reconcile Credit Statement

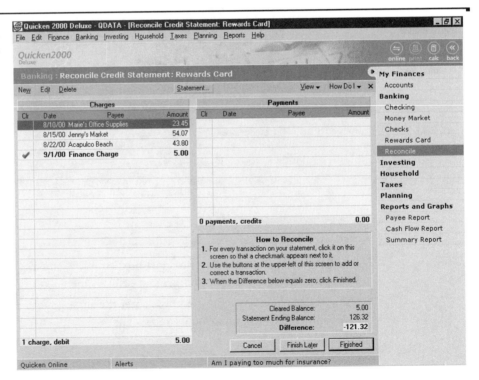

9. Review the list of transactions shown in the Reconcile Credit Statement, and highlight each of the transactions that has cleared. Quicken places a checkmark by each transaction you highlight. If you accidentally mark a transaction as cleared when it shouldn't be, click it again or press the spacebar to unmark it.

10. Select Finished when the difference between the cleared balance and the credit card statement balance is 0. Or click Finish Later if you would rather finish reconciling the credit card account at a later time.

As you indicate which transactions have cleared, Quicken continually recalculates a Cleared Balance figure. This figure is just your records' credit card account balance minus all the uncleared transactions. When the cleared balance equals the credit card statement balance, your account balances, or reconciles. In other words, when the uncleared transactions total explains the difference between your records and the credit card company's records, you've reconciled the account.

Figure 12.11 shows the Reconcile Credit Statement after reconciliation. When you select Finished, Quicken updates the cleared status of the transactions you marked as cleared by changing the asterisks to Rs. Then it displays a message box that asks if you want to make a payment on the credit card bill.

PART

II

Quicken and Your
Personal Finances

FIGURE 12.11

The Reconcile Credit Statement showing a Cleared Balance figure

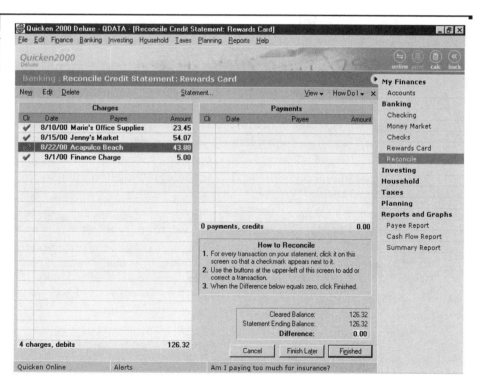

11. If you want to make a payment on the credit card bill, choose the bank account on which you'll write the check from the Bank Account drop-down list box.

12. Use the Payment Method option buttons to indicate whether you will hand-write the check or use Quicken to print it:

- Click the Printed Check option button to display the Write Checks area for the account you selected in step 11. Describe the check by filling out the text boxes in this area, and select Record Check.

- Click the Hand Written Check option button, then click Yes to display the bank account register for the account you selected in step 11. Complete the transaction as you would normally, and then select Enter.

Quicken also fills in the Category text box with the credit card account name; don't change this. When you pay off a portion of a credit card balance, you actually are transferring money from your bank account to the credit card company. Click Enter when you finish describing the payment transaction.

Recording Credit Card Charges with Online Banking

As long as you have either the Quicken credit card or a credit card issued by one of the banks that supports Quicken's Online Account Access feature, you can retrieve your credit card transactions from the credit card company through an online connection.

Setting Up Your Online Connection

Before you can begin to use any of Quicken's online financial services, you need to apply for online service. To do so, display the credit card register and click the Overview tab at the bottom. Then click the hyperlink to enable online account access. Quicken displays a series of dialog boxes for signing up for the service. These dialog boxes contain text boxes for entering your name and address, the password you use to connect to the service, and some information Intuit uses to identify you if the need arises.

 NOTE Quicken launches a Wizard to set up your modem whenever you attempt to use any online services, including online banking. If the modem setup doesn't work correctly, try choosing Edit ➢ Internet Connection Setup.

Retrieving a Credit Card Statement

Whenever you want to, you can retrieve your most recent credit card transactions from Intuit Services Corporation, the company that runs Quicken's online banking and bill payment services.

To update your credit card register, click the Reconcile command button. Quicken may ask you to go to the Online Center to get the latest data and update your accounts.

If you click Yes, Quicken displays the Online Center. Click Update/Send to retrieve the latest information. You can then click the Compare to Register button to compare your register's transactions to those the online credit card statement shows. When you do this, Quicken displays a list of the transactions shown in the online credit card statement. To accept all of the transactions shown on the online statement, click the Accept All button. To individually review transactions, select a transaction and then either click Accept or Delete. Note that when you review the online credit card statements by comparing them to what your register already shows, you're effectively reconciling the credit card statements.

What About Debit Cards?

You can also track debit cards in Quicken. The process varies from that used for tracking credit cards because a debit card isn't actually a liability. Rather, it's an asset, which makes it more analogous to a bank account, so you treat a debit card like another bank account. You can record debit card charges on the account in the same way that you record payments on a regular checking account. And you treat additions to the debit card account balance in the same way as deposits into a regular checking account.

 NOTE   A debit card attached to a regular bank account doesn't need a separate bank account. The debit card transactions can be recorded directly into the bank account's register.

Tracking Cash

Most people won't need to track the cash they hold (like what's in a wallet) or the cash they spend and receive. It's usually easy enough to monitor cash balances by looking in your pocket. And it's often possible to record the income and expense

categories associated with cash receipts and disbursements as part of cashing the
check you use to get the cash or as part of withdrawing money from the bank. If you
withdraw $100 from a bank account to spend on groceries, for example, you can cate-
gorize the $100 withdrawal as a Groceries expense.

Setting Up a Cash Account

To track your cash holdings, receipts, and expenditures more precisely than you can
with an informal approach, you can set up a cash account in the same way that you set
up other accounts: Display the Banking area and click the Create A New Account
hyperlink. When Quicken displays the Create New Account window, indicate that you
want to set up a cash account, and click Next. Then, when Quicken displays the Cash
Account Setup dialog box, click the Summary tab, give the account a name or simply
accept the default Cash, tell Quicken how much cash you're holding in the Balance
text box and when you want to start tracking it in the As Of box, and click Done.

To display a register that describes the cash account you've just set up, select the
cash account in the Account List and click the Open command button. Quicken displays the cash account version of the register, as shown in Figure 12.12.

FIGURE 12.12

*The cash version of the
account register with
sample receipt and
disbursement
transactions*

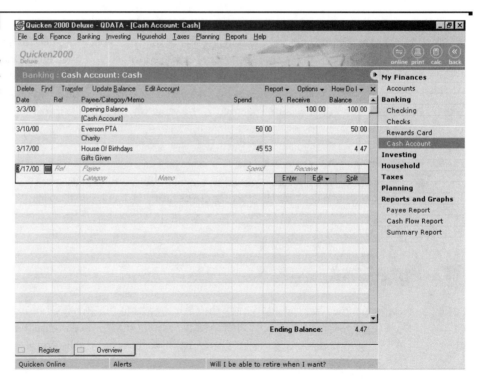

Recording Receipts and Disbursements

Recording cash receipts and disbursements is similar to recording bank account withdrawals and deposits. You begin by placing the cursor in the next empty row of the register or choosing Edit ➢ Transactions ➢ New. Then follow these steps:

1. Enter the cash receipt or disbursement date.

2. If you want a more detailed record, enter a cash receipt or disbursement reference number.

3. Name the person from whom you received or to whom you disbursed the cash.

4. Enter the receipt or disbursement amount. Use the Spend column for disbursements and the Receive column for receipts.

5. If you want to add more details, enter a memo description.

6. Categorize the receipt or disbursement transaction. (Increases in cash when you cash a check should be recorded as a transfer from your bank account to your cash account.)

7. Select Enter to record the receipt or disbursement. Quicken updates the cash balance and highlights the next empty row in the register.

 NOTE When a cash account register is displayed, click the Update Balance command button, and Quicken displays the Update Account Balance dialog box. You can use it to enter a cash transaction that adjusts the current balance to whatever actual cash you hold. The Update Account Balance dialog box provides text boxes for entering the correct account balance, the category to use for the adjustment transaction, and the adjustment date. You just fill in the blanks and click OK.

Creating a Debt-Reduction Plan

Quicken Deluxe includes a feature that helps you figure out the most painless way of reducing your present debts. To use the feature, you describe your debts in detail. With Quicken's help, you then develop a practical plan to repay your debts.

You open the Debt Reduction Planner by clicking the Planning QuickTab and then clicking the How Can I Get Out Of Debt? hyperlink. Quicken opens a window that resembles a file folder. Insert the Quicken CD in your CD-ROM drive and click Next. Quicken starts a multimedia presentation about debt reduction. If you want to skip ahead, click the Next button, and the window shown in Figure 12.13 appears.

FIGURE 12.13

List your debts here to create a debt-reduction plan.

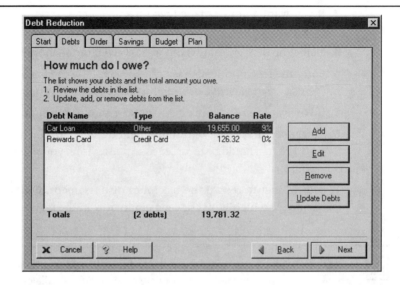

To add a debt to the list, click the Add button and fill in the blanks in the dialog box that Quicken displays. To edit the terms of a debt that is already listed (a debt for which you've set up an account in Quicken), click the debt, and then click the Edit button. Then make any required changes using the dialog box that Quicken displays. When you've described all of your debts, click Next.

Quicken next describes how long it will take for you to get out of debt if you keep going as you have in the past—in other words, if you continue to make the same payments. You continue to click the Next button to move through a series of dialog box tabs. During this process, Quicken alternatively runs multimedia presentations describing debt-reduction strategies and collects information about how much additional money you can free up from your existing expenditures and redirect to debt reduction.

When you get to the end of the step-by-step process and click Done, Quicken displays a window similar to the one shown in Figure 12.14. I've included some sample data, so that you can see the graph that Quicken creates.

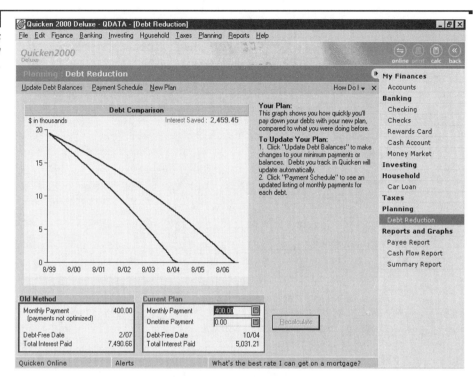

FIGURE 12.14

The graph represents your debt-reduction savings.

One line in the graph represents the amount of money you would pay if you continued on your present path; the other line represents how much less you would pay if you put your plan in action. It's usually pretty convincing.

If you want to adjust your plan, click the New Plan button. Then you can edit the previous plan and see the revised results.

MASTERING FINANCIAL SUCCESS

The Problem with Debt Reduction

Debt reduction can seem like a powerful personal financial concept. And that's particularly true when you look at the savings from early repayment of a long-term debt, such as a mortgage. Sometimes this is a good idea, particularly when you're borrowing money at high credit-card interest rates.

But early debt repayment doesn't always make sense. In some cases, instead of repaying the debt, you will be in better shape if you invest your money and earn a return that exceeds the interest rate. For example, you might want to take advantage of wonderful investment opportunities such as employer-sponsored 401(k) plans and 403(b) plans rather than opting for early repayment of a debt. In these types of plans, you save pre-tax money and also typically get an employer contribution that augments your savings.

How to Choose and Use Credit Cards

Credit cards are convenient, but they're also dangerous. A lot of people ruin their financial lives by turning the phrase "charge it" into a reflex. It's a real problem, and for that reason the rest of this chapter explains how to make good use of credit cards and how to choose a good credit card.

Selecting the Right Credit Card

Selecting a credit card is easy. If you don't carry charges forward from month to month, choose the card with the lowest annual fee. It doesn't matter to you if the credit card company charges a painfully high interest rate, since you pay only the annual fee if you pay your monthly credit card bill on time.

If you do carry a balance, it makes sense to choose the card with the lowest interest rate. Some credit card issuers play interest rate calculation tricks that make it very difficult to make apples-to-apples comparisons of credit cards. But if you choose the credit card rate with the lowest annual percentage rate, you're doing about as well as you can.

The Right Way to Use a Credit Card

You shouldn't use a credit card as a way to borrow money. That means always repaying the charges within the grace period. You want to be what the bank calls "a revolver," which is a person who always pays his or her credit card bills on time.

After a 401(k) or deductible IRA, the best investment you can make is to pay off credit cards that charge a high interest rate. Earning a tax-free interest rate of, say, 14 percent, which is what a 401(k) and deductible IRA pay, is too good to pass up.

Continued ▶

MASTERING FINANCIAL SUCCESS CONTINUED

Credit card interest rates are much too expensive. One reason they are so expensive is that consumer interest, which is what credit card interest is, is not tax-deductible. You can't deduct it from your gross income for income-tax purposes the way you can a mortgage interest payment. And even if you ignore income taxes, credit card interest rates are usually far above the interest rate on a car loan or a mortgage. Because you can use amortizing debt (*amortizing debt* is a regular loan on which you make payments on both the interest and the principal over time), any time it makes sense to borrow money, it's a safe bet that you should never borrow money using your credit card. If you carry a credit card balance, you often pay interest on both the old and new charges. In other words, there is no grace period for your charges.

Do Affinity Cards Make Sense?

An *affinity card* is a credit card that's issued by someone other than a bank—such as a car manufacturer, an airline, a professional group, and so forth. Affinity cards typically combine the usual features of a credit card with some extra benefit connected to the issuer. In the case of a General Motors card, for example, you accumulate dollars in a rebate account by virtue of what you spend with the affinity card.

In general, an affinity card—especially one that doesn't charge a fee—is a good deal as long as the interest rate is competitive. For example, I have a General Motors credit card that includes a 5 percent rebate account. In other words, five cents of every dollar I charge on the card goes into a rebate account that I can use toward purchasing a new General Motors car. How big your rebate gets depends on the type of affinity card you have. For example, as of this writing the regular General Motors credit card lets you accumulate up to $500 a year to a maximum of $3,500. The General Motors gold credit card lets you accumulate up to $1,000 a year to a maximum of $7,000.

There are many different affinity cards. Ford has one. Most of the major airlines have them, too. Airline affinity cards let you accumulate frequent flier miles based on the credit card charges. In the plans I've seen, you usually get a mile a dollar.

The one sticky part of using affinity cards, however, is that getting even a 5 percent rebate isn't worth it if having the card makes you spend more money. Some studies show that you spend 23 percent more when you use a credit card. The same is very likely true of affinity cards.

If you're one of those people who spends more when you have a card in hand, you won't save any money by using an affinity card. Even if you get a new General Motors car for free or a handful of free airline tickets to Europe, you pay indirectly for your new car or airline tickets with all the extra charging you do. If you don't make use of the rebate, the situation is even worse. You've charged more, perhaps paid hefty annual fees, and you've received nothing in return.

Continued

MASTERING FINANCIAL SUCCESS CONTINUED

How to Save Money on Credit Cards

Fortunately, you can use a bunch of different tactics to save money on credit cards. Some suggestions follow:

Leave Home without It

If you're like most people, you spend more money if you carry a credit card around. As I mentioned, some studies show that credit card holders spend 23 percent more on average even if they don't carry a balance on the credit cards. No investment pays an instantaneous 23 percent rate after taxes. Despite what American Express says, you're really better off if you leave home *without* it.

Cancel Unnecessary Credit Cards

If you don't carry credit card balances, cancel credit cards that charge an annual maintenance fee. Lighten your wallet by canceling all the cards you don't use, for that matter. You'll only spend more if you use them, anyway.

Ask Your Bank to Waive Its Annual Fee

Call your bank and explain that, because of the annual fee, you might cancel your credit card. Tell the bank you think it should waive its annual fee. Your current credit card issuer will probably gulp and then waive the fee. For a two-minute telephone call, you'll be ahead by $20 or $30. (By the way, most credit card issuers don't waive the fee on a gold card.)

Consider an Affinity Card

If you travel on business a lot, you can easily run up $10,000 or more on a credit card as you pay for airline tickets, hotels, and rental cars. In this case, it's well worth it to pay $50 for an affinity card. Once you have the card, charge all your purchases on it (your employer will likely reimburse you anyway). When you accumulate a whopping rebate, use it for a family vacation or a new car.

One caution here, however: Talk to your tax advisor, because there's a good chance your rebate will be considered taxable income if you go this route. On the other hand, if you charge only personal purchases on the affinity card, you can make a good case that the rebate isn't taxable income but is an adjustment in the price of the goods you bought.

Continued

Cancel Credit Insurance If You Have Any

Credit life insurance is usually a big waste of money. But before you cancel it, read through the primer in Chapter 16, which is about making life insurance decisions. You might need credit life insurance if you know your estate will collect and you can't get a better kind of insurance.

Credit disability insurance is usually another big waste of money. But, as with credit life insurance, you may need this insurance if you require disability insurance and you can't get better insurance.

Cancel Credit Card Protection Insurance If You Have It

Credit card protection insurance is another waste of money. If some nefarious type steals your credit card and runs up huge charges, you are liable for only the first $50 or so as long as you tell the credit card issuer that the credit card was stolen.

Never Make the Minimum Payment

Pay more than the minimum payment. Paying off high-interest-rate credit cards is one of the two best investments you can make. (The other is contributing money to a 401(k) plan in which the employer matches a portion of your contribution.) If you make minimum payments only, your credit card debt quickly balloons. *Very* quickly balloons, I should say. Soon you are paying massive monthly finance charges.

Get Rid of Your Gold Card

You're paying for the privilege and prestige of that gold card. But you knew that, right? You can probably save yourself at least $40 or $50 just by having an old, boring, regular Visa or MasterCard.

PART

II

Quicken and Your
Personal Finances

CHAPTER <u>13</u>

Loans and Mortgages

Earlier chapters described how you can use Quicken to track items such as bank accounts and credit cards and the ways you earn and spend your money. You can also use Quicken to track your debts and what they cost you. Performing this record keeping lets you more closely monitor your liabilities. And if you keep records of all your assets, Quicken lets you track your net worth as well.

Before You Begin

What you need to know to track loans and mortgages depends on what you want to do:

- To track any loan or mortgage, you need to know the current loan balance. You can probably get this information from the most recent loan statement or by telephoning the lender.

- To have Quicken break down loan payments into the interest and principal components, you need to know the loan's annual interest rate and the remaining number of payments. You can get this information from the loan contract or perhaps by telephoning the lender.

Using the Loan Calculator

The Loan Calculator introduced in Chapter 12 works well for experimenting with possible loan balances and payments. You can use this tool to see, for example, what the loan payment would be on that car you're eyeing or what size mortgage you can afford, given a specific payment amount.

To use the Loan Calculator for these tasks, follow these steps:

1. Choose Planning ➤ Financial Calculators ➤ Loan to display the Loan Calculator dialog box, as shown in Figure 13.1.

2. Tell Quicken which loan variable you want to calculate: Click the Loan Amount option button in the Calculate For section to calculate a loan payment given the loan amount, or click the Payment Per Period option button to calculate the loan amount given a loan payment.

3. If you've indicated you want to calculate a loan payment, enter the loan balance in the Loan Amount text box.

PART

II

Quicken and Your
Personal Finances

FIGURE 13.1

*The Loan Calculator
dialog box can calcu-
late either the loan
amount or the
payment.*

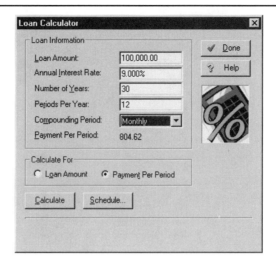

4. Enter the loan's annual interest rate in the Annual Interest Rate text box. If a loan charges 9 percent annually, for example, type **9**.

5. Using the Number of Years text box, enter the number of years over which you will repay the loan. For a 30-year mortgage, for example, type **30**.

6. Enter the number of payments you'll make each year into the Periods Per Year text box. In Figure 13.1, this text box shows 12, which indicates monthly payments.

7. If you indicated in step 2 that you want to calculate a loan balance, enter the loan payment you want to or will make in the Payment Per Period text box.

Once you complete these steps, click the Calculate button, and Quicken calculates the variable you said you wanted to calculate. Figure 13.1, for example, shows that the monthly payment on a $100,000, 30-year mortgage bearing 9 percent annual interest equals $804.62.

To create an amortization schedule that shows the periodic payments, the interest and principal portions of these payments, and the loan balance after each payment, click the Schedule command button. Quicken produces an amortization schedule report and displays it in its own dialog box, as shown in Figure 13.2. You can print the amortization schedule by clicking the dialog box's Print command button.

FIGURE 13.2

*The Approximate
Future Payment
Schedule*

Pmt	Principal	Interest	Balance
		9.0%	100,000.00
1	54.62	750.00	99,945.38
2	55.03	749.59	99,890.35
3	55.44	749.18	99,834.91
4	55.86	748.76	99,779.05
5	56.28	748.34	99,722.77
6	56.70	747.92	99,666.07
7	57.12	747.50	99,608.95
8	57.55	747.07	99,551.40
9	57.98	746.64	99,493.42
10	58.42	746.20	99,435.00
11	58.86	745.76	99,376.14
12	59.30	745.32	99,316.84
13	59.74	744.88	99,257.10
14	60.19	744.43	99,196.91

Saving Money with Early Repayment

You can often save enormous sums by repaying a loan early. In the preceding section, for example, I referred to a $100,000, 30-year mortgage bearing 9 percent annual interest. Although such a mortgage loan would call for monthly payments of $804.62, suppose a borrower could afford to increase the payment amount by $20 to $824.62—and the lender doesn't charge prepayment penalties. By making the larger payment each month, the borrower would save $24,135.56. No, you didn't misread the amount. An extra $20 a month results in roughly $24,000 of interest savings!

You can calculate how much money you'll save by early repayment of a loan such as a mortgage. To do this, calculate the total regular-sized payments you would have made according to the loan contract and the total new-but-bigger payments you're now planning to make. The difference between these two amounts equals the interest savings from the new payment.

Making the Early Repayment Calculations

The calculations just described require several steps, so I've created a simple worksheet you can use to work through the numbers. It is shown in Table 13.1. The worksheet's left column of numbers shows how you would calculate the interest rate savings by adding an extra $20 to a monthly payment of $804.62 when you have a $100,000, 30-year mortgage bearing 9 percent interest. The worksheet's right column provides blank spaces that you can use to calculate the actual interest rate savings you would receive via early loan repayment.

TABLE 13.1: THE EARLY LOAN REPAYMENT SAVINGS WORKSHEET

Input Description	Example Loan	Your Loan
Line 1: Regular payment amount	804.62	_____
Line 2: Number of remaining regular payments	360	_____
Line 3: Total regular payments (line 1 × line 2)	289,663.20	_____
Line 4: New payment amount	823.13	_____
Line 5: Number of remaining new payments	324	_____
Line 6: Total new payments (line 4 × line 5)	266,694.12	_____
Line 7: Repayment savings (line 3 − line 6)	22,969.08	_____

PART

II

Quicken and Your
Personal Finances

To complete the worksheet, follow these steps:

1. Enter the regular payment amount on line 1.

2. Enter the remaining number of payments on line 2. If you've just closed on a 30-year mortgage with monthly payments, for example, you have 360 monthly payments remaining. If you're halfway through repaying the same loan, you have 180 monthly payments remaining.

3. Multiply line 1 by line 2 to calculate the total remaining payments (you can use the Quicken calculator) and enter the result on line 3. To calculate the total remaining payments when the regular monthly payment equals $804.62 and there are 360 months of payments left, for example, multiply $804.62 by 360 months for a result of $289,663.20.

4. To set up the Loan Calculator so it's ready for calculating the number of new, larger payments you'll need to make, display the Loan Calculator dialog box and click the Payment Per Period radio button. Enter the remaining loan balance in the Loan Amount text box, the loan's interest rate in the Annual Interest Rate text box, and the number of payments per year (probably 12) in the Payments Per Year text box.

5. To estimate the number of years you'll make the new, larger payment, just keep entering new, smaller values in the Number of Years text box until you find the Number of Years value that results in a calculated loan payment that's close to your new payment; you probably won't be able to get a Number of Years value

that produces a payment amount exactly equal to your new planned payment. In the example, setting the Number of Years to 27 produces a payment amount equal to $823.13, even though I've indicated that $824.62 is really the new payment planned. This means I need to calculate the early repayment savings stemming from a monthly payment of $823.13, not $824.62.

6. Enter the new payment in the Loan Calculator dialog box on line 4 of the worksheet. In this case, this amount is $823.13. Actually, you will probably make the $824.62 payment because that figure equals the extra $20 plus the regular payment of $804.62. Unfortunately, you can't calculate the early repayment savings that stem from an $824.62 payment, only from an $823.13 payment.

7. Calculate the number of new, larger payments you'll need to make, and enter this value on line 5 of the worksheet. Do this by multiplying the value in the Number of Years text box by 12. If you'll make 27 years of monthly payments, for example, you calculate the number of payments as 324 (27 × 12).

8. Calculate the total new payments you'll make, and enter this value on line 6 of the worksheet. To calculate the total remaining payments when the new monthly payment equals $823.13 and there are 324 months of payments left, for example, multiply the monthly payment of $823.13 by 324 months for a result of $266,694.12.

9. Calculate the difference between the total regular payments and the total new payments, and enter this value on line 7 of the worksheet.

In the example, this difference of $22,969.08 represents the interest savings stemming from early repayment of the loan using the payment amount shown on line 4. If a borrower actually paid an amount larger than the monthly payment shown on line 4, the early repayment savings would exceed those shown in the worksheet.

Should You Always Repay Early?

When you work through the numbers, the savings that stem from early repayment of a loan can seem almost too good to be true. Can a few dollars a month really add up to, for example, $25,000 of savings?

When you save money over long periods of time and let the interest compound, the amount of interest you ultimately earn becomes very large. In effect, when you pay an extra $20 a month on a 9 percent mortgage, you're saving $20 each month in a savings account that pays 9 percent. By "saving" this $20 over more than 25 years, you earn a lot of interest. In the earlier example, this monthly $20 really would add up to roughly $23,000.

But you can't look just at the interest savings. If you placed the same $20 a month into a money market fund, purchased savings bonds, or invested in a stock market mutual fund, you would also accumulate interest or investment income.

How can you know whether early repayment of a loan makes sense? Simply compare the interest rate on the loan with the interest rate (or investment rate of return) you would earn on alternative investments. If you can place money in a money market fund that earns 6 percent or repay a mortgage charging you 9 percent, you'll do better by repaying the mortgage. Its interest rate exceeds the interest rate of the money market account. But if you can stick money in a small company stock fund and earn 12 percent or repay a mortgage charging you 9 percent, you'll do better by putting your money in the stock fund.

One complicating factor, however, relates to income taxes. Some interest expense, such as mortgage interest, is tax-deductible. What's more, some interest income is tax-exempt, and some interest income isn't tax-deferred. Income taxes make early repayment decisions a little bit complicated, but here are three rules of thumb:

- Usually, if you have extra money that you can tie up for a long time, you'll make the most money by saving your money in a way that provides you with an initial tax deduction and where the interest compounds tax free, such as a 401(k) plan or an individual retirement account (IRA). (Opportunities in which an employer kicks in an extra amount by matching a portion of your contribution are usually too good to pass up—if you can afford them.)

- If you've taken advantage of investment options that give you tax breaks and you want to save additional money, your next best bet is usually to pay off any loans or credit cards that charge interest you can't deduct, such as credit card debt. Start with the loan or credit card charging the highest interest rate and then work your way down to the loan or credit card charging the lowest interest rate. For this to really work, of course, you can't go out and charge a credit card back up to its limit after you repay it.

- If you repay loans with nondeductible interest and you still have additional money you want to save, you can begin repaying loans that charge tax-deductible interest. Again, you should start with the loan charging the highest interest rate first.

Understanding the Mechanics

Successful saving relies on a simple financial truth: You should save money in a way that results in the highest annual interest, including all the income tax effects.

It's tricky to include income taxes in the calculations, however. They affect your savings in two ways. One way is that they may reduce the interest income you receive or the interest expense you save. If interest income is taxed, for example, you need to multiply the pretax interest rate by the factor (1–*marginal tax rate*) to calculate the after-income-taxes interest rate. And if interest expense is tax-deductible, you need to multiply the interest rate by the factor (1–*marginal tax rate*) to calculate the after-income-taxes interest rate.

For example, suppose you have four savings options: a credit card charging 12 percent nondeductible interest, a mortgage charging 9 percent tax-deductible interest, a tax-exempt money market fund earning 6 percent; and a mutual fund earning 12 percent taxable interest income. To know which of these savings opportunities is best, you need to calculate the after-income-taxes interest rates. If your marginal income tax rate equals 33 percent—meaning you pay $.33 in income taxes on your last dollars of income—the after-income-taxes interest rates are as follows:

- 12 percent interest on the credit card
- 8 percent interest on the mutual fund
- 6 percent interest on the mortgage
- 6 percent interest on the tax-exempt money market fund

In this case, your best savings opportunity is the credit card; by repaying it you save 12 percent. Next best is the mutual fund because even after paying the income taxes, you'll earn 8 percent. Finally, the mortgage and tax-exempt money market fund savings opportunities produce 6 percent.

 TIP The difference between percentages such as 12 percent and 6 percent may not seem all that large. But choosing the savings opportunity with the highest after-income-taxes rate delivers big benefits. If you invest $20 each month in something paying 6 percent after income taxes, you'll accumulate $5,107 over 25 years. But if you invest $20 each month in something paying 12 percent after income taxes, you'll accumulate $13,848 over 25 years.

The second complicating factor stems from the tax deduction you sometimes get for certain kinds of investments, such as IRAs and 401(k) plans. When you get an immediate tax deduction, you actually get to boost your savings amount by the tax deduction. This effectively boosts the interest rate.

For example, if you have an extra $1,000 to save and use it to repay a credit card charging 12 percent, you will save $120 of interest expense (12% × $1,000).

If you save the $1,000 in a way that results in a tax deduction, such as through an IRA, things can change quite a bit. Say your marginal income tax rate is 33 percent. In this case, you can actually contribute $1,500 ($1,000 / the factor [1–*marginal tax rate*]). The arithmetic might not make sense, but the result should. If you have $1,000 to save but you get a 33 percent tax deduction, you can actually save $1,500, because you'll get a $500 tax deduction ($1,500 × 33%).

What's more, by investing in a tax-deferred opportunity, you avoid paying income taxes while you're earning interest. (A tax-deferred investment just lets you postpone paying the income taxes.) If you invest in a stock mutual fund earning 10 percent, for example, you can keep the whole 10 percent as long as you leave the money in the stock mutual fund. If you work out the interest income calculations, you would find that you earn 10 percent on $1,500, or $150. So the tax deduction and the tax-deferred interest income mean you'll earn more annually on the stock mutual fund paying 10 percent than you will save on the credit card charging 12 percent.

Be aware that ultimately you pay income taxes on the money you take out of a tax-deferred investment opportunity, such as an IRA. In the example, you would need to pay back the $500 income tax deduction, and you would also need to pay income taxes on the $150. (At 33 percent, you would pay $50 of taxes on the $150 of interest income, too.)

In general, however, if you're saving for retirement, it usually still makes sense to go with a savings opportunity that produces a tax deduction and lets you postpone your income taxes. The reason is that the income taxes you postpone also boost your savings—and thereby boost your interest rate. (It's also possible that your marginal income tax rate will be lower when you withdraw money from a tax-deferred savings opportunity.)

Tracking Loans and Mortgages

You can keep detailed records of loan balances and the payments you make on the loan. First, however, you'll need to set up an account in Quicken. To create an account for a car loan, mortgage, or any other debt you owe, follow these steps:

1. Click the Banking QuickTab to display the Banking area, as shown in Figure 13.3.

2. Click the Create a New Account hyperlink to display the Create New Account dialog box, as shown in Figure 13.4.

FIGURE 13.3

The Banking area

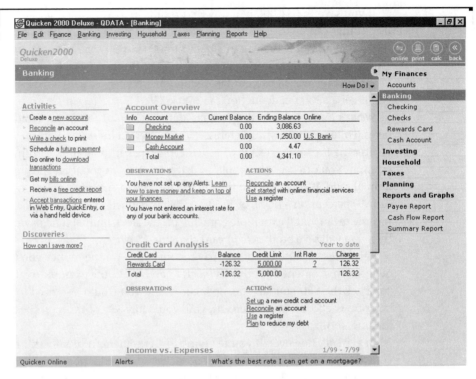

FIGURE 13.4

The Create New
Account dialog box

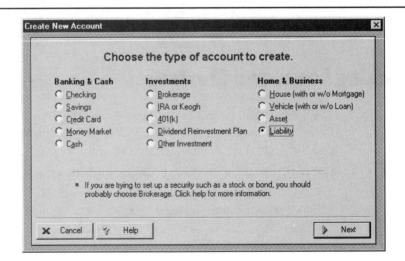

3. Click the Liability option button, click Next, and then click the Summary tab to display the Liability Account Setup dialog box, as shown in Figure 13.5.

FIGURE 13.5

The Liability Account Setup dialog box

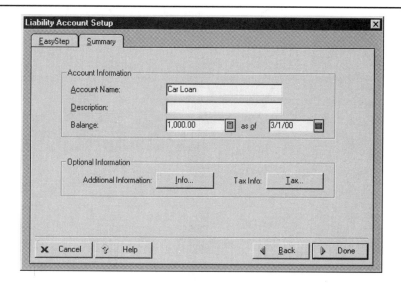

4. In the Account Name text box, enter an account name, such as **Mortgage** or **Car Loan**.

5. In the Description text box, enter a description of the loan or mortgage or additional information, such as the loan number or the lender's name.

6. In the Balance text box, enter the account balance on the day you'll start keeping records for the loan.

NOTE You can enter the loan balance as of the last statement date, but this figure won't include the payments made since the last statement. You will need to enter any transactions that have occurred since then.

7. Enter the date on which you start keeping records for the loan in *MM/DD/YY* format. For example, enter July 4, 2000, as **7/4/00**.

8. Click Done to tell Quicken that the Liability Account Setup dialog box is complete.

9. When Quicken asks if you would like to set up an amortized loan, answer the question by clicking either the Yes or No command button.

- If you answer this question with the No button, you're finished with the liability account setup and can skip the rest of the steps listed here.

- If you answer this question with the Yes button, be sure to click the Summary button. Quicken displays the Loan Setup dialog box, as shown in Figure 13.6.

FIGURE 13.6.

The Loan Setup dialog box

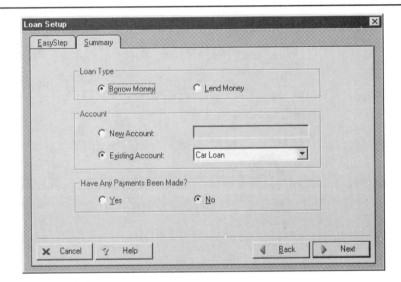

10. Because our example is set up as a Car Loan account, the Loan Type is Borrow Money, and the account is an existing car loan account. Since the account is new, no payments have been made; so click the No radio button. Click Next, and Quicken displays the next stage of the Loan Setup dialog box, as shown in Figure 13.7.

11. The Opening Date text box shows the date you entered in the Create New Account list. Confirm the original amount of the loan in the Original Balance text box. Note that you can display a pop-up calculator by clicking the button at the right end of the Original Balance text box.

12. Use the Original Length boxes to specify how long you'll make payments on the loan. Enter the number of years or months in the first text box. Then use the second box (a combo box) to specify whether you've entered the length in years or months.

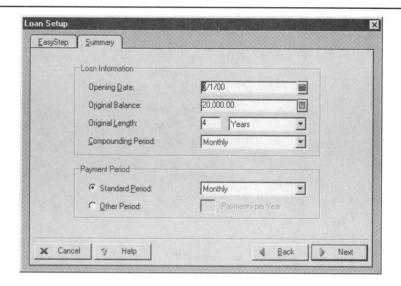

13. Use the Payment Period option buttons and boxes to indicate how often you'll make loan payments. The default payment period is a standard payment made monthly. You can select another payment period by selecting another period from the Standard Period drop-down list box—Monthly, Bi-Monthly, Semi-Monthly, and so on. You can also use the Other Period button and box to specify a different period.

14. Click Next when you finish providing Quicken with the Loan Information and Payment Period information. Quicken displays a new set of buttons and boxes, as shown in Figure 13.8.

15. If your loan includes a balloon payment, use the Balloon Information options to describe the loan's balloon payment. Enter the number of months or years (or some other time period) that the lender used to amortize the loan balance and to calculate the regular payments. Then indicate how you've specified this amortization term: months, years, or some other time period. (If your loan includes a balloon payment and you don't know the amortization term but you do know the regular payment amount, you can mark the Calculate button in the Balloon Information options to have Quicken determine the balloon payment for you.)

16. Enter the loan's interest rate in the Interest Rate text box.

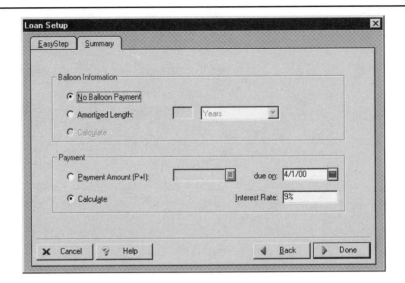

FIGURE 13.8

*Part 3 of the Loan
Setup dialog box*

NOTE Don't use the annual percentage rate figure as the annual interest rate, even though it is required by truth-in-lending laws in the United States and the United Kingdom (and maybe elsewhere). The annual percentage rate (APR) expresses all the costs of obtaining credit, including the loan interest, any fees, things like loan origination costs, and so on. APRs are an excellent way to compare the overall costs of one loan with another. But you can't use an APR to calculate loan payments because it's not the loan interest rate. The annual interest rate is documented in your loan agreement.

17. What you do next depends on whether you will make a balloon payment:

- If you haven't specified that Quicken should calculate the balloon payment, mark the Payment option's Calculate button. Then click Done to have Quicken calculate the loan payment. Quicken presents a dialog box saying that it has estimated the amount of the payment and asking you to click OK and then Done to accept the estimate.

- If you did tell Quicken to calculate the balloon payment, use the Payment Amount button and boxes to provide the regular principal and interest payment you'll make and the date of the first payment. Then click Done to have Quicken calculate the balloon payment.

TRACKING LOANS AND MORTGAGES

18. Click Done again. Quicken displays a message telling you it has estimated the amount of the next payment for this loan. Click OK to return to View Loans. Click Done, and Quicken displays the Set Up Loan Payment dialog box, as shown in Figure 13.9.

FIGURE 13.9

The Set Up Loan Payment dialog box

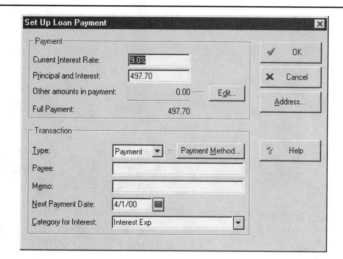

19. If you'll pay other amounts with the loan payment, such as $25 a month for private mortgage insurance, click the Edit command button to display the Split Transaction Window, as shown in Figure 13.10. This is the same window you see whenever you split a transaction among multiple categories.

20. Enter the category and amount of any other expenses you'll pay with the loan payment. For example, $25 of private mortgage insurance might be categorized as a Housing expense. Click OK, and Quicken redisplays the Set Up Loan Payment dialog box.

21. In the Transaction area of the Set Up Loan Payment dialog box, enter the information that will be used to complete the payment. In the Type drop-down list, choose Payment if you plan to write the payment from your checkbook, choose Print Check if you plan to use a Quicken memorized transaction to write the check, or select Online Pmt if you will use Quicken's online banking feature to make this payment. Enter the Payee for this payment.

22. Click the Address command button to open a dialog box you can use to enter the address to be printed on your check.

23. Click OK. Quicken displays a message asking if you would like to associate an asset with this loan. For now, click No. You're finished.

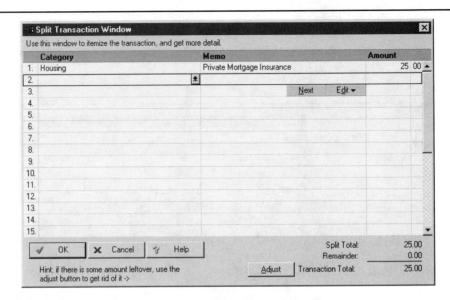

You have done a lot of work, but you won't need to do anything further except to make an occasional "tweak" if some element of your loan changes. We discuss ways to maintain and alter your loan in the following sections.

Making Payments

One of the final steps of setting up your new loan transaction is to use the Type drop-down list in the Set Up Loan Payment dialog box to specify whether your payment should be a scheduled, memorized, or repeating online payment transaction. Scheduled transactions are entered automatically on the date you specify. (Repeating online payment transactions are covered in Chapter 9.)

To use a memorized transaction, follow these steps:

1. Select the account you want to use to make your loan payment and open its register. Alternatively, you can start from the Write Checks area.

2. Enter the date, check number, and the payee name. You will find that a memorized transaction was created when you set up the loan. When you click Enter, Quicken opens a dialog box that lets you confirm that the principal and interest amounts are correct, as shown in Figure 13.11.

3. Confirm or change the amounts shown in the dialog box. Click OK to close the dialog box.

FIGURE 13.11

*Confirming a memo-
rized transaction*

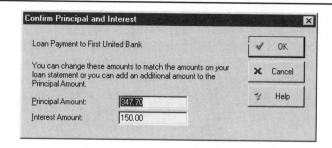

Maintaining Your Loan

Once you've set up a loan, you will want to track its progress and, if it is a variable-rate loan, change the interest rate from time to time. The View Loans area shown in Figure 13.12 is the key to these activities.

To display the View Loans area, choose Household ➤ Loans. This displays the details of the sample loan set up for this chapter. You can choose the loan to view from the drop-down list that appears when you click the Choose Loan command button at the top of the area. The Loan Summary tab shows the specifications of the loan, such as payee, term, and interest rate.

The Payment Schedule tab shows details about payments, and the Payment Graph tab shows a line graph that plots the loan balance.

Along the right edge of the View Loans area are four command buttons: Edit Loan, Edit Payment, Make Payment, and Rate Changes. Choosing the Edit Loan button opens the Edit Loan dialog box containing the details of the active loan. You can edit the loan information, retracing the steps covered in the preceding section on setting up a loan. If you choose the Edit Payment button, Quicken opens the Edit Loan Payment dialog box, in which you can edit the payment information.

Choosing Rate Changes opens the Loan Rate Changes dialog box shown in Figure 13.13. This dialog box displays a history of rate changes involving the selected loan. Right-click and choose Edit from the shortcut menu to change existing rates, or choose New to enter new ones. Quicken will calculate the necessary change in payment based on the new rate. When you change the interest rate or the payment in the Edit Interest Rate Change dialog box or in the Insert an Interest Rate Change dialog box, click OK, and then click Close in the Loan Rate Changes dialog box. Quicken recalculates the payment or loan length and applies the changes to the payment history section in the View Loans area.

FIGURE 13.12

The Loan Summary tab of the View Loans area

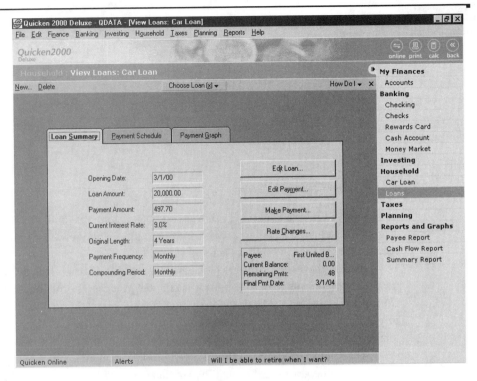

FIGURE 13.13

The Loan Rate Changes dialog box

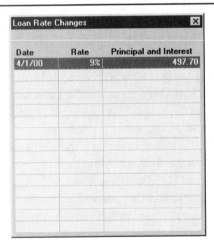

Adjusting Interest Calculations

It's possible that the interest calculation Quicken makes won't agree with the interest calculation a lender makes. Such discrepancies are common when you're talking about things besides mortgages: car loans, business loans, and so on. If you make a payment a few days early or a few days late, for example, or if there's a delay in the mail, the number of days of interest you calculate will differ from the number of days of interest the lender calculates.

 NOTE Interest calculation discrepancies aren't as much a problem with mortgage interest calculations because your lender probably calculates a month's worth of interest, even if you pay early or pay late. Of course, if you pay too late, the mortgage lender may also assess a late-payment penalty.

To adjust the Quicken interest calculations so that they agree with the lender's, display the loan's register, and then click on its Update Balance command button. When Quicken displays the Update Account Balance dialog box, you enter the loan balance as of the date you're making the correction (often the loan statement date), the interest expense category you're using to summarize interest expense on this loan, and the date you're making the correction.

Figure 13.14 shows the Update Account Balance dialog box with entries to adjust a loan balance to $19,655 on May 1, 2000. If the loan balance before this adjustment was shown as $19,652.30, Quicken will add an adjustment transaction to the loan's register that increases the loan balance by $2.70 and categorizes this change as interest expense. Figure 13.15 shows the adjustment transaction Quicken creates if you adjust the loan balance by $2.70.

FIGURE 13.14

The Update Account Balance dialog box allows you to make adjustments to the account.

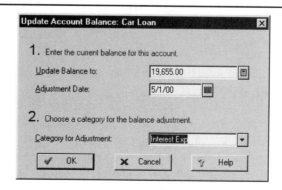

FIGURE 13.15

*The adjusting entry
makes your balance
match the lender's.*

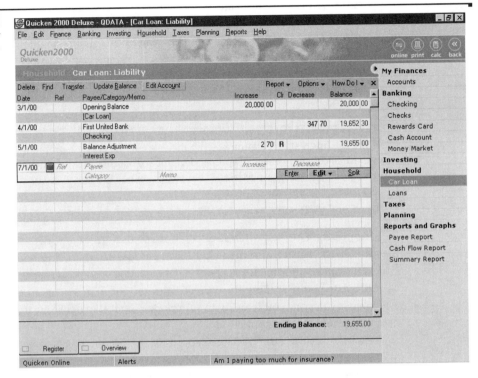

If it's confusing to you that the adjustment transaction is categorized as interest expense, remember this: When you set up an amortized transaction, Quicken splits all your loan payments between a principal category (which is actually a transfer to the liability account) and an interest category. If the liability account balance is wrong, it's because the split between principal and interest was wrong. And if the total principal splits are too low by, say, $2.70, it also means the total interest splits are too high by $2.70.

WARNING   If the interest expense you're recording in Quicken is tax deductible—probably because it's interest charged on a qualifying mortgage on a residence—you need to use the lender's total interest expense figure for your tax deduction, not the figure shown in your Quicken records. So, if you export Quicken's tax-deduction information to a tax-preparation package, be sure to adjust your loan balance and interest category total to whatever the mortgage lender shows on the annual loan statement information.

Scheduling a Transaction Using the View Loans area

If you have certain payments automatically deducted from a bank account, you set these up using the View Loans area. For example, you might well have your monthly mortgage payment automatically deducted from your checking account. To schedule these types of transactions, follow these steps:

1. Choose Household ➢ Loans to open the View Loans area.

2. Select the Payment Schedule tab, and click Edit Payment.

3. In the Edit Loan Payment dialog box, click the Payment Method button to open the Select Payment Method dialog box:

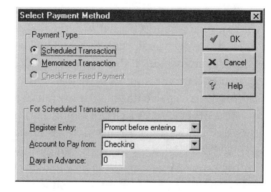

4. Click the Scheduled Transaction button and then record your preference for when to enter the transaction in the register, the account to use, and the number of days in advance you want to be reminded of the transaction.

5. Click OK.

At the appointed time, Quicken enters the transaction in the account. This happens as soon as you start Quicken on or following the next scheduled date.

Refinancing a Mortgage

There's one final loan transaction that's often tricky for people new to financial record keeping: recording a mortgage refinancing.

First, you need to set up a new liability account. The only difference is that you don't enter a balance for the new liability. You initially set the liability balance to zero by entering **0** into the Balance text box in the Liability Account Setup dialog box.

To record the starting loan balance, enter a transaction into the loan register. The amount of the transaction should be the loan amount. If the new loan equals the old loan, enter the category as the old, now-refinanced loan. If the new loan doesn't equal the old loan amount—say you borrowed a little more money as part of refinancing—you need to use the Split Transaction Window. One of the split transaction lines should show the old loan's account balance being transferred to the new loan's account balance. (This is really what you're doing—transferring a debt from one loan to another loan.) Any additional new loan amount you spend on items such as loan fees should be categorized using the appropriate expense. Finally, any cash you receive as part of the refinancing should be recorded as a transfer to the bank account into which you deposited the cash.

The rules of thumb people use in deciding whether or not to refinance are often useless. Calculating whether it makes sense to refinance a loan actually requires some very complicated analysis. Nevertheless, you can use some general rules in specific situations to easily determine when refinancing makes sense. First, you want to swap higher interest rate debt for lower interest rate. You can tell whether a new loan truly costs less when you include all the costs of obtaining credit by comparing its annual percentage rate (APR) with your existing loan's interest rate. The APR is the cost of borrowing money as a percentage of the loan. It includes not only the loan interest, but most of the other costs as well, including loan-origination charges, credit reports, escrow fees, and all the other ways the lender increases the cost of borrowing. If the new loan's APR is less than the old loan's interest rate, you will save interest—at least on a monthly basis—by swapping the new loan for the old loan.

You also want to make sure that you don't pay a lot more in interest on the new loan because its term is longer. For example, it probably doesn't make sense to swap a 9 percent, 15-year mortgage for an 8 7/8-percent, 30-year mortgage. Although with the new 30-year mortgage you'll pay a little less interest for the first 15 years, you'll make payments for an extra 15 years. To deal with this "years' interest is charged" issue, ask the lender to calculate the APR on the new loan assuming that you'll have the new loan paid off by the same time you would have had the old loan paid off. (This will make the APR higher, by the way.) You'll also want to make payments that are large enough to have the new loan paid off by the same time you would have had the old loan paid off.

NOTE If you are interested in refinancing your mortgage, Quicken's Refinance Calculator can compute the potential savings and time to recover the refinancing costs. See Chapter 15 for more information about this tool.

MASTERING FINANCIAL SUCCESS

How to Borrow and Repay Money

Get smart about the way you borrow and repay money, and you can dramatically improve your finances. Smart borrowing, however, is tricky. Dozens of big-dollar traps are out there waiting to snare you, and you have only a handful of money-saving tricks at your disposal.

Two Simple Rules

The following two simple rules for handling debt will take you a long way toward staying in the black.

Rule 1: Choose the Cheapest Debt You Can Find

By choosing the cheapest debt you can find—in other words, by finding the least expensive loan—you save money. It's that simple. Surprisingly, even small differences in interest rates can add up to big savings over time.

In the case of a fixed-interest-rate loan, choosing cheap debt is pretty easy to do. All you need to do is look for the loan with the lowest APR.

Finding a cheap loan is also relatively easy to do in the case of adjustable-interest-rate debt. With this type of debt, the interest rate is readjusted periodically, usually every six months or every year. Again, you can focus on the APR, but there is a slight problem with doing that: You want to make sure that you can bear the added risk of borrowing money at an unknown interest rate.

Rule 2: Repay the Loan before the Thing You're Buying Wears Out

You should repay a loan before the thing you're buying wears out. By doing so, you pay off the loan you borrowed to buy the first thingamajig before you buy the second thingamajig. A side benefit of this "quick repayment" approach is that you save substantial amounts in interest payments because you're not paying interest for two things, only one.

A debt, or loan, is a way to spread out the cost of something over the years that you use it, and it should be treated as such. By taking out a loan, you can purchase a house, purchase a car, or go to college, even though you don't have the cold, hard cash right now. For this privilege, you pay interest. But that doesn't have to be a bad situation as long as you're careful.

Continued

MASTERING FINANCIAL SUCCESS CONTINUED

Thirty-year home mortgages are, for example, perfectly reasonable. You pay off a 30-year mortgage for most of your adult life, but that's okay, because you're using the loan to buy something that will hold its value and will benefit you for the entire 30 years. Homes built today, if they are well maintained, can last for 100 years or more. Student loans, although they can take 10 or more years to pay off, are reasonable, because they provide long-term benefits such as preparation for a lifetime of employment.

To my mind, a 3-year car loan is pretty reasonable as long as the car lasts 5 or more years. Again, the car loan payments end long before the car wears out. An even better deal is saving the money first and then buying a car with cash, but often that can't be done.

Ways of Borrowing Money
Money is usually borrowed in one of two ways: with revolving credit debt or amortizing debt.

Revolving Credit
Revolving credit debt is the simpler approach. You probably have credit cards that fit into the revolving credit category. You borrow money on your credit card, interest is calculated on the amount you've borrowed, and at the end of the month, you pay the entire balance, a portion of the balance, or the interest for the month.

As a borrower, revolving credit offers more flexibility—and for this reason it is the most popular way to borrow money. The bank or credit card company sets minimum payment amounts and maximum credit limits, but within those guidelines, you borrow and repay as you please. Unfortunately, besides being the most flexible way to borrow money, revolving credit debt is also the most expensive.

Amortizing Debt
The other type of borrowing is *amortizing debt. Amortization* means paying off the balance on a loan in little increments over a period of time. Most home mortgages are of the amortizing variety: Each month you send the bank or mortgage company a check for the same amount. In the beginning, most of your payment goes toward interest. Over time, however, the little reductions in the loan balance begin to add up and thereby reduce the interest you're charged, so that a higher proportion of your payment goes toward reducing the principal.

Assuming you make regular payments, this amortization of the loan's balance results in a larger and larger portion of each month's payment going to pay off the loan balance. Home mortgages aren't the only types of debt that are amortizing. Most car loans are amortizing, and so are student loans.

Continued ▐▶

MASTERING FINANCIAL SUCCESS CONTINUED

Which Type of Debt Is Better?

Which type of debt is better, revolving credit debt or amortizing debt? This is a good question. Certainly, revolving credit is more flexible. It's easy to borrow money the instant you need it. Putting aside the convenience angle, however, you can almost always do better by using amortizing debt. It provides three important advantages:

- Amortizing debt is much tougher to use for impulse purchases. When you get the urge for a new car or item of clothing, you can't simply pull out your wallet or purse and, five minutes later, be even deeper in debt. Impulse purchases are a problem for some people. If you're one of them, you should definitely stay away from revolving credit cards.

- The lender makes sure you pay off the debt before the thing you're buying wears out.

- Amortizing debts almost always have lower interest rates than revolving credit debts, and that is their chief advantage.

Car Loans and Leases

A car is usually the second-largest purchase that people need to finance (the largest purchase, of course, is a home). Not surprisingly, car loans and leases are an area where borrowing decisions dramatically affect financial progress.

Choosing a Car

The first decision to make concerning a car loan is which car to buy. Choosing a car is largely a personal decision, not a financial one, but two points are worth noting about buying a car:

- Check the insurance and, if applicable, state and city taxes. (These can end up being big, unhappy surprises if you're not careful.)

- Reforecast your budget once you've picked a car to make sure that you can afford to spend as much money as you're planning to spend. (Remember that you can calculate a loan payment, including a car loan payment, by using the Loan Calculator, as described in this chapter.)

If you absolutely must have a luxury German or Italian import, consider getting a two-year-old car instead of a new one. Try to get a car that someone else owned for two years and then discovered he or she couldn't afford that car. New cars take the biggest drop in value over the first two years of their lives, even though most of their lives are still left. This advice, by the way, applies to just about any car. Buying a reasonably priced used car is usually an excellent way to purchase a car. Do have a mechanic you trust check the car first, however.

Continued

MASTERING FINANCIAL SUCCESS CONTINUED

If you want a new car and you don't need it immediately, you can usually get a better deal by waiting until the start of the new model year and buying one of last year's models.

Finally, be sure to "comparison-shop." Take notes. Don't go to just one dealer. And get whatever deal you're offered in writing. As a general rule, you can't rely on a promise made by a car salesman (or anyone else) unless the promise is made in writing.

Picking a Car Loan or Lease

Car loans work just like other loans. For this reason, all you need to do is pick the loan with the lowest APR.

Call a couple of banks before you head on down to the car dealer's showroom. Most car dealers offer financing for the cars on their lots. To know whether or not you're get-ting a good offer, you need to be able to compare what the dealer offers with what the bank offers.

You probably shouldn't lease a car. Almost always, it's a better deal to purchase one. The reason is that when you are finally finished making your car loan payments, you still have your car, but when you are finished making car lease payments, you don't. It's that simple.

More about Car Leases

Why do people lease cars if it's such a bad deal? There are two big reasons: The incep-tion fee you pay to get into a lease usually isn't as big as the down payment you're required to make on a regular car loan, and the monthly lease payment is usually less than the monthly loan payment. This makes sense, if you think about it for a minute. With a lease, you're really only renting the car for a couple years—maybe three. With a loan, you're buying the car.

Is there a good reason for leasing a car? You probably pay more money for automobile expenses if you do. Acquiring a car by means of a lease is inherently more expensive than getting a regular car loan. Another factor that makes leases more expensive—and this is just my intuition, since I haven't done a rigorous statistical study—is that people tend to get expensive cars when they lease.

These criticisms aside, however, I can think of several reasons why it makes sense to lease that shiny new car you've been eyeing. First, if you really, truly, absolutely must have a new car, leasing may be your only option if you're low on cash. If you have a job that requires having a better-than-average late-model car, it probably does make sense to spend, say, an extra $5,000 on a lease so you can keep your $40,000 a year sales job.

Continued

MASTERING FINANCIAL SUCCESS CONTINUED

Unless you're independently wealthy, your biggest investment is your job. Doing things that help you keep a good job or that let you get a better job can be very worthwhile.

How Car Leases Work

Car leases, in essence, amount to long-term rental agreements. To get into a car lease, you need to pay an inception fee and probably a deposit. Then, over the course of the lease, you make monthly lease, or rental, payments.

When the lease expires, you usually give the car back to the leasing company. There are a couple of possible catches, however. Most lease agreements state that you can't run up 100,000 miles on the car. If you put, say, ten years' worth of mileage on a car that you've leased for only two or three years, you must pay an extra charge for the extra miles you drove.

Another catch concerns damage done to the car: dings and dents, spilled milkshakes, and excess wear and tear. In all likelihood, you need to pay extra for damages.

There's also usually one other complicating factor: Most car leases give you the option of either re-leasing the car or purchasing the car at the end of the lease. Sometimes this is a great deal, and sometimes it isn't.

Picking a Mortgage

By making smart decisions about a mortgage, you can easily add tens of thousands of dollars to your net worth—and do it almost effortlessly. But to capture this easy source of wealth, you need to understand much more than most people do about choosing, refinancing, and ultimately repaying a mortgage. (The "How To Choose a Home and a Mortgage" section at the end of Chapter 19 describes the general rules that most mortgage companies and banks use to determine mortgage affordability.)

Perhaps the most important thing to do when you search for a mortgage is comparison shop. Borrowing money for a home is just like borrowing money for anything else. The main thing to do is find a mortgage lender that offers inexpensive loans. It's important to shop around and find the lowest APR.

Just for fun, I kept tabs on all the 30-year fixed mortgage interest rates that were available as I was writing this. The thing that struck me is how much the rates vary. From the lowest rate to the highest rate, there's a difference of roughly half a percent. On a $100,000 mortgage, that's equivalent to around $500 a year in payments for the first few years.

Fifteen-year and bi-weekly mortgages usually save you interest because you repay the mortgage earlier. (Usually, you save thousands of dollars.) But you shouldn't pay any

Continued |▶

PART

II

Quicken and Your Personal Finances

MASTERING FINANCIAL SUCCESS CONTINUED

thing extra for these types of mortgages. In fact, because you've reduced the lender's risk by paying bi-weekly or paying off the mortgage in 15 years, you should get a lower interest rate. You certainly don't need to pay some third party a special processing or handling fee, either, which is sometimes the case with a bi-weekly mortgage. If you want to get a 30-year mortgage paid off as quickly as you would pay off a bi-weekly mortgage, just add one-twelfth of your usual payment to your regular monthly payment. For example, if you're usually paying $1,200 a month in mortgage and interest, add another $100 a month to that payment. You can use Quicken's Loan Calculator to see how much money you save by repaying a loan early, as described earlier in the chapter.

Why You Should Consider an Adjustable-Rate Mortgage

With an adjustable-rate mortgage (ARM), the interest rate on the loan is adjusted every 6 months or every 12 months, and as a result, the amount you pay is adjusted too. The lender adjusts the rate by pegging, or tying, the mortgage interest rate to a well-known and respected interest rate *index.* For example, one such index is the 6-month or 1-year Treasury Bill rate. A typical ARM might adjust your mortgage interest rate to the 6-month Treasury Bill rate plus 2 percentage points. In other words, if the 6-month Treasury Bill rate is 5 percent, the interest rate on your loan is 7 percent.

The extra amount that gets added to the index (2 percent in this example) is called the *spread.* If interest rates rise or fall, the lender recalculates your payment by using the new interest rate plus the spread.

Tying the interest rate on a loan to an index sounds risky, but it's not quite as bad as it sounds, provided ARM interest rates are substantially lower than fixed-mortgage interest rates. In this situation, ARM payments are lower to begin with. The prospect of having your ARM payment bounce between $600 a month and $1,000 a month sounds risky indeed, but it isn't actually as risky as it seems if the alternative is an $800-a-month payment on a fixed-interest-rate mortgage. What's more, there's usually a *cap,* or maximum amount, above which rates on an ARM can't rise. If interest rates drop, then your mortgage interest rate drops too. However, mortgage interest rates don't drop as often as you might think because of teaser interest rates.

Teaser interest rates are artificially low starting interest rates. Teasers aren't bad, really. They save you money. But with a teaser interest rate, your payment often rises at the next adjustment date. Be sure to recalculate your loan payment using the current index and spread. You can do this by using Quicken's Loan Calculator, as explained in this chapter.

Continued

MASTERING FINANCIAL SUCCESS CONTINUED

Do ARMs make sense? Despite the risk of interest rates and payments climbing and dropping, ARMs can be good deals for borrowers when interest rates are high. They usually save borrowers money because they charge a lower interest rate in the long run. What's more, if the index rate drops, your mortgage rate and monthly payment drop as well, and you don't need to go through the rigmarole and cost of refinancing your mortgage.

The only problem with an ARM is that you bear extra risk: When interest rates rise, your monthly payment is adjusted upward.

Common sense says that you shouldn't take an ARM unless you know you can make the maximum payment. To find out what a maximum payment is, calculate your monthly payment using the interest rate cap—the highest interest rate you are forced to pay—on your ARM. If the payment looks pretty ugly, it probably doesn't pay to pick an ARM.

Here is a financial trick that an ARM borrower can use to reduce (and often reduce completely!) the risk of rising payments. Get an ARM but make the same payment you would make if you had a fixed-rate mortgage. In other words, if the ARM payment is $600 per month and the fixed-rate mortgage payment would be $800 per month, get the ARM and pay $800 a month. The extra amount that you pay each month quickly reduces the mortgage balance. What's more, you get accustomed to making larger payments in case the ARM interest rate does go up. If you're lucky and interest rates don't jump up dramatically in the first few years, you may never see your payment increase. The reason is that if you pay, say, an extra $100 to $200 a month over a 5- or 6-year period, the effect of the extra principal payments may more than offset the effect of a rise in interest rates.

Tips for Picking an ARM

If I've convinced you that an ARM is something you should look into, here are some smart shopping tips for picking one:

- Make sure the ARM has annual adjustment limit, or interest rate cap. There should be a cap on how much the mortgage lender can adjust your payments upward in a year. If the cap is a percent a year or half a percent every 6 months (these are the figures I look for), you won't get caught in a budget crunch if interest rates rise quickly. Instead, your payment will be adjusted over several adjustment dates.

Continued ▌▶

PART

II

Quicken and Your Personal Finances

MASTERING FINANCIAL SUCCESS CONTINUED

- Make sure there's no possibility of negative amortization. *Negative amortization* means your loan balance increases because your payment doesn't cover all of the loan interest. You shouldn't have a problem with negative amortization on a fixed-rate loan as long as the lender doesn't calculate your payment incorrectly. But negative amortization is a possibility when interest rate adjustments are made to an ARM more frequently than payment adjustments are made. Don't sign up for an ARM if this is the case.

- Compare spreads. If two ARMs are tied to the same index, go with the one that has the lower spread. Remember that the spread is the percentage point amount added to the index to calculate the ARM interest rate.

- Calculate the maximum payment. I know this isn't any fun. I know it may cause a big argument with your spouse about whether buying a house is a good decision. But you need to consider the risk of rising interest rates before, and not after, you're locked into them.

- Don't use an ARM to get a bigger house. The reason that most people get an ARM, or so an honest mortgage lender will tell you, is so they can buy a bigger home. I think this is a mistake. If you need to stretch yourself by getting an ARM, you're setting yourself up for trouble when interest rates rise. And rates *always* rise at some point in the future.

- Consider getting an ARM with annual adjustments. With annual adjustments, the chances of your getting a raise in salary or wages between adjustments are higher, and that raise could help with the increased payment. I should point out, however, that you usually pay a bit more in interest over the life of the loan if you go with annual adjustments. That's fair, however, since you're bearing less risk.

CHAPTER 14

Estimating and Preparing Income Taxes

Because Quicken largely (and perhaps completely) summarizes your financial affairs, much of the information you'll need to prepare your income tax return can and should be extracted from your Quicken accounts. What's more, Quicken provides an income tax planner that you can use to plan for your income tax expenses.

Building Appropriate Category Lists

There's only one real trick to using Quicken as a tool for income tax preparation: Use category lists that neatly tie to the tax form lines you need to fill in when you file your income tax return.

Although you won't actually know which tax form lines you'll use for the current year until the year is almost over, in Quicken you track your tax-related transactions throughout the year. Then, at the end of the year, you can create a report listing the category totals and use it to fill out your tax return forms and schedules.

Determining Which Categories You Need

In case you don't have last year's forms handy, you can take a look at the tax schedule in Figures 14.1 through 14.8. Use these forms as guides for indicating which categories you need to complete in the 1997 and 1998 forms. Each input line on each form that you'll use should have its own category or set of categories. Note that lines used for calculating subtotals and totals don't need their own category.

FIGURE 14.1

The 1040 form

Form **1040** Department of the Treasury–Internal Revenue Service
U.S. Individual Income Tax Return 1998 (99) IRS Use Only–Do not write or staple in this space.

For the year Jan. 1±Dec. 31, 1998, or other tax year beginning , 1998, ending , 19 | OMB No. 1545-0074

Label
(See instructions on page 18.)

Use the IRS label. Otherwise, please print or type.

L A B E L   H E R E

Your first name and initial | Last name | Your social security number

If a joint return, spouse's first name and initial | Last name | Spouse's social security number

Home address (number and street). If you have a P.O. box, see page 18. | Apt. no.

City, town or post office, state, and ZIP code. If you have a foreign address, see page 18.

▲ **IMPORTANT!** ▲
You **must** enter your SSN(s) above.

Presidential Election Campaign
(See page 18.)

Do you want $3 to go to this fund? . . . .
If a joint return, does your spouse want $3 to go to this fund? . . . .

Yes | No | Note: Checking ™Yes] will not change your tax or reduce your refund.

Filing Status

Check only one box.

1 Single
2 Married filing joint return (even if only one had income)
3 Married filing separate return. Enter spouse's social security no. above and full name here. ▶ _____
4 Head of household (with qualifying person). (See page 18.) If the qualifying person is a child but not your dependent, enter this child's name here. ▶
5 Qualifying widow(er) with dependent child (year spouse died ▶ 19). (See page 18.)

Exemptions

6a ☐ **Yourself.** If your parent (or someone else) can claim you as a dependent on his or her tax return, **do not** check box 6a. . . . .
b ☐ **Spouse** . . . .

c **Dependents:**

(1) First name Last name	(2) Dependent's social security number	(3) Dependent's relationship to you	(4) ✔ if qualifying child for child tax credit (see page 19)
			☐
			☐
			☐
			☐
			☐
			☐

If more than six dependents, see page 19.

d Total number of exemptions claimed . . . .

No. of boxes checked on 6a and 6b

No. of your children on 6c who:
• lived with you
• did not live with you due to divorce or separation (see page 19)

Dependents on 6c not entered above

Add numbers entered on lines above ▶

Income

Attach Copy B of your Forms W-2, W-2G, and 1099-R here.

If you did not get a W-2, see page 20.

Enclose, but do not staple, any payment. Also, please use **Form 1040-V.**

7 Wages, salaries, tips, etc. Attach Form(s) W-2 . . . . | 7
8a **Taxable** interest. Attach Schedule B if required . . . . . . | 8a
b **Tax-exempt** interest. DO NOT include on line 8a . . . | 8b |
9 Ordinary dividends. Attach Schedule B if required . . . . . | 9
10 Taxable refunds, credits, or offsets of state and local income taxes (see page 21) . . | 10
11 Alimony received . . . . | 11
12 Business income or (loss). Attach Schedule C or C-EZ . . . . | 12
13 Capital gain or (loss). Attach Schedule D . . . . | 13
14 Other gains or (losses). Attach Form 4797 . . . . | 14
15a Total IRA distributions . | 15a | b Taxable amount (see page 22) | 15b
16a Total pensions and annuities | 16a | b Taxable amount (see page 22) | 16b
17 Rental real estate, royalties, partnerships, S corporations, trusts, etc. Attach Schedule E | 17
18 Farm income or (loss). Attach Schedule F . . . . | 18
19 Unemployment compensation . . . . | 19
20a Social security benefits . | 20a | b Taxable amount (see page 24) | 20b
21 Other income. List type and amount–see page 24 ------------------------ | 21
22 Add the amounts in the far right column for lines 7 through 21. This is your **total income** ▶ | 22

Adjusted Gross Income

If line 33 is under $30,095 (under $10,030 if a child did not live with you), see EIC inst. on page 36.

23 IRA deduction (see page 25) . . . . | 23
24 Student loan interest deduction (see page 27) . . . | 24
25 Medical savings account deduction. Attach Form 8853 . | 25
26 Moving expenses. Attach Form 3903 . . . . . | 26
27 One-half of self-employment tax. Attach Schedule SE . | 27
28 Self-employed health insurance deduction (see page 28) | 28
29 Keogh and self-employed SEP and SIMPLE plans . | 29
30 Penalty on early withdrawal of savings . . . . | 30
31a Alimony paid b Recipient's SSN ▶ _____ | 31a
32 Add lines 23 through 31a . . . . | 32
33 Subtract line 32 from line 22. This is your **adjusted gross income** . . . . . ▶ | 33

For Disclosure, Privacy Act, and Paperwork Reduction Act Notice, see page 51. | Cat. No. 11320B | Form **1040** (1998)

PART
II

Quicken and Your Personal Finances

FIGURE 14.1

The 1040 form
(continued)

Form 1040 (1998)   Page **2**

Tax and Credits	34	Amount from line 33 (adjusted gross income)		34
	35a	Check if: ☐ **You** were 65 or older, ☐ Blind; ☐ **Spouse** was 65 or older, ☐ Blind. Add the number of boxes checked above and enter the total here . . . . ▶	35a	
	b	If you are married filing separately and your spouse itemizes deductions or you were a dual-status alien, see page 29 and check here . . . . . . ▶ **35b** ☐		
Standard Deduction for Most People	36	Enter the **larger** of your **itemized deductions** from Schedule A, line 28, **OR standard deduction** shown on the left. **But** see page 30 to find your standard deduction if you checked any box on line 35a or 35b **or** if someone can claim you as a dependent . . .		36
Single: $4,250	37	Subtract line 36 from line 34		37
Head of household: $6,250	38	If line 34 is $93,400 or less, multiply $2,700 by the total number of exemptions claimed on line 6d. If line 34 is over $93,400, see the worksheet on page 30 for the amount to enter .		38
Married filing jointly or Qualifying widow(er): $7,100	39	**Taxable income.** Subtract line 38 from line 37. If line 38 is more than line 37, enter -0-		39
	40	**Tax.** See page 30. Check if any tax from **a** ☐ Form(s) 8814 **b** ☐ Form 4972 . . ▶		40
	41	Credit for child and dependent care expenses. Attach Form 2441	41	
Married filing separately: $3,550	42	Credit for the elderly or the disabled. Attach Schedule R . .	42	
	43	Child tax credit (see page 31)	43	
	44	Education credits. Attach Form 8863	44	
	45	Adoption credit. Attach Form 8839	45	
	46	Foreign tax credit. Attach Form 1116 if required	46	
	47	Other. Check if from **a** ☐ Form 3800 **b** ☐ Form 8396 **c** ☐ Form 8801 **d** ☐ Form (specify) _____	47	
	48	Add lines 41 through 47. These are your **total credits**		48
	49	Subtract line 48 from line 40. If line 48 is more than line 40, enter -0- . . . . . . ▶		49
Other Taxes	50	Self-employment tax. Attach Schedule SE		50
	51	Alternative minimum tax. Attach Form 6251		51
	52	Social security and Medicare tax on tip income not reported to employer. Attach Form 4137		52
	53	Tax on IRAs, other retirement plans, and MSAs. Attach Form 5329 if required . . .		53
	54	Advance earned income credit payments from Form(s) W-2		54
	55	Household employment taxes. Attach Schedule H		55
	56	Add lines 49 through 55. This is your **total tax** . . . . ▶		56
Payments	57	Federal income tax withheld from Forms W-2 and 1099 . .	57	
Attach Forms W-2 and W-2G on the front. Also attach Form 1099-R if tax was withheld.	58	1998 estimated tax payments and amount applied from 1997 return .	58	
	59a	**Earned income credit.** Attach Schedule EIC if you have a qualifying child **b** Nontaxable earned income: amount ▶ and type ▶ _____	59a	
	60	Additional child tax credit. Attach Form 8812	60	
	61	Amount paid with Form 4868 (request for extension) . .	61	
	62	Excess social security and RRTA tax withheld (see page 43)	62	
	63	Other payments. Check if from **a** ☐ Form 2439 **b** ☐ Form 4136	63	
	64	Add lines 57, 58, 59a, and 60 through 63. These are your **total payments** . . . . ▶		64
Refund	65	If line 64 is more than line 56, subtract line 56 from line 64. This is the amount you **OVERPAID**		65
Have it directly deposited! See page 44 and fill in 66b, 66c, and 66d.	66a	Amount of line 65 you want **REFUNDED TO YOU** . . . . ▶		66a
	▶ b	Routing number		▶ c Type: ☐ Checking ☐ Savings
	▶ d	Account number		
	67	Amount of line 65 you want **APPLIED TO YOUR 1999 ESTIMATED TAX** ▶	67	
Amount You Owe	68	If line 56 is more than line 64, subtract line 64 from line 56. This is the **AMOUNT YOU OWE**. For details on how to pay, see page 44 . . . . ▶		68
	69	Estimated tax penalty. Also include on line 68 . . .	69	

Sign Here

Under penalties of perjury, I declare that I have examined this return and accompanying schedules and statements, and to the best of my knowledge and belief, they are true, correct, and complete. Declaration of preparer (other than taxpayer) is based on all information of which preparer has any knowledge.

Joint return?
See page 18.

Keep a copy for your records.

Your signature	Date	Your occupation	Daytime telephone number (optional)
▶			
▶ Spouse's signature. If a joint return, BOTH must sign.	Date	Spouse's occupation	( )

Paid Preparer's Use Only

Preparer's signature ▶	Date	Check if self-employed ☐	Preparer's social security no.
Firm's name (or yours if self-employed) and address ▶			EIN
			ZIP code

FIGURE 14.2

Schedule A

SCHEDULES A&B
(Form 1040)

Department of the Treasury
Internal Revenue Service (99)

Schedule A—Itemized Deductions

(Schedule B is on back)

► **Attach to Form 1040.** ► **See Instructions for Schedules A and B (Form 1040).**

OMB No. 1545-0074

19**98**

Attachment
Sequence No. **07**

Name(s) shown on Form 1040

Your social security number

Medical and Dental Expenses		**Caution:** *Do not include expenses reimbursed or paid by others.*	
	1	Medical and dental expenses (see page A-1)	1
	2	Enter amount from Form 1040, line 34 . [2]	
	3	Multiply line 2 above by 7.5% (.075)	3
	4	Subtract line 3 from line 1. If line 3 is more than line 1, enter -0-	4
Taxes You Paid (See page A-2.)	5	State and local income taxes	5
	6	Real estate taxes (see page A-2)	6
	7	Personal property taxes	7
	8	Other taxes. List type and amount ►	
	9	Add lines 5 through 8	8 / 9
Interest You Paid (See page A-3.)	10	Home mortgage interest and points reported to you on Form 1098	10
	11	Home mortgage interest not reported to you on Form 1098. If paid to the person from whom you bought the home, see page A-3 and show that person's name, identifying no., and address ►	
Note: Personal interest is not deductible.	12	Points not reported to you on Form 1098. See page A-3 for special rules	11 / 12
	13	Investment interest. Attach Form 4952 if required. (See page A-3.)	13
	14	Add lines 10 through 13	14
Gifts to Charity	15	Gifts by cash or check. If you made any gift of $250 or more, see page A-4	15
If you made a gift and got a benefit for it, see page A-4.	16	Other than by cash or check. If any gift of $250 or more, see page A-4. You **MUST** attach Form 8283 if over $500	16
	17	Carryover from prior year	17
	18	Add lines 15 through 17	18
Casualty and Theft Losses	19	Casualty or theft loss(es). Attach Form 4684. (See page A-5.)	19
Job Expenses and Most Other Miscellaneous Deductions (See page A-6 for expenses to deduct here.)	20	Unreimbursed employee expenses–job travel, union dues, job education, etc. You **MUST** attach Form 2106 or 2106-EZ if required. (See page A-5.) ►	20
	21	Tax preparation fees	21
	22	Other expenses–investment, safe deposit box, etc. List type and amount ►	22
	23	Add lines 20 through 22	23
	24	Enter amount from Form 1040, line 34 . [24]	
	25	Multiply line 24 above by 2% (.02)	25
	26	Subtract line 25 from line 23. If line 25 is more than line 23, enter -0-	26
Other Miscellaneous Deductions	27	Other–from list on page A-6. List type and amount ►	27
Total Itemized Deductions	28	Is Form 1040, line 34, over $124,500 (over $62,250 if married filing separately)?	
		NO. Your deduction is not limited. Add the amounts in the far right column for lines 4 through 27. Also, enter on Form 1040, line 36, the **larger** of this amount or your standard deduction. } ►	28
		YES. Your deduction may be limited. See page A-6 for the amount to enter.	

For Paperwork Reduction Act Notice, see Form 1040 instructions.

Cat. No. 11330X

Schedule A (Form 1040) 1998

PART

II

Quicken and Your Personal Finances

FIGURE 14.3

Schedule B

Schedules A&B (Form 1040) 1998   OMB No. 1545-0074   Page **2**

Name(s) shown on Form 1040. Do not enter name and social security number if shown on other side.

Your social security number

Schedule B–Interest and Ordinary Dividends

Attachment
Sequence No. **08**

Note: *If you had over $400 in taxable interest income, you must also complete Part III.*

			Amount
Part I **Interest** (See pages 20 and B-1.) **Note:** If you received a Form 1099-INT, Form 1099-OID, or substitute statement from a brokerage firm, list the firm's name as the payer and enter the total interest shown on that form.	1	List name of payer. If any interest is from a seller-financed mortgage and the buyer used the property as a personal residence, see page B-1 and list this interest first. Also, show that buyer's social security number and address ▶	**1**
	2	Add the amounts on line 1	**2**
	3	Excludable interest on series EE U.S. savings bonds issued after 1989 from Form 8815, line 14. You MUST attach Form 8815 to Form 1040	**3**
	4	Subtract line 3 from line 2. Enter the result on Form 1040, line 8a ▶	**4**

Note: *If you had over $400 in ordinary dividends, you must also complete Part III.*

			Amount
Part II **Ordinary Dividends** (See pages 21 and B-1.) **Note:** If you received a Form 1099-DIV or substitute statement from a brokerage firm, list the firm's name as the payer and enter the ordinary dividends shown on that form.	5	List name of payer. Include only ordinary dividends. Report any capital gain distributions on Schedule D, line 13 ▶	**5**
	6	Add the amounts on line 5. Enter the total here and on Form 1040, line 9 . ▶	**6**

			Yes	No
Part III **Foreign Accounts and Trusts** (See page B-2.)		You must complete this part if you **(a)** had over $400 of interest or ordinary dividends; **(b)** had a foreign account; or **(c)** received a distribution from, or were a grantor of, or a transferor to, a foreign trust.		
	7a	At any time during 1998, did you have an interest in or a signature or other authority over a financial account in a foreign country, such as a bank account, securities account, or other financial account? See page B-2 for exceptions and filing requirements for Form TD F 90-22.1		
	b	If ™Yes,∫ enter the name of the foreign country▶		
	8	During 1998, did you receive a distribution from, or were you the grantor of, or transferor to, a foreign trust? If ™Yes,∫ you may have to file Form 3520. See page B-2		

For Paperwork Reduction Act Notice, see Form 1040 instructions.   Schedule B (Form 1040) 1998

SCHEDULE C (Form 1040) Department of the Treasury Internal Revenue Service (99)	**Profit or Loss From Business** (Sole Proprietorship) ▶ **Partnerships, joint ventures, etc., must file Form 1065 or Form 1065-B.** ▶ **Attach to Form 1040 or Form 1041.** ▶ **See Instructions for Schedule C (Form 1040).**	OMB No. 1545-0074 1998 Attachment Sequence No. 09

Name of proprietor | Social security number (SSN)

A Principal business or profession, including product or service (see page C-1) | **B** Enter NEW code from pages C-8 & 9 ▶

C Business name. If no separate business name, leave blank. | **D** Employer ID number (EIN), if any

E Business address (including suite or room no.) ▶ ....
City, town or post office, state, and ZIP code

F Accounting method: **(1)** ☐ Cash   **(2)** ☐ Accrual   **(3)** ☐ Other (specify) ▶ ....
G Did you ™materially participate⌡ in the operation of this business during 1998? If ™No,⌡ see page C-2 for limit on losses . ☐ Yes   ☐ No
H If you started or acquired this business during 1998, check here .   .   .   . ▶ ☐

Part I   Income

1	Gross receipts or sales. **Caution:** *If this income was reported to you on Form W-2 and the ™Statutory employee⌡ box on that form was checked, see page C-3 and check here* . . . . . . ▶ ☐	1	
2	Returns and allowances	2	
3	Subtract line 2 from line 1	3	
4	Cost of goods sold (from line 42 on page 2)	4	
5	**Gross profit.** Subtract line 4 from line 3	5	
6	Other income, including Federal and state gasoline or fuel tax credit or refund (see page C-3) . .	6	
7	**Gross income.** Add lines 5 and 6 . . . . ▶	7	

Part II   Expenses. Enter expenses for business use of your home **only** on line 30.

8	Advertising	8		19	Pension and profit-sharing plans	19	
9	Bad debts from sales or services (see page C-3) . .	9		20	Rent or lease (see page C-5):		
					a Vehicles, machinery, and equipment .	20a	
10	Car and truck expenses (see page C-3)	10			**b** Other business property . .	20b	
11	Commissions and fees . .	11		21	Repairs and maintenance . .	21	
12	Depletion	12		22	Supplies (not included in Part III) .	22	
13	Depreciation and section 179 expense deduction (not included in Part III) (see page C-4) . .	13		23	Taxes and licenses . . .	23	
				24	Travel, meals, and entertainment:		
					a Travel	24a	
14	Employee benefit programs (other than on line 19) . .	14			**b** Meals and entertainment .		
15	Insurance (other than health) .	15			**c** Enter 50% of line 24b subject to limitations (see page C-6) .		
16	Interest:						
	a Mortgage (paid to banks, etc.) .	16a			**d** Subtract line 24c from line 24b	24d	
	b Other	16b		25	Utilities	25	
17	Legal and professional services	17		26	Wages (less employment credits) .	26	
18	Office expense	18		27	Other expenses (from line 48 on page 2)	27	
28	**Total expenses** before expenses for business use of home. Add lines 8 through 27 in columns . ▶					28	

29	Tentative profit (loss). Subtract line 28 from line 7	29	
30	Expenses for business use of your home. Attach **Form 8829**	30	
31	Net profit or (loss). Subtract line 30 from line 29. • If a profit, enter on **Form 1040, line 12,** and ALSO on **Schedule SE, line 2** (statutory employees, see page C-6). Estates and trusts, enter on Form 1041, line 3. • If a loss, you MUST go on to line 32.	31	
32	If you have a loss, check the box that describes your investment in this activity (see page C-6). • If you checked 32a, enter the loss on **Form 1040, line 12,** and ALSO on **Schedule SE, line 2** (statutory employees, see page C-6). Estates and trusts, enter on Form 1041, line 3. • If you checked 32b, you MUST attach **Form 6198.**	32a ☐ All investment is at risk. 32b ☐ Some investment is not at risk.	

For Paperwork Reduction Act Notice, see Form 1040 instructions.   Cat. No. 11334P   **Schedule C (Form 1040) 1998**

FIGURE 14.4

Schedule C (continued)

Schedule C (Form 1040) 1998 ▪ Page **2**

Part III   **Cost of Goods Sold** (see page C-7)

33   Method(s) used to value closing inventory: **a** ☐ Cost   **b** ☐ Lower of cost or market   **c** ☐ Other (attach explanation)

34   Was there any change in determining quantities, costs, or valuations between opening and closing inventory? If ™Yes,ʃ attach explanation . . . . ☐ **Yes**   ☐ **No**

35 Inventory at beginning of year. If different from last year's closing inventory, attach explanation . .	**35**	
36 Purchases less cost of items withdrawn for personal use	**36**	
37 Cost of labor. Do not include any amounts paid to yourself	**37**	
38 Materials and supplies	**38**	
39 Other costs	**39**	
40 Add lines 35 through 39	**40**	
41 Inventory at end of year	**41**	
42 **Cost of goods sold.** Subtract line 41 from line 40. Enter the result here and on page 1, line 4 . .	**42**	

Part IV   **Information on Your Vehicle.** Complete this part **ONLY** if you are claiming car or truck expenses on line 10 and are not required to file Form 4562 for this business. See the instructions for line 13 on page C-4 to find out if you must file.

43   When did you place your vehicle in service for business purposes? (month, day, year) ▶ ..../......../........ .

44   Of the total number of miles you drove your vehicle during 1998, enter the number of miles you used your vehicle for:

a Business .... **b** Commuting .... **c** Other ....

45   Do you (or your spouse) have another vehicle available for personal use? . . . . ☐ **Yes**   ☐ **No**

46   Was your vehicle available for use during off-duty hours?   . . . . ☐ **Yes**   ☐ **No**

47a Do you have evidence to support your deduction?   . . . . ☐ **Yes**   ☐ **No**

  b If ™Yes,ʃ is the evidence written?. ☐ **Yes**   ☐ **No**

Part V   **Other Expenses.** List below business expenses not included on lines 8±26 or line 30.

---	
48 **Total other expenses.** Enter here and on page 1, line 27 . . . . **48**	

⊕

FIGURE 14.5

Schedule C-EZ

**SCHEDULE C-EZ
(Form 1040)**

Department of the Treasury
Internal Revenue Service   (99)

Net Profit From Business
(Sole Proprietorship)

▶ **Partnerships, joint ventures, etc., must file Form 1065 or 1065-B.**

▶ **Attach to Form 1040 or Form 1041.** ▶ **See instructions on back.**

OMB No. 1545-0074

19 98

Attachment
Sequence No. **09A**

Name of proprietor

Social security number (SSN)

Part I   **General Information**

**You May Use
Schedule C-EZ
Instead of
Schedule C
Only If You:**

▶

- Had business expenses of $2,500 or less.
- Use the cash method of accounting.
- Did not have an inventory at any time during the year.
- Did not have a net loss from your business.
- Had only one business as a sole proprietor.

And You:

▶

- Had no employees during the year.
- Are not required to file **Form 4562**, Depreciation and Amortization, for this business. See the instructions for Schedule C, line 13, on page C-4 to find out if you must file.
- Do not deduct expenses for business use of your home.
- Do not have prior year unallowed passive activity losses from this business.

A   Principal business or profession, including product or service

B   Enter NEW code from pages C-8 & 9
▶

C   Business name. If no separate business name, leave blank.

D   Employer ID number (EIN), if any

E   Business address (including suite or room no.). Address not required if same as on Form 1040, page 1.

City, town or post office, state, and ZIP code

Part II   **Figure Your Net Profit**

1   Gross receipts. **Caution:** *If this income was reported to you on Form W-2 and the ™Statutory employee⌡ box on that form was checked, see **Statutory Employees** in the instructions for Schedule C, line 1, on page C-3 and check here* ▶ ☐ | **1** |

2   Total expenses. If more than $2,500, you **must** use Schedule C. See instructions . . . . . | **2** |

3   Net profit. Subtract line 2 from line 1. If less than zero, you **must** use Schedule C. Enter on **Form 1040, line 12,** and ALSO on **Schedule SE, line 2.** (Statutory employees **do not** report this amount on Schedule SE, line 2. Estates and trusts, enter on Form 1041, line 3.) . . . . . | **3** |

Part III   **Information on Your Vehicle.** Complete this part **ONLY** if you are claiming car or truck expenses on line 2.

4   When did you place your vehicle in service for business purposes? (month, day, year) ▶ ....../....../...... .

5   Of the total number of miles you drove your vehicle during 1998, enter the number of miles you used your vehicle for:

a Business ....   **b** Commuting ....   **c** Other ....

6   Do you (or your spouse) have another vehicle available for personal use? . . . . ☐ **Yes**   ☐ **No**

7   Was your vehicle available for use during off-duty hours? . . . . ☐ **Yes**   ☐ **No**

8a   Do you have evidence to support your deduction? . . . . ☐ **Yes**   ☐ **No**

b If ™Yes,⌡ is the evidence written? . . . . ☐ **Yes**   ☐ **No**

For Paperwork Reduction Act Notice, see Form 1040 instructions.   Cat. No. 14374D   **Schedule C-EZ (Form 1040) 1998**

**PART
II**

**Quicken and Your
Personal Finances**

FIGURE 14.5

Schedule C-EZ (continued)

Schedule C-EZ (Form 1040) 1998   Page **2**

Instructions

You may use Schedule C-EZ instead of Schedule C if you operated a business or practiced a profession as a sole proprietorship and you have met all the requirements listed in Part I of Schedule C-EZ.

Line A

Describe the business or professional activity that provided your principal source of income reported on line 1. Give the general field or activity and the type of product or service.

Line B

Enter the **new** six-digit code that identifies your principal business or professional activity. See pages C-8 and C-9 for the list of codes.

Line D

You need an employer identification number (EIN) only if you had a Keogh plan or were required to file an employment, excise, estate, trust, or alcohol, tobacco, and firearms tax return. If you need an EIN, file **Form SS-4**, Application for Employer Identification Number. If you do not have an EIN, leave line D blank. **Do not** enter your SSN.

Line E

Enter your business address. Show a street address instead of a box number. Include the suite or room number, if any.

Line 1

Enter gross receipts from your trade or business. Include amounts you received in your trade or business that were properly shown on **Forms 1099-MISC.** If the total amounts that were reported in box 7 of Forms 1099-MISC are more than the total you are reporting on line 1, attach a statement explaining the difference. You must show all items of taxable income actually or constructively received during the year (in cash, property, or services). Income is constructively received when it is credited to your account or set aside for you to use. Do not offset this amount by any losses.

Line 2

Enter the total amount of all deductible business expenses you actually paid during the year. Examples of these expenses include advertising, car and truck expenses, commissions and fees, insurance, interest, legal and professional services, office expense, rent or lease expenses, repairs and maintenance, supplies, taxes, travel, 50% of business meals and entertainment, and utilities (including telephone). For details, see the instructions for Schedule C, Parts II and V, on pages C-3 through C-7. If you wish, you may use the optional worksheet below to record your expenses.

If you claim car or truck expenses, be sure to complete Part III of Schedule C-EZ.

Optional Worksheet for Line 2 (keep a copy for your records)

a Business meals and entertainment	**a**		
b Less: 50% of business meals and entertainment subject to limitations (see the instructions for lines 24b and 24c on pages C-5 and C-6) .	**b**		
c Deductible business meals and entertainment. Subtract line **b** from line **a**	**c**	
d	**d**	
e	**e**	
f	**f**	
g	**g**	
h	**h**	
i	**i**	
j **Total.** Add lines **c** through **i.** Enter here and on line 2	**j**	

FIGURE 14.6

Schedule D

SCHEDULE D **(Form 1040)** Department of the Treasury Internal Revenue Service (99)	OMB No. 1545-0074

Capital Gains and Losses

▶ Attach to Form 1040.   ▶ See Instructions for Schedule D (Form 1040).

▶ Use Schedule D-1 for more space to list transactions for lines 1 and 8.

19**98**

Attachment Sequence No. **12**

Name(s) shown on Form 1040

Your social security number

Part I — Short-Term Capital Gains and Losses–Assets Held One Year or Less

(a) Description of property (Example: 100 sh. XYZ Co.)	(b) Date acquired (Mo., day, yr.)	(c) Date sold (Mo., day, yr.)	(d) Sales price (see page D-6)	(e) Cost or other basis (see page D-6)	(f) GAIN or (LOSS) Subtract (e) from (d)	
1						

2   Enter your short-term totals, if any, from Schedule D-1, line 2 . . . .   **2**

3   **Total short-term sales price amounts.** Add column (d) of lines 1 and 2 . . .   **3**

4   Short-term gain from Form 6252 and short-term gain or (loss) from Forms 4684, 6781, and 8824 . . . .   **4**

5   Net short-term gain or (loss) from partnerships, S corporations, estates, and trusts from Schedule(s) K-1 . . . .   **5**

6   Short-term capital loss carryover. Enter the amount, if any, from line 8 of your 1997 Capital Loss Carryover Worksheet . . . .   **6** (   )

7   **Net short-term capital gain or (loss).** Combine lines 1 through 6 in column (f). . . . . ▶   **7**

Part II — Long-Term Capital Gains and Losses–Assets Held More Than One Year

(a) Description of property (Example: 100 sh. XYZ Co.)	(b) Date acquired (Mo., day, yr.)	(c) Date sold (Mo., day, yr.)	(d) Sales price (see page D-6)	(e) Cost or other basis (see page D-6)	(f) GAIN or (LOSS) Subtract (e) from (d)	(g) 28% RATE GAIN or (LOSS) * (see instr. below)
8						

9   Enter your long-term totals, if any, from Schedule D-1, line 9 . . . .   **9**

10   **Total long-term sales price amounts.** Add column (d) of lines 8 and 9 . . .   **10**

11   Gain from Form 4797, Part I; long-term gain from Forms 2439 and 6252; and long-term gain or (loss) from Forms 4684, 6781, and 8824 . . . . .   **11**

12   Net long-term gain or (loss) from partnerships, S corporations, estates, and trusts from Schedule(s) K-1 . . . .   **12**

13   Capital gain distributions. See page D-2 . . . .   **13**

14   Long-term capital loss carryover. Enter in both columns (f) and (g) the amount, if any, from line 13 of your 1997 Capital Loss Carryover Worksheet . . .   **14** (   ) (   )

15   Combine lines 8 through 14 in column (g) **15**

16   **Net long-term capital gain or (loss).** Combine lines 8 through 14 in column (f). . . . . ▶   **16**

    Next: Go to Part III on the back.

***28% Rate Gain or Loss** includes **all** ™collectibles gains and losses∫ (as defined on page D-6) and up to 50% of the eligible gain on qualified small business stock (see page D-5).

For Paperwork Reduction Act Notice, see Form 1040 instructions.   Cat. No. 11338H   Schedule D (Form 1040) 1998

PART

II

Quicken and Your Personal Finances

FIGURE 14.6

Schedule D (continued)

Schedule D (Form 1040) 1998

Page **2**

Part III	**Summary of Parts I and II**

17 Combine lines 7 and 16. If a loss, go to line 18. If a gain, enter the gain on Form 1040, line 13   **17**

    Next: Complete Form 1040 through line 39. Then, go to **Part IV** to figure your tax if:
- Both lines 16 and 17 are gains, **and**
- Form 1040, line 39, is more than zero.

18 If line 17 is a loss, enter here and as a (loss) on Form 1040, line 13, the **smaller** of these losses:
- The loss on line 17; **or**
- ($3,000) or, if married filing separately, ($1,500) . . . .   **18** (   )

    Next: Complete Form 1040 through line 37. Then, complete the **Capital Loss Carryover Worksheet** on page D-6 if:
- The loss on line 17 exceeds the loss on line 18, **or**
- Form 1040, line 37, is a loss.

Part IV	**Tax Computation Using Maximum Capital Gains Rates**

19 Enter your taxable income from Form 1040, line 39 . . . . **19**

20 Enter the **smaller** of line 16 or line 17 of Schedule D **20**

21 If you are filing Form 4952, enter the amount from Form 4952, line 4e   **21**

22 Subtract line 21 from line 20. If zero or less, enter -0- **22**

23 Combine lines 7 and 15. If zero or less, enter -0- **23**

24 Enter the **smaller** of line 15 or line 23, but not less than zero . . . **24**

25 Enter your unrecaptured section 1250 gain, if any (see page D-7) . **25**

26 Add lines 24 and 25 . . . . **26**

27 Subtract line 26 from line 22. If zero or less, enter -0- **27**

28 Subtract line 27 from line 19. If zero or less, enter -0- **28**

29 Enter the **smaller** of:
- The amount on line 19, **or**
- $25,350 if single; $42,350 if married filing jointly or qualifying widow(er); $21,175 if married filing separately; or $33,950 if head of household } **29**

30 Enter the **smaller** of line 28 or line 29 . . . . **30**

31 Subtract line 22 from line 19. If zero or less, enter -0- **31**

32 Enter the **larger** of line 30 or line 31 . . . . **32**

33 Figure the tax on the amount on line 32. Use the Tax Table or Tax Rate Schedules, whichever applies . . . . ▶ **33**

34 Enter the amount from line 29 . . . . **34**

35 Enter the amount from line 28 . . . . **35**

36 Subtract line 35 from line 34. If zero or less, enter -0- **36**

37 Multiply line 36 by 10% (.10) . . . . ▶ **37**

38 Enter the **smaller** of line 19 or line 27 . . . . **38**

39 Enter the amount from line 36 . . . . **39**

40 Subtract line 39 from line 38 . . . . **40**

41 Multiply line 40 by 20% (.20) . . . . ▶ **41**

42 Enter the **smaller** of line 22 or line 25 . . . . **42**

43 Add lines 22 and 32 . . . . **43**

44 Enter the amount from line 19 . . . . **44**

45 Subtract line 44 from line 43. If zero or less, enter -0- **45**

46 Subtract line 45 from line 42. If zero or less, enter -0- **46**

47 Multiply line 46 by 25% (.25) . . . . ▶ **47**

48 Enter the amount from line 19 . . . . **48**

49 Add lines 32, 36, 40, and 46 . . . . **49**

50 Subtract line 49 from line 48 . . . . **50**

51 Multiply line 50 by 28% (.28) . . . . ▶ **51**

52 Add lines 33, 37, 41, 47, and 51 . . . . **52**

53 Figure the tax on the amount on line 19. Use the Tax Table or Tax Rate Schedules, whichever applies **53**

54 **Tax on taxable income (including capital gains).** Enter the **smaller** of line 52 or line 53 here and on Form 1040, line 40. . . . . ▶ **54**

FIGURE 14.7

Schedule E

SCHEDULE E (Form 1040)	Supplemental Income and Loss	OMB No. 1545-0074
Department of the Treasury Internal Revenue Service (99)	(From rental real estate, royalties, partnerships, S corporations, estates, trusts, REMICs, etc.) ▶ Attach to Form 1040 or Form 1041. ▶ See Instructions for Schedule E (Form 1040).	1998 Attachment Sequence No. 13

Name(s) shown on return   Your social security number

Part I   Income or Loss From Rental Real Estate and Royalties Note: *Report income and expenses from your business of renting personal property on* **Schedule C** *or* **C-EZ** *(see page E-1). Report farm rental income or loss from* **Form 4835** *on page 2, line 39.*

1 Show the kind and location of each **rental real estate property:**

A ....

B ....

C ....

2 For each rental real estate property listed on line 1, did you or your family use it during the tax year for personal purposes for more than the greater of:
- 14 days, **or**
- 10% of the total days rented at fair rental value?

(See page E-1.)

	Yes	No
A		
B		
C		

Income:		Properties			Totals
		A	B	C	(Add columns A, B, and C.)
3 Rents received	3		3		
4 Royalties received	4				4
Expenses:					
5 Advertising	5				
6 Auto and travel (see page E-2)	6				
7 Cleaning and maintenance	7				
8 Commissions	8				
9 Insurance	9				
10 Legal and other professional fees	10				
11 Management fees	11				
12 Mortgage interest paid to banks, etc. (see page E-2)	12				12
13 Other interest	13				
14 Repairs	14				
15 Supplies	15				
16 Taxes	16				
17 Utilities	17				
18 Other (list) ▶	18				
19 Add lines 5 through 18	19				19
20 Depreciation expense or depletion (see page E-3)	20				20
21 Total expenses. Add lines 19 and 20	21				
22 Income or (loss) from rental real estate or royalty properties. Subtract line 21 from line 3 (rents) or line 4 (royalties). If the result is a (loss), see page E-3 to find out if you must file **Form 6198**.	22				
23 Deductible rental real estate loss. **Caution:** *Your rental real estate loss on line 22 may be limited. See page E-3 to find out if you must file* **Form 8582**. *Real estate professionals must complete line 42 on page 2.*	23	( )(	)(	)( )	

24 **Income.** Add positive amounts shown on line 22. **Do not** include any losses . . . . | 24 | |

25 **Losses.** Add royalty losses from line 22 and rental real estate losses from line 23. Enter total losses here | 25 | ( ) |

26 Total rental real estate and royalty income or (loss). Combine lines 24 and 25. Enter the result here. If Parts II, III, IV, and line 39 on page 2 do not apply to you, also enter this amount on Form 1040, line 17. Otherwise, include this amount in the total on line 40 on page 2 . . . . | 26 | |

For Paperwork Reduction Act Notice, see Form 1040 instructions.   Cat. No. 11344L   **Schedule E (Form 1040) 1998**

PART II

Quicken and Your Personal Finances

FIGURE 14.7

Schedule E (continued)

Schedule E (Form 1040) 1998   Attachment Sequence No. **13**   Page **2**

Name(s) shown on return. Do not enter name and social security number if shown on other side. | **Your social security number**

Note: *If you report amounts from farming or fishing on Schedule E, you must enter your gross income from those activities on line 41 below. Real estate professionals must complete line 42 below.*

Part II   **Income or Loss From Partnerships and S Corporations**   Note: *If you report a loss from an at-risk activity, you MUST check either column (e) or (f) on line 27 to describe your investment in the activity. See page E-5. If you check column (f), you must attach* **Form 6198.**

27	(a) Name	(b) Enter P for partnership; S for S corporation	(c) Check if foreign partnership	(d) Employer identification number	Investment At Risk? (e) All is at risk	(f) Some is not at risk
A						
B						
C						
D						
E						

	Passive Income and Loss		Nonpassive Income and Loss		
	(g) Passive loss allowed (attach **Form 8582** if required)	(h) Passive income from **Schedule K±1**	(i) Nonpassive loss from **Schedule K±1**	(j) Section 179 expense deduction from **Form 4562**	(k) Nonpassive income from **Schedule K±1**
A					
B					
C					
D					
E					
28a Totals					
b Totals					

29	Add columns (h) and (k) of line 28a	29	
30	Add columns (g), (i), and (j) of line 28b	30 (	)
31	Total partnership and S corporation income or (loss). Combine lines 29 and 30. Enter the result here and include in the total on line 40 below	31	

Part III   **Income or Loss From Estates and Trusts**

32	(a) Name	(b) Employer identification number
A		
B		

	Passive Income and Loss		Nonpassive Income and Loss	
	(c) Passive deduction or loss allowed (attach **Form 8582** if required)	(d) Passive income from **Schedule K±1**	(e) Deduction or loss from **Schedule K±1**	(f) Other income from **Schedule K±1**
A				
B				
33a Totals				
b Totals				

34	Add columns (d) and (f) of line 33a	34	
35	Add columns (c) and (e) of line 33b	35 (	)
36	Total estate and trust income or (loss). Combine lines 34 and 35. Enter the result here and include in the total on line 40 below	36	

Part IV   **Income or Loss From Real Estate Mortgage Investment Conduits (REMICs)–Residual Holder**

37	(a) Name	(b) Employer identification number	(c) Excess inclusion from **Schedules Q**, line 2c (see page E-6)	(d) Taxable income (net loss) from **Schedules Q**, line 1b	(e) Income from **Schedules Q**, line 3b

38	Combine columns (d) and (e) only. Enter the result here and include in the total on line 40 below	38	

Part V   **Summary**

39	Net farm rental income or (loss) from **Form 4835.** Also, complete line 41 below	39	
40	TOTAL income or (loss). Combine lines 26, 31, 36, 38, and 39. Enter the result here and on Form 1040, line 17 ▶	40	

41	**Reconciliation of Farming and Fishing Income.** Enter your **gross** farming and fishing income reported on Form 4835, line 7; Schedule K-1 (Form 1065), line 15b; Schedule K-1 (Form 1120S), line 23; and Schedule K-1 (Form 1041), line 14 (see page E-6)	41	
42	**Reconciliation for Real Estate Professionals.** If you were a real estate professional (see page E-4), enter the net income or (loss) you reported anywhere on Form 1040 from all rental real estate activities in which you materially participated under the passive activity loss rules . . .	42	

FIGURE 14.8

Schedule F

SCHEDULE F
(Form 1040)

Department of the Treasury
Internal Revenue Service   (99)

Profit or Loss From Farming

▶ Attach to Form 1040, Form 1041, Form 1065, or Form 1065-B.

▶ See Instructions for Schedule F (Form 1040).

OMB No. 1545-0074

1998

Attachment
Sequence No. **14**

Name of proprietor

Social security number (SSN)

A Principal product. Describe in one or two words your principal crop or activity for the current tax year.

B Enter NEW code from Part IV
▶

D Employer ID number (EIN), if any

C Accounting method: **(1)** ☐ Cash   **(2)** ☐ Accrual

E Did you ™materially participate∫ in the operation of this business during 1998? If ™No,∫ see page F-2 for limit on passive losses. ☐ Yes ☐ No

Part I Farm Income–Cash Method. Complete Parts I and II (Accrual method taxpayers complete Parts II and III, and line 11 of Part I.)
Do not include sales of livestock held for draft, breeding, sport, or dairy purposes; report these sales on Form 4797.

1	Sales of livestock and other items you bought for resale	**1**		
2	Cost or other basis of livestock and other items reported on line 1	**2**		
3	Subtract line 2 from line 1			**3**
4	Sales of livestock, produce, grains, and other products you raised			**4**
5a	Total cooperative distributions (Form(s) 1099-PATR)	**5a**	5b Taxable amount	**5b**
6a	Agricultural program payments (see page F-3)	**6a**	6b Taxable amount	**6b**
7	Commodity Credit Corporation (CCC) loans (see page F-3):			
a	CCC loans reported under election			**7a**
b	CCC loans forfeited	**7b**	7c Taxable amount	**7c**
8	Crop insurance proceeds and certain disaster payments (see page F-3):			
a	Amount received in 1998	**8a**	8b Taxable amount	**8b**
c	If election to defer to 1999 is attached, check here ▶ ☐		8d Amount deferred from 1997	**8d**
9	Custom hire (machine work) income			**9**
10	Other income, including Federal and state gasoline or fuel tax credit or refund (see page F-3)			**10**
11	**Gross income.** Add amounts in the right column for lines 3 through 10. If accrual method taxpayer, enter the amount from page 2, line 51 ▶			**11**

Part II Farm Expenses–Cash and Accrual Method. Do not include personal or living expenses such as taxes, insurance, repairs, etc., on your home.

12	Car and truck expenses (see page F-4–also attach **Form 4562**)	**12**		25	Pension and profit-sharing plans	**25**
13	Chemicals	**13**		26	Rent or lease (see page F-6):	
14	Conservation expenses (see page F-4)	**14**		a	Vehicles, machinery, and equipment	**26a**
15	Custom hire (machine work)	**15**		b	Other (land, animals, etc.)	**26b**
16	Depreciation and section 179 expense deduction not claimed elsewhere (see page F-5)	**16**		27	Repairs and maintenance	**27**
				28	Seeds and plants purchased	**28**
				29	Storage and warehousing	**29**
17	Employee benefit programs other than on line 25	**17**		30	Supplies purchased	**30**
18	Feed purchased	**18**		31	Taxes	**31**
19	Fertilizers and lime	**19**		32	Utilities	**32**
20	Freight and trucking	**20**		33	Veterinary, breeding, and medicine	**33**
21	Gasoline, fuel, and oil	**21**		34	Other expenses (specify):	
22	Insurance (other than health)	**22**		a		**34a**
23	Interest:			b		**34b**
a	Mortgage (paid to banks, etc.)	**23a**		c		**34c**
b	Other	**23b**		d		**34d**
24	Labor hired (less employment credits)	**24**		e		**34e**
				f		**34f**

35	**Total expenses.** Add lines 12 through 34f ▶	**35**
36	**Net farm profit or (loss).** Subtract line 35 from line 11. If a profit, enter on **Form 1040, line 18**, and ALSO on **Schedule SE, line 1.** If a loss, you MUST go on to line 37 (estates, trusts, and partnerships, see page F-6).	**36**
37	If you have a loss, you MUST check the box that describes your investment in this activity (see page F-6). • If you checked 37a, enter the loss on **Form 1040, line 18**, and ALSO on **Schedule SE, line 1.** • If you checked 37b, you MUST attach **Form 6198.**	37a ☐ All investment is at risk. 37b ☐ Some investment is not at risk.

For Paperwork Reduction Act Notice, see Form 1040 instructions.   Cat. No. 11346H   Schedule F (Form 1040) 1998

PART
II

Quicken and Your
Personal Finances

FIGURE 14.8

Schedule F (continued)

Schedule F (Form 1040) 1998   Page **2**

Part III   **Farm Income–Accrual Method**   (see page F-7)

Do not include sales of livestock held for draft, breeding, sport, or dairy purposes; report these sales on Form 4797 and do not include this livestock on line 46 below.

38	Sales of livestock, produce, grains, and other products during the year	**38**
39a	Total cooperative distributions (Form(s) 1099-PATR) **39a** **39b** Taxable amount	**39b**
40a	Agricultural program payments . . . . . **40a** **40b** Taxable amount	**40b**
41	Commodity Credit Corporation (CCC) loans:	
a	CCC loans reported under election	**41a**
b	CCC loans forfeited . . . . **41b** **41c** Taxable amount	**41c**
42	Crop insurance proceeds	**42**
43	Custom hire (machine work) income	**43**
44	Other income, including Federal and state gasoline or fuel tax credit or refund	**44**
45	Add amounts in the right column for lines 38 through 44	**45**

46	Inventory of livestock, produce, grains, and other products at beginning of the year	**46**		
47	Cost of livestock, produce, grains, and other products purchased during the year	**47**		
48	Add lines 46 and 47	**48**		
49	Inventory of livestock, produce, grains, and other products at end of year	**49**		
50	Cost of livestock, produce, grains, and other products sold. Subtract line 49 from line 48*			**50**
51	**Gross income.** Subtract line 50 from line 45. Enter the result here and on page 1, line 11 . . . . ▶			**51**

*If you use the unit-livestock-price method or the farm-price method of valuing inventory and the amount on line 49 is larger than the amount on line 48, subtract line 48 from line 49. Enter the result on line 50. Add lines 45 and 50. Enter the total on line 51.

Part IV   **Principal Agricultural Activity Codes**

Caution: File **Schedule C** *(Form 1040), Profit or Loss From Business,* or **Schedule C-EZ** *(Form 1040), Net Profit From Business,* instead of Schedule F if:

• *Your principal source of income is from providing agricultural services such as soil preparation, veterinary, farm labor, horticultural, or management for a fee or on a contract basis, or*

• *You are engaged in the business of breeding, raising, and caring for dogs, cats, or other pet animals.*

These **new** codes for the Principal Agricultural Activity classify farms by the type of activity they are engaged in to facilitate the administration of the Internal Revenue Code. These six-digit codes are based on the new North American Industry Classification System (NAICS) and do not resemble prior year codes.

Select one of the following new codes and enter the six-digit number on page 1, line B:

Crop Production

111100	Oilseed and grain farming
111210	Vegetable and melon farming
111300	Fruit and tree nut farming
111400	Greenhouse, nursery, and floriculture production
111900	Other crop farming

Animal Production

112111	Beef cattle ranching and farming
112112	Cattle feedlots
112120	Dairy cattle and milk production
112210	Hog and pig farming
112300	Poultry and egg production
112400	Sheep and goat farming
112510	Animal aquaculture
112900	Other animal production

Forestry and Logging

113000	Forestry and logging (including forest nurseries and timber tracts)

NOTE Despite what some people say, the business income tax laws don't actually have very many "gray areas." You need to know two basic rules. First, all business income is taxed—unless it's specifically excluded. Second, any business expense that's ordinary and necessary is deductible. The bottom line is that it's pretty clear whether a particular amount that flows into the business needs to be counted as income. (It almost always does.) And it's pretty clear whether a particular expenditure is deductible. (Ask yourself the question, "Is this expense ordinary and necessary for the business?")

Telling Quicken If You Want Tax-Schedule-Specific Information

Quicken lets you tag categories for entry onto specific lines of specific tax forms. It's this ability that makes it possible to export information from Quicken for use in another tax-preparation program (such as TurboTax or TaxCut).

If you want to associate tax schedules and lines with your categories, follow these steps:

1. Choose Edit ➢ Options ➢ Quicken Program to display the General Options dialog box.

2. Click the General tab.

3. Mark the selection Use Tax Schedules with Categories, as shown in Figure 14.9.

4. Click OK.

FIGURE 14.9

*The General tab of the
General Options
dialog box*

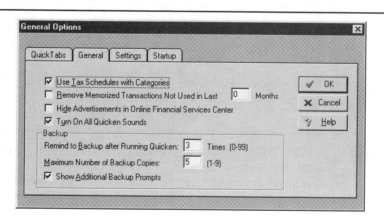

Modifying the Category List

When you create a new Quicken file, Quicken sets up a category list for you based on the general information you provide. You may need to make changes to this original category list in order to better support your income tax preparation. You can make changes to the list from the Category & Transfer List, as shown in Figure 14.10. To display this area, choose Finance ➤ Category & Transfer List. From here, you can add, edit, and delete categories, as described in the following sections.

FIGURE 14.10

The Category & Transfer List

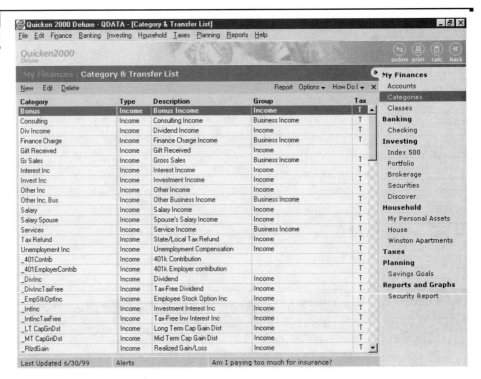

 WARNING Quicken sets up special categories for tracking investments when you create your first investment account. To identify these categories, Quicken starts each category name with an underscore character. You shouldn't change any of the investment categories.

Adding a Category for Income Taxes

To add a new category to the category list, follow these steps:

1. Click the New command button in the Category & Transfer List to display the Set Up Category dialog box, as shown in Figure 14.11.

2. Enter a name for the category in the Name text box.

3. Enter a description for the category. Quicken uses the description along with the category name on its reports to identify the category's total. If the description is left blank, only the name is used.

FIGURE 14.11

The Set Up Category dialog box

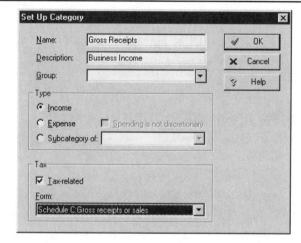

4. Use the Type option buttons to indicate whether the new category tracks income or expense or is a subcategory of a category that tracks income or expense.

5. If you clicked the Subcategory Of option button, activate the Subcategory drop-down list box and select the category that the subcategory's total gets rolled up into. You can have subcategories that roll up into other subcategories. To do this, select as a primary category the subcategory that the new subcategory's total will get rolled up into from the Subcategory drop-down list.

6. Mark the Tax-related checkbox to indicate that you'll use this category for tracking taxable income or tax-deductible expense items. This tells Quicken that the category total should appear on a Tax Summary Report.

7. Indicate on which tax form and tax form line the category total is reported: Activate the Form drop-down list box and select the list entry that names the correct form (or schedule) and the form (or schedule) line. For example, if you want to set up a category for tracking the gross receipts or sales figure that will ultimately be entered on line 1 of the Schedule C form, select the Schedule C: Gross Receipts or Sales entry.

 NOTE Quicken doesn't display the Form drop-down list box in the Set Up Category dialog box until you mark the Use Tax Schedules with Categories checkbox in the General Options dialog box.

8. Click OK. Quicken adds the category you described to the Category & Transfer List and closes the dialog box.

9. Repeat steps 1 through 8 for each tax category you want to add.

Editing a Category for Income Taxes

To edit an existing category so it works (or works better) for tracking taxable income and tax-deductible expenses, follow these steps:

1. Select the category in the Category & Transfer List and click the Edit command button to display the Edit Category dialog box, as shown in Figure 14.12.

2. If you need to, change the category name. Quicken will update the transactions that used the old category name so they show the new category name.

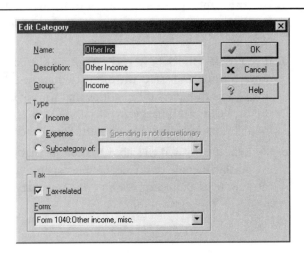

3. If you need to, edit the description for the category.

4. Use the Type option buttons to indicate whether the category tracks income or expense or is a subcategory of a category that tracks income or expense.

 TIP You can change a category into a subcategory and a subcategory into a category using the Type option buttons. If you demote a category, you must also complete step 5.

5. If you mark the Subcategory Of option, select the parent category in which you want the subcategory included from the Subcategory Of drop-down list box.

6. Mark the Tax-related checkbox to indicate that you'll use this category for tracking taxable income or tax-deductible expense items, or deselect the checkbox if the category is currently being treated as taxable or tax-deductible but shouldn't be.

7. If the category is tax-related, indicate on which tax form and tax form line the category total is reported: From the Form drop-down list box, select the list entry that names the correct form (or schedule) and the form (or schedule) line.

8. Click OK when the Edit Category dialog box is complete. Quicken makes the changes and closes the dialog box.

9. Repeat steps 1 through 8 for each category you want to modify.

Deleting Extraneous Categories

You can remove any categories that you don't want on the category list. (This is a good idea if you want to eliminate the chance that someone—perhaps you—will accidentally use an incorrect category to summarize taxable income or a tax-deductible expense.)

To remove unneeded categories, select the category in the Category & Transfer List and click the Delete command button. Click OK when Quicken asks you to confirm the deletion. Quicken removes the category from the Category & Transfer List and erases the contents of the Category text box for existing transactions that use the category.

 TIP If you want to delete a category but want transactions that use the old category to use another category—I'll call this the *new category*—make the old category you want to delete a subcategory of the new category. Then delete the old category. Click Yes when Quicken asks if you want to merge the subcategory with the parent. Quicken will use the parent category to summarize the transactions.

PART

II

Quicken and Your
Personal Finances

Using Quicken's Tax Reports

Quicken provides two reports for helping you prepare your income tax returns more easily: the Tax Summary and Tax Schedule reports (see Chapter 4 for details about viewing, printing, and customizing Quicken's reports).

If you haven't connected taxable income categories and tax-deductible expense categories to tax schedule lines, use the Tax Summary report (choose Reports ➤ Taxes ➤ Tax Summary, complete the Create Report dialog box to include the correct dates in the report, and click Create). Use the data in this report to enter the taxable income and tax-deductible expense category totals into the appropriate tax form or schedule input lines. You would, for example, enter the TOTAL Charity figure shown in Figure 14.13 on the "Gifts by cash or check" line (line 15) of the Schedule A form (see Figure 14.2).

FIGURE 14.13

The Tax Summary report lists all taxable income categories and tax-deductible expense categories (as long as you've set up your category list correctly).

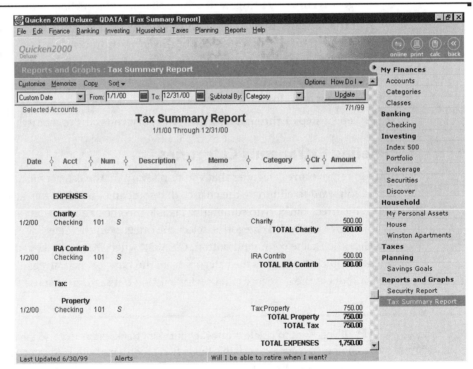

If you have connected taxable income categories and tax-deductible expense categories to tax schedule lines, use the Tax Schedule report (choose Reports ➤ Taxes ➤ Tax Schedule, complete the Create Report dialog box to include the correct dates in the report, and click Create). Enter the report's tax schedule line totals on the corresponding tax schedule lines. Figure 14.14 shows a portion of a Tax Schedule report. This example is tax-deductible expenses.

FIGURE 14.14

The Tax Schedule report lists all taxable income categories and tax-deductible expense categories summarized by input lines on a tax schedule form.

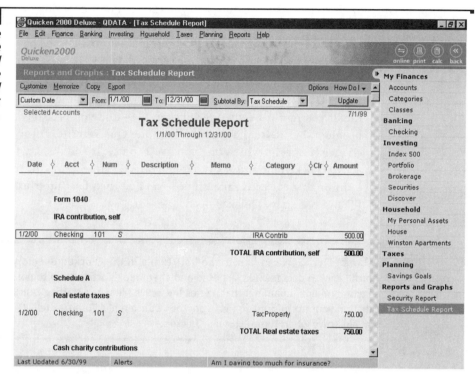

Exporting to a Tax-Preparation Package

Quicken lets you export taxable income and tax-deductible expense information to a tax-preparation program, such as TurboTax or TaxCut. If you've collected accurate taxable income and tax-deductible expense information in Quicken and have decided to use a tax-preparation program, you'll want to consider using the export feature.

TIP As a reader of this book, you're entitled to a free booklet I've written, "The Quicken Users Guide to TurboTax." To get this free booklet, visit the SYBEX Web site at www.sybex.com.

PART

II

Quicken and Your Personal Finances

Exporting to TurboTax

The TurboTax for Windows program is so clever about the way it uses your Quicken data that all you need to do is start TurboTax and tell it you want to import data from Quicken. (If you've installed TurboTax, you can start it by choosing Taxes ➤ TurboTax.) TurboTax then starts Quicken, tells it to create a Tax Schedule report for the appropriate year, and uses the Tax Schedule report information to fill in the open tax return.

There are only two tricks to exporting Quicken data to TurboTax:

- The Quicken file with the tax information you want to use needs to be the active Quicken file, so that when TurboTax starts Quicken, it gets the correct file. If you're using only one Quicken file—and you probably are—this isn't a problem. But if you have more than one Quicken file, TurboTax gives you a chance to specify which one you want to use. It will display the name of the active Quicken file and ask you if it's correct, before it imports the data. You can indicate that the active file isn't correct and then tell TurboTax which Quicken file it should have Quicken open.

 NOTE TurboTax can look at the Q3.DIR file in the Quicken directory to determine which Quicken data file was last used and, therefore, is active. It's also possible to include a command-line parameter that names the active file when starting Quicken. If you indicate that your tax information is in another Quicken file, TurboTax tells Quicken to make that file active when TurboTax starts Quicken.

- Make sure that you use the correct version of TurboTax. If you use the 1999 version of TurboTax, for example, the Tax Schedule report that TurboTax has Quicken produce includes the transaction date range January 1, 1999, through December 31, 1999. Presumably, if you use the 2000 version of TurboTax, the Tax Schedule report that TurboTax has Quicken produce includes the transaction date range January 1, 2000, through December 31, 2000. (I say "presumably" because the 2000 version of TurboTax isn't available as I'm writing this.)

This rigid transaction date-range feature makes perfect sense, of course. Because the tax laws and tax tables change, you can't use the 1999 version of TurboTax to do your 1998 or your 2000 taxes. (You can't, for example, use this automatic importing feature to "guesstimate" what your 1999 income taxes will be using 1999 data and the 1998 version of TurboTax.)

Exporting to Other Tax-Preparation Programs

You can export the information shown in a Tax Schedule report to a Tax Exchange Format, or TXF, file. Almost any tax-preparation program you work with, including TurboTax, will import the data contained in this file and use it to fill in the lines of a tax return.

 NOTE You don't need to first export your Quicken data to a TXF file if you're working with TurboTax. TurboTax will retrieve Quicken data automatically.

To export the information shown in a Tax Schedule report, you first produce the report: Choose Reports ➤ Taxes ➤ Tax Schedule, complete the Create Report dialog box, and click Create. (Figure 14.14, earlier in the chapter, shows a Tax Schedule report.)

Once you've created the Tax Schedule report, take these steps to export the tax schedule information to a TXF file:

1. Click the Export command button on the button bar of the report to display the Create Tax Export File dialog box, as shown in Figure 14.15.

FIGURE 14.15

Name the export file in the Create Tax Export File dialog box.

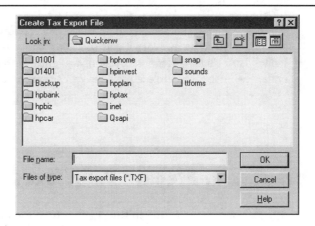

2. Use the File Name text box to name the TXF file. You don't need to specify TXF as the file extension; Quicken adds it for you. If you don't specify a path, Quicken puts the file in the current directory, which is probably the Quicken data directory.

3. If you want to put the file in some other folder, such as the TurboTax folder, use the Look In drop-down list in the dialog box to navigate to the destination folder. Then click OK. Quicken creates the TXF file.

To use the TXF file, import it into the tax-preparation package you'll use to complete your return. Refer to that product's documentation or user's guide for information about how you do this. If you're working with TaxCut, for example, choose File ➢ Import in TaxCut. Then complete the dialog boxes supplied by the tax-preparation program to answer questions about where the TXF file is located.

MASTERING TROUBLESHOOTING

Quicken and Tax-Preparation Programs

You need to be careful when you export Quicken data to a tax-preparation program for a couple of reasons:

- The numbers you enter on your tax form need to match the numbers shown on the W-2, 1099, or 1098 forms that you receive—even if your Quicken reports show different numbers. (If the information on one of these forms is wrong, you need to have the issuer of the information correct the return.)

- To determine which taxable income or tax-deduction transactions should be counted for a particular year, Quicken and the tax-preparation program can look only at the transaction date. If the transaction date shows the income or deduction amount falling in the tax year, it gets counted for that year. This sounds correct, but it often isn't. Usually, some transactions you enter at the very beginning of the calendar year really relate to the previous year's tax return.

Using TurboTax to Prepare Your Taxes

TurboTax, as mentioned earlier in the chapter, is an income tax-preparation program. Because TurboTax is another Intuit program and because many Quicken users will be interested in knowing just a bit more about this program, let's take a closer look at its features and suitability for different situations.

TurboTax is relatively easy to use (although not as easy as Quicken). You can use it in a couple of ways. If you're familiar with what forms you need to fill out to complete your federal and state income tax returns, you can display on-screen forms that mirror the actual forms you file. Using this approach, you just fill in the blanks.

If you're not sure about income tax laws and accounting, you can tell TurboTax you want to be "interviewed." The program will ask you a series of questions that you answer by filling in text boxes and clicking buttons. Based on your answers, TurboTax then fills out your tax return. You can print a copy of your tax return directly from TurboTax, and you can file your federal tax return electronically if you want.

The Benefits of Using TurboTax

Is TurboTax a good product? Yes, it is. In fact, I do my own tax returns with TurboTax, so I really like the program. You benefit in a couple of big ways from using a tax-preparation package. First, being able to print an entire return with TurboTax means never having to worry about whether you have all the right tax forms and schedules. If you need to file a particular form or schedule, TurboTax can print it. (Before Turbo-Tax, I always found myself running over to the local public library or calling the IRS to get some obscure form or schedule I needed.)

 TIP If you have an Internet connection and a Web browser, you can get almost any tax form you need from the IRS Web site: www.irs.ustreas.gov. You can download tax forms in a variety of formats.

A second benefit of TurboTax is that you can easily make changes to your return. For example, when I used to prepare my return manually, I would invariably complete the entire return, think I was finished, and then find a missing deduction or income amount I needed to report. Because of this, I would need to input the new figure and then recalculate a bunch of different figures. With TurboTax, redoing your return for last-minute input is a breeze. You just start up TurboTax, input the new figure, and then tell the program to recalculate the return.

Who Should Use TurboTax?

Does this mean everyone should go out and buy a tax-preparation program? No, I don't think so.

If you pay a tax preparer to do your taxes now, I don't think you can use TurboTax as a substitute for that professional. TurboTax automates and expedites the tax-preparation process, but it still requires you to answer a series of questions having to do with your income taxes.

If you file a really simple return, you probably don't need TurboTax. For example, if you're a single taxpayer with no itemized deductions whose only income is from a job, your taxes are fairly simple in the first place. It wouldn't make sense in your situation to get TurboTax only to have it make a few calculations automatically. You won't actually save any tax-return preparation time, because you'll need to install the program and learn the ropes.

Purchasing TurboTax

You need to buy a new copy of tax-preparation programs such as TurboTax every year because the tax rates and, sometimes, the tax laws change. Unfortunately, tax rate changes and tax law changes don't occur until the very end of the year. For this reason, there are always two versions of tax-preparation programs: an early-bird version that's available late in the year and useful only for making estimates, and a final version that you need to actually prepare and print your return. Early-bird purchasers always get a free upgrade to the final version, but you still need to be aware of the difference between the two versions. You don't, for example, want to purchase an early-bird version on April 15, thinking you'll have time to install the software and then prepare the return.

If you want to purchase a new copy of TurboTax, in Quicken, choose Finance ➢ Quicken On The Web ➢ Quicken Store. From this Web site, you can order Turbo Tax or download the retail version or a free trial of the program. Once you install Turbo-Tax, you can choose Taxes ➢ TurboTax from Quicken to start it.

Using the Tax Planner

Quicken 2000 comes with a handy income tax expense estimator, built by the same people who produce TurboTax. This tool is called the Tax Planner. Based either on inputs you enter directly into a worksheet or on Quicken data, the Tax Planner gives you an accurate estimate of what you'll pay in income taxes for a particular year.

You may want to print a copy of the Tax Schedule report before you estimate your income taxes. To do this, choose Reports ➢ Taxes ➢ Tax Schedule, complete the Create Report dialog box, and click Create. Then click the Print button to print the report.

Estimating Your Income Taxes

To use the Tax Planner, follow these steps:

1. Choose Taxes ➢ Tax Planner. Quicken displays the Quicken Tax Planner dialog box, as shown in Figure 14.16.

FIGURE 14.16

The Quicken Tax
Planner dialog box

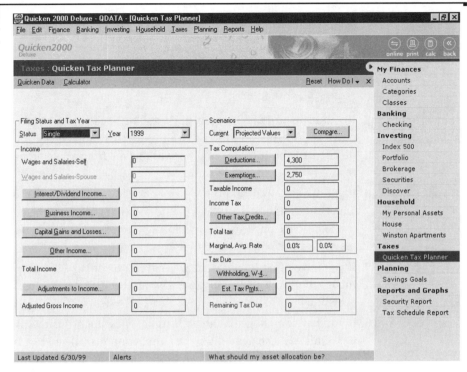

2. Activate the Status drop-down list box and select the appropriate filing status: Single, Married-Joint, Married-Sep, Head of House, or Qual.Widow. (If you have questions about your filing status, refer to the IRS instructions that came with last year's return.)

3. Activate the Year drop-down list and select the year for which you're estimating your income tax expenses. (Picking the right year is important because the tax rate schedules are annually adjusted for things like tax law changes and inflation.)

 NOTE The Scenarios choices in the Tax Planner dialog box let you store up to three sets, or scenarios, of inputs to the Tax Planner and compare them. See the "Comparing Different Income Tax Scenarios" section later in the chapter for more information.

4. Enter your total wages in the Wages and Salaries-Self text box.

PART

II

Quicken and Your
Personal Finances

5. Enter your spouse's total wages (if you're married) in the Wages and Salaries-Spouse text box.

6. If you have interest or dividend income, click the Interest/Dividend Income button. Quicken displays a worksheet dialog box that contains labeled text boxes you use to describe your interest and dividends. Fill in the text boxes and select OK.

7. If you have business income, click the Business Income button. Quicken displays a worksheet dialog box that contains labeled text boxes you use to describe any business income, such as income from a sole proprietorship. Fill in the text boxes and select OK.

8. If you have capital gains or losses, click the Capital Gains and Losses button. Quicken displays a worksheet dialog box that contains labeled text boxes you use to describe any investment capital gains or losses you've realized. Fill in the text boxes and select OK.

9. If you have other income that you haven't recorded elsewhere, click the Other Income button. Quicken displays a worksheet dialog box. Use it to describe this other income.

10. If you have any adjustments to income, click the Adjustments to Income button. Quicken displays a dialog box that contains labeled text boxes you use to describe any adjustments, such as IRA or Keogh contributions, alimony payments, self-employment deductions, and early withdrawal penalties. Fill in the text boxes and select OK.

11. Click the Deductions button. Quicken displays a worksheet dialog box you use to estimate your itemized deductions. Fill in the text boxes and select OK. (Quicken uses the larger of your total itemized deductions or the standard deduction.)

Quicken 2000 now comes with an Itemized Deduction Estimator, which you can use to figure out how to maximize your deductions and to see the effects deductions have on your tax bill. To start the Itemized Deduction Estimator, choose Taxes ➤ Tax Activities ➤ How Can I Maximize My Deductions? To navigate through the Itemized Deduction Estimator, click hyperlinks in the far-left frame to display forms in the middle frame, which you can use to enter data. The Tax Projection Data frame on the right shows how your tax liabilities change with the deductions you take.

12. Click the Exemptions button. Quicken displays a worksheet dialog box you use to specify the number of exemptions you're entitled to claim. Fill in the Dependents text box provided and select OK.

13. If you pay other federal taxes or are entitled to claim any income tax credits, click the Other Tax Credits button. Quicken displays a worksheet dialog box you use to specify any other taxes you pay, such as self-employment income tax, or any income tax credits. Fill in the text boxes and select OK.

With the information you provide in steps 2 through 13, the Tax Planner estimates your total federal tax bill and also calculates both your marginal income tax rate and your average income tax rate.

 TIP Your marginal income tax rate is a useful piece of information. It allows you to convert pre-tax investment yields and interest rates to after-tax investment yields and interest rates. All you do is multiply the pre-tax rate by 1 minus the marginal income tax rate. For example, to convert a 10 percent pre-tax rate to an after-tax rate if the marginal tax rate is 28 percent, make the following calculation: 10 percent x (1 – 28 percent). This formula returns 7.2 percent.

---

14. Click the Withholding, W-4 button. Quicken displays a worksheet dialog box you use to describe the federal income taxes you (and your spouse if you're married) have already had withheld and how much you'll probably have withheld over the remaining payroll periods in the year. Fill in the text boxes and select OK.

 Quicken 2000 comes with a Tax Withholding Estimator that you can use to project your tax bill and find out if you are under-withholding or over-withholding. If your withholding is too high or low, Quicken's Alerts can also notify you of this. To use the Tax Withholding Estimator, choose Taxes ➢ Tax Activities ➢ Am I Under Or Over Withholding? To navigate through the Tax Withholding Estimator, click hyperlinks in the far-left frame to display forms in the middle frame, which you can use to enter data. The Tax Projection Data frame on the right shows how your year-end tax situation changes when you withhold different amounts.

15. Click the Est. Tax Pmts button. Quicken displays a worksheet dialog box you use to describe any estimated taxes you (and your spouse if you're married) have made and will make. Fill in the text boxes and select OK.

With the completion of steps 14 and 15, the Tax Planner calculates the remaining federal taxes you'll still owe at the end of the year after all your estimated withholding and any estimated income taxes.

To print a summary of the tax-planning calculations, click the Print button. Quicken displays a Print dialog box, which mirrors the Print dialog boxes you use to print reports.

If you've printed a report or two—presumably you have by this point—you'll have no trouble completing the Tax Planner's version. (See Chapter 4 if you need more information about printing reports.)

Click the Calc button to display Quicken's calculator. You can use this to make quick calculations for your income tax estimating. You can also use the Ctrl+C and Ctrl+V commands to copy and paste values to and from the calculator and the Tax Planner.

To remove the Quicken Tax Planner dialog box and at the same time save your inputs, click the close button. To erase your inputs in the Quicken Tax Planner dialog box, click the Reset button.

Using Tax Data from Account Registers

In general, the best way to approach the tax-planning process is by entering values directly into the Tax Planner's text boxes and worksheets. You have another choice, however. If you are using categories that connect to specific lines in your tax return, as described earlier in the chapter, you can tell Quicken it should instead use the data from your account registers. To do this, click the Quicken Import button in the Tax Planner. Quicken then looks through your registers, collects and tallies any transactions that should go into one of the Tax Planner text boxes or into a worksheet, and lists these transactions.

 WARNING If there are Tax Planner text boxes and worksheets that are not filled in when you tell the Tax Planner to use account register data—perhaps you haven't yet entered the taxable income or tax-deduction information in a register—you'll need to fill in these inputs manually. See the steps in the previous section, "Estimating Your Income Taxes."

 If you don't track all of your finances in Quicken but use TurboTax to prepare your taxes, you can import your tax data directly from TurboTax so that your tax plans are more accurate. To do this, choose Taxes ➢ Tax Activities ➢ Import Personal Profile From TurboTax. Then use the Import TurboTax File dialog box to locate your Turbo-Tax file.

Comparing Different Income Tax Scenarios

You can store as many as four sets of inputs in the Tax Planner: the projected values set and then three alternative scenarios: Scenario 1, Scenario 2, and Scenario 3. Typically, you first create a projected-values case scenario. You can create alternative first, second, and third scenarios by selected the appropriate scenario from the Scenarios box. When you select Scenario 1, 2, or 3, Quicken asks if you want to copy the current inputs as a starting point for the new scenario. If you want to do this—and you probably do—click Yes.

You can compare the inputs and the income tax calculations for your four scenarios by clicking the Compare button. Quicken displays a dialog box that summarizes the filing status, tax year, adjusted gross income, deductions and exemptions, taxable income, total tax, and tax rates for each scenario.

Estimating Capital Gains Taxes

You can use Quicken's Capital Gains Estimator to estimate the capital gains taxes you'll owe for investments you sell. In order to use the Capital Gains Estimator, you must have an investment account set up in Quicken. To start the Capital Gains Estimator, choose Taxes ➢ Other Tax Activities ➢ Capital Gains Estimator. To add securities to the Proposed Sales plan, select the securities you're considering selling. If you don't want to select specific lots, select the security in the Current Holdings Excluding Tax-Deferred Accounts pane, then click Add. In the Add to Scenario dialog box, enter the number of shares you'll sell and the sale price you expect to receive for them. Quicken assumes you'll sell the oldest shares first. If you want to select specific lots, select the folder icon next to the security in the Current Holdings Excluding Tax-Deferred Accounts pane to display the individual lots. Select the lot(s) you want to sell and click Add.

 NOTE Click the Rates button to specify your long- and short-term capital gains tax rate. Click Current Prices to reset the sale price to its current value as last recorded or downloaded. The bottom of the Proposed Sales pane displays the effects of your proposed sales on your capital gains taxes, as well as displaying the net gain from the sale. You can use the other Scenario tabs to set up other sale scenarios. The Capital Gains Estimator cannot estimate the tax deductions for capital losses. It alerts you to losses by displaying the words LT Loss or ST loss in the Approx. Tax column for the security.

Finding Tax Deductions

A feature in Quicken Deluxe helps you to find tax deductions that you may have missed in your planning and also checks your eligibility for the deductions. Choose Taxes ➤ Deduction Finder, and the Introduction to Deduction Finder dialog box appears. Click OK to move to the window shown in Figure 14.17.

You begin by choosing a Deduction Type in the drop-down list box, then clicking a possible deduction in the Choose a Deduction list. Answer the Yes or No questions in the third section by clicking the appropriate checkboxes. When you answer all of the questions, the Deduction Finder tells you whether or not you may be eligible for that particular deduction.

 WARNING After you have consulted the Deduction Finder, be sure to talk over the information with your tax advisor before making any final decisions.

The Deduction Finder also keeps track of the deductions you have tried and develops an Action Plan for you, based on the results. Click the Summary and Action Plan tabs to see the Deduction Finder's records.

FIGURE 14.17

Quicken can help you find tax deductions.

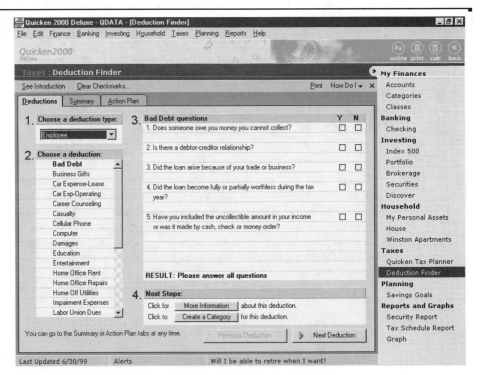

Reviewing Quicken's Other Tax Tools

At this point, this chapter has described the most important and commonly used tax features of Quicken. However, as even a quick review of the Tax menu will indicate, Quicken provides several other noteworthy tax tools. There isn't space here to describe each of these other tools in detail, but before I move on to a discussion of how you solve common tax and tax-preparation problems, let me quickly review these other features:

Tax Center The Tax Center command displays Quicken's Tax Activity Center. It provides hyperlinks to other tax-planning tools, tax-related articles, and even reports and charts that summarize your current tax sitation. It's probably well worth your time to spend a few minutes exploring this self-explanatory activity center.

Tax Link Assistant The Tax Link Assistant displays a dialog box you can use to tell Quicken which categories belong with which tax form lines. You might use this feature if you didn't provide tax form and line number information when you set up a category and want to directly export Quicken information to TurboTax. However, as we discuss in the next section of this chapter, "Common Tax-Preparation Problems and Solutions," directly exporting from Quicken to TurboTax opens up a can of worms.

Tax Profile The Tax Profile command displays a form you use to provide tax-payer information about yourself, including your filing status. If you let it, Quicken collects and then uses this information to make tax-planning suggestions and to initially fill out the Tax Planner dialog box, which is described earlier in this chapter. Note that Quicken builds a tax profile for you as you work with the program based on the way you use the program and the way you set it up.

WebTurboTax and TurboTax The Web TurboTax and TurboTax commands let you access either the Web version of TurboTax, which is of course called WebTurboTax, or the regular version of TurboTax.

Tax Activities The Tax Activities command displays submenu of 10 additional commands that amount to a grab bag of tax planning tools. The Tax Activities submenu supplies commands for downloading a free, trial version of TurboTax, for accessing a capital-gains estimator, for comparing the yields of taxable and tax-exempt investments, and so on.

Common Tax-Preparation Problems and Solutions

There are some potential pitfalls to using your Quicken data as the one and only source of all your taxable income and tax-deductible expense information. This doesn't mean you shouldn't use Quicken; it just means that you need to be careful—you can't blindly automate the process.

Discrepancies between Your Records and Informational Returns

When the IRS processes your return, one of the things the processors will do is verify that any informational returns they've received match up with your return. They will compare the W-2 information provided by your employer (or employers) with what you enter on the "Wages, Salaries, Tips, etc." line, and they will compare the 1099-INT and 1099-OID statements provided by almost anyone who has paid you interest with what you enter on your 1040 or Schedule B. (Schedule B summarizes your dividend and interest income when you have more substantial amounts of either.)

Any difference between what one of these informational returns shows and what you enter on a line of a tax schedule of your income tax return will almost certainly trigger a review of your return. In this case, the IRS will write you a letter asking for an explanation of the discrepancy. You'll then need to review your records to determine whether your return's number was the correct one or—and this is probably more likely—the informational return's number was the correct one. Then you'll need to fix the mistake.

This sequence of events points out a potential trouble spot. You can use Quicken to collect your taxable income and, in some cases, your tax-deductible expense information. But it may just be that there's another, more accurate source of the taxable income or tax-deductible expense numbers you need to enter on your tax return. When this is the case, it makes the most sense to use this other source for preparing your tax return. And even if you do record the information provided by this other source into Quicken, you may make an error entering the data.

For this reason, it's easiest and most accurate to get your salaries and wages information from employer-provided W-2s and to get interest and dividend information from the 1099 informational returns your broker or bank prepares.

Timing Differences

Another opportunity for error concerns timing differences. You may be required to report some item of income or deduct some expense in one year, although you did not record the information into a Quicken register until a subsequent year. For example, if you're a partner in a business, you may be required to include in your taxable income a share of partnership profits earned in one year but paid in the following year. Or if you've invested in a long-term certificate of deposit, you may be required to report any accrued interest for the year as income. (The CD issuer may send you a 1099-OID statement of your interest earnings.)

To use Quicken to keep records of taxable income and tax-deductible expenses like this, you need to use a transaction date that places the transaction in the year that the transaction affects taxable income or tax-deductible expenses, which won't necessarily be the same year you make a deposit or write a check.

What to Do If You Get Audited

Although your chances of being audited are probably remote, some of the people who read this chapter will be audited. Here are some things you should do—and shouldn't do—if you get audited.

Quicken Tasks You Should Complete

The Quicken Tax Summary report lists and tallies each of the taxable and tax-deductible transactions included on your return. Since the audit will probably consist of the agent reviewing these transactions and deductions, you'll want to have a listing of the transactions. A Tax Summary report gives this information.

If you know beforehand that a specific tax deduction is being questioned, be sure to bring all the source documents that evidence the pertinent transactions. For example, if the IRS is questioning your charitable contributions deduction, bring any canceled checks you used to make your contributions.

 WARNING Don't bring a laptop computer with Quicken to the audit. The IRS agent may appreciate your enthusiasm, but remember that your Quicken file largely summarizes your financial life. And Quicken's reports make it easy for the agent to quickly review every nook and cranny, searching for income you may have missed or deductions you shouldn't have taken.

Other Audit Preparation Tasks

There are a couple of other things you should be sure to do before you attend the audit:

- Make sure that you understand all the numbers on your return, and remember that you signed it under penalty of perjury.

- You may want to consider asking your tax preparer to represent you at the audit. There are a variety of reasons for doing this. If you don't understand your return but your preparer does, it makes sense to have the preparer at the audit.

 NOTE Sometimes, it also makes more sense to have a tax preparer represent you because he or she knows (or should know) quite a lot about the income tax laws but relatively little about your financial life. I know a tax attorney who follows this approach because the tax preparer can honestly answer many IRS questions by saying, "I don't know." The tax attorney feels that the "I don't knows" tend to terminate many spontaneous inquiries.

Things to Do during the Audit

An audit doesn't have to be a bad experience. All that really happens is that the IRS agent will ask you to explain and document items that the IRS doesn't understand.

Nevertheless, let me provide you with two final suggestions. First, if the agent identifies himself or herself as a special agent, ask to terminate the interview so you can reschedule it. A special agent investigates criminal tax code violations, so you'll probably want a tax attorney present at any meetings.

Another thing I suggest is that you be very reserved in your comments. Don't lie, of course, but don't volunteer extra information. If you have questions about some deduction or how to treat some income item, ask a tax preparer or telephone the IRS's taxpayer assistance line, but don't expect the IRS agent auditing your return to answer tax-preparation questions. (My feeling is that there's a very strong tendency for the auditor to look only for things that increase your income tax bill and not for things that decrease your bill.)

MASTERING FINANCIAL SUCCESS

How to Plan for and Save on Taxes

Understanding the conceptual framework of the federal income tax codes can help when you plan for and prepare your taxes. Also, understanding the significance of marginal income tax rates is important when you're working on personal finance planning issues. So let's look at each of these topics in turn.

Federal Income Taxes

Essentially, the federal income tax forms take you through the following formulas when you calculate your taxable income:

adjusted gross income = total income – adjustments

taxable income = adjusted gross income – the standard deduction amount or itemized deductions – personal exemptions

Total Income

Your *total income* includes wages, salaries, interest and dividend income, capital gains, and gambling winnings. In other words, it includes just about anything you receive that has value. Exceptions include tax-exempt interest income on state and local government obligations, insurance proceeds, and gifts from others.

The IRS allows certain adjustments to total income. One of the most popular is the individual retirement account (IRA) deduction. IRAs let you save money for retirement and not count the money you've saved as part of your total income. Other examples of adjustments (all of which are shown on the 1040 form) include alimony and penalties on early withdrawal of savings.

Adjusted Gross Income

Finding your *adjusted gross income* is an intermediate but important step in calculating your income taxes. Several itemized deductions for personal expenses, such as medical expenses, are allowed, but only to the extent that they exceed a certain percentage of your adjusted gross income. You either take the standard deduction or subtract the total of your itemized deductions from your adjusted gross income.

Most people don't itemize. It's easier to simply take the standard deduction because itemizing requires you to add up several categories of personal expenses, including home mortgage interest, state and local property taxes, state income tax, charitable

Continued

MASTERING FINANCIAL SUCCESS CONTINUED

contributions, and other expenses. The income tax forms are relatively straightforward in explaining what to enter on each line, but you need to read the instructions carefully because the rules for itemized deductions have become more complex in the past few years. What's more, if you have an adjusted gross income that's above $100,000 or so, you may not be able to take all the deductions you want.

Personal Exemptions

To arrive at your taxable income, you subtract what are called personal exemptions from your adjusted gross income. You get one personal exemption of roughly $2,700 for each person in your family during the tax year, as long as your adjusted gross income doesn't exceed roughly $125,000 if you're filing single, $155,000 if you're filing head of household, $187,000 if you're married filing jointly, and $93,000 if you're married filing single. These are rough amounts rounded to the nearest thousand, and the $2,700 personal exemption figure is adjusted annually for inflation. If your adjusted gross income does exceed the limits just mentioned, you lose some portion of your personal exemptions.

Calculating What You Owe

To calculate the taxes on your taxable income, you multiply the taxable income by the tax rates. It's a little tricky because different rates apply to different parts of your income. For example, you might pay a 15 percent tax on one part of your income, a 28 percent tax on another, and 31 percent tax on still another part. For example, a married couple with $50,000 of taxable income would pay a 15 percent income tax on the first roughly $40,000 of income and a 28 percent tax on the remaining income.

To calculate the actual income taxes you are required to pay on your taxable income and the amount of the additional payment you'll make or the refund you'll get, use the following formula:

tax before credits = taxable income × tax rates

The tax before credits minus the tax credits equals your total income tax bill. From your total bill, you subtract withholding and estimated tax payments to arrive at a refund if the result is negative or a payment if the result is positive.

Currently, five income tax rates are in effect: 15, 28, 31, 36, and 39.6 percent. In recent years, however, Congress has continued to add more and more rates, and this trend might continue. One other tricky point is that the parts of your income to which the

Continued

MASTERING FINANCIAL SUCCESS CONTINUED

rates apply aren't the same for everybody. Any of five breakdowns might apply to your situation, depending on the following:

- If you're a widow or widower
- If you have dependents
- If you're married or single
- If you're married, and you and your spouse file a combined, or joint, return
- If you're married, and you and your spouse file separate returns

Five different tax rate schedules show which dollars are taxed at which rates; each schedule corresponds to a filing status, as listed above.

Tax Credits

After you calculate the taxes you owe by using the tax rates, you calculate your tax credits. *Tax credits* are reductions in the amount of your income taxes. Tax credits include the earned income credit, the child-care and dependent-care credit, and the HOPE and Lifetime Learning credit.

 NOTE Don't confuse tax credits with tax deductions. Both reduce the taxes you pay, but credits are more powerful. Deductions reduce only your taxable income; tax credits reduce the amount of taxes you pay.

After subtracting any tax credits from the taxes on your taxable income, you arrive at the actual income taxes you owe. If this amount is more than you paid or withheld over the year, you pay the government additional money. If the amount is less than you paid or withheld, you get a refund. (Generally, income taxes are paid throughout the year, either when your employer withholds an amount and passes it along to the IRS or when you make quarterly estimated income tax payments.)

That, in a nutshell, is how the personal federal income tax calculations and laws work. Actually, the mathematics isn't very difficult. But a lot of little nuances and subtleties exist.

Continued

PART

II

**Quicken and Your
Personal Finances**

MASTERING FINANCIAL SUCCESS CONTINUED

Alternative Minimum Tax

As you plan for and prepare your federal income tax return, you need to be aware of the alternative minimum tax. This tax is reached by yet another set of rules and methods for income calculation. If you have what the tax laws describe as "tax-preference items," such as accelerated depreciation deductions on rental property or tax-exempt interest on private-purpose municipal bonds, you need to calculate the alternative minimum taxes you owe. You pay whichever is more: the taxes you owe using the regular income tax rules or the taxes you owe using the alternative minimum tax rules. If you think you might be subject to alternative minimum taxes, confer with a tax accountant or a tax attorney.

Marginal Income Tax Rates

Personal financial planning professionals and investment advisors talk a lot about marginal income tax rates. These rates are very important, so you'll benefit by understanding what marginal income tax rates are.

Marginal income tax rates let you calculate the income that you either pay or save as a result of changes in your income or changes in your income tax deductions. For example, suppose that you're considering buying a home and the mortgage interest you will pay will increase your itemized deductions by $10,000. To calculate the effect of this additional income tax deduction, you need to know the difference the deduction will make in your taxable income and, therefore, in your income taxes. Before you start thinking that marginal income tax rates are too messy to worry about, let's look at a quick example. After you see an example, the logic and arithmetic of marginal tax rates should be clearer to you.

If you were single in 1999, you paid income taxes of 15 percent on the first $25,750 of your taxable income, 28 percent on income over $25,750 but not over $62,450, 31 percent on income over $62,450 but not over $130,250, 36 percent on the income over $130,250 but not over $283,150, and 39.6 percent on income over $283,150. As explained earlier, different tax rates and brackets apply to different people. I'm using the single status to provide the simplest example, but the basic logic is the same for each filing status.

What happens if you're single and your taxable income is $50,000? Suppose you're considering a mortgage that will add $10,000 to your itemized deductions. In this case, taking on the mortgage will reduce your taxable income from $50,000 to $40,000.

Continued ▐▶

MASTERING FINANCIAL SUCCESS CONTINUED

Because all those dollars are taxed at a marginal rate of 15 percent (everything between $25,750 and $64,450 is taxed at 28 percent), you can calculate the tax savings you'll enjoy by multiplying the marginal tax rate of 28 percent by the change in your taxable income of $10,000. The result is $2,800, so $2,800 is the income tax amount you will save.

Let's look at another quick example: Suppose you're single, your taxable income is $150,000, and you're considering putting $10,000 in a tax-deductible retirement plan such as a SEP/IRA. (A SEP/IRA is a special type of individual retirement account for employees of small businesses.) By identifying the marginal income tax rate—36 percent in this example—you can tell what amount of income taxes you'll save by making this contribution. In this example, the tax savings can be calculated as 36 percent times $10,000 (0.36 × 10,000), which equals $3,600 of savings.

CHAPTER **15**

Planning Your Personal Finances

Quicken's record-keeping abilities are fabulous. In fact, that's probably the reason Quicken is so popular. But personal financial success requires more than just good record keeping. You need to intelligently monitor and plan your personal finances. This chapter describes the tools that Quicken provides to help you plan.

 NOTE To use most of the planning tools described in this chapter, you must have the Deluxe, Home & Business, or Suite version of Quicken 2000. Most of the planners are not available in Quicken Basic 2000.

Setting Savings Goals

Quicken lets you set savings goal amounts, calculate the periodic saving required to reach the goal, and track your progress toward the goal. While you don't need to use Quicken to achieve your savings goals, it can make the whole process much easier (by quantifying exactly what you need to do) and increase your chances of success (by focusing attention on your progress).

Creating a Savings Goal

To create a savings goal, choose Planning ➤ Savings Goals. Quicken displays the Savings Goals area. The window won't list any savings goals because you have not yet described any. To set up a goal, click the New command button. Quicken displays the Create New Savings Goal dialog box.

 NOTE If you don't find the Savings Goals item on your Planning menu, this planner is not implemented in your version of Quicken.

Describe your savings goal by filling in the text boxes in the Create New Savings Goal dialog box. Enter a name for the goal (perhaps the item you're saving for) in the Goal Name text box. In the Goal Amount text box, enter the amount you want to accumulate. Using the Finish Date combo box, give the date by which you want to reach your goal. Figure 15.1 shows an example. When you enter your information and click OK, Quicken returns you to the Savings Goals area, which now lists the goal you described. Figure 15.2 shows an example.

FIGURE 15.1

The Create New
Savings Goal
dialog box

In the box in the top half of the Savings Goals area, Quicken lists each of the savings goals you've described. (In Figure 15.2, the list shows only one goal: European Vacation.) In the box in the bottom half of the Savings Goals area, Quicken draws a bar chart that depicts your progress toward the goal. (In Figure 15.2, the bar doesn't appear because zero progress has been made toward the goal.)

At the bottom of the Savings Goals area, a number appears ($384.61 in Figure 15.2). This is the monthly amount you need to save in order to reach your goal by the finish date. Quicken calculates this figure by dividing the savings goal amount by the number of payments. (Quicken assumes that you won't earn any interest on your savings.

FIGURE 15.2.

The Savings Goals
area lists your
savings goals.

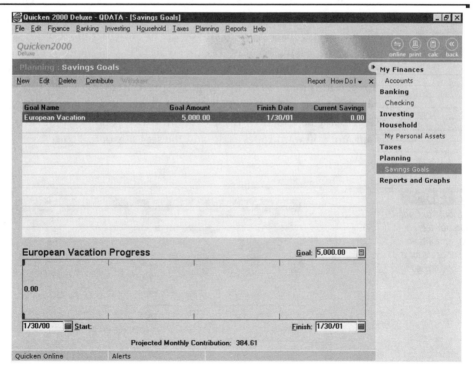

PART

II

Quicken and Your
Personal Finances

From the Savings Goals area, you can take the following actions:

- You can print your savings goals by choosing File ➣ Print Goal.
- By clicking Report, you can get a printable report that shows your progress toward your goals.
- You can change a savings goal's description by selecting the goal and clicking Edit. In the Edit Savings Goals dialog box, you can change the goal amount or finish date.

 NOTE The Planning Center includes a Special Purpose Planner wizard that helps you strategize about how you might save more money or save money more easily. To start this planning wizard, choose Planning ➣ Special Purpose Planner. Then follow the onscreen instructions.

Saving Money toward a Goal

Using a savings goal is easy. When you set up a savings goal, what Quicken actually does is create a special type of account called a savings goal account. This account works like a separate compartment you use to earmark funds you've stored in, say, your regular checking account. In other words, you might have $1,000 in your checking account, but $384.61 of this money may be earmarked for a savings goal.

To set aside money for a savings goal, open the Savings Goals area and click Contribute. (Quicken assumes that all contributions will be monthly.) In the Contribute to Goal dialog box, identify the account in which you'll set aside savings goal money, the amount you want to set aside, and the set-aside date. Figure 15.3 shows an example.

FIGURE 15.3

The Contribute to Goal dialog box lets you describe amounts you want to set aside for a savings goal.

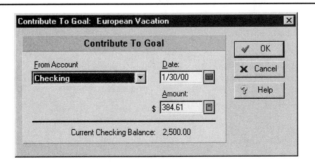

The transaction will appear as a transfer in the register of whatever account you have chosen. The money will remain in the account but will not be shown in your balance figure. Figure 15.4 shows a transaction recording a transfer to the European Vacation account.

NOTE Savings goal transactions don't have any effect on bank account reconciliations. When you reconcile a bank account with savings goal transactions, Quicken hides all the savings goal transactions.

Deleting a Savings Goal

To delete a savings goal, display the Savings Goals area (choose Features ➢ Planning ➢ Savings Goals), select the goal, and click Delete.

Quicken returns the money to the source account and asks what to do with the account it created for the savings goal. You can tell Quicken to delete the account or to save the account. You might want to save the account, for example, if you really did purchase the item you were saving for and now you want to keep the account for tracking the appreciation or depreciation of that item (Quicken creates an asset account for the item).

NOTE The Planning Center also includes a Save More Planner wizard that helps you strategize about how you might save more money or save money more easily. To start this planning wizard, choose Planning ➢ Save More Planner. To use this simple wizard, just follow the onscreen instructions. Note, though, that if you postpone using this wizard until after you've been using Quicken for a bit, the wizard will base some of its suggestions on actual data.

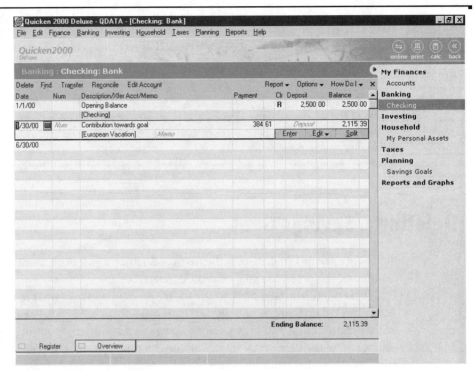

Category Groups for Closely Monitoring Finances

Category Groups are just groups of categories you want to monitor especially closely. A family that's closely monitoring its finances and cash flow might want to track its discretionary spending. A business with several sources of income might want to track its monthly revenue. You can perform this kind of monitoring by using Category Groups.

Creating a Category Group

To create a Category Group, display the Category & Transfer List by choosing Finance ➢ Category & Transfer List. Then choose Options ➢ Assign Category Groups to open the Assign Category Groups dialog box, as shown in Figure 15.5.

PART

II

Quicken and Your
Personal Finances

FIGURE 15.5

*The Assign Category
Groups dialog box lets
you create groups of
categories to monitor.*

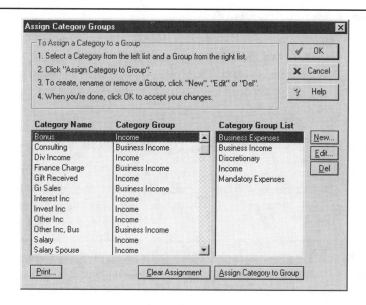

In this dialog box, click the New button. When Quicken prompts you with the Create Category Group dialog box, enter a name and click OK.

To assign categories to a Category Group, follow these steps:

1. Select the categories you want to place into a Category Group by clicking each one. To select more than one category at a time, hold down the Ctrl key as you click the categories.

2. Select the Category Group you want to use to tally and track these categories.

3. Click the Assign Category to Group button.

4. Click OK.

Monitoring a Category Group

Quicken lets you summarize your financial data by category groups. Chapter 4, "Tracking Your Finances with Reports," describes how you prepare reports. Quicken also lets you budget by categories, as described in the next section of this chapter, "Setting Up A Budget."

Setting Up a Budget

There's a lot written about budgeting, and most of the advice isn't all that bad—although it may not be too insightful. Mostly, the process is mechanical. You sit down, look at what you'll make, and then come up with a plan for spending the money that meets your needs.

Two Tricks for Successful Budgeting

You can read an entire book about budgeting, but I'm assuming you would prefer some quick tips on how to use budgets and budgeting to make it easier to manage your personal financial affairs, as described in the following sections.

 NOTE Much of the information discussed at the end of this chapter, "How to Achieve Financial Independence," directly relates to personal budgeting.

Start with a Categorized Report

You need to start some place, and the best place is with an itemized list of what you've already been making and spending. In fact, it's probably most accurate to start by planning to spend in the future what you've been spending in the past.

If you've already been tracking your income and spending with Quicken, you can print an itemized category report to get the information you need.

 TIP If you can, look at an entire year's income and spending. It's too easy for an individual month's category total to be significantly higher or lower than average—for example, if you've been paid for a lot of overtime or if you pay more for heating costs in the winter.

Don't Plan to Spend Every Dollar You Make

One of the bigger mistakes you can make in your budgeting is to plan how you'll spend every dollar that you'll make. Two problems exist with this approach:

- You probably will have some unexpected expenses during the year—the water pump on your car may need to be replaced, or you may have some unexpected medical expenses not covered by insurance.

- You probably will find some new ways you want to spend money during the year. You might see something six months from now that you need or want: chairs for summer nights in the backyard or perhaps even a book about Quicken.

If you leave yourself some extra money to pay for these things, they don't have to be financial emergencies. To do this, you might want to set up an Unbudgeted Expenses or Miscellaneous Emergencies category to track and tally just these sorts of expenditures. Then you'll be able to take the extra $150 needed for the car repair out of the Unbudgeted Expenses category.

Using a Budgeting Spreadsheet

Once you've figured out or estimated what you'll make and what you'll want to spend, you can record this information in Quicken in a budgeting spreadsheet. In fact, since Quicken will do a lot of the math for you, you may want to use this budgeting spreadsheet as a tool for building your budget.

 TIP When you tell Quicken that you want to create your first budget, the program grabs all of your Quicken data and enters it in the budget so that you can use this data as your starting point. So it makes sense to have all of your accounts up to date before you begin budgeting.

To get to the Quicken budgeting spreadsheet so you can begin entering your budget, choose Planning ➢ Budgeting. Quicken displays the Budget area, as shown in Figure 15.6. You'll use this area to describe the income and expense you plan by category group or by category.

 NOTE To indicate whether you want to budget by category or category group, you click the Options button and then choose the Show Category Groups command. This command works like a toggle switch you turn on and off by choosing the command. When the switch is on—Quicken indicates this by placing a checkmark in front of the command—Quicken shows category groups in the Budget area. When the switch is off, Quicken doesn't.

FIGURE 15.6

The Budget area

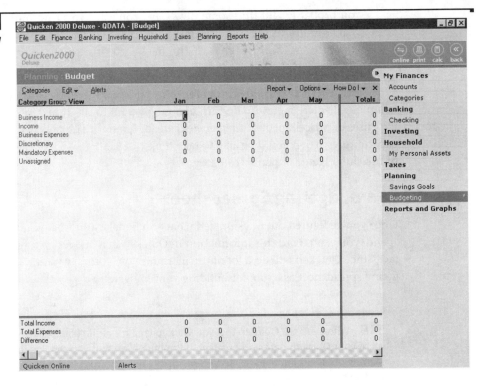

Entering Income and Expense Budget Data

As you can see from Figure 15.6, the budgeting spreadsheet presents each month's data in a separate column. It uses a separate row for each income category and each expense category. The budgeting spreadsheet also includes subtotals for income and expenses and the difference between the total income and expenses.

 TIP Use the horizontal and vertical scroll bars to move left and right and up and down in the spreadsheet if you can't see all the columns or rows.

The simplest way to enter a monthly income or expense budget amount is to highlight the area where you want to place the amount and type the number. To budget the January Income as $3,000, for example, highlight the January Income amount and type **3000**. When you move to the next field, Quicken updates the January Total Income amount and the Difference amount.

If you want to budget by income and expense subcategories, click the category name or the folder icon that appears in front of the category name. Quicken displays any subcategories in that category. You can click the category name or button again to indicate that you don't want to budget these subcategories.

For a more sophisticated budget presentation, use the features that become available when you click the Options button on the Budget button bar. Choosing that command opens the following menu:

If you want to see your Category Groups, choose Show Category Groups. The next time you click the Options button, Quicken places a check next to it to tell you that the Show Category Groups option is on.

To hide any unused budget categories or other categories with zero balances, click Categories to open the Select Categories to Include dialog box. Uncheck the categories you don't want, and then click OK. This will improve the clarity of your reports and make your screens easier to read.

Budgeting by the Quarter or by the Year

Normally, you'll want to budget on a monthly basis, but you can also budget by the quarter or by the year. To indicate which time period you want to budget, click the Options button in the Budget area and choose Display Months, Display Quarters, or Display Current Year. Quicken reconfigures the columns for the new budgeting time periods and also converts the existing budget data. If you switch from monthly budgeting to quarterly budgeting, for example, Quicken creates quarterly budget amounts from the monthly data you've already entered. January, February, and March, for example, are rolled together into the first-quarter budget amount.

Budgeting Biweekly Expenses

If an income or expense item doesn't fit neatly into monthly, quarterly, or annual time periods, you can budget the item by two-week intervals. You tell Quicken the biweekly amount, and Quicken calculates how much of the income or expense item goes into each budgeting period.

For example, if you get paid biweekly, you can budget your payroll checks as coming every two weeks. Quicken then calculates how many payroll checks you receive each month. In months with more than 28 days, you'll occasionally receive three paychecks.

To budget biweekly expenses, select the Income or Expense category in the Budget area and click the Edit command button. From the menu that opens, choose the command 2-Week. Quicken displays the Set Up Two-Week Budget dialog box, as shown in Figure 15.7.

FIGURE 15.7

The Set Up Two-Week Budget dialog box

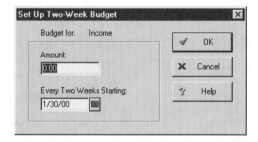

Enter the biweekly amount in the Amount text box. Then enter the date of the first day you receive the biweekly income item or you pay the biweekly expense item and click OK.

Data-Entry Tricks

You can reach several helpful data-entry commands from the menu that opens when you select the Budget area's Edit command button. These commands let you copy, fill, and clear entries rapidly.

You can copy the budgeted amount for one budgeting period's income or expense category into future periods using the Fill Row Right command. To use this command, select the budgeted income or expense amount you want to use for the budgeting periods that follow. Then click Edit and select Fill Row Right. To copy the January Salary Income amount into each of the months that follow, for example, select the January Salary Income amount, click Edit, and select Fill Row Right.

You can copy an entire period's budgeted income or expense category amounts into future periods using the Fill Columns command. To do this, select a budgeted income or expense amount in the budgeting period column you want to copy, click Edit, and select Fill Columns. To copy the July budget into each of the months that follow, for example, select a budget amount in the July column, click Edit, and select Fill Columns.

The Copy All command lets you copy material you have highlighted to the Windows Clipboard. From there, you can paste it into another program, such as a spreadsheet.

The Clear Row command removes all entries from the row containing the highlight. Clear All removes every entry from the entire Budget area, leaving you with a clean slate.

Building a Budget with Last Year's Data

It's often a good idea to use last year's actual income and expense information as a budget or as the starting point for a budget.

To use the previous year's income and expense category information to build your budget, click the Edit command button and then choose the Autocreate command to display the Automatically Create Budget dialog box.

Use the From and To date text boxes to indicate the months in the previous year from which data should be retrieved. For example, to get the entire previous year's income and expense data if it's now 2000, type **1/99** in the From text box and **12/99** in the To text box.

Use the Round Values to Nearest drop-down list box to tell Quicken how to round off the budgeted amounts created using the actual data: to the nearest dollar, to the nearest ten dollars, or to the nearest hundred dollars. You can use this approach, for example, to copy last year's actual category information for July and use it as this year's July budget.

The Use Monthly Detail option button will tell Quicken to copy the indicated budget month by month, category by category. If your budgeted amounts have changed on a monthly basis (say, allowing for higher heating costs during the winter months), you might use this option. However, if you click the Use Average for Period option button, Quicken fills each of the budgeting periods for the year with the previous year's average amounts for the periods you specified in the From and To text boxes. For example, if you based the budget on 1999, the budget entry for Groceries would be the average of grocery expenses for all 12 months in 1999.

Figure 15.8 shows an example of a filled-in Automatically Create Budget dialog box.

FIGURE 15.8

*The Automatically
Create Budget
dialog box*

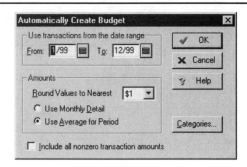

Saving Your Budget

Choose Options ➢ Save Budget to save your budget entries to a file on your computer's hard disk. The Close button (marked with an *X* in the upper-right corner of
the window) does the same thing, but it also closes the Budget area.

Working with More Than One Budget

In Quicken, you can work with more than one budget. You might do this, for example, if you're performing a what-if analysis and having two separate budgets helps you
explore the ramifications of your decisions. You might also have more than one budget to assess the effect of a major change in your financial affairs. For example, if you
are moving to a new home, if your spouse is going back to work, or if you are tem-
porarily unemployed, you might create two budgets.

To create multiple budgets, click Options ➢ Other Budgets to open the Manage
Budgets dialog box, as shown in Figure 15.9. This dialog box lists the budgets you've
created. Once you've created more than one budget, you can use this dialog box to
choose which budget you want to work with.

FIGURE 105.9

*The Manage Budgets
dialog box*

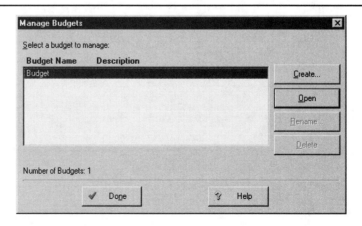

To create a new budget, click the Create command button. Quicken displays the Create Budget dialog box.

You can name and describe the budget with the Name and Description text boxes, of course. You use the Create Budget Options option buttons to tell Quicken how it should create the new budget:

Autocreate Budget Automatically creates the budget based on a prior year's actual income and spending. If you select this option and then click OK, Quicken displays the Automatically Create Budget dialog box (see Figure 15.8), which works as described earlier in this chapter.

Copy Current Budget Tells Quicken to copy the numbers in the currently open budget.

Figure 15.10 shows an example of a filled-in Create Budget dialog box.

PART

II

Quicken and Your
Personal Finances

FIGURE 15.10

*The Create Budget
dialog box*

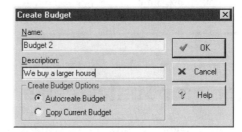

Using the Manage Budgets dialog box (see Figure 15.9), you can rename or delete a budget, as long as it isn't the budget currently open. To rename a budget, select it, click the Rename command button, and then use the dialog box that Quicken displays to provide a new name or description. To delete a budget, select it and then click the Delete command button.

Monitoring Your Success in Achieving a Budget

The information you enter into the budgeting spreadsheet is valuable in its own right. You can use it to plan your income and spending in a way that makes the most sense for you and your family.

But this budget information can be even more valuable. You can use it to compare your actual income and spending with the budget. To do this, you produce a Budget report using the Reports ➤ Planning ➤ Monthly Budget command (see Chapter 4 for information about creating and printing Quicken reports).

Note that the last two commands on the Options menu—this is the menu of commands that appears when you click the Options button on the Budget area—also provide tools you can use to monitor your budgeting success. If you choose the Save Budget Alerts Options command, for example, Quicken displays the Save As Alerts dialog box, which you can use to tell Quicken how and when it should alert you when your spending approaches or exceeds some budgeted amount. If you choose the Monthly Expenses command, Quicken displays the Set Up Alerts dialog box, which you can use to tell Quicken that it should alert you when your spending exceeds some specified amount. Note that the "specified amount" used for the Monthly Expenses command isn't the same as your budgeted amount. It's an amount you set in addition to or as a replacement for the budgeted amount.

 TIP After you create a budget, you can use the Save More Planner to come up with ways to make more out of the money you make. To use the Save More Planner, choose Planning ➢ Save More Planner.

Quicken's Tools for Strategic Planning

Savings goals, Category Groups, and budgeting are important elements of successful personal financial planning. But while such budgeting improves your financial affairs on a short-term basis, it doesn't address your long-term, or strategic, objectives.

Presumably, there are financial objectives you want to achieve. Someday, for example, you may want to quit working—or at least quit working for a paycheck. You may also want to send your children or your grandchildren to college.

Quicken provides several tools for addressing just these types of strategic financial planning issues, including a Retirement Planner, a College Savings Planner, and a generalized Savings Planner.

 NOTE If you don't find these items on your Planning menu, these planners are not implemented in your version of Quicken.

Giving Quicken the Basic Information

Before you can make use of Quicken's planners, you need to tell Quicken a little about yourself. To do this, choose Planning ➤ Assumptions. This displays the Planning Assumptions dialog box. Click hyperlinks on the left side of the dialog box to enter information regarding that particular aspect about you, your plans, or your finances. Click an Edit hyperlink on the right side to display a dialog box you can use to enter or edit specific values. Quicken uses the information you enter about yourself and your finances when formulating your financial plans for the future.

If you have trouble deciding what to enter for one of the assumptions, for instance if you haven't yet decided the age at which you'll retire, the timing of large purchases, or the type of investment you'll make and return you can expect, go ahead and enter your best guesses. You can then use Quicken's What-If Even Scenarios to see how changes in these variables affect your financial picture. To use Quicken's What If Event Scenarios, choose Planning ➤ What If Event Scenarios. Then select a goal type from the Choose A Goal Type drop-down list box. Click a hyperlink in the What If I section for the variable you're considering changing. Quicken displays a dialog box you can use to edit the assumption information. After you make the change, you can see the effects of it on your financial forecast using the graph on the right. If you want to adopt the modified plan, click the Save What If As Plan button. If you don't like the effects of the change and want to edit it or make a different change, click the Reset What If button.

Planning for Retirement

For most workers, early financial planning for retirement delivers enormous benefits. And for today's younger workers—people who are middle-aged and younger—it's imperative to do at least some financial planning for retirement. Early in the next century, the social security system will be under enormous pressure as the ratio of workers paying social security to retirees receiving social security drops to two-to-one. (Currently the ratio is more than three-to-one.) And the growth in federal entitlement programs like social security almost dictates that at some point in the future upper-middle-class recipients will lose benefits.

What's more, with a shift from defined benefit plans to defined contribution plans, thoughtful workers will benefit by making forecasts of future total retirement savings and the investment income generated by those savings. Quicken's Retirement Financial Calculator and its Retirement Planner let you do this.

NOTE A defined *benefit* retirement plan pays a specified benefit—for example, 50 percent of your last year's salary. A defined *contribution* plan contributes specified amounts to a retirement account—such as $2,000 a year.

Using the Retirement Calculator to Forecast Your Retirement Income

To use Quicken's Retirement Calculator to estimate the retirement income you'll have, given your current savings plans, follow these steps:

1. Choose Planning ➤ Financial Calculators ➤ Retirement to display the Retirement Calculator dialog box, as shown in Figure 15.11.

2. Make sure the Annual Retirement Income option button is marked in the Calculate For area of the dialog box.

3. Enter the amount you've already saved for retirement in the Current Savings text box. Include amounts saved in employer-defined contribution retirement plans, such as deferred compensation programs and 401(k) plans, as well as amounts you've saved in things such as individual retirement accounts (IRAs) and Keogh plans.

4. In the Annual Yield box, enter the average annual yield you expect your investment portfolio to generate over your working years.

 TIP As a frame of reference, the stock market's annual return over long periods of time is about 10 percent, the average annual return on long-term corporate bonds over long periods of time is just shy of 6 percent. These are gross return numbers, so if you invest in a way that results in investment expenses—such as a mutual fund that charges fees—you may want to adjust the historical return.

5. Enter the annual amount you'll contribute in the Annual Contribution text box. For example, if you plan to contribute $2,000 a year to an employer's 401(k) plan, type **2000**. If someone else, such as your employer, will contribute to your retirement savings, include this extra amount. Some employers, for example, match 401(k) contributions as a way to encourage employee retirement saving. If your employer will add 50 percent to your $2,000-per-year contribution, the total annual contribution you enter should be $3,000.

FIGURE 15.11

*The Retirement
Calculator dialog box*

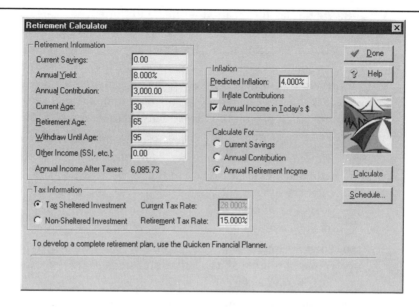

6. Enter your age in the Current Age box, the age you want to retire in the Retirement Age box, and the age through which you want to withdraw money in the Withdraw Until Age box.

TIP A reasonable way to build in a financial cushion for retirement is to assign a Withdraw Until Age value that's several years beyond when you expect to live. I do my retirement planning calculations, for example, assuming I will withdraw money through age 95, even though I may well run out of steam long before that.

7. Use the Other Income text box to indicate how much other retirement income you'll have available. For example, you may be eligible for social security benefits, or you may have invested in a defined-benefit retirement plan that promises to pay you some monthly amount.

TIP You can get an estimate of your future social security benefits by filling out a simple form (called an SS-4) and sending the form to the Social Security Administration. To get the form you need, you can call the local social security office, or you can request the information online at http://s00dace.ssa.gov/pro/batch-pebes/bp-7004home.shtml. You may be surprised by the social security benefit you're slated to receive. Social security benefits are paid according to a complicated formula that allows people with modest incomes (or only a few years of earnings) to get a benefit that's a much larger percentage of their current earnings than people who make a lot of money.

8. Use the Tax Information settings and Current Tax Rate text box to describe the income taxes you'll pay on your retirement savings. If you will use investment options like IRAs and 401(k)s that allow for deferral of income taxes, click the Tax Sheltered Investment option button. If you will use investment options that result in your paying taxes on the investment income earned by your savings, click the Non-Sheltered Investment option button. Then enter the marginal tax rate you'll pay on the investment income in the Current Tax Rate text box.

9. If you want to estimate your after-income-taxes retirement savings account withdrawals, you can estimate the income tax rate in effect over the years you're retired and enter the figure in the Retirement Tax Rate text box. Alternatively, enter the Retirement Tax Rate as **0**. With this input, the Planner calculates the pre-tax withdrawal you'll make. (This is simpler and will probably work better for you anyway.)

10. Enter the inflation rate you expect over the years you'll work and be retired. As a frame of reference, the inflation rate over the twentieth century averaged slightly over 3 percent.

11. If you will make annual contributions and will adjust these amounts for inflation over the years you work, mark the Inflate Contributions checkbox. With 4 percent inflation and $1,000-per-year contributions, for example, Quicken assumes you contribute $1,000 the first year, $1,040 the second year ($1,040 is 104 percent of $1,000), $1,081.60 the third year ($1081.60 is 104 percent of $1,040), and so on.

12. Make sure the Annual Income in Today's $ checkbox is marked to tell Quicken to estimate an annual retirement income figure that uses the same size dollars you make and spend today. (If you don't mark this checkbox, Quicken estimates an annual retirement income figure using inflated dollars you'll actually receive, say, in 30 years.)

13. Click the Calculate button.

14. Click the Schedule command button to see a scrollable list of the annual amounts you'll contribute or withdraw, the annual interest earnings, and the retirement savings balance. Figure 15.12 shows a Deposit Schedule depicting retirement savings activity in a schedule.

FIGURE 15.12

The Deposit Schedule details the progress of your plan.

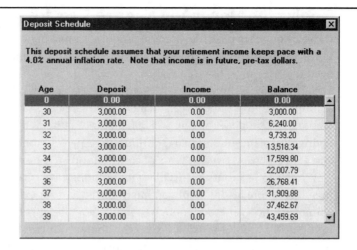

Deposit Schedule

This deposit schedule assumes that your retirement income keeps pace with a 4.0% annual inflation rate. Note that income is in future, pre-tax dollars.

Age	Deposit	Income	Balance
0	0.00	0.00	0.00
30	3,000.00	0.00	3,000.00
31	3,000.00	0.00	6,240.00
32	3,000.00	0.00	9,739.20
33	3,000.00	0.00	13,518.34
34	3,000.00	0.00	17,599.80
35	3,000.00	0.00	22,007.79
36	3,000.00	0.00	26,768.41
37	3,000.00	0.00	31,909.88
38	3,000.00	0.00	37,462.67
39	3,000.00	0.00	43,459.69

15. Once you've entered all the needed information and told Quicken how it should make the calculations, you can scroll down and look at the Income column for your indicated retirement age. It shows the estimated annual retirement income you'll receive based on your forecasting assumptions.

16. To close the Deposit Schedule box, click the Close button. To remove the Retirement Calculator dialog box when you're finished with it, select Done.

Figuring Out How Much You Should Save

The preceding discussion calculates how much you'll have in the way of retirement income, given your current savings and your plans about how you'll save in the future. If instead you want to provide for a specific level of retirement income, you can calculate the current savings you must already have accumulated in order to reach your retirement income goal. Or, you can calculate how much you need to be saving on a regular basis in order to reach that income goal.

To calculate how much you already need to have saved, given all the other retirement information, go back to the Retirement Calculator (see Figure 15.11) and click the Current Savings option button. To calculate how much you need to save on an annual basis, given all the other retirement information, click the Annual Contribution option button. Once you've indicated what savings figure you want to accumulate, enter the annual retirement income you want in the Annual Income After Taxes text box. Then fill in each of the remaining text boxes and mark the appropriate option buttons and checkboxes.

Finding the Money You Need to Save for Retirement

It can be more than a little discouraging to start making retirement planning calculations. You'll usually find that to achieve the annual retirement income you want, you need to be saving a lot more than is practical.

Suppose, for example, that the Retirement Calculator calculates an annual savings amount equal to $5,200 a year—which is the same as $450 a month. (This savings amount will produce roughly $15,000 a year of retirement income if you start with $0 savings, increase your annual contributions 3 percent each year because of inflation, and earn 9 percent over 20 years of contributions.)

While $450 a month seems like a lot of money, you may be able to come up with this figure more readily than you might think. Say, for example, that you work for an employer who's generous enough to match your 401(k) contributions by 50 percent. In other words, for every dollar you contribute, your employer contributes $.50. Also suppose that you pay federal and state income taxes of 33 percent and that you can deduct your 401(k) contributions from your income. In this case, the actual monthly out-of-pocket amount you need to come up with equals $200, not $450.

Here's how the arithmetic works. You need to come up with $300 a month to have $450 a month added to your retirement savings because of your employer's 50 percent matching, as shown here:

Amount you contribute	$300
Employer's matching amount	$150
Total 401(k) contribution	$450

However, if your last dollars of income are taxed at 33 percent, the $300 tax deduction you'll receive because of your $300 401(k) contribution will save you $100 in income taxes. So the actual amount you need to come up with on a monthly basis equals $200, as shown here:

Amount you contribute	$300
Income taxes saved	(100)
After-tax contribution	$200

Admittedly, $200 a month is still a lot of money. But it's also a lot less than the $450-per-month savings figure that the Retirement Calculator calculations suggest.

These calculations also suggest a couple of tactics to consider using when you save for retirement. If an employer offers to match your contributions to something like a 401(k) plan, it will almost always make sense to accept the offer—unless your employer is trying to force you to make an investment that is not appropriate for you.

TIP If you do want to contribute $300 a month to a 401(k) plan and need to reduce your income taxes withheld by $100 a month to do so, talk to your employer's payroll department for instructions. You may need to file a new W-4 statement and increase the number of personal exemptions claimed.

What's more, any time you get a tax deduction for contributing money to your retirement savings, it's almost certainly too good a deal to pass up. As described in the preceding example, you can use the income tax savings because of the deduction to boost your savings so they provide for the desired level of retirement income.

While people often have an emotional aversion to locking money away in tax-sheltered investments, there are only three situations in which it may be a poor idea to use tax-sheltered investments:

- You need (or may need) the money before retirement. In this case, it may not be a good idea to lock away money you may need before retirement because there is usually a 10 percent early-withdrawal penalty paid on money retrieved from a retirement account before age 59 1/2. But you will also need money after you retire, so the "What if I need the money?" argument is more than a little weak. Yes, you may need the money before you retire, but you will absolutely need the money after you retire.

- You've already saved enough money for retirement. Using retirement planning vehicles, such as IRAs, may be a reasonable way to accumulate wealth. And the deferred taxes on your investment income do make your savings grow much more quickly. Nevertheless, if you've already saved enough money for retirement, it's possible that you should consider other investment options as well as estate-planning issues. This special case is beyond the scope of this book, but if it applies to you, I encourage you to consult a good personal financial planner— preferably one who charges you an hourly fee, not one who earns a commission by selling you financial products you may not need.

- You'll pay more income taxes when you're retired than you do now. The calculations get tricky, but if you're only a few years away from retirement and you believe income tax rates will be going up (perhaps to deal with the huge federal-budget deficit or because you'll be paying a new state income tax), it may not make sense for you to save, say, 15 percent now but pay 45 percent later.

Read This If You Can't Possibly Save Enough for Retirement

It's relatively easy to save for retirement when you're still young. Five thousand dollars set aside for a new baby grows to an amount that generates over a $100,000 a year in current-day dollars if the money earns 12 percent annually and inflation runs at 3 percent.

NOTE The data is a little sketchy, but small-company stocks probably deliver average returns of around 12 to 13 percent over long periods of time. Small-company stocks are, however, very risky over shorter periods of time.

The flip side of this is that it becomes difficult to save for retirement if you start thinking (and saving) late in your working years. If you're 60, haven't started saving, and want $25,000 a year in income from your retirement savings at age 65, you probably need to contribute more annually than you make.

Say you're in your 50s—or even a bit older. With the kids' college expenses, or perhaps a divorce, you don't have any money saved for retirement. What should you do? What can you do? This situation, though unfortunate, doesn't need to be untenable. There are some things you can do.

One tactic is not to retire—or at least, not yet. After all, you save for retirement so the earnings from those savings can replace your salary and wages. If you don't stop working, you don't need retirement savings to produce investment income.

Note, too, that "not retiring" doesn't mean you need to keep the same job. If you've been selling computers your whole life and you're sick of it, do something else. Get a job teaching at the community college. (Maybe you'll get summers off.) Join the Peace Corps and go to South America. Get a job in a daycare center and help shape the future.

A second tactic is to postpone retirement a few extra years, which, of course, also reduces the number of years you're retired. Rather than working to age 62 or 65, for example, working until age 67 or 69—a few more years of contributions and compound interest income—will make a surprising difference, and you'll boost substantially the money you receive from defined-benefit retirement plans. If you're paying a mortgage, maybe you can pay that off in those few extra years, too.

A third and more unconventional tactic is to decide that less is more and tune into the art and philosophy of frugality. A good book on this subject is *Your Money or Your Life* by Joe Dominquez and Vicki Robin (Viking Penguin, 1992). And if you decide to live on less while you're still working, you'll end up saving a lot more over the remaining years you work.

 NOTE If it's not too bold, let me also say that I've written a book entitled the *Millionaire Kit*, which provides strategies and software tools you can use to come up with money you need or want to save for retirement. If you're interested in learning about that book, you can read reviews available at the online bookstores like amazon.com, borders.com, and barnesandnoble.com.

Using the Retirement Planner

Quicken2000 Deluxe also supplies a brand new Retirement Planner. The Retirement Planner, which you start by choosing the Planning ➤ Retirement Planner command, walks you through a rather thorough discussion of many of the same issues I've just covered in the preceding paragraphs (see Figure 15.13). To use Quicken's Retirement Planner, simply follow the onscreen instructions.

FIGURE 15.13

The Quicken Retirement Planner helps you construct a more formalized retirement savings plan.

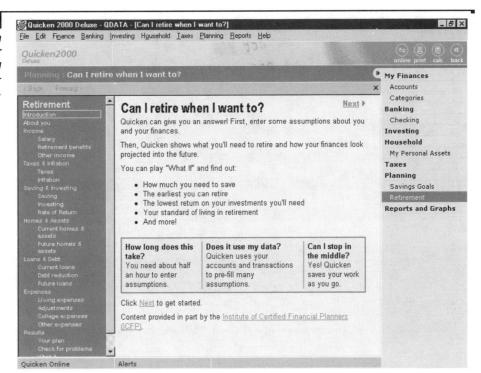

Planning for a Child's College Expenses

Quicken provides two handy tools you can use to plan for a child's college expenses: the College Financial Calculator, which I'll describe first because it's the easiest and fastest to use, and a College Planner wizard, which is much more powerful and insightful, but also more work and more time-consuming to use.

Using the College Financial Calculator

Quicken provides another financial calculator, similar to the Retirement Calculator, which helps you prepare for the expenses of a child attending college.

To use the College Financial Calculator, follow these steps:

1. Choose Planning ➤ Financial Calculators ➤ College to display the College Calculator dialog box, as shown in Figure 15.14.

FIGURE 15.14

The College Calculator dialog box

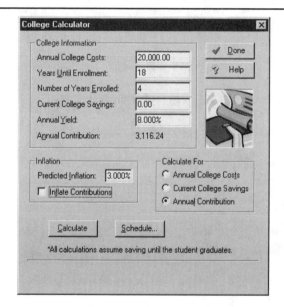

2. Make sure the Annual Contribution option button is marked in the Calculate For area at the lower-right corner of the dialog box.

3. Enter the current annual costs of college in the Annual College Costs text box. (If you don't know for sure which college your child will attend, enter a figure that's representative.)

4. Enter the number of years until the child enrolls in college in the Years Until Enrollment text box.

5. Indicate how many years the child will attend college. For example, if you assume the child will enroll in a regular four-year undergraduate program, type **4**.

6. Enter the amount you've already saved for college in the Current College Savings text box.

7. In the Annual Yield box, enter the annual average annual yield you expect the college savings money to generate and the inflation rate you expect.

 NOTE As noted earlier, the inflation rate over the last century or so has averaged slightly over 3 percent. College tuition, however, has risen much faster than inflation. (Some recent studies show average tuition hikes in the 7 percent neighborhood!) It seems unlikely that college costs will continue to outpace inflation because few people will be able to afford college if the percentage increases continue to be more than double the inflation rate. For this reason, I use a 3 percent inflation rate in my calculations—and cross my fingers.

---

8. If you will adjust your college-savings contributions for inflation, mark the Inflate Contributions checkbox. For example, with 4 percent inflation and $1,000-per-year contributions, Quicken assumes you contribute $1,000 the first year, $1,040 the second year, $1,081.60 the third year, and so on.

9. Click the Calculate button.

10. Click the Schedule command button to see a summary of the annual amounts you'll contribute or withdraw, the annual interest earnings, and the college-savings balance.

Once you've entered all the needed information and told Quicken how it should make the calculations, you can look at the Annual Contribution field. It shows the estimated annual contribution you'll need to make each year until your child finishes college, based on your forecasting assumption.

The preceding discussion calculates how much you need to save annually to be able to pay for college. You can also calculate the current savings you must already have accumulated in order to pay for college. And you can calculate the college costs you can afford given your current and planned savings.

To calculate how much you need to have already saved, click the Current College Savings option button, then click Calculate. To calculate what college costs you can afford, click the Annual College Costs option button. Indicate what figure you want to calculate, fill in the dialog box's remaining text boxes, and mark the appropriate option buttons and checkboxes. Then click Calculate. (For help with a text box entry or in deciding whether to mark an option button or checkbox, see the discussion about using the Retirement Calculator earlier in this chapter.)

PART

II

Quicken and Your
Personal Finances

What You Should Know About Income Taxes and College Savings

There's a minor flaw in the way the college-savings calculations work: The College Calculator doesn't make any allowance for income taxes, but the interest income the college savings earn will be subject to income taxes.

To deal with this deficiency, you can increase your annual contributions to pay the income taxes (or assume the child pays the income taxes). For example, if you have $10,000 of college savings earning a respectable 9 percent, you'll be taxed on $900 of investment income. If the marginal income tax rate is 33 percent, you'll need to come up with an extra $300 for income taxes (33 percent of $900 is $300), so you would need to contribute an extra $25 a month.

You can also consider giving the money to the child in the form of a trust account so the child is taxed, not you. The benefit is that much, and perhaps all, of the investment income earned probably won't be taxed because of the standard deduction the child gets. In 1999, for example, a minor less than 14 years of age who is claimed as a dependent on someone else's return gets a standard deduction of about $700, which allows the child to escape taxes on at least the first $700 of investment income. What's more, in 1999, the next $700 of investment income gets taxed at the low 15 percent marginal income tax rate. After that, the child's investment income gets taxed at the parent's marginal tax rate.

After a child reaches age 14, the 1999 standard deduction amount jumps to roughly $4,300, which means the child can earn up to $4,300 in either wages or investment income without paying any taxes or much taxes. In other words, taxing the child allows you to avoid much of the income taxes you would otherwise have to pay.

There is a drawback to having the child rather than the parent pay the income taxes: The savings need to be given to the child for the investment income earned by the savings to be taxed to the child. This means, for example, that the $8,000 you've scrimped and saved for and put into an account for college may ultimately get spent on what the child decides—which might be a sports car instead of a college education. By putting the money in a trust, you, as the custodian of the trust, retain control of the trust as long as the child is a minor. But when the child reaches the age of majority, the child can spend the money any way he or she wants.

Using the College Planner

Quicken Deluxe 2000 also supplies a brand new College Planner. The College Planner, which you start by choosing the Planning ➢ College Planner command discusses many of the same issues I've just covered in the preceding paragraphs (see Figure 15.15). To use Quicken's College Planner, simply follow the onscreen instructions.

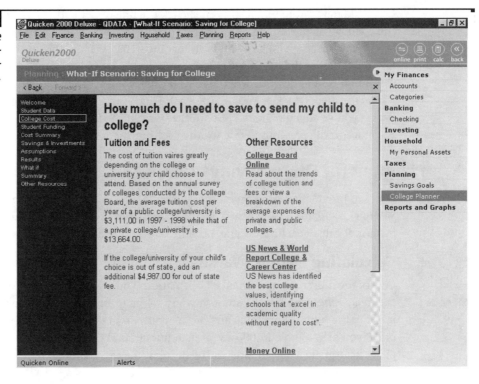

FIGURE 15.15

The Quicken College Planner helps you construct a detailed college savings plan.

Cash Flow Forecasting

You can create a cash flow forecast to see how changes in income and expense items affect your cash flow over a range of time. To create a cash flow forecast, choose Planning ➤ Cash Flow Forecast. The first time you create a forecast, Quicken asks you to enter the historic date range on which you want to base the forecast amounts. If you've already created a forecast, you can edit this range by clicking the Options button and choosing Update Forecast.

 NOTE To create a forecast based on a budget you've already created, click the Advanced button in the Automatically Create Forecast dialog box and click the From Budget Data option button.

To edit income or expense items currently included in the forecast, click the Income Items or Expense Items button and change the values in the Amount column. You can also click the Delete button to exclude an item from the forecast. Click Done when you're finished.

To add new future financial events, click the line under Future Financial Events in the Cash Flow Forecast area. Quicken displays the Create New Expense Item dialog box. If the future financial event is an income item, click the Income option button. Enter a name for the item in the Description box, enter an amount for the item in the Amount box, and describe when and how often the event occurs. Click Done when you're finished. Quicken updates the Cash Flow Forecast. To follow the effects of events you've added or edited out another year in the future, click the Next button. To return to the previous year, click the Prev button.

Planning for Other Savings Goals

Quicken provides another financial-planning tool you'll sometimes find helpful: the Savings Calculator. The Quicken Savings Calculator works like a regular financial calculator. It calculates future value, present value, and payment amounts.

Calculating a Future Value

One of the most common financial calculations you make when you plan savings is the *future value*, which is the amount your savings or investment will be worth at some point in the future—including any profits you've reinvested or left invested. For example, if you plan to save $2,000 a year in a mutual fund for 25 years and expect to earn 9 percent annually, you can forecast the future value of the mutual fund investment.

To perform a future-value calculation, follow these steps:

1. Choose Planning ➤ Financial Calculators ➤ Savings to display the Investment Savings Calculator dialog box, as shown in Figure 15.16.

FIGURE 15.16

The Investment Savings Calculator dialog box

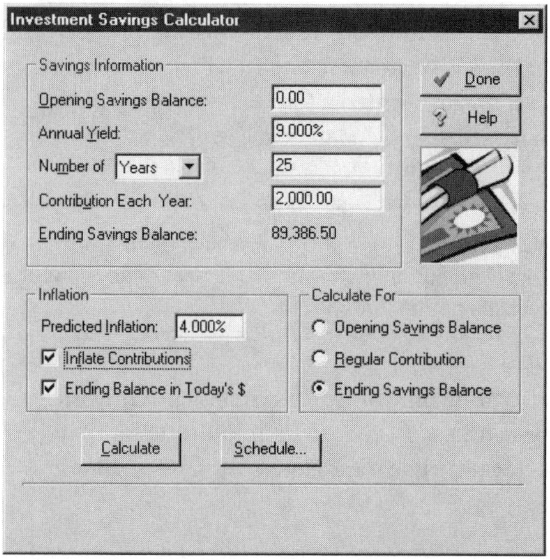

2. Click the Ending Savings Balance option button in the Calculate For area in the lower right of the dialog box.

3. Enter the starting savings balance in the Opening Savings Balance text box. If you haven't yet saved anything because you're just starting, type **0**.

4. In the Annual Yield box, enter the annual yield you expect your savings to earn. If you've invested in a mutual fund you expect will earn 9 percent, type **9**.

5. Use the Number Of drop-down list box to indicate how often you'll add to the investment—each week, each month, each quarter, or each year—and use the Number Of text box to indicate the number of terms you'll make contributions. For example, if you'll contribute $2,000 to an IRA for 25 years, select Years from the Number Of drop-down list box and type **25** in the Number Of text box.

6. Use the Contribution Each text box to indicate how much you'll contribute. For example, if you'll contribute $2,000 to an IRA for 25 years, type **2000** in the Contribution Each text box.

7. Enter the annual inflation rate you expect over the years you will save in the Predicted Inflation text box.

8. If you will increase your contributions for inflation over the years you save, mark the Inflate Contributions checkbox. With 4 percent annual inflation, for example, and $100-per-month contributions, Quicken assumes you contribute $100 the first month, $100.33 the second month, $100.67 the third month, and so on. (Quicken calculates the monthly inflation by dividing the annual inflation by 12.)

9. Make sure the Ending Balance in Today's $ checkbox is marked to tell Quicken to estimate an ending balance figure that uses the same size dollars you make and spend today. (If you don't mark this checkbox, Quicken estimates a future-value figure using inflated dollars you'll actually accumulate, say, in 25 years.)

10. Click Calculate.

11. Click the Schedule command button to see a scrollable list of the annual amounts you'll save, the annual interest earnings, and the ending savings balance. When you've finished viewing the schedule, select Close.

Once you've collected all the necessary information, Quicken calculates the ending balance. Figure 15.16, for example, shows that in today's dollars, you accumulate almost $90,000 by contributing $2,000 annually.

PART

II

Quicken and Your
Personal Finances

NOTE The Savings Calculator calculations assume that you make your contributions at the end of the year, quarter, month, or week. (This is called an ordinary *annuity*.) If you make your contributions at the beginning of the period, you earn an extra period of interest. (This is called an *annuity due*.)

Calculating a Contribution

If you don't know the regular savings, or contribution, amount, you can calculate it by setting the ending savings balance. To do this, you follow the same basic steps you use for calculating a future value, with just a couple of exceptions. In this case, you click the Regular Contribution option button rather than the Ending Savings Balance option button, and you enter the ending savings balance, not the regular contribution amount. When you click Calculate, Quicken calculates the regular contribution amount.

When do you calculate the regular contribution? You calculate the contribution when you want to accumulate a specific future-value amount—say $1,000,000—and you want to know how much you need to be contributing to achieve your future-value goal.

 NOTE If you don't know the opening savings balance but you know everything else, you can calculate the opening savings balance, too. To do this, mark the Opening Savings Balance option button.

Planning a Mortgage Refinancing

Favorable mortgage rates in recent years have prompted a rush of mortgage refinancing. If you find yourself in a position to refinance, Quicken's Refinance Calculator, shown in Figure 15.17, can rapidly compute the potential savings and time to recover the refinancing costs. When you fill in the text boxes, Quicken calculates the costs and savings automatically. To use this feature, follow these steps:

1. Choose Planning ➤ Financial Calculators ➤ Refinance to display the Refinance Calculator dialog box, as shown in Figure 15.17.

2. Enter your current monthly principal and interest payment in the Current Payment text box.

3. Enter any additional amounts you pay into an escrow or impound account each month in the Impound/Escrow Amount text box. (These amounts might include property taxes and insurance, for example.)

4. Enter the new, refinanced mortgage amount in the Principal Amount text box. For example, if the new mortgage balance will equal $115,000, enter that figure into the Principal Amount text box.

5. Enter the number of years you'll be making the mortgage payments in the Years text box. For a 30-year mortgage, for example, you need to enter **30**.

6. Enter the annual interest rate in the Interest Rate text box.

FIGURE 15.17

The Refinance Calculator dialog box

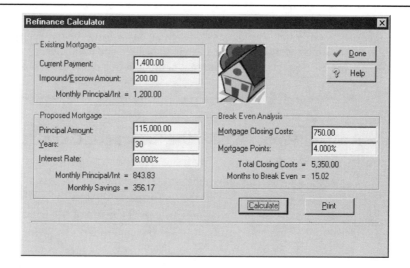

PART

II

Quicken and Your Personal Finances

NOTE The annual interest rate isn't the same thing as the annual percentage rate. The annual interest rate is what the lender uses to calculate your monthly payments. The annual percentage rate is a rate that lets you compare the total costs of borrowing between lenders. An annual percentage rate includes the interest costs of borrowing as well as all the other costs of borrowing, such as loan fees and discount points.

7. Enter the closing costs—appraisals, loan processing fees, and the like—into the Mortgage Closing Costs text box.

8. Enter the total loan fee and discount points in the Mortgage Points text box. If the loan fee is 2 percent and you'll pay 2 percent in discount points, for example, enter **4** in the Mortgage Points text box.

9. Click Calculate.

Once you enter all the Refinance Calculator inputs, you use the Monthly Savings output, the Total Closing Costs output, and the Months to Break Even output to assist you in your decision. In Figure 15.17, for example, the calculations show monthly savings of about $350 and a pay-back period of roughly 15 months.

 TIP Use the Home Purchase Planner to find out how much of a house you can afford. To start the Home Purchase Planner, choose Planning ➤ Home Purchase Planner. The Home Purchase Planner describes the different types of mortgages and helps you weigh the expected expenses (such as property taxes and homeowner association dues) against the expected income (such as rent or profit from the sale of the property if it appreciates in value).

A Minor Problem with the Refinance Calculator

There is one minor problem with the way the Refinance Calculator works: It tells you whether your monthly payment will go down and how many months it will take to recoup your closing costs, but that information doesn't really let you determine whether or not you're saving monthly over the life of the mortgage.

To understand this point, consider the case of a person who has only one year left on a $20,000, 30-year mortgage and is considering refinancing over the next 30 years. On the face of it, this refinancing makes sense because the monthly mortgage payment will go way down and it will take only a month or two to recoup the closing costs. But by refinancing, the homeowner has 29 extra years of payments! That means, over the long haul, the homeowner pays much more interest by refinancing. In this case, the imprudence of refinancing is clear, but the reasonableness of refinancing gets rather murky if you're considering whether to refinance a mortgage for which you have 24 years of payments.

Fortunately, you can apply a couple of rules to make sure you save money by refinancing. You need to make sure that the APR on the new loan is lower than the interest rate on the old loan. You also need to get the new loan paid off just as quickly.

MASTERING FINANCIAL SUCCESS

How to Achieve Financial Independence

For most people, wealth doesn't have to be an impossible dream. With the right strategies and the appropriate tools, you can achieve financial independence. In fact, I truly believe that many, and maybe most, of the people who buy this book can become millionaires if they want to.

Building a fortune, however, is very similar to building a house. You need time. You need a plan. Of course, you also need the right tools. In most cases, people have the time. And if you have Quicken, you have all the tools you need. All you need after that to enjoy financial independence is a plan.

The Three Routes to Riches

Let me talk for a minute about the various ways you can achieve financial independence. In a nutshell, there are really only three routes to riches: instant wealth, entrepreneurial wealth, and investment wealth.

Instant wealth is the wealth one acquires by winning a lottery, receiving a monstrous inheritance, or making an overnight killing on some wildly speculative investment. Everyone has heard stories about people who have become rich this way: the factory worker who wins a $20-million state lottery, the woman who receives an unexpected inheritance from an uncle she never knew she had, or the neighbor who repeatedly tells how he made an overnight killing on a shady real-estate deal.

Unfortunately, there aren't any guaranteed "get-rich-quick schemes." You know that. Very few people actually get rich playing the lottery. Even if you have a rich uncle or aunt, you can't be sure that your name is in the will. And wildly speculative investments produce losses more often than they produce profits.

 NOTE People spend more on postage to enter the Publishers' Clearing House sweepstakes than the sweepstakes sponsor gives away in prizes.

Continued

PART

II

Quicken and Your
Personal Finances

MASTERING FINANCIAL SUCCESS CONTINUED

Despite what some would-be entrepreneurs think, entrepreneurial wealth amounts to a "get-rich-slow" scheme. Sometimes, of course, it can work out very well. However, entrepreneurial wealth isn't the best route to riches for most people. There's a much simpler, safer way to achieve financial independence if your financial aspirations are more modest.

This simpler, safer way is to invest prudently and wisely. You need to become a disciplined saver and a smart investor. If you do these things, you will become rich by taking the third path to financial independence—the investment-wealth route.

No doubt, at this point, you're thinking one of two things. If you're a bit of a cynic, you're thinking, "If it's so easy, how come everybody isn't doing it?" Well, my response is that many, many people are—some of them without realizing it. What's more, a surprising number of people have already become millionaires.

 NOTE The best figures available estimate that there are more than 1,000,000 millionaires in the United States. The same figures also estimate that there are more than 80,000 decamillionaires, persons worth $10 million or more.

Another point is that it's a lot easier to say, "Oh, you just need to save religiously and invest smartly," than it is to actually do it. I want to be candid with you: You need to be a disciplined saver. And the older you are, the more serious you need to be about saving. But with time and discipline, it's truly amazing what you can accumulate.

What's more, to earn really impressive investment profits, you need to become a savvy, street-smart investor. You need to learn about taxes, inflation, and the right way to measure investment profits. You need to learn about stocks and bonds and real estate. And you need to make sure that once you start making money you don't start losing it.

 NOTE If a "pack-a-day" 20-year-old quits smoking and stashes the cigarette money in a savings account, he or she can accumulate roughly $150,000 by age 65. If the same "pack-a-day" smoker invests the cigarette money in an employer-sponsored 401(k) plan, he or she can accumulate as much as $1,000,000 in uninflated dollars.

Continued

MASTERING FINANCIAL SUCCESS CONTINUED

No, it isn't easy to accumulate a personal fortune. But it isn't all that difficult, either. The trick is to take the necessary time, have a plan, and use the right tools.

Obstacles to Attaining Wealth

I should point out that there are some major obstacles to achieving financial independence. The biggest obstacle, at least in my opinion, is the looking-rich trap. The very first thing you need to realize if you do choose the investment route to riches is that looking rich is far different than becoming or actually being rich. Looking rich requires you to live in a fancy neighborhood. Looking rich requires you to drive an expensive car. Looking rich requires you to wear designer clothes. But looking rich isn't the same as being rich. Most millionaires drive American cars and live in middle-class neighborhoods.

Television and the movies show the rich jetting to places like Paris to shop, slurping champagne, and gorging themselves on caviar. Here's the problem with this patently false image: This sort of consumption invariably prevents you from ever becoming rich. You end up spending all your money trying to look rich and there isn't any leftover money for saving and investing.

False affluence isn't the only obstacle to becoming rich. Another is the "I may die tomorrow" syndrome. People who fall into this trap generally don't think it's worthwhile to postpone enjoying the finer things in life. "Don't put off until tomorrow what you can enjoy today," is their motto and philosophy. I'll be the first to admit that you can't always live for the future. But there is a problem with this business of focusing just on today: Chances are, you won't die tomorrow, and that means that you need to prepare for the future. If you have children, you probably want them to attend college. Someday, presumably, you will retire. To do these sorts of things, you need to prepare financially by accumulating wealth.

Most of the obstacles to acquiring riches are illusory, but one obstacle is almost insurmountable: You may not have enough time. The problem is that the engine that powers wealth creation is something called compound interest. (I explain compound interest at the end of Chapter 17, which covers mutual fund investments.) You need time for the compound-interest engine to work its magic. You can't use the compound-interest engine to become rich in a year or two.

This doesn't mean that you can't enjoy the benefits of financial success in the coming weeks and months, though. Rather, it means that years must pass before your wealth gives you complete independence from a job. Meanwhile, you have to settle for things like financial peace of mind, financial progress, and a worry-free financial future.

Continued ▮▶

MASTERING FINANCIAL SUCCESS CONTINUED

How Much Is Enough: Picking a Wealth Target

All this talk leads quite naturally to a discussion about how much is enough. People always throw around the figure of a million dollars. But do you really need a million dollars? It depends. Usually, you don't need that much money. Let's take a hypothetical case to illustrate why. Say you're 40 years old and that you're making $40,000 a year. Further, suppose that you want to achieve financial independence by age 65. Do you need enough investment wealth to generate $40,000 of income? Probably not. You may currently be spending money on a mortgage that will be paid off by the time you retire. Presumably, you'll receive some money in social security or pension benefits. If that is the case, you won't need $40,000 a year by the time you retire.

Here is another example to make the whole thing clearer: Say you are making $40,000 a year; you currently pay $7,500 a year in mortgage payments, but your mortgage will be paid off by the time you retire; and you will receive $7,500 a year in social security and pension benefits. Once your mortgage is paid and you're eligible for pension benefits, you can live as well on $25,000 of investment income as you currently live on $40,000 in wages. What you need is enough wealth to produce an investment income of $25,000, because the $25,000 of investment income will make you financially independent.

 NOTE As I noted earlier in the chapter, you can find out exactly how much social security you'll receive by calling your local social security office, asking them to send you an SS-4 form, and then filling out and returning the form. I also gave you a URL from which you can request this information online.

Your next step is to determine how much wealth you need to produce $25,000 a year of investment income. In general, you need twenty dollars of investment wealth to produce a dollar of investment income. To generate $25,000 of income, therefore, you need $500,000 of investment wealth, because 20 times $25,000 equals $500,000. But you can and should make a more precise determination with the Retirement Planner. (I described the Retirement Planner earlier in this chapter.)

Looking at the Big Picture

I want to conclude this discussion about financial independence with what will seem like a digression but with what is really the most important point of all. I honestly

Continued

MASTERING FINANCIAL SUCCESS CONTINUED

believe you will be happier if you prepare for and eventually achieve financial independence, but I also believe wealth should not be an end-all, be-all goal. I respectfully suggest that you consider financial independence one of your minor life objectives. It certainly shouldn't be your only objective.

This may seem like strange advice coming from someone who makes his living by writing, thinking, and advising people about money. But my activities give me a rather unique vantage point. Because of the work I do, I get to meet a number of very wealthy individuals. I'll let you in on a little secret: having great gobs of money doesn't make the difference you might think. All that will happen, if you do accumulate these great sums of money, is that you'll acquire more expensive habits, hobbies, and friends. You'll still argue with your spouse or children about how you should spend money. You'll still encounter rude neighbors, dangerous drivers, and incompetent sales clerks. And you'll still have to answer all the big questions about life and love and death.

I don't think this perspective conflicts with the idea that you should accumulate a certain amount of wealth. Having a million dollars in wealth isn't essential to your happiness. I don't think it's bad, either. If you want to make financial independence your goal in life, great. My point is that, when you get right down to the specifics of your situation, $200,000 may be as good a target as $1,000,000 or $2,000,000. In any case, $200,000 is a lot easier to achieve.

PART

II

**Quicken and Your
Personal Finances**

CHAPTER 16

Making Better Insurance Decisions

Quicken supplies two useful tools for insurance purposes. One is the Savings Calculator, which lets you make a sophisticated estimate of how much life insurance you should have in place. The other tool is an asset-account type of register, which helps you to build useful lists of the items you've insured.

 NOTE There are no prerequisites for using Quicken to make better insurance decisions.

Determining How Much Life Insurance You Need

When considering life insurance, you're planning and preparing for an event most of us would rather not think about. But life insurance represents a critical step in managing your personal finances and ensuring your family's well-being.

The Two Approaches to Life Insurance

You can use one of two approaches to estimate how much life insurance you should buy: the needs approach or the replacement-income approach. Using the needs approach, you calculate the amount of life insurance necessary to cover your family's financial needs if you die. Using the replacement-income approach, you calculate the amount of life insurance you need to equal the income your family will lose. Let's look briefly at each approach.

 NOTE At the end of this chapter, you'll find tips on making decisions about obtaining life insurance.

The Needs Approach

Using the needs approach, you add up the amounts that represent all the needs your family will have after your death, including funeral and burial costs, uninsured medical expenses, and estate taxes. However, your family depends on you to pay for other needs, such as your child's college tuition, business or personal debts, and food and housing expenses over time.

The needs approach is somewhat limiting. The task of identifying and tallying family needs is difficult, and separating the true needs of your family from what you want for them is often impossible.

The Replacement-Income Approach

Using the replacement-income approach for estimating life insurance requirements, you calculate the life insurance proceeds that would replace your earnings over a specified number of years after your death. Life insurance companies sometimes approximate your replacement income at four or five times your annual income. A more precise estimation considers the actual amount your family members need annually, the number of years for which they will need this amount, and the interest rate your family will earn on the life insurance proceeds, as well as inflation over the years during which your family draws on the life insurance proceeds.

Using the Savings Calculator to Estimate Life Insurance Needs

Using the Quicken Savings Calculator, you can calculate what life insurance you need to replace earnings over a specified number of years. You can then add to this figure any additional needs-based insurance. The total insurance would be the amount calculated by Quicken as necessary to replace earnings plus the amount calculated by you as necessary to pay for any additional needs.

Be careful not to count items twice. For example, if you consider paying off your mortgage on the family home to be a final expense, your estimate of the annual living expenses should reflect this. Similarly, if you include the costs of a spouse's returning to and finishing law school as a prerequisite for supporting the family, reduce the number of years your family will need replacement income.

To use the Quicken Savings Calculator to estimate the life insurance necessary to replace earnings over a specified number of years, follow these steps:

1. Choose Planning ➤ Financial Calculators ➤ Savings to display the Investment Savings Calculator dialog box, as shown in Figure 16.1.

2. Click the Opening Savings Balance option button in the Calculate For section (in the lower-right corner of the dialog box).

3. In the Annual Yield text box in the Savings Information section (at the top of the dialog box), enter your estimate of the annual interest rate you expect your savings, investments, and life insurance proceeds to earn when they are invested. Because this money might need to provide basic living expenses for your family, you might want to assume that this money is invested in conservative, lower-risk investments, which means you should expect lower interest rates.

4. In the Number Of drop-down list box, select Months.

5. In the Number Of text box, enter the number of months you will use the life insurance proceeds and the interest earned on those proceeds to replace earnings of the insured. You might need replacement income only until a child completes an education or until your spouse returns to work.

FIGURE 16.1

You can use the Investment Savings Calculator dialog box to estimate insurance needs.

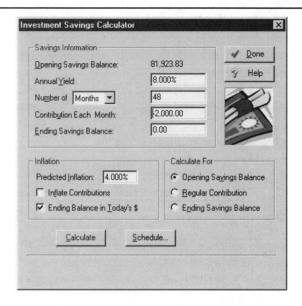

6. In the Contribution Each Month text box, enter the monthly amount your family members will withdraw from the life insurance savings money at the end of each month to supplement their living expenses. For example, if you want your family to be able to withdraw $2,000 at the end of each month, enter **–2000**. (You enter the amount as a negative number because your family will be withdrawing this amount from your savings, not adding it.)

TIP If you have children and pay social security taxes, there's a good chance that social security survivors' benefits will provide several hundred dollars a month. Call your local social security office for more information.

7. Enter the Ending Savings Balance as **0**.

8. In the Predicted Inflation text box, specify the annual inflation rate you expect over the years your income needs to be replaced.

9. Mark the Inflate Contributions checkbox to tell the Investment Savings Calculator that you want the monthly amounts withdrawn from the life insurance savings money to grow each month by the monthly inflation rate.

10. Make sure that the Ending Balance in Today's $ checkbox is marked.

As you enter the values, Quicken calculates an Opening Savings Balance, which equals the amount of life insurance needed to produce enough money to support or supplement the support of your family over the number of months you specified. The assumption is that your family will place the life insurance in a savings account or an investment that will produce the annual return you forecasted and, at the end of each month, withdraw a monthly amount to replace your income.

To see a schedule that shows the monthly withdrawals and the end-of-month life insurance proceeds balance, click the Schedule command button. Quicken displays the Deposit Schedule dialog box, as shown in Figure 16.2. The Number column identifies the months. The Deposit column actually shows the withdrawals. (This is confusing, but remember you're using the Investment Savings Calculator to do something the folks at Intuit never intended.) The Total column shows the balance after the monthly withdrawal.

NOTE   The monthly withdrawal amounts increase every month by the monthly inflation rate. Allowing for increasing withdrawal amounts is important if you want to replace earnings over a long period of time.

If you use the approach described here to plan life insurance needs, remember that you must add any additional special needs (such as final expenses or extraordinary debts) to the opening savings balance amount in order to come up with a life insurance amount that both replaces earnings and provides for special needs.

PART

II

Quicken and Your
Personal Finances

FIGURE 16.2

The Deposit Schedule dialog box shows potential monthly withdrawals.

Deposit Schedule

The effect of 4.0% annual inflation over the period of 48 months will make $0.01 worth $0.00 in terms of today's purchasing power.

Number	Deposit	Total
0	0.00	81,923.83
1	-2,000.00	80,469.99
2	-2,000.00	79,006.46
3	-2,000.00	77,533.17
4	-2,000.00	76,050.05
5	-2,000.00	74,557.05
6	-2,000.00	73,054.10
7	-2,000.00	71,541.13
8	-2,000.00	70,018.07
9	-2,000.00	68,484.86
10	-2,000.00	66,941.42

Using Quicken to Build Property Insurance Lists

There's one other insurance-related task you can do with Quicken: You can build a list of the items that you have insured or will insure with property insurance. You simply use an asset account to build a list of items and values. This list is not only useful for your records, but your insurance agent or property insurer may also want to see a copy.

One benefit of this kind of list is that you'll get an idea of how much property insurance you should really have. You can compare the total value of the items on such a list with the personal property limit on your homeowner's or renter's policy. Another benefit is that, should something destroy your personal property, you'll have a record of what you've lost.

If you have the Deluxe version of Quicken, you can use the Quicken Home Inventory program to create a list of your personal property, insurance policies, and pending claims. If you don't have Quicken Deluxe, you can just use a separate file and account. Both approaches are detailed in the paragraphs that follow.

Using the Home Inventory Program

The Quicken Home Inventory program provides tools for making a complete personal inventory of all your property. Such an inventory might come in handy in any situation where you may need to have a record of what you own. For instance, if you were robbed and needed to tell the police what had been taken, a home inventory would be useful in making sure that you did not forget anything.

You begin Quicken Home Inventory by choosing Household ➣ Quicken Home Inventory ➣ Quicken Home Inventory. Then click Continue. Quicken opens a window that, after you add a few items, looks similar to Figure 16.3.

Here's how you compile your home inventory list:

1. Choose a room in the View By Location drop-down list box.

2. Click the first blank Item Description box and type the name of the item.

 TIP If the Suggested Items For scroll box lists an item you own, you can double-click it, and Quicken will add the item to your current list, along with its best guess as to the Replace Cost and Resale Value. If Quicken's guess is inaccurate, highlight the incorrect amount by double-clicking it, then type the correct amount.

---

3. Use the Item Category drop-down list box to categorize the item.

FIGURE 16.3

The Quicken Home Inventory helps you keep track of your belongings in case of emergency.

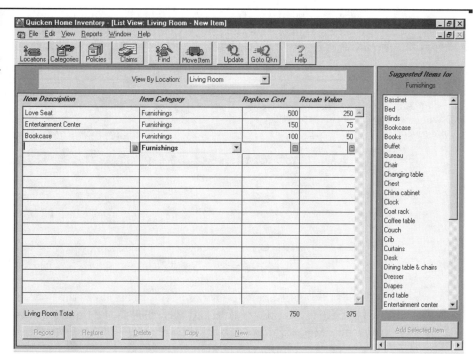

4. Click the Replace Cost box and type in the amount that it would cost to buy an exact replacement of the same item.

5. The Resale Value is the amount you would get if you sold the item today. Quicken assumes that it would be half of the Replace Cost. If it isn't, drag through the amount to highlight it, then type the correct amount.

6. Click Record.

Repeat this process for each item of value.

 TIP You should also keep a list of any unique identifying marks with this information. For example, note the make and serial and model numbers of the item, whether you have etched an ID number somewhere on the item, whether you once scratched it when you dropped it, and similar information. If the item is stolen and recovered, this information may be the difference between getting the item back or not.

Quicken Home Inventory also allows you to track your insurance policies, including special riders, using its Policies list. To see this list, click the Policies button. Figure 16.4 shows an example of the Policies window.

FIGURE 16.4

The Policies list helps you keep your insurance current.

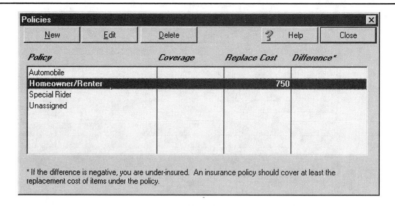

To describe an insurance policy once you've displayed the Policies window, click the policy that you want to edit, and then click the Edit button. When Quicken displays the Edit Policy dialog box, as shown in Figure 16.5, fill in the text boxes with the appropriate information, and then click OK.

FIGURE 16.5

The Edit Policy dialog box lets you describe an insurance policy.

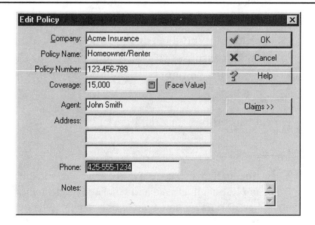

Note that along the top edge of the Quicken Home Inventory, a row of buttons appears. Three of these buttons are worth briefly mentioning:

Locations   Click the Locations button to display a dialog box you can use to add or change the Quicken Home Inventory program's list of locations. If you have an attic loft, for example, where you also store items, you would use the Locations dialog box to add this storage place.

Categories   Click the Categories button to display a dialog box you use to add or change the categories that the Quicken Home Inventory program uses to organize your items.

Claims   Click the Claims button to display a dialog box you can use to document and monitor outstanding claims you've filed.

Creating a New File for Your Property List

If you have Quicken Basic and so don't have access to the Quicken Home Inventory Organizer, consider putting the asset account that lists the property in a separate file, especially if you've listed items such as clothing that have a substantial replacement value or cost (which is why you've insured them) but don't have much market value. This way, the value of things you've insured won't get included in your net worth.

Figure 16.6 shows an asset property list. To create such a list, create an asset account and open its register. Then simply enter a transaction for each item you've insured. The dollar amount is the insured replacement value. Don't categorize the transactions. You may want to use the Memo text box to cross-reference some other piece of information (such as the model number of the insured item or the merchant from whom you purchased the item).

To create a separate file, choose the File ➤ New command to display the Creating New File: Are You Sure? dialog box. Click the New Quicken File option button, and then click OK. When Quicken displays the Create Quicken File dialog box, use the File Name text box to give the file a name and then click OK. Quicken creates the new file in the Quicken directory. It is to this file that you'll add the asset list account.

To switch between your two Quicken files, choose the File ➤ Open command. When Quicken displays the Open Quicken File dialog box, select the file you want to work with from the File Name list box.

PART

II

Quicken and Your
Personal Finances

FIGURE 16.6

*An asset register that
lists insured property*

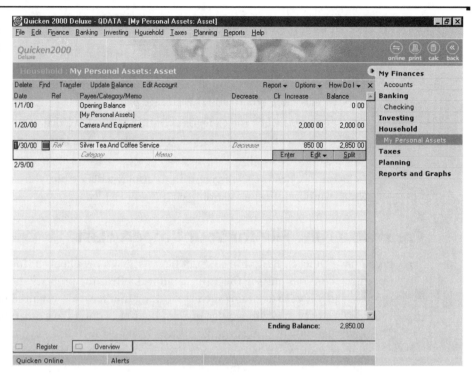

 TIP   Keep a backup record of any property records away from your property. If something happens, you don't want whatever destroys your property to also destroy your records.

Creating Your Property List

To create an asset list account for property insurance records, follow these steps:

1. Choose Finance ➢ Account List to display the Account document area.

2. Click the New command button. Quicken displays the Create New Account dialog box, as shown in Figure 16.7.

3. Click the Asset command button in the dialog box, and then click Next. Quicken displays the Asset Account Setup dialog box, as shown in Figure 16.8.

FIGURE 16.7

You can choose the type of new account you want to set up.

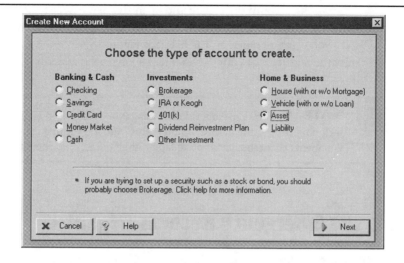

FIGURE 16.8

The Summary tab of the Asset Account Setup dialog box collects the information you need to create an account for listing insured property.

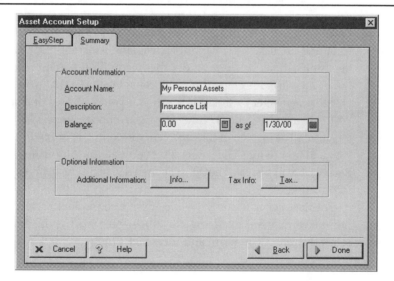

4. Click the Summary tab.

5. Complete the Asset Account Setup dialog boxes by entering a name for the account, a description, a zero (0) balance, and a starting date.

6. Click Done.

PART

II

Quicken and Your
Personal Finances

From the account list, locate and open the new asset account that you just created. Quicken displays the asset register in a document window. Enter a transaction for the item you want included on the list. (See Figure 16.6, shown earlier, for an example of how the register looks after several items have been added.)

 NOTE If you can, make a video of things you've stored in all the rooms of your house, including closets, the garage, and the attic. And if the video camera records sound, add comments about the items you're taping, their prices, and where you got them.

Using the Emergency Records Organizer

Quicken Deluxe supplies an Emergency Records Organizer. The Emergency Records Organizer essentially creates a report that describes where your personal documents (such as wills, birth certificates, trust documents, passports, and so on) are located. The Emergency Records Organizer also collects and creates a report that summarizes personal and financial information, such as family member physicians, bank accounts, safe deposit locations, and dozens of other pieces of important information. In short, the Emergency Records Organizer produces a document that would be absolutely invaluable in an emergency situation (such as if you're injured or a family member dies).

To use the Emergency Records Organizer, choose Household ➢ Emergency Records Organizer. The first tab of the Emergency Records Organizer displays information about why and how to use this feature. After you read the information, click the Create/Update Records tab. In this tab, shown in Figure 16.9, fill in the fields to collect your personal information.

The Emergency Records Organizer can also produce reports that summarize your personal and financial affairs. Click the Report tab, use the drop-down list box to select the report you want, and then click Print.

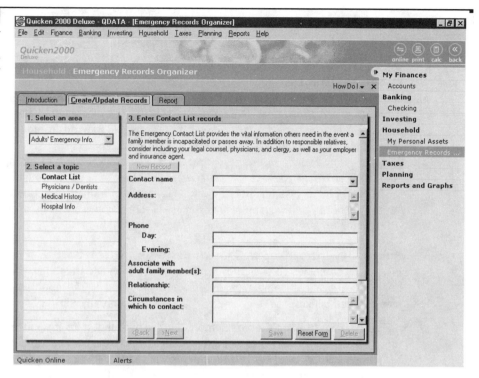

FIGURE 16.9

The Emergency Records Organizer collects information about your personal and financial affairs.

MASTERING FINANCIAL SUCCESS

How to Get the Right Insurance Policy

A lot can be said about making smart decisions when it comes to getting insurance. Rather than write a lengthy and encyclopedic description of how insurance policies work, I want to focus on eight general rules for buying insurance of any kind. Then I'll explain how to buy the two kinds of insurance that most everyone needs: life insurance and health insurance.

Eight Rules for Buying Insurance of Any Kind

By following the eight rules explained here, you can save money, and just as important, you can save yourself from making serious mistakes when you shop for and acquire insurance policies.

Continued

Rule 1: Buy Insurance Only for Financial Risks You Can't Afford to Bear on Your Own

The purpose of insurance is to cover catastrophes that would devastate you or your family. Don't treat insurance as a chance to cover all your losses no matter how small or insignificant, because if you do you'll fritter away money on insurance you really don't need. For example, if your house caught fire and burned down, you would be glad you had homeowner's insurance. Homeowner's insurance is worth having, because you likely can't—and you certainly don't want to—cover the cost of rebuilding a house. On the other hand, insuring an old clunker is a waste of money if the car is only worth $800. You would be throwing away money for something you could cover yourself if you had to.

Rule 2: Buy from Insurers Rated A or Better by A.M. Best

Insurance companies go bust, they are bought and sold, and they suffer the same economic travails that all companies do. Between 1989 and 1993, 143 insurance companies declared bankruptcy. You want to pick a reliable company with a good track record.

A.M. Best is an insurance company monitoring service that rates insurance companies on reliability. Look for insurers rated A or better by A.M. Best, and periodically check to see whether your insurer is maintaining its high rating. If your insurer goes down a notch, consider finding a new insurance company. You can probably get A.M. Best's directory of insurance companies at your local public library, and you can find A.M. Best on the Web at www.ambest.com.

Rule 3: Shop Around

There are many, many, many kinds of insurance policies, and insurers don't advertise by price. You need to do some legwork to match your needs with the cheapest possible policy. Talk to at least two brokers to start with. Look for no-load insurance companies—companies that sell policies directly to the public without a broker taking a commission—since they usually offer cheaper prices.

Rule 4: Never Lie on a Policy Application

If you fib and get caught, the company can cancel your policy. If you lie on an application for life insurance and die during the first three years you hold the policy, the company will cancel your policy, and your beneficiaries will receive nothing. Health, life, and disability insurers run background checks on applicants through the Medical Information Bureau, so you can get caught lying. The medical examination you take for life insurance can also turn up a lie. For example, if you smoked tobacco in the previous year, it will come up in the test.

Continued ▌▶

MASTERING FINANCIAL SUCCESS CONTINUED

Rule 5: Don't Buy Specific-Risk Policies—Buy General Policies Instead

When it comes to insurance, you want the broadest coverage you can get. Buying insurance against cancer or an uninsured motorist defeats the purpose of having an insurance policy. If you have ulcers, your cancer insurance will not help you. Get comprehensive medical coverage instead.

Uninsured motorist insurance is supposed to protect you if you get hit by someone who doesn't have car insurance or doesn't have adequate car insurance. But, in my opinion, you don't need it if you have adequate car insurance yourself, as well as health, disability, and life insurance. I should point out that some attorneys advise you to carry uninsured motorist insurance because, by doing so, you may be able to recover damages for "pain and suffering."

Rule 6: Never Cancel One Policy until You Have a Replacement Policy in Place

If you cancel a policy without getting a replacement, you will be uninsured for however long it takes to get a new policy. And if disaster strikes during this period, you could be financially devastated. This rule goes for everyone, but especially for people getting on in years, since older folks sometimes have trouble getting health and life insurance.

Rule 7: Get a High Deductible

You save money by having insurance policies with high deductibles. The premium for high-deductible policies is always lower. Not only that, but you save yourself all the trouble of filing a claim and needing to haggle with insurance company representatives if you have a high deductible and you don't need to make as many claims.

People who buy low-deductible policies usually do so because they want to be covered under all circumstances. But the cost, for example, of a $400 fender-bender is usually worth paying out of your own pocket when compared to the overall cost of being insured for $400 accidents. Statistics show that most people have a fender-bender once every ten years. The $400 hurts to pay, but the cost of insuring yourself for such accidents over a ten-year period comes to far more than $400.

One other thing: If you have a low deductible, you will make more claims. That means you become an expensive headache for the insurance company. That means your rates will go up, and you don't want that to happen.

Continued

MASTERING FINANCIAL SUCCESS CONTINUED

Rule 8: Use the Money You Save on Insurance Payments to Beef Up Your Rainy Day Account

While you can save money on your insurance premiums by following the rules mentioned earlier, it's probably a big mistake to use that money for, say, a trip to Hawaii. Instead, use any savings to build a nice-sized rainy day fund that you can draw on to pay deductibles. A big enough rainy day fund can cover both periods of unemployment and your insurance deductibles.

Buying Life Insurance

Not everyone needs life insurance. The first thing to do is make sure you need it. Life insurance is really meant for your family members or other dependents who rely on your earnings. You buy life insurance so that, if you die, your dependents can live the same kind of life they live now. Strictly speaking, then, life insurance is only a means of replacing your earnings in your absence. If you don't have dependents (say, because you're single) or you don't have earnings (say, because you're retired), you don't need life insurance. Note that children rarely need life insurance because they almost never have dependents and other people don't rely on their earnings.

If you do need life insurance, you should know that it comes in two basic flavors: *term insurance* and *cash-value insurance* (also called "whole life" insurance). Ninety-nine times out of 100, what you want is term insurance.

Term life insurance is simple, straightforward life insurance. You pay an annual premium, and if you die, a lump sum is paid to your beneficiaries. Term life insurance gets its name because you buy the insurance for a specific term, such as 5, 10, or 15 years (and sometimes longer). At the end of the term, you can renew your policy or get a different one. The big benefits of term insurance are that it's cheap and it's simple.

The other flavor of life insurance is cash-value insurance. Many people are attracted to cash-value insurance because it supposedly lets them keep some of the premiums they pay over the years. After all, the reasoning goes, you pay for life insurance for 20, 30, or 40 years, so you might as well get some of the money back. With cash-value insurance, some of the premium money is kept in an account that is yours to keep or borrow against. This sounds great. The only problem is that cash-value insurance usually isn't a very good investment, even if you hold the policy for years and years. And it's a terrible investment if you keep the policy for only a year or two. What's more, to really analyze a cash-value insurance policy, you need to perform a very sophisticated financial analysis. And this is, in fact, the major problem with cash-value life insurance.

Continued

MASTERING FINANCIAL SUCCESS CONTINUED

While perhaps a handful of good cash-value insurance policies are available, many—perhaps most—are terrible investments. And to tell the good from the bad, you need a computer and the financial skills to perform something called discounted cash-flow analysis. If you do think you need cash-value insurance, it probably makes sense to have a financial planner perform this analysis for you. Obviously, this financial planner should be a different person from the insurance agent selling you the policy.

What's the bottom line? Cash-value insurance is much too complex a financial product for most people to deal with. Note, too, that any investment option that's tax-deductible—such as a 401(k), a 401(b), a deductible IRA, a SEP/IRA, or a Keogh plan—is always a better investment than the investment portion of a cash-value policy. For these two reasons, I strongly encourage you to simplify your financial affairs and increase your net worth by sticking with tax-deductible investments.

If you do decide to follow my advice and choose a term life insurance policy, be sure that your policy is noncancelable and renewable. You want a policy that cannot be canceled under any circumstances, including poor health. (You have no way of knowing what your health will be like ten years from now.) And you want to be able to renew the policy even if your health deteriorates. (You don't want to go through a medical review each time a term is up and you need to renew.)

Buying Health Insurance

Everybody needs health insurance. With medical costs skyrocketing, you simply can't pay for this stuff on your own. Too many families get wiped out by a stroke, a car accident, or some other major medical emergency because they didn't have medical coverage and were forced to pay for the surgeries and hospital visits themselves. Even worse, if you don't have health insurance, you may not be able to get the treatment that you need to save your life.

The problem, however, is that heath insurance is very expensive. Fortunately, there are some good ways to save money on health insurance.

Buy Major Medical Coverage and Self-Insure the Minor Stuff

The amounts of your deductible and co-payments are the biggest determining factors in how much you pay in premiums. If you have a large deductible, your premiums will fall accordingly. If you co-pay the first $2,000 to $5,000 in medical bills—that is, if you pay a certain percentage of these bills, usually 20 to 50 percent—your premiums drop dramatically.

Continued

PART

II

Quicken and Your
Personal Finances

MASTERING FINANCIAL SUCCESS CONTINUED

The surest way to save money on health insurance is to get a high deductible and a large co-payment. Under this plan, you pay for checkups and minor cuts and scrapes. The insurance company starts paying only when your bills soar due to a major medical emergency. Follow this plan only if you're healthy and you have enough tucked away in a rainy day account to pay the deductible and make the co-payments. You don't want to be stuck in a hospital bed wondering how you can make co-payments or pay a deductible.

Investigate Preferred Provider Plans

Several major health insurance companies offer discounted insurance plans if you agree to see your family doctor first for all of your medical care. You select a primary care physician from a list of participating doctors in your area, and then you agree to see only this physician, except in the case of an emergency. If this physician cannot provide you with the help you need, he or she can refer you to a specialist. Usually, the insurance company pays for specialist services only if you have a referral from your family doctor.

Don't Get One-Disease Insurance

Some insurers prey on people's fears by offering them cancer or other types of one-disease insurance. The problem with cancer insurance is that it won't do you any good if you get ulcers, the gout, athlete's foot, or any other disease except cancer. Buy broad health insurance that covers all the illnesses you might get. One-disease insurance is too expensive, and it can too easily leave holes in your coverage.

Make a Living Will

A *living will* tells the doctor and your family that, if you're dying, you don't want your life extended by aggressive life-support measures. Although a living will seems like a strange topic for anyone who's healthy, drawing up a living will is a really smart thing for you to take care of now. For a set of blank living-will documents you can fill in, write to Society for the Right to Die, 250 West 57th St., New York, NY 10107. Include a self-addressed, stamped envelope and a small donation to pay for the forms and the shipping. You can also order living will software by going to www.easylegalforms.com/list.htm.

Skip Maternity Coverage—As Long As Your Policy Covers Complications from Pregnancy and Newborn Care

Having a baby is expensive. But even so, maternity coverage usually isn't a good deal. If you work out the numbers, you need to have a baby about every year or every other year just to break even on the extra cost (the premiums, in other words) of having this benefit.

Continued

MASTERING FINANCIAL SUCCESS CONTINUED

You do need to be very careful about skipping maternity coverage if there's even the slightest chance that you or your spouse will have a baby in the near future. If there are any complications from the pregnancy or if your newborn needs special care, the costs of having the baby can increase astronomically. Ideally, you want a policy that either includes all maternity benefits or one that doesn't cover delivery, but does cover pregnancy complications and newborn care. If you choose the latter policy, you may save some money in the long run, but make sure you have enough money in your rainy-day fund to pay the delivery costs out of pocket.

Compare Doctor and Hospital Prices

It would be great if doctors wore prices on their foreheads the way that used cars have prices on their windshields. Comparing doctor and hospital prices is not easy, but it can be done simply by asking.

Look for a Doctor Who Accepts Assignment If You're on Medicare

Accepting assignment means that the doctor charges no more than what Medicare deems appropriate. You still pay the deductible and the co-payment, but you can rest assured that the bill will not go above that.

Ask for Generic Drugs

Once you take the tiny little words off the capsules or pills, brand name drugs are exactly the same as their generic counterparts. Did you know that generic drugs and name brand drugs are often made in the same laboratories? Always opt for generic drugs, and use the money you save to see a good movie.

Use 24-Hour Emergency Clinics instead of Hospital Emergency Rooms

Clinics are much cheaper than hospital emergency rooms. Cheaper still is seeing your own doctor. Most doctors' offices have an after-hours telephone number that puts you in contact with the physician or nurse on call. If you get sick or injured at a time during which your doctor's office is closed, and you are not sure if you need to go to an emergency clinic, call the after-hours telephone number to find out if your condition can wait until you can see your doctor.

Get a Guaranteed Renewable Policy

You should be able to renew your policy without needing to pass a medical exam. A nonrenewable policy defeats the purpose of having health insurance. You buy health insurance in case you get sick. You don't buy it for when you're healthy.

PART

II

Quicken and Your
Personal Finances

PART III

Quicken for Investors

LEARN TO:

- *Track Mutual Fund Investments*

- *Keep Records of Stocks, Bonds, and Other Common Investments*

- *Monitor Home and Rental Property Investments*

CHAPTER **17**

Mutual Fund
Investments

Mutual funds are an excellent way to invest. Even with relatively small amounts of money, you get tremendous diversification. Without mutual funds, if you had only a small amount of money to invest, you could buy shares of just one or two stocks. This would be a risky venture, because the success or failure of a single business (versus a group of 50 to 5,000 or more businesses) could have disastrous effects on your investment returns. If you have only one egg, you have no other option but to put it in one basket, but if you get together with a bunch of people, the people can put their eggs in a pile and divide them among several baskets!

Investing in mutual funds is a good idea, but mutual-fund record keeping can be tricky. When the profits you earn from a mutual fund investment are taxable, the profit calculations—in particular, the capital gain or loss calculations—quickly become cumbersome. Fortunately, Quicken can help you with these calculations, as well as your other mutual-fund tracking activities.

 TIP Even if you don't invest using mutual funds but instead invest directly in stocks and bonds, this chapter is a good place to start learning. Quicken's stock and bond record-keeping features represent an extension of its mutual fund record-keeping features. So read through this chapter and then continue onto the next one, which covers stock and bond record keeping.

Before You Begin

Here are the prerequisites for tracking a mutual fund investment in Quicken:

- You need to keep records that document the mutual fund shares you've purchased and sold. Quicken is, after all, a record-keeping tool. If you don't have the raw data you want to record in Quicken, you can't use Quicken.

- You should know the mechanics of using the Quicken register. To keep records of investments, you use many of the same windows and commands you do to keep records of bank accounts, credit cards, and other assets and liabilities.

What to Do about IRA and 401(k) Mutual Fund Investments

It probably doesn't make sense to track tax-deferred mutual fund investments in Quicken. There's no harm in doing so, but you don't get anything extra for your effort.

If your mutual fund investing is through tax-deferred accounts such as employer-sponsored 401(k) accounts, IRAs (individual retirement accounts), and self-employed pension plans like SEPs (Simplified Employee Pension Plans) and Keogh plans, your investment profits aren't taxed. Dividends and interest aren't taxed, capital gains aren't taxed, and capital losses aren't tax-deductible.

Instead, money you withdraw from the account is taxed. Restated in terms of Quicken mechanics, when you deposit money that has been withdrawn from, say, your IRA account into a bank account, you just categorize the bank account deposit as income. (The income category could be named something like IRA Distribution.)

Because you don't need to keep records for the purpose of tracking your mutual fund profits, there's little reason to go to the extra work of keeping mutual fund investment records in Quicken. You can easily obtain information about these accounts in several ways:

- If you want to know the current value of your mutual fund investment, you can just look at your last statement from the mutual fund investment management company or give that company a telephone call. The big mutual fund management companies have toll-free numbers that give fund price and account value information. You can also look up the fund on the Web.

- If you want to see what taxable income you have because of the mutual fund, you can look at your bank accounts and summarize the deposits you've made into these accounts.

- You can get the annual return on the investment by looking at the annual report the mutual fund management company sends you at the end of the year.

There are other, similar situations in which it doesn't make sense to track a mutual fund investment with Quicken because you don't get any new information or added value from your record-keeping effort. Suppose you have retirement money in a mutual fund, you don't buy and sell shares, and you don't reinvest your mutual fund profits (because you live on these profits). In this case, it doesn't make sense to track your mutual fund investments in Quicken. You can keep a record of the mutual fund profits by using appropriate income categories when you deposit the dividend, interest, or capital gains distributions check into your bank account. And you can get investment activity and current market value information by looking at a recent statement or by telephoning the mutual fund investment company.

That much said, if you feel compelled to set up an account for an IRA or 401(k), follow these steps:

1. Display the Account List by choosing Finance➤ Account List.

2. Click the New button to tell Quicken you want to create a new account.

3. Click the 401(k) option button, and click Next twice.

4. Enter a name for the 401(k) account in the Account Name text box and, optionally, add a description in the Description text box. Click Next.

5. Enter the ending date from your last statement and whether your statement includes the number of shares you own of each security in the dialog box Quicken provides, then click Next.

6. In the next dialog box, specify whether your employer contributes to your 401(k) account, and make any changes to your securities as necessary. Click Next, and then click Done.

7. For each fund, enter a name for the fund, your ending share balance, and its market value, as shown in Figure 17.1. Click Next to proceed to the next fund.

Once you have set up a 401(k) account, you can use the Paycheck Wizard (described in Chapter 2) to describe any 401(k) contributions you deduct directly from your paycheck.

FIGURE 17.1

The 401(k) Setup dialog box

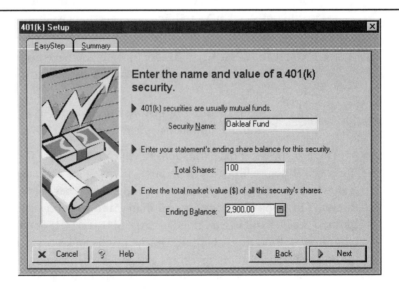

Setting Up a Mutual Fund Account

If you do decide to track a taxable mutual fund investment in Quicken, you need to set up an investment account. It will be into this account that the mutual investment transactions are recorded. You'll set up one investment account for each mutual fund in which you own shares.

To set up a mutual fund account, follow these steps:

1. Choose Finance ➢ Account List to display the Account List.

2. Click the New command button to display the Create New Account dialog box.

3. Click the Other Investment option button, click Next, and then click the Summary tab to display the Investment Account Setup dialog box, as shown in Figure 17.2.

4. Enter an account name in the Account Name text box. You can use the mutual fund's name as your account name. If you have shares of the Vanguard Index 500 trust fund, for example, you might choose to name the account Vanguard or Index 500.

5. If you want to further describe or collect additional information about an account, use the Description text box. You can enter a maximum of 54 characters.

6. Mark the Account Contains a Single Mutual Fund checkbox to tell Quicken that you'll use the account for a single mutual fund investment.

FIGURE 17.2

The Summary tab of the Investment Account Setup dialog box

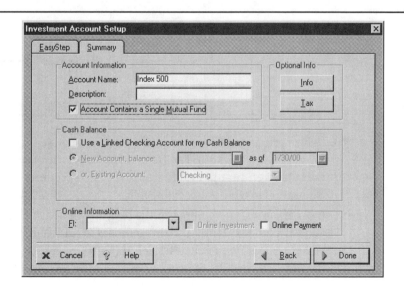

PART

III

Quicken for Investors

TIP If you own shares in more than one mutual fund and want to track all of your investments in a single account, follow the approach for setting up accounts described in this chapter, but don't mark the Account Contains a Single Mutual Fund checkbox. Then refer to Chapter 18 for more information about working with accounts containing more than one investment.

7. Leave the Use a Linked Checking Account for My Cash Balance checkbox unmarked. This feature doesn't apply to mutual fund accounts (as I'm suggesting you use and set them up here).

8. If you want to store additional information about an account, click the Info command button to display the Additional Account Information dialog box. You can use it to further describe the mutual fund management company in the Bank Name text box, the mutual fund account number in the Account Number text box, and so on. (Some of these fields don't make sense for an investment account; Quicken uses the same Additional Account Information dialog box for all account types.) Click OK to close this information dialog box.

9. Click the Tax command button to display the Tax Schedule Information dialog box, as shown in Figure 17.3.

FIGURE 17.3

The Tax Schedule Information dialog box

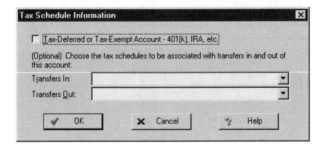

10. If the mutual fund account won't produce taxable income or tax-deductible capital losses, mark the Tax-Deferred or Tax-Exempt Account checkbox. This tells Quicken that it should not count this account's income and expense amounts as taxable or tax deductible.

11. If the transfers into and out of the investment account should be reported on your income tax return, use the Transfers In and Transfers Out drop-down list boxes to identify on which tax return form or schedule (and on which line on the form or schedule) these transfers should be reported. In the case of a mutual fund investment that's part of your IRA, for example, transfers to the account are reported as IRA contributions.

12. Click OK to close the Tax Schedule Information dialog box.

13. Click Done in the Investment Account Setup dialog box. Quicken displays the Set Up Mutual Fund Security dialog box, as shown in Figure 17.4.

FIGURE 17.4

The Set Up Mutual Fund Security dialog box

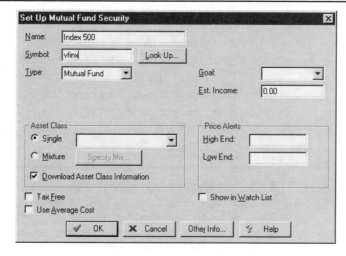

14. If you will update the mutual fund's share prices by using Quicken's Online Quotes feature, enter the security symbol for the mutual fund in the Symbol text box.

 TIP If you don't know the security symbol for your mutual fund and you have an Internet connection, you can click the Look Up button. This connects you to a page on the Quicken.com Web site, where you can get help in determining the correct mutual fund symbol. (See Chapter 11 for more information about the Quicken.com Web site.) If you still can't find the symbol, or if you don't have an Internet connection, you can use the Mutual Fund Finder (if you have the Deluxe version of Quicken) to find the symbol. Just click the Name button in the Mutual Fund Finder window, enter the name of the investment company, and click Search. When the Mutual Fund Finder displays the list of funds, select the fund and click the Fund Details button. The ticker symbol for the fund appears in the upper-left corner. (See the last section of this chapter, "Selecting Mutual Funds with the Mutual Fund Finder," for more information about the Mutual Fund Finder.)

PART

III

Quicken for Investors

15. Activate the Type drop-down list box and select the Mutual Fund entry.

16. If you want to segregate your investments by investment goal, activate the Goal drop-down list box and select one of the goals listed.

17. If you want to monitor your mutual fund investments by the type of investments made, activate the Asset Class drop-down list box and select the asset class that most closely matches the mutual fund's principal investments.

18. Click OK. Quicken adds the mutual fund account to the account list and redisplays the Account List.

19. Select the investment account from the Account List and click the Open command button. Quicken displays the Create Opening Share Balance dialog box, as shown in Figure 17.5. Usually, you don't want to use this dialog box because it doesn't allow you to enter the actual cost data that is useful for tax calculations. Don't enter anything into the Number of Shares and Price Per Share text boxes here. You will enter the opening shares and price information later.

 NOTE You can enter the date, number-of-shares, and price-per-share information in the Create Opening Share Balance dialog box if you won't use the data for calculating the tax basis and, as a result, for calculating taxable profits or tax-deductible losses. But if you don't need to calculate taxable investment profits or tax-deductible losses, you also don't need to use Quicken for your investment record keeping.

FIGURE 17.5

The Create Opening Share Balance dialog box

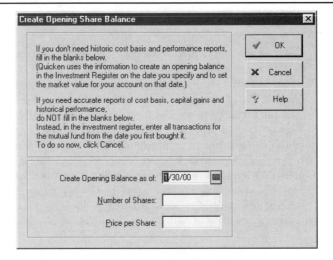

20. Click Cancel to close the dialog box and display the investment account version of the register, as shown in Figure 17.6.

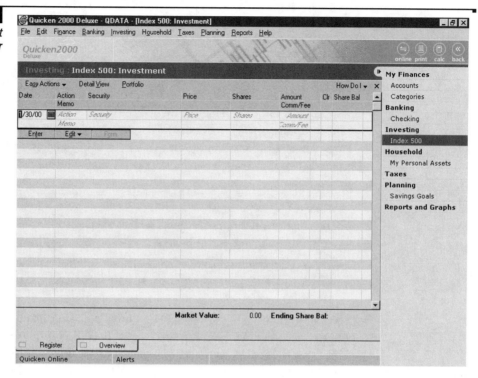

Describing the Mutual Fund Shares You Buy

The first mutual fund transaction you record is the purchase of shares. This is easy as long as you have your monthly statement or confirmation slip. You'll need to know the number of shares purchased, the price per share (or the transaction total), and the commission paid (if any).

Quicken provides two methods for recording transactions such as share purchases:

- You can enter a purchase transaction directly into the register.

- You can use an investment form dialog box to collect the share purchase transaction and then have Quicken enter the purchase transaction into the register for you.

Both methods work in the same way. Which one you choose depends on which window you're currently working in.

Entering a Purchase Directly into the Register

To enter the first and any subsequent purchases of mutual fund shares directly into the register, follow these steps:

1. Display the investment register and move to the first empty row of the register.

2. Enter the purchase date in the Date text box. Be sure to enter the actual purchase date and not the date you mailed the check to the mutual fund management company or the broker or the date you recorded the purchase. Quicken categorizes any capital gain or loss as short-term or long-term based on the difference between the purchase and sales dates shown in the register.

3. Enter the action, as follows:

   - *If you made this purchase sometime in the past,* enter the action as ShrsIn. Place the cursor in the Action combo box and type **ShrsIn** or select the ShrsIn entry from the Action list box.

   - *If this is a purchase you're currently making,* enter the action as BuyX. Type **BuyX** in the Action combo box or select that entry from the Action list box.

4. Press Tab to move past the Security text box. Quicken fills in the Security text box with whatever you named the mutual fund account. (You specified this name using the Set Up Mutual Fund Security dialog box as part of setting up the mutual fund.)

5. Enter the price per share you paid in the Avg. Cost or Price text box. (Quicken changes the name of the box that holds the share price data from Avg. Cost to Price if you record a BuyX transaction.) You can enter the share price in dollars and cents, such as 10.125, or in dollars and eighths, such as 10 1/8.

6. Enter the number of shares you purchased in the Shares text box or the total amount you paid in the Basis or Amount text box. (Quicken changes the name of the box that holds the total price from Basis to Amount if you record a BuyX transaction).

Quicken calculates whatever piece of data you didn't enter. For example, if you enter the price as $10.00 and the number of shares as 100, Quicken calculates the total as $1,000.00.

7. If you want to record some additional piece of information, such as the order number, use the Memo box.

8. If you're recording a BuyX action, use the XFer Acct combo box to show which account you used to pay for the purchase.

 NOTE If you enter an account name in the XFer Account field, Quicken records a payment transaction in the account equal to the value you enter in the XFer Amt text box.

9. If you're recording a BuyX action, either enter the amount you paid for the mutual fund shares and any commission in the XFer Amt text box or enter the commission you paid in the Comm Fee text box. (If you purchased shares of a no-load mutual fund, the commission equals 0.)

Quicken calculates whatever piece of data you didn't enter. For example, if you enter the total paid for the mutual fund shares as $1,000.00 and the commission as $50.00, Quicken calculates the XFer Amt as $1,050.00.

 TIP You don't need to pay commissions, or *loads*, when you purchase mutual fund shares. To purchase shares of a mutual fund without paying a commission, you simply purchase shares of a no-load mutual fund. Use the Mutual Fund Finder in Quicken to find no-load mutual funds (described in the last section of this chapter), or if you have an Internet connection, choose the Finance ➢ Quicken on the Web ➢ Quicken.com command and click the Investments hyperlink to search for no-load mutual funds.

10. Click Enter to record the transaction.

Quicken records the transaction into the investment register and moves to the next empty row of the register so you can enter another transaction. If you entered the Action as BuyX, Quicken also records a payment transaction in the XFer Acct. Figure 17.7 shows the investment register with two transactions: a ShrsIn transaction for $2,000 and a BuyX purchase for $5,000.

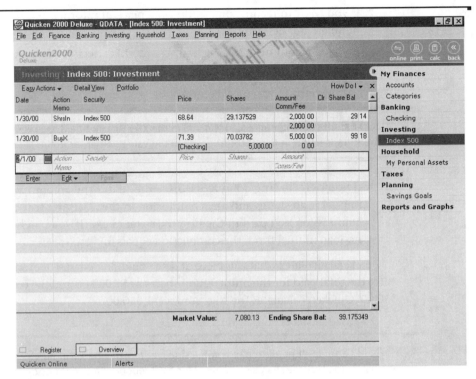

FIGURE 17.7

An investment register with some share purchases

Using a Form to Record a Purchase

Instead of recording information directly into the investment register, you can use the Buy/Add Shares dialog box to record a current purchase or an earlier purchase of mutual fund shares. A current purchase is one for which you not only want to record the purchase of the mutual fund shares, but also need to record the corresponding payment transaction (probably the check you wrote to purchase the shares). An earlier purchase is one for which you want to record only the purchase of the mutual fund shares but not the corresponding payment transaction. Here's how both transactions work:

1. Display the investment account in a register, move the cursor to the next empty row of the investment register, and click the Easy Actions button to display the Easy Actions menu. Choose the Buy/Add Shares command to display the Buy/Add Shares dialog box.

2. Click the Summary tab of the Buy/Add Shares dialog box. This tab is shown in Figure 17.8.

3. Enter the purchase date in the Date text box.

4. Press Tab to move past the Security and Account text boxes. Quicken fills in the Security text box and the Account text box with whatever you named the mutual fund account. (You specified this name in the Set Up Mutual Fund Security dialog box as part of setting up the mutual fund.)

FIGURE 17.8

The Summary tab of the Buy/Add Shares dialog box

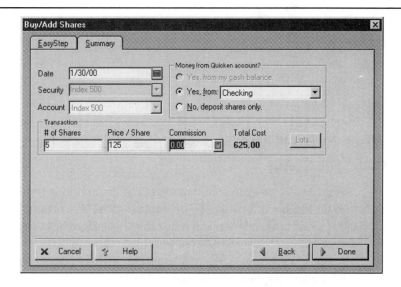

5. Enter the shares you purchased in the # of Shares text box, the price per share you paid in the Price/Share text box (in dollars and cents or dollars and eighths), and the commission you paid, if any, in the Commission text box.

6. If you're recording a current purchase, mark the Yes, From option button in the Money from Quicken Account? section of the dialog box, and then use the Yes, From drop-down list box to identify the account from which the payment was made.

7. If you're recording an earlier purchase, mark the No option button in the Money from Quicken Account? section of the dialog box.

8. Click Done.

Quicken uses the information you've entered in the Buy/Add Shares dialog box to record a current purchase or an earlier purchase in the investment account register.

PART

III

Quicken for Investors

Describing Mutual Fund Profit Distributions

Periodically, a mutual fund distributes profits to the shareholders. On a monthly basis, for example, a money market or bond mutual fund may distribute interest income. On a quarterly basis, a stock mutual fund probably distributes dividend income. And on an annual basis, most mutual funds make distributions of capital gains or losses.

 NOTE A capital gain occurs when the fund sells a stock, bond, or other security held by the fund for more than the security originally cost. A capital loss occurs when the fund sells a security held by the fund for less than the security originally cost.

What to Do When You Receive a Check from the Mutual Fund Manager

With Quicken, you can record mutual fund distributions you receive either directly into the register or by using an investment form. The advantage to using the investment form is that it lets you describe the distribution just once. When you record the amount directly into the register, you must sequentially describe each type of distribution separately: the dividend distribution, the short-term capital gain distribution, the long-term capital distribution, and so on.

To record a mutual fund distribution you receive by check using an income form, follow these steps:

1. Display the investment account's register, move the cursor to the next empty row of the register, click the Easy Actions button, and then choose the Record an Income Event command. You see the Record Income dialog box, as shown in Figure 17.9.

2. Enter the distribution date in the Date text box. Be sure to enter the actual distribution date, not the date you received the distribution or the date you recorded the distribution. The date you enter determines in which year's income the distribution is counted. For example, if you receive a distribution of 1999 capital gains in 2000, you need to enter the distribution date as 1999 so that the capital gains are counted in 1999's taxable income and not in 2000's taxable income.

FIGURE 17.9

*The Record Income
dialog box*

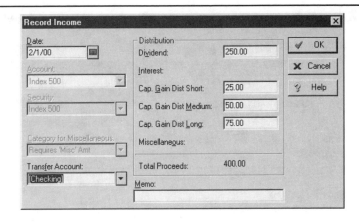

3. Press Tab to move past the Account and Security boxes to accept the mutual fund security name.

4. Enter the dividend income amount in the Dividend text box. (The mutual fund statement will give the amount of each type of distribution.)

5. Enter the short-term capital gain amount in the Cap. Gain Dist Short text box, and the long-term capital gain amount in the Cap. Gain Dist Long box.

6. Enter the name of the account into which you'll deposit the distribution check in the Transfer Account combo box.

7. If you need to collect any additional information, use the Memo text box.

8. Click OK.

Quicken takes the information entered in the Record Income dialog box and records transactions into the investment register. Quicken records one transaction for each type of distribution. Figure 17.10 shows the investment register with a $250 dividend distribution (the fourth transaction). The figure also shows a $25 short-term capital gain distribution, a $50 medium-term capital gain distribution, and a $75 long-term capital gain distribution.

As noted earlier, you don't need to use the Record Income dialog box to enter income distribution transactions into an investment register, but it makes things easier. To record them directly into the register, enter each distribution individually, as in Figure 17.10.

PART

III

Quicken for Investors

FIGURE 17.10

*How Quicken records
an income distribution
into the register*

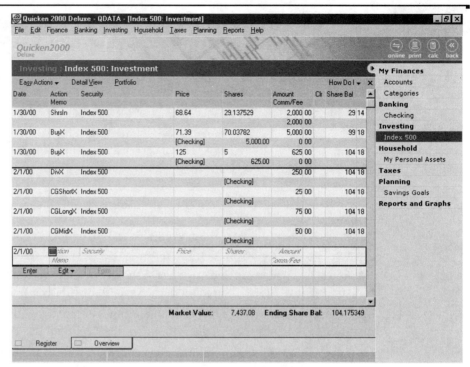

FIGURE 17.10

*How Quicken records
an income distribution
into the register*

What to Do When You Reinvest a Mutual Fund Distribution

When you reinvest a mutual fund distribution by buying additional shares, you essentially combine two of the transactions already described in this chapter: receiving a distribution and buying shares. You can record this sort of transaction directly into the register, but as with income distributions you don't reinvest, the easiest approach is to use an investment form.

To record a reinvested mutual fund distribution using the investment form, follow these steps:

1. Display the investment account's register, move the cursor to the next empty row of the register, click the Easy Actions button, and choose the Reinvest Income command. Quicken displays the Reinvest Income dialog box, as shown in Figure 17.11.

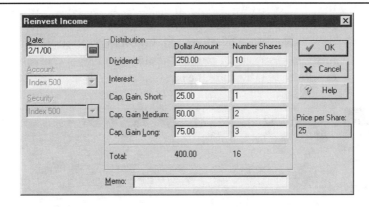

2. Enter the distribution and reinvestment date in the Date text box.

3. Press Tab to move past the Account and Security boxes to accept the mutual fund security name.

4. Enter the dividend income amount in the Dividend Dollar Amount text box.

5. Enter the number of shares purchased with the reinvested dividend in the Dividend Number Shares text box. (The mutual fund statement will give the amount of each type of distribution.)

6. Enter the interest income amount in the Interest Dollar Amount text box.

7. Enter the number of shares purchased with the reinvested interest in the Interest Number Shares text box, the short-term capital gain amount in the Cap. Gain Short Dollar Amount text box, the number of shares purchased with the reinvested short-term capital gains in the Cap. Gain Short Number Shares text box, the long-term capital gain amount in the Cap. Gain Long Dollar Amount text box, and the number of shares purchased with the reinvested long-term capital gains in the Cap. Gain Long Number Shares text box.

Quicken calculates the total dollar amount of the reinvested distribution, the total number of shares purchased, and the average price per share based on the information you entered in steps 4 through 7. These totals and the average price values will agree with what your mutual fund statement shows if you've correctly completed these steps.

8. If you need to collect any additional information, use the Memo text box.

9. Click OK.

Quicken takes the information you entered in the Reinvest Income dialog box and records transactions into the investment register. As with an income distribution

PART

III

Quicken for Investors

that isn't reinvested, Quicken records one transaction for each type of distribution. Figure 17.12 shows an investment register with a $250 reinvested dividend distribution, as well as a $25 reinvested short-term capital gain distribution, a $50 reinvested medium-term capital gain distribution, and a $75 reinvested long-term capital gain distribution. (These are the last four transactions shown in Figure 17.12.)

FIGURE 17.12

How Quicken records an income distribution into the register when the money is reinvested

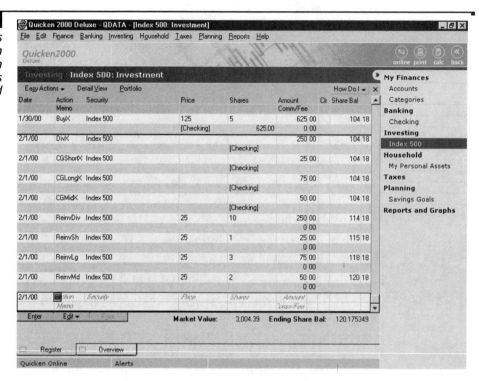

Again, you are not required to use an investment form—in this case, the Reinvest Income command and dialog box—to enter the reinvested distribution transactions. You can enter the transactions shown in Figure 17.12 directly into the register, one transaction at a time; just be sure to specify the correct action for each transaction.

Describing the Mutual Fund Shares You Sell

At some point, you'll probably sell the mutual fund shares you originally purchased with a check or that you acquired by reinvesting the dividends or capital gains. As with the other types of mutual fund transactions you record, this is easy as long as you have the necessary information: the number of shares sold, price per share (or transaction total), and commission paid (if any).

Again, you have two ways to record the sale of mutual fund shares: directly into the register or through an investment form. However, for this task, both record-keeping approaches are fast and convenient, and they are described in the following sections.

Recording the Sale Directly into the Register

To record the sale of mutual fund shares directly into the register, follow these steps:

1. Place the cursor in the next empty row of the register and enter the sales date in the Date text box. Be sure to enter the actual sales date. Quicken categorizes any capital gain or loss as short-term or long-term, based on the difference between the purchase and sale dates shown in the register.

2. Enter the Action as follows:

   - *If this is a sale you made sometime in the past*, enter the Action as ShrsOut.

   - *If this is a sale you're currently making*, enter the Action as SellX.

3. Press Tab to move past the Security text box to accept the mutual fund security name.

4. Enter the sales price per share you received in the Price text box, and enter the shares you sold in the Shares text box or the total amount you sold in the Amount text box.

Quicken calculates whatever piece of data you didn't enter. For example, if you enter the price as $10.00 and the number of shares as 100, Quicken calculates the total as $1,000.00.

5. If you want to record some additional piece of information, such as the sales order number, use the Memo text box.

6. If you're recording a SellX action, use the XFer Acct combo box to show the account into which you will deposit the check you receive from the sale of the shares.

If you enter an account name in the XFer Account text box, Quicken records a deposit transaction in the account equal to the value you enter in the XFer Amt text box.

7. If you're recording a SellX action, either enter the amount you received for the sale of the mutual fund shares less any commission you paid in the XFer Amt text box or enter the commission you paid in the Comm Fee text box. Again, Quicken calculates whatever piece of data you didn't enter.

8. Select Enter to display a message box that asks if you want to specifically identify the shares you're selling.

Specific identification of the shares you sell gives you control over the capital gain or loss stemming from the sale. People often use this control to minimize or postpone capital gains taxes and accelerate or maximize deductible capital losses. For example, by selling the most expensive shares first, you minimize the capital gain or maximize the capital loss on the sale of these shares. If you don't use specific identification, Quicken assumes that the first shares you purchased are the first shares you sell. You may have heard this costing assumption referred to by its initials, FIFO (first in first out).

9. If you don't want to specifically identify the shares, click Cancel, and you're finished.

10. If you want to use specific identification, click Specify Lots. Quicken displays a dialog box similar to the one in Figure 17.13. You can indicate which lots or parts of lots you're selling (a *lot* is just a set of shares you purchased at the same time). As you make your selections, Quicken shows you how many shares you've said you'll sell and how many you've identified. If you make a mistake in your specific identification and want to start over, choose Clear. When you've specifically identified as many as you've said you'll sell, click OK.

   - To specify a lot, click it or highlight it and click OK.

   - To select a portion of a lot, highlight it and enter the number of shares in the Total Selected box. Quicken displays a message box that asks for the number of shares from the lot you want to sell. You can enter some number of shares or accept Quicken's suggestion. (Quicken suggests you sell as many shares as you need to complete the specific identification.)

   - To tell Quicken to pick lots that minimize your capital gain (and therefore your capital gains taxes), click the Minimum Gain command button.

   - To tell Quicken to pick lots that maximize your capital gain (and therefore your capital gains taxes), click the Maximum Gain command button.

   - To tell Quicken to sell the oldest lots first, click the First Shares In command button.

   - To tell Quicken to sell the newest lots first, click the Last Shares In command button.

Quicken records the transaction into the investment register and selects the next empty row so you can enter another transaction. If you entered the action as SellX, Quicken also records a deposit transaction in the XFer Acct. Figure 17.14 shows 100 shares of the Vanguard Index 500 Trust being sold on February 1 at $28 a share.

FIGURE 17.13

This dialog box lets you tell Quicken which shares you're selling.

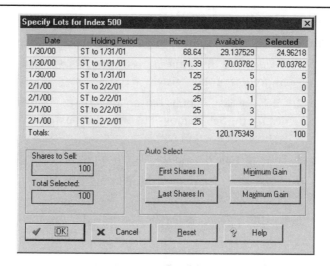

FIGURE 17.14

An investment register with a sale transaction

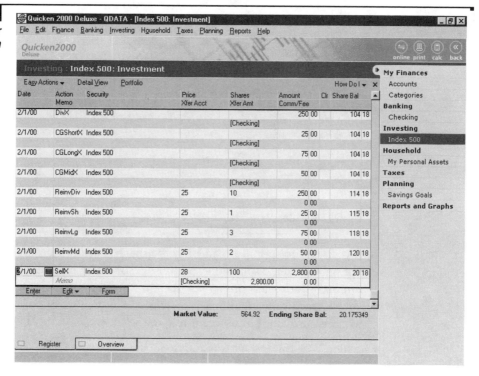

Using a Form to Record a Sale

To record the sale of shares using an investment form, follow these steps:

1. Display the investment account's register and place the cursor in the next empty row of the register.

2. Click the Easy Actions button and choose the Sell/Remove Shares command to display the Sell/Remove Shares dialog box. Then click the Summary tab, which is shown in Figure 17.15.

3. Enter the sale date in the Date text box.

4. Press Tab to move past the Security and Account boxes to accept the mutual fund security name.

5. Use the # of Shares text box to indicate how many shares you are selling.

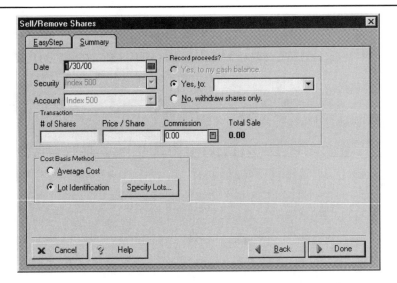

FIGURE 17.15

The Summary tab of the Sell/Remove Shares dialog box

6. If you want to specifically identify the shares, click the Specify Lots command button. Quicken displays the Specify Lots For dialog box (see Figure 17.13). You can make your selections as described in step 10 in the previous section. When you've specifically identified as many shares as you've said you'll sell, click OK to close the dialog box and return to the Sell/Remove Shares dialog box.

If you don't use the Specify Lots command button to specifically identify the shares you're selling, Quicken uses a first-in, first-out costing assumption to calculate the capital gain or loss on the sale. In other words, it assumes the shares you sell are always those you've held the longest.

7. Enter the share sales price in the Price/Share text box and the sales commission you are paying, if any, in the Commission text box. Quicken calculates the total amount of the sale.

You need to enter only three of the following four inputs: number of shares, price, commission, and total. Quicken can use any three of these inputs to calculate the fourth input.

8. If you're recording a current sale, indicate the account into which you'll deposit the sales proceeds by marking the Yes, To option button in the Record Proceeds? section of the dialog box. Then select the account from the Yes, To drop-down list box.

9. If you're recording an earlier sale and don't want to adjust a bank account balance for the sale, mark the No option button in the Record Proceeds? section of the dialog box.

10. Click Done. Quicken records the sale and enters a transaction describing the sale into the register.

Account Fees, Stock Splits, and Reminders

The preceding sections described various record-keeping actions for a mutual fund account. There are three additional mutual fund transactions you may need to record. Probably the most common is an account fee transaction (such as a mutual fund management company might charge for an IRA). The other two actions are StkSplit, which you use to record mutual fund share splits, and Reminder, which you use to put reminder notes in the investment register.

Recording Account Fees

Some mutual funds periodically levy account fees. For example, I used to have an IRA in a T. Rowe Price mutual fund. T. Rowe Price charged me an annual IRA custodian fee of $10. To pay the custodian fee at the end of every year, I could either write a $10 check to T. Rowe Price Company or let T. Rowe Price sell $10 worth of the mutual fund shares.

When You Write a Check to Pay the Account Fee

If you write a check to pay an account fee, you don't need to do anything special in the investment register. You just write the check in the usual way.

Categorize the check that pays an account fee as investment expense or a similar expense category. Items such as IRA account and custodial fees are miscellaneous deductions. At the time I'm writing this, a miscellaneous deduction in excess of 2 percent of your adjusted gross income may be used as an itemized deduction.

When You Sell Shares to Pay an Account Fee

If you sell shares (or, more likely, the mutual fund manager sells shares) to pay an account fee, you need to do a little more work to record the account fee. You need to record a SellX transaction in the investment register, as described in the section "Describing the Mutual Fund Shares You Sell" earlier in this chapter.

There's a slight trick to recording this type of SellX transaction. The entry for the commission or fee equals the total sales amount. For example, if you record the sale of $10 of mutual fund shares to pay for, say, a $10 account fee, both the Total Amount and Comm/Fee text boxes show 10. The XFer Amt text box, as a result, shows as 0. (When you record this transaction, Quicken sets the Price text box value back to 0, so both the Price and XFer Amt text boxes show 0.)

If you use the Sell/Remove Shares dialog box (displayed when you choose the Sell/Remove Shares command from the Easy Actions menu) to record an account fee transaction, you enter the number of shares you need to sell to pay the account fee, the sales price per share, and the commission. If you've correctly entered these inputs, the total sale shows as 0 because the commission—really the account fee—consumes the entire sales proceeds.

 WARNING Check with your tax advisor concerning investment expenses such as account maintenance fees paid for by selling shares. While the approach described here is the only one you can easily do in Quicken, it causes your account maintenance fees to show up as capital losses equal to whatever you originally paid for the shares. Unfortunately, this overstates your capital loss by the amount of the account fee and understates your investment expenses by the amount of the account fee. On your tax return, therefore, you need to adjust your capital losses or gains and your investment expenses (a possible miscellaneous deduction) for this discrepancy.

Recording a Mutual Fund Share Split

A share split occurs when the mutual fund company gives each current shareholder new shares. In a two-for-one split, for example, a shareholder receives one new share for each share already held. Someone who holds 100 shares prior to the split, for example, holds 200 shares after the split. You can record share splits directly into the register or with an investment form.

Recording the Share Split Directly into the Register

To record a mutual fund share split directly into the register, follow these steps:

1. Place the cursor in the next empty row of the register and enter the split date in the Date text box.

2. In the Action combo box, enter **StkSplit** as the action.

3. Press Tab to move past the Security text box to accept the suggested security, the mutual fund name.

4. If you want to update your mutual fund price per share data, enter what the price per share will be after the split in the Price text box.

5. Enter the number of new shares you'll receive for a specified number of old shares in the New Shares text box. (When you indicate the action as StkSplit, Quicken replaces the Number of Shares text box with the New Shares text box.)

6. If you want to record some additional piece of information about the split—perhaps to cross-reference the mutual fund statement that explains or reports the split—use the Memo text box.

7. Enter the number of old shares you'll give up to receive a specified number of new shares using the Old Shares text box. (When you indicate the action as StkSplit, Quicken replaces the XFer Account combo box with the Old Shares text box.)

8. Select Enter.

Quicken records the transaction into the investment register and adjusts the number of mutual fund shares you're holding according to the new-shares-to-old-shares ratio. Then it selects the next empty row of the investment register so that you can enter another transaction. Figure 17.16 shows the investment register with a stock split transaction (the selected transaction shown in the figure).

FIGURE 17.16

*An investment register
with a stock split
transaction*

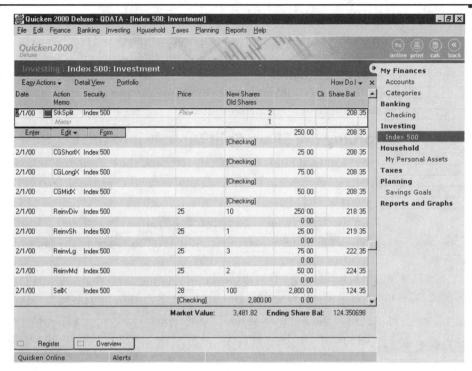

Using a Form to Record a Share Split

To record a share split transaction using an investment form, follow these steps:

1. Display the investment account in a register and move the cursor to the next empty row of the investment register.

2. Click the Easy Actions button and choose the Stock Split command to display the Stock Split dialog box, as shown in Figure 17.17.

FIGURE 17.17

*The Stock Split
dialog box*

3. Enter the split date in the Date text box.

4. Press Tab to move past the Account and Security boxes to accept the mutual fund security name.

5. Enter the number of new shares equal to one old share in the New Shares text box.

6. Enter the number of old shares in the Old Shares text box.

7. If you want to update the share price information, enter the price per share after the split in the Price after Split text box.

8. If you want to describe some additional piece of information about the stock split, use the Memo text box.

9. Click OK. Quicken uses the information you've entered to record a stock split transaction for the investment account.

Storing Reminders in the Investment Register

Your investment activities may require you to do things by certain dates—cash a certificate of deposit by June 3, for example. You can use the investment register to store reminder messages, which alert you about these types of events.

To enter a reminder message directly into an investment register, just enter the date by which you want to be reminded in the Date text box, enter the action as Reminder, and then type your message in the Description text box. If you wanted to remind yourself about a certificate of deposit that needs to be either cashed or rolled over by February 1, 2000, for example, set the date as 2/1/00 and the action as Reminder. You might enter the text **Cash Big National CD** in the Description text box and any other notes to yourself about this transaction in the Memo text box.

To enter a reminder message with an investment form, click the Easy Actions button and then select Advanced ➤ Reminder Transaction. Quicken displays the Reminder dialog box shown in Figure 17.18, which collects the date and the reminder message.

PART

III

Quicken for Investors

FIGURE 17.18

The Reminder dialog box

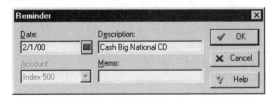

To stop Quicken from reminding you, you can delete the reminder message transaction or enter a **c** in the Clr text box to mark the reminder message as cleared.

Editing Mutual Fund Transactions

Just as with the transactions that appear in any other account, you can edit investment account transactions. There are two ways to do this:

- Highlight the incorrect transaction in the register, and then fix the incorrect pieces of the entry. Be sure to click the Enter button after you've made your changes.

- Use an investment form to make your corrections. First, select the transaction that needs to be edited, and then choose the Form button. Quicken displays an investment form like the one you might have used originally to record the transaction, but the dialog box is already filled out with the transaction's information. Make your changes and click OK.

Success Strategies for Mutual Fund Record Keeping

Once you're familiar with the mechanics, you'll find it very easy to use Quicken to keep records of your mutual fund investments. When you use Quicken for your mutual fund record keeping, there are some strategies to consider, as described in the following sections.

ShrsIn and ShrsOut versus BuyX and SellX

It can be confusing to choose between the ShrsIn and BuyX actions and between the ShrsOut and SellX actions. Follow this basic rule: Use the ShrsIn and ShrsOut transactions when the cash effect of an investment purchase or sale has already been recorded, and use the BuyX and SellX transactions when the cash effect of an investment purchase or sale hasn't yet been recorded.

In general, you should use the ShrsOut and ShrsIn actions when you're entering old investment transactions so that you have a historical record. And this raises an important question: Is it worth it to go back and enter historical records? I think it is if you're dealing with a taxable mutual fund, which is a mutual fund that's not being used as an IRA or a 401(k) plan account.

One of the biggest benefits of using Quicken for your mutual fund record keeping is that it lets you more easily track the tax basis, or cost, of the mutual fund shares you've acquired through the years. When you sell the mutual fund shares, you need to report the capital gain or loss stemming from the sale on a Schedule D tax form.

And to do this, you'll need to know not only the sales proceeds, but also the cost of the shares you sell.

 TIP Quicken's reports and charts provide a handy means of summarizing and organizing the investment information stored in the investment account registers. See Chapter 4 for details on producing Quicken's investment reports and Chapter 8 for more information about Quicken's charting capabilities.

Tracking Market Values

You can store current share price information about investments. By doing so, you'll be able to track the market value of your mutual fund investments over time. You'll also be able to calculate the performance of your mutual fund investment over any time period. Your mutual fund probably provides the quarterly and annual returns of the fund in its quarterly and annual reports. If you invested sometime other than at the start of the year or the start of the quarter, however, these performance figures don't actually give the performance of your shares.

 WARNING When Quicken produces a Net Worth or Balance Sheet report, it uses the most recent market price per share to calculate the value of an account balance. This approach is probably fine for personal net worth reports as long as the valuation method is clearly disclosed, but reporting securities at their fair market value on a business's balance sheet isn't the accepted convention unless the fair market value is less than the original cost.

Entering Market Price Information

To provide the current price-per-share information to Quicken, follow these steps:

1. In the investment account register, display the Portfolio View of the investment account by clicking the Portfolio button at the top of the register or by choosing Investing ➤ Portfolio View. Figure 17.19 shows this view.

The Portfolio View lists each of the securities you hold within each account. An *e* shows next to the prices of those security prices that are only estimates. (In the Investment Portfolio Value report, this *e* changes to an asterisk.)

2. If the date shown beneath the Portfolio View's button bar isn't the current date, use the Calendar button located just to the right of the date display to select the current date.

FIGURE 17.19

The Portfolio View displays investment information by security.

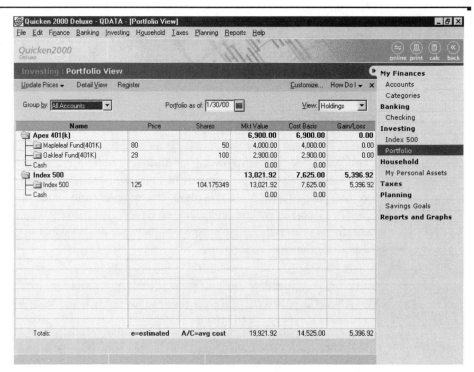

3. If you want to reorder the list, use the Group By list box to specify how you want Quicken to arrange your investment portfolio information: by account, security, security type, investment goal, asset class, or watch list.

4. Select the security for which you want to record the current market price.

5. Enter the current market price in the Price column. Typically, you can enter mutual fund prices in dollars and cents, such as 13.87, but you can also use fractional prices, such as 8 7/8. (Use the + and – keys to incrementally adjust the price by one-eighth.) If the estimated price is correct, you can just press the asterisk key.

6. Repeat steps 4 and 5 to enter the current market price for each of the other mutual funds shown in the Portfolio View. You will see the results of each adjustment as you move your cursor to the next security.

7. If you want to return to the register, click the Register button.

NOTE In general, a mutual fund will have only one security. You can, however, put more than one mutual fund security in an account—for example, if you invest in a mutual fund family.

Creating Custom Portfolio Views

You can create customized portfolio views that show the information and calculations that you specify. To customize the view, click the Customize button in the Portfolio View to open the Customize Portfolio dialog box, as shown in Figure 17.20. This dialog box provides a set of list boxes for specifying which investment information and which calculation results a custom view should display. You can click the Date Range button to display another dialog box that lets you specify the time period for which the investment returns are calculated.

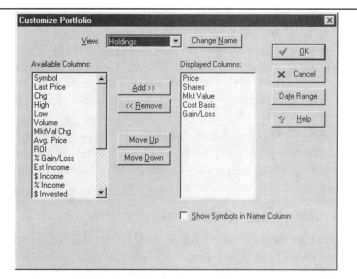

Updating Prices Online

You can quickly and easily retrieve security price information using Quicken's Online Quotes feature. If you have an Internet connection and have entered ticker symbols for all of the securities you want to track, Quicken can update the price and adjust the market value automatically. Simply click the Update Prices button in the Portfolio View and choose the Get Online Quotes & News command. Click the Update Now button or the Customize button to display the Customize Investment Download dialog box (not shown in a figure). Here you can specify for which securities you want to get updated prices. Click OK, then click Update Now to connect to the Internet and download the information you requested. As you do this, you will see a series of messages as Quicken connects, transmits, and receives information over the Internet.

NOTE In order to use Quicken's Online Quotes & News feature, you need to have entered ticker symbols for each of the securities you want to track. If you want to go back and do this, select the investment in the Detail View and click the Properties button. Then enter the ticker in the Symbol text box and click OK.

You can also update quotes online by choosing the Online ➢ One Step Update command. Just select the information you want to update from the dialog box Quicken displays and click Update Now.

Updating Prices Manually

If you don't have an Internet connection, you can enter price updates manually. Updating prices manually usually doesn't take much more time than downloading price information, so you may want to update prices by hand even if you do have an Internet connection (especially if you infrequently track a small number of mutual funds).

To update prices, display the Portfolio View and click the Price column. Then enter the current price, and press Enter. (You can get daily prices from your local paper or from the *Wall Street Journal*.) Quicken updates the Mkt Value amount to reflect the new price.

Editing Price History Information

You may want to enter or edit historical price data for a security. To do this, display the Portfolio View and select the security. Then choose the Update Prices command button and select Edit Price History. Quicken displays the Price History, as shown in Figure 17.21.

FIGURE 17.21

The Price History

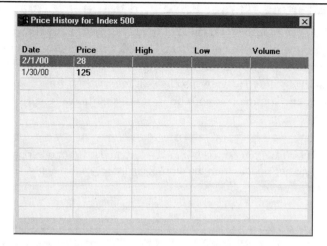

To enter a new price, right-click a price (so that Quicken displays a shortcuts menu) and then choose the New command. Quicken displays the New Price For dialog box, as shown in Figure 17.22.

FIGURE 17.22

The New Price For
dialog box

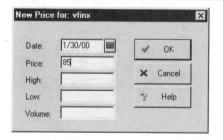

This dialog box provides five text boxes: Date, Price, High (Price), Low (Price), and Volume. To add a new price to the history, enter the date and price and click OK. Optionally, enter the daily high price, daily low price, and trading volume for that day. When you click OK, Quicken adds the price to the Price History.

To correct a price that already shows in the Price History, right-click a price and then choose the Edit command. Quicken displays the Edit Price dialog box, which asks what the correct share prices and volume should be for the selected date. To correct the prices or volume shown, enter this data and click OK. Quicken updates the Price History.

You can also delete a price from the Price History. To do this, right-click the price and then choose Delete.

PART

III

Quicken for Investors

Charting Market Price and Value Information

You can plot the total value of the investment in the Portfolio View as well as the price per share and other data. Just click the Detail View button. Quicken displays a window like the one shown in Figure 17.23. The Security Detail View shows the total market value. The view also lists all transactions for a security using a scrollable list box and summarizes your holdings of a particular security.

 NOTE You can view your investment data from other perspectives by selecting other viewing options from the drop-down list boxes that appear above the graph.

FIGURE 17.23

The Security Detail View plots account values in charts and provides other investment information.

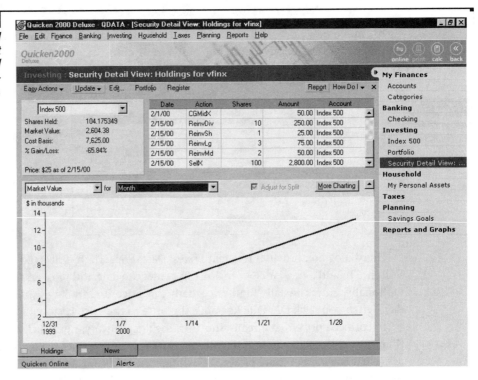

You can record investment activity when the Security Detail View is displayed. This approach doesn't make as much sense for mutual funds as it does for brokerage investment accounts, but you should know that the capability exists. To record investment transactions when the Security Detail View is displayed, click the Easy Actions button to display the Easy Actions menu and use its menu commands to display the appropriate investment form dialog box. Then fill in the dialog box's text and combo boxes. For example, to record the purchase of mutual fund shares, click the Easy Actions button, choose the Buy command, and use the Buy/Add Shares dialog box to describe the purchase.

You can expand the size of the investment graphs by clicking the up arrow that appears above the top-right corner of the graph. Figure 17.24 shows the expanded graph.

You can print the graphs by clicking the Print button that appears in the upper-right corner of the area or by choosing the File ➤ Print Graph command.

FIGURE 17.24

The Security Graph area shows an expanded version of the same graphs shown by the Security Detail View.

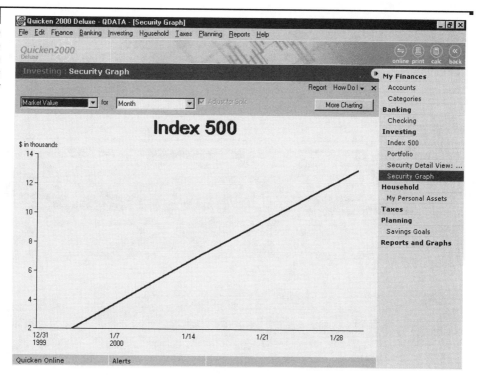

Using the Mutual Fund Finder

Quicken.com, Quicken's Web site, provides a handy Mutual Fund Finder. In essence, what the Mutual Fund Finder does is help you select mutual funds based on your feelings about the risks you're willing to bear and the rewards you hope to achieve.

 NOTE If you have an Internet connection, Quicken.com provides a rich variety of other investment research information, too. You'll find it both enjoyable and educational to spend some time exploring what the Quicken.com Web site offers.

Selecting Mutual Funds with the Mutual Fund Finder

To start the Mutual Fund Finder, start Quicken and then choose Investing ➤ Investment Research. Quicken displays the Investment Research Web page on the Quicken.com Web site, as shown in Figure 17.25. (You need to have a working Internet connection, obviously, for this to work.)

FIGURE 17.25

The Investment Research Web page provides a mutual fund finder.

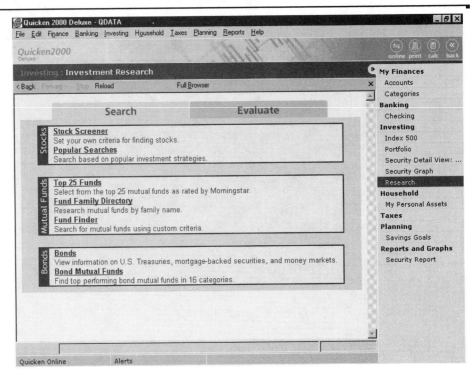

To use the Mutual Fund Finder, click the Search tab and then the Fund Finder hyperlink. (You may need to scroll down the page a bit to see this hyperlink.) Quicken displays the Web form shown in Figure 17.26. It provides buttons and boxes that let you describe how you want to locate a mutual fund: by searching based on fund characteristics (Search by Criteria) or by searching for a particular fund name (Search by Name).

FIGURE 17.26

The Quicken.com Web site provides this Web form, which you can use to describe the characteristics of the mutual fund you want.

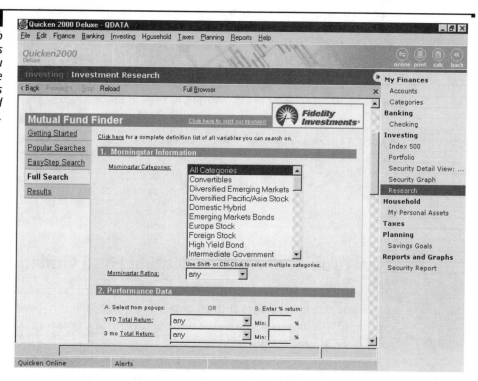

To continue a search, click the Submit Search button. (You may need to scroll down a bit to see this button.) Quicken then displays the first page of a list of mutual funds meeting your selection criteria, as shown in Figure 17.27. You will need to click the Next Page hyperlink to move to the subsequent pages of the list. If you want to start a new search, you can scroll down the Web page until you get the Web form that lets you describe the mutual fund characteristics you're looking for. To print the contents of this window, click the Full Browser button to display the Web page in your default browser and then choose its Print button.

PART

III

Quicken for Investors

MASTERING THE OPPORTUNITIES

Index and Callan-Screen Funds

An *index fund* is one that buys all the stocks in a particular stock market index or bond market index. The return from an index fund basically matches the index the fund attempts to mimic, but falls slightly short of the actual index's return because the index fund must pay expenses. However, because there aren't expensive professional money managers to pay, index fund expense ratios are typically very low—often 0.2 percent.

Index funds are popular because, over time, roughly two-thirds of the actively managed funds fall short of the index for the market they invest in. By investing in an index fund, therefore, you know you won't beat the market; in fact, you'll trail the market by the expense ratio. You probably will beat the majority of the actively managed funds, however.

A *Callan-screen fund* is a fund that meets specific mutual fund criteria developed by Callan and Associates, including mutual fund size and adherence to the stated invest-ment philosophy.

Practical Problems with the Mutual Fund Finder

The Mutual Fund Finder is a wonderful tool. And it's much better than the alterna-tives, such as throwing darts at the mutual fund page of the *Wall Street Journal* or read-ing some "This-month's-hot-mutual-funds" article in *Money Magazine.* But it bases its analyses on at least two suspect notions.

The most suspect notion, at least in my opinion, is the idea that a fund's past per-formance provides a clue about how it will do in the future. This implicit assumption is understandable, but almost all academic research supports the view that, in the securities markets, the past is no predictor of the future.

In fact, there is a strong tendency toward "regression to the mean." If you're not familiar with this statistical truism, let me explain. Over long periods of time, a fund's average annual return "averages out" to the historical average of the stock market. If a fund has done two percent better on average than the market over the last ten years, for example, it probably will do about two percent worse on average over the next ten years. As a practical matter, chasing last year's winners more likely finds next year's losers, not next year's winners.

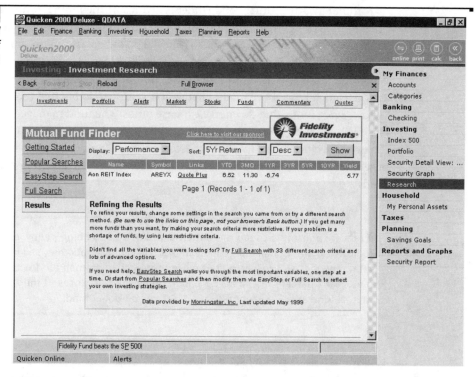

FIGURE 17.27

The Mutual Fund Finder's list of mutual funds

There are exceptions to the regression-to-the-mean truism, but exceptions are few and far between. If you're reading this, you probably know the funds and the names of fund managers who have defied the truism: Peter Lynch and the Fidelity Magellan Fund, John Templeton and the Templeton Growth Fund, John Neff and the Vanguard Windsor Fund, and others. But these are the exceptions, not the rule. And knowing now that 25 years ago you should have invested with Lynch or Neff or Templeton isn't relevant. What you need to find is the next Lynch, the next Neff, or the next Templeton.

There's also another problem with the Mutual Fund Finder: The expense ratio data can be misleading. One of the most important elements in picking a mutual fund is the fund's expense ratio. If you pick a mutual fund with a low expense ratio, you're likely to do better over the long haul, all other factors being equal.

TIP To its credit, the Mutual Fund Finder suggests that you find no-load mutual funds with annual expense ratios of less than 1 percent.

Fortunately, the Mutual Fund Finder lets you sort the mutual funds it finds in order of increasing expense ratios. But if you do this, you may find that the first funds listed don't have expense ratios at all. They all show up as zero-expense ratio funds.

Technically, this is correct. These funds don't have expense ratios. But the reason is that the funds will invest in other funds that do have expense ratios. For example, a fund from T. Rowe Price might charge no expense ratio because it invests in other T. Rowe Price funds that do charge expense ratios. The fund manager isn't trying to cheat you here; it's his or her way of being fair. You shouldn't, after all, need to pay the expense ratio twice. But the zero-expense ratios of mutual funds that invest in other mutual funds make it more difficult to search for the lowest priced mutual funds.

 TIP If choosing a cheap mutual fund strikes you as being penny-wise and pound-foolish, remember that a big fund with a small expense ratio may still be able to pay its fund manager and research staff more money than a small fund with a big expense ratio. A 0.2 percent fee on a $1.5 billion dollar fund produces as much revenue to the mutual fund as a 2 percent fee on a $150 million dollar fund.

 MASTERING FINANCIAL SUCCESS

How to Be a Smart Investor

A lot of people think smart investing means complicated investing. That's not true. Smart investing is usually simple investing. In fact, the most important things you can do relate to the way you go about investing, not the specific investments you pick. Here, I offer five secrets that can help you become a smart investor.

The First Secret: Compound Interest

Compound interest represents the first secret. Does that seem strange? Compound interest doesn't seem very powerful at first blush. You put, say, $1,000 into an investment that returns a 10 percent profit. The first year, the $1,000 earns $100. Let's say you leave the $100 in the savings account and add another $1,000. The second year, you earn $210. If you continue saving this way (every year putting $1,000 into the account), you earn $330 in the third year.

Continued

MASTERING FINANCIAL SUCCESS CONTINUED

Compound interest produces a very interesting result. Your interest earnings grow because you continue to add to your investment. Some of the addition comes from additional savings. But more and more of the interest earnings come from the interest you're earning on the interest—what's called compound interest.

By year seven, for example, you typically earn more in interest than the regular amount you annually save. And the interest earnings continue to grow and grow. After 25 years, you earn around $10,000 a year in interest. After 35 years, you earn around $27,000 a year in interest. After 45 years, you earn around $72,000 a year in interest. And all of this from a $1,000-per-year savings plan.

Nothing is tricky about compound interest. You need to be able to save some money and then reinvest the interest. And you need to be able to earn a decent interest rate or investment rate of return (which is basically the same thing). By meeting these simple requirements, you can grow rich.

How quickly you grow rich depends on the interest rate and your savings. The higher the interest rate and the bigger the savings, the faster and more impressive the compounding.

The Second Secret: Opt for Tax-Deductible, Tax-Deferred Investment Choices

You need to use tax-deductible, tax-deferred investment vehicles such as IRAs or, even better, an employer's 401(k) or 403(b) plan. Let me show you how powerful these two tools are.

To provide a backdrop against which to discuss your future investing, let's suppose that your personal wealth target requires you to save $6,000 a year. And just to make things fun, let's also pretend that $6,000 is an absolute impossibility. Let's say that you're currently spending every dollar you make and you couldn't come up with an extra $500 a month unless your life depended on it.

Here's the secret of meeting the $6,000-per-year goal: Tax-deductible investments let you borrow a huge chunk of the money from the federal and state government. Suppose, for example, that you're working with an employer who provides a 401(k) plan but doesn't contribute any matching money. You want to save $6,000 a year because that amount will ultimately allow you to become financially independent. By using a tax-deductible investment such as a 401(k), you would, in effect, be able to borrow roughly $2,000 a year. Here's why: If you stick $6,000 in your 401(k) plan, you will save about

Continued ▐▶

$2,000 in income taxes. Of the $6,000 in annual savings, then, $4,000 would come from your pocket and $2,000 would come from the federal and state government.

Notice what you've already accomplished by using the powerful concept of tax-deductible investing: You've cut your out-of-pocket cash by around a third.

Things get even better if you happen to work for an employer who matches a portion of your 401(k) contribution. Let's say, for example, that your employer matches your contributions by contributing $.50 to your savings for every $1.00 you contribute. The math gets a little tricky in this case. If you contribute $4,000, you get another $2,000 from your employer. You also get roughly $1,500 in government contributions in the form of tax savings. The bottom line is that you need to come up with only about $2,500 of your own money to reach your $6,000-per-year savings goal.

If you work for an employer who generously matches a portion of your 401(k) contributions, most of the money you need to achieve financial independence will come from your employer and the government. That's right—*most of the money comes from your employer and the government.*

In a tax-deferred investment vehicle like a 401(k) or an IRA, income taxes on your interest or investment profits are deferred. For this reason, you effectively earn a much higher rate of interest inside a tax-deferred account. The reason is that the federal and state income taxes you pay on interest and investment income wipe out anywhere from 15 to 40 percent of your profit, with most people paying about a 30 percent tax on their profits. But inside a tax-deferred investment vehicle like a 401(k) or an IRA, you might earn compound interest at the annual rate of 10 percent. Outside a tax-deferred investment vehicle, on the other hand, you might earn around 7 percent.

Those differences may not seem very big, but over time they have a cumulative impact on compound interest calculations. For example, suppose that you are a 20-year-old adult just entering the work force and you're trying to decide how to invest $2,000 a year for retirement at age 65. If you compound interest using a 7 percent annual rate, you end up with around $570,000 by the time you retire. If you instead compound interest using a 10 percent annual rate, you end up with around $1,400,000—roughly $800,000 more.

To sum things up, tax-deductible, tax-deferred investment vehicles are the best and most effective method of accumulating wealth. There is no better method for moving toward financial independence—none. You can save up to roughly $10,000 a year by using a 401(k) or 403(b) plan.

Continued

MASTERING FINANCIAL SUCCESS CONTINUED

What If You're Unlucky?

The financial power of tax-deductible, tax-deferred investment choices such as 401(k)s begs an important but awkward question. Let's say your employer doesn't offer a 401(k) plan, 403(b) plan, or an equivalent tax-deductible, tax-deferred savings program. Is this whole tax-deductible, tax-deferred investing business such a big deal that you should consider switching employers?

First, if you're serious about achieving financial independence, I recommend moving to a new employer with a 401(k) or equivalent, tax-deductible, tax-deferred investment plan. The wealth-creation benefits are just too enormous to pass up. Likewise, if your employer does offer a matching plan, well, free money is free money. I'm not saying that you should keep a job you hate, but I would think long and hard about leaving an employer who has put you on a fast track toward financial independence.

What if you're working where there isn't a 401(k)? If I were you, I would start by talking to other employees and gauging their interest. Then, assuming you're not alone in your feelings, I would approach management. A simple 401(k) plan for a small company costs a few thousand dollars a year. As you know now, such a plan delivers enormous benefits. If it were me, I would rather have a 401(k) plan than a fancy holiday party or a summer picnic. If the truth be told, I would even forgo part of my next raise.

I should note here, too, that you may be eligible to contribute up to $2,000 a year in a tax-deductible IRA. (IRA earnings on allowable contributions are always tax-deferred.) If you're married and your spouse works, you both may be able to contribute $2,000 a year. Even if your employer doesn't provide a 401(k) plan, it may be worthwhile to save several thousand dollars a year by using tax-deductible investment choices. They may be all you need to progress toward your wealth target.

The Third Secret: Work Your Money Hard

Most people don't make their money work very hard. Not surprisingly, their profits reflect this. They earn returns of 3 or 5 percent. By working their money harder, they could double or triple their returns and earn 9 percent, 10 percent, or more.

You make your money work harder by investing in riskier investments. If the idea of investing in, say, the stock market, scares the living daylights out of you, you've made way too big a deal out of stock market risks.

Let's start by discussing the concept of risk. What you mean by risk, I'll venture, is really two things: volatility and the fear of losing your investment.

Continued

PART

III

Quicken for Investors

MASTERING FINANCIAL SUCCESS CONTINUED

As for the volatility of the stock market, some days the market is up, and some days the market is down. Up and down, up and down. It's enough to make some people sick. However, people make way too big a deal over day-to-day fluctuations in the weather. Stock prices are like the weather. Some days it's warmer, and some days it's colder. Some days the market is up, and some days the market is down. This up and down business gives the nightly news anchor something to talk about, but it's only so much blather. It's pseudo-news.

You don't let day-to-day temperature fluctuations bother you. The fact that it was two degrees colder last Thursday doesn't matter. Neither should you let day-to-day stock market fluctuations bother you. It's just plain silly. The only thing that really matters is the change in price between the time you buy a stock and the time you sell it.

The other feeling about risk, based on the fear of volatility, is that what you buy today for, say, $1,000, won't be worth $1,000 when you sell it. You have only to look at day-to-day fluctuations in the market to realize that. However, if you take the long view, you will see that the general trend in the stock market is always up. You can't buy a handful of stocks today and be certain that they will increase in value over the coming weeks, but you can be certain that they will grow in value over a decade or, even better, over two or three decades.

"Well, even so," you're thinking, "I'll still stick with something a little safer. All that bouncing about makes me nauseous." Unfortunately, there is a simple problem with so-called safe investments: They appear to be safe because their values don't jump around, but they aren't profitable. Your money doesn't earn anything or much of anything.

Here are a few simple facts: In this century, common stocks have delivered about a 10 percent return. Long-term corporate bonds have delivered about a 5.5 percent return. U.S. Treasury Bills over the same time period have delivered just under a 4.0 percent return.

If you adjust the historical long-term bond return for inflation and income taxes, you just break even. If you adjust the historical U.S. Treasury Bill return for inflation and income taxes, you lose about a percent a year. These two options, remember, are so-called safer investments.

History teaches investors two lessons. One is that you profit by sticking your money in riskier investments such as stocks and real-estate—ownership investments. The other is that you don't make any real profit by loaning your savings to the government, a corporation, or a local bank. To profit from your investments, you need to be an owner, not a loaner.

Continued

MASTERING FINANCIAL SUCCESS CONTINUED

"Now, wait a minute," you're thinking. "That may be true over recent history. But the world is a far more dangerous place today. We can't be sure things will run so smoothly in the future."

Actually, I agree with you. But I would say that the last century hasn't been smooth. The stock market collapsed. The world suffered a global recession. We had two world wars. We saw the first use of nuclear weapons. We had a 50-year cold war that, for peace, relied upon the threat of thermonuclear exchange.

The world *is* a dangerous place, but it's been a dangerous place for a long time. And yet, despite all the terrible things that have happened, ownership investments have been profitable. For that reason, I firmly believe that the only way to achieve financial independence—the only way to accumulate any significant amount of wealth—is by investing money in ownership investments such as stocks or real estate.

The Fourth Secret: Broadly Diversify

There is one other point of which you need to be aware, and it's a very quick point but crucially important: You need to be well-diversified. Ideally, in fact, you should have a couple dozen, equal-sized investments in different areas.

You should also make sure that you're not heavily dependent on a single industry or tied to a particular geographical location. You don't, for example, want to own 20 rental houses in the same town. And you wouldn't want to own 20 bank stocks.

This business about broadly diversifying is a statistical truth. Unfortunately, the statistics are too daunting—and darn unpleasant—to explain here. Suffice it to say, the only way you can hope to achieve the average returns I've talked about in the preceding secret is by having enough individual investments so that they "average out" to the historical average.

Diversification has a really interesting ramification, by the way. Even with several thousand dollars of savings a year, you need, as a practical matter, to invest in mutual funds. To own a portfolio of, say, 20 or 25 common stocks and to keep your commission costs reasonable, you would probably need to be able to invest $40,000 or $50,000 at a time. That way, you can purchase round, 100-share lots of stocks, thereby lowering your expenses. To own a portfolio of 20 or 25 rental houses, you probably need to invest several times that much. You also have the challenge of geographically diversifying yourself. It is much harder, obviously, to own houses in many different parts of the country than it is to own stocks in many different places. So picking a mutual fund is the way to go.

Continued ▮▶

PART

III

Quicken for Investors

MASTERING FINANCIAL SUCCESS CONTINUED

Picking a stock mutual fund isn't tough. But rather than try to give you a bird's-eye view of this subject, I encourage you to read a wonderful book on the subject by Richard D. Irwin, called *Bogle on Mutual Funds* (Richard D. Irwin, Inc., 1994). John C. Bogle was chairman of The Vanguard Group of Investment Companies. This easy-to-read book provides hundreds of pages of worthwhile and honest advice on picking mutual funds.

The Fifth Secret: You Don't Have To Be a Rocket Scientist

None of this investment business requires anywhere near as much know-how as is needed to be a rocket scientist. All you need to know is the following, which is a summary of what I've explained in the preceding pages:

- Compound interest is a mathematical truth that says you should regularly save and reinvest your profits.

- Use tax-deductible and tax-deferred investment choices such as 401(k)s and IRAs. These investment vehicles boost your savings and the interest rate you earn on your investments.

- The case for investing in ownership investments is simple: It's the only real way to make money over time.

- Diversification is important because it increases the probability that investment profits closely match the stock market's historical returns. However, for diversification to work, you must invest for long enough periods of time.

CHAPTER **18**

Stocks, Bonds, and Other Equity and Debt Securities

FEATURING:

If you invest in common stocks through a brokerage account, you can set up a special investment account that tracks all the securities you hold in the brokerage account. In addition, this special investment account keeps a record of the brokerage account's cash balance if the account includes an associated cash or money market account.

Tracking stocks and other equity securities with Quicken works very much like tracking mutual funds, as described in Chapter 17. The main difference is that Quicken provides a lengthier list of investment actions for stocks and other equity securities since these transactions can affect the cash account associated with a brokerage account or your regular bank account.

 TIP You can track shares of mutual funds that invest in stocks and shares of publicly traded real estate investment trusts in the same way that you track stocks. You may want to set up securities for these other equity investments too.

Before You Begin

Here are the prerequisites for tracking stock investments in Quicken:

- You need to have records that document the stock you've purchased and sold (the raw data you want to record in Quicken).
- You need to know the mechanics of using the Quicken investment register. To keep records of stock investments, you use many of the same windows, dialog boxes, and commands you do to keep records of mutual funds (see Chapter 17).

Setting Up a Brokerage Account

You'll need to set up a separate investment account for each brokerage account you have. If you have one brokerage account with a full-service broker and another with a discount broker, you need two investment accounts. If you also hold stocks (and other securities) outside a brokerage account, you can set up another investment account for these.

TIP A good rule of thumb is to set up an investment account for each brokerage statement you receive.

Setting Up the Quicken Investment Account

To set up an investment account for tracking stocks and other securities, follow these steps:

1. Choose Finance ➢ Account List to display the Account List.

2. Click the New command button in the Account List or choose Edit ➢ Account ➢ New to display the Create New Account dialog box.

3. Click the Brokerage button, click Next to display the Investment Account Setup dialog box, and then click the Summary tab, which is shown in Figure 18.1.

4. Enter an account name in the Account Name text box.

5. If you want to enter a description of the brokerage account or additional account information, such as the account number, use the Description text box.

6. Be sure that the Account Contains a Single Mutual Fund checkbox is not marked. This tells Quicken that you'll use the account for tracking multiple securities.

FIGURE 18.1

The Summary tab of the Investment Account Setup dialog box

Investment Account Setup

EasyStep | Summary

Account Information
  Account Name: Brokerage
  Description:
  ☐ Account Contains a Single Mutual Fund

Optional Info
  Info
  Tax

Cash Balance
  ☐ Use a Linked Checking Account for my Cash Balance
  ○ New Account, balance: as of 1/30/00
  ○ or, Existing Account: Checking

Online Information
  FI: ▾ ☐ Online Investment ☐ Online Payment

✕ Cancel   ⚡ Help   ◀ Back   ▶ Done

PART

III

Quicken for Investors

7. If your brokerage account includes a cash account or cash management account (it probably does), mark the Use a Linked Checking Account for My Cash Balance checkbox. If your investment account uses a linked cash account, Quicken assumes that any time an investment action affects cash, the cash goes into or comes out of the linked cash account.

8. If you need to set up a new account for the linked account, mark the New Account button. Specify the account balance using the New Account Balance text box and the transaction date Quicken should use for the opening balance transaction using the As Of box.

9. If you will use an existing checking account for the linked account, mark the Or Existing Account option button and then select the account from the drop-down list box.

10. Click Tax. Quicken displays the Tax Schedule Information dialog box, as shown in Figure 18.2.

11. If the investments in the brokerage account won't produce taxable income or tax-deductible capital losses, mark the Tax-Deferred or Tax-Exempt Account checkbox. This tells Quicken that it should not count this account's income and expense amounts as taxable or tax deductible.

FIGURE 18.2

The Tax Schedule Information dialog box

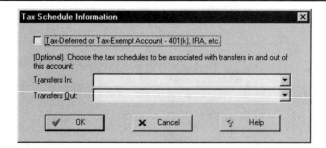

12. If the transfers into and out of the investment account should be reported on your income tax return, use the Transfers In and Transfers Out drop-down list boxes to identify on which tax return form or schedule (and on which line on the form or schedule) these transfers should be reported. Then click OK.

13. If you want to store additional information about an account, click the Info command button to display the Additional Account Information dialog box. You can use it to further describe the brokerage firm in the Bank Name text box, the brokerage account number in the Account Number text box, and so on. (Some of these fields don't make sense for an investment account because

Quicken uses the same Additional Account Information dialog boxes for all account types.) Then click OK.

14. Click Done in the Investment Account Setup dialog box.

Quicken next displays the Security Setup dialog box, which you can use to describe the securities (individual stocks and bonds) that you'll track with the account. However, I recommend, rather than using the Security Setup dialog box, that you individually set up securities on your own, as described in the next section. If you want to follow my suggestion, click Cancel to close the Security Setup dialog box, and then click Yes. Alternatively, to use the Security Setup dialog box, just follow the on-screen instructions.

Describing the Stocks You Already Hold

Once you've set up the brokerage account, you're ready to describe the stocks you hold in the account. To do this, you record the individual stocks or securities and provide the number of shares and original purchase price information.

Naming the Stocks or Securities You Hold

To name the stocks or securities you hold once you've provided the starting cash balance, display the brokerage account's register. Then follow these steps:

1. Choose Investing ➤ Security List to display the Security List, as shown in Figure 18.3.

2. Click the New command button in the Security List to display the Set Up a New Security dialog box, as shown in Figure 18.4.

3. Indicate what type of security you're adding to the list. To do this, click the option button that corresponds to the type of security you're adding. If you're adding a stock, for example, click Stock. Then, click Next.

4. Enter the name of the security in the Name text box (see Figure 18.5).

5. If you want to use Quicken's Online Quotes feature to download security prices with your modem, enter the symbol used to identify the stock in the Ticker Symbol text box. Then, click Next.

6. When Quicken asks you to describe the class of investment, do so using the option button and boxes provided. For example, if you're purchasing a small capitalization stock, select Small Cap Stock from the Type drop-down list box. Then click Next.

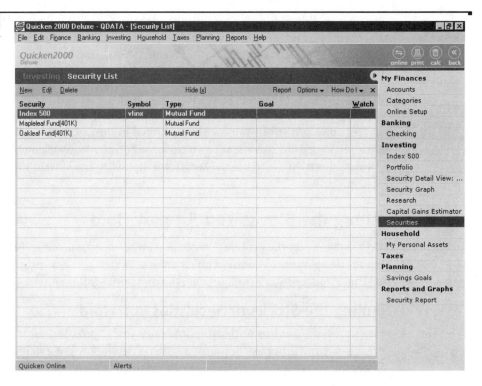

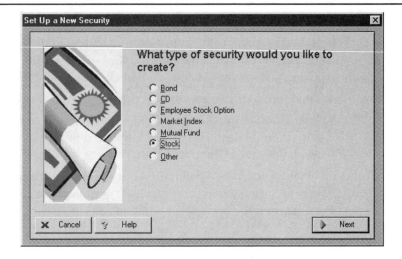

FIGURE 18.5

*The second Set Up
Security dialog box*

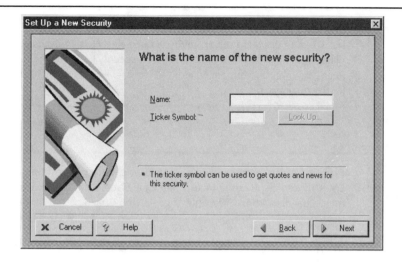

7. When Quicken asks you to how you want to account for the costs of your security, mark either the Lot Identification or Average Cost button (see Figure 18.6). If you're tracking investments in a taxable account, you want to use the Lot Identification button because lot identification gives you the most control over the timing of capital gains and losses. Click Next when you're finished.

FIGURE 18.6

*The fourth Set Up
Security dialog box*

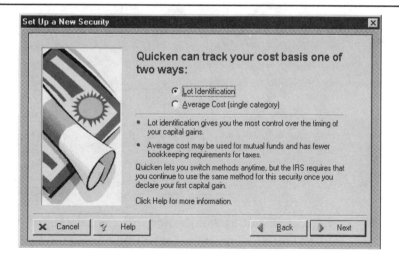

PART

III

Quicken for Investors

NOTE You can create your own security type by choosing Investing ➢ Security Type List. Quicken displays the Security Type List. Select New to display the Set Up Security Type dialog box. Then enter a name for the new security type into the Type text box and use the Price Display option buttons to indicate whether you want to use cents or fractional dollars for the security's price.

 NOTE You can create your own goal by choosing Investmenting ➢ Investment Goal List. Quicken displays the Investment Goal List. Select New to display the Set Up Investment Goal dialog box. Then enter a goal in the Goal box.

8. When Quicken asks how you want to track the security, click the Track My Holdings button (see Figure 18.7). This tells Quicken you'll be tracking a security for, among other reasons, tax purposes. (If you want to track a security you're considering, you can instead mark the Put It on the Watch List button.)

FIGURE 18.7

The fifth Set Up a New Security dialog box

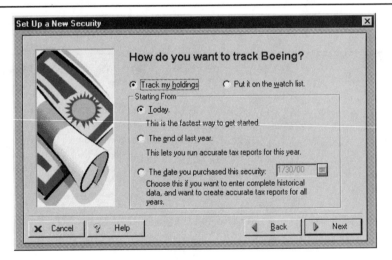

9. Click the Starting From button that corresponds to when you want to begin tracking this information. For taxable investments, you generally want to begin at the very beginning since that gives you the cost data you'll ultimately need for calculating capital gains. This would mean that you'll want to click the The Date You Purchased This Security button and then enter the purchase date into the accompanying text box. If you're working with a nontaxable investment—such as securities you hold in a self-directed IRA—you might choose to mark one of the other option buttons. Then click Next.

10. When Quicken displays the next Set Up a New Security dialog box, use the Account Name drop-down list box to specify which investment account will hold this security. Then click Next.

11. When Quicken displays the next Set Up a New Security dialog box, provide the cost, number of shares, and the commission for the security. Then click Next.

12. Quicken adds the security to your list and then asks if you want to add another security. If you do, click Yes and then repeat steps 3 through 9**.**

TIP If you want to use Lot Identification, you treat each lot as a separate security. This creates extra work, but the work is generally worth the effort because specific lot identification lets you control the timing of capital gains and losses—and usually minimize or delay taxes.

13. Once you indicate you're finished adding securities, Quicken asks if you want to download historical price information about the securities you've set up. If you want to do this, click Yes. Quicken retrieves historical price information and then and redisplays the Security List.

When you're finished, close the Security List. At this point, you've described both your securities and your current holdings.

NOTE If you hold mutual funds in a brokerage account, you can treat them as stocks for purposes of your investment record keeping.

Keeping Records of Your Stock Purchases, Sales, and Profits

Once you've set up the brokerage account records, you're ready to begin recording stock purchases, sales, and any profits. If you've used Quicken for mutual-fund record keeping (as described in Chapter 17), you'll notice many similarities in the way stock-investment record keeping works.

Describing the Shares You Buy

Whenever you buy additional shares of a stock, you'll need to record the purchase. To do this, you name the security as described earlier in the chapter and record the purchase of shares. You can record the purchase of new shares either directly into the register or by using the Easy Actions menu's Buy/Add Shares command. To record the purchase of shares using the Buy/Add Shares command, follow these steps:

1. Click the Easy Actions menu and choose Buy/Add Shares to display the Buy/Add Shares dialog box. Click its Summary tab (see Figure 18.8).

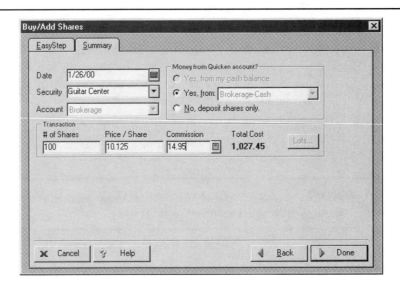

FIGURE 18.8

The Summary tab of the Buy/Add Shares dialog box

2. Enter the purchase date, stock name, number of shares purchased, and the price per share you paid in the appropriate boxes.

3. Enter the sales commission or transaction fee paid in the Commission text box.

4. If you are using cash from an account besides the brokerage account, mark the Yes, From button and then use the combo box to show from which account you wrote the check to pay for the purchase.

 NOTE   If you enter an account name in the Yes, From combo box, Quicken records a payment transaction in the account. If you don't enter an account name, Quicken reduces the cash held in your brokerage account.

---

5. Click Done. Quicken records the transaction into the investment register.

Describing Dividend Interest and Capital Gains Distributions

Many companies disburse a quarterly dividend to their shareholders, and sometimes they even disburse special dividends—as the result of a particularly good year, perhaps. And mutual funds, which you can also track in a brokerage account, may pay interest or capital gains.

You can record these sorts of investment profits either directly into the register (as described in Chapter 17) or by using an investment form. The investment form approach is easier, and it is the one described here.

 TIP   You don't need to worry about which kind of distribution is which. The 1099 statement, and probably your brokerage statement, will tell you what kind of distribution you've received.

To record a dividend, interest, or capital gains distribution using an investment form, follow these steps:

1. Click the Easy Actions button and then choose the Record An Income Event command to display the Record Income dialog box, as shown in Figure 18.9.

2. Enter the distribution date, stock name, amount of the dividend, interest payment, short-term capital gain payment, medium-term capital gain payment, and long-term capital gain payment in the appropriate text boxes.

3. Enter the amount of any other payment in the Miscellaneous text box. Use the Category for Miscellaneous combo box to show how the miscellaneous payment

PART

III

Quicken for Investors

should be categorized. (Quicken doesn't show this combo box until you enter an amount in the Miscellaneous text box.)

FIGURE 18.9

*The Record Income
dialog box*

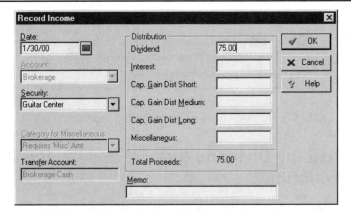

4. If you will deposit the distribution in another account (in other words, not the brokerage account), use the Transfer Account combo box to identify the other account. (This combo box isn't available unless you're using an account that doesn't have a linked cash account.)

5. If you need to record some additional piece of information—for example, to cross-reference the source that documents the distribution—use the Memo text box.

6. Click OK.

Recording Reinvestment Transactions

You may reinvest investment profits by purchasing additional shares of a stock or mutual fund. Some companies even have formal reinvestment programs called *DRIPs* (Dividend Reinvestment Programs). With a DRIP, you can buy additional shares of a company using your dividends, often without needing to pay any commissions or transaction fees.

To record reinvested investment profits, you can use either the register or an investment form, but the investment form approach is easier and more efficient. (To learn how to record reinvestment transactions directly into the register, see Chapter 17.) Follow these steps to use a form:

1. Choose Easy Actions ➢ Reinvest Income to open the Reinvest Income dialog box, as shown in Figure 18.10.

2. Enter the reinvestment date and stock name in the appropriate text boxes.

3. Use the Dividend Dollar Amount and Number Shares text boxes to describe the dividends you reinvested and the number of shares acquired with the dividends.

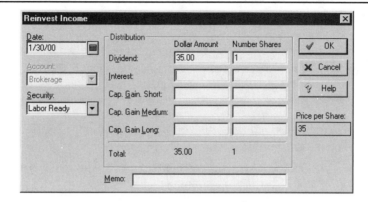

4. Use the Interest Dollar Amount and Number Shares text boxes to describe the number of shares acquired with the interest.

5. Use the Cap. Gain Short Dollar Amount and Number Shares text boxes to describe the short-term capital gains you reinvested and the number of shares acquired with the capital gains money.

6. Use the Cap. Gain Medium Dollar Amount and Number Shares text boxes to describe the medium-term capital gains you reinvested and the number of shares acquired with the capital gains money.

7. Use the Cap. Gain Long Dollar Amount and Number Shares text boxes to describe the long-term capital gains you reinvested and the number of shares acquired with the capital gains money.

Using the values you enter in the Dollar Amount and Number Shares text boxes, Quicken calculates the total dollar amount reinvested, the total number of shares purchased by reinvesting, as well as the average price per share you're paying.

8. If you need to record additional information about the reinvestment, use the Memo text box.

9. Click OK. Quicken records the distribution and the purchase of new shares.

PART

III

Quicken for Investors

Describing the Shares You Sell

As with the other types of stock transactions you record, describing the shares you sell is easy as long as you have the necessary information: the number of shares sold, the price per share (or the transaction total), and the commission paid (if any).

 NOTE You can record a short-sale transaction. Quicken asks you to confirm your action, however, since it knows you don't hold the stock you're selling.

You can record stock sales either directly into the register or by using an investment form, but the investment form approach is easier. Just follow these steps:

1. Choose Easy Actions ➤ Sell/Remove Shares to open the Sell/Remove Shares dialog box. Click the Summary tab.

2. Enter the sale date in the Date text box. Be sure to enter the actual sale date. Quicken categorizes any capital gain or loss as short-term or long-term based on the difference between the purchase and sale dates shown in the register.

3. Name the stock you're selling using the Security combo box.

4. Enter the number of shares you sold in the # of Shares text box.

5. Enter the sales price per share you received in the Price/Share text box.

6. Enter the sales commission or transaction fee in the Commission text box.

7. If you will deposit the sales proceeds in some account other than the brokerage one, click the Yes, To button and use the combo box to show the account. Alternatively, mark the No button if you don't want to record the proceeds. (By default, Quicken assumes that you will deposit proceeds into a cash, or linked, account.)

8. If you want to use specific identification, click the Lot Identification command button in the Cost Basis Method section, and then click Specify Lots. In the Specify Lots dialog box, identify the lots you want to sell. (For more information about specific identification of shares, see the section "Describing the Mutual Fund Shares You Sell" in Chapter 17.)

9. Click Done. Quicken records the transaction.

Stock Splits, Dividends, and Reminders

Chapter 17 explained how you record stock split transactions and investment reminder transactions in mutual fund accounts. These two transactions work the same way for brokerage accounts.

Stock dividends are really just stock splits. With a stock dividend, a company increases the number of shares held by each shareholder by a set percentage. A company, for example, might give current shareholders a 10 percent stock dividend. In this case, the company increases the number of shares held by each shareholder by 10 percent.

To record dividends, enter the ratio of old shares to new shares. If a company issued a 10 percent dividend, for example, the ratio is 1 to 1.1. In other words, for every old share, a stockholder receives 1.1 new shares.

 TIP Quicken also provides a special advanced action for stock dividends. To use this action, click the Easy Actions command button, choose Advanced, and then choose Stock Dividend (non-cash dividend). Quicken displays a dialog box that collects the information it needs to record a stock split transaction that shows the effect of the stock dividend.

Recording Brokerage Account Fees

Many brokerage accounts levy annual fees. Some also charge exit fees when you close the account. Recording these account fees isn't difficult, but how you record them depends on the type of investment account you've set up.

If you've set up an investment account that has a linked cash account, you record these fees directly into the linked cash account's register as an account withdrawal. When you record the withdrawal, you categorize the expense as falling into an investment expense category. This process works in the same way as recording bank service charges for a regular bank account.

If you've set up an investment account that doesn't have a linked cash account, you can record the fees either directly in the investment register or by using an investment form. Using an investment form is easier. To record one of these fees using an investment form, follow these steps:

1. Choose Easy Actions ➤ Miscellaneous Expense to open the Miscellaneous Expense dialog box.

2. Enter the date the fee is charged in the Date text box.

3. If the fee is tied to a specific stock or you have only one stock in the account, enter the stock's name in the Security text box.

4. Enter the amount of the fee in the Amount text box.

5. In the Category drop-down list, select the expense category you use to track and tally investment expenses. (Investment expenses may be deductible as miscellaneous deductions.)

6. If you want to further describe the fee—for example, to note that a fee is charged annually for account maintenance—use the Memo text box.

7. Click OK. Quicken records the account fee and adjusts the brokerage account's cash balance accordingly.

 NOTE If you write a check to pay an account fee, you don't need to do anything special in the investment register. You just write the check in the usual way—probably by using the Write Checks area or the register. Be sure, however, to categorize the check that pays an account fee as investment expense since it may qualify as a miscellaneous deduction.

Recording Cash Balance Interest and Miscellaneous Brokerage Account Income

It's likely that you'll earn interest or other income on the cash balances you hold in your brokerage account. To record this interest or income, choose Easy Actions ➤ Record an Income Event, and then fill out the Record Income dialog box as described earlier in the chapter. The only difference in recording cash balance interest and miscellaneous brokerage account income rather than stock income is that you don't identify a specific security.

 NOTE The 1099 or brokerage account statement will indicate what kind of distribution the check is for.

Reconciling Investment Accounts

You can reconcile mutual fund investment accounts and brokerage investment accounts. In a mutual fund, you reconcile just the shares. In a brokerage account, you reconcile shares and the cash balance.

Mechanically, reconciling an investment account works like reconciling a bank account. After you've read Chapter 5 of this book and performed a few bank account reconciliations, you'll have no trouble reconciling investment accounts.

Handling Tricky Stock Investment Transactions

The earlier portions of this chapter describe the most common investment transactions you need to record for common stocks you hold in a brokerage account. There are, however, several additional transactions you may need to record, particularly if you're an aggressive investor (one who's willing to bear increased risk in the pursuit of greater returns). These transactions involve short sales, margin loans and interest, call and put activities, employee stock options, and corporate reorganizations. The following sections briefly describe how you record these other types of transactions.

Short Sales

A *short sale* occurs when you sell stock you don't actually hold. The logic of a short sale is that rather than buying low and later selling high, you first buy high and then sell low. (To effect the transaction, you actually borrow the stock from your broker.)

To record a short sale transaction in Quicken, you just sell a stock you don't own. To show that these are shares you actually owe your broker, Quicken displays the number of shares and the current market value as negative amounts in the Portfolio View.

To record the transaction in which you close out your short position by buying the stock you've previously sold, you record a stock purchase in the usual way.

Margin Loans and Margin Interest

If you purchase a security and the total purchase cost exceeds the cash balance in a brokerage account, Quicken assumes that you've borrowed the needed cash on margin from your broker. To show the margin loan, it displays the cash balance as a negative value.

To record margin loan interest in cases where you have a linked cash account, you record the margin loan interest as an expense when you record the withdrawal from the linked cash account that pays the margin interest.

To record margin loan interest in cases where you don't have a linked cash account, choose Easy Actions ➤ Advanced ➤ Margin Interest Expense. When Quicken displays the Margin Interest Expense dialog box, use it to describe the margin interest.

Calls and Puts

A *call* is an option to buy a share of stock. A *put* is an option to sell a share of stock. You may write, buy, or exercise calls and puts.

Writing Calls and Puts

When you write a call or put, what you really do is collect money from someone in return for promising the person the option, or chance, to buy or sell a share of stock at a specified, or *strike*, price by some future date.

When a call or put expires without being exercised—and this is the usual case— recording the transaction is simple. If you're the one writing the call or put, just record the transaction as miscellaneous income.

Buying Calls and Puts

If you're the one buying the call or put, you just record the option purchase the way you do any other stock purchase. If the call or put expires and becomes worthless, just record the sale as a stock purchase with the amount set to 0. (This is the most common case.)

If, on the other hand, you sell the call or put before the expiration date because the call or put can be profitably exercised, you record the sale as a stock sale with the amount set to whatever you sell the option for.

Exercising Calls and Puts

You probably won't actually exercise a call or put. You'll probably sell it, as described above. If you do exercise a call or buy option, however, you need to record two transactions.

To record the exercise of a call option, first record a transaction that sells the call option for 0. Then record a transaction that purchases the optioned number of shares at the option price.

To record the exercise of a put option, first record a transaction that sells the put option for 0. Then record a transaction that sells the optioned number of shares at the option price.

 TIP For income tax purposes, what you pay for a call needs to be counted as part of the purchase price if you exercise the call option and purchase shares. What you receive for a put needs to be counted as part of the sales price if you exercise the put and sell shares. This can get complicated, so you may want to consult your tax advisor.

Employee Stock Options

 You can track the value of employee stock options in the same way that you track shares of stock. (The purchase price in this case is 0 if you don't pay anything for the option.) And Quicken 2000 even includes a special investment type button for indicating that an investment you're setting up holds employee stock options. The value of the option, of course, is the difference between the exercise price and the fair market value of the vested shares.

The income tax accounting for stock options can get a little tricky, depending on whether the options are part of a qualified incentive stock option plan or a nonqualified stock option plan. You may have a taxable gain when you are granted or when you exercise the option, or you may have a taxable gain only later when you sell the shares. If you have questions about the income tax treatment, consult your tax advisor. You'll need to show him or her the stock option plan document, so be sure to bring that with you.

Dealing with Corporate Reorganizations, Mergers, and Spin-Offs

Several of the commands on the Advanced submenu of the Easy Actions menu are useful for investment actions that stem from corporate reorganizations, mergers, or spin-offs:

Transfer Shares between Accounts   Lets you move securities between investment accounts.

Corporate Name Change   Lets you change the name of a security without losing any of your financial records for the security.

Corporate Securities Spin-Off Lets you describe new securities you're adding to an account as coming from existing securities you already own. In this way, your rate-of-return calculations don't ignore "spun-off" securities in their calculations of investment profits.

Corporate Acquisition (Stock for Stock) Lets you record stock-for-stock corporate mergers.

Stock Dividend (Non-Cash Dividend) Lets you record a stock dividend, which is essentially a type of stock split.

Bonds and Other Debt Securities

To keep records for bonds and other debt securities, you use the same brokerage account described earlier in the chapter. Tracking these securities works very much like tracking stocks.

Getting Ready for Bond Record Keeping

You'll need to set up a separate investment account for each brokerage account you have. If you have one brokerage account with a full-service broker and another with a discount broker, you need to set up two investment accounts. If you also hold stocks and bonds outside a brokerage account, you can set up another investment account for these.

Once you've set up the brokerage account, you're ready to describe the bonds and any other debt securities you hold in the account. This process works the same way for bonds and debt securities as it does for stocks and mutual funds.

 NOTE Bond prices are quoted as a percentage of their face, or *par*, value. A $1,000 par value bond that sells for $950, for example, has a price of $95. Because Quicken calculates the total security amount as the price times the quantity, however, you can't enter the bond price as a percentage. Instead, you need to enter the actual dollar price. To describe a bond you've purchased for $950, for example, you enter the price as $950.

Keeping Records of Your Bond Purchases, Sales, and Profits

Once you've set up the brokerage account records, you're ready to begin recording bond purchases, sales, and any profits. If you've used Quicken for stock investment record keeping, you'll find that bond record keeping works pretty much the same way.

Describing the Bonds You Buy

Whenever you buy additional bonds, you need to record the purchase and any accrued interest, so you actually record two transactions. As with stocks and mutual funds, you can record bond purchases directly into the register or by using an investment form. Because the investment form approach is easier, it's the one I'll describe here. To learn how to record transactions directly into the register, see Chapter 17. It describes how you record mutual fund transactions directly into the register, but the same basic approach works for stocks and bonds.

Recording a Bond Purchase   To record a bond purchase, follow these steps:

1. Choose Easy Actions ➤ Buy/Add Shares to open the Buy/Add Shares dialog box, and then click the Summary tab (see Figure 18.8, earlier in the chapter).

2. Enter the purchase date in the Date text box, the bond name in the Security combo box, and the quantity of bonds you purchased in the # of Shares text box.

3. Enter the dollar price per bond you paid in the Price/Share text box. Remember that Quicken expects you to enter the actual dollar price you paid, not the price as a percentage of the bond's face, or par, value.

 NOTE   You don't include the accrued interest in the bond price in step 3. You record that bit of information later.

4. Enter the brokerage commission you paid in the Commission text box.

You can enter any three of the following four inputs: number of shares, price, commission/fee, or total of sale. Using the three values you do enter, Quicken calculates the fourth value.

5. If you will use cash from some other account for the purchase instead of cash from the brokerage account, mark the Yes, From button and use the combo box to add the account. Do this only if you're not using a linked cash account.

6. Click Done. Quicken records the transaction.

Recording Accrued Interest   After you record the bond purchase, you usually need to record accrued interest paid to the previous holder. In effect, what you're really doing by paying accrued interest is giving the previous bond holder his or her share of the next interest payment. To record this accrued interest, follow these steps:

1. Choose Easy Actions ➤ Return of Capital to open the Return of Capital dialog box, as shown in Figure 18.11.

2. Enter the purchase date in the Date text box and the bond or lot name in the Security text box.

3. In the Amount text box, enter the accrued interest you paid as a negative number.

FIGURE 18.11

The Return of Capital dialog box

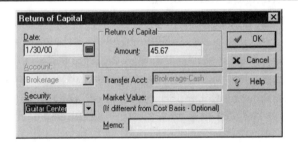

4. If you want to identify the transaction as an accrued interest adjustment, use the Memo text box.

5. Click OK. Quicken records the accrued interest transaction.

Describing Bond Interest and Return of Capital Distributions

Most bonds pay monthly or semi-annual interest. In addition, some bonds—for example, mortgage-backed securities such as GNMA bonds—return a portion of the bond principal with each interest payment.

TIP Don't worry about which kind of distribution is which. The 1099 statement, and probably also your brokerage statement, tells you what kind of distribution you've received.

As with other investment transactions, you have a choice as to how you record bond interest and return of capital transactions. You can enter these transactions directly into the register, as discussed in Chapter 17, or you can use an investment form.

To record an interest payment, choose Easy Actions ➢ Record an Income Event. In the Record Income dialog box, identify the interest payment date, the security paying the interest, and the amount. Fill in the Record Income dialog box's text and combo boxes as described in Chapter 17 and earlier in this chapter. The steps for recording bond income are similar to those for recording stock or mutual fund income.

To record a return of capital distribution, including the payment of interest you previously accrued, choose Easy Actions ➢ Return of Capital. In the Return of Capital dialog box, give the interest payment date, name the security paying the interest, and indicate the amount of previously accrued interest you're now receiving.

Recording Accrued Interest Shown on a 1099-OID

You aren't always paid the interest that you've earned. If you purchase a negotiable certificate of deposit (CD), for example, the bank issuing the CD may accrue the interest you've earned through the end of the year and then add this amount to the CD's value. If you purchase a zero-coupon bond, you don't receive periodic interest payments at all. Rather, the bond issuer accrues interest each year and then repays the bond and the total accrued interest at maturity. Even though you aren't paid interest, however, you need to record the interest you've earned because you need to report the accrued interest as taxable income. Fortunately, in most cases the bond issuer sends a 1099-OID form that reports the amount of accrued but not paid interest.

 NOTE Bond issuers also report the amortization of original-issue discounts on 1099-OID forms. In fact, OID stands for Original Issue Discount. Because original-issue discounts effectively increase the annual interest earnings, you also need to record these.

To record accrued interest, you actually record two transactions, as described in Chapter 17 and earlier in this chapter:

- Choose Easy Actions ➢ Record an Income Event, and then complete the Record Income dialog box.

- Choose Easy Actions ➤ Return of Capital, and fill in the Return of Capital dialog box. Describe the accrued but unpaid interest as a negative return of capital. (This is the same technique used earlier in the chapter to deal with accrued interest paid with the bond purchase.)

 TIP By entering the return of capital as a negative number, Quicken increases the bond cost, or carrying value, by the accrued interest amount.

 MASTERING TROUBLESHOOTING

Accrued Interest and the 1099-OID Form

Accrued interest income can get messy when, for income tax purposes, you need to record accrued interest that isn't reported on a 1099-OID form. The reason is that you're required to report the accrued interest—even though you won't get a 1099-OID amount. Later on, when you ultimately do get a 1099-INT or 1099-OID that includes the previously recorded accrued interest, you need to adjust this figure so it doesn't double-count the accrued interest.

Many people don't report accrued interest income until it's reported on a 1099-OID form or actually paid and reported on a 1099-INT form. With this simplified approach, you don't evade income taxes on the interest income, but you do delay paying the income taxes. Once the interest is accrued, the IRS does insist that you pay income taxes. If this applies to your situation, talk to your tax advisor.

Describing the Bonds You Sell

Describing the bonds you sell is easy as long as you have the necessary information: the number of bonds sold, the price per share (or the transaction total), and the commission paid (if any). You also need to know the amount of accrued interest you will be paid.

As with other investment transactions, you can record bond sales either directly into the register or by using an investment form; using an investment form is easier. To record a bond sale, choose Easy Actions ➤ Sell/Remove Shares. In the Sell/Remove

Shares dialog box, select the Summary tab. Enter the sales date, name the bond being sold; give the sales amount and sales commission; and indicate where you'll deposit the money. (Chapter 17 and earlier sections in this chapter describe how investment sale transactions work.)

After you record the bond sale, you need to record the amount of accrued interest you're being paid. In effect, the bond purchaser pays you your share of the next interest payment. To do this, choose Easy Actions ➤ Record an Income Event, and fill out the Record Income dialog box so that it describes the accrued interest being paid. From your perspective, it's irrelevant that the bond purchaser rather than the bond issuer pays the interest, so recording this accrued interest payment works just like recording a regular interest coupon payment, as described earlier in this chapter.

Recording Early Withdrawal Penalty Transactions

Early withdrawal penalties on certificates of deposit are a special type of tax-deductible expense. Like IRA contributions, alimony, and a few other items, these penalties are deductions from your total income and are used to calculate your adjusted gross income. Because of this, be sure to record any early withdrawal penalties you pay with a separate transaction. If you're using an investment account with a linked cash account, record the early withdrawal penalty as if it were paid from the cash account. If you're not using an investment with a linked cash account, use the Easy Actions menu's Miscellaneous Expense command. In either case, when you do record the early withdrawal penalty, categorize the early withdrawal penalty expense in a way that lets you easily report this penalty on your income tax return. (You might want to set up a new expense category called Early Withdrawal Penalty.)

Tips for Tracking Other Debt Securities

You can use Quicken to keep records of most other debt securities. Here's a list of some of the other common debt securities, along with suggestions for how you can treat them in Quicken:

Debt Security	How to Handle It
Certificates of deposit	Treat negotiable certificates of deposit like bonds. (Mechanically, jumbo negotiable CDs are almost identical to corporate and government bonds.) Consider treating non-negotiable certificates like bank accounts.

Debt Security	How to Handle It
U.S. Savings Bonds	Treat these as you do a regular bond. You won't record interest payments, but you will need to accrue interest.
Zero-coupon bonds	Treat these the same way as U.S. Savings Bonds. You won't need to record interest payments (the bond won't pay these), but you will need to accrue interest.

Understanding Quicken's Annual Return Calculations

Quicken's Investment Performance report calculates an internal rate of return for each security, as described in Chapter 4. Here I'll describe why you use the internal rate of return (IRR) tool and show how it compares with the other standard performance measurement tools.

What Is an IRR?

The IRR tool calculates the annual profit an investment delivers as a percentage of the investment's value at the start of the year. For example, in a simple case, if you buy an investment for $100 and the investment pays $10 in dividends at the end of the year and then is sold for $95, your IRR is 5 percent.

There are actually two steps to making this calculation:

- You need to calculate the annual profit. You can do this by combining the $10 of dividends with the $5 capital loss (calculated as $95–$100) for a result of $5 of annual profit.

- You divide the $5 of annual profit by the $100 investment value at the start of the year. $5/$100 equals 5 percent, and that's the IRR.

By calculating an IRR, you can quantify the performance of a stock that you've purchased and of your investment portfolio as a whole. This is particularly true with individual stocks and brokerage accounts because you often don't really know how your stock picks, your broker's picks, and your portfolio have done and are doing relative to the market as a whole and relative to other investments.

> **NOTE** In comparison, you usually have a pretty good idea as to how well a mutual fund does on a quarterly or at least an annual basis. The fund manager will report to you on the quarterly and annual returns.

Some Mechanical Problems with the IRR

Now that you understand the basic logic of the IRR tool, you should know that the IRR, for all of its usefulness, isn't flawless. Quicken (and every other investment record-keeper's computer program) calculates a daily IRR and then multiplies this percentage by the number of days in a year to get an equivalent annual IRR.

This sounds right, but it presents problems in the case of publicly traded securities because a short-term percentage change in a security's market value—even if modest—can annualize to a very large positive or negative number. If you buy a stock for $10^1/8$ and the next day the stock drops to $10, the annual return using these two pieces of information is a whopping –98.9 percent! If you buy a stock for $10^1/8$ and the next day the stock rises to $10^1/4$, the annual return using these two pieces of information is an astronomical 8,711 percent.

To minimize the problems of annualizing short-term percentage changes, you probably want to refrain from measuring IRRs for only short periods of time. An annualized daily return can be very misleading.

One other thing to note is that the IRR calculation becomes more difficult when you try to calculate the average annual profit percentage, or IRR, for a series of years when the starting value is changing from year to year. The basic problem is that the IRR formula is what's called an nth root polynomial (n is the number of days in the IRR calculation). A one-year IRR calculation is a 365th root polynomial. (Remember that Quicken calculates daily IRRs and then annualizes these daily percentages.)

The problem with an nth root polynomial is that, by definition, it can have up to n real and imaginary solutions. An annual IRR calculation could theoretically have 365 correct IRRs. You would not normally have this many solutions, but you could still have several correct solutions. So you can see that by using IRR-based return calculations, there's an opportunity for real confusion. Quicken, recognizing these problems, does not attempt to calculate IRRs for investments that look like they may have more than one IRR. You'll know for which investments you can't calculate an IRR, but you won't know how those investments did.

PART

III

Quicken for Investors

Online Investing with Quicken

Quicken supports online investing for many (perhaps most) of the popular online brokerage services. What this means is that you don't have to record the transactions you effect with an online investment account. Instead, you can tell Quicken to retrieve these transactions directly from the online investment broker.

To tell Quicken that you want it to work with your online investment account, choose the Investing ➤ Online Investing Setup. Then follow the on-screen instructions for setting up your account.

To download investment instructions from your online investment service, choose the Investing ➤ Online Investing command and then click the Update/Send command. Note that the Online Investing command doesn't appear on the Investing menu until you've successfully set up an account for online service. For more information about how to work with any online account—including an investment account—refer to Chapter 9.

 WARNING As you've probably already noticed on your monthly brokerage account statement, your brokerage may record many more transactions in your account to reflect some purchase or sale than you would. Predictably, then, you'll find your Quicken registers much fuller if you download transactions from your online broker. This doesn't cause any problems. It can be a little disconcerting the first time you see this.

Quicken's Quicken.com Web site provides several online services to make it easier for you to use Quicken and to expand the work you can do with Quicken. One of these services, Online Quotes, helps with your investment record keeping by providing you with recent securities prices for investments such as stocks and mutual funds.

Using Online Quotes is easy. In the Portfolio View, choose Update Prices ➤ Get Online Quotes Only.

As long as you've provided symbols for each of your securities (you do this as you describe the securities), when you click Update Prices, Quicken connects you to the Internet and retrieves share price data for the securities you selected. (This is the same information you get from the stock page of your local newspaper or from the *Wall Street Journal*.) When you use Quicken's Online Quotes feature, Quicken enters the price history data for you so that you don't need to do this manually.

TIP If you want to track a stock you don't own, you simply indicate that you want the stock added to your "watch list" when you set up the security. To view the downloaded information, display the Portfolio View and choose Watch List from the Group By drop-down list box and Quotes from the View drop-down list box.

 MASTERING FINANCIAL SUCCESS

How to Avoid Investment Mistakes

Smart people sometimes make dumb mistakes when it comes to investing. Part of the reason for this, I guess, is that most people don't have the time to learn what they need to know to make good decisions. Another reason is that oftentimes when you make a dumb mistake, somebody else—an investment salesperson, for example—makes money. Fortunately, you can save yourself lots of money and a bunch of headaches by not making bad investment decisions.

Don't Forget to Diversify

At the end of Chapter 17, I mentioned that the average stock market return is 10 percent or so, but to earn 10 percent you need to own a broad range of stocks. In other words, you need to diversify.

Everybody who thinks about this for more than a few minutes realizes that it is true, but it's amazing how many people don't diversify. For example, some people hold huge chunks of their employer's stock but little else. Or they own a handful of stocks in the same industry.

To make money on the stock market, you need around 15 to 20 stocks in a variety of industries. (I didn't just make up these figures; the 15 to 20 number comes from a statistical calculation that many upper-division and graduate finance textbooks explain.) With fewer than 10 to 20 stocks, your portfolio's returns will very likely be something greater or less than the stock market average. Of course, you don't care if your portfolio's return is greater than the stock market average, but you do care if your portfolio's return is less than the stock market average.

By the way, to be fair I should tell you that some very bright people disagree with me on this business of holding 15 to 20 stocks. For example, Peter Lynch, the outrageously successful manager of the Fidelity Magellan mutual fund, suggests that individual

Continued

MASTERING FINANCIAL SUCCESS CONTINUED

investors hold 4 to 6 stocks that they understand well. His feeling, which he shares in his books, is that by following this strategy, an individual investor can beat the stock market average. Mr. Lynch knows more about picking stocks than I ever will, but I nonetheless respectfully disagree with him for two reasons. First, I think that Peter Lynch is one of those modest geniuses who underestimate their intellectual prowess. I wonder if he underestimates the powerful analytical skills he brings to his stock picking. Second, I think that most individual investors lack the accounting knowledge to accurately make use of the quarterly and annual financial statements that publicly held companies provide in the ways that Mr. Lynch suggests.

Have Patience

The stock market and other securities markets bounce around on a daily, weekly, and even yearly basis, but the general trend over extended periods of time has always been up. Since World War II, the worst one-year return has been −26.5 percent. The worst ten-year return in recent history was 1.2 percent. Those numbers are pretty scary, but things look much better if you look longer term. The worst 25-year return was 7.9 percent annually.

It's important for investors to have patience. There will be many bad years. Many times, one bad year is followed by another bad year. But over time, the good years outnumber the bad. They compensate for the bad years too. Patient investors who stay in the market in both the good and bad years almost always do better than people who try to follow every fad or buy last year's hot stock.

Invest Regularly

You may already know about *dollar-average investing*. Instead of purchasing a set number of shares at regular intervals, you purchase a regular dollar amount, such as $100. If the share price is $10, you purchase ten shares. If the share price is $20, you purchase five shares. If the share price is $5, you purchase twenty shares.

Dollar-average investing offers two advantages. The biggest is that you regularly invest—in both good markets and bad markets. If you buy $100 of stock at the beginning of every month, for example, you don't stop buying stock when the market is way down and every financial journalist in the world is working to fan the fires of fear.

The other advantage of dollar-average investing is that you buy more shares when the price is low and fewer shares when the price is high. As a result, you don't get carried away on a tide of optimism and end up buying most of the stock when the market or the stock is up. In the same way, you also don't get scared away and stop buying a stock when the market or the stock is down.

Continued ▏▶

One of the easiest ways to implement a dollar-average investing program is by participating in something like an employer-sponsored 401(k) plan or deferred compensation plan. With these plans, you effectively invest each time money is withheld from your paycheck.

To make dollar-average investing work with individual stocks, you need to dollar-average each stock. In other words, if you're buying stock in IBM, you need to buy a set dollar amount of IBM stock each month, each quarter, or whatever.

Don't Ignore Investment Expenses

Investment expenses can add up quickly. Small differences in expense ratios, costly investment newsletter subscriptions, online financial services (including Quicken Quotes!), and income taxes can easily subtract hundreds of thousands of dollars from your net worth over a lifetime of investing.

To show you what I mean, here are a couple of quick examples. Let's say that you're saving $7,000 per year of 401(k) money in a couple of mutual funds that track the Standard & Poor's 500 index. One fund charges a 0.25 percent annual expense ratio, and the other fund charges a 1 percent annual expense ratio. In 35 years, you'll have about $900,000 in the fund with the 0.25 percent expense ratio and about $750,000 in the fund with the 1 percent ratio.

Here's another example: Let's say that you don't spend $500 a year on a special investment newsletter, but you instead stick the money in a tax-deductible investment such as an IRA. Let's say you also stick your tax savings in the tax-deductible investment. After 35 years, you'll accumulate roughly $200,000.

Investment expenses can add up to really big numbers when you realize that you could have invested the money and earned interest and dividends for years.

Don't Get Greedy

I wish there was some risk-free way to earn 15 or 20 percent annually. I really, really do. But, alas, there isn't. The stock market's average return is somewhere between 9 and 10 percent, depending on how many decades you go back. The significantly more risky small company stocks have done slightly better. On average, they return annual profits of 12 to 13 percent. Fortunately, you can get rich earning 9 percent returns. You just need to take your time. But no risk-free investments consistently return annual profits significantly above the stock market's long-run averages.

Continued

PART

III

Quicken for Investors

MASTERING FINANCIAL SUCCESS CONTINUED

I mention this for a simple reason: People make all sorts of foolish investment decisions when they get greedy and pursue returns that are out of line with the average annual returns of the stock market. If someone tells you that he has a sure-thing investment or investment strategy that pays, say, 15 percent, don't believe it. And, for Pete's sake, don't buy investments or investment advice from that person.

If someone really did have a sure-thing method of producing annual returns of, say, 18 percent, that person would soon be the richest person in the world. With solid year-in, year-out returns like that, the person could run a $20-billion investment fund and earn $500 million a year. The moral is: There is no such thing as a sure thing in investing.

Don't Get Fancy

For years now, I've made the better part of my living by analyzing complex investments. Nevertheless, I think that it makes most sense for investors to stick with simple investments: mutual funds, individual stocks, government and corporate bonds, and so on.

As a practical matter, it's very difficult for people who haven't been trained in financial analysis to analyze complex investments such as real estate partnership units, derivatives, and cash-value life insurance. You need to understand how to construct accurate cash-flow forecasts. You need to know how to calculate things like internal rates of return and net present values with the data from cash-flow forecasts. Financial analysis is nowhere near as complex as rocket science. Still, it's not something you can do without a degree in accounting or finance, a computer, and a spreadsheet program (like Microsoft Excel or Lotus 1-2-3).

CHAPTER 19

Tracking Real Estate Investments

FEATURING:

Quicken isn't really set up specifically for tracking real estate investments. Yet because it's probably the place where you'll keep all your other financial records, and because real estate often amounts to one of your most valuable assets, you may want to use it for real estate record keeping. In this chapter, I describe how you can use Quicken to keep tax records for your home and income property investments.

Tracking Your Home as an Investment

Tracking the value and cost of a home delivers one of two benefits:

- You can track your home in a way that lets you include your home's value in your net worth report.

- You can track your home in a way that lets you minimize the capital gains tax you may ultimately pay when you sell your home.

This chapter will help you decide whether it's worth more to you to focus on and track your home's market value or worth more to save capital gains taxes at some point in the future.

Focusing on Your Home's Market Value

To track your home's market value and, as a result, the home equity you've accumulated, you need to set up an asset account for your house and a liability account for your mortgage. Chapter 13 explains how to set up liability accounts for mortgages. Here, I'll explain how to set up an asset account for your house.

Setting Up the House Account

To set up an asset account for tracking your home's value, follow these steps:

1. Display the Account List and click the New command button.

2. Select the House button to indicate that you want to set up an asset account for your house, and then click Next to display the Asset Account Setup dialog box.

3. Click the Summary tab.

4. Enter a name for the new account (such as House) in the Account Name text box (see Figure 19.1).

FIGURE 19.1

*The Summary tab of
the Asset Account
Setup dialog box used
to set up a house
account*

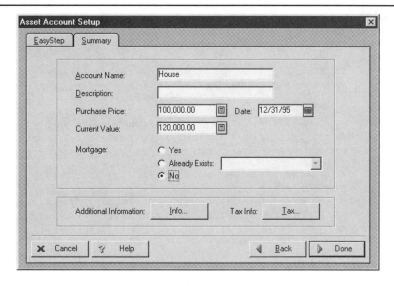

5. If you want to provide an additional description, such as the street address, use the Description text box.

6. Enter the purchase price of your home into the Purchase Price text box, the purchase date into the Date box, and then the current market value of the house in the Current Value text box.

7. Use the Mortgage option buttons—Yes, Already Exists, and No—to indicate whether you need to also set up a Mortgage Liability account. If you select the Yes button, Quicken walks you through the steps for setting up a mortgage liability account. If you have questions about this process, refer to Chapter 13.

8. Click Done. Quicken adds the new account and then asks if you want to retrieve recent house sales information near your home. If you do, you supply your house street address, city, state, zip code, and estimated square footage. Then you click Go Online. Quicken retrieves this information, displaying it in another window (see Figure 19.2). If you don't want to retrieve this information, obviously, you don't need to fill in the text boxes or click Go Online.

PART

III

Quicken for Investors

Quicken retrieves comparable sales data like that shown in this window.

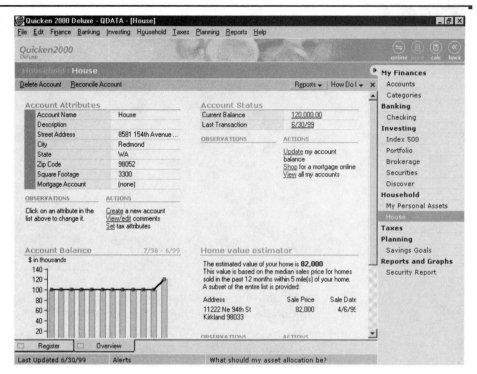

Updating Your Records for Changes in the Market Value

To update your records for changes in your home's market value, follow these steps:

1. In the Account List, select the house account and click Open to display the house account information in its own register, as shown in Figure 19.3.

2. Click the Update Balance button to display the Update Account Balance dialog box, as shown in Figure 19.4.

3. Enter the current market value in the Update Balance To text box, enter the date as of which the current market value is correct in the Adjustment Date text box, and click OK.

4. Clear the Category for Adjustment text box, and click OK. (By convention, you don't include changes in a home's market value in your income and expense summaries.)

FIGURE 19.3

The House account in its own register

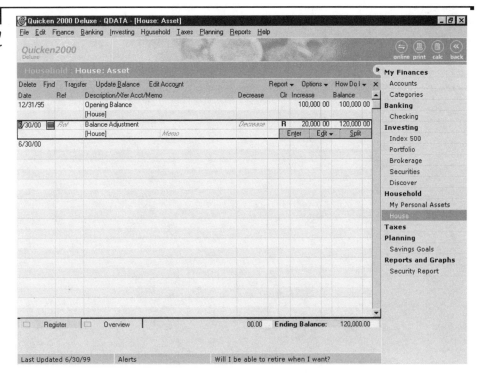

FIGURE 19.4

The Update Account Balance dialog box

Quicken adds an adjustment transaction to the register that changes the house account balance to whatever you specified in step 3. Figure 19.5 shows a house asset account register with two adjustment transactions.

FIGURE 19.5

The House asset account register with an adjustment transaction that decreases a home's value to $110,000

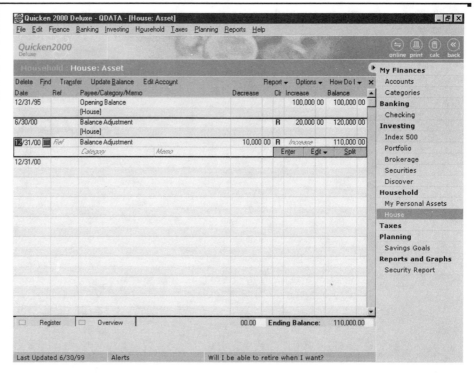

MASTERING FINANCIAL SUCCESS

What's Wrong with the Current Market Value Approach

The current market value approach presents a problem: It's difficult to pick the correct current market value. You could periodically have your home appraised, of course, but appraisals are expensive and imprecise. You might be able to get reasonable estimates of your home's value from your annual property tax assessment if it's based on the estimated market value, but again, this number is only an estimate. In my experience—and admittedly the feature is very new so I've had limited experience with it—the Quicken comparable sales data provides only a ballpark estimate.

If you do use the assessed value as your current market value, one advantage is that you'll have a piece of paper that documents and triggers the current market value adjustment. Every year, when you get the assessment notice, you'll know it's time to adjust the market value.

But realize that the only way to truly ascertain your home's market value is to find someone who is interested in buying your house.

Focusing on Saving Capital Gains Taxes

A second approach for keeping financial records of your investment in a home is to track the home's *adjusted cost basis,* which is the initial home purchase price plus the cost of any home improvements you've made: new cabinetry, landscaping, an addition, and so on.

By tracking a home's adjusted cost basis, you may be able to save capital gains taxes when you someday sell the home.

To keep financial records that will minimize the capital gain you ultimately pay when you sell a home, you set up an asset account as described in the previous section, but you set the starting balance to the home's initial purchase price. Be sure to include any of the related costs you incurred to purchase the home, such as escrow and closing fees, appraisals, and so on.

Then, whenever you make an improvement to the home, record the improvement as an increase in the house account's balance.

 TIP Usually it's easiest to just categorize the check you write to pay for the improvement as a transfer to the house account.

As long as the home improvements are considered capital improvements, they increase the home's tax basis. Since the capital gain on which you'll ultimately be taxed when you sell the home is based on the difference between the home's sale price and the home's tax basis, the larger the home's tax basis, the smaller the capital gains tax.

If you sell your home, be sure to show a copy of your house account register to your tax advisor, who can review each of your increase transactions and make sure they can be counted as capital improvements. If you have specific questions about deferring or avoiding capital gains on the sale of a home, confer with a tax advisor. Your advisor will be aware of nuances in the law that apply to your specific situation. In addition, it's always possible that Congress will once again change the income tax laws relating to calculation of capital gains on sales of a principal residence.

MASTERING FINANCIAL SUCCESS

What's Wrong with the Saving Capital Gains Taxes Approach

I used to recommend that everybody use the "saving capital gains taxes" approach, and I still think it's a pretty good idea, but the approach isn't perfect. Here's the problem: The approach doesn't necessarily save you any capital gains taxes. Why? Because you may be able to avoid capital gains taxes on the sale of your home by taking advantage of any one of several loopholes.

You may never need to pay income taxes on a home sale—even if you've made a lot of money—because the federal income tax laws include two interesting provisions related to the capital gains taxes owed on the sale of your principal residence (the place you live most of the time):

- You can take an exemption of up to $250,000 ($500,000 for married couples filing joint returns) for any gain on the sale of your principal residence. This probably means that you stand a good chance of never having to pay income taxes on gains from home ownership.

- For purposes of calculating the capital gain on an asset held in your future estate, including your home, the estate's trustee will probably subtract the asset's value at the date of your death from the sales price. This means that if you never sell your home and just leave it in your estate for your heirs, your estate won't need to pay capital gains taxes (although the estate may be required to pay federal and state estate taxes).

Because of these factors, it's possible that you won't get anything for tracking the cost of your home plus any improvements. For the "saving capital gains taxes" approach to actually save you money, you'll need to be someone who can't avoid a capital gain on the sale of a home (perhaps because the home isn't a principal residence) and who can't avoid the capital gains tax by using the exemption.

Tracking Rental Property

Quicken's account registers and categories provide a handy format for tracking real estate investments such as income property. By using Quicken for this record keeping, you can prepare summaries of income and expenses by property for monitoring your individual real estate investments. You can also easily complete the Schedule E income tax form you use.

Moreover, if you set up asset accounts for each of the individual real estate properties you hold and then use these to record both capital improvements and any depreciation, you can easily calculate any capital gains or capital losses stemming from the sale of a piece of real estate.

Describing Your Real Estate Holdings

To track income and expense by individual real estate property, you need to do two things:

- Set up the income and expense categories needed to describe this income and expense. As noted in Chapter 14, make sure that whatever income and expense categories you set up support completion of the Schedule E tax form.

- Set up a class for each individual real estate property, and then, whenever you categorize an income or expense item for a particular property, identify the property by providing the class.

 NOTE   If you have only a single real estate investment and you know for certain that you'll never add another real estate investment to your portfolio, you don't need to set up classes.

Setting Up Classes for Real Estate Investments

To set up classes for your real estate investments, follow these steps:

1. Choose the Lists ➢ Class command to display the Class List, as shown in Figure 19.6.

FIGURE 19.6

The Class List

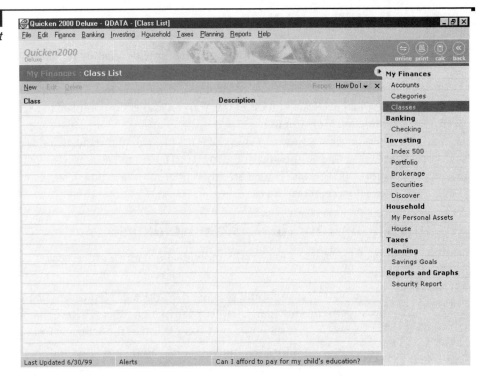

2. Click the New command button to display the Set Up Class dialog box, as shown in Figure 19.7.

FIGURE 19.7

The Set Up Class dialog box

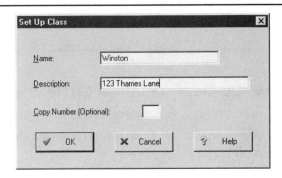

3. Use the Name text box to provide a brief name for the real estate property. For example, if you're setting up a class for a rental property and the property has the name Winston Apartments, you might shorten this to **Winston**.

4. If you need to describe the property in more detail, such as noting the street address, use the Description text box.

5. Click OK. Quicken adds the new class to the Class List.

Repeat steps 2 through 5 for each real estate property you'll track as an investment using Quicken.

Setting Up Subclasses for Real Estate Investments

You might also want to set up subclasses, which are simply classes used to classify the components of a class, for your real estate investments. For example, if you set up a class for Winston Apartments but want to separately track income and expenses related to a certain type of tenant, such as low-income tenants, you could create two subclasses: Qualified, for tenants who qualify as low-income tenants, and Nonqualified, for tenants who don't qualify. (You might need to do this, for example, if you're claiming federal low-income housing credits for a property and therefore need to track tenants by class, too.)

To set up a subclass, you take the same steps you use to set up a class. Keep in mind, however, that you can use only 31 characters to enter categories, subcategories, classes, and subclasses. All this information goes into the Category combo box, so use short names. For example, you might use **Qual** and **Nonq** for Qualified and Nonqualified.

 NOTE Quicken lets you use subclasses and classes interchangeably: You can use a class as a subclass and a subclass as a class. Therefore, if you do choose to use subclasses, you need to be more careful in your data entry.

Tracking Income and Expenses by Property

Once you've set up classes for each of your individual properties, you're ready to begin tracking income and expenses by property. To do this, simply enter both the income or expense category and the class name in the Category text box, separating the category from the class with a slash.

To record a rent check from one of your Winston Apartments tenants when Rental Income is the income category and Winston is the class name, for example, type **Rental Income/Winston** in the Category combo box.

If you've used subclasses, such as Qual and Nonq for Qualified and Nonqualified to identify tenants as qualified and nonqualified (low-income) tenants, follow the class name with a colon and then the subclass name. To record a rent check from one of your

Winston Apartment "qualified" tenants when Rental Income is the income category and Winston is the class name, for example, type **Rental Income/Winston:Qual** in the Category combo box.

 NOTE Classes can be a little tricky for a couple of reasons. You can flip-flop the classes and subclasses because Quicken doesn't track your classes and subclasses separately. From its perspective, they're both the same. And you can't tell Quicken to always remind you to enter a class, which you can do for categories. So be careful to always use classes and subclasses, and if you find that a report shows unclassified amounts, use QuickZoom to locate the unclassified transactions you need to fix.

When you want to print an income and expense report by property, produce the Job/Project report by choosing Reports ➤ Business ➤ Job/Project and then clicking the Create button. (For more information about how to produce and print reports, refer to Chapter 4.)

Setting Up Real Estate Investment Accounts

You can use Quicken accounts to track the adjusted cost basis of individual real estate investments. You calculate the gain or loss upon sale by subtracting the adjusted cost basis of a property from the net sales price. To do this, set up an asset account for individual real estate properties the same way you do for your home if you're keeping records to minimize any future capital gains taxes, as described earlier in this chapter.

As with a home, whenever you make an improvement to the property, record the improvement as an increase in the property's balance. Usually, the easiest way to do this is to just categorize the check you write to pay for the improvement as a transfer to the house account.

 NOTE As with a home capital gain calculation, be sure to show a copy of your property account register to your tax advisor, who can review each of your increase transactions and make sure that they can be counted as capital improvements.

You can also record the periodic depreciation you'll use for calculations of the taxable profit or loss on the real estate investment. To do this, first set up a depreciation expense category, such as Depreciation. Then record an annual depreciation expense transaction that decreases the property's account balance.

To record a depreciation on Winston Apartments when Depreciation is the expense category and Winston is the class name, for example, type **Depreciation/Winston** in the Category text box.

You can't see the complete Category text box entries because only part of the class name shows, but Figure 19.8 shows an asset account register for the fictitious real estate investment, Winston Apartments. Note that I've recorded more than a single year's depreciation. For income tax purposes, the adjusted cost basis is the account balance at the date of sale.

 TIP You can learn what depreciation expense is allowable on a property for tax purposes by consulting your tax advisor or telephoning the IRS.

FIGURE 19.8

The asset account register for Winston Apartments

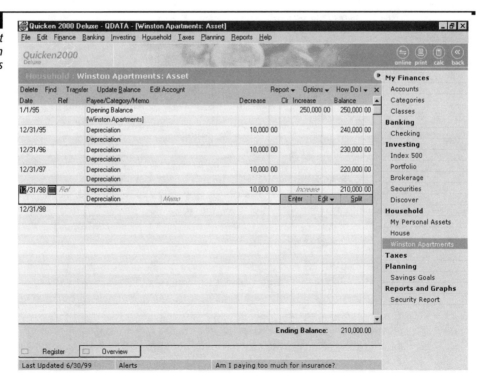

MASTERING FINANCIAL SUCCESS

How to Choose a Home and a Mortgage

Home ownership is usually considered the most important part of the so-called American Dream. Many consider home ownership the national birthright. It's often called the average American's best investment. And, usually, it results in the single largest debt a person takes on, in the form of a 30-year mortgage. Given these major financial characteristics, it makes sense to talk about home ownership. Here, I'll discuss some important aspects of home ownership: the decision to purchase a home, home affordability, and how to choose a mortgage.

Deciding Whether to Buy or Rent

The first decision you need to make, of course, is whether to buy a home or rent one. This decision isn't an easy one to make, at least if you look at the impact of a home in purely economic terms.

Since World War II, a single-family home has been, on the average, a very reasonable investment. Calculating the profits of home ownership is quite complicated, but I can sum things up quite nicely by stating that home ownership produces two benefits: rent savings and appreciation. Home ownership has been profitable for people because these benefits have more than paid the average homeowner's property ownership expenses and mortgage interest. When you boil down home ownership to its financial essence, it's really that simple.

A few years ago, an economist at the Mortgage Banking Association did a national survey of the investment returns of home ownership. He found that, on average, home ownership produced returns of around 10 to 12 percent. This figure is very respectable in light of the stock market's 50-year average of 10 percent and the 12 to 13 percent average of small-company stocks.

Before you trot off and use this bit of real estate trivia in your decision-making, however, it's important to understand the fundamental reason why home ownership has been a good investment. Suppose a person is considering two options: renting a three-bedroom house for, say, $600 a month or purchasing the same house for $100,000 with a $95,000 (9.25 percent) mortgage. Initially, the renter pays just $600 a month, while the homeowner pays a mortgage payment equal to $780 plus another $220 in property taxes and maintenance. So, renting costs $600 a month and owning costs $1,000 a month. With gradual inflation, however, things change over time. Assume that there's a 3 percent inflation rate, for example (3 percent is the historical average of this century).

Continued

MASTERING FINANCIAL SUCCESS CONTINUED

After 10 years of 3 percent inflation, the renter pays around $800 a month in rent; after 20 years, the renter pays around $1,080 in rent; after 30 years, when the homeowner's mortgage is presumably paid off, the renter pays around $1,460 a month in rent. Even when the homeowner has paid off the mortgage in 30 years, he or she would still pay about $530 a month in property taxes and maintenance, but this figure is still roughly $900 a month less than what the renter pays.

The following graph shows this financial reality by comparing monthly housing costs when you purchase versus monthly housing costs when you rent. At first, purchasing is more expensive. Gradually, over time, however, the costs of renting and purchasing converge and then flip-flop. The big change, however, comes when the homeowner finally pays off his or her mortgage. In the graph, this is when the homeowner line drops. At that point, the homeowner pays only property taxes and maintenance costs. The renter, meanwhile, is still writing a monthly check to a landlord.

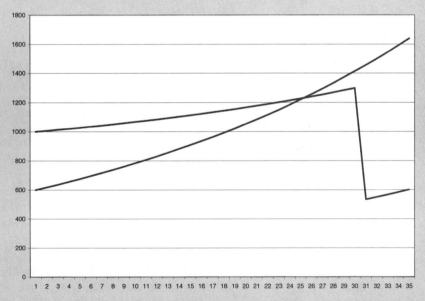

If you understand this graph, you understand why home ownership can be a good investment. In recent history, rents and real estate values have inflated at annual rates in excess of the 3 percent average. People who purchased their own homes locked in, or froze, the major portion of their housing expenses. With higher inflation, of course, the two lines cross much earlier. In the 1970s, when the nation suffered double-digit inflation, it didn't take long at all for buying to be cheaper than renting.

Continued

PART

III

Quicken for Investors

MASTERING FINANCIAL SUCCESS CONTINUED

However, as you might know, one of the very best ways to boost your investment profits is to take advantage of investment vehicles that either increase your investment (such as the matching that employers sometimes provide to their employees with 401(k) plans) or that produce immediate tax savings (such as tax-deductible individual retirement accounts). Home ownership produces neither of these benefits. Employers don't pay more to homeowners. And you can't claim your down payment as a tax deduction. A home ownership investment is probably a respectable investment, but it doesn't hold a candle to a 401(k) plan (especially if there's employer matching!) or tax-deductible IRAs (individual retirement accounts).

About the Tax Benefits of Home Ownership

Many people claim that mortgage interest deductions are a tax benefit, but this isn't always true. For most people, the interest on a mortgage is an itemized deduction that reduces taxable income and therefore income taxes. But the same thing is usually true of interest on a loan used to purchase an investment. Deductible mortgage interest really isn't a tax benefit when you're talking about the investment qualities of buying a home versus, say, the investment qualities of putting money into a mutual fund.

One loophole that may benefit homeowners, however, concerns the gain on the sale of a principal residence (the place where you live most of the time). As I mentioned earlier in the chapter, you might be able to postpone indefinitely paying income taxes on any appreciation in the value of your house. If you sell your home, you can take an exemption of up to $250,000 ($500,000 for married couples filing joint returns) for any gain on the sale of your principal residence.

The Problems of Home Ownership as an Investment

As an investment, however, home ownership isn't flawless. Financially, you must consider several things if you're trying to decide whether to buy or to rent. Perhaps the first thing to consider is this: Home ownership is very illiquid. In other words, it's very difficult to turn an investment in a home into cash. The value of liquidity is debatable. Suppose that you need money for an unexpected expense, perhaps because you've lost your job. An investment in a publicly traded stock or a stock mutual fund takes only minutes to convert to cash. Equity in a home takes weeks or months to reach. (This illiquidity business, by the way, is the reason it's not really a good financial idea to repay debts such as mortgages, despite what some of the popular financial writers say.) Another problem with real estate as an investment is that the transaction costs are extremely high. To buy a home, for example, you must pay for things like loan fees and

Continued ▎▶

appraisal expenses. To sell a home, you usually need to pay a real estate broker a commission that can be as much as 7 percent of the home's value. Due to high transaction costs, home ownership loses its investment shine if you frequently buy and sell homes. In fact, if a home appreciates, say, 3 percent a year and your transaction costs amount to 9 percent, as they easily can, it takes three years of steady 3 percent inflation just to pay for the 9 percent transaction costs of trading homes.

One final problem that's more important than most people realize is the financial principle of diversification. When you store a large chunk of your financial wealth in one place—your home—it's much easier for a single event to damage or destroy your financial situation. It's easy to think of these sorts of "single events" as hurricanes, tornadoes, or fires. But when you're thinking about a home as an investment, the real danger (if you want to call it that) is that your home won't appreciate in value or, even worse, that its value will depreciate. Take another quick look at the housing costs graph shown earlier. If you look closely at the data, you'll see that it takes more than 20 years of steady 3 percent inflation before home ownership becomes less expensive on a monthly basis than renting. If home values fall or they just don't rise in value for a few years, home ownership isn't a good investment. In fact, it becomes a very poor investment.

One final problem of home ownership as an investment is that it's a leveraged purchase. *Leverage* simply means you borrow much of the money you use to make the purchase. Financial leverage can dramatically impact the goodness or badness of an investment, including a home.

The problem of financial leverage is a simple one. You owe the mortgage company the money you borrowed plus any accrued interest regardless of whether the home you purchased with the borrowed money increases in value or decreases in value. Suppose that you borrow $95,000 to purchase a $100,000 home. If the home increases in value a mere 10 percent to $110,000, you still only owe $95,000, so your $5,000 investment grows to $15,000—a 200 percent return. On the other hand, if the home decreases in value a mere 10 percent to $90,000, you still owe $95,000, and you've actually lost your entire investment—the down payment. You need to come up with an additional $5,000 if you sell the home.

What's the Bottom Line?

Focusing entirely on the financial issues, you can draw several conclusions. First, be sure to take advantage of superior investment options such as employer-sponsored 401(k) plans and deductible IRAs before you invest in a home. You probably need a certain amount of money for things like retirement. A home isn't the best way to accumulate the financial wealth you need when you no longer work.

Continued

MASTERING FINANCIAL SUCCESS CONTINUED

If you have exhausted the superior investment opportunities available (like 401(k) plans and deductible IRAs), home ownership is usually a very prudent investment. It is prudent if you will be able to live in the home for at least five years and preferably ten to twenty years. As a diversification measure, a real estate investment in home owner-ship nicely balances retirement savings invested in the stock market. Real estate often represents a reasonable hedge against inflation. What's more, most of the problems of real estate, such as illiquidity and leverage, aren't serious if you're willing to live some-place for a long time and you have other savings.

Don't, however, make the mistake of believing that the bigger a house is, the better the investment is. People often and erroneously justify a larger, more expensive home because "it's a good investment." Admittedly, I haven't seen a lot of good data that con-clusively disproves this particular theory. There is evidence, however, that suggests mod-est and middle-class housing is the better investment. What's more, luxury housing is often much more illiquid.

Maybe the most important thing to say, after all of this, is that if you can't afford a home, don't worry about it. There are better investments. Not owning a home means being far more mobile than you would be if you owned one. Remember, too, that it takes renters years and years before they spend more for housing than their home-owning friends. Finally, even when your home-owning friends have repaid their mortgages, you'll be in very good shape if you've been salting money away in things like 401(k)s or IRAs.

Can You Afford It?
A home costs more than you probably have in your checking account, so to buy one you need to borrow money from either the seller or a lender. It's impossible to gener-alize about what an individual seller might do. In fact, most of the creative financing schemes available today, including most of the "nothing down" schemes, rely on a seller doing what a regular lender won't do: take a down payment in a form other than cash, trade properties, loan money at below-market interest rates, and so on.

Regular lenders, such as banks and mortgage companies, usually follow three rules to determine how much money to lend and how much house you can afford: the hous-ing expenses rule, the long-term debt payments rule, and the down payment rule.

The Housing Expenses Rule
Typically, a lender suggests that your total monthly housing expenses should not exceed 25 to 28 percent of your gross monthly income. Monthly housing expenses include mortgage payments and insurance, property taxes, maintenance, and utilities. Your

Continued ▐▶

MASTERING FINANCIAL SUCCESS CONTINUED

gross monthly income might include your wages (before taxes), investment income, and miscellaneous income items such as pension benefits or alimony. (In some areas of the country, higher standards apply because housing expenses in general are very high.)

Because the loan calculations are complicated without a financial calculator, I created a table that rates how many "dollars" of 30-year mortgage a "dollar" of income supports at various interest rates. The figures all suppose that you can spend 25 percent of your monthly gross income on a mortgage payment. This really means that a lender will be applying the 28 percent rule and that the extra 3 percent will go for the non-mortgage payment part of your housing expenses.

Mortgage Interest Rates (%)	Mortgage Dollar Per Income Dollar
7.00	$3.13
7.25	$3.05
7.50	$2.98
7.75	$2.91
8.00	$2.84
8.25	$2.77
8.50	$2.71
8.75	$2.65
9.00	$2.59
9.25	$2.53
9.50	$2.48
9.75	$2.42
10.00	$2.37
10.25	$2.32
10.50	$2.28
10.75	$2.23
11.00	$2.19

Using the numbers in this table, if interest rates are 8 percent, for example, someone making $25,000 a year would be able to qualify for a mortgage of $2.84 times $25,000, or $71,000.

Continued

PART

III

Quicken for Investors

Long-Term Debt Payments Rule

This loan qualification rule sets a limit on the amount of long-term debt you can have. The general rule is that long-term debt payments shouldn't exceed 33 to 36 percent of your monthly gross income. Lenders want to be sure that you can comfortably bear the total debt burden you'll have after you get the mortgage. Long-term debt includes mortgage payments and any other debt borrowers still have in 10 to 12 months.

As long as your long-term debts don't exceed about 10 percent of your income, the long-term debt rule usually isn't the limiting factor that determines how large a mortgage you can afford. If you have a lot of long-term debt—car payments, student loans, and so on—you may have a problem finding a mortgage you can afford.

The Down Payment Rule

In addition to the rules that have to do with the size of the mortgage, there's another rule for determining affordability. Lenders typically do not lend the full purchase price of homes. Most lenders want the borrower to pay 10 to 20 percent of the purchase price, although some might require as little as 5 percent down. Federal Housing Administration and Veterans Administration loans allow even smaller down payments, from 0 to 5 percent. However, if you put down less than 20 percent, you need to pay private mortgage insurance. This type of insurance protects the lender against loss if you default on your mortgage payments.

Another way to look at the down payment business is by expressing the mortgage you can have as a percentage of the price of the house. With a 20 percent down payment, for example, a lender puts up 80 percent of the purchase price in the form of a mortgage; with a 10 percent down payment, a lender puts up 90 percent; and with a 5 percent down payment, a lender puts up 95 percent.

To take our earlier example, if interest rates are 8 percent and your family gross income is $25,000, you can't go out and buy a house for $71,000, because the lender doesn't want to put up 100 percent of the purchase price. You need to pay part of the purchase price—at least 5 percent in most cases—in the form of a down payment.

By the way, lenders aren't concerned only with the percentage of the purchase price that you can supply. Usually, the lender is also interested in how you come up with the down payment. From a lender's perspective, some sources are acceptable and some are not. Acceptable sources include savings, investments, and gifts from parents and relatives. Unacceptable sources include draws on credit cards and loans (not gifts) from parents and relatives.

Continued

A Final Word about Affordability

The rise in home values in many parts of the country has made it very difficult for many people to afford a home. If you've spent time working through the numbers and found yourself thinking that owning a home is more like the impossible dream than the American dream, don't give up for a couple of reasons.

- Don't depend too much on what I've said here. Lender guidelines often vary, so you should place a telephone call to your local bank.
- Interest rates have a dramatic impact on home affordability. They bounce up and down. Although you can't afford a home today, a lower interest rate next month or next year might mean you can afford a home then.

Choosing a Mortgage

Choosing a mortgage is easier than you might think, thanks to federal truth-in-lending laws. You basically have two choices: a fixed-interest rate loan or an adjustable-interest rate loan. The first question to ask yourself is whether you should go with a fixed-interest rate or an adjustable-interest rate mortgage. I explained how adjustable-rate mortgages and fixed-rate mortgages work at the end of Chapter 13. Here, I'll briefly review the pros and cons of each type of mortgage.

Fixed-Rate versus Adjustable-Rate Mortgages

Some financial writers and perhaps most of your neighbors think ARMs are worse than bad. To be quite blunt, their advice is influenced more by fear and emotion than by the hard facts. Several studies have shown that, for the most part, ARMs cost homeowners with mortgages less money. This cost-savings feature is particularly true of ARMs with capped, or increase-limited, interest rates in which the rate of interest cannot rise above a certain rate.

The cost-savings can add up quickly. As you may know, in the early years of a mortgage, very little of the mortgage payments are actually applied to reducing the principal. This fact suggests an interesting money-saving and risk-reduction technique. Suppose a homeowner chooses an ARM and then uses the interest rate savings (as compared to a fixed-rate mortgage) to reduce the cost of the mortgage. In other words, the borrower gets an ARM but makes the larger fixed-interest rate payment. If interest rates don't jump up for at least a few years, the homeowner is very unlikely to lose money because the mortgage balance ends up getting reduced so quickly.

Continued ▮▶

MASTERING FINANCIAL SUCCESS CONTINUED

As part of writing this chapter, in fact, I constructed a little computer-based model that did just this. My model calculates what happens if a person looking for a $90,000 mortgage chooses an adjustable-rate 7 percent mortgage with a $598-per-month payment but then makes the $724.16-per-month payment that would be required on the alternative 9 percent fixed-rate mortgage. In this case, the extra payment amount—roughly $125—is applied directly to principal.

Here's the interesting thing about all this: It turns out that even if interest rates rise by a full percent each year, you would pay less with an ARM than you would with a fixed-rate mortgage until the fourth straight year of rising interest rates. At this point, the ARM borrower ends up paying about an extra $50 a month.

However, if interest rates don't immediately rise but stay level for even a few years, the person with the ARM saves a bundle of money. And even if interest rates skyrocket later on, this person will never pay more than the person with the fixed-rate mortgage because the extra monthly principal payments made early on so quickly reduced the mortgage balance.

Another thing to consider about all this is that if interest rates are rising rapidly, as you would assume if you're seeing back-to-back interest rate increases, it probably means that inflation has kicked up again. With strong inflation, it's very possible that your wages or salary will be adjusted annually for inflation and that your house will be inflating in value as well.

Given these characteristics, many people really should consider an ARM rather than a fixed-rate mortgage when ARM interest rates are significantly below fixed-rate mortgage interest rates. Sure, there's a little more risk, as there always is in any financial investment. But with a limit on the year-to-year increases a lender can make (such as 1 percent) and on the total increases a lender can make (such as 5 percent), you are more likely to save money by going with an ARM.

If fixed-interest mortgage rates are low, fixed-interest mortgages certainly are worth considering. What's more, to truly reduce the financial risk of an ARM, you need to be the sort of person (or the sort of family) who has the discipline to always add that extra amount to the payment.

It's not a good idea to use an ARM because it's the only mortgage you can afford. The reason for this—and, admittedly, I'm pretty conservative—is that if this is the case, it likely means that you can't afford an increase in your mortgage payments, and that is what

Continued ▐▶

MASTERING FINANCIAL SUCCESS CONTINUED

will happen the next time interest rates jump up. By picking an ARM when that is the only kind of mortgage you can afford, you're almost certain to have the unpleasant task of someday trying to figure out how to pay for something you can't really afford.

Note, too, that many ARM lenders use what are called *teaser rates*. Teaser rates amount to a marketing ploy where a lender offers a special, temporary, lower-than-normal interest rate. The problem with a teaser rate is that even if the underlying interest rate index doesn't change, your payment still increases the next time it's recalculated because the lender used a special rate to entice you. Teasers aren't bad, by the way. They do save you money. It's just that you need to be ready for the payment bump that occurs when the teaser interest rate is adjusted.

Comparing Mortgages

Once you make the fixed-rate versus adjustable-rate decision, the rest is easy. To compare fixed-interest rate mortgages, all you need to do is compare the annual percentage rates, or APRs. Then pick the one that's lowest. That's it.

APRs measure the total cost of a mortgage, including the periodic mortgage interest you need to pay and all other costs of obtaining credit, such as the loan origination fee and processing costs. By comparing APRs, you don't need to get bogged down wondering whether, for example, an 8.5 percent mortgage with a 2 percent fee is a better deal than a 9 percent mortgage with no fee. The APR combines all the costs into one easy-to-understand number that, in effect, expresses all the loan costs as an effective interest rate.

ARMs also can be compared by using APRs. Unfortunately, it's often more difficult to get the lender to provide an APR because the calculation is more complicated. Nevertheless, you should still be able to get an APR if you press the lender for it.

PART

III

Quicken for Investors

PART IV

Quicken in a Small Business

LEARN TO:

- **Prepare Payroll Checks and Taxes**

- **Track Accounts Receivable and Accounts Payable**

- **Monitor Cash Flow and Business Profits**

CHAPTER 20

Payroll

You can use Quicken to prepare payroll checks, calculate payroll taxes, and expedite the preparation of federal and state payroll and payroll tax returns. In this chapter, you'll learn how to set up payroll categories and liability accounts for your record keeping. You'll also learn how to prepare payroll checks and payroll tax returns and how to memorize and schedule payroll-related transactions.

 NOTE At the end of this chapter, you'll find information about what you need to do before you hire your first employee to address federal and state payroll tax collection and reporting requirements. Be sure to read that material to make sure that you're ready to start processing a payroll with Quicken.

Setting Up Payroll Categories and Accounts

Once you take care of the federal and state payroll and employment prerequisites (and you do need to take care of these items first), you're ready to set up Quicken to prepare payroll checks and tax returns. To do this, you set up categories (or subcategories) for each payroll expense that you, the employer, pay. For example, you set up a Payroll Expense category to track wages, Social Security, Medicare, and federal unemployment taxes, as well as any state payroll taxes you pay (such as state unemployment and workers' compensation).

You also need liability accounts for every payroll tax liability (amount you owe someone) you incur, such as the amounts you owe the IRS for the federal income, Social Security, and Medicare taxes you withhold from the employee's payroll check, as well as the federal payroll taxes, Social Security, and Medicare taxes you pay as an employer. (Social Security and Medicare taxes are paid by both the employer and the employee.)

Setting Up Payroll Categories

The easiest way to set up payroll categories is to set up a Payroll expense category and then create subcategories for each of the types of payroll expense you actually pay: wages, Social Security, Medicare, federal unemployment, state unemployment, and so on. The following sections explain how to create the main category and subcategories.

Setting Up a Payroll Expense Category

To set up an expense category for payroll, follow these steps:

1. Choose Finance ➤ Category & Transfer List to open the Category & Transfer List. Click the New command button to display the Set Up Category dialog box, as shown in Figure 20.1.

FIGURE 20.1

*The Set Up Category
dialog box*

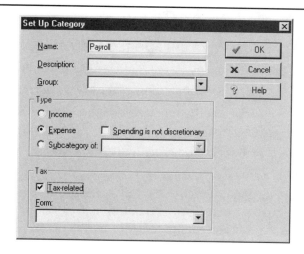

2. Enter **Payroll** in the Name text box. (You'll use this as the main expense category for payroll.)

3. If you want to describe the payroll expense category in more detail, use the Description text box.

4. Be sure the Expense option button is marked.

5. If you're going to be processing payroll that is or may be a tax-deductible expense, mark the Tax-Related checkbox and choose the appropriate entry from the Form drop-down list box. Here are some suggestions:

   • If you're a sole proprietor who uses Schedule C, select Schedule C: Wages Paid.

   • If you're a farmer who uses Schedule F, select Schedule F: Labor Hired.

   • If you're a parent preparing to process payroll for an employee providing child care, select 2441: Qualifying Childcare Expenses.

TIP If you don't see the Form drop-down list box, go ahead and click OK to set up your account. Then choose Edit ➤ Options ➤ Quicken Program. When Quicken displays the General Options dialog box, click the General tab and mark the Use Tax Schedules with Categories checkbox. Click OK, and then choose Taxes ➤ Tax Link Assistant to open the Tax Link Assistant dialog box and assign a tax form to the category you just created.

6. Click OK. Quicken adds the Payroll expense to the Category & Transfer List window.

Setting Up Payroll Expense Subcategories

You need at least three payroll subcategories to handle the payroll:

- A gross wages subcategory to track what an employee really earns
- A Social Security subcategory to track the Social Security taxes that you owe as an employer
- A Medicare subcategory to track the Medicare payroll taxes that you owe as an employer

If your employees are subject to federal unemployment tax, you also need a subcategory to track that expense. Finally, you need subcategories to track any state payroll taxes that you are required to pay as an employer.

NOTE You don't need any subcategories to track amounts that an employee pays through payroll deductions.

To set up the subcategories you use to track the various types of payroll expenses, take these steps:

1. In the Category & Transfer List, click the New command button to display the Set Up Category dialog box (see Figure 20.1).

2. Enter the name for the payroll subcategory in the Name text box. (You can use an abbreviation such as Wages, SS, MCARE, or FUTA.) Do not use the same names that you will use for your liability accounts. Quicken does not allow duplication of names in accounts and categories.

3. If you want to describe the payroll expense subcategory, use the Description text box. For example, if you abbreviated the payroll expense in the Name text box, you can enter the full payroll expense subcategory name in the Description text

box. You might describe the Wages subcategory as "Gross Wages," the SS subcategory as "Social Security," the MCARE subcategory as "Medicare," the FUTA subcategory as "Federal Unemployment Taxes," and so on.

4. Click the Subcategory Of option button and enter the name of the Payroll expense category into the text box. (If you've followed the instructions so far, the expense category's name will be Payroll.)

5. If you're going to process payroll that is or may be a tax-deductible expense, mark the Tax-Related checkbox.

6. Click OK. Quicken adds the payroll expense subcategory to the Category & Transfer List.

Repeat steps 2 through 6 for each of the payroll expense subcategories that you need to create.

Setting Up Payroll Liability Accounts

The next task is to set up liability accounts to track the amounts you owe the federal and state governments. You should set up payroll tax liability accounts for federal income taxes withheld, state income taxes withheld, Social Security owed, and Medicare taxes owed. If there are other significant payroll tax liabilities, set up payroll-tax liability accounts for these too. If a payroll tax liability is very small (federal unemployment taxes, for example, can equal 0.08 percent), you may want to skip tracking the liability. In this case, just categorize the check that pays the tax using a payroll tax category.

To set up the payroll liability accounts you need, follow these steps:

1. Display the Account List by choosing Finance ➤ Account List.

2. Click the New button. Quicken displays the dialog box for creating new accounts.

3. Click the Liability button, and then click Next.

4. When Quicken displays the Liability Account Setup dialog box, click the Summary tab. This tab is shown in Figure 20.2.

5. In the Account Name text box, enter an account name for the payroll liability. Make *Payroll* the first word in the account name. For example, you might use the name Payroll-FWH to track the federal withholding amounts, Payroll-SS to track the Social Security taxes owed, and Payroll-MCARE to track the Medicare taxes owed.

FIGURE 20.2

*The Summary tab of
the Liability Account
Setup dialog box*

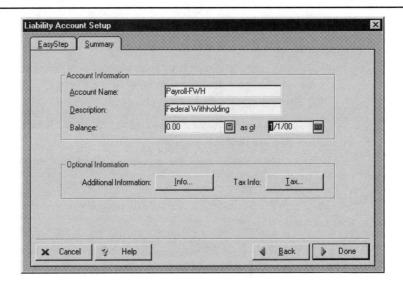

 TIP You should start each payroll liability account's name with the word *Payroll* so that you can easily prepare a report of payroll transactions and account balances. The Payroll report on the Business submenu does just this; it summarizes transactions that use categories and accounts starting with the word *Payroll*.

6. If you want to describe the payroll liability account in more detail, use the Description text box. For example, if you abbreviated the liability name for the account name, you might enter the full payroll liability name as the description.

7. In the Balance text box, enter the amount you currently owe on the payroll liability.

8. In the As Of text box, enter the date for which you owe the amount entered in step 7.

9. Click Done. When Quicken asks if you want to set up an amortized loan for the account, select No. Quicken adds the new payroll liability account.

Repeat steps 2 through 9 for each of the other payroll tax liability accounts you want to add.

Preparing a Payroll Check

Once you've set up your payroll categories and accounts, you're ready to use Quicken to prepare employee payroll checks. To do this, you first calculate the employee's wages and the payroll taxes you and the employee pay based on those wages. Second, you record a transaction in the Quicken register that summarizes the payroll check and the related payroll taxes.

Calculating an Employee's Wages and Payroll Taxes

There are really two parts to figuring out what a payroll transaction is supposed to look like:

- Calculate the employee's gross wages and the payroll taxes you, the employer, owe. (This is usually the easiest part.)
- Describe the payroll deductions you withhold from the check.

Calculating Gross Wages and Employer's Payroll Taxes

Calculating an employee's wages and payroll taxes starts with the actual gross wages calculation. For example, if an employee works 40 hours and you pay $7.50 an hour, you owe the employee $300, calculated as 40 times $7.50. If an employee works for a month and you've agreed to pay $1,000 a month, you owe the employee $1,000.

 NOTE In the following payroll tax examples, I use round numbers to keep things simple. The wages you pay as an employer might be much more or less than the numbers used in the examples.

Once you know the employee's gross wages, you can calculate the payroll taxes you owe as a result of wages. Just multiply the payroll tax rate by the gross wages amount. (You can start the Quicken calculator by clicking the Calculator button, which appears in the upper-right corner of the Quicken program window.)

Suppose, for example, you owe an employee $1,000 for a month of work. To calculate the Social Security taxes you owe because of the $1,000, multiply the $1,000 by the Social Security taxes percentage, which is currently 6.2 percent. (The *Employer's Tax Guide* usually prints this information on the first or second page of the *Guide*, but you can also consult a table in the *Guide* to find out what number is 6.2 percent of $1,000.)

NOTE To order a printed copy of the *Employer's Tax Guide* or to access it online, go to the Internal Revenue site at www.irs.gov.

To calculate the Medicare taxes you owe because of the $1,000, either multiply the $1,000 by the Medicare taxes percentage, which is currently 1.45 percent, or consult the table in the *Guide* to find out what number is 1.45 percent of $1,000.

If you owe an employee $1,000 in gross wages but need to pay 6.2 percent in Social Security taxes and 1.45 percent in Medicare taxes, the total payroll expenses you incur are equal to those shown in Table 20.1.

 NOTE Each of the payroll expenses in Table 20.1 should be recorded using a separate payroll expense subcategory.

TABLE 20.1: SAMPLE PAYROLL EXPENSES

Description	Amount
Gross wages	$1,000.00
Social Security	$62.00
Medicare	$14.50
Total payroll expenses	$1,076.50

If you owe other federal and state payroll taxes, such as a 1 percent state unemployment tax paid by the employer, calculate them in the same way, obtaining the data you need from your state's equivalent of the *Employer's Tax Guide*.

Calculating the Payroll Deductions

An employee doesn't get paid the gross wages amount. You, the employer, are required to deduct from the employee's gross wages amount for federal income taxes, Social Security, and Medicare. You may also be required or allowed to deduct amounts for other payroll taxes.

The amount an employee pays for Social Security and Medicare taxes through a payroll deduction is calculated in the same way as the amount an employer pays for

Social Security and Medicare taxes: You just multiply the appropriate tax rate by the gross wages amount. In the case of a $1,000 monthly paycheck, Social Security taxes equal $62.00 (calculated as 6.2 percent of $1,000), and Medicare taxes equal $14.50 (calculated as 1.45 percent of $1,000). If there are other payroll taxes paid by the employee, you calculate these in the same way.

The amount of federal income taxes you withhold is dictated by the IRS. You look at the employee's W-4 to obtain the filing status and the number of personal exemptions claimed. Then you look up (in the *Employer's Tax Guide*) the employee's gross wages amount in the appropriate pay-period table for the employee's filing status. For example, to determine the amount of federal income taxes to withhold for an employee who makes $1,000 a month and files a tax return using the Married Filing Jointly status, you use the Married Persons—Monthly Payroll Period table. Figure 20.3 shows this page from the *Employer's Tax Guide*.

WARNING Don't use the information shown in Figure 20.3! You need to get your own *Employer's Tax Guide* to make sure you're using the most up-to-date income tax rates.

Look down the first column of the table until you find the gross wages row for monthly wages equal to $1,000. Then look across that row until you get to the withholding amount specified for the claimed number of withholding allowances. For example, if the employee claimed two exemptions on the W-4 form, the table in Figure 20.3 says you should withhold $4 in federal income taxes. Table 20.2 summarizes the calculation.

TABLE 20.2: A SAMPLE NET WAGES CALCULATION

Description	Amount
Gross wages	$1,000.00
Social Security	$(62.00)
Medicare	$(14.50)
Federal income taxes	$(4.00)
Net wages	$919.50

FIGURE 20.3

The Married Persons–
Monthly Payroll Period
table from the
Employer's Tax
Guide

MARRIED Persons– MONTHLY Payroll Period

(For Wages Paid in 1999)

If the wages are±		And the number of withholding allowances claimed is–										
At least	But less than	0	1	2	3	4	5	6	7	8	9	10
		The amount of income tax to be withheld is–										
$0	$540	0	0	0	0	0	0	0	0	0	0	0
540	560	2	0	0	0	0	0	0	0	0	0	0
560	580	5	0	0	0	0	0	0	0	0	0	0
580	600	8	0	0	0	0	0	0	0	0	0	0
600	640	12	0	0	0	0	0	0	0	0	0	0
640	680	18	0	0	0	0	0	0	0	0	0	0
680	720	24	0	0	0	0	0	0	0	0	0	0
720	760	30	0	0	0	0	0	0	0	0	0	0
760	800	36	2	0	0	0	0	0	0	0	0	0
800	840	42	8	0	0	0	0	0	0	0	0	0
840	880	48	14	0	0	0	0	0	0	0	0	0
880	920	54	20	0	0	0	0	0	0	0	0	0
920	960	60	26	0	0	0	0	0	0	0	0	0
960	1,000	66	32	0	0	0	0	0	0	0	0	0
1,000	1,040	72	38	4	0	0	0	0	0	0	0	0
1,040	1,080	78	44	10	0	0	0	0	0	0	0	0
1,080	1,120	84	50	16	0	0	0	0	0	0	0	0
1,120	1,160	90	56	22	0	0	0	0	0	0	0	0
1,160	1,200	96	62	28	0	0	0	0	0	0	0	0
1,200	1,240	102	68	34	0	0	0	0	0	0	0	0
1,240	1,280	108	74	40	5	0	0	0	0	0	0	0
1,280	1,320	114	80	46	11	0	0	0	0	0	0	0
1,320	1,360	120	86	52	17	0	0	0	0	0	0	0
1,360	1,400	126	92	58	23	0	0	0	0	0	0	0
1,400	1,440	132	98	64	29	0	0	0	0	0	0	0
1,440	1,480	138	104	70	35	1	0	0	0	0	0	0
1,480	1,520	144	110	76	41	7	0	0	0	0	0	0
1,520	1,560	150	116	82	47	13	0	0	0	0	0	0
1,560	1,600	156	122	88	53	19	0	0	0	0	0	0
1,600	1,640	162	128	94	59	25	0	0	0	0	0	0
1,640	1,680	168	134	100	65	31	0	0	0	0	0	0
1,680	1,720	174	140	106	71	37	3	0	0	0	0	0
1,720	1,760	180	146	112	77	43	9	0	0	0	0	0
1,760	1,800	186	152	118	83	49	15	0	0	0	0	0
1,800	1,840	192	158	124	89	55	21	0	0	0	0	0
1,840	1,880	198	164	130	95	61	27	0	0	0	0	0
1,880	1,920	204	170	136	101	67	33	0	0	0	0	0
1,920	1,960	210	176	142	107	73	39	4	0	0	0	0
1,960	2,000	216	182	148	113	79	45	10	0	0	0	0
2,000	2,040	222	188	154	119	85	51	16	0	0	0	0
2,040	2,080	228	194	160	125	91	57	22	0	0	0	0
2,080	2,120	234	200	166	131	97	63	28	0	0	0	0
2,120	2,160	240	206	172	137	103	69	34	0	0	0	0
2,160	2,200	246	212	178	143	109	75	40	6	0	0	0
2,200	2,240	252	218	184	149	115	81	46	12	0	0	0
2,240	2,280	258	224	190	155	121	87	52	18	0	0	0
2,280	2,320	264	230	196	161	127	93	58	24	0	0	0
2,320	2,360	270	236	202	167	133	99	64	30	0	0	0
2,360	2,400	276	242	208	173	139	105	70	36	1	0	0
2,400	2,440	282	248	214	179	145	111	76	42	7	0	0
2,440	2,480	288	254	220	185	151	117	82	48	13	0	0
2,480	2,520	294	260	226	191	157	123	88	54	19	0	0
2,520	2,560	300	266	232	197	163	129	94	60	25	0	0
2,560	2,600	306	272	238	203	169	135	100	66	31	0	0
2,600	2,640	312	278	244	209	175	141	106	72	37	3	0
2,640	2,680	318	284	250	215	181	147	112	78	43	9	0
2,680	2,720	324	290	256	221	187	153	118	84	49	15	0
2,720	2,760	330	296	262	227	193	159	124	90	55	21	0
2,760	2,800	336	302	268	233	199	165	130	96	61	27	0
2,800	2,840	342	308	274	239	205	171	136	102	67	33	0
2,840	2,880	348	314	280	245	211	177	142	108	73	39	5
2,880	2,920	354	320	286	251	217	183	148	114	79	45	11
2,920	2,960	360	326	292	257	223	189	154	120	85	51	17
2,960	3,000	366	332	298	263	229	195	160	126	91	57	23
3,000	3,040	372	338	304	269	235	201	166	132	97	63	29
3,040	3,080	378	344	310	275	241	207	172	138	103	69	35
3,080	3,120	384	350	316	281	247	213	178	144	109	75	41
3,120	3,160	390	356	322	287	253	219	184	150	115	81	47
3,160	3,200	396	362	328	293	259	225	190	156	121	87	53
3,200	3,240	402	368	334	299	265	231	196	162	127	93	59

Producing the Payroll Check

Now you're ready to prepare the payroll check and record it. The instructions here assume that you'll print the check in Quicken by using the Write Checks area to record it. If you don't want to print the check, you can record it directly in the register.

To record gross wages, deductions, and net wages, follow these steps:

1. In the Write Checks area, enter the payroll date in the Date text box, the employee's name in the Pay to the Order of text box, and the net wages amount in the $ text box.

2. If you'll mail the check in a windowed envelope, type the employee's address in the Address block.

3. If it will help you or the employee identify the payroll period, enter additional information in the Memo text box.

4. Click the Split command button to display the Split Transaction Window.

5. Enter the gross wages amount on the first split transaction line. In the Category field, type **Payroll** followed by a colon (:) and the name of the gross wages subcategory. (If you use Wages as the name of the gross wages subcategory, for example, type **Payroll:Wages**.) Then type the gross wages amount in the Amount field.

6. Enter the Social Security tax deduction on the second split transaction line. In the Category field, type the name of the payroll liability account you set up to track what you owe for Social Security. If you used Payroll-SS as the liability account name, for example, you enter **[Payroll-SS]**. In the Amount field, enter the Social Security taxes paid by the employee as a negative number.

 WARNING Be sure that you use payroll liability accounts in steps 6, 7, and 8. You don't want to use payroll subcategories. By using the payroll liability accounts, you show that it's the employee who is paying these amounts. If you incorrectly use payroll subcategories, you show that it's you, not the employee, who is paying these amounts.

7. Enter the Medicare tax deduction on the third split transaction line. In the Category field, type the name of the payroll liability account you set up to track what you owe for Medicare. In the Amount field, enter the Medicare taxes paid by the employee as a negative number.

8. Enter the federal income taxes withheld from the employee's payroll check on the fourth split transaction line. In the Category field, type the name of the payroll liability account you set up to track what you owe for federal income taxes withheld. Then enter the federal income taxes withheld as a negative number in the Amount field.

Figure 20.4 shows an example of the Split Transaction Window after entering the gross wages and the Social Security, Medicare, and federal income taxes withholding information. If the employee pays other payroll taxes through deductions, you record these in the same way as you record federal income taxes.

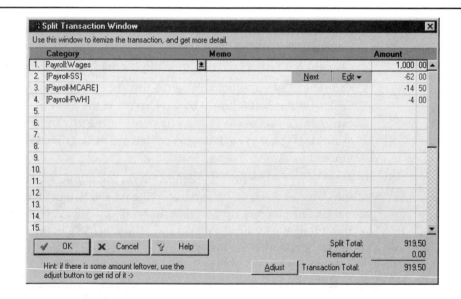

 NOTE In steps 9 through 12, you record the Social Security and Medicare payroll taxes that you as the employer must pay. This is the information shown in Table 20.1.

9. Move to the seventeenth line of the Split Transaction Window (since only the first 15 lines of the split transaction detail appear on check stubs, the employer's payroll taxes won't appear there) and enter the employer's Social Security taxes expense on that line. In the Category field, type **Payroll** followed by a colon (:) and the name of the Social Security taxes subcategory. (For example, if you use

SS as the Social Security subcategory name, type **Payroll:SS**.) Then enter the Social Security taxes amount in the Amount field.

10. Enter the employer's Social Security taxes liability (because of the Social Security taxes expense) on the eighteenth split transaction line. In the Category drop-down list box, select Transfer to [the Social Security liability account]. Then enter the Social Security taxes amount as a negative number in the Amount field.

Figure 20.5 shows an example of the Split Transaction Window after entering the employer's Social Security taxes expense and Social Security taxes liability.

FIGURE 20.5

The Split Transaction Window with Social Security taxes expense and liability information

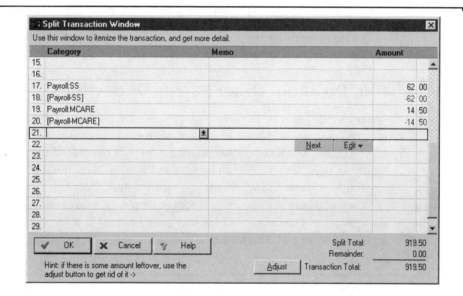

NOTE You use the same liability account to track both the amounts you owe for Social Security because you withheld money from an employee's check and the amounts you owe for Social Security because of the Social Security payroll tax.

11. Enter the employer's Medicare taxes expense on the nineteenth split transaction line. For example, if you use MCARE as the Medicare subcategory name, type **Payroll:MCARE** in the Category field. Then enter the Medicare taxes amount in the Amount field.

12. Enter the employer's Medicare taxes liability (because of the Medicare taxes expense) on the twentieth split transaction line. In the Category drop-down list box, select Transfer funds to [the Medicare liability account]. Then enter the Medicare taxes amount as a negative number in the Amount field.

NOTE You use the same liability account to track both the amounts you owe for Medicare because you withheld money from an employee's check and the amounts you owe for Medicare because of the Medicare payroll tax.

13. Click OK to close the Split Transaction Window, and then click Record Check.

Quicken records the payroll check and related payroll taxes into the Quicken register. Then it scrolls the just-completed check off your screen so you can write another one.

What to Do about Other Payroll Deductions

Other amounts may be deducted from an employee's check, for items like state income taxes, a 401(k) plan, and other employee-paid amounts. You can record these payroll deductions too. Just treat them as you treat the federal income taxes that the employee pays: Set up a payroll liability account for the deduction and transfer an amount to this account whenever you subtract the deduction from the gross wages.

When you later pay the amount for the employee, you categorize the check paying the amount as a transfer to the liability account—just as when you pay the IRS amounts you've withheld for federal income taxes.

WARNING The payroll net wages and payroll tax calculations described in the preceding sections work well for most small businesses and for household employees. But be aware of a potential problem: Some payroll taxes and payroll deductions apply to salaries and wages only up to a specified limit. Social Security taxes, for example, are levied on roughly only the first $70,000 of income. This rule means that for more highly paid employees, you need to first verify that the employee still owes or that you, the employer, still owe the tax. You can do this manually (with a pencil and a scratch pad), but if you need to track things like the net wages subject to Social Security, get a full-featured payroll program or go to an outside service bureau.

Using Memorized and Scheduled Transactions

You can memorize the payroll transactions you regularly record. Then, the next time you want to record the same or almost the same transaction, you can recall the transaction from the memorized transactions list. Quicken uses the memorized transaction's information to fill in the text boxes of the transaction.

Memorizing a Transaction

To memorize a transaction, you can start from either the Write Checks area or the register. In the Write Checks area, display the payroll check you want to memorize. In the register, select the payroll check (or any other transaction). Then choose Edit ➤ Transaction ➤ Memorize to display a message box asking if you want to memorize the split amounts as percentages of the transaction total shown in the Write Checks area. Since you want to memorize the split amounts and not the split percentages, select No. When the "This transaction is about to be memorized" message appears, click OK. Quicken adds the selected payroll transaction to its memorized transactions list.

 TIP It's likely that Quicken is automatically memorizing transactions as you create them. To check on this, click the Options button to display the Check Options dialog box and then click the QuickFill tab. If the Auto Memorize New Transactions checkbox is marked, Quicken is automatically memorizing all your transactions as you record them.

Reusing a Memorized Transaction

To reuse a memorized transaction, follow these steps:

1. Display an empty check in the Write Checks area or select the new empty row in the register.
2. Choose Bankings ➤ Memorized Transaction List to display the Memorized Transaction List, as shown in Figure 20.6.
3. Select the memorized transaction you want to reuse and click the Use command button. Quicken uses the memorized transaction to fill in the text boxes in the Write Checks area or in the selected row of the register.

FIGURE 20.6

*The Memorized
Transaction List*

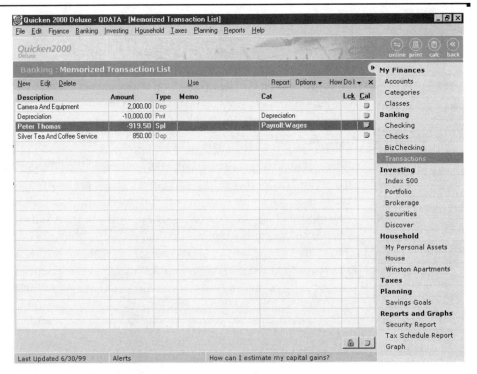

 TIP Quicken automatically reuses a memorized transaction if you haven't turned off that option in the QuickFill tab. To check this, choose Edit ➢ Options ➢ Register and click the QuickFill tab. If the Recall Memorized Transactions checkbox is marked, Quicken is automatically recalling transactions. All you need to do is enter the payee name and press Tab.

Using Scheduled Transactions to Speed Payroll

If you have employees whom you pay, without fail, every week, Quicken's scheduled transactions feature can help you. To tell Quicken that it should automatically record a memorized transaction, you *schedule* the transaction in one of two ways: with the Banking ➢ Scheduled Transaction List command or by using the Financial Calendar.

Scheduling a Transaction Using the Financial Calendar

To schedule one of the memorized transactions shown in the Financial Calendar, follow these steps:

1. Choose Finance ➤ Financial Calendar to display the Financial Calendar, as shown in Figure 20.7.

PART

IV

Quicken in a Small Business

FIGURE 20.7

The Financial Calendar

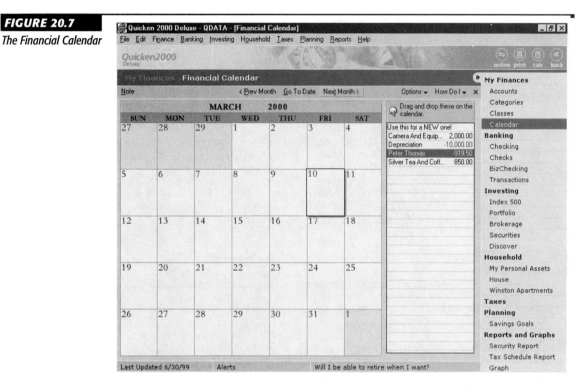

The main part of the Financial Calendar shows the current month's calendar. You can move backward and forward a month at a time by clicking the Prev Month and Next Month buttons. The list box on the right half of the area shows the memorized transactions.

 NOTE If you want to show transactions from only a selected group of accounts, choose Options ➤ Calendar Accounts to display the Calendar Options dialog box, click its Accounts tab, and then mark and unmark the accounts you want to see by clicking them.

2. Display the first month you want to schedule the transaction by using the Prev Month or Next Month button.

3. Select the memorized transaction by clicking it. Then drag the transaction to the first day it should be scheduled. Quicken displays the New Transaction dialog box, as shown in Figure 20.8. The information displayed in the dialog box describes the transaction you've just dragged.

FIGURE 20.8

The New Transaction dialog box

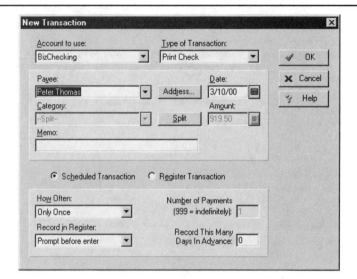

4. Activate the Account to Use drop-down list box and choose the account into which the transaction should be recorded.

5. Activate the Type of Transaction drop-down list box to indicate whether you want Quicken to record a check, a deposit, or another type of transaction.

6. Use the next section's drop-down lists and text boxes to change any part of the recurring transaction.

7. Mark either Scheduled Transaction for a repeating transaction or Register Transaction for a one-time-only transaction.

 NOTE If you mark the Scheduled Transaction option, other options are displayed in the lower half of the New Transaction dialog box.

8. Activate the How Often drop-down list box to indicate the frequency of the transaction: Only Once, Weekly, Every Two Weeks, Twice a Month, or another time period.

9. If you want to schedule more than one occurrence of this payment, use the Number of Payments text box to enter the number of payments you want Quicken to enter.

10. Use the Record in Register drop-down list box to specify whether you want Quicken to automatically enter the transaction or prompt you to enter the transaction.

11. If you want Quicken to remind you of unprinted checks, investment reminder notices, and scheduled transactions, use the Record This Many Days In Advance text box to specify the number of days of advance warning you want for this scheduled transaction.

12. Click OK.

NOTE Quicken automatically displays the Reminder area when you start Quicken if there's something it wants to remind you about. You can also display this area by choosing Finance ➤ Reminders.

Quicken schedules the transaction. To show the scheduled transaction, it puts the payee name on the calendar for each day the transaction will be recorded.

Using the Scheduled Transaction List

If you want to delete or edit a scheduled transaction, choose Banking ➤ Scheduled Transaction List. Quicken displays the Scheduled Transaction List, which lists all your scheduled transactions.

To delete a scheduled transaction, select it, click Delete, and click OK. To edit a scheduled transaction, select it, click Edit, and make your changes using the Edit Scheduled Transaction dialog box. You can also add new scheduled transactions using the Scheduled Transaction List's New command button.

Using the Financial Calendar's Reminder Notes

The Financial Calendar provides one other useful feature for managing and monitoring your payroll activities. You can post notes on calendar days. For example, you might add a note that says, "Payroll tax deposit due." Quicken then uses the note text to remind you that the payroll tax deposit is due.

To post a note, follow these steps:

1. In the Financial Calendar, select the day you want to be reminded.

2. Click the Note command button to display the Note dialog box.

3. Type your note, and then click Save.

 TIP Yellow is the traditional color for reminder notes, but you can change the color Quicken uses. To pick another color, select one from the Note Color drop-down list box in the Note dialog box.

Quicken saves your note and adds a yellow square to the calendar day to show you that there's a calendar note for the date. (To see the note, click the yellow square.)

Customizing the Financial Calendar

When you click the Options down arrow in the upper-right corner of the Financial Calendar, you have six choices.

To display a chart beneath the Calendar that shows your daily account balances, choose Options ➤ Show Account Graph. To display or hide the Memorized Transaction List, choose Options ➤ Show Memorized Transaction List. To edit the Memorized Transaction List, choose Options ➤ Edit Memorized Transaction List to open the Memorized Transaction List.

To display recorded or scheduled transactions or both in the Calendar, choose Options ➤ Show Recorded Transactions in Calendar or Options ➤ Show Scheduled Transactions in Calendar.

Preparing Payroll Tax Returns and Paying Payroll Taxes

There are two other payroll tasks that you need to complete on a regular basis:

- You need to pay the IRS both the amounts you've withheld from employee checks and the amounts you owe for payroll taxes.

- You need to prepare payroll tax returns, usually on both a quarterly and an annual basis.

What to Do When You Write the Check

The rules for remitting federal tax deposits change frequently, but one useful piece of information concerns how much you owe. For example, as I'm writing this, if you owe less than $500, you are not required to pay a tax deposit until the end of the quarter. (If you owe more than $500, your best bet is to pay what you owe immediately.)

But how do you know how much you owe the IRS? It's simple: You know by looking at the payroll liability accounts. The balances in these accounts are the amounts you owe for various employer payroll taxes and employee payroll deductions.

 TIP   Read through the section in the *Employer's Tax Guide* that describes the rules for depositing taxes. It describes how quickly you'll need to make deposits, including information such as the fact that you should allow time for the check to clear. It also describes the penalty you must pay if you're delinquent.

Along with your check, you need to send a Federal Tax Deposit (Form 8109) coupon. This coupon gives your Federal Tax Identification number. The IRS should send you a booklet of these forms a few weeks after you apply for your employer identification number. The booklet of Federal Tax Deposit coupons has instructions about how you fill out the form and where you mail it.

As an example, let's say you currently owe the amounts shown in Table 20.3. The payroll tax liability account balances shown in Table 20.3 equal the amounts you will owe if you have prepared one payroll check for $1,000 of gross wages, as described earlier in the chapter. The $4 in federal taxes is the amount withheld from the employee's check. The $124 is the total Social Security owed, including both the $62 paid by the employee as a payroll deduction and the $62 Social Security payroll tax paid by the employer. The $29 is the total Medicare tax owed, including both the $14.50 paid by the employee as a payroll deduction and the $14.50 Medicare payroll tax paid by the employer.

TABLE 20.3: SAMPLE PAYROLL LIABILITY ACCOUNT BALANCES

Description	Amount
Social Security	$124.00
Medicare	$29.00
Federal income taxes	$4.00
Total taxes owed	$157.00

To record a check that makes the federal tax deposit for the payroll tax liabilities shown in Table 20.3, write a check for $157. To show that your payment reduces the payroll tax liability account balances, use the Split Transaction Window to record transfers to the liability accounts in the amount shown in Table 20.3. Figure 20.9 shows the Split Transaction Window that records this federal tax deposit.

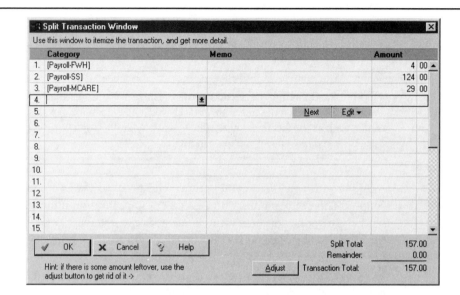

FIGURE 20.9

The Split Transaction Window that records a federal tax deposit

 NOTE   When you make a federal tax deposit, you use the depository's name for the payee.

Preparing Payroll Tax Returns

To get the payroll information you need to fill out a payroll tax return, produce the Business Payroll Report by selecting Reports ➢ Business ➢ Payroll. Figure 20.10 shows an example of the Payroll Report. (For more information about how to produce and customize Quicken's reports, see Chapter 4.)

FIGURE 20.10

First page of the
Payroll Report

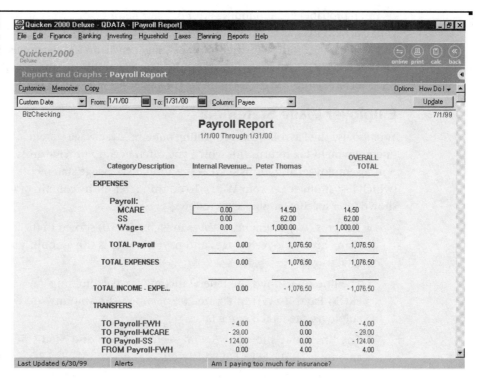

Quarterly and Federal Payroll Tax Returns

Most, and maybe all, of the quarterly and federal payroll tax returns you file will simply ask for the total gross wages you've paid for the quarter or for the year. In Figure 20.10, you get this number from the Wages (for gross wages) row in the Overall Total column. (This is $1,000 in Figure 20.10, and it includes only the $1,000 paid to one employee.) The trick to getting a quarterly or annual gross wages total is using the appropriate Report From and To date ranges.

You can tell the total federal income taxes you've withheld by looking at the TRANS-FERS FROM Payroll-FWH row in the Overall Total column. (It is $4 in Figure 20.10.)

Most of the other numbers you fill in on a quarterly or an annual report for items like Social Security taxes, Medicare, and unemployment taxes are calculated by multiplying the tax rate by the gross wages total. For example, if you fill out the quarterly 942 form (which you use to show Social Security and Medicare taxes for household employees such as a nanny), you multiply the gross wages total by 12.4 percent to calculate the total Social Security taxes owed, and you multiply the gross wages total by 2.9 percent to calculate the total Medicare taxes owed.

You'll probably get a rounding error of a few pennies, but you can double-check your calculations—at least roughly. Whatever you calculate as the Social Security tax and Medicare tax for the quarter or year should be within a few pennies of the TRANSFERS FROM amounts shown for the payroll liability accounts you've set up to track Social Security ($124 in Figure 20.10) and Medicare ($29 in Figure 20.10).

Employer Wage Statements

You also use the Payroll Report for filling out employee wage statements for state unemployment tax returns (for which you often need to provide gross wages information by employee) and forms such as the annual W-2 wage statements and the W-3 (which just summarizes your W-2s). To do this, refer to the column of information shown for a specific employee, as follows:

- The gross wages amount (Wages in Figure 20.10) shown in the column summarizing an employee's wages and payroll taxes is the amount you report as the total wages.

- The line that shows the federal income tax withholding amount (TRANSFERS FROM Payroll-FWH in Figure 20.10) shows the amount you withheld for the employee's federal income taxes.

- The lines that show the Social Security taxes and Medicare taxes transfer amounts (TRANSFERS FROM Payroll-SS and TRANSFERS FROM Payroll-MCARE in Figure 20.10) provide the raw data you need to figure out how much in Social Security and Medicare taxes to withhold from an employee's gross wages. Simply take one-half of these amounts.

NOTE   Both the employer and employee pay equal amounts for Social Security and Medicare taxes, so one-half of the total Social Security taxes and one-half of the Medicare taxes equal the amount withheld from the employee's payroll check.

Saving Payroll Tax Deposit Money

You may want to set aside the payroll tax money you owe and the amounts you deduct from employee wages. You can do this by using another bank account or a savings goal account. Which type of account you use depends on the way you actually save, or set aside, the money.

If you will save the money in another bank account, such as a savings account, just set up another bank account in Quicken. Then, when you deposit money into this other account, you record an account transfer transaction (see Chapter 2).

If you won't save money in another bank account but want to show that some of the money you have in, say, your checking account is really payroll tax deposit money, set up a savings goal account (see Chapter 15). Then, whenever you want to set aside money for the payroll tax deposits, you transfer the money to this savings goal account in the same way that you record any transfer. Quicken then records the decrease in your bank account and the increase in your savings goal account, so your account records show the bank account balance minus the payroll tax deposit money. The savings goal account will show the payroll tax deposit money you've accumulated.

There is one big difference about using a savings goal account: Account transfers to and from a savings goal account don't show up as real transactions during a reconciliation, nor do they show up as account transfers on Quicken reports. For purposes of reconciling and reporting, Quicken just ignores any transfers to a savings goal account.

 MASTERING FINANCIAL SUCCESS

How to Handle Federal and State Payroll Paperwork

Few things are as exciting—or as scary—as hiring your first employee. Whether you're a small business that is doubling its work force (from one employee to two employees!) or a busy professional hiring your first household employee, it's a big step to suddenly assume the responsibility of regularly meeting a payroll.

Unfortunately, in addition to all the other issues that you now need to address—whether you can afford new employees, picking the best person for a job, and so on—you also have mounds of new paperwork to deal with.

I can't describe all this new paperwork, but I can give you an overview of what you need to collect and prepare for the federal and state governments. If you have questions about all this, I suggest you confer with an accountant or a bookkeeper who specializes in helping small businesses prepare their payroll and payroll tax returns.

Continued

MASTERING FINANCIAL SUCCESS CONTINUED

When You Become an Employer…

As an employer, you need to do the following:

- Request and receive a Federal Tax Identification number from the IRS. To do this, fill out IRS form SS-4 (call the IRS to request one or visit the IRS Web site at http://www.irs.gov to download one) and return it to the IRS. The IRS will send you a Federal Tax Identification number.

NOTE You can also receive a Federal Tax Identification number over the telephone. Just tell the IRS agent how you filled out the SS-4 form, and he or she will enter it into the IRS computer and give you the number. You still need to send or fax in the SS-4 form, however.

- Obtain a copy of the *Employer's Tax Guide,* commonly referred to as a Circular E, from the IRS. This pamphlet tells you how much federal income tax you need to withhold from a person's check and what Social Security and Medicare taxes you and the employee pay.

- If your state requires it, get an employer identification number from your state for filing state payroll tax returns, such as unemployment taxes, workers' compensation, and so on.

- If you intend to withhold state income taxes, obtain your state's equivalent of Circular E. It tells how much state income tax to withhold from an employee's payroll check.

- Obtain federal and perhaps state tax deposit coupons so that you can remit federal and state tax deposits to the IRS and the equivalent state revenue agency. (Ask for these if you don't get them automatically.)

- At the end of the first quarter during which you employ people, obtain the appropriate federal and state quarterly payroll tax return forms. For federal payroll taxes, businesses should use the 941 form, and household employers (if you've hired a nanny, for example) should use the 942 form. You also probably need to file equivalent state quarterly payroll tax returns.

Continued

MASTERING FINANCIAL SUCCESS CONTINUED

- At the end of the year, obtain the appropriate federal and state annual payroll tax returns. For federal unemployment tax returns, for example, you need the 940 or the 940EZ form, and again, you probably need the equivalent state form for annual payroll tax returns.

When You Hire a New Employee...

Whenever you hire a new employee, the employee must fill out a W-4 form. This form provides you with the employee's Social Security number, filing status, and personal exemptions. You need both the filing status and the personal exemptions to determine the amount of federal income taxes to withhold, and you need the employee's Social Security number so you can prepare a year-end W-2 statement.

You will very likely have other requirements, which are not related to income taxes, to meet. For example, you may need to verify to the Immigration and Naturalization Service (INS) that the person you're employing either is a U.S. citizen or has a valid work permit. Be sure to check for this type of requirement. The IRS's *Employer's Tax Guide* and the equivalent state information guide can supply most of the information you need.

CHAPTER 21

Accounts Payable and Accounts Receivable

Accounts receivable are simply the amounts your customers or clients owe you. Accounts payable are the amounts you owe your vendors. Because Quicken is basically a checkbook-on-a-computer program, it doesn't provide the same tools for managing accounts receivable and accounts payable that a full-featured accounting package provides. But you can still use Quicken to track the amounts customers owe and the amounts you owe vendors.

 NOTE To use Quicken for tracking accounts receivable or accounts payable, you simply need to know how to work with the Quicken register, which is the method that this chapter describes. You should know (if you haven't already purchased Quicken) that Intuit also sells a special version of Quicken, Quicken Home & Business, that provides special features for small businesses. Quicken Home & Business lets you invoice customers, for example, and track amounts your customers owe. The newest version of Quicken Home & Business also provides a special payroll feature, QuickPayroll, and supports invoice e-mailing.

Tracking Accounts Payable

Tracking accounts payable with Quicken is easy. You simply enter payment transactions for the amounts you owe using the Write Checks area. You enter the check date as the date the payment is due. Then, whenever you want to see what you owe your vendors, you can produce an A/P by Vendor report. To create this report, select the Reports ➤ Business ➤ A/P by Vendor command. (See Chapters 3 and 4 if you need help using the Write Checks area or producing a report.)

Figures 21.1 and 21.2 illustrate how accounts payable tracking works in Quicken. Figure 21.1 shows a register with several unprinted checks. Notice that Quicken identifies the unprinted check transactions as checks by putting Print in the Num field. Quicken assigns a number when you print the checks. Figure 21.2 shows an onscreen A/P by Vendor report that summarizes the unprinted check information from Figure 21.1.

If you use unprinted checks for tracking accounts payable, be sure to enter the same name for every transaction with a particular vendor. When you produce the A/P by Vendor report, it summarizes your unprinted check transactions by payee names. You can easily keep payee names consistent by using the QuickFill feature, which automatically completes the entry of a payee name it recognizes (see Chapter 2 for a description of how QuickFill works). Another good approach is to select the payee name from the Payee drop-down list box.

FIGURE 21.1

The Quicken register
with unprinted check
transactions

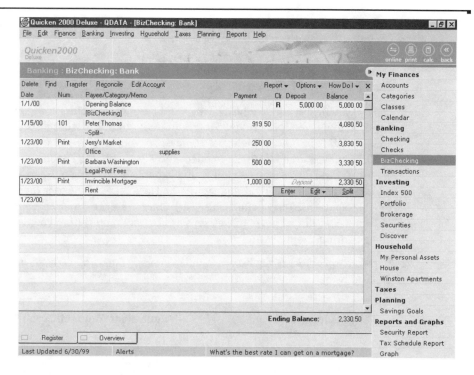

FIGURE 21.2

An A/P by Vendor
report summarizing
the unprinted check
information from
Figure 21.1

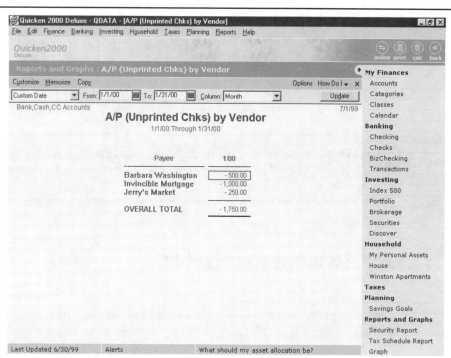

MASTERING FINANCIAL SUCCESS

Early Payment Discounts

Early payment discounts, which many vendors offer, are often too good to pass up. Suppose that a vendor bills you $100 but offers you a 2 percent discount if you'll pay within 10 days instead of the usual 30 days. So, you can pay $98 on, say, March 10, or $100 if you wait until March 30. In effect, the 2 percent (or $2) early payment discount is interest. And while this may not sound like much, charging a 2 percent interest rate for 20 days works out to an annual rate of more than 36 percent (because there are roughly eighteen 20-day periods in a year). Since there are usually cheaper ways to borrow money, it almost never makes sense to borrow money from your vendors by foregoing early payment discounts.

Here are the precise equivalent annual interest rates for early payment discounts allowed by paying a vendor 20 days early:

Early Payment Discount	Equivalent Annual Interest Rate
1%	18.43%
2%	37.24%
3%	56.44%
4%	76.04%
5%	96.05%

TIP To display information about the unprinted checks that need to be paid, choose Finance ➢ Reminders. Click the Print Checks command button in the dialog box that appears.

Tracking Accounts Receivable

To use Quicken to keep accounts receivable records, you first need to set up a separate asset account. You then use this account to keep a list of the amounts customers or clients owe. As your customers or clients pay their bills, you need to update the list with their payments. For your efforts, you get the ability to produce a list of the accounts receivable by customer, organized by due date.

Setting Up a Receivables Register

To create an accounts receivable register, set up an asset account by following these steps:

1. In the Account List, click the New command button to display the Create New Account dialog box.

2. Click the Asset option button, and then click Next.

3. In the Asset Account Setup dialog box, click the Summary tab. This tab is shown in Figure 21.3.

4. Enter a name for the accounts receivable account, such as **AcctRec**, in the Account Name text box.

5. Enter a brief description of the new account, such as **Accounts Receivable**, in the Description text box.

6. Enter **0** in the Balance text box. (You calculate the accounts receivable balance later by entering the individual customer invoice amounts in the accounts receivable register.) Quicken adds the decimal point and the zeros.

7. Leave the As Of text box entry (probably the current system date) as is. You don't need to change this date.

8. Click Done. Quicken adds the new account and redisplays the Account List.

FIGURE 21.3

Setting up an asset account for accounts receivable

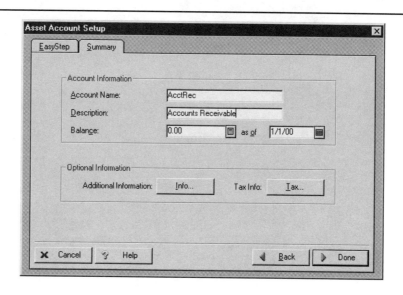

Building a List of Accounts Receivable

To build a list of the accounts receivable your customers or clients owe, follow these steps every time you issue an invoice:

1. Display the accounts receivable register, as shown in Figure 21.4.

2. Delete the Opening Balance transaction, which shows as 0 (click the Delete button, and then click Yes to confirm). Quicken removes the transactions and selects the first (now empty) row in the register.

3. Enter the invoice date and invoice number in the appropriate text boxes.

4. Enter the name of the customer or client in the Payee combo box. If this is the first time you've recorded an invoice to this person or business, type the name. If you've previously recorded an invoice to this person or business, select the person's or business's name from the Payee drop-down list.

5. Enter the invoice amount in the Increase text box.

6. If you want to add a memo description—for example, to cross-reference a customer's or client's purchase order number—use the Memo text box.

FIGURE 21.4

An asset account version of the register, which you use for tracking accounts receivable

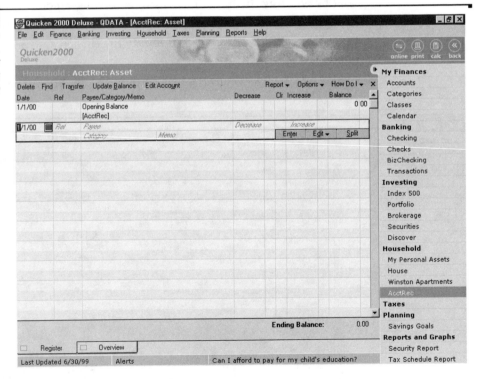

7. Click Enter. If Quicken asks, confirm that you don't want to use a category. (In a cash-basis accounting system, you don't categorize accounts receivable transactions as income; you categorize as income the customer deposit that pays an account receivable.) Quicken updates the account balance and moves the cursor to the next empty row in the register.

Repeat steps 3 through 7 to record each invoice your customers need to pay. Figure 21.5 shows an accounts receivable register with several unpaid customer invoices.

FIGURE 21.5

An accounts receivable register showing unpaid invoices

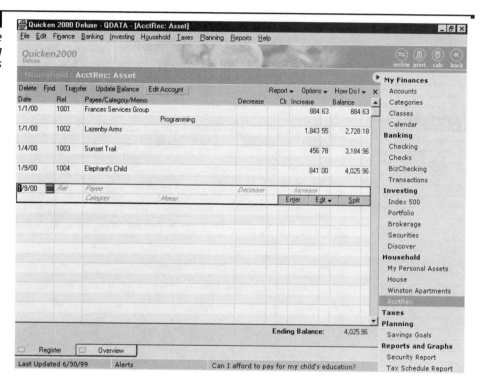

Producing an Accounts Receivable Report

To see a report that summarizes accounts receivable by customer and ages accounts receivable by invoice date, follow these steps:

1. Choose Reports ➤ Business ➤ A/R by Customer and click Yes to display the Customize A/R By Customer dialog box, shown in Figure 21.6.

2. Select a reporting period and click Create to display the A/R by Customer report.

3. Click Customize, and then click the Accounts tab of the Customize A/R by Customer dialog box. This tab is shown in Figure 21.7.

4. Quicken initially selects each of the asset accounts for inclusion in the A/R by Customer report. (If you have only one asset account—the accounts receivable account—it is the only one selected.)

5. Select accounts to add or delete from the report by clicking them or by pressing the spacebar. When the proper accounts are selected, click Create to return to the Report area. Figure 21.8 shows an A/R by Customer report.

6. Choose File ➢ Print Report or click the Print command button in the Report area to print a paper copy of the accounts receivable report as it is displayed.

You can further customize the report by using the options in the Customize A/R by Customer dialog box. See Chapter 4 for a discussion of report customization options.

FIGURE 21.6

The Display tab of the Customize A/R by Customer dialog box

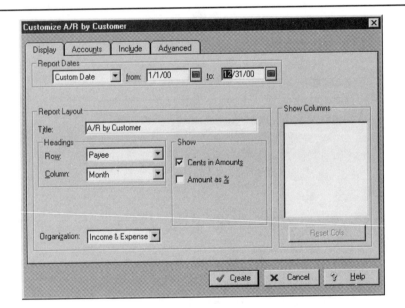

FIGURE 21.7

The Accounts tab of the Customize A/R by Customer dialog box

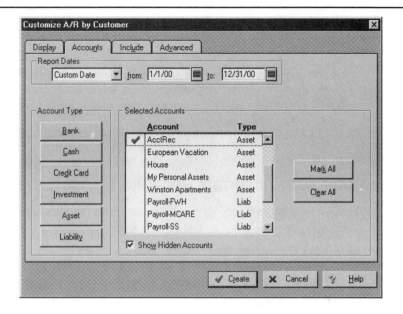

FIGURE 21.8

An A/R by Customer report

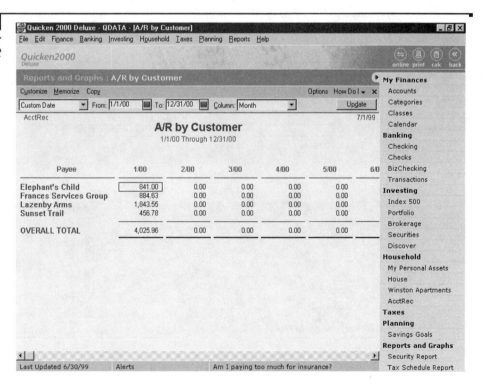

TIP You can—and probably should—use the A/R by Customer report as a guide to your collection activities. When a customer owes amounts from a previous month, for example, you might want to verify that the customer received the invoice and that payment is forthcoming. When a customer owes amounts that are from the months before the previous month (meaning at least one invoice is one or more months past due), you might want to consider more aggressive collection measures, such as a letter from you, your attorney, or even a collection agency.

Keeping Your Accounts Receivable List Current

The A/R by Customer report lists all the uncleared transactions in the selected account, summarized by payee name. An easy way to keep track of which customer invoices have and haven't been paid is to use the Split Transaction Window to keep a record of the original invoice amount and the payments a customer or client makes. The original invoice amount should show as the first split transaction detail line, and payments should show as negative values on the subsequent lines, as shown in Figure 21.9. One tricky aspect of using the Split Transaction Window is that after you enter a customer-payment amount, you need to select Adjust so that the transaction amount shown in the accounts receivable register equals the balance still owed on the invoice.

FIGURE 21.9

The Split Transaction Window filled out to record customer payments on an invoice

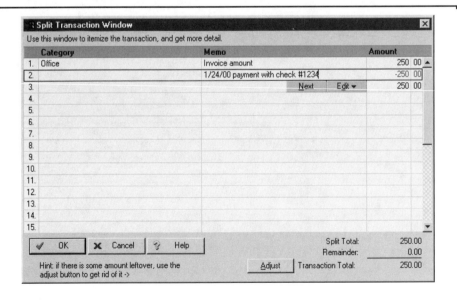

MASTERING FINANCIAL SUCCESS

How to Be a Good Bookkeeper with Quicken

If you're a bookkeeper for a small business, or you do the bookkeeping for a small business even though you're not really a bookkeeper, this part of the chapter is for you. It describes what you need to know about your computer to be a bookkeeper, what you need to know about Windows, and what you need to know about Quicken. It also explains how to perform financial record keeping in a small business and where to get additional help if you need it.

What You Need to Know about Quicken and Windows

Remember that accounting systems do three things: They let you calculate profits, they generate business forms, and they let you keep records of assets and liabilities. Quicken lets you calculate profits by tagging bank account deposits as income and bank account withdrawals as expense. If this approach doesn't work for the small business you're keeping the books for, you need to use another program. Quicken lets you generate only one business form: a check. If you need other business forms, such as invoices, you need to use another program. Also, Quicken keeps detailed records of bank accounts only. If you need to keep detailed records of other business assets, such as inventory, you need to use another program.

You need to know how to work within the Windows operating environment to use Quicken; the more you know about Windows, the easier you'll find using Quicken. You can read the first part of this book and get most of the useful information, and you can also read the Microsoft Windows documentation.

Spend a few days—maybe even a week or two—working with Quicken. Be sure you've entered a series of checks and deposits, and experiment with Quicken's reports. If things still don't click for you, you may be trying to do too much with Quicken.

What You Don't Need to Know

As a bookkeeper, you need to know how to keep financial records that let your employer assess profitability and cash flow; how to keep records for a bank account and reconcile the account; and, in some cases, how to prepare payroll checks and returns. But there is also a list of things you don't need to know—information that goes beyond the scope of your job:

- You don't need to be an expert on federal or state income taxes. It's helpful if you know a few things, but, for example, your boss shouldn't expect you to understand

Continued

MASTERING FINANCIAL SUCCESS CONTINUED

the income tax rules for employee fringe benefits, asset depreciation, or partnership taxation. Your boss can get this type of information and analysis from a CPA or from an attorney who specializes in income tax planning.

- You don't need to be a computer genius. Yes, you need to know how to work with Windows and Quicken, but you don't need to know how to drop an Ethernet card into a computer or reformat the hard disk. A local computer retail or repair shop can take care of these things.

- You also don't need to (and shouldn't) provide legal advice to your employer. An employer who wants to incorporate, deal with an employee's legal threats, or determine whether a contract is fair should talk to an attorney.

A Weekly Bookkeeping Checklist

Use the following list of tasks as a checklist at the end of each week:

- Enter all the payment and deposit transactions for the week (see Chapters 1 and 2).

- Back up the Quicken file to a floppy disk so that you won't lose the data if there's a computer problem or a human error (see Chapter 7).

- Check to see if you should remit any payroll tax deposit money by looking at the payroll tax liability account balances (see Chapter 20).

- Print a copy of the check register for the week and store it as a permanent financial record (see Chapter 2).

A Monthly and Quarterly Bookkeeping Checklist

Here is a checklist of tasks you should usually complete at the end of each month:

- Reconcile all your bank accounts (see Chapter 5).

- Print monthly Cash Flow and Profit & Loss Statement reports. Give a copy to the owner for assessing the month's profitability and cash flow, and put another copy in a permanent financial reports file (see Chapter 4).

- Prepare any monthly or quarterly payroll tax reports. Most businesses prepare the quarterly 941 payroll tax statement (see Chapter 20).

- Make quarterly estimated tax payments for the owner, or remind the owner to make the estimated tax payments. A small business owner is typically required to make quarterly payments of estimated taxes owed on April 15, June 15, September 15, and January 15.

Continued ▐▶

MASTERING FINANCIAL SUCCESS CONTINUED

An Annual Checklist

Here are the things you should do at the end of each year:

- Print annual Cash Flow and Profit & Loss Statement reports. Give one copy to the owner for assessing the year's profitability and cash flow, and put another copy in a permanent financial reports file (see Chapters 4 and 22).
- Prepare a Tax Summary and Tax Schedule report (see Chapter 14).
- Consider creating a disk version of the Tax Schedule report so that the Quicken data can be exported to a tax-preparation package (see Chapter 14).
- Prepare any annual payroll tax reports. Most businesses prepare the annual 940 payroll tax statement and W-2 employee wage statements (see Chapter 20).
- Archive a copy of the previous year's financial records (see Chapter 7).

Two Things Bookkeepers Should Never Do

There are a couple of things you should never do. If you're not careful, doing either of these two things can, quite literally, lead to financial ruin.

Don't Borrow Payroll Tax Deposit Money

Don't ever borrow the payroll tax deposit money, and don't ever help the business owner borrow the payroll tax deposit money. Handling payroll tax deposits was discussed in Chapter 20. The important thing is that the IRS takes a very dim view of mishandling this money. If you're the bookkeeper and you've actively participated in borrowing the payroll tax deposit money, the IRS can collect the money from you. (The IRS assumes that this borrowing amounts to stealing and that, as an accomplice to the theft, you may as well be the one to pay.)

If you've already been doing this, my advice is that you stop immediately. If the small business you keep the books for owes payroll tax money it can't repay, I suggest you confer with a tax attorney.

Don't Participate in Misrepresentation

Financial misrepresentation occurs when you (or the business owner with your help) juggle a few of the financial figures to make the business look a little more profitable or a little healthier. Although the practice may seem innocent enough, it's a serious crime. Never participate in misrepresentation.

Continued

MASTERING FINANCIAL SUCCESS CONTINUED

A business owner might juggle the figures to get a bank or a vendor to lend money or to get an investor to contribute money. When this happens, the bank, vendor, or investor contributes money because of a lie. If the bank, vendor, or investor loses money or discovers you've lied, both you and the business owner can end up in serious trouble. People do go to jail for this.

If you've been participating in financial misrepresentation or are being asked to participate, I suggest that you try to find a new job and that you talk with an attorney to see if there is some way you can extricate yourself from the mess.

Income tax evasion is basically just another form of financial misrepresentation. In this case, however, it's the IRS that's being lied to rather than a bank or an investor.

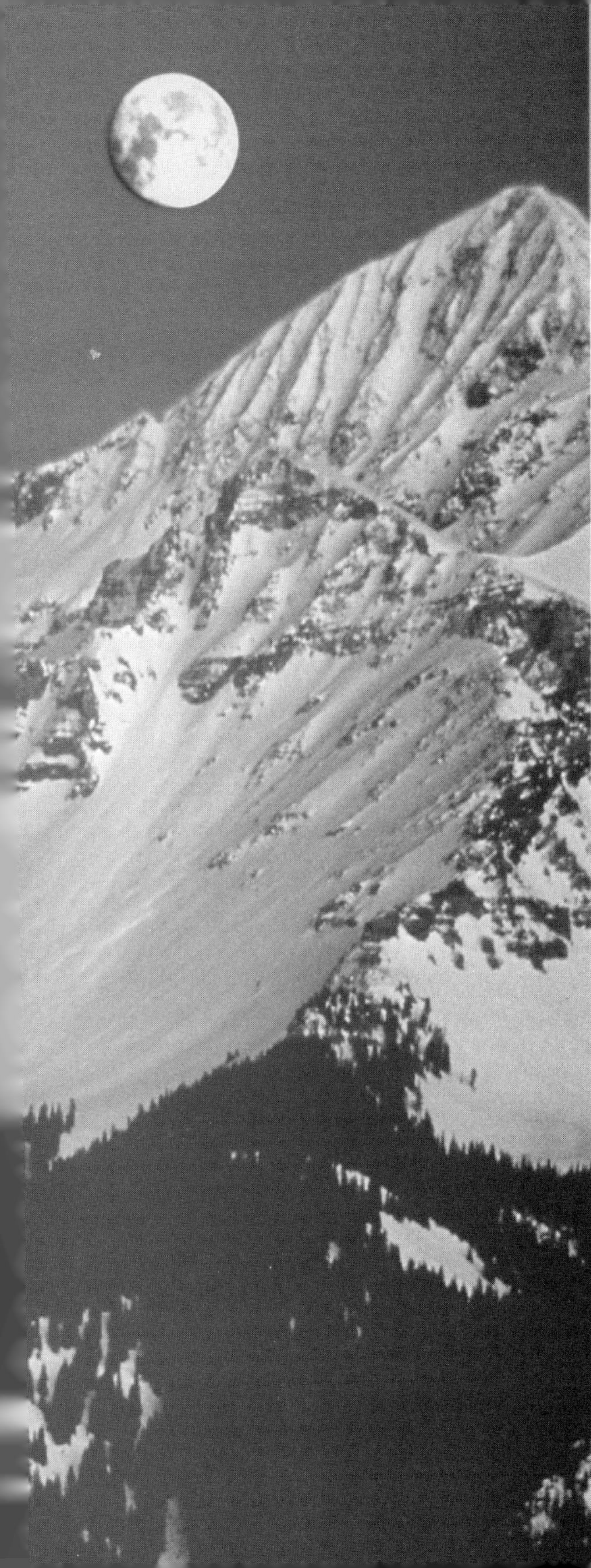

CHAPTER 22

Measuring Cash Flows and Profits

FEATURING:

B y collecting bank account payment and deposit information in Quicken registers, you can easily track the cash flows of a business. All of your business cash flows move into and out of your bank accounts. Although Quicken's registers provide a wonderful structure for monitoring your cash flows, there is more work to do if you want to accurately measure your profits with these same registers.

Before You Begin

To measure cash flows, you need to set up Quicken bank accounts for each of the actual bank accounts you have. You should also know how to use income and expense categories to summarize payments and deposits (see Chapters 1 and 2).

To measure profits, you need to know how to set up asset and liability accounts (see Chapters 13 and 21), as well as how to record account transfers (see Chapter 2).

Measuring Cash Flows

To monitor a business's actual cash flows in Quicken, choose the Reports ➢ Business ➢ Cash Flow Report command. Quicken displays the Cash Flow Report shown in Figure 22.1. Note, however, that if you're using Quicken for both your personal and business financial record keeping, you'll want to make sure that your business cash flow report shows only business cash flows.

If you use a separate bank account for your business—and this is probably a good idea—click the Customize button to display the Customize Cash Flow Report dialog box. Then click the Accounts tab and select your business bank account or accounts, as shown in Figure 22.2. If you don't use a separate business bank account or set of accounts, you'll need to indicate which categories you're using for tracking business income and spending. To do this, click the Include tab and then use it to select your business categories.

As Figure 22.1 shows, a Cash Flow Report summarizes by income and expense category the money flowing into and out of bank accounts and cash accounts. A checkbook program like Quicken does a better job of describing and summarizing cash flows than any of the full-featured, double-entry bookkeeping systems because it uses the cash-basis method of accounting.

FIGURE 22.1

A Cash Flow Report

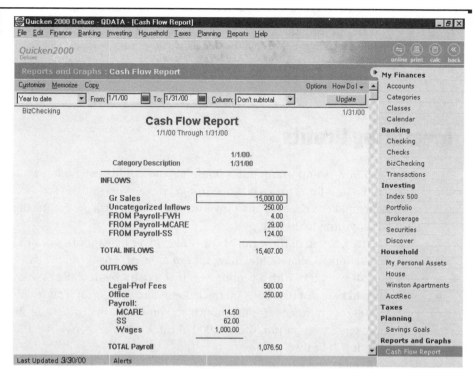

FIGURE 22.2

*The Accounts tab of
the Customize Cash
Flow Report dialog box*

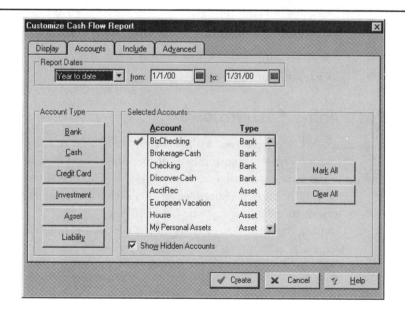

TIP Because Quicken summarizes income and expense cash flows, you budget by cash flows too. This means that the Budget window really amounts to a cash-flow budgeting spreadsheet.

Measuring Profits

Cash flow is important, but it doesn't always indicate whether a business is profitable. Cash flows into a business, for example, when a bank loans you money, a customer makes a deposit, or an investor contributes cash—yet none of these actions has anything to do with profit.

Often, a cash outflow can't be included in a single month's or single year's profit calculations. A shareholder draw, for example, isn't really an expense. Neither is a deposit you make with a vendor. And if you're in the trucking business, for example, the purchase of a new $50,000 truck doesn't actually mean you should include the $50,000 as an expense for the month you purchase the truck. (It probably makes more sense to apportion the $50,000 of truck cost as expense over the months or years it will be used.)

To measure your profits precisely, you need to enter transactions that adjust cash flows. To adjust the cash flow data, you need to know how to do the following:

- Postpone cash inflows so that they are counted as future income.
- Postpone cash outflows so that they count as future expense.
- Count future cash inflows as current income.
- Count future cash outflows as current expense.

Postponing Cash Inflows

Suppose that you receive a $10,000 deposit from a customer and that deposit is a down payment for work the customer wants performed next year. If you record this deposit in the usual way—by categorizing it as income—you end up counting the deposit as income in the current year. However, it really makes more sense to record the $10,000 as income in the following year.

To postpone cash flows so that they're counted as future income, you need to set up a liability account. Name the liability account something like **Def. Rev.**, and give the account a description such as **Deferred Revenue**.

When you record a deposit that really represents income for a future year, record the deposit as a transfer to the deferred revenue account. In effect, by doing this you record the increase in the bank account that stems from depositing the $10,000, and you record the fact that you actually owe the customer $10,000 because you've taken a deposit but haven't yet performed the work. (Think about it this way: If you take a $10,000 deposit from a customer, you may not owe the customer $10,000 in cash, but you do owe the customer $10,000 of products or services.)

When you earn the income you've previously deferred, record a transaction in the deferred revenue account that reduces the account balance by the amount of revenue earned. Categorize this transaction using the appropriate income category.

Figure 22.3 shows a liability account with two transactions: a $10,000 increase in the liability account, such as would occur if you deferred $10,000 of revenue, and a $10,000 decrease in the liability account, with the decrease categorized as income.

FIGURE 22.3

How a deferred revenue liability account might look

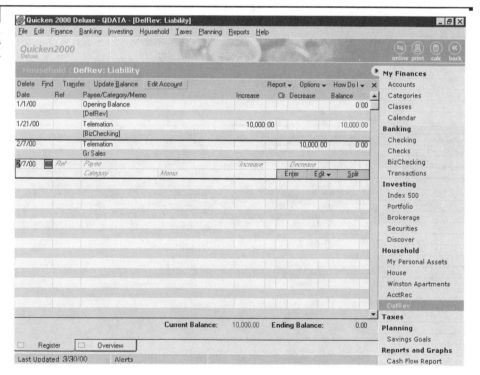

PART

IV

Quicken in a Small Business

Postponing Cash Outflows

In some cases, you may want to postpone counting all or part of a cash outflow as an expense. Say you purchase a $50,000 truck. If you will use the truck for five years, it probably makes sense to allocate, or depreciate, the truck's cost over those five years. (In this case, you might want to record $10,000 of truck expense in each of the five years.)

To postpone cash outflows so that they're counted as future expenses, you need to set up an asset account. In the case of a truck, for example, you would set up an account for the truck.

When you record the payment that really represents expenses for a future year or for future years, record the payment as a transfer to the new asset account. (Think about it this way: The amounts you pay for future years' expenses add up to prepaid expenses.)

Then you enter decrease transactions for each of the years you want to record an expense. Categorize this transaction using the appropriate expense category.

Figure 22.4 shows a truck asset account with six transactions—a $50,000 increase in the truck account, which would occur if you purchased a $50,000 truck, and five $10,000 decreases in the truck account, with the decreases categorized as truck depreciation expense.

FIGURE 22.4

How a deferred cost asset account might look if the asset is a truck you're depreciating

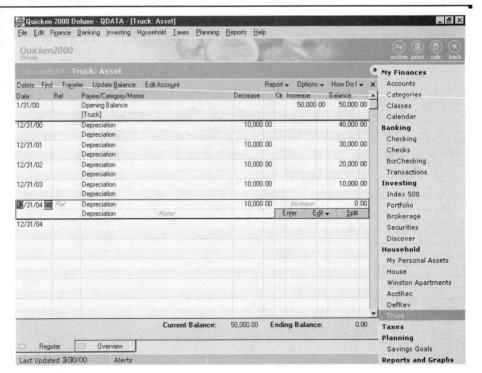

Counting Future Cash Inflows as Current Income

In Chapter 21, you learned how you can use an asset account to build a list of accounts receivable. Although the approach described there works if you're willing to record income whenever you deposit cash, you need to use a slightly more sophisticated approach if you want to record income when you earn it.

For example, if you perform $5,000 of consulting for a client, you might want to correctly count the $5,000 as income in the year you perform the consulting services rather than wait until you collect the cash.

To count future cash inflows as current income, you need to set up an accounts receivable asset account for each customer.

When you want to record income, enter an increase transaction in the appropriate customer's or client's accounts receivable account, and categorize the increase by using an income category.

When you ultimately collect the income, you record a deposit in the appropriate bank account. But you categorize the deposit as a transfer from the customer's or client's accounts receivable account using the Split Transaction Window for the invoice transaction in the accounts receivable account.

Preparing a Profit & Loss Statement Report

To prepare a Profit & Loss statement that includes the sorts of adjustment transactions I've described, choose Reports ➢ Business ➢ P&L Statement Report. Figure 22.5 shows a Profit & Loss Statement.

A Profit & Loss Statement differs from the Cash Flow Report shown in Figure 22.1 in one important way: The Profit & Loss Statement category totals include transactions from all the accounts in the Quicken file. For example, if you've set up an asset account for recording depreciation expense, the Profit & Loss Statement shows that expense. (In comparison, a Cash Flow Report's category totals include only those transactions from bank and cash accounts.)

 NOTE Although the adjustment techniques described should let you better measure your profits, you may still want to prepare your income tax return using cash-based accounting. If this is the case, you need to prepare your income tax returns using the information shown in the Cash Flow Report, not the Profit & Loss Statement. (You may want to confer with your CPA about this.)

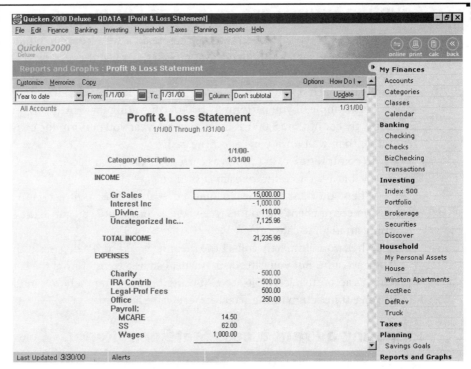

FIGURE 22.5

A Profit & Loss Statement

If Quicken Doesn't Work for Your Accrual-Based Accounting...

Quicken isn't really set up to handle accrual-based accounting, which is what you're doing when you try to record income when you earn it and expenses when you incur them.

If your business needs the increased precision of accrual accounting and you can't practically or successfully employ the techniques described here, it may be time to consider one of the other, more powerful—but more complicated—accounting programs, such as Intuit's QuickBooks (which is relatively easy to use) or Peachtree Accounting for Windows (which is slightly more challenging to use but also much more powerful).

Forecasting Profits and Cash Flows

Quicken comes with a Forecasting tool that lets you estimate your future cash flows and profits by extrapolating past information. In essence, what Quicken does is look at your register and scheduled transactions, assume that these transactions will occur in the future, and then create *pro forma* registers for producing cash flow and income statement reports.

NOTE This forecasting tool can also be used for personal financial management for someone whose personal finances are very complex. Using the forecasting tool in this way is probably overkill, however, for most individuals.

Creating a Forecast

The steps for creating a forecast are relatively simple:

1. Choose Planning ➢ Cash Flow Forecast. Quicken displays the Forecast–Base Scenario area. If necessary, click Create to display the Automatically Create Forecast dialog box, shown in Figure 22.6.

2. Use the Date Range to Read text boxes, From and To, to describe the period of time that should be used to create the forecast.

3. Click the Advanced button to access the Forecast Items to Create option buttons, and then use these buttons to indicate the type of transactions Quicken should use as the basis for the forecast:

   - **Known Items** (from Scheduled Txns) tells Quicken to use scheduled transactions to create the forecast.

   - **Estimated Items** tells Quicken to forecast future income and expense amounts by using average income and expense amounts from either your register or your budget.

   - **Create Both** tells Quicken to use scheduled transactions and average income and expense amounts.

4. Use the From Register Data or From Budget Data option buttons to indicate whether Quicken should create estimates using the register transactions or your budget.

FIGURE 22.6

The Automatically Create Forecast dialog box

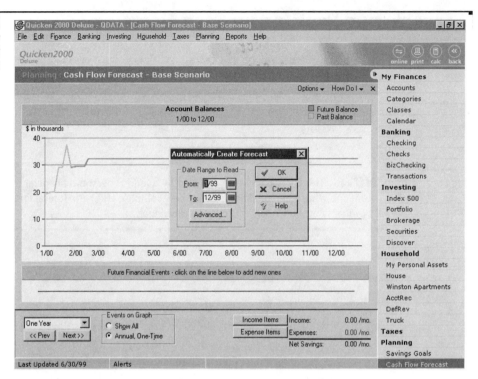

5. If you want Quicken to forecast only certain income and expense categories, click the Categories command button. Quicken displays the Select Categories to Include dialog box. Indicate which categories you want to forecast by marking them (mark and unmark categories by clicking them), and then click OK.

6. If you want Quicken to forecast only certain account balances, click the Accounts command button. Quicken displays the Select Accounts to Include dialog box. Indicate which accounts you want to forecast by marking them (mark and unmark categories by clicking on them), and then click OK.

7. Click Done to save your advanced options.

8. Click OK in the Automatically Create Forecast dialog box. Quicken displays the Forecast–Base Scenario window, as shown in Figure 22.7.

FIGURE 22.7

The Forecast–Base Scenario window

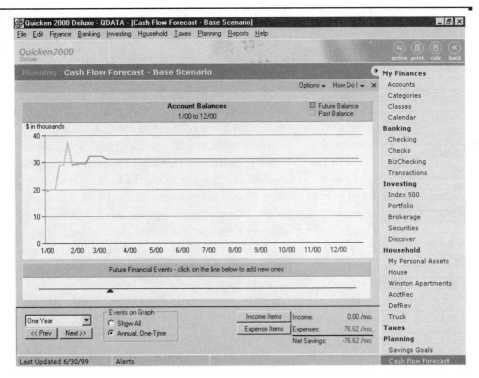

Reading a Forecast

The line chart shows the forecasted account balance in either all or a selected group of accounts. You can select which accounts to include in the account balances line by clicking the Accounts button. When Quicken displays the Select Accounts to Include dialog box, mark the accounts you want to include. (You can mark and unmark accounts by clicking them.)

You can change the forecasting interval—to month, half-year, full-year, and so on—by activating the drop-down list box in the lower-left corner of the window. You can change the forecasting period, such as from April to May if you've selected months as the period, by clicking the left and right arrow buttons. Clicking the left arrow button displays the account balances line chart for the previous period. Clicking the right arrow button displays the account balances line chart for the next period.

If you click the Track button, you can build a budget based on your forecast. (You may need to provide additional data to Quicken in order for it to build a budget in this manner.)

Updating a Forecast

To change the parameters used to create the forecast, click the Create button. Quicken redisplays the Automatically Create Forecast dialog box (Figure 22.6). From here you can change any of the parameters you initially supplied to Quicken.

In the lower-right corner of the Forecast area, Quicken summarizes the forecasted income and expense totals. If you want to see the income and expense details that Quicken uses to forecast the account balance, click the Income Items and Expense Items buttons. Quicken displays a list of the forecasted income or expense categories and the forecasted amount. Quicken also shows the frequency and forecasting method. A monthly frequency, for example, means Quicken is forecasting one transaction a month. A Date column entry of Average tells you that Quicken is forecasting the category by looking at past averages.

You can change any of the forecasted amounts by clicking the amount and then entering a new value. (You can flip-flop between the income and expense forecasts by clicking the Income Items and Expense Items option buttons that are located in the upper-left corner of the Forecast Income or Expense Items dialog box.) If you want to add new forecasted events, click the New button and then fill in the dialog box that Quicken displays. You can change existing forecasted events by clicking the Edit button and then filling in the dialog box that Quicken displays. To remove a forecasted event, select it and click Delete. To save your changes to these forecasted items, click Done.

The Events on Graph option buttons in the Forecast window tell Quicken whether you want to see all the financial events for a forecasting interval or just those that occur on a one-time or annual basis.

Creating Multiple Forecast Scenarios

You can work with multiple forecasts, or scenarios, by clicking Options ➢ Manage Scenarios in the Forecast–Base Scenario window. Quicken displays the Manage Forecast Scenarios dialog box, as shown in Figure 22.8. To name and save the current forecast, click the New button and enter a name for the scenario when Quicken displays the Create New Scenario dialog box. (By default, when you create a new scenario, the Copy Current Scenario button is checked and Quicken actually makes a copy of the current scenario.) When you click OK to save this scenario name, you go back to the

Manage Forecast Scenarios dialog box. To later display a forecast, choose the Scenario button and simply select it from the Scenario Data drop-down list. You can also edit and delete scenarios by using the Edit and Delete command buttons.

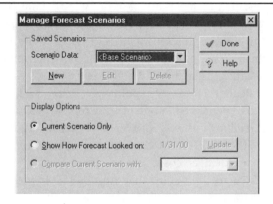

FIGURE 22.8

The Manage Forecast Scenarios dialog box lets you work with multiple forecasts.

If you create a baseline scenario that you always want to show, create a comparison line. To do this, first make sure the scenario you want is the one currently shown. (You may need to use the Scenario Data drop-down list box to activate the scenario.) Then click New and enter a name in the dialog box that Quicken displays.

Calculating a Business's Break-Even Points

Break-even analysis allows you to determine the income necessary to pay all your expenses. Break-even analysis is a simple and powerful financial-management technique related to business profits. At the break-even point, a business doesn't make any money, but it also doesn't lose any money. In general, you want to know a business's break-even point because it represents a sales level you must surpass to make money.

The Trick to Calculating Break-Even Points

To calculate a business's break-even point, you need to determine the total fixed costs of a business and its gross profit margin as a percentage.

A business's fixed costs are those expenses a business must pay regardless of the sales volume. In a retailing business, for example, fixed costs probably include rent, salaries of sales clerks, and other overhead expenses such as utilities and insurance. If a business's fixed costs include $2,000 in monthly rent (which also includes utilities and property insurance) and $4,000 in salaries, the business's fixed costs equal $6,000 a month.

A business's gross profit margin percentage is the difference between sales and its variable costs expressed as percentage of sales. You can calculate the gross margin percentage either on a per-unit basis or by using total sales and total variable costs. Suppose you want to calculate the gross profit margin on a per-unit basis. If you own a retailing business that sells T-shirts for $15 and the T-shirts cost you $3, your gross profit margin per unit is $12 or, restated as a percentage, your gross profit margin is 80 percent, calculated as $12 divided by $15.

To calculate a break-even point, you figure out how much gross profit margin needs to be generated in order to pay for the business's fixed costs. In the case of the T-shirt retailing business with $6,000 of fixed costs and an 80 percent gross profit margin, the retailer must sell enough T-shirts so that the gross profit earned on the T-shirts pays the fixed costs.

To calculate the T-shirts that must be sold to break even, use the following formula:

Break-even point = (fixed costs/gross profit margin)

In the case of the T-shirt retailing business, for example, you can calculate the number of T-shirts that must be sold to break even like this:

Break-even point in units = ($6,000 fixed costs/80 percent)

When you divide the $6,000 by 80 percent, you calculate the sales necessary to break even: $7,500. (At $15 a T-shirt, this works out to 500 T-shirts.) You can test this number by creating a worksheet that describes the income and expenses expected if the retailer sells 500 T-shirts, as shown here:

Income	$7,500	Calculated as 500 T-shirts @ $15 each
T-shirt expenses	$1,500	Calculated as 500 T-shirts @ $3 each
Fixed expenses	$6,000	
Profit (Loss)	0	

Using Quicken to Make Break-Even Calculations Easier

The preceding discussion described how you can determine your business's break-even point if you know your fixed costs and your gross profit margin. As a practical matter, however, you probably don't know these two figures—at least not right off the bat. Does not knowing them mean you can't calculate your break-even point? No, you can easily use Quicken to develop the raw data you need.

To collect the raw data you need for your break-even analysis, you set up a couple of classes: one named Fixed, for tracking your fixed costs, and one named Variable, for tracking your variable costs.

Setting Up the Fixed and Variable Cost Classes

To set up classes for segregating your fixed and variable costs, follow these steps:

1. Choose the Finance ➢ Class List command to display the Class List, as shown in Figure 22.9.

2. Click the New command button to display the Set Up Class dialog box, shown in Figure 22.10.

3. Use the Name text box to enter the class name, **Fixed**.

4. If you want to further describe the cost classification, use the Description text box.

FIGURE 22.9

The Class List

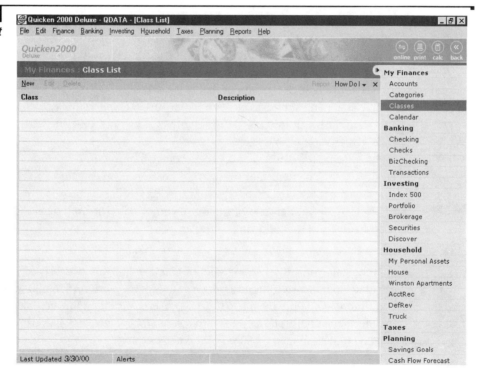

FIGURE 22.10

*The Set Up Class
dialog box*

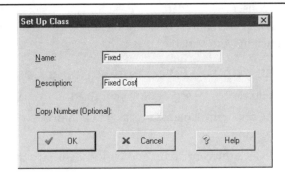

5. Click OK. Quicken adds the new class to the Class List.

Repeat steps 2 through 5 to set up the Variable class. You can set up subclasses in the same way.

Collecting the Break-Even Raw Data

Once you set up the Fixed and Variable cost classes, classify each cost you incur as either fixed or variable. Things such as rent, utilities, insurance, and salaries are probably fixed; items such as sales commissions, costs of products or services you sell, and delivery or freight charges are probably variable.

To classify an expense as either fixed or variable, follow the expense category with a forward slash and the class name. Figure 22.11 shows a register with transactions classified as Variable and Fixed.

To see what fixed and variable costs you've incurred in a year or month, produce a Profit & Loss Statement that summarizes costs by both category and class. This will give you the total fixed costs—one of the pieces of data you need.

To calculate your gross profit margin, you can use the total sales and total variable costs figures and the following formula:

Gross profit margin = (sales–variable costs)/sales

If the data you collect shows sales of $20,000 and variable costs of $16,000, you calculate your gross profit margin percentage as 80 percent ($16,000/$20,000). Then you simply divide the fixed costs by the gross profit margin percentage to calculate the break-even point. If the fixed costs were $6,000, your break-even point would be $7,500 ($6,000 divided by 80 percent equals $7,500).

FIGURE 22.11

Transactions that are both categorized and classified

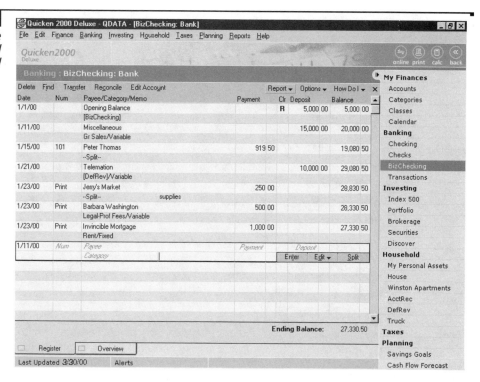

MASTERING FINANCIAL SUCCESS

How to Be a Better Business Owner

If you're a business owner, this part of the chapter is for you. The earlier chapters of this book provided information about using Quicken in a small business setting. This chapter takes a slightly different tack by discussing some issues that are specific to business owners who use Quicken.

Thinking about Security

You're going to use Quicken for an important and, possibly, confidential job: managing your financial affairs. Here are some things you can do to increase the security of the financial-management system:

- Set up a password to restrict access to the Quicken system and your financial records if the PC running Quicken is used by employees who don't work with Quicken (see Chapter 7).

Continued ▌▶

- Lock up the business forms you use, such as the Quicken checks. You don't want to allow anyone to steal check forms that can later be used in a forgery.

- Be sure you (or an employee) regularly enter payment and deposit transactions. You can't run a successful business without knowing how much cash you have and whether you're making money. With Quicken, getting this information should take only a few minutes a day.

- Be sure you regularly back up your Quicken data files. This protects you from hard disk failures and human error (see Chapter 7).

- Be sure you reconcile your bank accounts on a monthly basis. This will help you catch the errors that people make (see Chapter 5).

The Problem of Embezzlement

Employee theft is extremely common. People steal office supplies in the fall (to use as school supplies for the children), deal with vendors who provide kickbacks (often in the form of expensive gifts and services), and sometimes even find clever ways to steal inventory and pilfer cash.

Most people don't steal, but it does happen; so it makes sense for you to consider what you can do to minimize your employees' opportunities to steal.

Sign Checks Yourself

It's a good idea to sign all checks—even small ones—yourself. This can be a lot of work (as a corporate controller, I used to sign about $100,000 in checks every week), but you can have an employee prepare the checks for your review and signature. The benefit of signing all your checks is that your signature will be a requirement for money to leave the business. No cash will be deducted from the business bank account without your knowing about it.

If you sign all checks, an employee who wants to steal cash from you might try to convince you to write a check that the employee can cash. (You wouldn't write out, say, a $1,000 check to the employee without asking questions.) This means that the employee would need to set up a fictitious vendor and then convince you to pay this vendor some amount. Or the employee might have you pay someone the employee needs to pay anyway. (I saw an employee have the employer write a check that paid the employee's Visa bill.) By carefully reviewing the checks that you sign, you minimize the employee's opportunities for committing these crimes.

Continued

MASTERING FINANCIAL SUCCESS CONTINUED

If you'll be on vacation for, say, a couple of weeks, the business will probably need to pay some bills while you're away. You can deal with this in a couple of ways. You can decide to trust an employee enough to leave behind a signed check or two; the employee can then use these signed checks to pay for things such as an unexpected C.O.D. shipment. Or you can decide to simply require vendors to wait. If you leave signed checks, be sure to leave specific instructions as to what these checks should be used for, and review the checks when they come back from the bank to be sure that your instructions were followed.

Review Canceled Checks

Be sure to intercept the bank statement when it comes and review the canceled checks. (An easy way to do this is to have the bank send the bank statement to your home.) This way, you can make sure that no one is forging your signature and writing a check or two for nonbusiness reasons. This might seem unlikely, but if your business writes a hundred checks a month totaling tens of thousands of dollars, would you really notice an extra check or two if the amounts were "only" a few hundred dollars?

Separate Mailroom Duty from Bank Deposit Duty

One of the most common ways to embezzle money from an employer is called *lapping.* To lap, an embezzler skims a little bit of the cash that comes in each month and then adjusts the books to hide the skimming. As long as the person skimming the cash also maintains the checkbook, it's easy for the theft to go unnoticed. The embezzler simply ignores or hides the fact that, for example, the $500 Customer A owes you has been paid. You can minimize the opportunities for lapping if you have one employee open the mail and make a list of the incoming cash and another employee enter the bank deposit information into the checkbook. For this approach to work, you simply compare the list of incoming cash maintained by the mailroom person with the bank deposit information shown in the check, and you contact customers about past-due payments. This way, you can discover, for example, that Customer A actually paid the $500 owed and that the check has cleared the bank.

Protect Other Valuable Assets

From an embezzler's perspective, cash is the most convenient item to steal. It's portable, easy to store, and easy to convert to other things an embezzler might want. Because cash is usually watched so closely, however, embezzlers often steal other items of value, such as office equipment, inventory, and supplies.

Continued

MASTERING FINANCIAL SUCCESS

You can follow a couple of general rules to minimize losses such as these. You can keep a record of the things that your business owns and periodically compare what your records show you have with what you actually hold. If you buy and sell inventory, for example, keep a record of what you buy and sell. Then, once a month or once a year, compare what your records show with what you have in your warehouse or storeroom.

NOTE If you buy and sell inventory in your business, Quicken will not meet your needs. Consider upgrading from Quicken to a small business accounting system that tracks inventory, such as Intuit's QuickBooks Pro for Windows or Peachtree Accounting for Windows.

You can also restrict access to any valuable assets that the business owns. Warehouses and storerooms should be locked. Access should be limited to people who really need what is being kept behind lock and key. If you have items of high value in a storeroom, for example, and several employees have access, it's also a good idea to make it a rule that people go into the storeroom only in pairs. (A dishonest employee is less likely to steal if someone else is present who may see and report the theft.)

Require Vacations

There's a final embezzlement prevention tool that many big businesses use and that you should probably consider: Require regular vacations of a week or two. (Banks almost always do this.)

Here's the rationale: Some embezzlement schemes are so clever that they're almost impossible to catch. The one typical weakness of these super-clever schemes, however, is that they usually require ongoing maintenance on the part of the embezzling employee. By making the employee take a vacation, you can see what happens if the employee's not around. Here are a couple of examples.

One embezzler who managed a concession stand had a simple but clever technique: He always pocketed a few hundred dollars of cash sales each week. This scheme worked for years. The owner assumed that cash sales were typically about $4,000 a week, even though they were really quite a bit more than that, and that he was losing about $200 a week of ice cream cones, soda pop, and popcorn because of spoilage

Continued

MASTERING FINANCIAL SUCCESS CONTINUED

and, perhaps, a little shoplifting. The concession stand manager never did take a vacation, but he did eventually have a heart attack. And a funny thing happened. Cash sales increased overnight (literally). Even more dramatic, profits jumped because sales increased while expenses stayed level. When the owner looked into the situation in the employee's absence, he figured out that sales and profits had increased because the employee was no longer pilfering cash from the till.

Another embezzler who got tripped up by a vacation requirement was a salesman selling profitable remodeling jobs for a company I'll call XYZ Construction. His scheme was to have every fourth or fifth job done by a company he had set up, which I'll call ABC Remodeling. He regularly used the resources and reputation of XYZ Construction to sell a remodeling job for ABC Remodeling and thereby collect the 40 percent profit his employer (XYZ Construction) would have made rather than his usual 10 percent sales commission. As long as he stayed in town, his little ploy worked reasonably well. He could answer all his telephone calls—both those from XYZ Construction customers and those from ABC Remodeling customers—and handle any problems that surfaced for either set of customers. When he went on vacation, however, the whole thing blew up as soon as an ABC Remodeling customer called XYZ Construction to ask about a remodeling project in progress.

Finding Good Bookkeeping Help

In any business, it's a challenge to find and keep good people. It can be even more difficult to find good people to do something such as bookkeeping when you are not particularly knowledgeable about the subject, but there are some guidelines you can follow.

First, if you're hiring someone who simply is going to keep your checkbook, that person needs to know basic arithmetic, of course, but doesn't need to know how to use Quicken. If Quicken works well for you and you have no plans to upgrade to a more powerful program, the person can learn to use Quicken on the job. It will help if the employee already knows a thing or two about computers and has worked with Windows or a program that runs under it, such as WordPerfect for Windows.

One other thing: You'll do well to find someone who knows how to do payroll net wages and payroll tax calculations. Mechanically, preparing payroll is one of the more complicated things you do in Quicken. An employee who understands these procedures will have an easier time using Quicken for payroll.

Continued ▐▶

MASTERING FINANCIAL SUCCESS CONTINUED

 NOTE The IRS and many state revenue agencies sponsor free small-business tax-payer education programs (sometimes referred to as STEP workshops) that explain how things such as payroll taxes work. If a bookkeeper needs to learn how to do payroll, find out if there are any such workshops in your area.

How to Tell if You've Outgrown Quicken

Small-business accounting systems (Quicken is one when you use it in a small-business setting) are supposed to do three things:

- Measure your profits and cash flow so that you can prudently manage your business.
- Track the assets and liabilities of the business so that you know what you own and what you owe.
- Generate the business forms that you use to transact business.

As long you keep these three accounting system tasks in mind, you'll find it easy to tell when you've outgrown Quicken and should move up to a more full-featured small-business accounting system.

Quicken measures income and expenses using cash-based accounting, so you generally record income when you deposit money into a bank account and record expenses when you write a check. In comparison, accrual-based accounting measures profits more precisely. With this type of accounting, you record income when you earn revenue and record expense when you incur costs. If you want to do accrual-based accounting rather than cash-based accounting, you can't use Quicken. You'll need a more full-featured accounting system, such as QuickBooks from Intuit or Peachtree Accounting for Windows.

To keep detailed records of assets besides cash and your investments, you also need to use a small-business accounting system. For example, if you buy and sell inventory items and want to track those items, you need an accounting system that includes inventory-management features. (Most small-business accounting packages provide these features.) If you own a lot of depreciable assets and want to track them, you need an accounting system that includes a fixed-assets module. (This is a less-common feature, by the way.) If you want job costing, point-of-sale accounting, or other special features, you also need to upgrade to a more powerful accounting system.

Continued

MASTERING FINANCIAL SUCCESS CONTINUED

One other issue is business forms. Quicken produces check forms, but you probably need to produce other business forms, such as invoices, customer statements, purchase orders, and other types of forms. If you want to automate production of these other forms with an accounting system rather than prepare them manually, you need to upgrade to a more powerful system.

Before you purchase a new accounting system to take care of the tasks I've just described, there are a couple of things to keep in mind. First, no accounting system is perfect. I've seen more than one business waste enormous amounts of time, energy, and money pursuing the perfect accounting system. If you have a system that works reasonably well, lets you gauge the performance of your business, and in general does most of the things you need it to do, you may create more problems than you solve by converting to a more complicated new system.

Also, the more powerful small-business accounting systems generally require you (or someone who works for you) to know a lot more about accounting than you need to know to operate Quicken. When you get right down to it, all you need to know to operate Quicken is how to use a checkbook and enter payments and deposits into a check register. In comparison, to use a full-featured small-business accounting system, you (or your employee) should know how to perform double-entry bookkeeping, understand the tricks and techniques used in accrual-based accounting (accruals, deferrals, reversing journal entries, and so on), and be able to read and use the financial information contained in a standard set of accrual-based financial statements (income statements, balance sheets, and cash flow statements). Note that the cash-flow statement produced by an accrual-based accounting system won't look anything like the Cash Flow Report produced by Quicken.

Two Things Business Owners Should Never Do

As a business owner, you know that there are plenty of things that you should do. Here, I'll point out two things that you should never do.

Misrepresent Your Financial Affairs

You should never misrepresent your financial condition and your business's financial performance. You may think that you would never do this, but let me tell you how it always seems to start. You go to the bank for a loan (perhaps a home mortgage). The bank loan officer looks at your Quicken Profit & Loss Statement and then tells you that you're not making quite enough money or that your debts seem a bit high.

Continued ▶

MASTERING FINANCIAL SUCCESS CONTINUED

It appears that a fair number of business owners go home, mull things over, and then think, "What if I made more money?" Asking and answering this question leads quite naturally to a careful review of the Quicken register, and suddenly the business owner has recategorized a series of business transactions as personal expenses. This has the nice effect of increasing the business profits. When the bank loan officer looks at your new Quicken Profit & Loss Statement, the loan is approved.

This may seem like a harmless solution, but misrepresenting your finances subjects you to two extremely serious risks. First, by misrepresenting your finances, you've committed a felony because you fraudulently obtained your loan. In a worst-case scenario, the bank can probably force you to repay the loan immediately. Many of the laws that normally protect you if you're a borrower don't protect you if you've fraudulently obtained a loan. (In a bankruptcy proceeding, for example, you probably can't escape repayment of fraudulently obtained loans.)

Another serious risk you run by misrepresenting your finances occurs if the IRS audits your return. If the IRS agent sees that expenses you claimed as business deductions on your tax return are later described as personal expenses on a Profit & Loss Statement, the IRS can probably disallow the business deductions. If you assured the bank that $3,000 of travel expenses were for a personal vacation, you'll need to do a lot of backpedaling to convince the IRS that the $3,000 was really for business travel.

Borrow Payroll Tax Deposit Money

Never borrow the money you've deducted from an employee's payroll check for taxes, and never spend the money you've set aside for the payroll taxes that you owe as the employer. If for any reason you can't repay the money, the IRS will pursue you with merciless vigor.

If you get to the point where you can't continue business without dipping into the payroll tax deposit money, don't compound your problems by getting into trouble with the IRS. It doesn't matter what you want to use the money for. If you can't make payroll, can't get a supplier to deliver goods, or can't pay the rent without borrowing a bit of the payroll tax deposit money, you simply can't make payroll, receive the goods, or pay the rent. If you did, you would be stealing from the IRS. And when the IRS finds out, the IRS may padlock your business some afternoon, thereby putting you out of business; seize any valuable personal assets you own, including your home; and garnish your wages if you get another job. In short, the IRS will do anything it legally can to collect the money you should have paid.

Because of all this, I can't imagine a situation in which it makes sense to "borrow" the payroll tax deposit money. If things are so bad that you can't go on without taking the payroll tax deposit money, it's time for you to consider drastic action—perhaps closing the business, filing for bankruptcy, laying off employees, or finding an investor.

Glossary of
Accounting and
Financial Terms

401(k) plan   A retirement plan, sponsored by an employer, that allows employees to set aside some of their wages or salary for retirement. The set-aside money is not taxed. Some employers match 401(k) contributions.

AAA   The highest rating that can be given to a municipal bond. Bonds with this rating are considered a safe investment by banks and other financial institutions.

ABA transit number   The number that identifies the bank against which a check is drawn. Every check has an ABA (American Bankers Association) transit number, usually in the upper-right corner. The number—actually two numbers separated by a hyphen—identifies the bank's location and the bank's name.

abusive tax shelter   A tax shelter is considered "abusive" when its organizers knowingly misrepresent its tax benefits or value. The IRS imposes special penalties on abusive tax shelters.

access code   The password or number you punch in at an automatic teller machine (ATM) to make deposits and withdrawals. Also called *personal identification number* (*PIN*).

account   The record of transactions in a checking, savings, securities, trust, or charge account, including the account's up-to-date balance.

account number   The number that identifies the holder of an account. All accounts must have an account number.

accountant's opinion   The results of an audit of a company's records and books.

accrual basis   An accounting method in which income and expenses are recorded as they occur, not when they are completed. For example, a check you write on March 1 is subtracted from your balance on that day, not the day the check is cashed. With the *cash-basis* method, transactions are recorded when money actually changes hands.

accrued interest   Interest earned on a bond or certificate of deposit, but paid at some future date—such as when the bond or certificate of deposit is sold.

actuary   The person who determines what your annual insurance payments are.

ad valorem   Latin for *to the value*. Sales and property taxes are calculated ad valorem, as a percentage of the property value or the thing being sold.

adjustable-rate mortgage (ARM)   A mortgage whose interest rate is adjusted periodically, usually every six months. ARMs are usually tied to some sort of money index, like the prime lending rate or the cost of Treasury Bills. When the index goes up or down, so does the monthly mortgage payment.

adjusted gross income   Your annual income after you've subtracted retirement contributions, alimony, and other deductions allowed by the IRS.

adjuster   The insurance company representative who decides how much insurance settlements should be.

affidavit   A signed statement promising that you will fulfill an obligation. Affidavit means *has pledged his faith* in Latin.

affinity card   A credit card issued by an organization or by a bank in cooperation with an organization. Affinity cards typically combine the usual features of a credit card with some extra benefit connected to the issuer. For example, in the case of an airline card, you accumulate frequent flyer miles by virtue of what you spend with the affinity card. In the case of a card issued by a bank on behalf of a charitable organization, the bank gives part of the interest income from the card to the charity.

aggregate demand   A measure of how well the economy is doing. The aggregate demand is the monthly total spent by consumers, governments, and investors for goods and services.

allonge   When there isn't enough room to write endorsements, a piece of paper attached to a check, draft, bill, or promissory note for writing endorsements.

altered check   A check whose signature, date, payee name, or amount has been changed or erased. Banks can refuse to honor altered checks.

alternative minimum tax   A flat-rate tax that trusts, corporations, and wealthy individuals must pay, regardless of how much or how little tax they owe. The alternative minimum tax ensures that wealthy people and companies pay at least some tax.

American Bankers Association (ABA)   The professional association of U.S. banks. The ABA sponsors conferences and lobbies before Congress, among other activities.

American depository receipt (ADR)   A security issued by a U.S. bank on behalf of a foreign corporation.

American Stock Exchange (AMEX)   America's second-largest stock exchange, where the stocks of medium- to small-sized companies are traded.

amortization   The gradual paying off of a debt or a loan.

amortization schedule   A schedule for making payments on a mortgage. The schedule shows the number of payments, when payments are due, how much of each payment goes toward the principal and how much goes toward paying interest, and the declining amount of money owed on the loan as payments are made.

annual cap   Adjustable-rate mortgages usually have an annual cap—a percentage rate above which mortgage payments cannot rise, no matter how much interest rates rise.

annual percentage rate (APR)   The cost of a loan, expressed as a percentage of the amount of the loan.

annual percentage yield (APY)   The amount of interest income that an account will earn in a year, expressed as a percentage rate.

annual report   A report showing the financial status of a corporation. Public corporations are required to issue annual reports to their shareholders.

annuity   A sum of money paid to policyholders or shareholders either annually or at regular intervals.

appraisal   An estimate of the current market value of an asset.

appreciation   The amount that an asset has increased in value over its value in an earlier period. Appreciation is expressed as a percentage or as a monetary value. For example, a house that cost $200,000 five years ago, if it increases in value to $220,000, has appreciated by $20,000, or 10 percent, in five years.

arbitrage   Buying items in one market and selling them in another in order to profit on the difference between the two market prices. For example, if the U.S. dollar cost 1.5 deutsche marks (DM) in New York but only 1.45 DM in London, a trader could simultaneously buy deutsche marks in London and sell them in New York, thereby earning a profit.

arbitration   Submitting a dispute to a third party for settlement instead of to a court of law. If the arbitration is *binding*, the parties involved are required to agree to the settlement.

arm's-length transaction   A transaction made between a buyer and seller who have no relationship to one another. Transactions made between subsidiary companies of the same parent company are not arm's-length transactions because the companies may not be acting in their own self-interest but in the interest of a parent company.

arrears   Being behind in payments. You are in arrears if you have one or more unpaid debts.

asked price   The price at which a seller offers an item. The asked price is often different from the bid price, which is the most anyone will pay for the item being offered. Also called *asking price*.

assessed valuation   For tax purposes, the value of a property. Usually, property taxes are paid as a percentage of the assessed valuation of the property.

assessment   The amount charged, such as for property taxes.

asset   Any property that has value. Real estate, personal items, and even trademarks are examples of assets. The value of all your assets is called your *total assets*.

asset-based lending   A lending method in which a company's accounts receivable and inventory are used as collateral for the loan and as the basis for determining whether the company is worthy of receiving a loan.

asset dividend   A dividend paid as property instead of cash. For example, in lieu of cash, a corporation might pay dividends in the form of stock certificates to its stockholders.

assumable mortgage   A mortgage in which the borrower, if he or she subsequently sells the property, has the right to pass on the unpaid portion of the mortgage to the new buyer. With an assumable 30-year mortgage, if one person buys a house and sells it 10 years later, the subsequent buyer assumes payments for the remaining 20 years of the mortgage.

attorney-in-fact   A person hired to act in the name of another person. Also called *power of attorney*.

audit   A formal examination of the accounts, assets, liabilities, and transactions of a company or an individual.

auditor's opinion   The results of an audit of a company's records and books.

automated teller machine (ATM)   A machine that allows bank patrons to make withdrawals, deposits, and transfers and inquire about account balances without entering a bank. In order to use an ATM, you need a credit, debit, or bank card, and you need to know the *personal identification number (PIN)* for the card you use.

available balance   The amount of money in a bank account after all deposits are cleared. You can make withdrawals and write checks up to the amount of your available balance. When you deposit a check, it is entered on your balance, but you cannot make use of the money until the check has cleared and become part of your available balance.

average annual yield   The interest income you can earn on a certificate of deposit (CD) or bank account, expressed as a percentage.

back-end load   A sales commission that the investor pays to the broker only if the investor sells or disposes of mutual funds. With a *front-end load*, the investor pays the sales commission when purchasing the funds from an investment house.

bad check   A check that a bank refuses to honor. A check is considered "bad" if it is not filled out completely, if it does not have the proper endorsement signatures, or if there are not sufficient funds to cover the check.

balance of payments   The total payments of the businesses, people, and government of one country, less the total payments made by all other countries. A country with a favorable balance of payments receives more money than it pays out to other countries.

balance of trade   The difference between the amount of goods a country imports and exports. If a country imports more than it exports, it has a negative balance of trade. If it exports more, it has a favorable balance.

balloon maturity   A bank loan in which the last payment is a large lump-sum payment.

balloon mortgage   A mortgage in which the last payment is much larger than the other payments. Typically, a balloon mortgage is given to home buyers who anticipate a large appreciation of their property and who intend to sell before the mortgage matures. Balloon mortgages are also given to borrowers whose incomes are likely to rise.

balloon payment   A large lump-sum payment made as the last payment on a loan.

bank   A somewhat stodgy institution that loans money, takes deposits, and performs other financial services. Banks figure prominently in western movies, where they are often robbed. The old ones have marble floors and brass hand rails.

bank discount rate   The rate that banks charge customers for the use of banker's acceptances and other financial instruments.

bank draft   A check written by a bank that draws on funds that the bank holds in another bank. For example, if a customer in Las Vegas needed funds immediately, a bank in Boston might issue a bank draft on its account in Las Vegas so that the customer could get the money more quickly. Banks charge for this service.

bank holiday   A day in which banks are closed, whether to observe a holiday or by order of the federal government.

bank reserves   The actual cash on hand and assets held by a bank that can be turned into cash quickly.

bank run   When many depositors try to withdraw their money from a bank at short notice. When depositors fear that a bank is failing or otherwise lose confidence in a bank, a bank run can result.

banker's acceptance   A short-term credit instrument used by importers and exporters to speed international trade. The exporter sends a bill of exchange to a bank in the United States, which accepts the bill of exchange and agrees to pay it if the importer cannot pay.

bankruptcy   The legal procedure for deciding how to handle the debts of a business or individual who cannot meet credit obligations. If the debtor is declared insolvent, the property is put under the control of a trustee or receiver so it can be distributed to creditors.

base rate   For indexing purposes, the interest rate used to establish the price of bank loans. For example, many banks use the prime rate—the rate banks charge their most trustworthy customers for commercial loans—as the base rate for determining mortgage rates.

basis   The original cost of an asset, used to calculate capital gains and capital gains taxes.

basis point   0.01 percent, the smallest percentage point for quoting bond yields. If a bond yield changes from 6.00 to 6.85 percent, it has moved 85 basis points in yield.

bear   A securities or stock market investor who believes that the market will decline. The opposite of a bear is a *bull*.

bear bond   A bond expected to rise in value with rising interest rates.

bear market   A market, usually a stock market, in which the price of shares is declining. The opposite of a *bull market*.

bearer bond   A bond that belongs to the person who has it in hand. Bearer bonds are not registered to individuals or institutions. To receive payment, the bearer must present the bond. By contrast, owners of registered bonds are sent payments automatically when they fall due.

bearer instrument   A financial instrument, such as a bearer bond, payable to the person who possesses it. Bearer instruments are not registered to any party and do not need to be endorsed before payment is made.

beneficiaries   The people who benefit, or receive annuities, from a life insurance policy when the policyholder dies.

bequest   A gift of money or personal items made in a will.

beta   A measure of how volatile the price of an investment or stock is, as compared with the entire market. If the price changes dramatically, the investment has a "high beta." If the price is stable, it has a "low beta."

bid   The highest price that prospective buyers will pay for an item. The bid is often different from the asked price, which is the price at which a seller offers an item.

bid and asked   In the over-the-counter market, refers to the price range of quotes for a security, the bid price being the highest price a prospective buyer will pay, and the asked price being the owner's offering price.

Big Board   The New York Stock Exchange.

bill of exchange   A financial instrument by which one party instructs another party to pay a third party. Also called a *draft*.

biweekly mortgage   A mortgage payment schedule requiring payments every two weeks instead of once a month. Biweekly mortgages can be paid off in about 17 years, nearly half the 30 years required for a typical mortgage.

blank endorsement   A check or bill of exchange in which the "Pay to the order of" line is left blank.

blanket mortgage   A mortgage that covers more than one piece of property.

blanket policy   An insurance policy that covers more than one piece of property or that offers insurance of more than one type for a single piece of property.

blue-chip stock   Stock in a well-established company noted for its stability and reliable earnings.

blue-sky laws   State laws governing how securities are issued and traded. Blue sky laws are meant to prevent fraudulent transactions.

board of directors   Advisors elected by stockholders to manage a public company. The board of director's job is to represent stockholder interests. The board makes recommendations to the company's chief executive officer (CEO).

boiler room   A term to describe an out-of-the-way place in which shady salespeople sell fraudulent securities over the telephone.

bond   An interest-bearing certificate of public or private indebtedness. Bonds pay a fixed interest rate and are redeemable after a certain time period.

bond, bull   A type of bond that does well when interest rates are falling. Bull bonds are mortgage-backed, principal-only bonds. When mortgage rates fall, people refinance their homes, making bull (mortgage-backed) bonds more attractive.

bond, discount   A bond sold for less than the value its issuer promises to pay when the bond reaches maturity.

bond, fidelity or surety   Binding promises that "principal(s)" will perform certain acts to "obligee(s)," with the obligee(s) being paid sums of money if the principal(s) do not fulfill their obligations. Fidelity bonds pay employers in case their bonded employees prove to be dishonest. Surety bonds guarantee that the principal, often an employer, will fulfill certain duties.

bond issue   Bonds of the same type of class offered at the same time.

bond, premium   A bond sold for more than the value its issuer promises to pay when the bond reaches maturity.

bond prices   Prices quoted as percentages of their principle amount. For example, a $500 bond quoted at 95 would sell for $475. One quoted at 105 would sell for $525.

bond rating   A ranking system for assessing the financial solvency of bonds. AAA is the highest ranking. Bonds are ranked by Standard & Poor's and Moody's Investor's Service, among others.

book value   The original value of an asset less the cumulative depreciation. The book value is the value of an asset on the balance sheet. The book value is different from the market value.

borrowed stock   Stock borrowed from a broker in order to complete a *short sale* (selling a stock one does not own, with the idea of making a profit by rebuying the stock later when the price goes down).

bridge loan   A short-term loan provided while long-term financing is being finalized. Homeowners who have purchased a new home but have yet to sell the old one can get a bridge loan to tide themselves over until the old home is sold and the proceeds from the old home arrive.

broker   Someone who negotiates the buying and selling of stocks, securities, commodities, insurance, or real estate for a fee or a commission.

brokerage firm   A business that negotiates the buying and selling of stocks, securities, commodities, insurance, or real estate for a fee or a commission.

bull   A securities or stock market investor who is very optimistic about the future success of a market, stock, or commodity. The opposite of a bull is a *bear*.

bull market   A market in which prices are on the rise and brokers are confident of its future success. The opposite of a *bear market*.

bullet loan   A loan for which the interest and principal are paid in one payment, in one lump sum.

bullion   Uncoined gold or other precious metals in bars or ingots.

business plan   A plan explaining to loan officers how a new business or a business that is restructuring will use the loan money.

cable   A bank draft sent from one bank to another by cable.

call   A demand for payment of a loan. A lender can make a call if the borrower has failed to make timely payments or has breached a contractual agreement regarding the loan.

call option   An option to purchase shares of a stock at a specific price in a certain time period. Brokers exercise a call option if the price of the stock rises above the option price during the option period.

callable bonds   Bonds that issuers can pay off before the maturity date is reached.

callable preferred stock   Stock that can be called in by the issuer and redeemed for cash at any time. Stockholders of callable preferred stock are required to give back their shares when the issuer asks them to do so. Also called *redeemable preferred stock*.

calls and puts   Options to sell or buy stock shares at a certain price within a certain time. The holder of a put can require a buyer to buy an option, within the agreed-upon time period, at the specified price. The holder of a call can demand that a seller sell an option, within the agreed-upon time period, at the agreed-upon price. Investors buy put and call options as a hedge against large declines or rises in stock prices.

canceled check   A check that has been endorsed by a payee and paid by the bank from which it was drawn.

capital   All items of value owned by an individual or corporation, including cash, inventory, and property.

capital gain (or loss)   The difference between the purchase price of an asset and the resale price. If the resale price is higher than the purchase price, a capital gain results. If the resale price is lower than the purchase price, that represents a capital loss. Capital gains are subject to taxation. Capital losses are tax-deductible.

capital lease   For accounting purposes, a lease that is treated as an owned asset. Equipment is often leased to companies on a capital basis. The company leasing the asset enjoys the tax benefits of ownership, including deductions for maintenance expenses. When the lease expires, the company leasing the asset is usually allowed to purchase it.

capital market   A general term referring to stock markets and bond markets where governments and corporations can sell securities, stocks, and bonds in order to raise capital.

cash   Money that can be used for financial transactions, including funds held in checking accounts.

cash basis   An accounting method in which income and expenses are recorded when money actually changes hands. For example, a check you write on March 1 is not subtracted from your balance until the day the check is cashed. With the *accrual-basis* method, the check is subtracted on the day you write it, regardless of when it is cashed.

cash dividend   Stock dividends paid in cash, not in shares of stock.

cashier's check   A check written by a bank against its own funds. Cashier's checks are guaranteed to be redeemable, since they are drawn on banks.

cash surrender value   The amount of money that a life insurance policy pays if the holder gives up the policy or cancels it. The cash surrender value of a life insurance policy can be used as collateral on a loan.

caveat emptor   Latin for *let the buyer beware*. This saying means that buyers should not rely on sellers to present goods in their true light, but should investigate goods themselves before buying.

caveat venditor   Latin for *let the seller beware*. Refers to the obligation on the part of the seller to deliver goods as described in the sales contract.

central bank   A bank, usually operated by a government, that controls a nation's banking system and acts as the fiscal agent of the government.

certificate of deposit (CD)   A bank deposit that pays a fixed rate of interest over a stated period of time. Most CDs cannot be redeemed until a maturity date is reached.

certified check   A check that has been guaranteed by a bank and can be considered as good as cash. Before giving its acceptance, the bank makes sure enough money is in the account to cover the check and that the signature is valid.

certified public accountant (CPA)   A person who has been certified by the state to keep or inspect the financial records of businesses or individuals and also to prepare tax and financial reports for businesses or individuals.

charitable contribution   A contribution to a charity that can be deducted for income tax purposes.

charitable gift annuity   An annuity purchased from a charitable organization for more than the annuity's market value. The amount paid over and above the market value is considered a charitable donation.

chartist   A securities broker who bases purchasing decisions on graphs and charts of past sales activity.

chattel mortgage   A lien on personal property as a security against a loan. *Chattel* refers to personal property such as jewelry or equipment. In a chattel mortgage, the collateral is in the form of personal property, not real estate.

cheap money   Low-interest credit made available because interest rates are low.

check   A written order instructing a bank to pay a sum to a third party.

check kiting   An illegal scheme for fraudulently inflating the account balance of checking accounts. For example, a man with two checking accounts, one in Bank A and one in Bank B, writes a check on account A for $5,000 to his Bank B account. He deposits the check in Bank B. Until the check clears, he has $5,000 in both Bank B and Bank A. Next, he writes a check on account B for $5,000 to his Bank A account. He deposits this check, too. Until the checks clear, he has $10,000 in his Bank A account and $5,000 in his Bank B account. On paper he has $15,000; actually; he has only $5,000.

Chinese Wall   The name for the division between a bank's trust department and its credit department. The departments are not supposed to talk to one another, since one is engaged in extending credit and the other in making investments, and communication between the two might be a conflict of interest.

churning   Unnecessarily trading on a customer's account for the purpose of acquiring broker's commissions.

claim   A demand for money from an insurance company. You file a claim when you believe you are entitled to compensation from an insurer.

class action   A lawsuit filed on behalf of a group of people who have been wronged in the same way.

clear   To settle or discharge an account. Checks are cleared when they are redeemed for cash.

clearing house   A convenient place where banks in a given area exchange checks written against one another. Clearing houses make it easier for banks to clear and settle checks, since bank representatives can meet in a central place without needing to visit one anothers' banks.

Clifford trust   A trust established for ten or more years whereby assets are transferred from one individual to another and then back again when the ten or more year period is over. Before laws governing Clifford trusts were changed in 1986, they were often used to transfer assets, such as college funds, to children, who are taxed at a lower tax rate than adults. After the ten-or-more-year period, the adult could reclaim the trust.

closed-end fund   A fund that issues a fixed number of shares instead of continuously offering new shares to buyers.

closing price   The final price of a stock or commodity at the time the exchange closes for the day.

cloud on title   A title that cannot be transferred to someone else because liens, court judgments, or other impediments prevent the owner from selling it.

co-insurance   A percentage amount for which an insurance policyholder must be covered. For example, if a fire insurance policy has a 70 percent co-insurance clause, the insured must be covered for at least 70 percent of the value of his or her home.

collar   A device that protects the lender and the borrower from fluctuations in interest rates. The collar consists of the *floor*, which is the lowest the interest rate on the loan can go, and the *cap*, which is the highest interest rate that the bank can charge the borrower.

collateral   As part of a loan agreement, the property or securities that the borrower pledges to the lender in case the borrower cannot pay back the loan.

collateral loan   A loan given on the strength of the borrower's collateral, as opposed to the borrower's good standing in the community or good character.

collateral trust bond   A bond backed by the issuer's collateral. With this type of bond, the issuer pledges assets in the event that the bond cannot be paid when it falls due.

collateralized mortgage obligation (CMO)   A bond backed, or collateralized, by one or more real estate mortgages.

collateral value   The value of the properties and securities that a prospective borrower has pledged when applying for a loan.

collection agency   An organization whose job it is to collect outstanding debts from individuals on behalf of companies and businesses.

collection letter   A letter, always very polite but vaguely threatening, asking you to please pay an overdue bill.

collusive bidding   When bidders agree among themselves to offer one (usually low) bid. Collusive bidding always results in a lower bid than competitive bidding, in which the bidders do not know one another's bids.

commercial bank   A full-service bank owned by stockholders that makes loans, accepts deposits, and offers other commercial financial services.

commercial paper   Promissory notes, such as checks, drafts, and IOUs, that constitute a debt of some kind. Commercial paper is negotiable and can be traded.

commission   The fee that brokers and agents charge for their services. A commission is often a percentage of the total value of a sale.

commodity exchange   A marketplace where dealers and traders can meet to buy and sell goods.

common law   The body of law developed in England, based on precedents and custom, that forms the basis for the legal system in all states except Louisiana, where Napoleonic law is practiced.

common stock   Securities that represent ownership in a corporation. By law, holders of common stock can receive dividends only after claims by preferred stockholders, creditors, and bondholders have been satisfied. Common stockholders are the last to be paid if a corporation goes bankrupt.

compensating balance   A minimum balance that borrowers who wish to secure a loan from a bank must keep on deposit with the bank.

compound interest   Interest calculated on the original principal of a deposit plus all accrued interest.

condominium   An individual unit in an apartment house or other multi-unit building. Condominiums are different from apartments or flats in that they can be owned. Usually, condominium owners belong to a tenant association that is responsible for upkeep and maintenance, as well as for determining how much property tax each tenant owns.

consent decree   A judicial decree in which the parties settle their differences by agreeing to change their practices rather than by litigation.

conservator   A person appointed by a court to manage the affairs of an estate or the affairs of a person deemed incompetent.

consignment   An arrangement in which the manufacturer or person who made the goods is paid only after the goods are sold (referred to as *sold on consignment*).

construction loan   A loan covering construction costs, paid out at intervals as the construction project is completed. Also called a *construction mortgage*.

constructive notice   A notice published in a newspaper announcing some action, such as a lien or the confiscation of property by the state. By law, some actions must be "given constructive notice" so that anyone objecting can take action.

consumer credit   Credit given to individuals so they can buy personal things.

consumer-credit protection act An act passed by Congress in 1969 requiring lenders to be truthful about how they compute finance charges. Under the consumer-credit protection act, finance charges must be expressed as an annual percentage rate (APR) of the loan amount. Also called *truth in lending*.

consumer durables Items that consumers purchase infrequently and use over a period of years, such as televisions and washing machines. Also called *durable goods*.

consumer lease The lease of a consumer item, such as a car, with a value under $25,000.

consumer price index An index that measures the cost of living in the United States. The U.S. Labor Department is responsible for monitoring the consumer price index.

contract A legally binding agreement between two or more parties, where the responsibilities of each are clearly outlined.

conventional mortgage A mortgage not backed by the Federal Housing Administration (FHA).

convertible An adjustable-rate mortgage (ARM) that the holder can exchange for a fixed-rate mortgage. Usually, the holder must make the conversion, if he or she opts to do so, in the first few years of the mortgage.

Convertible currency Currency that is easy to exchange for the currency of another nation. Countries whose currency is not convertible set restrictions on how their currency can be traded.

co-payment In a health insurance plan, a percentage of a medical bill that you pay (the insurer covers the rest). Typically, you co-pay bills until you reach a certain dollar limit. After that point, the insurer pays 100 percent of your medical bills.

corpus Latin for *body*. The corpus is the principal of a fund or estate, as distinguished from the interest or other income it generates.

co-signer A joint signer of a promissory note. Co-signers are jointly responsible for paying back loans.

cost-of-funds index (COFI) An index that banks use to help determine the cost of adjustable-rate mortgages (ARMs). If the index goes up, so do ARM payments.

cost-of-living increases Payment increases that pensioners and social security recipients get to offset rising costs brought about by inflation.

counterfeit Money, bank cards, or checks that look real but are not.

countersign A signature that asserts the authenticity of a document already signed by another. In most companies, large checks require a countersign. Also called *countersignature*.

country risk The risk that an economic or political upheaval in a country will deplete its foreign reserves and prevent the country from paying back international loans.

coupon A certificate attached to a bond stating how much interest is due. When the coupon is presented, the interest payment is made.

coupon bond Bond with a coupon attached that states when interest payments are due and how much the payments are.

covenant A written agreement between parties that has been sealed from public disclosure.

credit Money a bank or other lending institution places at your disposal when you agree to pay it back at a later date.

credit agency   An agency that obtains data about the credit history of individuals and companies and offers the data to creditors and others.

credit application   A request to obtain credit. Most lenders require applicants to provide information about their creditworthiness.

credit card   A plastic card you can use to pay for things. It seems magical until the monthly bill arrives, at which point you realize you're charging too much and you wish you didn't have a credit card.

credit clinic   Slang term for an organization that claims to help consumers clear up unfavorable credit ratings. By law, creditors have 60 days to respond to credit challenges. If 60 days pass without a response, the challenger's creditworthiness is restored automatically. All a credit clinic does is advise people to contest all unfavorable ratings. The idea is that creditors will not respond within the 60-day period and will need to restore the challenger's favorable credit rating.

credit counseling   A service for companies or individuals who wish to get out of debt.

credit insurance   Insurance purchased by banks as a defense against large credit losses.

credit limit   The most that a consumer or company can borrow at one time from a bank or other creditor.

credit line   The maximum amount of money that a creditor will extend to an individual or company.

credit rating   A lender's appraisal of a borrower's ability to pay back loans. Credit ratings are based primarily on the borrower's past history of paying back loans.

credit risk   The risk that a borrower will not be able to pay back a loan.

credit slip   A notice removing a credit card charge from a cardholder's bill. If you return something you've purchased with a credit card, you are issued a credit slip in the amount of the charge to reverse its effect on your credit card balance.

creditor   A bank or other agency that extends credit to borrowers. The opposite of a creditor is a *debtor*.

creditworthiness   The ability of a person to pay back loans. Creditworthiness is judged according to your past history of loan payments, how long you have been employed, and other criteria.

cross-collateral   Collateral that backs up several loans, not just one, as arranged by agreement with the lender.

currency   Paper money in circulation. Also refers to the paper money issued by a nation. The dollar is the currency of the United States.

currency basket   Currency unit composed of currency from different nations. International transactions are sometimes made in basket currency to protect against one currency being devalued. For example, a payment made in U.S. dollars as well as Japanese yen retains more of its value if the yen or dollar happens to fall in value.

currency swap   An agreement between companies to exchange equivalent amounts of one type of currency for another. Companies engage in currency swaps, for example, to diversify their portfolios. At the end of the agreement, the currencies are swapped back.

currency translation   Changing balance sheet entries and totals from one currency to another. Multinational corporations perform currency translations on their balance sheets as a way of measuring financial performance. Some countries require corporations to do currency translations when reporting their income.

current account   The imports and exports, as well as transfer payments, between two countries. A country that has a surplus current account with another country has exported more goods and made more payments than it has received. A deficit current account means the country has imported more and received more payments than it has exported or paid out.

current assets   Assets that can easily and readily be converted into cash.

current yield   The annual interest rate paid by a bond or other security, expressed as a percentage of the principal.

cushion   The time between the date a bond is issued and its first call date; that is, the day it can be redeemed either in whole or in part.

custodian   An institution or a broker that oversees the management of a group of assets.

custody account   A bank account held in trust by a parent or guardian on behalf of a minor.

customs   Taxes placed on goods being imported.

cycle billing   Billing one set of customers from a customer list on specific days of the month. For example, customers whose last names begin with *A* would be billed on the first of the month, *B* on the second day, and so on. The idea is to spread out the paperwork over a month and keep bill payments coming in regularly.

daily interest   Interest compounded daily on a bank deposit. Although the interest is compounded daily, it is deposited in accounts at weekly, biweekly, or monthly intervals.

dealer   A person who trades in securities on his or her own. Dealers trade with their own money and take the risks themselves; brokers trade on behalf of others.

debentures   Unsecured bonds backed by the general credit of the issuer, not by the issuer's assets.

debit   An entry, made on the left side of a balance sheet, that records an expense.

debit card   A bank card that draws directly on the holder's bank accounts, not on a credit line. Charges made on a debit card are subtracted immediately from the user's checking or savings account.

debt   Money owed.

debt limit   The most that a government can legally borrow. State legislatures and constitutions decide the debt limits of state and local governments. The federal government can raise its debt limit as it pleases, since its limit is decided by Congress.

debtor nation   A nation that is behind in its interest or principal payments to banks.

debt service   Interest or principal payments on a mortgage. Debt service usually describes either the monthly payments or the total annual payment.

decedent   Legal term for a person who has died.

deductible   The part of a bill that your pay out of your own pocket. The insurer pays the rest.

deed A signed document describing a legal agreement or contract.

deed of trust A legal document giving the bearer title to a property. Banks usually hold the deed of trust until the borrower has paid the mortgage in full. After that, title is given over to the borrower.

default To fail to pay back a loan or meet an obligation.

default risk The risk that a bond issuer will not be able to pay either the interest or principal.

deferred annuity An annuity whose payments, by agreement, will begin in the future.

deferred compensation Earnings to be received in the future, not when they are earned. Deferring compensation sometimes has tax advantages.

deferred gifts Gifts to a charity or nonprofit organization that are to be given at the time of the giver's death. Arrangements for giving deferred gifts are sometimes written into wills.

deferred payment A privilege sometimes offered to renters, credit-card holders, and others to skip or postpone payments. Deferred payments are usually offered as a sign-on incentive.

deficiency The amount by which a taxpayer fails to fulfill tax obligations. For example, if you underpay by $500, that is a $500 deficiency.

deficiency judgment A court order giving a lender authority to collect part of the proceeds from a sale of property, when the seller of the property has defaulted on a mortgage or other financial obligation.

deficit The amount that a business's total assets fall below its total liabilities.

deficit financing The federal government's fiscal policy of borrowing to cover its deficit.

defined benefit plan A retirement plan set up for a corporation's employees. These plans pay no taxes on their investments and must be managed according to federal standards.

defined contribution plan Blanket term for various plans by which employees can make tax-deferred contributions to retirement plans.

deflation A decline in prices. *Inflation*, a rise in prices, is the opposite of deflation.

delinquency Failure to fulfill a financial obligation. Loans with two or more payments overdue are considered delinquent.

demand deposit Any deposit account that can be withdrawn at a moment's notice. A checking account is a demand deposit.

demand draft A written request to a bank to pay a third party (in other words, a check).

demand loan A loan that can be paid back at any time and has no maturity date. Interest is paid until the principal has been paid off.

deposit Money entered in a bank account.

deposit insurance Insurance on bank deposits to protect depositors in the event of a bank failure. The Federal Deposit Insurance Corporation (FDIC), a government agency, insures bank accounts up to $100,000.

depository A bank where funds and securities are deposited.

depreciation The decline in value of an asset. Assets depreciate as they are used or as they become obsolete.

deregulation   A loosening of government regulations concerning business activity. Deregulation is supposed to stimulate business competition and make for a more prosperous economy.

derivative   A security whose value is based on, or derived from, a stock or bond. Options to buy and sell stocks are derivatives, for example.

derivative mortgage-backed security   A derivative whose value is based on securities, usually bonds, that are collateralized by real estate mortgages.

devaluation   The decline in value of a currency relative to a standard, such as another country's currency or the price of gold.

direct deposit   Depositing paychecks automatically in employees' banks accounts. Many companies now offer their employees direct deposit.

direct placement   Selling a security issue to one group of investors without the use of underwriters. Long-term securities are sometimes sold to institutions this way.

discharge of bankruptcy   A court order giving a bankrupt debtor release from all debt obligations. The debtor is no longer responsible for the debts, although the record of bankruptcy remains on the debtor's credit record for ten years.

disclosure   Information about the annual percentage rate (APR), method of computing interest, and minimum monthly payment that banks must give to mortgage customers. Federal law requires banks to disclose this information.

discount   A reduction in price. In the bond market, the discount is the difference in price between what a bond costs today and its face value (what it will cost at maturity).

discount brokerage   A brokerage firm that executes buy and sell orders without giving investment advice.

discount point   One percent of the principal of a mortgage. Home buyers typically pay the lender 1 discount point when their loans close.

discount rate   Rate used to measure the value of money over time. As a practical matter, a discount rate is the same thing as an interest rate.

discount yield   Method for computing Treasury Bill yields, in which the par value is computed instead of the purchase price. The formula for computing discount yields is the discount, divided by the par value amount multiplied by 360, divided by the number of days to maturity.

discounted cash flow   A mathematical technique used by financial analysts in which future-day dollars are converted into present-day dollars by adjusting for inflation and compound interest. A company's overall value (its share price times the number of shares outstanding) is typically calculated using discounted cash flow calculations.

discounting   Converting future-day dollars into present-day dollars by adjusting for inflation and compound interest. Because discounting calculations are cumbersome, one typically uses a computer to perform the actual calculations.

disinflation   Refers to Federal Reserve policies meant to prevent inflation. In order to do this, the Federal Reserve slows down the money supply, leaving less money for credit.

disintermediation   When investors pull their money out of interest-earning bank accounts and reinvest it in other places, such as stocks and money market funds.

disposable income   The money left over for buying things or investing after taxes are paid.

diversification   Investing in many different areas—real estate, stocks, and bonds, for example—as a hedge against decline in one area. Diversification really means not putting all your eggs in one basket.

divest   To sell off assets or businesses because they are unprofitable or because they don't fit in a company's plans for the future.

dividend   A profit share paid out to a stockholder.

dividend reinvestment plan   A plan allowing corporate stockholders to be paid in cash or in stock.

double taxation   Refers to federal taxes on corporate earnings and how these earnings are taxed twice: once in the form of corporate taxes and again when earnings are distributed to shareholders.

dower   The right of a widow to inherit all or part of her deceased husband's property.

Dow-Jones Industrial Average   An index used to measure price changes in the stock market.

Dow theory   A stock market analysis method that, like all such methods, tries to detect price trends in the market and sometimes even succeeds.

down payment   Part of the full price of an item, paid at the time of delivery, with the rest to be paid later.

draft   A financial instrument by which one party instructs another party to pay a third party. Also called a *bill of exchange*.

drawee   The bank on which a check is drawn.

drawer   The person who writes, or *draws*, a check that is to be paid by the drawee. The *drawee* is the bank where the check writer keeps a checking account.

due diligence   The responsibility of bank officers to evaluate loan applications in a prudent and forthright manner. Due diligence is a credo of the banking industry.

dumping   Selling large amounts of stock in order to make share prices drop or the market itself decline.

Dun & Bradstreet (D&B)   A company that rates corporations' financial performance for the benefit of investors.

durable goods   Items that consumers purchase infrequently and use over a period of years, such as televisions and washing machines. Also called *consumer durables*.

duration   For a fixed-income security, the average time it takes to collect all payments of interest and principal.

Dutch auction   Gradually lowering the price of a security until a buyer is found. The Dutch auction system is used in securities underwriting.

duties   Tax on imported or exported items.

E bond   A U.S. government bond issued before 1980.

early-withdrawal penalty   A fee charged to depositors if they withdraw their certificates of deposit (CDs) or saving deposits before the CDs or savings deposits reach maturity.

earnest money   A sum of money paid for property to assure the seller that the buyer is sincere. When the sales transaction is completed, the earnest money is counted toward the purchase price of the property.

earning asset   Any asset that generates interest income.

earnings per share   The amount that each stock share earns in dividends after both preferred stockholders and taxes have been paid.

EE bond   A U.S. government bond issued after 1980.

effective annual yield   What a depositor earns on a certificate of deposit (CD) or savings account on a yearly basis, provided the money is not withdrawn.

efficient market   Refers to an economic theory that says that today's prices for securities and commodities are a measure of what investors think their prices will be in the future.

electronic funds transfer (EFT)   Transferring money by electric wire instead of by traditional paper means, such as check writing.

embargo   Keeping ships from entering port or leaving port by government decree.

embezzlement   Fraudulently appropriating money for personal use.

eminent domain   The right of a government to take private property and use it for the public good.

Employee Retirement Income Security Act (ERISA)   Federal act describing how managers of profit-sharing funds and private pension funds may invest those funds. ERISA sets guidelines for fund managers.

employee stock ownership plan (ESOP)   A plan allowing employees to buy stock in the company they work for.

encumbrance   A claim against property that keeps the property from being sold. A lien is an encumbrance, for example.

endorsement   A signature that allows for the transfer of a negotiable item. The signature on the back of a check, for example, is an endorsement.

endowment insurance   A type of life insurance policy in which the insurance money is paid when the policyholder dies or when the term of the policy is finished.

equity kicker   An amount, in addition to interest, that a lender receives from the borrower. Equity kickers are common in large commercial real estate mortgages.

escrow   An agreement whereby a deed, a bond, or property is held in trust by a third party until some obligation is fulfilled.

estate   A deceased's property at the time of death. An estate is passed to the deceased's heirs if he or she left a will. If not, the matter of how to divide the estate is decided by a probate court.

estate tax   Taxes levied by federal and state governments on the transfer of property from an estate to its beneficiaries. Estate taxes are paid by the estate. Inheritance taxes—taxes the heirs pay for the property they receive—are paid by heirs.

estoppel   A legal bar preventing a witness in court from denying a fact he or she previously stated as the truth.

Eurobonds   Bonds issued in a currency other than the currency of the country where the bonds are being issued. Eurobonds got their name when corporations and governments in Europe began issuing bonds in U.S. dollars.

Eurodollar   Refers to U.S. dollars held in banks outside the United States.

European Monetary System   A system of balanced exchange rates for the national currencies of Europe. The system was set up by the European Economic Community to help stabilize exchange rates.

exchange rate   The rate that the currency of one country is trading against the currency of another. For example, an exchange rate of 118.18 yen to the dollar means that one U.S. dollar purchases 118.18 Japanese yen.

Exchange Stabilization Fund   Fund managed by the Federal Reserve System, set aside to be spent to help stabilize the dollar and other international currencies.

excise taxes   Taxes on acts, not property. For example, sales of liquor are subject to excise taxes.

executor   The institution or person named in a will to manage the estate of the deceased. The executor pays taxes, distributes the estate's assets, and pays estate debts.

exempt securities   Securities that are not subject to the reporting rules of the Securities and Exchange Commission (SEC).

Export-Import Bank   A federally run bank set up to help U.S. companies export their products. The bank provides loans to U.S. companies who cannot otherwise find commercial loans.

exposure   The likelihood that market fluctuations will cause financial losses or ruin. Also refers to credit extended to a borrower.

external audit   An audit of a business conducted by an outside auditor to determine its financial soundness. Outside auditors have no stake in the business being audited and therefore can be considered a disinterested party.

face value   The principal of a stock, bond, or other security. Also the principal of an insurance policy. Face value is sometimes called *par value*.

fair market value   The reasonable price of an asset. Fair market value is the price that a willing seller and buyer would negotiate for an asset, given that both know all the facts and are not under compulsion to buy or sell.

Fannie Mae   Nickname of the Federal National Mortgage Association (FNMA), a publicly owned organization that buys mortgages from banks and resells them to investors.

Farmer Mac   Nickname of the Federal Agricultural Mortgage Corporation, a government agency that guarantees farm loans.

Federal Deposit Insurance Corporation (FDIC)   Federal agency that insures bank accounts against bank failures. The FDIC insures accounts to $100,000.

federal funds   Money purchased by commercial banks from the Federal Reserve.

federal funds rate   Interest rate charged to commercial banks for purchasing federal funds. The federal funds rate is the benchmark for many commercial credit rates, including short-term business loans.

Federal Government securities   U.S. government bonds, which represent the debt of the U.S. government.

Federal Home Loan Bank System   Name for the 11 regional banks in charge of selling money to U.S. Savings & Loan institutions.

Federal Housing Administration (FHA)   Federal housing agency set up to aid home financing. The FHA insures home mortgages made by commercial banks.

Federal Insurance Contributions Act   The federal program that gives retirees, the disabled, and surviving spouses benefit payments. Also known as *Social Security*.

Federal Open Market Committee (FOMC)   Committee responsible for setting the Federal Reserve Board's short-term monetary policies. The chief job of this committee is to take actions that control the supply of credit.

Federal Reserve Bank   One of the 12 regional banks that serve as creditors to commercial banks.

Federal Reserve Board (FRB)   Board of governors of the Federal Reserve System. Members are appointed by the President and must be confirmed by the Senate.

Federal Reserve Notes   U.S. paper money. (It says so right at the top of the bills—"Federal Reserve Note"—check it out.)

Federal Reserve Regulations   Rules establishing how banks may operate in the United States. There are 30 regulations, named A through DD.

Federal Reserve System   The central bank of the United States, whose job is to regulate and control the supply of credit to the nation's bank.

Federal Unemployment Tax   Tax paid on wages and salaries to pay for federal and state unemployment programs.

fiat money   Money not backed by gold.

fidelity bonds   Bonds that bankers purchase from insurance companies to protect themselves against robbery, employee fraud, and other wrongdoings. In some states, banks are required to purchase fidelity bonds.

fiduciary   A person who manages someone else's investments.

finance charge   The cost of interest payments, filing fees, and other costs apart from the actual cost of an item. The finance charge is what you pay when you finance a purchase.

finance company   A private company that issues loans.

Financial Accounting Standards Board (FASB)   The board that establishes rules for certified public accountants (CPAs). This board also determines the generally accepted accounting principles.

financial institution   An institution, public or private, that collects money from depositors and loans it out or invests it.

financial planning   Counseling by financial planners to help individuals get the highest returns for their investments.

fiscal policy   The financial policies of the federal government, including its taxation policies and spending.

fiscal year   A period of 12 months for which a company plans its budget and reports on its financial activity. The fiscal year and the calendar year often do not coincide; the fiscal-year can begin at any point in the calendar year.

fixed asset   A tangible asset, such as equipment, that a company cannot dispose of without interrupting normal business activities.

fixed-rate loan   A loan whose rate of interest does not change.

fixture   Personal property that becomes part of real property because of the way in which it is used. Fixture is a legal term. If you build shelves into a wall in your rented apartment, they become a fixture; that is, they are a part of the rental property.

float   To place a bond on the market.

floating exchange rate   Exchange rate between currencies that is allowed to change as the market dictates. In a fixed exchange rate, governments or banks determine the exchange rates between currencies.

flood insurance   Insurance against damage from floods. Flood insurance, like earthquake insurance, is often hard to get or very expensive, except in areas where flooding rarely occurs.

floor   The minimum interest rate that borrowers can pay on a variable-rate loan. By placing a floor on the interest rate, lenders can be assured that interest rates do not fall below an unprofitable margin. The ceiling is the maximum rate borrowers can pay on a variable-rate loan.

floor limit   The most a merchant can accept as a credit card charge without seeking confirmation from the credit card issuer.

floor trader   A trader on a stock exchange floor.

forbearance   Not seeking penalties against a borrower in default, on the condition that the borrower will fulfill obligations in the future.

foreclosure   Legal proceeding in which a lender attempts to obtain the collateral that was secured for a defaulted loan.

foreign exchange   Converting the currency of one country into its equivalent in the currency of another country.

foreign trade   Importing and exporting goods between nations.

foreign trade zone   A place where goods can be imported and exported without being subject to customs duties or taxes. Foreign trade zones are meant to encourage trade.

forged check   A check whose drawer signature or endorsement signature is not valid.

forgery   Fraudulently altering a document, such as a check.

Form 10K   The form used to file an annual financial report with the Securities and Exchange Commission (SEC). Large corporations are required to file the form.

Form 1099   The disclosure form filed with the IRS that lists all unearned income from stocks, bonds, interest, and the like.

forward exchange contract   A contract by which two parties agree to trade currencies at a date in the future. Forward exchange contracts allow banks to protect themselves against currency fluctuations, since the money is paid for at the current exchange rate, not the future exchange rate.

forward market   A market in which traders agree to deliver stocks, bonds, commodities, or other tradable items at a future date. Forward markets allow traders to protect themselves against future price hikes, since the items are paid for at the time of sale, not the time of delivery.

franchise   A business arrangement whereby one party is allowed to use another party's name for a fee. Fast-food eateries are the best examples of franchises.

franchise tax   A tax imposed by a state on a business headquarters outside the state that does business in the state.

fraud   Intentional deception undertaken to trick someone else into parting with something of value. No legal definition of fraud exists.

front-end load   A sales charge paid to a broker when purchasing mutual funds.

frozen account   An account whose funds cannot be withdrawn, pending a judicial ruling.

full faith and credit   The commitment of a government to pay the interest and principal on a bond. Municipal bonds and U.S. Treasury Bills are backed by full faith and credit.

full-service broker   A brokerage firm that offers investment advice as well as executing buy and sell orders.

fundamentalist   A securities analyst who bases investment decisions on the bond issuer's financial position. By contrast, a *chartist* bases decisions on the trends in the bond market.

funds transfer   Moving funds between accounts held by the same party.

fungible   A security of the same value as another that can be exchanged easily with the other.

future value   The value that a stock, bond, or commodity will attain in the future.

futures   Commodities to be delivered and paid for at a future date at a price agreed upon by the buyer and seller.

garnishment   Court judgment ordering a lender to be given part of the wages or salary of a borrower who has defaulted on a loan.

generally accepted accounting principles (GAAP)   The rules and guidelines that certified public accountants (CPAs) use when preparing financial statements.

general-obligation bond   A bond issued to pay for public works projects, issued by a state or municipal government. Also called *G-O bond*.

general partner   A co-owner of a business. General partners receive a share of the business's profit and are partly responsible for its debts and liabilities.

gift tax   A tax on gifts of cash or property. Gift taxes are paid by the donor.

GI loan   Name for special mortgage loans available to veterans of the U.S. armed services.

gilt-edged   Name for low-risk AAA corporate bonds that have proven earnings.

Ginnie Mae   Nickname for Government National Mortgage Association (GNMA), the government corporation that backs securities associated with Department of Veterans Affairs and the Federal Housing Administration. Securities backed by Ginnie Mae are considered very safe investments.

going concern   Name to describe a business that is in operation and is expected to remain so in the future.

gold card   A credit card with a credit line of at least $5,000.

gold certificate   A certificate giving the bearer title to gold in the U.S. gold reserve.

gold standard   A monetary system in which currencies are backed by gold; paper bills can be exchanged for gold at any time.

government bonds   U.S. savings bonds, which the government issues to pay its debts. The bonds have high ratings and are sold in small denominations.

grace period   The period of time during which a loan payment is to be paid. If the payment is not made during the grace period, it is overdue.

graduated payment mortgage (GPM)   A mortgage with lower payments in the early years and higher ones as time goes by. GPMs are sold to borrowers whose incomes are expected to rise, the idea being that these borrowers will be able to make the higher payments in years to come.

grantor   A person who writes a deed passing property from one party to another.

gross estate   The property in an estate before debts, taxes, and other expenses are paid. The *net estate* is what remains after these expenses are paid.

Group of Ten   The ten leading industrial countries and members of the International Monetary Fund. They are France, Japan, Italy, Sweden, England, Belgium, Canada, Germany, Holland, and the United States.

growing-equity mortgage (GEM)   A fixed-interest mortgage with monthly payments that rise instead of decline, the idea being to pay off the mortgage faster.

growth stock   A stock in a company that is expected to grow quickly. Investors like growth stock, since it is expected to increase in value faster than other stock.

guaranteed bond   A bond whose principal and interest are backed by a corporation other than the issuer.

guarantor   A person or corporation that guarantees a debt will be paid if another party defaults. Guarantors are considered co-endorsers of a debt and are therefore liable for the debt.

guaranty   A promise on the part of an individual or corporation that it will pay the debt of another party if the other party defaults on a debt.

H bond   A U.S. government bond, or savings bond.

hard currency   The currency of a developed nation that is easy to convert to other currencies.

hedging   Buying and selling commodities in a futures market to protect against price fluctuations.

HH bond   A U.S. government bond, or savings bond. HH bonds are sold in denominations of $500 to $10,000.

high-grade bond   A bond with AAA or AA rating, considered a secure investment.

home-equity loan   A loan backed by the equity in the borrower's home.

humped yield curve   When medium-term rates are higher than both short- and long-term rates. If you drew this on paper, you would have a humped curve.

hyperinflation   Very high inflation. Hyperinflation is usually defined as inflation higher than 600 percent a year.

illiquid   Refers to assets that are not easy to liquidate; that is, to convert into cash.

impaired credit   A bank loan that is not likely to be repaid.

import taxes   Taxes levied on certain imported items. Most nations have import taxes to protect domestic markets from foreign competition.

income statement   A report describing a corporation's activities, its profit, and its losses over a fixed period.

indemnity   An obligation to pay all costs of damage, pain, or suffering.

indenture   A document that states the terms under which a bond is issued. The indenture declares the maturity date, the interest, and other information.

independent agent   An insurance agent who represents more than one company.

independent bank   A commercial bank that draws depositors from and serves the residing area. Independent banks, which are scarce and getting scarcer, are not branches of large commercial banks.

index   A numerical measurement that compares past and present economic activity. The Dow Jones Industrial Average is an index of stock performance. The Consumer Price Index measures the price of consumer goods.

individual retirement account (IRA)   A retirement account to which individuals can deposit up to $2,000 (or $2,250, if their spouse is not working) of their annual earnings. IRAs provide two significant income tax benefits: IRA contributions may reduce an individual's taxable income, and IRA earnings are not taxed. Withdrawals from an IRA can be made after age 59½ at which time the withdrawals are taxed as normal income.

individual retirement account rollover   Rule allowing holders of individual retirement accounts (IRAs) to pass on the accumulated savings in one IRA to another IRA, provided that they do so within the first 60 days of closing the first IRA.

industrials   Securities of mining, manufacturing, construction, and other companies whose work is producing commodities or services.

inflation   Rises in prices. Inflation is caused by excess purchasing power among the general populace and by increasing production costs, which producers pass on to consumers.

inheritance tax   Tax that heirs must pay in order to receive property from an estate. Not all states have inheritance taxes.

inside director   A member of a corporation's board of directors who also works inside the corporation as a manager.

insider information   Information available to managers and others in a corporation that could be used to make sweet stock deals. Insider information is not available to the general public. The Securities and Exchange Commission (SEC) forbids corporation directors and principals from buying or selling stock based on insider information.

insider trading   Trading stock with insider information not known to the general public. Insider trading is forbidden by the Securities and Exchange Commission (SEC).

insiders   Corporate managers, directors, principals, and officers are considered insiders.

insolvency   Being unable to pay debts.

installment contract   Agreement to pay for goods in fixed installments—for example, weekly or monthly.

installment credit   A loan that is repaid in monthly payments of the same amount.

institutional investor   A corporation that invests many of its assets, even though its chief purpose is not to make investments. For example, insurance companies provide insurance, but they also make many investments. Institutional investors make up a large portion of the securities investment market.

insufficient funds   What you have if you try to write a check for $10 and you only have $7.50 in your checking account, or if you try to withdraw $20 from a savings account with $18 in it.

insurance agent   A representative of an insurance company.

insurance broker   Someone who sells insurance policies.

insurance contract   A contract between an individual and an insurance company, in which the individual promises to pay premiums and the company promises to pay a certain amount of money if the individual loses life, limb, or property.

intangible assets   The assets of a company that aren't property but are assets nonetheless. For example, an established clientele is an intangible asset.

interest   Amount of money paid to borrow capital. Typically, the interest is expressed as a percentage of the principal that was borrowed.

interest-only loan   A loan that requires the borrower to pay only interest for the term of the loan. Loan payments on an interest-only loan do not reduce the loan balance. At the end of the loan, the borrower makes a balloon payment equal to the original loan (and ending) loan balance.

interest rate   The price of borrowing money. The interest rate is usually expressed as a percentage of the total principal borrowed, although sometimes the rate of interest on a loan is tied to an index of some kind.

interest rate cap   A fixed limit on the amount that a borrower must pay in interest on a loan.

interest-sensitive assets   Assets whose value rises and falls with changes in interest rates. Treasury Bills and variable-rate mortgages are examples of interest-sensitive assets.

interim report   A report showing stockholders how a company is doing. An interim report appears before the company's annual report.

interim statement   A statement regarding account balances that you can get from an automatic teller machine (ATM). Interim statements are not as detailed as monthly statements.

interlocking directorate   When members of the board of directors of one corporation also sit on the board of another, competing organization.

internal rate of return (IRR)   The profit that an investment earns expressed as a percentage. Typically, IRRs are stated as annual profit percentages. On an investment that pays interest and for which there is no change in value, such as a bank savings account, the interest rate is the IRR.

interstate banking Expansion of banks across state lines, as they acquire subsidiaries in other states.

interstate commerce Commercial trading of goods across state lines.

intervention When central banks buy or sell currency in order to influence exchange rates. By selling currency, a central bank can flood the market and lower the value of the currency. By buying currency, a central bank can create a seller's market and increase the currency's value.

inter vivos trust Latin for *between the living*. An inter vivos trust gives one person's property to another person.

intrinsic value The benefit to the holder of an option contract if he or she doesn't exercise the option. The intrinsic value is the exercise price less the option price.

inventory In a business, a list of a stock on hand, with the value of each item and the total value of all items by category.

investment advisor A person or agency paid to research investments and make investment recommendations for another person or institution. Investment advisors are required to disclose any conflict of interest recommendations to the Securities and Exchange Commission (SEC).

investment banker A person or corporation who buys and sells stocks, bonds, other securities, and even whole companies or that assists others in these activities.

investment club A group of individuals that studies investment opportunities together. Sometimes the individuals pool their funds and make investments.

investment companies Companies that buy securities from other companies and then sell shares in those securities to investors.

investment counselor A person who researches investments, makes recommendations, and invests on behalf of others. Investment counselors must register with the Securities and Exchange Commission (SEC).

involuntary bankruptcy A petition by creditors asking a bankruptcy court to declare a firm bankrupt, the firm having failed to pay its debts and meet its financial obligations. Also called a *creditor's opinion*.

involuntary lien A lien made by the judgment of a court, without the consent of the property owner.

irrevocable trust A trust that cannot be revoked without the approval of the beneficiary. An irrevocable trust cannot be changed in any way without the beneficiary's approval.

joint account A savings or checking account in the name of two or more people.

joint annuity An annuity that is paid out to two or more people.

joint custody When authorization is required by two or more people to undertake an action. For example, the customer and bank have joint custody of a safe deposit box. Opening a box requires authorization of the customer and a bank officer.

joint endorsement A check requiring the endorsement of two or more signers.

joint tenancy When two or more people inherit an estate, and each has equal interests. When one of the joint tenants dies, the estate passes automatically to the survivor or survivors.

joint tenants with right of survivorship   The usual arrangement between a married couple, in which each has the right to shared property, and the property passes to the other in the event that one dies.

joint venture   A business initiative undertaken by two different businesses, each working toward a common goal. Companies engage in joint ventures to pool their resources and help overcome the high cost of entering new markets.

jointly and severally   A legal term meaning that, when two or more people take out a loan together, all are liable. If they default, the lender can take legal action against all of them or specific individuals.

judgment   The official decision of a court of law.

judgment lien   A court order placing a lien on the property of a debtor.

judicial sale   A sale of property, as ordered by a court, to satisfy a debt. A foreclosure is an example of a judicial sale.

jumbo certificate of deposit   A certificate of deposit (CD) with a principal of $100,000 or more.

junior mortgage   A second or subsequent mortgage on a property. If the property is in default, junior mortgages are paid only after the first mortgage has been paid.

junk bond   A bond whose creditworthiness is very low. Junk bonds usually have a rating of BB or below. To attract investors, junk bonds pay a higher interest rate than do other bonds, since the bonds carry a high risk of default.

Keogh plan   Retirement plan that allows you to set aside some of your wages or salary for retirement. Keogh plans are more complex to set up and to administer than SEP/IRA (Simplified Employee Pension Plan/individual retirement account) plans, but they may allow larger contributions.

kicker   An extra condition imposed by a lender before the lender will approve a loan. Part ownership in the property or a share of its proceeds are examples of kickers.

kiting   See *check kiting*.

lagging indicator   An economic indicator that usually reflects not where the economy is headed, but where it has been. For example, the gross national product (GNP) is a lagging indicator, since increases or declines in the GNP aren't registered until after the fact.

land flip   A real estate scam in which property is sold repeatedly, usually within a matter of months, with the value of the property increasing with each sale until the last sucker buys it at an overvalued price and is stuck with it.

late charge   A charge for tardiness in paying a bill or a mortgage payment.

laundered money   Large cash deposits, often acquired by illicit means, accepted by banks as normal deposits. To prevent money laundering, banks are required to report any cash deposit of more than $10,000.

leading indicators   Economic indicators that usually reflect where the economy is headed. For example, when the number of new investments—a leading indicator—goes up, it usually means that the economy is healthy.

lease   A contract that gives an individual or business the right to use a property for an agreed-upon price and time period.

leasehold   The right of occupancy that tenants enjoy as part of a lease.

legal tender   Money that is valid legally for the payment of debts. A dollar bill is legal tender, as noted just northwest of George Washington's head, where it says, "This note is legal tender for all debts, public and private."

lender of last resort   The bank from which all money flows initially, the Federal Reserve Bank.

letter of credit (L/C or LOC)   A document from a bank giving authority for payments to be made to a third party from the bank on behalf of a bank's customer.

leverage   Credit acquired in order to improve an individual's or company's ability to invest or speculate.

leveraged buyout   When one company takes over another and uses the acquired company's assets in order to pay back the loans that were taken out in order to take over the company in the first place.

liability   All debts and obligations of a business.

liability insurance   Insurance protecting the policyholder against financial losses resulting from injury done to others.

lien   A charge against real or personal property to secure the repayment of a debt.

life estate   An estate that gives income to a beneficiary until the time of the beneficiary's death, at which time the estate passes to another party. The beneficiary cannot sell any property belonging to the estate.

limitations   The conditions under which an insurer will either make limited payments or make no payments at all on a policy claim.

limited partnership   A partnership in which profits and responsibility for liabilities and debts are shared according to how much of the business each partner owns.

line of credit   A commitment on the part of a bank to lend up to a certain amount of money to a borrower.

liquidity   Turning assets such as property into cash. An asset with "good liquidity" can be sold or converted into cash easily.

liquidity preference   Refers to people's innate preference for liquid assets, such as cash, over hard assets, such as property. Liquid assets are easier to spend.

litigation   Contesting a dispute in a court of law.

living trust   A trust giving one person's property to another person. Also called an *inter vivos trust*.

load   The commission that an investor pays to a broker when purchasing mutual funds. In a back-end load, the commission is paid when the investor sells the funds. In a front-end load, it is paid when the investor purchases the funds from the investment house.

load fund   A mutual fund whose purchase price includes a commission. *No-load funds* do not charge commissions.

loan   Money lent at interest, to be repaid by a specific date.

loan committee   A bank committee that reviews applications for large loans above what a loan officer has the authority to review.

loan shark   A lender who charges exorbitant fees for loans. With the exception of some credit card issuer banks, which charge upward of 15 percent annually in interest on their cards, most loan sharks do not work out of commercial banks.

lock-in period   The 30- to 60-day period during which a lender must keep mortgage rates to the figure quoted in the loan application. The lock-in period protects borrowers in case interest rates rise before the mortgage is approved.

London Interbank bid rate   The rate at which banks in the London Interbank Market borrow from one another.

London Interbank offered rate (LIBOR)   The rate at which the biggest banks in London lend money to one another. LIBOR is used as an index by some banks for pegging the interest rate charged to borrowers.

long position   Broker's term for a security owned free and clear, including all interest, income, and dividends. For example, a commodities dealer who owns 500 units of pork bellies outright could say, "I am long in 500 pork bellies," and he would be right.

long-term   In financial terms, *long-term* refers to a security that matures in ten or more years.

lump-sum distribution   A single payment to the beneficiary of a retirement plan. For tax purposes, the lump-sum may be treated as if it had been received over ten years, depending on the beneficiary's age and other conditions.

M1, M2, M3   Ways of measuring the *money supply*. M1, the narrowest measure, includes only money held in hand by the public. M2 encompasses M1's definition, but also includes money in savings accounts and certificates of deposit (CDs). M3, the widest measure, encompasses M2 but also includes money market funds and other long-term holdings.

maker   The writer of a check.

management report   A report describing company performance, prepared monthly for the officers of a corporation.

margin   Money given to a broker that serves as a pledge to pay for securities. Investors are required to put up 50 percent of the cost of their investments as a margin, although some brokers require more.

margin call   A demand by a securities broker for a client to put up more cash or collateral to back up investments. If the call is not met, the broker can sell existing collateral.

margin trading   Buying securities with credit provided by a broker.

market   In financial terminology, a place where traders gather to exchange commodities, securities, or stocks.

market risk   The likelihood that the price of items will rise or fall as economic conditions change.

Massachusetts trust   A business association, owned by stockholders and managed by trustees. Many mutual funds are Massachusetts trusts.

maturity   The date when the borrower is obliged to pay back the loan.

maximum out-of-pocket   The most you can pay for insurance in a year. Usually, the maximum out-of-pocket is the sum of the premium, the deductible, and all co-payments.

mechanic's lien   A lien on real property made by a contractor or builder for payment overdue. A builder can request a mechanic's lien if he or she has not been paid according to the contract to build or improve the property.

merger   When two or more corporations pool their common stock and become one corporation.

minimum balance   The least amount of money that can be kept in a savings or checking account. Letting the balance drop below the minimum sometimes incurs a service charge.

minimum payment   The smallest payment that can be made on a monthly credit card bill without incurring a service charge.

minor   In most states, a person under age 18. Minors do not have all the legal rights of adults, nor the legal responsibilities.

mint   Where money is coined and printed. Mints are operated by the U.S. Treasury Department.

mobile-home certificate   A certificate representing ownership of an investment in mobile home loans insured by the Federal Housing Administration (FHA).

monetarist   One who believes that controlling the supply of money is the best way to control inflation and make the economy grow at a stable rate.

monetary policy   Refers to the Federal Reserve Board's policies to promote the economic health of the United States. The Federal Reserve Board sets monetary policies designed to control inflation, increase employment, and achieve other such goals.

money-center bank   A bank located in an important commercial city that does business both domestically and internationally.

money laundering   Depositing large amounts of cash, often acquired illicitly, in banks as though they were normal deposits. To prevent money laundering, banks are required to report any cash deposit of more than $10,000.

money market   A market in which short-term investment funds are traded. The money market is not organized like a stock exchange, but is the loose-knit organization of buyers and sellers of money market funds.

money market certificate   A certificate of deposit (CD) representing a debt security. Money market certificates must have a denomination of at least $2,500. The individual institutions that issue them set the rate of interest and maturity date.

money market deposit account (MMDA) Money market funds managed through a commercial bank. Bank customers can make deposits directly into their MMDAs from their banks.

money market fund (MMF)   A mutual fund that invests in Treasury Bills, certificate of deposits (CDs), and other short-term debt instruments. Investors own shares in the fund and receive regular interest payments.

money market rates   The rate of return paid by individual money market funds.

money supply   The total sum of money available in an economy for spending and investing. Money supply is usually defined in one of three ways called *M1*, *M2*, and *M3*.

monopoly   When an individual or corporation has complete control over a market, through ownership of source materials, ownership of distribution in a certain area, or ownership of the means by which the product is made.

moratorium When a borrower officially declares that he or she can't pay back a loan.

mortgage A deed giving ownership of a property to a borrower on the condition that the borrower makes all interest and principal payments to a lender. The lender owns the mortgage until the borrower pays in full, after which the borrower becomes sole owner of the property.

mortgage-backed securities Securities backed by mortgages and deeds of trust.

mortgage banker A banker who sells mortgages or pools of mortgages to investors.

mortgage broker A broker who helps people who want to acquire mortgages find willing lenders. Brokers work on commission.

mortgage payable An account in a ledger recording mortgage payments for a company asset.

mortgage REIT (real estate investment trust) A trust that supplies capital to real estate developers who want to build new housing.

mortgagee Name for the lender who supplies mortgages and collects mortgage payments.

mortgagor On a mortgage, the borrower who must pay the interest and principal.

municipal bond A bond issued on behalf of a municipality, such as a city, state, or government agency, to cover its debts.

municipal bond insurance Insurance against the failure of a municipal bond. Private companies provide the insurance and agree to buy the bonds in the event of a default.

mutual fund An investment company that trades in bonds, stocks, Treasury Bills, securities, real estate, and other items, on behalf of its stockholders. Shares in a mutual fund are offered on a continual basis, and investors can always buy in.

mutual insurance company An insurance company that is owned by its policyholders. Company earnings are paid to policyholders as dividends.

mutual savings bank A savings bank, similar to a cooperative, in which bank assets belong to depositors and dividends are paid to depositors.

mutual wills Wills written by two people each naming the other as beneficiary.

national currency The official currency of a nation. The national currency of the United States is the dollar; the national currency of Greece is the drachma.

national income All earnings from production in a nation, including earnings from interest, rental income, and business profits. The U.S. Department of Commerce publishes a monthly report on national income.

natural guardian The mother or father of a child, who acts by law as the child's guardian. Children who do not have natural guardians are appointed guardians by a court.

negotiable Capable of being transferred from one party to another. Checks, drafts, securities, and commercial paper are negotiable.

negotiable certificate of deposit (CD) A CD issued by a commercial bank. Negotiable CDs are large-denomination CDs of $100,000 or more. Typically, they are held by institutional investors.

negotiable instrument A written order promising to pay a certain amount to the bearer upon demand or at a certain date. Checks, promissory notes, and bills of exchange are examples of negotiable instruments.

negotiable order of withdrawal (NOW) account   A combination checking and savings account. Like a savings account, a NOW pays interest; like a checking account, checks can be written against a NOW.

nest egg   Money not needed for day-to-day spending, set aside in a savings account. Also savings for retirement.

net-asset value   The total value of a share in a mutual fund. The net-asset value is what each share would be worth if all shares were suddenly paid out.

net worth   The total value of the assets of a business less the liabilities.

netting   When banks or corporations settle debts with each other by balancing out what they owe instead of paying each other in full. For example, if company A owed $20,000 to company B, and B owed $25,000 to A, B could pay A $5,000 straight up instead of each company paying its debt in full.

New York Stock Exchange (NYSE)   The "Big Daddy" of stock exchanges, located on Wall Street in New York, New York; the oldest and biggest stock exchange between the Atlantic and Pacific Oceans.

next of kin   The nearest blood relative to another person. The next of kin inherits a dead person's property if no will was left behind.

no-load fund   A mutual fund that charges no sales commission.

no-load insurance   Insurance sold directly to consumers without the aid of a broker. No-load insurance is usually cheaper because the buyer does not need to pay a sales commission.

nolo contendere   Latin for *I do not contend it.* By pleading nolo contendere, a defendant admits to the facts of the case but does not admit guilt, thereby freeing that person to contest the charge at another time.

nonaccrual loan   A loan for which interest is not being paid because the borrower cannot pay the interest.

noncallable   A bond or stocks that cannot be redeemed, or "called in," before a pre-agreed date or the date of maturity.

nonprofit corporation   An organization that does not distribute its profits, if there are any, to owners. Profits are plowed back into the nonprofit's capital fund.

nonrecourse   Refers to the lack of a legal claim against a party to a contract. In a nonrecourse arrangement, one or both parties are not liable if the contract is not fulfilled. The "wronged" parties, therefore, have no recourse to the law.

nonrecourse indebtedness   Indebtedness for which the borrower is not liable.

nonrecourse loan   A loan for which the lender will be repaid by proceeds generated by the loan. For example, a loan for a housing development would be a nonrecourse loan if the builder intended to pay back the loan with proceeds from the sale of the completed project. The loan is called *nonrecourse* because if the borrower defaults, the lender has no recourse except to foreclose on the borrower's collateral.

notary public   A public officer who attests to the authenticity of deeds, affidavits, and depositions.

note   A written promise to pay a debt or sum of money.

notes payable   In a general ledger, an account showing the business's liability for promissory notes.

notes receivable   In a general ledger, an account showing the business's promissory notes received from customers.

not sufficient funds (NSF)   What you have if you try to write a check for $10 and you have only $7.50 in your checking account, or if you try to withdraw $20 from a savings account with $18 in it.

novation   An agreement to remove one party from a contract and replace that party with another. All parties in the contract must agree to the novation substitute.

odd lots   Lots not being traded in the usual number. For example, stock is usually traded in lots of 100 on stock exchanges, so an odd lot would be 50 or 75 shares.

off-board   Describes transactions of stock not listed in a stock exchange, but traded directly by brokers and dealers.

offer   The lowest price that a seller will accept for stock.

offering price   The per-share price of a new stock offering or securities offering.

online banking service   A service offered by a bank that allows you to download bank statements and make electronic fund transfers using a home computer and a modem.

online bill payment service   A service offered by a bank or another company that allows you to send electronic payment instructions to a computer. This computer then withdraws the appropriate funds from your account and writes and sends a check to pay the bill.

online investing   Buying and selling securities such as stocks, bonds, and mutual funds through an Internet Web site run by a stock broker or mutual fund management company.

open-end lease   A car lease requiring monthly payments, at the end of which the borrower can make a large balloon payment to buy the car outright, or return the car to the lender.

open market   A market where securities and commodities are traded freely by competitive bidding. In open markets, bidding is not limited to members.

open-market rates   The interest rates paid on negotiable certificates of deposit (CDs), Treasury Bills, commercial paper, and other money market negotiables in the secondary trading market.

operating lease   A lease covering a time period shorter than the economic life of the asset. Operating leases can be canceled at any time.

opportunity cost   Income that could be saved or earned by investing in another, more attractive endeavor. For example, if you had $10,000 in mutual funds paying $500 in dividends annually, and you knew you could earn $750 in dividends from stock, the cost of staying with your original investment—your opportunity cost—would be $250.

option   A contract giving a dealer or broker the right to buy or sell a security during a certain time period at a certain price.

original issue discount (OID)   The difference between what a bond costs when it was issued and what its price is at maturity.

original maturity The time between the day a bond was issued and the day it reaches maturity. The current maturity is the time between today's date and the date the bond reaches maturity.

origination fee The fee that lenders charge loan applicants to handle loan applications and to conduct credit investigations.

overdraft The amount that a check exceeds what is in the checking account it was written against. If you write a check for $20 and you have only $15 in your checking account, you have a $5 overdraft.

overdraft protection A service offered by banks to their customers in which the bank pays overdrawn checks up to a certain amount.

over-the-counter Securities not listed with a stock exchange are traded over-the-counter by dealers and brokers.

paper gain/loss Name for capital gains or losses in an investment portfolio that have yet to be realized.

participating bond A bond that entitles the bearer to minimum interest payments and proceeds from the profits of the company, as stated by the terms of a contract.

partnership A business with two or more owners, who share equally in the profits as well as the liability for debts.

passbook A book for recording deposits and withdrawals in a savings account. Some banks require the passbook to be presented when money is deposited or withdrawn.

patent An exclusive right to sell, make, and use an invention. Patents are awarded by the U.S. Patent Office.

pay to bearer Refers to bonds and other negotiables that are paid to the person who has them in hand, not necessarily to the person named on the bond or negotiable.

pay to order Refers to bonds and other negotiables, such as checks, that are to be paid to the person named, not necessarily to the one who has them in hand.

payee The person or party to whom a check is written.

payment shock When payers of adjustable-rate mortgages (ARMs) make their first high payment after the introductory payment period, they are said to experience "payment shock."

payroll taxes Taxes on a payroll, including social security taxes and employment insurance taxes.

pegging Indexing the price of mortgage rates and other lending rates with a rate charged by a major bank or important banking institution. For example, mortgage rates are often pegged to the prime rate, which is the rate banks charge their most reliable customers for credit.

penalty clause The clause in many banking contracts stating that customers must pay a penalty for late mortgage payments, early withdrawals of savings accounts, and the like.

penny stocks Stocks whose offering price is less than a dollar per share. Penny stock prices are sometimes extremely volatile.

pension fund   A fund set up by a corporation to provide for its employees in retirement. Typically, employees contribute a portion of their paychecks to the fund. The fund is used to make investments as part of the company's pension plan.

pension plan   A plan by which a company provides for its employees in retirement. Employees—sometimes with matching contributions from employers—contribute to a pension fund, which is used to make investments as part of the plan. Managers of pension plans must follow strict investment guidelines.

perfect title   A title to a property that is free of debts, liens, prior claims, and other encumbrances.

perfected lien   A lien that has not only been filed by the lien holder but is also in force.

periodic rate   The price of credit, expressed as a percentage and charged at periodic intervals. For example, a credit card that charges a 12 percent annual rate for outstanding debt would charge a 1 percent periodic rate if it billed customers monthly (12 times a year). If it only billed customers 6 times a year, it would charge a 2 percent periodic rate.

permanent financing   A long-term mortgage, typically used to finance construction projects, covering all requirements of the project from legal costs to building materials.

perpetual bond   A bond that has no maturity date. Owners of the bond collect income as long as they hold it. Also called an *annuity bond*.

personal banker   An employee of a bank who manages a customer's accounts and acts as a financial counselor.

personal identification number (PIN)   The password or number you punch in at an automatic teller machine (ATM) to make deposits and withdrawals. Also known as an *access code*.

personal loan   A loan, usually for under $5,000, for the personal use of the customer, not for business use.

personal property   Items and things, as opposed to *real property*, such as buildings and land. By definition, personal property is not "immovable"; in other words, it can be moved. A baseball card is personal property; a baseball field is real property.

personal property tax   Tax on valuable personal property, such as jewelry, cars, and yachts. Also called a *luxury tax*.

personal residence   For tax purposes, the home you live in most of the year. Each taxpayer has one personal residence. Capital gains stemming from sales of a personal residence often receive preferential treatment.

personal trust   A trust created for individuals or families. Personal trusts are set up for a variety of reasons, such as for the tax benefits or to benefit grandchildren.

pit   The floor of a commodity or stock exchange, where brokers and dealers make hand gestures and scream at one another.

pledge   Placing property or collateral with a lender in order to secure a loan. For example, a watch left with a pawnbroker in return for a loan is a pledge.

plus sign (+)   In a newspaper report, a plus sign next to a stock or mutual fund price means that it rose that day. In a bond or Treasury note price, a plus sign means that the price is expressed in sixty-fourths of a percentage point. For example, a par value of 89.52 means 89 and $52/64$ of par.

plus tick   Refers to when a security is resold at a higher value. Also called an *up tick*.

point   In stock prices, a point equals one dollar; in bond prices, a point equals ten dollars.

Ponzi scheme   To swindle by paying early investors with money from later investors, not with earned income. Eventually, the incoming investment money cannot keep up with payments to investors, and the whole deal collapses. Named for Charles A. Ponzi, a well-known swindler.

pool   When securities of a similar type are combined and bought and sold as a group. Securities can also be pooled as collateral.

portfolio   The term for the total assets and investments held by an individual, company, or institution. For reporting and tracking purposes, a portfolio can be divided into smaller portfolios, such as the loan portfolio, land portfolio, and so on.

positive yield curve   The curve that demonstrates how securities held longer yield a higher rate of return. Because interest rates are higher for long-term securities than they are for short-term ones, rates of return rise the longer a security is held.

posting   Recording accounting entries in a general ledger.

power of attorney   A legal document that lets someone you trust run your financial affairs if you become unable to do so.

preapproved credit   The credit extended automatically to prospective credit-card holders. Preapproved credit is used as an incentive to get customers to apply for cards. By custom, the amount of preapproved credit being offered is printed in bold red letters on the envelope in which the credit card application comes.

preemptive right   The right of the Federal Reserve Board to overrule state laws concerning the regulation of banks. Also, the right of stockholders to buy new stock offerings before they are put on the general market.

preexisting condition   A sickness or injury that a person has before applying for health insurance. Most insurers will not cover preexisting conditions immediately upon the issuance of a new health insurance policy. Instead, preexisting conditions are covered only after the expiration of a waiting period.

preference   The selling or transfer of property within 90 days of filing for bankruptcy.

preferred stock   The dividend-paying stock in a corporation that gives its holders advantages over holders of common stock. Preferred stockholders are paid before common stockholders. If the corporation goes bankrupt, preferred stockholders are paid from the assets of the corporation before common stockholders but after any creditors.

premium   The sum above the face value of a bond when the bond is purchased at an above-par price. In insurance, the amount you pay for insurance coverage.

present value   The current-day equivalent of some future amount, or future value. In converting future values to present values, one adjusts for compound interest and for inflation.

price/earnings ratio   The ratio between the current price of a stock and the earnings it will make over a specific period of time. Investors use the price/earnings ratio to measure the value of stocks.

primary market   The market where loans are awarded to borrowers. Once a loan is made, it can be sold on the *secondary market*, where pools of mortgages are bought and sold by investors.

prime rate   The rate banks charge their most trustworthy customers for commercial loans.

principal   The actual money borrowed in a loan, as distinguished from the *interest*, the price of buying the loan. Also a deposit as distinguished from the interest it earns.

private banking   Banking services for wealthy customers, including investment counseling and lending services.

private placement   Selling the entire issue of a security to one group of investors.

privity   In a property, the relationship between all parties with mutual interests, such as the donor and recipient, or a landlord and tenant. Privity is a legal concept and is used in court to determine where fault, negligence, and conflicting interests arise.

probate   When a court examines a will to determine if it is valid. During probate, the court also assigns an *executor* to the will.

problem bank   A bank with a large number of loans in default.

profit-sharing plan   A plan by which employees share in the profits of a company, either by receiving bonuses or having their profit shares put in a trust. Profit-sharing plans encourage employees to be more productive and more loyal to their companies.

profit-taking   In stock trading, when investors sell shares after several days of rises in the market. A rising stock market encourages investors to sell and take advantage of higher prices; in other words, it encourages them to "profit-take."

progressive tax   Tax rate that rises along with the amount being taxed, the idea being that everyone should share equally in the tax burden.

promissory note   A written promise to pay a sum of money at a future date to a specific person or to the bearer of the written promise. Also known as an *IOU*.

property taxes   Taxes on property, including real estate and stocks.

proprietorship, sole   When a business is owned by one person. Sole proprietorship is one of three types of business organizations; the other two are a *partnership* and a *corporation*.

prospectus   Latin for *prospect*. A statement designed to attract investors to a newly formed corporation. A prospectus usually includes the corporation's goals, a plan for how it will turn a profit, and an explanation of how investments will be used.

protectionism   Giving domestic industries protection against foreign competition by levying taxes on foreign goods, using quotas, and other means.

proxy   A person who has authority to vote on behalf of a stockholder.

prudent-man rule   Name of the law requiring trustees to invest only in securities that a prudent man or woman would buy. Trustees, who are legally responsible for others' money, may be held responsible under this rule if they make unwise investments.

public offering   A bond issue offering to the general public.

puts and calls   Options to sell or buy stock shares at a certain price within a certain time. The holder of a put can require a buyer to buy an option, within the agreed-upon time period, at the specified price. The holder of a call can demand that a seller sell an option, within the agreed-upon time period, at the agreed-upon price. Investors buy put and call options as a hedge against large declines or rises in stock prices.

pyramiding   In real estate, pyramiding means to finance property purchases with property that is already mortgaged. In banking, pyramiding means to use loans to pay off interest debt.

qualified opinion   When omissions in bank records prevent auditors from doing a thorough review of a bank's books, auditors give a qualified opinion, which is a best-available assessment of the bank's financial health.

quiet title action   A legal action meant to resolve all claims against a property.

quorum   The minimum number of people who must be present at a corporate meeting to conduct business.

quote   The highest bid to buy and the lowest offer to sell a security or commodity. Also called a *quotation.*

rate of return   Money made on invested capital.

real-estate investment trust (REIT)   A trust that owns real estate and sells shares from the profits of that ownership to investors.

real-estate owned   Term to describe real estate that a lender has acquired through foreclosure.

real income   Income measured for what it can buy, not in dollars-and-cents terms. For example, the real income of a low wage earner might be higher than that of someone who earns high wages, if the low wage earner lives in a region where goods and housing are inexpensive.

real-interest rate   The interest rate that takes into account how interest yields are reduced by inflation. To get the real interest rate, you subtract the inflation rate in a given period from interest earnings in the same period.

real property   Land and buildings on the land, as opposed to personal property, which comprises movable items such as jewelry and equipment.

real money   Coins and actual currency. Checks and bank drafts, by comparison, are not considered real money.

real rate of return   The rate of return on an investment that takes into account how rates are affected by inflation. The real rate of return is the rate of return less the rate of inflation over the length of the investment.

realized profit/loss   The cash profit or loss from the sale of a security.

rebate   A return of part of a payment, made after the payment is received. Rebates are offered as incentives for consumers to buy or use products.

receiver   A person assigned by a court to help a bankrupt business reorganize its finances, satisfy its creditors, and become profitable.

receivership   A bankrupt business to whom a receiver has been assigned is *in receivership.*

record date   For payment of dividends, the date fixed by a board of directors for determining who will receive dividends.

record owner of stock   According to the records of a corporation, the individual or institution that owns shares of its stock.

recourse   Being able to compel a debtor to cover debts.

redeemable bonds   Bonds that issuers can repurchase if they so choose.

redeemable preferred stock   Stock that can be called in by the issuer and redeemed for cash at any time. Stockholders of redeemable preferred stock are required to give back their shares when the issuer asks them to do so. Also called *callable preferred stock*.

redemption   Exchanging bonds for cash when the bonds reach maturity.

redemption price   The price a corporation pays to bondholders when they redeem its bonds. Corporations pay the principal if the bonds are redeemed on their maturity date; they pay the principal and a premium if the bonds are called in before they reach maturity.

red herring   On page one of a prospectus, a statement printed in red saying that the material inside is not an offer to sell but is instead a public disclosure of facts. Also, a distraction from the true issue at hand, originating from the practice of placing a smoked red herring across a path to confuse hunting dogs.

redlining   Discriminating against minority and poor neighborhoods by declining to consider offering mortgages there. The name comes from the former practice of drawing red lines around these neighborhoods on maps.

refinancing   Exchanging one mortgage for another, in order to take advantage of better interest rates, for example.

regional stock exchange   A stock exchange that chiefly trades the stocks of corporations in the surrounding region.

registered bond   A bond registered to an individual or institution at the time of sale. Owners of registered bonds are known to the issuer and are sent payments automatically when the bonds fall due. Owners of bearer bonds, on the other hand, are not known to the issuer and must present their bonds in order to receive payment.

registered check   A check purchased at a bank and backed by the bank that can be presented as payment to a third party. Registered checks work like money orders.

Regulation 9   Regulation allowing national banks to have trust departments and manage the investments of customers.

Regulation A   Federal Reserve regulation establishing how Federal Reserve Banks advance money to financial institutions.

Regulation AA   Federal Reserve regulation governing how banks should handle customer complaints.

Regulation B   Federal Reserve regulation establishing guidelines for processing credit applications.

Regulation BB   Federal Reserve regulation requiring banks to serve the communities they reside in.

Regulation C   Federal Reserve regulation requiring lending institutions to disclose the locations where they lend money.

Regulation CC   Federal Reserve regulation streamlining how banks handle the return of unpaid checks.

Regulation D   Federal Reserve regulation requiring banks to keep a certain amount of money in reserve.

Regulation DD   Federal Reserve regulation establishing truth-in-lending laws.

Regulation E   Federal Reserve regulation setting rules for electronic fund transfers.

Regulation F   Federal Reserve regulation limiting the risks banks can take in dealing with other banks.

Regulation G   Federal Reserve regulation requiring lenders to report large credit extensions to brokers and dealers.

Regulation H   Federal Reserve regulation establishing membership requirements for banks in the Federal Reserve System.

Regulation I   Federal Reserve regulation stating how much stock member banks must purchase in the Federal Reserve Bank.

Regulation J   Federal Reserve regulation establishing how checks are collected and accounted for.

Regulation K   Federal Reserve regulation governing international banking.

Regulation L   Federal Reserve regulation governing interlocking directorships.

Regulation M   Federal Reserve regulation governing leasing companies.

Regulation N   Federal Reserve regulation governing bank transactions.

Regulation O   Federal Reserve regulation establishing how much credit banks may extend to their executive officers.

Regulation P   Federal Reserve regulation establishing security guidelines for banks.

Regulation Q   Federal Reserve regulation governing how banks must deal fairly with customers.

Regulation R   Federal Reserve regulation building a better *Chinese Wall* in banks.

Regulation S   Federal Reserve regulation establishing how government agencies may seek information about bank customers.

Regulation T   Federal Reserve regulation governing how dealers and brokers may extend credit to customers.

Regulation U   Federal Reserve regulation governing how banks may extend credit for margin securities.

Regulation V   Federal Reserve regulation governing how banks may deal with firms in the defense industry.

Regulation X   Federal Reserve regulation applying Regulations G, T, and U to foreigners applying for credit in the United States.

Regulation Y   Federal Reserve regulation governing how banks may establish holding companies.

Regulation Z   Federal Reserve regulation establishing protections for consumers seeking credit.

remittance slip   Attached to a check, a list of all deductions, corrections, discounts, taxes, or other information, along with the net amount of the check.

reorganization   After a business has declared bankruptcy, the restructuring of its assets in order to make it profitable again.

repossession   Seizing the collateral for a loan due to inability to pay the interest or principal. Repossession is usually the last recourse for failure to pay a debt.

reserve   Funds put aside for anticipated future costs.

reserve requirements   Reserves that banks are required to keep on hand for their basic operations. These reserves are deposited at the bank's district Federal Reserve Bank.

residual value   The value an asset has when the asset's user or owner is finished using it.

Resolution Trust Corporation (RTC)   A government institution established after the 1980s Savings & Loan debacle to sell off the assets of failed Savings & Loans. The RTC is attempting to recover some of the $500 billion lost to U.S. taxpayers during the freewheeling 1980s.

restraint of trade   Refers to the concept, ingrained in U.S. law and in the American tradition, that no restrictions should be placed on the free flow of commerce.

restrictive covenant   A clause in an agreement or contract prohibiting a party or parties from taking certain actions. The most common restrictive covenant in business is one that prohibits a seller of a business from engaging in the same business for a certain number of years.

retained earnings   Business profits that are used for expansion, not paid in dividends to stockholders or added to capital funds.

return of investment   When the earnings derived from a piece of capital equipment equal the price paid for the piece of equipment, you have a perfect return on your investment.

return on assets   A company's profits as a percentage of its assets. Return on assets is one way to measure a company's profitability.

revenue   The total income from a given endeavor. Also gross income from an investment.

revenue bond   A municipal bond for which the principal and interest are paid for by the project the bond finances. For example, a municipal bond issue for a harbor would be paid for by berth fees.

reverse mortgage   A mortgage in which a lender makes payments to a borrower, with the understanding that the lender will take possession of the borrower's property at some later date. Retired people who need more income sometimes have reverse mortgages on property for which they possess the equity. These types of mortgages are rare.

reverse split   When stockholders exchange stock such that each owns the same number of shares. Reverse splits are undertaken so that stockholders all own the same percentage of a corporation.

revocable trust   A trust giving property to heirs that can be changed or revoked at any time by the person who originates the trust. Under this arrangement, the property is transferred to the heirs on the death of the trust originator, and the estate does not need to go through probate.

revolving credit   A form of credit in which the account holder is given a credit line, runs up a bill, and pays off the amount owed in monthly payments. If the amount owed is not paid off monthly, interest charges are made. A minimum monthly payment is usually required on outstanding credit loans. Most credit card accounts are revolving credit accounts.

rigging   Manipulating the price of a security to give it a false value.

right of foreclosure   The right of a lender to foreclose on a mortgaged property if the borrower cannot meet mortgage obligations.

right of redemption   The right of a debtor to buy a property at a sale of foreclosure if he or she has the means to do so. To redeem the property this way, the debtor must pay the interest and principal on the defaulted mortgage, as well as all foreclosure costs incurred by the lender.

right of survivorship   The right of surviving spouses to inherit the property of deceased spouses.

risk   In financial terms, the possibility that an investment will not be repaid and that the method of investment will be rendered unprofitable by market conditions.

rollover   The automatic renewal of a certificate of deposit (CD) at present rates of interest. Also, the automatic reinvestment of money market funds.

Roth-IRA   An individual retirement account that, while not allowing for tax deductibility of initial contributions, also doesn't tax withdrawals.

round lot   A basic unit of common stock, usually 100 shares, bundled together for trading purposes.

Rule of 72   A way of determining how long it will take for a sum of money to double at a specific interest rate, by dividing 72 by the interest rate. For example, a savings account earning 6 percent interest will double in 12 years, since 72 divided by 6 equals 12.

run   When many depositors try to withdraw their money from a bank at short notice. When depositors fear that a bank is failing or otherwise lose confidence in a bank, a bank run can result.

safe deposit box   A small safe in a bank vault that can be rented for storing valuables and important papers.

salary-reduction plan   A retirement plan in which money is taken automatically from employees' salaries and put in a retirement fund, such as a 401(k).

sales tax   A tax levied by state and local governments, usually as a percentage of retail sales.

savings account   A deposit bank account that yields interest. Cash can be deposited or withdrawn at the discretion of the holder.

savings bank   A bank that accepts deposits from customers and invests it in mortgages and securities.

savings bond   A U.S. government bond, issued to finance the debt of the U.S. government. Savings bonds earn variable interest and are sold in denominations from $50 to $10,000.

seasonal adjustment   Adjusting data collected throughout the year to an annual rate for the purposes of analysis. For example, retail sales rise in December when people shop for the holidays. Retail sales figures for December, therefore, need to be adjusted downward.

seasonal credit   The line of credit extended to businesses during peak manufacturing and sales cycles.

seasonal variations   Term for differences in economic statistics that repeat themselves year to year. For example, manufacturing rates decline in the winter due to cold weather, but rise again in the spring in any given year.

seat   A membership on a stock exchange. Members of a stock exchange are said to have a "seat" on the exchange.

second mortgage   Another mortgage on a property, usually taken out to provide capital for home improvements or to finance a business. The obligations due the lender of a second mortgage are subordinate to the obligations owed the lender of a first mortgage.

secondary mortgage market   A market where first mortgages, or residential mortgages, are pooled and sold to investors. The secondary mortgage market serves as a capital fund for the mortgage originators, who sell their mortgages for the secondary market.

secured credit card   A credit card that is backed by a savings account. Issuers of secured credit cards can draw on cardholders' savings accounts if cardholders are unable to pay their credit card bills.

securities   Stocks, bonds, and other financial instruments that can be traded in a securities market.

Securities and Exchange Commission (SEC)
The regulatory agency charged with overseeing laws regarding the buying and selling of securities. Companies selling securities, and brokers and dealers who trade in them, must register with the SEC.

securitization   The conversion of loans and other bank assets into securities that can be traded in the securities market. Securitization enables banks to obtain capital.

security agreement   A document that gives a lender a claim to the assets that the borrower has put up as collateral for a loan. The security agreement must be signed by the borrower to be valid.

security interest   The claim of a lender to assets that the borrower has pledged as collateral to back up a loan.

self-directed IRA   An individual retirement account (IRA) that allows its owner to decide how the funds should be invested.

self-insurance   A rainy day fund set aside for emergencies, illness, and periods of unemployment.

self-liquidating loan   A loan whose purpose is to give the borrower capital to acquire or manufacture goods, the sale of which will help repay the loan. For example, a loan to a farmer for seed money could be a self-liquidating loan, since the farmer would pay back the loan with revenue from the sale of crops.

seller's market   Raising demand and raising the price that sellers can offer goods in short supply.

selling against the box   Selling a stock with the idea of making a profit by rebuying the stock later when the price goes down. Selling against the box works like this: The seller, believing that the stock will fall in price, has his or her broker "borrow" shares of the stock from one of the broker's clients. At the same time, the seller buys shares of the stock for himself or herself. Now all the stock is sold and the buyer of the stock gets the shares. Meanwhile, with luck, the stock drops in value. The seller buys the stock at the reduced price and returns the shares through the broker to the person they were borrowed from. The seller keeps the profits from shares of the stock he or she borrowed through the broker. However, if the stock went up instead of down after it was "borrowed," the seller does not make a profit. Fortunately, the seller did buy shares of stock for himself or herself, and these now serve their purpose as a hedge against the stock's rise.

senior lien   When two or more liens have been placed on a property, the senior lien takes precedence over other liens and must be satisfied first. The senior lien is the first mortgage on the property.

serial bonds   Bonds from the same issue that mature at different times. This way, the bonds do not all fall due at once and strain the finances of the issuer.

service charge   A bank charge, such as the charge issued when an account is overdrawn or a check bounces.

settlement date   The actual date of the transfer of a security from the buyer to the seller.

severally but not jointly   In a stock offering, when the people selling the stock are each responsible for selling their part, but not for selling the entire offering. In a *jointly but severally* arrangement, all parties are responsible for the sale of the offering.

shared appreciation mortgage (SAM)   A short-term mortgage offered at a low fixed rate of interest. In exchange for providing such favorable terms, the lender gets to benefit from the appreciation of the property's value.

sheriff's sale   An auction of a borrower's property as part of a foreclosure. The proceeds go to help pay the borrower's debts.

short sale   Selling a stock one does not own with the idea of making a profit by rebuying the stock later when the price goes down. A short sale works like this: The short seller, believing the stock will fall in price, has his or her broker "borrow" the stock from one of the broker's clients. The stock is sold. The buyer of the stock gets the shares the broker borrowed. Meanwhile, with luck, the stock drops in value. The short seller buys the stock at the reduced price and returns the shares through the broker to the person they were borrowed from. The short seller keeps the profits, unless of course the stock went up instead of down after it was "borrowed." If the stock went up, the short seller still must buy the shares in order to return them to the person they were borrowed from, and the short seller must buy the shares at the higher price.

short-term financing   A loan that falls due in less than one year.

short-term gain   For the purpose of determining capital gains and losses, a gain on an investment that was held for less than a year. Whether an investment gain is short-term or long-term is important because long-term capital gains sometimes receive preferential treatment.

signature card   A card that depositors fill out when they open a bank account.

signature loan   A loan given without collateral, but with only the borrower's promise to pay and his or her signature on a promissory note. Such loans are given on the basis of the good standing of the borrower.

Simplified Employee Pension Plan (SEP)   A retirement plan for small businesses. It allows small business people to set aside up to 15 percent of their gross income for retirement.

sinking fund   A savings fund that accumulates money to pay off bonds or purchase a large asset.

sinking fund bond   A bond for which the bond issuer has provided a sinking fund. All other factors being equal, a sinking fund reduces the chance that bond purchasers will not be repaid.

skip payment privilege   An incentive clause giving a borrower the right to skip one or more payments.

slump   A slowdown in business activity. Also called a lull, an adjustment period, a valley, a slight downturn, a leveling off, a slow time, an introspection, and a gut check.

Small Business Administration (SBA)   An agency of the federal government that helps provide credit to small businesses.

smurf   A money launderer.

social security   Insurance benefits provided by the federal government for old age, disabilities, and unemployment.

sole proprietorship   When a business is owned by one person. Sole proprietorship is one of three types of business organization; the other two are a *partnership* and a *corporation.*

sovereign risk   The risk that a foreign government will default on its debt payments. Sovereign risks present special risks to banks, since collecting debt from a foreign government is virtually impossible.

special offering   A block of securities so large it cannot be offered on the trading floor without depressing prices. Instead of being traded on the floor, special offerings are traded through members of the exchange, who sell them on their own.

specialist   A broker or dealer who specializes in trading a single commodity or security.

specie   Coins, not paper money.

specific identification method   In an inventory, when each item is identified and accounted for. In some other types of inventorying methods, similar items are grouped.

speculation   Trading at a greater risk in order to obtain a fast profit.

speculator   A person who trades in commodities, stocks, or bonds with the idea of making a quick profit by taking many risks.

spin-off company   A semi-independent company headed by members of the original corporation and drawing on the capital and expertise of its parent company. A corporation might create a spin-off company, for example, when it sees an opportunity to branch into a new but related field.

split   The dividing of existing stock into more shares. Individual stocks lose value, but the total value of the stock stays the same. Stock splits are often undertaken to make the stock easier to trade when companies are bought and sold.

spot   In trading lingo, refers to the immediate delivery of orders or goods.

spot commodity   In a commodity exchange, a good offered for immediate delivery.

spot market   A market for goods that are delivered and paid for immediately, not at some future date.

spot prices   Commodity prices in present-day prices, as opposed to trading in future prices.

spread   Covering the spread means to buy and sell the same commodity in a futures market as a hedge against price rises or declines. With orders to buy and sell, the trader is insured against market fluctuations.

squeeze   A shortage of funds in the money market, which causes a demand for money and a hike in interest rates.

stabilization   The selling or buying of currency by a central bank in order to stabilize rates of exchange. When its currency is overvalued, a central bank sells its currency to flood the market and lower prices. When its currency is undervalued, the bank buys currency to increase competitive bidding and raise the price.

stale check   A check that is more than six months old.

stamp taxes   Taxes in the form of stamps, which manufacturers must buy and stick on their products or securities before they can be sold. You can see tax stamps on some brands of whiskey, for example.

Standard & Poor's   The advisory service that rates securities for their creditworthiness.

standard of living   The goods and services that a social group requires for its well-being. The standard of living is an abstract term and cannot be measured against an index.

statute of frauds   A legal statute that says a contract cannot be enforced unless it has the signature of the person against whom it is being enforced. In the case of a mortgage or other assumable debt, the signature of the borrower is required. The statute of frauds should never be confused with the statue of frogs.

statute of limitations   A limit on the time within which a legal action can be brought or a file claimed.

stock certificate   A written document giving title to a share or shares of stock.

stock exchange   A market where stocks are traded.

stock purchase option   A benefit offered to employees, giving them the option to buy stock in the companies they work for. Usually, the stock is offered at a reduced price.

stock split   The dividing of existing stock into more shares. Individual stocks lose value, but the total value of the stock stays the same. Stock splits are often undertaken to make the stock easier to trade when companies are bought and sold.

stop order   An order to buy or sell a stock or commodity when it reaches a certain price.

stop payment   To inform a bank not to honor a check. Even after a check is written and delivered, a bank customer can stop payment on it if he or she thinks the check was written in error.

straddle   To order a call and put option at the same time, at the same date, with the same price. Such an order would be made to take advantage of severe fluctuations in the market.

Street   Nickname for Wall Street in New York, New York, the address of the New York Stock Exchange, and the place where so many financial decisions are made by men in tasseled loafers.

street name   A security registered in the name of a bank or brokerage firm, not in the owner's name.

strike price   The price that the holder of a put option can sell a security, or the holder of a call option can buy one, as stated in the option contract.

subject order   An order requiring confirmation.

subsidiary corporation   A company that is owned wholly or partly by another company, called the *parent company*. The parent company usually owns a majority of the stock in the subsidiary.

super NOW account   A three-in-one checking account, savings account, and money market fund account.

supply-side economics   An economic theory that says that lowering the tax rates drastically will put more capital in the hands of businesses, which will in turn create more jobs and more business activity. As the economy is stimulated this way, revenues will increase, which will increase the tax base and compensate for revenue lost by tax cuts.

surcharge   An extra charge for people who pay with credit cards instead of cash. The surcharge pays for the extra costs of processing credit card payments.

surety   A guarantee that a debt will be repaid. Also, a person who is legally responsible for a debt.

surety bond   An agreement that if a housing development cannot be completed, an insurance company will take charge of the project, settle all disputes, and finish the project if necessary. Municipal development projects require surety bonds.

surplus   The amount by which a company's assets exceed its liabilities and capital stock, as shown on the company's balance sheet.

surtax   An added tax on income that has already been taxed once.

syndicate   An association of investment bankers formed to distribute an issue of new securities.

tape   Nickname for the ticker tape that shows price quotations in securities and commodities markets.

tariff   Taxes on import goods, levied to protect domestic industries or to raise revenue.

tax-deferred savings   Tax-free savings that can be put in an individual retirement account (IRA) or other retirement plan. Taxes are not imposed on the interest or principal until funds are withdrawn at age 59½ or later.

tax-exempt bond   A municipal bond that is free of all taxes.

tax-free rollover   The automatic renewal of a certificate of deposit (CD), tax-free at present rates of interest. Also, the automatic tax-free reinvestment of money market funds.

tax lien   A lien on property for failure to pay property taxes.

tax sale   An auction of property to raise money for the payment of delinquent taxes.

taxable estate   The part of an estate that is subject to taxes. The taxable estate is what is left after all debts, funeral expenses, and taxes are paid.

taxpayer identification number (TIN)   For taxation purposes, the number that identifies corporations, nonprofits, associations, and partnerships to the IRS. Sole proprietors and individuals are identified by their social security numbers.

teaser rate   A low mortgage rate offered to borrowers as an incentive. Typically, the rate is brought up to normal mortgage rates after a few months or years.

technical analysis   A method, like charting and fundamental analysis, of predicting trends in the stock, securities, and commodities markets. Technical analysts examine volume, supply and demand, and other factors.

teller's check   A check written by a bank against its own funds. Teller's checks are guaranteed to be redeemable, since they are drawn on banks.

tenancy at will   A lease that the landlord or tenant can terminate whenever he or she so desires.

tenancy by the entirety   An estate held by a wife and husband that cannot be terminated without both people's consent.

tenancy in common   An estate held by two or more people. If a partner in the estate dies, his or her share of the estate goes to the heirs.

term   The time it takes for a loan or deposit to mature. The term is usually expressed in months.

testator   A person who dies leaving a will.

thin market   Said of a sluggish market with few offers and bids.

third-party check   A check transferred by the endorser to another party. The endorser writes "pay to the order of" and then the third party's name on the check, making it redeemable by the third party.

tick $1/32$ of a percentage point, the unit for measuring price changes in securities, bonds, and Treasury Bills.

tight money   When the Federal Reserve tightens credit in order to raise interest rates and prevent inflation.

time deposit   A deposit in a bank that pays a fixed rate of interest and cannot be withdrawn without penalty until a certain maturity date is reached.

time-value of money   A general rule that says a dollar today is worth more than a dollar a year from today because if you have a dollar today you can invest it and earn interest over the next year.

title   Having ownership of real property. A deed, bill of sale, or certificate is required to prove title.

title company   A company that determines who has ownership of a property. Having conducted a title search, the company issues a certificate of title to the owner.

title defect   A claim, obstruction, or other condition that makes it difficult to determine who the owner of a property is.

total lease obligation   As required by the Federal Reserve, an accounting of all costs associated with a lease, including rent and interest payments, as well as the value of the leased property at the end of the lease.

trade date   The day an order is made to buy or sell securities.

trader   Someone who buys and sells stocks, securities, and commodities, on his own behalf or on the behalf of others.

trading range   The price range between the lowest bid and the highest offer for a stock, commodity, or security in an exchange market during a specific time period.

treasurer   A financial officer of a corporation whose job is, among other duties, to manage cash payments and deposits, procure and budget funds, handle the payroll, and discharge tax liabilities.

Treasury Bill   A short-term bill issued by the U.S. government to cover its debt. Treasury Bills are in $10,000 denominations. They mature in periods of 13, 26, or 52 weeks.

Treasury bond   A long-term bond issued by the U.S. government to cover its debts. Treasury bonds are sold in denominations of $10,000 or more.

treasury stock   A stock that has been repurchased by the issuer.

troubled bank   A bank with a large number of loans in default.

trust   Property held by one person or persons for the benefits of others.

trustee   The person who administers a trust.

trustor   The person who establishes a trust.

truth-in-lending law   Federal Reserve regulation (Regulation DD) establishing what information lenders must disclose to borrowers, including how finance charges are imposed, when additional charges will be made, and when a borrower may acquire a security interest in a property.

underlying lien   A lien to which other liens and property claims are subordinate. A first mortgage, for example, is an underlying lien.

underwriter   The person at an insurance company who processes applications for insurance and decides who gets insurance and who doesn't get insurance.

underwriting   In securities, when brokers and dealers buy securities in order to resell them. In banking, examining a credit application to see if the prospective borrower is worthy of receiving a loan.

unearned income   Income earned from investments and interest.

unemployment insurance   A federal and state run program that provides an income to unemployed workers. Contributions to unemployment insurance are deducted from salaries and wages.

Uniform Commercial Code (UCC)   Standardized state laws that establish rules for contracts, including how to prepare negotiables and handle deeds of title.

Uniform Consumer Credit Code   A law applicable in some states outlining how lenders and borrows should treat consumer loans under $25,000. The code sets guidelines for fair lending practices and describes how lenders can recoup defaulted loans.

Uniform Gift to Minors Act   A law applicable in some states regarding how property is to be transferred to minors. The act makes the minor responsible for property taxes and stipulates that a guardian be appointed for the minor.

uninsured depositor   A depositor with a savings or checking account larger than $100,000. Accounts above that amount are not insured by the *FDIC*.

unlisted securities   Securities not listed with a stock exchange and traded over the counter by dealers and brokers.

unrealized profit/loss   A profit or loss for securities that has been recorded but has yet to be collected.

unsecured creditor   A creditor who is owed a debt by a borrower who has declared voluntary bankruptcy. To be an unsecured creditor, the creditor cannot have a security interest in the borrower's assets.

unsecured loan   A loan given without the borrower posting collateral or providing any other security.

up tick   Refers to when a security is resold at a higher value. Also called a *plus tick*.

U.S. savings bond   A U.S. government bond, issued to finance the debt of the U.S. government. Savings bonds earn variable interest and are sold in denominations from $50 to $10,000.

usury   The lending of money at an exorbitant rate of interest. By law, usury is defined as charging an interest rate above the legal limit.

variable annuity   An annuity paid out at a variable rate, depending on interest accrued on a principal.

variable-rate certificate   A certificate of deposit (CD) yielding a variable rate of interest.

variable-rate loan   A loan whose rate of interest changes. The rate is determined by a standard index, such as the *prime rate*.

variable-rate mortgage   A mortgage whose interest rate is adjusted periodically. These mortgages are usually tied to some sort of money index, such as the prime lending rate or the cost of Treasury Bills. When the index goes up or down, so does the monthly mortgage payment. Also called an *adjustable-rate mortgage* (*ARM*).

venture capital   Capital available for new enterprises and startup companies.

vested interest   In financial terminology, a stake in something that will give you money in the future. For example, employees have a vested interest in the prosperity of their company pension plans.

veteran's loan   A mortgage backed partially or wholly by the Department of Veterans Affairs. Veterans are eligible for these loans, which are easier to acquire and service than conventional mortgages.

void   Null and no longer applicable, such as a voided check.

volume of trading   The total number of shares traded on a stock market. Trading volume is a measure of market activity.

voluntary bankruptcy   When a debtor declares bankruptcy in order to gain relief from creditors.

voluntary trust   A living trust in which the beneficiary has title and possession of a property, but the legal title stays in the hands of the one who set up the trust.

voting stock   Stock in a corporation that entitles the owner to vote on matters important to the running of the corporation.

wage earner plan   Part of a bankruptcy agreement, where the debtor agrees to pay some of the debt to creditors in installments.

wage garnishment   A court judgment ordering a lender to be given part of the wages of a borrower who has defaulted on a loan.

Wall Street   The famous street in New York, New York, the address of the New York Stock Exchange, and the place where so many financial decisions are made by men in tasseled loafers.

ward   A minor whose financial affairs are managed by a guardian appointed by a court. Incompetent people also can be wards of a court.

warrant   A certificate allowing the bearer to purchase stock at a fixed price at some future date.

warranty   A guarantee that what is written in a contract is indeed true.

warranty deed   A deed by which the seller of a property guarantees that the property is free of liens and encumbrances.

wash sale   A stock-manipulation scheme in which traders buy and sell shares repeatedly in a short period of time to give the impression that the stock is a hot item, when really it is not.

watch list   A list of banks that bank examiners need to "watch" because they are earning poorly or are undercapitalized.

wholly owned subsidiary   A subsidiary completely owned by its parent company.

will   A legal document stating how a person wants his or her property disposed of after death.

window dressing   Changing how accounts are organized to give a more favorable impression of a business's financial position without actually changing that position.

wire transfer   Transferring money electronically, as opposed to by check or by means of another type of paper transfer.

withholding   Taking deductions from income to cover taxes or liabilities.

without recourse   Refers to the fact that the buyer of a promissory note is the one who takes the risk that it will not be paid. The buyer has no recourse to make the seller make good on the note.

with right of survivorship   A right by which joint owners of an asset inherit the asset if one or the other dies. The asset does not go to the heirs of the deceased.

working control   Control of a corporation by right of owning at least 51 percent of its stock.

workmen's compensation insurance   By state law, insurance paid by employers in case of injury on the job.

write-off   Removing an item from an account ledger, because the item has been fully depreciated or deemed worthless.

wraparound mortgage   A refinanced mortgage in which the new rate of interest reflects both the rate on the old mortgage and current market rates. In this way, the old mortgage is "wrapped" with the new one.

yield curve   A graph comparing the yields at maturity of different securities.

yield to call   The annual return, expressed as a percentage, of a bond or note if it is redeemed at the first possible call.

yield to maturity   The annual return, expressed as a percentage, of a bond or note redeemed at maturity.

zero-coupon bond   A bond issued without coupons and without a statement of its rate of interest.

zero-coupon security   A security that pays no interest until maturity, when the interest is paid in a lump sum.

APPENDIX <u>A</u>

Installing Quicken and Setting Up Your First Account

This appendix describes how to install Quicken 2000 and set up your first bank account in Quicken.

Installing Quicken under Windows 95, Windows 98, or Windows NT

To install Quicken under Windows 95, Windows 98, or Windows NT, follow these steps:

1. Close any running applications.

2. Insert the Quicken CD-ROM into your CD-ROM drive. When your computer detects the CD-ROM, it displays the AutoRun Windows Application message box. Click Yes to launch the Quicken Setup program, shown in Figure A.1.

 NOTE If nothing happens when you insert the Quicken CD-ROM, you can install Quicken the way you install any other Windows application, by using the Add/Remove Programs tool in the Control Panel.

3. Click Next to begin the installation.

4. Read Intuit's licensing terms and click Yes.

5. Quicken suggests a folder in which to install the program, as shown in Figure A.2. If you agree with Quicken's suggestion, click Next. To select another folder, click Browse and select a different folder.

6. If you don't have a previous version of Quicken installed, the default folder for Quicken doesn't exist. Click Yes when asked if you want to create it.

7. The installation program asks questions about the type of installation you want, as shown in Figure A.3. You can choose between an Express or Custom installation and between the U.S. or Canadian version of Quicken. Mark your choices (or just accept the defaults if you're not sure), and then click Next.

FIGURE A.1

*The Quicken Setup
program*

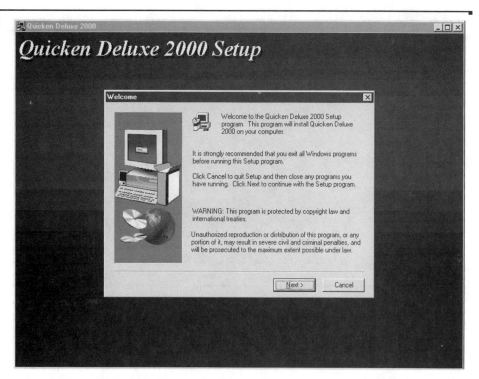

FIGURE A.2

*The Choose
Destination Location
dialog box*

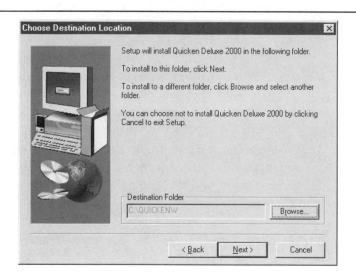

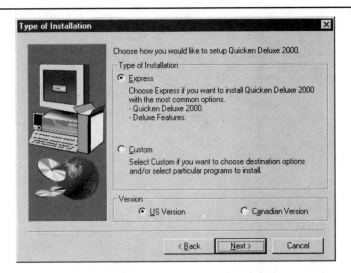

NOTE If you choose to install the Canadian version of Quicken, see Appendix B for information about using Quicken in Canada.

8. If you selected the Express installation, the Quicken installation program will begin to install Quicken and Microsoft Internet Explorer. Click Start Copying to begin the installation.

9. If you selected the Custom installation, you can choose which components you want to install, as well as accept the default folder location for Quicken or specify another folder. (You should use the default location unless you have a good reason for designating a different one, such as if you are installing Quicken on an external drive.) To define a new path, click Browse, select or type the name of the path you want Quicken to use, and then click OK. When the path is correct, click Next. Then click Start Copying.

10. When the Quicken installation program finishes, it displays a dialog box telling you that the installation is not complete until your computer has been restarted and asks if you wish to restart now or later. Remove any disks from their drives, select the Yes, I Want To Restart My Computer Now option button, and click Finish.

11. Double-click the Quicken 2000 icon on the desktop.

12. Quicken asks if you want to register Quicken, which you probably want to do. To register, click Register. Then fill in the information Quicken asks for, such as your name, address, and use of the program. If you select to register online, Quicken asks you to select your connection and the Web browser you want to use with the program.

 TIP Intuit wants your name for its mailing list, of course. But even though you probably have an aversion to junk mail, it's a good idea to register. By registering, you're notified of product updates and add-on products. (Sometimes existing users get special, discount prices on upgrades!) And in the unlikely event of a serious bug, you will be notified.

Setting Up Your First Account

Installing a record-keeping system like Quicken isn't just a matter of copying program files to your computer's hard disk. You also need to set up your first accounts.

If you've been using an earlier version of Quicken, Quicken upgrades your data when you first start up Quicken 2000. Simply click OK at the Welcome screen. In the process, Quicken creates a backup of your data.

If you haven't used Quicken before, Quicken runs the New User Setup Wizard when you start Quicken for the first time. Simply follow the on-screen instructions to set up your first account, and then turn to Chapter 1 to start using that account and Quicken.

APPENDIX B

Using the Canadian Version of Quicken

I f you live in Canada and want to use Quicken to track your finances, you can take advantage of several features included in the Canadian version of Quicken. This appendix describes how you set up Windows and Quicken for use in Canada and outlines special features included in the Canadian version of Quicken.

Reconfiguring Windows and Quicken

If your system is not already set up for Canadian use, your first task is to reconfigure Windows with settings for Canada. This is quite easy to do:

1. Click the Start button and choose Settings.

2. Choose Control Panel.

3. When the Control Panel window opens, double-click the Regional Settings icon. The Regional Settings Properties dialog box appears, as shown in Figure B.1.

4. On the Regional Settings tab, use the drop-down list box to choose English (Canadian). Now Canadian English is the default for your system, as is the Canadian date style of *DD/MM/YY*.

5. Click OK.

After configuring Windows for Canadian use, you must also configure Quicken with the settings for Canada. If you've already installed Quicken on your computer, you will need to reinstall it. If you have not yet installed Quicken, you need to choose the Canadian configuration during the installation process. (This option is selected by default if you have configured Windows for Canadian use.) In either case, install Quicken according to the instructions in Appendix A of this book. When you get to the Type of Installation window, click the Canadian Version radio button, as shown in Figure B.2. Then complete the installation, as described in Appendix A.

FIGURE B.1

The Regional Settings Properties dialog box

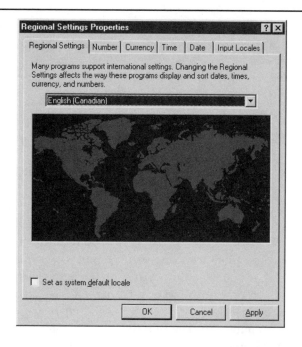

FIGURE B.2

Choosing the Canadian version of Quicken

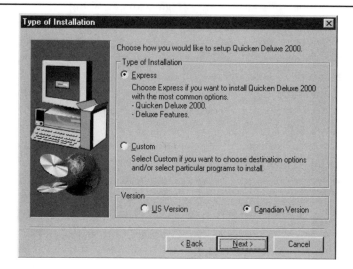

TIP To see whether you've installed the Canadian version of Quicken, choose Help ➤ About Quicken. The words *Canadian Quicken* should appear in the dialog box Quicken displays.

Using Canadian Categories

Before you start processing transactions, you need to be aware of the ways in which the Canadian version differs from the U.S. version. One of the major differences has to do with the categories you use for your record keeping.

As explained in Chapter 2 of this book, when you create a new file for keeping financial records, you are given the opportunity to choose which kinds of categories you want: various home categories, business categories, or both. When you tell Quicken to configure the program for use in Canada, in addition to including almost all the categories for Quicken users in the United States, Quicken adds income categories unique to Canada.

For example, Quicken adds the CPP-QPP category for describing Canada or Quebec Pension Plan benefits, the Old Age Sec. category for describing Old Age Security income, the RRIF Income category for describing registered retirement income fund payments, and the RRSP Income category for describing registered retirement savings plan payments. Quicken also adds several categories for describing expenses, such as the Private and Prov H-care categories for describing health care expenses, the RPP Contrib category for describing Registered Pension Plan contributions, as well as tax subcategories for tracking employment insurance premiums and Canada Pension Plan contributions. These categories become essential when you begin describing transactions.

If you specify in the installation that you want to include business categories in your category list, Quicken also adds categories for tracking the federal goods and services tax (GST) and provincial retail sales taxes (PST). Of all the provinces, only Alberta does not collect retail sales taxes. Likewise, neither the Yukon nor Northwest Territories collect retail sales taxes. New Brunswick, Nova Scotia, and Newfoundland collect a harmonized sales tax (HST). If the default category list does not include the categories you need for tracking business income or expenses in your province or territory in Canada, you can easily add and delete categories, as described in Chapter 14 of this book.

TIP To order QuickTax, Intuit's Canadian personal tax-preparation program, visit the Quicken.com Web site and look for a hyperlink about Quicktax.

Tracking Business Finances

Tracking GST and PST becomes a necessity when you use Quicken to track business finances. Accurate records are extremely important when you're dealing with taxes, and this is where Quicken can save you a lot of time.

Rather than using the GST and PST categories in your banking transactions, create separate liability accounts for them. This way, you can get up-to-the-minute reports on the status of those accounts and separate any GST you collect from the amounts that are reported as your net worth in reports.

First, create a GST (and, if necessary, a PST) liability account as described in Chapter 20 of this book. Be sure to name the account or accounts appropriately. Figure B.3 shows the Summary tab of the Liability Account Setup dialog box filled out to create a GST account. After you click Done, answer No when Quicken asks whether you want to set up an amortized loan to go with the account.

APPX

B

Using the Canadian
Version of Quicken

FIGURE B.3

*Setting up a GST
liability account*

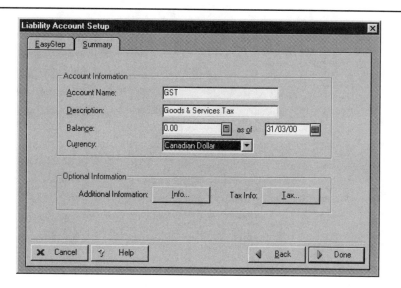

After you've set up the necessary liability accounts, you can use them for your split transactions. For example, suppose that you sold 1,000 widgets to Bob's Widget Warehouse. To record this sale, you put the information in your business account as you would normally. The amount you charge for the widgets, in this case, is $600, which you can write in the Amount box of the register. You then split the categories and include lines that transfer the tax amounts to the appropriate liability accounts (*not* the categories), as shown in Figure B.4.

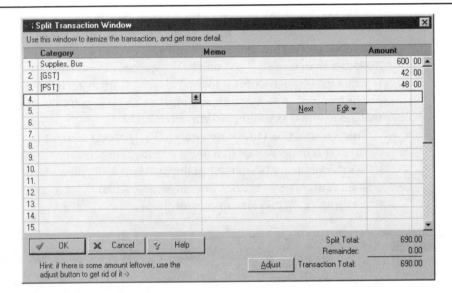

When you are recording a business *purchase* you have made, however, the PST you pay should *not* be credited to you, although the GST should be credited to you. Because the amount of the PST should not appear as a credit in your liability account, when you record a business purchase, process the transaction by using the PST *category* and not as a transfer to the PST *liability account* in the Split Transaction Window.

To pay the GST and PST to the tax authorities, find out how much you owe for each tax by looking at the ending balances of the tax liability accounts. Then write a check to the tax authority from a bank account, entering a transfer to the tax payable account in the Category field. This reduces the balance of the liability account.

Describing Canadian Mortgages

Installing the Canadian version of Quicken also allows you to set up loan accounts with semiannual compounding. Most Canadian mortgages are compounded semi-annually. This means that interest is added to the principal every six months instead of monthly, as is predominant in the United States.

For example, if you were to take out a $10,000 loan, with a 10 percent annual interest rate compounded annually, the interest payment is $1,000 per year. With a 10 percent interest rate compounded semiannually, the interest payments total $1,025 per year, meaning that the effective annual interest rate is 10.25 percent. With a 10 percent interest rate compounded monthly, the interest payments total $1,047.13 per year, meaning that the effective annual interest rate is 10.47 percent.

Investing in Canada

The Canadian version of Quicken includes a couple of special features for investors as well. If you report capital gains, Quicken uses the average cost basis of your investment to calculate your capital gains, as is required for Canadian taxpayers.

 WARNING Do not use Quicken's lot-handling features (described in Chapter 18 of this book) to specify lots. Doing so makes the Capital Gains report amounts incorrect.

Quicken 2000 also allows you to download security prices from Canadian exchanges. To specify Canadian exchanges, you need to precede the stock ticker symbol with T: for Toronto, V: for Vancouver, or M: for Montreal in the Symbol text box when you set up your investments.

INDEX

Note to the Reader: Page numbers in **bold** indicate the principal discussion of a topic or the definition of a term. Page numbers in *italic* indicate illustrations.

Numbers and Symbols

R

T

Get
Rocket-Fast

Internet Access With All the Perks!

- Unlimited Internet access at speeds up to 56k

- Local access nationwide and international roaming capabilities

- Free, reliable email

- Free 6MB of webspace for your own Web site

- A fully customizable Personal Start Page℠

- 24/7 toll-free customer service and tech support

- Free subscription to bLink™, Earthlink's member magazine

- Free software like QuickTime™, RealPlayer®, and Shockwave®

And much more!

Earthlink Sprint launches you into the Web with unlimited access at speeds up to 56k and more local access numbers than any other ISP.

www.earthlink.net
EarthLink
Sprint

Call Now!
1-800-Earthlink (327-8454)

Mention Reg. #400037787

Visit Marco's Delphi Developer Web Site

The book's author, Marco Cantù, has created a site specifically for Delphi developers, at www.marcocantu.com. It's a great resource for all of your Delphi programming needs.

The site includes:

- The source code of the book (also available on the Sybex site)
- Extra examples and tips
- A number of Delphi components, wizards, and tools built by the author.
- The online book *Essential Pascal*
- Delphi reference material not found in the Help file
- Some papers the author has written about Delphi, C++, and Java
- Extensive links to Delphi-related Web sites and documents
- Other material related to the author's books, the conferences he speaks at, and his training seminars

The site also hosts a newsgroup, which has a specific section devoted to the author's books, so that readers can discuss the book content with him and among themselves. There are also other sections of the newsgroup for discussing Delphi programming and general topics.

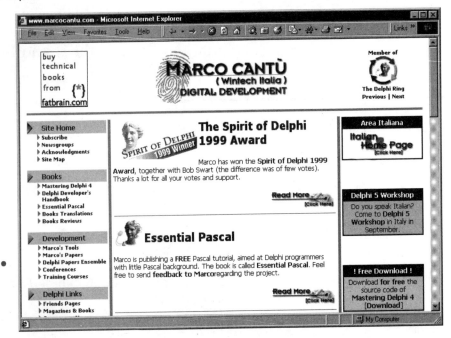